My Life in Athletics

By

Mel Watman

My Life in Athletics
Mel Watman

© Melvyn Watman 2017

The right of Melvyn Watman to be identified as author of this work had been asserted by him in accordance with the Copyright, Designs & Patent Act 1988.

Paperback ISBN **978-1-907953-69-9**

First published by Melvyn Watman in 2017
13 Garden Court
Stanmore
HA7 4TE, UK
(melvynwatman@gmail.com)

Printed by Lightning Source UK Ltd, Milton Keynes, UK

CONTENTS

INTRODUCTION

It's impossible to prove, but there is a strong possibility that I have written more words on athletics than anyone else. Since my first by-lined article appeared in *Athletics Weekly* in July 1954 I must have tapped out several million words and in this book I'm adding another quarter-million or so in an attempt to recapture the privilege and pleasure I've experienced in reporting and documenting the sport which has dominated my life. As I head towards my 80th birthday in May 2018 I thought it was time to reflect on the momentous events and wonderful personalities I have written about over the years. How incredibly lucky I have been: happily married since 1973 to my darling Pat (whose love and support has made it possible for me to continue working for so long), achieving my schoolboy ambition of editing *Athletics Weekly* and spending more than 60 fulfilling years as a professional journalist, historian and statistician – all the while managing to retain the enthusiasm I had as a teenager.

The events and people mentioned in these memoirs are set out more or less in chronological order although from time to time I go on to explain what may have transpired later. In order to recall my words, opinions and emotions at the time I have reprinted numerous extracts (in italics) from my reports and features, primarily from *Athletics Weekly* (my thanks to editor Jason Henderson for permission to reproduce so much material), *Athletics Today* and *Athletics International*, and dating from the late 1950s to the present day. Although it's a record of my personal involvement in the sport, this book could be viewed as a selective history of athletics over the last six decades. During that time I have witnessed and commented on huge changes in the sport at the elite level with the advent of officially approved professionalism, although at club level it remains essentially amateur and dependent upon an army of unpaid volunteers.

I would like to take this opportunity to thank my family for their interest and encouragement, all my colleagues over the years, the enthusiasts who have continued to read my outpourings, and of course the athletes. I might have been on the sidelines observing and chronicling their deeds but I was always, and remain, a fan first and foremost.

Mel Watman
October 2017

1. WAR & EARLY SCHOOLDAYS (1938-1950)

Although I was born in the East London borough of Hackney (on May 26 1938), which just about qualifies me as a cockney, my first memories are of Bedford where my mum, sister Benita and I were evacuated during the war. My dad, who was away in the army, used to claim he was a sprinter who ran occasionally at Paddington Recreation Ground, but athletics played no part in my early life although, decades later, I discovered a remarkable connection. Harold Abrahams, the 1924 Olympic 100m champion of *Chariots of Fire* fame and an important influence on my career, was born at 30 Rutland Road, Bedford on December 15 1899 (in 2012 a blue plaque to mark the event was unveiled there) .... and, some 42 years later, when I was aged four, we moved into a house just a couple of doors away!

It may have been wartime but I knew nothing different and I experienced an idyllic childhood, the strict sweet rationing (no more than two ounces a week) being the only serious deprivation that I can recall. I enjoyed school, the children's playground in Russell Park, riverside walks along the embankment by the River Great Ouse, listening to such radio comedy shows as ITMA, Much Binding In The Marsh, Variety Bandbox, and – in those pre-television days – going to the cinema two or three times a week, with Roy Rogers westerns, Hollywood musicals and the Bob Hope/Bing Crosby/Dorothy Lamour series of Road films among my favourites.

A trip to the cinema in those far-off days was so different to today's multi-screen, fixed performance time and single feature format. For a couple of shillings or so my mum, sister and I would spend at least three hours in one of Bedford's "picture palaces". A torch-wielding usherette would find you seats and more often than not we would settle down in the middle of the main film, trying to puzzle out what it was all about. It didn't matter too much because, after an interval in which a mighty Wurlitzer organ would rise from the depths and we would be treated to a medley of contemporary hits, that would be followed by a newsreel, a cartoon and a second feature, and then we could catch up with what we had missed from the main feature. "This is where we came in" would be the signal for us to leave and walk home. We certainly got our money's worth. And there was more cinema-going for me, as I would never miss a Saturday matinee show just for children, featuring a feast of goodies such as cartoons, Laurel & Hardy, Charlie Chaplin and the ever thrilling Flash Gordon serial, plus a spot of community singing. Everything seemed so innocent at that time even though outside our cocooned existence a terrible war was raging.

Bedford suffered two German bomber attacks in July 1942. I think I saw the bombs drop, but to be honest I may have imagined it. The main benefit of wartime Bedford, as Benita and I saw it, was that the town was a base for American servicemen, driving around in their Jeeps. We adored those guys, forever offering us packs of chewing gum (my sister, four years older than me, was still much too young for nylons!), and they all looked like Hollywood film stars in their smart uniforms. One Christmas we were driven over to their base and allowed to pick any present we wished – heaven! No wonder I've always had a love affair with America, and would go on to spend over two years of my life there in segments of a week or two at a time. Since 1958 I must have flown the Atlantic and back at least 60 times.

My final memory of Bedford was on VE Day (May 8 1945), just before my seventh birthday. It was a magical occasion with fairy lights strung along The Embankment and I recall my Uncle Ben, a former professional violinist who had been invalided out of the services, hoisting me on his shoulders to allow me a better view. Within weeks we packed up and the next phase of my life began back in my native city of London.

Mum, Benita and I moved initially to a council house in Wilberforce Road, Finsbury Park – a fairly nondescript area of North London although, as with Rutland Road in Bedford, Wilberforce Road was the birthplace of a great celebrity, in this case the ballet dancer Dame Alicia Markova (born plain Lilian Alicia Marks). Less than a mile away in Highbury was the Arsenal Football Stadium – so no prize awarded for guessing which football team I have supported ever since. I attended the local London County Council primary school nearby in Blackstock Road and, being more advanced than my classmates in most subjects as a result of my sister teaching me what she had learnt, I was considered a high flier and was told that I could qualify for a scholarship to the prestigious Christ's Hospital in Horsham, Sussex. The prospect of going to a boarding school filled me with horror for although I was a voracious reader of the exploits of Billy Bunter of Greyfriars School and the pupils at the Red Circle School (which I seem to recall included a stopwatch obsessed embryonic track nut) there was no way I was prepared to move away from home.

I was always a studious, rather shy boy with his nose invariably in a book or comic, and my earliest obsession involved London's red buses. When I grew up I wanted to become a bus conductor, now a vanished species but in those days every bus had an employee on board dispensing multi-coloured tickets dependent on the cost of your journey, from a penny upwards. I collected as many of those tickets as I could, often dipping my hand into the used ticket box situated on every bus, and would play at being a conductor. We couldn't afford much in the way of toys (I never did get the Hornby Dublo model railway I yearned for) but I did acquire a few Dinky Toy buses and cars. Perhaps the most memorable moment of my time in Finsbury Park, as it remains so vivid, was accompanying mum to the Fish & Cook stationers in Blackstock Road to buy some pencils or whatever. As we were leaving I noticed a pile of London Transport bus maps. I pleaded with mum to buy me one … and when we took it to the till we were told it was free! That map immediately became my most prized possession as I would trace every bus route from no 1 upwards, acquiring an almost encyclopaedic knowledge of the network. I eventually wore out that map but was content in the knowledge that I could replace it by applying to London Transport's HQ at 55 Broadway.

6

A note here about my Jewish heritage, of which I am very proud. My parents, Alf (a barber, back home with us in 1946 after six years' army service) and Flora (a part-time milliner), were born in London but my two grandfathers came to England from what was then Russia in around the year 1900. One hailed from Pinsk (now in Belarus), the other from Bialystok (now in Poland), and both fled from the grim prospect of pogroms (unprovoked violent, often murderous, attacks on Jews) and/or enforced military service in the Imperial Russian Army. Outside of school hours, when I would have preferred to be kicking a ball or playing marbles or flicking cigarette cards, I went to Hebrew classes as preparation for my barmitzvah at age 13, an important rite of passage even though my family was mainly non-observant.

In 1948 we moved to the upstairs section of another council house a mile or so away in Bethune Road, Stoke Newington. Living just up the road was a girl a year older than me by the name of Barbara Deeks, who was eventually to become Dame Barbara Windsor. A change of school was required and I was accepted by Avigdor High School on the basis that it was geographically the closest to our home and its educational standards were impressive. It was a mistake. Certainly it was academically excellent (I was learning Latin at age nine) but it was an orthodox Jewish school and Benita and I were virtually the only pupils who were not from deeply religious families.

However, my two years there did yield something that would shape the rest of my life. I discovered I was a pretty good runner and my love of athletics developed from that. Earlier in 1948 I recall my dad asking whether I was interested in going to the Olympics, which were to be staged at Wembley that summer, and I have to confess I didn't know what the Olympic Games were and my only spark of interest was in the rowing events because they were to take place at Henley-on-Thames and that would be a nice train journey away, railways (having superseded buses) being my passion in those days. Anyway, nothing came of it and it would be another 12 years before I had the opportunity of attending an Olympics.

My first success (one of very few!) as a runner came in an inter-schools match at the Parliament Hill track in July 1949. I was very lightly built in those days (see photos of Seb Coe at that age of 11, only that was where the resemblance ended!) and I found that my forte was at the longer distances. In the 880 yards event, all my opponents tore off at the start while instinctively I began cautiously, aware that two laps of the cinder track was quite a long way, and as my rivals inevitably flagged I overtook one after another to win by a big margin. On my certificate I scribbled 'time of about 3 minutes' but I've no memory of whether I was actually timed. I returned to Parliament Hill for a schools "cross country" race early in 1950. The course was actually a downhill run on muddy grass of around 600 yards, finishing at the entrance to the track, and I won that too.

A month or two later I left Avigdor and was accepted as a late entrant for the first form at Hackney Downs Grammar School (formerly known as Grocers'), which at that time was an outstanding school which *The Times* once described as "a prestigious hothouse for bright East End boys." Years later, as a comprehensive with many of its pupils being immigrants for whom English was not their first language, it was designated a failed school but thankfully it has since risen from the ashes as the successful Mossbourne Community Academy, its GCSE and A Level results placing it among the country's top 1%. Anyway, in my case it was a shrewd move as I would now be receiving a fine mainstream education without undue emphasis on Jewish studies and I thrived in this new environment. My four years at Hackney Downs also were vital in shaping my future ... thanks to my physical education teacher Leslie Mitchell. That my life and athletics were to become forever intertwined was largely due to his influence.

2. HACKNEY DOWNS & WHITE CITY (1950-1954)

Hackney Downs was probably unique in that, through Mr Mitchell's influence, athletics was the school's major sport, outranking even football and cricket. Mr Mitchell was a huge athletics fan, his study at the gym adorned with such memorabilia as a signed photo of star miler Bill Nankeville, and thanks to his enthusiasm I was persuaded to join a party he was taking to the 1950 AAA Championships at the White City Stadium in West London. That visit changed my life.

Watching the likes of McDonald Bailey, Arthur Wint and Roger Bannister got me hooked on the sport. Fortuitously, a week or two later, I happened to spot a magazine entitled *Athletics Weekly* at the Hackney Downs station bookstall. In fact there were two issues on display and I was offered the pair for the price of one (all of sixpence or 2.5p!). How could I resist?

AW, which was originally called *Athletics* as a monthly magazine established by Jimmy Green in December 1945, had only gone weekly at the start of 1950 and comprised just 16 small format pages. I was in heaven, reading and re-reading every line, every result. I may have been only 12 but already a dream was starting to take shape. English was my best subject at school and I knew I wanted to become a journalist. Better still, how about writing on my new love, athletics? That was it – my goal in life was not only to work for AW but eventually to become its editor. Seventeen years later that dream would become reality as Jimmy handed the editorial reins to me.

I spent the rest of 1950 learning all I could about athletics. I was especially fascinated by the sport's history and thanks to my local library I was able to read Captain Webster's marvellous *Great Moments in Athletics*. That was one hugely influential work; another, published in 1951, was *Get To Your Marks!* by Norris and Ross McWhirter. As well as following the fortunes of those athletes active in the early fifties I was now getting acquainted with the exploits of such great stars of the past as Paavo Nurmi and Jesse Owens.

My second visit to the White City, off my own bat this time, was on a cold, damp, misty afternoon in March 1951. The occasion was the annual Oxford v Cambridge clash. A barrel chested redhead by the name of Chris Chataway won the mile for Oxford in 4:16.4 and looked like a star in the making ... but who could have predicted that the rather ungainly Cambridge runner who finished a distant second in the 3 miles in 14:41.8 would, five years later, win an Olympic gold medal? It was Chris Brasher.

The crowd wasn't much bigger for the Women's AAA Championships in July but it was a very special occasion for me as I witnessed my first world record when Sheila Lerwill, the pioneering female straddle jumper, went clear at 1.72m. One of my heroes, Arthur Wint, came close to setting a world record in the AAA Championships, his 880 yards time of 1:49.6 falling just 0.4 sec short of the mark shared by Sydney Wooderson and Mal Whitfield, and later that season – at the White City's first floodlit meeting – Wint and John Parlett dead-heated in a wonderful race which I can still recall vividly all these years later.

Two weeks after that, on September 26, Parlett anchored a British team to a world record in the 4x880 yards relay while an English women's team set new world figures at 4x220 yards, the anchor being Olympic 100m silver medallist Dorothy Hall (née Manley) who many years later would become Mrs Parlett!

Apart from being much longer, the British season in the 1950s was so different from today's. Top athletes now are rarely seen on home soil but then there was a logical structure to an athlete's year. It started at the county championships, then on to the inter-counties at Whitsun, area championships, AAA and Women's AAA Championships, followed by international championships and matches. Officially the sport was strictly amateur in those days, prizes restricted to canteens of cutlery and the like, although "shamateurism" flourished with a few highly successful athletes secretly rewarded for boosting gate receipts by their appearance.

Tracks were either cinder or grass. All-weather surfaces were not introduced until the late 1960s and today's runners can have no conception of competing on flooded or muddy tracks, their kit and bodies caked with the grit that was thrown up. Starting blocks were the preserve of the elite; most club athletes were still using a trowel to dig holes for their feet. There were no soft landing beds for the vertical jumpers ... this was long before the Fosbury Flop and fibre glass poles revolutionised those events.

As for the women, they were dreadfully restricted. At the 1948, 1952 and 1956 Olympics the longest track event, ludicrously, was 200m. The WAAA did include 400m/440y, 800m/880y and mile as championship events but no one then could have dreamt of a time when women would run the marathon and steeplechase, pole vault, triple jump or throw the hammer – and, if they so wished, wearing little more than a bikini! In those days there were strict rules about women's athletic clothing – modest tops and dark coloured shorts being mandatory.

It all sounds a little primitive now, but athletics was an immensely popular sport then with the big White City meetings often attracting crowds of around 40,000. Even the newspapers, in contrast to today's football-obsessed sports pages, provided extensive coverage. Each had its own dedicated athletics correspondent, the *News of the World* – the sport's major sponsor – even having two in miling stars past and present, Joe Binks and Doug Wilson. On a Monday during the track season *The Times* would feature columns of domestic results. Oh how, literally, the times have changed!

I have vivid memories of the Olympic year of 1952. By that time I had got my closest circle of school friends interested also in athletics and we would take the Tube together to the White City. I even invented "table athletics", adapting a horse racing board game called Totopoly and compiling a chart of times for various distances based on the roll of the dice. My school friends and I would play this as an alternative to our Subbuteo table football tournaments, table tennis or pontoon sessions and on one memorable occasion my horse representing Herb McKenley clocked under 44 sec for 400m (the real world record then was 45.8) thanks to a phenomenal sequence of fives and sixes!

I also caught the autograph hunting bug. Not only did I station myself outside the White City dressing rooms, but I also fired off fan letters to various American stars c/o their university athletic departments. I could hardly wait for the post to arrive (three deliveries a day then, would you believe!) and I nearly passed out from excitement when an envelope from Fresno State University dropped on the mat ... it was from pole vaulting legend Cornelius Warmerdam. I ended up with a fabulous collection, including numerous Olympic champions from 1952 and earlier.

It was in 1952 that Norris and Ross McWhirter launched their wonderful monthly magazine, *Athletics World*, crammed full of news, results and statistics from around the globe. Each issue was such a feast that I would not allow my eyes to stray over the page. Instead, to savour the contents to the full and prolong the suspense, I would cover up the rest of the page and reveal one line at a time. I was so proud when in 1954 the twins published a little survey of mine declaring Davis as the most successful surname in athletics. *Athletics World's* coverage of the 1952 Olympics was absolutely superb and remains unsurpassed in my opinion.

There were no TV pictures from those Games in Helsinki and I relied on the BBC radio reports from Harold Abrahams, whose commentaries and factual summaries were commendable, and Rex Alston, who would drive me wild with his long-winded descriptions of the stadium and weather instead of the results I yearned for.

Because there were no British winners in athletics, certain sections of the British press were vicious in their condemnation of the team's performance. In fact the journalists concerned were merely displaying their own ignorance and arrogance. Without doing the homework to be aware of the quality of the opposition, they had in many cases led their readers to expect a glut of gold medals when that was never a realistic prospect. In fact, the team performed up to reasonable expectations. Sheila Lerwill won the high jump silver medal, and there were bronze medals for McDonald Bailey in the 100m, John Disley in the steeplechase, Shirley Cawley in the long jump and the women's 4x100m relay squad. There were six fourth places, including Roger Bannister in the 1500m – who was heavily criticised despite breaking the British record in a final he was ill-prepared for as a result of an extra round of heats being inserted at short notice. The athlete who received the most acclaim, and rightly so, was Emil Zátopek. He was responsible for shattering the dreams of Olympic glory of such athletes as Gordon Pirie, Chris Chataway and Jim Peters, but even the most fanatical British supporter could not begrudge the Czech's phenomenal success. No one before had ever won the 5000m, 10,000m and marathon – and no one will ever do so again. For those of my generation, Emil was – and remains – "the greatest".

Much as I revelled in Zátopek's extraordinary achievement, I felt nothing but anguish for Jim Peters, a non-finisher in the Olympic marathon. The previous month I had been at the Polytechnic Stadium in Chiswick to see Jim complete his journey from Windsor in the staggering time of 2:20:43. That may not sound anything special these days – after all, Paula Radcliffe has run five minutes faster – but in June 1952 that was considered absolutely amazing. Until then, no one had covered the marathon distance quicker than 2:25:39 by a Korean in the 1947 Boston event. Stan Cox, who like Peters was coached by 1928 Olympic 5000m finalist 'Johnny' Johnston, was second in 2:21:42 and sceptics raised doubts about the length of the course. Yes, it wasn't the universally accepted distance of 26 miles 385 yards ... it was remeasured as 26 miles 645 yards!

An emotional event at the tail-end of 1952 was Arthur Wint's farewell lap of honour at the White City. What a remarkable athlete, and man, he was ... a giant in every sense. I recall, with amusement, his frustration at an experimental indoor meeting at the Harringay Arena in March of that year. He had the utmost difficulty negotiating the impossibly tight bends of the unbanked 152-yard track, nevertheless winning the 600 yards. Outdoors, though, his enormous nine-foot stride swallowed up the ground at an extraordinary rate and the fans never failed to gasp at the sight of him in full flow. The first Jamaican to become an Olympic champion, his medal tally was two golds (1948 400m, 1952 4x400m) and two silvers (at 800m behind his great American rival, Mal Whitfield). Although he represented his native island at the Olympics, Arthur did run for Britain in international matches and the former RAF fighter pilot graced the UK athletics scene from 1946 until his retirement at the age of 32. During that time he qualified as a doctor (later as a surgeon), and from 1974 to 1978 held Jamaica's most prestigious diplomatic post as High Commissioner to London. A dignified and caring man, he was an outstanding ambassador for his country. Many years later, in 2012, I was privileged and moved to attend the unveiling in London's Earls Court area of a blue plaque indicating he lived at that particular house from 1949 to 1960. The ceremony took place 20 years after his death in Jamaica at the age of 72.

The other great West Indian athlete who had been such an influence in my early days in the sport was McDonald Bailey. He was the most stylish as well as most consistent of sprinters, winning the AAA 100/220 yards double seven times between 1946 and 1953, equalling the 100m world record of 10.2 (first set by Jesse Owens in 1936) in 1951 and going so frustratingly close to capturing the Olympic title in 1952. While Lindy Remigino and Herb McKenley dipped for the tape, he maintained his classic upright form through the finish line. As he remarked ruefully: "It was one of those times when if I'd stuck out my chest I might have won." A native of Trinidad, 'Mac' – like his Polyechnic Harriers clubmate Arthur Wint – volunteered for wartime service in the RAF. During the post-war period the pair of them were among the most popular athletes ever to set foot on a British track and great role models. 'Mac' finally hung up his spikes in 1953, aged 32, in order to turn, briefly as it transpired, to rugby league. He eventually returned to Trinidad and died there in 2013, four days before his 93rd birthday.

Athletics Weekly and *Athletics World* satisfied most of my appetite for news and results. But in 1952 I also began subscribing to *Track & Field News*.

The US athletics scene had long fascinated me. There was so much glamour attached to such names as Harrison Dillard, Glenn Davis, Bob Richards, Parry O'Brien and Bob Mathias, and TFN stimulated my interest and admiration even further. Little did I know that many years later I would come close to being appointed the magazine's editor!

Another hugely important addition to my fast growing store of athletics literature was the second (1952) edition of the *International Athletics Annual* by the Association of Track & Field Statisticians, the editors being Fulvio Regli, the ATFS secretary from Switzerland, and Roberto Quercetani, the president from Italy. The ATFS had been founded in Brussels during the 1950 European Championships by a group of 11 track nuts with the aim, in Quercetani's words, of "documenting the present and recovering the past, in order to commit to future memory the efforts of thousands of athletes, men and women, who have given lustre to the sport all over the world. Our aim was to promote such a work at both national and international levels." Actually, the women's side of the sport was barely covered in that publication, just 17 pages out of 217, but otherwise there was every statistic one could crave for: world, European and national records, first three places in 1951 national championships and such events as the inaugural Pan American Games, results of the international matches which were then so prevalent, and deep world and European year lists. The national records of 36 countries were included, from Argentina to Yugoslavia, but not such future powerhouses as Kenya, Ethiopia, Cuba, Jamaica or China. The only Africans to appear in the world list were white South Africans, French West Africans Papa Gallo Thiam (high jump) and M'Baye Malic (hop, step and jump as the triple jump was known then), and UK-based Nigerian long jumper Sylvanus Williams.

Harold Abrahams was the ATFS honorary president and Norris McWhirter a founding member. The next Britons to be invited to become members were Ross McWhirter, Jack Barlow and Teddy O'Neill in 1952, Richard Szreter in 1954, and then in 1958 Neil Allen, Stan Greenberg, Bob Sparks and myself ... but that's getting way ahead of this narrative.

A word here about Roberto Quercetani. For "nuts" like myself, RLQ is the maestro. His pioneering work revolutionised the collection of statistics and over the years his output has been prodigious, including a series of wonderfully researched and written historical books. It has indeed been a privilege to have corresponded, and on occasion spent time, with a man who has certainly been a major inspiration. And what longevity. Here is someone who witnessed Luigi Beccali setting an Italian 800m record in Florence during the half-time interval of a football match in 1933 ... and published his final (?) book, *Intriguing Facts & Figures from Athletics History*, in 2015 at the age of 93!

The most memorable athlete of 1953 for me was Gordon Pirie, Britain's answer to Emil Zátopek. Like his Czech hero, the young South London Harrier trained incredibly hard, causing some observers to warn that he would soon burn himself out. That didn't happen as he went on to enjoy a long career at or near the top, although he might have been even more successful had he eased off a little prior to major races. He started his fabulous 1953 campaign by winning the national cross country title by over a minute from Frank Sando, while on the track he competed in 32 individual races ranging from 800m to 10,000m, won 27 of them, set world records for 6 miles (28:19.4 at the AAA Championships) and 4x1500m relay, and smashed British records at various distances including 3000m, 3 miles, 5000m and 10,000m. The tall, crewcut "thin man of athletics" was seemingly always in conflict with officialdom and the press but the fans loved him and he inspired a whole generation of runners, some (including myself) believing that by blowing out their cheeks as Pirie did it would help make them run faster! Never one to doubt his ability, he proclaimed that he would eventually run 5000m in 13:40. The world record stood then at 13:58.2 and such a time was the stuff of science fiction, it would seem ... but, sure enough, in 1956 he ran 13:36.8 on a rain-sodden Norwegian track, defeating Vladimir Kuts into the bargain.

Going back to 1953, though, Pirie's most memorable race was the inaugural Emsley Carr Mile at the White City. British athletics' most important sponsor, the *News of the World*, spared no expense in promoting this race at their traditional August British Games. Named in memory of a former editor of the newspaper, the race was preceded by what Norris McWhirter described as "a motorised lap of honour for four of the greatest milers of the past in an open Lagonda." The passengers were none other than former British record holder Joe Binks (79) and world record breakers Paavo Nurmi (56), Sydney Wooderson (38) and Gunder Hägg (34). The race itself could have been an anti-climax after that, but it turned out to be a thriller as Pirie, who had never run faster than 4:11.0, produced a 58.4 last quarter-mile lap to win in 4:06.8 a stride or two ahead of American star Wes Santee, a 4:02.4 performer who would go on to clock 4:00.5 in 1955. I'm unsure whether it actually happened or not but I have a recollection of hats being tossed into the air as Pirie crossed the line for an unexpected victory. In fairness to Santee, it should be noted that this was his 27th race in 40 days, outclassing even Pirie in his appetite for competition (and expenses).

Unfortunately, like Nurmi and Hägg among others, Santee was discovered to have transgressed the strict amateur rules of that era and his career came to a premature end. What a tragedy and farce those rules – framed in class conscious Victorian times – were. Why shouldn't top athletes, whose arduous training and dedication to perfecting their talent was just as intense as an opera singer, ballet dancer, concert pianist or violinist, not be rewarded materially for attracting a paying audience? Instead, for decades, there was what was known as "shamateurism" whereby certain distinguished athletes would receive undercover payments. It was a shabby arrangement and hypocritical too as officials must have known how widespread the practice was but only occasionally did they make an example of someone by banning them for life. Pirie somehow managed to maintain his amateur status and as late as 1960 finally fulfilled one of his most nagging ambitions by running a 3:59.9 mile.

Meanwhile, my own ever modest running career was progressing as in 1953 I made the school team for the first time. One of my races was a 440 yards handicap in which, off 70 yards, I was caught just before the finish by an "old boy" of the school, Harry Kane – a name rather better known today as a prolific goal scorer for the Spurs. The original Harry Kane, one of the sport's great characters, was destined the following year to break Lord Burghley's 22 year-old British record for 400m hurdles with 51.5. A somewhat lesser achievement over one lap of the track in 1954 was my under-16 victory in the North East London Grammar Schools championships at Eton Manor (now part of the London Olympic complex), reducing my best 440 yards time by three seconds. The cinders were those transported from the Wembley Olympic track, and so I was running on the same surface as my hero Arthur Wint when winning the 1948 400m gold medal in 46.2! A couple of weeks later I lined up at the White City for the North London finals. Inspired by the venue I placed fourth in another big personal best. Having improved from 66 sec at 14 to 57 at 15 I was convinced that within a few years, as I grew bigger and stronger, I would surely break 50 sec. It didn't happen. I never ran as fast again as I gradually moved up in distance.

I used to train on Sunday mornings at Victoria Park in East London and was star-struck at sharing the track, so to speak, with several international athletes from Essex Ladies, most notably Jean Desforges who in 1954 won the European long jump title and married Ron Pickering. Many years later the Pickerings became good friends of mine.

That year of 1954 was a notable one for the Watman family as on April 4 my dear sister Benita, aged 20, was married to Charles Sharon, who by coincidence happened to be a road runner with the Oxford & St George's Boys' Club in the East End.

It was a memorable year for me too, and could have been even more so had I not had to sit my GCE French Oral examination on May 6. I had a feeling that Roger Bannister might become the world's first sub-four minute miler in Oxford that day and but for that exam I would have played truant from school and caught a coach to Oxford. Unlike Edith Piaf, I still have regrets! Still, it was so exciting to hear about the record and watch film of it on television that night. I had been following Bannister's career closely since my first glimpse of him four years earlier; he was like a Greek god in action and no one was ever able to match his finishing kick.

I can still recall the suspense as to who would be the first to reach that particular milestone in sporting history. Bannister was the favourite to succeed, particularly when it was revealed that shortly before the 1952 Helsinki Olympics he had clocked the sensational time of 2:52.9 in a three-quarter mile time trial. Ironically, it was his "failure" to win the Olympic 1500m title which would lead to his very special place in athletics history. Had he been crowned Olympic champion he would have retired and concentrated immediately on his medical career. Instead he decided to give himself two more years in pursuit of the sub-four minute mile.

That he would get there first was by no means sure, but he was certainly spurred on by the news in December 1952 that Australia's John Landy, who had been eliminated in the heats of the Olympic 1500m and 5000m, had suddenly improved from 4:10.0 to 4:02.1 – a time bettered only by the Swedish duo of Gunder Hägg (4:01.3 in 1945) and Arne Andersson (4:01.6 in 1944). The race was on!

I was staggered by the speed of Landy's progress. I had seen him compete at the White City earlier in 1952 and although I recall his being quite an elegant runner I had no inkling then that he would quickly become Bannister's main rival for miling immortality. Although the British newspapers would run a few lines on Landy's performances "down under" I relied on AW's Australian correspondent Joe Galli for in-depth accounts of his races. Any scepticism about Landy's time was swept away in January 1953 when, in cold and windy conditions, he clocked 4:02.8. Later that month, on a grass track, he won the Australian title in 4:04.2 ... although Galli's comment that "this must stamp this boy as the greatest miler ever" was somewhat premature!

Landy did not come to Europe in the summer of 1953, so Bannister had the stage to himself – or almost. Paced by Chris Chataway at Oxford in May, he broke Wooderson's British record of 4:04.2 with 4:03.6 in windy conditions, and the following month at Motspur Park he was timed at 4:02.0. That mark was never ratified as it was in effect an illegally paced time trial inserted into a schools meeting, but the target was getting closer. However, a few days earlier another contender joined the race in the person of American college student Santee who ran 4:02.4, covering the second half in an unprecedented 1:57.1. Now there were three genuine candidates eager to snatch the prize.

Landy had the best chance of getting below four minutes first as his opening serious mile race of the new Australian campaign would take place in December 1953. And what a start: winning by over 200 yards he clocked 4:02.0. He followed with a 4:02.4 and 4:02.6, but that was it in terms of fast times. The spotlight now turned on Bannister and Santee. In April 1954 Santee ran 4:03.1 and in late May he improved to 4:01.3, equal to Hägg's old record, but by then it was too late ... for Bannister had pre-empted him and every other miler who had dreamt of being the first to break four minutes. He achieved that feat in his first race since the previous August. Chris Brasher towed him through the first lap in 57.4 and passed halfway in 1:58.0. Chris Chataway then took over and reached the three-quarter mark in 3:00.4, a tenth of a second ahead of Bannister. A last lap of 59.4 was required for eternal glory, and Bannister's lungs and long strides were up to the challenge. Almost unconscious as he snapped the tape, the watches stopped at 3:59.4. He had covered the laps in 57.5, 60.7, 62.3 and 58.9. I was in seventh heaven when I heard the news that evening and, for the first of countless times, watched on TV the film of this epic run. It wasn't a race; as with the 4:02.0 effort it was essentially a paced time trial but as the pacemakers completed the distance the time was accepted for record purposes.

Now the question was how good a racer was Bannister, and we would soon find out as he and Landy – who broke the world record in Finland on June

21 with a stunning 3:57.9 – were due to clash at the British Empire & Commonwealth Games in Vancouver in August. This was billed as the "mile of the century" and it certainly lived up to the hype. It was a classic confrontation between the front runner and the kicker. As someone who has always been a front running fan, an admirer of the courage required to cut out a scorching pace in an attempt to burn off an opponent's superior finishing speed, I should have willed Landy to victory. But patriotism prevailed and I was elated when Bannister caught and passed his rival to win in the British record time of 3:58.8. Landy had been almost ten yards up at halfway but Bannister gradually narrowed that deficit so that at the bell he was within a stride's length. On the final bend the Australian shot a nervous glance to his left ... at the precise moment that the Englishman overtook on the right. Yes, Bannister had proved himself a formidable man v man racer, not simply a great runner against the clock, and he brought his athletics career to an end three weeks later with a sublime performance over 1500m at the European Championships in Bern where an unheard of final 200m covered in just 25 sec demolished the best that continent could offer. He had fulfilled his ambitions as an athlete, went on to become a distinguished neurologist and in 1975 was knighted for services to medicine.

Joy and despair are two emotions familiar to athletes striving for success, and in Vancouver while the crowd was still excitedly discussing that epic mile, the mood changed at the sight of poor Jim Peters entering the stadium literally miles ahead of the opposition in the marathon but barely conscious. Having typically refused to compromise with the searing heat that day, Peters became seriously dehydrated and proceeded to horrify the spectators for the next eleven minutes as he repeatedly fell over while groggily attempting to cover the last few hundred yards of track. The agony came to an end, at least for the crowd, just 200 yards from the mirage of the finishing tape when officials, unable to stand by helplessly any longer, carried him off. Peters never raced again, lucky to stay alive, and for the rest of his life he was afflicted by headaches and giddiness from that ordeal in the sun. The winner was Scotland's Joe McGhee but just as the 1908 Olympic marathon will for ever be remembered for the name of the loser, Dorando Pietri, so this race will always be associated with Jim Peters. He later received a special gold medal from the spectating Duke of Edinburgh inscribed: "To J Peters as a token of admiration for a most gallant marathon runner."

I was not in Vancouver, but I had witnessed three of Jim's greatest triumphs. He was tenacity personified, someone who had trained so hard to transform himself from a moderate long distance track runner into the man who revolutionised marathon standards of performance. In 1952, 1953 and 1954 I was privileged to have been at the finish line at the Polytechnic Stadium in Chiswick, West London to see him smash the world record, first with 2:20:43 and then with 2:18:41 and 2:17:40. In those days a marathon field would number less than 200 hardened former track runners who had moved up in distance as their speed deteriorated, and it would have been utterly impossible to imagine that around 40,000 runners would one day contest something called the London Marathon – the brainchild of Peters' 1952 Olympic team-mates Chris Brasher and John Disley!

For the last few decades not just the marathon but middle and long distance running, including the steeplechase, has been dominated by runners from East Africa, specifically Kenya and Ethiopia. Yet, prior to 1954, there was no indication of what was to come. You would look in vain at the deep 1953 world lists in the *International Athletics Annual* for any names from that region, but I was fortunate enough to witness the start of the African running revolution at the 1954 AAA Championships. The 3 miles featured a terrific scrap with Freddie Green holding off Chris Chataway by inches as both were credited with a world record of 13:32.2. More significant, in historical terms, was the performance by the distant third finisher in 13:54.8, Nyandika Maiyoro of Kenya. He held a lead of some 45 yards after a seemingly suicidal first mile of 4:23.4 and was still on world record pace as he traded strides with Chataway and Green at 2 miles in 9:01.6 before dropping away. As Jimmy Green enthused in his report for AW: "His action was the nearest to the ideal I have yet seen for a track distance runner, so effortless, so economical, yet so effective. Never again shall we nurse the idea that the coloured races are no good at anything beyond a mile." Maiyoro went on to run 13:43.8 for fourth place in Vancouver behind the English trio of Chataway, Green and Frank Sando, while fellow Kenyan Lazaro Chepkwony finished seventh in the 6 miles, which saw another clean sweep by England thanks to Peter Driver, Sando and Jim Peters (seven days before that fateful marathon).

The seed was sown and in 1960 Abebe Bikila of Ethiopia, running barefoot, won the Olympic marathon in world record time. He retained the title in 1964, again with a world record, and at the Mexico City Games of 1968, a high altitude venue which clearly favoured runners from the Rift Valley, Kenya got into the act with gold medals in the 1500m, 10,000m and steeplechase while the marathon was won by an Ethiopian for the third time. Since then, East Africans have won the Olympic 800m five times, 1500m three times, 5000m and 10,000m five times, marathon four times and steeplechase (all Kenyans) an astonishing ten times! Back in 1954 no one even thought about African women athletes (other than white females from South Africa and Rhodesia) but athletes from Mozambique, Kenya, Ethiopia and South Africa have since 1992 collected numerous Olympic titles at distances between 800m and the marathon.

The week after Jim Peters' final marathon world record, an important milestone was reached in my fledgling athletics writing career. I had already contributed various odds and ends to AW but in the July 3 1954 issue Jimmy Green published my first by-lined article, on American decathlon great Bob Mathias. I was on cloud nine. A few weeks later I left school. I had the GCE passes I needed to qualify for a career in journalism and I couldn't wait to get started.

3. LEARNING MY TRADE (1954-1957)

It wasn't that easy. As soon as I realised I would not need to return to school (all my closest friends were staying on to the sixth form and ultimately university) I began writing to just about every local newspaper in the London area seeking employment as a trainee reporter, but to no avail. My English and careers master Joe Brearley, who some years earlier had nurtured the literary talents of one Harold Pinter, had warned me it would be difficult to break into journalism and he and my cautious parents advised a "safe" career in banking, insurance, shipping and the like. The thought appalled me. Fortunately, a lifeline was offered by the Westminster Press Provincial Newspapers Group, whose London office was situated in Fleet Street – the "street of adventure" which then was the home of most of Britain's national newspapers. The job wasn't really what I wanted – it was as an "editorial messenger" or in effect an office boy – but at least it would give me a foothold in a journalistic environment. It was up to me as to what I could make of the opportunity.

In fact I did make the most of what might have been a dead-end job. I started work in September 1954 and although I did run errands occasionally for the sub-editors I was based mainly in the reference library. There I was in contact all the time with reporters coming in to check facts and consult the shelves of reference books and newspaper files. My primary duty was to clip out, label and file newspaper and magazine items designated by the two librarians for use by reporters researching stories, and to help them find what they required from such works of reference as *Who's Who*, *Burke's Peerage* and *Hansard*. On occasion I would be transferred to the City office to work out rises and falls in share prices and – best of all – I would link up most Saturdays with sports reporter Ted Hart, a former even-time sprinter (i.e. 10 sec for 100 yards) who was a joy to work with. I would dictate his reports from top football matches, including the 1955 FA Cup Final (Newcastle United 3, Manchester City 1), to a copy-taker back in Fleet Street. How I envied Ted's job!

While I continued to hunt for a proper trainee journalist post on a suburban paper, but was still getting nowhere, I used my initiative to drum up some freelance work at the Westminster Press. My starting wage was a princely three pounds a week (equivalent to £75 in today's money) but I was soon augmenting that as I seized the opportunity to contribute items for the "London Letter" column which was syndicated to all the group's titles, which included the *Oxford Mail*, *Northern Echo*, *Yorkshire Observer*, *Birmingham Gazette* and countless others. Better still, once the London sports editor realised I had a good knowledge of athletics he relied on me, from February 1955, to provide previews and reports on major events. I still have a scrapbook containing those yellowing articles, including an on-the-spot report from the White City on a world mile record in May 1955 by Birmingham's Diane Leather. I was now gaining invaluable experience of dictating my own live reports down a telephone line and I am perpetually grateful to that sports editor, Albert Shaw, for his trust and confidence in a 16 year-old kid. In fact I was contributing so many pieces to the newspaper group that the accounts department was querying why an office junior on £3 per week was often collecting more than double that!

One stirring athletics occasion which came too early for me to report on was the celebrated London v Moscow floodlit meeting at the White City in October 1954. I had only been working for a few weeks and following a frantic Tube journey after clocking off at 5 pm I just managed to get into the stadium before the gates were closed. The atmosphere that night was electric and of course the highlight was the 5000m clash between Chris Chataway and Vladimir Kuts. As with Landy against Bannister, I should have been supporting the front-running Soviet sailor but Chataway, the charismatic 'red fox' of British athletics, had long been one of my favourites and I cheered myself hoarse on his behalf. Even now, well over 60 years later, that race remains among the most thrilling I've ever witnessed. After a fabulous duel Chataway managed to snap the tape just ahead in a world record shattering 13:51.6 and the packed stadium went wild.

That run by Chataway created such a strong impression that a few weeks later he won the inaugural BBC Sports Personality of the Year award, beating his good friend Bannister, for whom he had been such a valuable pacemaker early in the season. And what a long season it had been, starting for Chataway at Oxford on May 6 and climaxing at White City on October 13. Chataway continued his running career until the 1956 Olympics but there were other fields to conquer. In September 1955 he became ITV's first newscaster and later worked for the BBC's Panorama. He became a Conservative MP in 1959, in his maiden speech recommending that the England cricket team should refuse to play in apartheid South Africa, and between 1970 and 1974 he served first as Minister for Posts & Telecommunications and later as Minister for Industrial Development. This renaissance man then left politics for a distinguished career as a merchant banker and in 1991 was appointed chairman of the Civil Aviation Authority, being knighted in 1995 for services to aviation.

Surprisingly, for someone who trained lightly and enjoyed a cigarette, Chataway maintained a remarkably high level of fitness all his life, running a 5:36 mile when he was 64 and clocking 1 hr 52 min for the Great North Run half marathon when he was 79. He died in 2014, aged 82. By way of contrast, Kuts put on an immense amount of weight after he stopped running in 1959, became an alcoholic and died at 48. Pirie, one of his great rivals, always maintained that Kuts was on drugs in his racing days but that was never proven.

The year of 1955 proved a notable one for me on many levels. I journeyed abroad for the first time, wrote my first (and only) travel article and finally landed a job as a trainee journalist.

I had always wanted to travel but my first destination abroad was an unusual one … Warsaw. The occasion was a World Youth Festival which incorporated a star-studded five-day athletics meeting. As soon as I learned that my hero Emil Zátopek was due to race there in the 5000m and 10,000m I was determined to sign up for a tour (£29 all-in) organised by Stan Levenson, who I didn't know at the time but who ultimately became a valued colleague as the athletics correspondent and sports editor of the *Daily Worker* (later *Morning Star*). Originally two or three of my closest friends were going to accompany me but they opted instead for a school trip to Austria. The festival was overtly political, celebrating communism, and among the 500 British participants I was probably the only one who didn't toe the party line. I was certainly a Labour Party supporter in those days but no admirer of the Soviet system. However, I was curious to see at first hand a communist country although my priority was to witness a top class athletics meeting.

That it was, and my extensive report filled several pages of AW, a momentous decision (for me) by editor Jimmy Green as normally he would have left the coverage to his Prague-based correspondent Armour Milne but I beat him to it. Zátopek did indeed win the 10,000m but later, sitting next to him while we watched the women's long jump, he told me "I am no good this year." The star turn actually was the one western athlete present, the glamorous 1952 Olympic 80m hurdles champion Shirley de la Hunty (née Strickland), who not only won her speciality but set a world record of 11.3 for 100m. After standing up repeatedly to the Soviet national anthem at the victory ceremonies I felt really proud when the strains of "God Save The Queen" drifted over the loudspeakers to mark the Australian's wins.

As there were no printed programmes and the announcements were in Polish, I had to rely on the newspapers to copy out the results. However, at one session I was greatly assisted by a group of Polish "nuts" sitting behind me. They jotted down the times and measurements for me and in return I showed them a copy of the *1955 International Athletics Annual*, which had them chattering excitedly. They were astounded to read of an 81.29m javelin throw by the USA's Bill Miller in California in August 1954 – they had heard nothing about it and the "chief nut" was himself a 60m javelin thrower.

Never mind the athletics, it was an extraordinary experience to go behind the Iron Curtain at the height of the Cold War. As a non-believer in the Soviet bloc's political system I was forever having heated but stimulating discussions with those who felt that Marxism was the only way forward. "Anyway," I wrote in my diary of the trip, "there was a good deal of tolerance on both sides – this was the period of goodwill immediately following the original Geneva Summit." The talks were aimed at reducing international tension and although the Cold War would linger until 1991 they were an important step in preventing World War Three.

The 1400 mile journey to Warsaw was an epic in itself. We left London's Victoria Station at 8.20 am on July 30 and following the Dover-Ostend ferry crossing a specially chartered steam-powered train drew away from the Belgian port. The train was packed and my home for the next two days was a wooden seat! We crossed into Germany at Aachen and reached Nuremberg at 7.15 am on July 31. We had five hours to kill and I spent the morning walking around the city. I noted in my diary that the girls in our group, dressed in jeans and slacks, were looked upon with disapproval by the locals, most of whom made clucking noises. Obviously Sunday mornings in Bavaria were no time for frivolity. We crossed the Czechoslovak border at Cheb and there, and during subsequent stops in Pilsen and Prague, we were greeted enthusiastically by hundreds of people. My feeling was that the Czechs, and later the Poles, were not cheering us because most of us were communist sympathisers but because they thought we were a typical cross-section of British youth eager to see and learn about their countries and thus contribute a little towards international peace and understanding. The Polish border (Zebrzydowice) was reached at 8 am on August 1 and at last we steamed into Warsaw at 3.35 pm.

The festival was a more lavish affair than I had expected. Just walking down the street was a memorable experience as Russians, Arabs, Chinese, delegates from all parts of the world, would file past. Even Hollywood could not have matched the scene around the hideous Soviet-style Palace of Culture each evening as young men and women, dressed mostly in national costume, mingled together. National, racial and religious barriers appeared to be non-existent ... it was a glimpse of a Utopian world, although I realised that almost without exception these joyful men and women were distrustful of the western democracies.

During my 11-day stay I met a journalist of about 40 who talked freely to me in English. He vividly described what life was like in (or rather under – in the sewers) Warsaw during the wartime occupation by the Nazis. He explained why cats and dogs were nowhere to be seen. When people are starving to death they will eat anything. That he survived such hardship was miraculous, but I knew he was not exaggerating. Andrzej Wajda's great film *Kanal*, which came out in 1957, bore out his experiences. As I wrote in my diary: "I was only a fortnight older than when I had set out, but I think I gained about ten years in experience."

Keen to share my impressions of war-torn Warsaw and its courageous inhabitants, I wrote an article which was published in such Westminster Press titles as the *Swindon Evening News* (headline: "Warsaw – The World's Most Austere City") and *Shields Gazette* ("Blasted, Burnt Warsaw Still Stands In Its Ruins"). I reported that London, Berlin and Hiroshima had suffered terribly during the Second World War but ten years later had recovered almost completely and once again were noisy, thriving cities. But nearly half of Warsaw was still in ruins. When the city had been liberated in January 1945 more than three-quarters had been reduced to rubble and its pre-war population of 1,300,000 had shrunk to a pitiful 100,000. The once large Jewish community had been completely exterminated.

I wrote: "Now Warsaw can boast a million inhabitants again. Yet not more than 60% of the city has been rebuilt, with the result that many families live in very bad conditions. True, Warsaw lives again but communist propaganda stating that Warsaw is completely rebuilt, due entirely to the virtues of socialism, is so much nonsense."

It was in October 1955 that I left the Westminster Press, having learned so much during my year there. Opportunity had knocked at last and I was employed as a trainee journalist with the *Hatfield & Potters Bar Gazette*, a brash local weekly tabloid which hadn't long been in existence and was fighting an ultimately losing battle against two well entrenched and conservative rivals in the *Barnet Press* and *Herts Advertiser*. Unlike my closest school friends (and future wife) I never attended university but I reckon my three years on the *Gazette* taught me more about life and people than any academic institution.

Mind you, I came perilously close to missing out on the *Gazette* ... and indeed on the next 60-odd years. The week before I started my new job I happened to be in Potters Bar to attend a lecture on "Britain's place in world athletics" by one of my heroes (journalistically if not politically), Norris McWhirter. I already knew Norris and his twin brother Ross from my Fleet Street days as they produced the wonderful magazine *Athletics World* nearby and each month I would call in to collect an advance copy. After the lecture, Norris offered to give me and Don Vanhegan, an all-round thrower of repute, a lift in his Mercedes. As we sped down Stagg Hill towards Cockfosters we skidded clean off the road and ended up in a field on the other side. We were lucky to escape death or serious injury and, after checking we were all in one piece and some careful manoeuvring back onto the road south, the journey was completed at a more sedate pace. Norris, of course, was the man who the previous year had – with a great show of suspense – announced to the crowd at Iffley Road that his friend Roger Bannister had dipped below four minutes, and it was in 1955 that the brothers produced the first edition of the ground-breaking *Guinness Book of Records*.

My first editor at the *Gazette*, David Pryke, was a bright and breezy type who had touching (reckless?) faith in his new 17 year-old recruit as within the first few weeks I was trusted with covering court cases, inquests and local council meetings as well as chasing up all manner of news stories, making regular visits to the Potters Bar police and fire stations and dropping in each week to all the local churches for details of fetes and whatever. Other tasks included attending the occasional Women's Institute meeting ... alas, there were no Calendar Girls in the strait-laced fifties! In time I became the paper's drama critic and sports editor, my duties including following the Hatfield Town football team home and away. I worked all hours for very little money, but I loved it all and there was one welcome perk. In return for publicising the latest film releases I was given a free pass to cinemas in Potters Bar and Barnet. Next to athletics, the cinema was my greatest passion during my teenage years. I would not only watch practically every American and British film, Hollywood musicals like *Singin' In The Rain, An American in Paris, Oklahoma!, On The Town, Seven Brides for Seven Brothers, Carousel, Guys and Dolls* and *South Pacific* being among my absolute favourites, but I would also appreciate subtitled foreign language classics from France, Italy, Sweden, Russia and Japan.

Of course, donning my sports editor's hat, I devoted plenty of space to the activities of Potters Bar Athletic Club. The 1956 edition of the club's well supported under-21 road relay was started by none other than Tom Hampson, the 1932 Olympic 800m champion and world record breaker. It was a thrill to meet him, as it was to talk with the referee, Stan Tomlin, the Empire Games 3 miles champion of 1930. Stan would later become a work colleague when we started a St Albans edition of the paper and he – a talented journalist who edited his own athletics magazine – was on the staff as a reporter. I also got to know the club's honorary secretary, Barry Willis, who would go on to become a long serving (1965-1982) and highly respected honorary secretary of the Amateur Athletic Association.

Speaking of the AAA, an amusing insight into the ridiculous and draconian amateur laws of the time was provided when I had to register with Ernest Clynes, then the honorary secretary, declaring that I was a full-time professional journalist. Only on that basis could I retain my amateur status as an athlete. Had I earned money writing on athletics as a sideline I would have been banned!

During my time on the *Gazette*, the easy-going John Winder succeeding David Pryke as editor, I also had to attend a weekly course for young journalists at what was then the North West London Polytechnic in Kentish Town but which later was upgraded to the University of North London and is now part of London Metropolitan University. A group of us learning our trade on local newspapers were instructed in such subjects as English literature, economics, British institutions and law for journalists. Pitman's shorthand was an option but I gave that up after a while, preferring to employ my own system of abbreviations (and later making good use of miniature tape and cassette recorders), while my typing gradually got faster and more accurate from constant practice. In May 1959 I passed the National Council for the Training of Journalists' Proficiency Test. I was now a fully qualified journalist, an enthusiastic member of the National Union of Journalists and proud possessor of the NUJ's Press card which ensured that never again would I have to pay to attend an athletics meeting! There was only one snag ... the *Gazette* had ceased publication a few weeks earlier and I was out of a job.

But we are leaping ahead of ourselves, for much was happening in the world of athletics and athletics journalism while I was still with the paper. Let's return to 1955, because that summer, while competing for Grafton Athletic Club in an inter-club match at Parliament Hill, I happened to eavesdrop on a conversation in the dressing room between two older clubmates I had not met before. Stan Greenberg and Alf Wilkins were talking about the German sprinter Heinz Fütterer, who the previous year had equalled McDonald Bailey's European 100m record of 10.2. I knew about his exploits and butted in. They were surprised someone so young would even have heard of Fütterer, and a friendship was formed which has lasted for over 60 years.

Alf, a chartered accountant, became a successful coach in his spare time and Stan went on to become sports editor of the *Guinness Book of Records* and for several years was BBC Television's athletics statistician. Far in the future, Stan would be the best man at my wedding in 1973 and barely a day goes by without one of us phoning the other to discuss the latest results. For many years we have sat together in the press box at major meetings, two elder statesmen of athletics all too reminiscent of Statler and Waldorf in *The Muppet Show*!

That encounter with Alf and Stan was one of several steps which led towards the creation of the NUTS (National Union of Track Statisticians), of which more later.

Ever since I attended the 1950 edition of the AAA Championships I have missed only a couple over the years and the 1956 meeting at the White City was interesting in that Britain's only gold medallist later that year at the Melbourne Olympics was steeplechaser Chris Brasher and yet at the AAA Championships he placed only third (9:02.6) way behind Eric Shirley (8:51.6) and John Disley (8:53.4). The British team selectors have not always been over generous, and could have opted to pick just the top two, but on this occasion they did well to include Brasher who – at the Games – ran an inspired race, knocking six seconds off his previous best with a British and Olympic record of 8:41.2. He never set world records like Roger Bannister and Chris Chataway but of the trio who planned and executed the first sub-four minute mile he alone became an Olympic medallist. As Chataway once remarked of Brasher: "He is 5 per cent ability and 95 per cent guts." Someone else, less charitably, referred to him as the original Achilles heel!

Just after the Games, in December 1956, I had a letter published in AW, extolling the promise of Elliott Denman, who at 22 had finished 11th for the USA in the 50 kilometres walk in Melbourne. I had a particular interest in Elliott's career, for we had been pen friends for the past few years. It all started with a letter from Elliott in *World Sports*, a great British magazine long since gone, concerning Lindy Remigino, the unexpected winner of the 1952 Olympic 100m. As Elliott's New York address was printed, I wrote to him … and that was the beginning of a transatlantic friendship that has flourished ever since. In those early days we would exchange magazines, clippings etc and any package postmarked New York would be a cornucopia of delights. Later in this story I will tell of my momentous first visit to the USA as the guest of Elliott and his parents.

I had an obsessional interest in all things American. I was brought up, of course, on Hollywood movies but I also read voraciously such authors as John Steinbeck and Ernest Hemingway, loved jazz and the music of George Gershwin and his contemporaries, and many of my favourite TV shows were imports from across the pond. I would visit the US Embassy in London to read American newspapers and I subscribed to the *New Yorker* magazine as well as occasionally buying *Time Magazine*, *Newsweek* and *The Saturday Evening Post*.

Looking back all those years, I don't know how I found the time or energy to pursue so many interests. I had a demanding job with long hours and, still a junior and now a sub-5 minute miler, I trained when I could. Victoria Park in East London, a track my club Grafton AC shared with Victoria Park Harriers, was where I had always done my track sessions but from early in 1957 I would take a long bus journey across London most Sunday mornings to Tooting Bec where I would train alongside Derek Ibbotson (or rather my training would constitute his warm-up as he might run 20 to 25 quarters in 60 sec each with a 50 sec recovery!) and his wife Madeline, herself an international half miler and future English cross country champion.

I certainly can't claim any credit but "Ibbo" went on to have a fantastic year in 1957. Previously best known as a three miler, who had beaten Chataway in a thrilling AAA title battle in 1956, he astonished everyone (like Gordon Pirie in 1953) in the Emsley Carr Mile that summer. His best official time was 4:07.0 although he had clocked 4:04.4 in training, and had only entered because Madeline wanted an extra ticket for the post-meeting banquet. He created a sensation by winning in 3:59.4, with Ireland's Ron Delany – destined to win the Olympic 1500m crown in Melbourne some months later – a distant third. The ever jaunty Ibbotson, now dubbed "The Four Minute Smiler", thought he could have won that title but was instead selected for the 5000m where he collected the bronze medal behind Kuts and Pirie.

In June 1957 (two months after I became an uncle when my sister Benita gave birth to Sandra) Derek celebrated the birth of his first child by setting a European mile record of 3:58.4 in Glasgow, second only to John Landy's 3:57.9 from 1954, and the following month at the White City he ran the race of his life to break the world record with 3:57.2, destroying a great field in the process. Such was his zest for competition and popularity with meeting promoters and fans that he went on to race too frequently and he never reached those sublime heights again.

It was during 1957 that I got increasingly involved with AW. It was a case of being in the right place at the right time. Jimmy Green recognised my youthful enthusiasm and encouraged me to contribute more to the magazine. I was particularly keen to develop the statistical and international aspects of the publication and in February I sent in coverage of the American indoor season, and from March there was a 'World News by Melvyn Watman' section in practically every issue. This was because Teddy O'Neill, who had compiled the overseas news and results for several years, was about to retire and Jimmy needed someone to succeed him. I was delighted to oblige. I may have been paid peanuts but I didn't mind; I would gladly have done it for nothing. Apart from a break during my National Service I would continue to provide AW's overseas coverage for most of the next 30 years.

I even managed in March 1957 to get my name in the classified results section for the first and only time, as winner of the Grafton AC 4 miles road handicap. I can't imagine who would have taken the trouble to submit that result.

What I desired most of all was to be asked to report on British meetings for AW and my chance came at the London v New York match in July 1957. Jimmy Green, who until then practically monopolised such coverage, wrote about the first day's proceedings, including Ibbotson's world record, but left me to cover the second day. There I was, up in the White City press box at last, rubbing shoulders with famous (in some cases infamous?) Fleet Street reporters for the first time. I must have worked fast on my report, and popped it into the post, because that very evening I was on my way to Yugoslavia! Although I had left Hackney Downs three years earlier, I joined in a school trip organised by Les Mitchell and Joe Brearley as three of my closest school friends – Stan Posner, Hugh Harvey and Harold Heller – had signed up for it. After a thousand mile train journey through Belgium, Germany and Austria, we arrived in Ljubljana (now the capital of Slovenia) where our guide was Luba Andelkovic, a former 400m international. Yes, there was always an athletics connection wherever I went! Luba introduced me to several of the country's leading athletes, forming the basis for an article on Yugoslav athletics that was published in AW. During the next fortnight we took excursions to some of the most beautiful places imaginable, including Lake Bled and the Lakes of Plitvice (now in Croatia), while it was fascinating to tour the caves of Postojna. The last couple of days of our tour were spent in fabulous Venice, sleeping in a convent!

Always keen to provide AW with new material, at the end of the season I compiled a multi-part series "The Outstanding Athletes of 1957", setting out the achievements during the year of the top 6-12 in the world in each event, and another statistical breakthrough was the appearance of the deepest yet UK year lists (top 50) compiled by Norris McWhirter, Stan Greenberg and myself. From then on the NUTS would take over that role.

4. NUTS & THE BIG APPLE (1958-1959)

Officially the NUTS began life in London on January 31 1958, the founder members in descending order of age being Len Gebbett 35, Stan Greenberg, Alf Wilkins and Martin James 26, 400m star Chris Lindsay 24, ace walker Colin Young 23, Bob Sparks 20 and myself the baby of the group at 19. Some 60 years later Messrs Greenberg, Wilkins, Young and Watman remain committee members, which is fine in terms of experience and commitment ... but where are today's young statisticians?

Bob Sparks, whose son Paul is married to Stan's daughter Karen, tragically passed away in 2003 aged only 65 after a long and courageous battle against leukaemia. His contribution to the NUTS, to the ATFS (of which he was president for 25 years), athletics announcing (at 37 consecutive AAA Championships for example), and the scrupulous collection and scrutiny of results was immense. One of his most valuable services to the sport was examining photo finish prints and it was due to his attention to detail that, although the Olympic authorities have chosen not to make any official amendment, we know it was Shirley Strickland (later de la Hunty) of Australia and not Audrey Patterson of the USA who actually finished third in the 1948 200m final, and it was Bob's eagle eye that determined Daley Thompson had clocked 14.33 and not 14.34 in the 110m hurdles during the 1984 Olympic decathlon, that one extra point enabling him to equal the world record score of 8798, rising under a later version of the scoring tables to 8847 points, which looks like remaining the British record until the end of time.

How did the NUTS come about? It all started when Len, Alf and Stan met up on the ship home from the Helsinki Olympics. Stan pinpoints the fateful rendezvous as in the middle of the Baltic Sea on August 4 1952. The trio realised they shared an interest not only in watching athletics but in collecting facts and figures. They agreed to get together at British meetings and gradually the circle of like enthusiasts who would gather at the White City and other venues to discuss the results widened.

Initially, at a time when various pressure groups were campaigning for the athletics establishment to improve conditions for the athletes and give them more say in the running of the sport, the NUTS was regarded with suspicion by some key figures like Jack Crump, the all-powerful British Board honorary secretary and team manager, for being too youthful and potentially subversive. Individually we may have held radical views on the administration of British athletics but collectively our mission was apolitical; it was to co-ordinate and rationalise the collection and publication in booklet form of the deepest UK year lists ever compiled. The election of Harold Abrahams as our president allayed the fears of Crump and others. The 1924 Olympic gold medallist, then aged 60, was as establishment a figure as you could get but as a pioneering statistician and historian in his own right he was an enthusiastic father figure for us all. He was a hands-on president, happy to attend practically every committee meeting, and it was through his good offices, persuading the British Board to underwrite the costs, that we were able to publish the early editions of the Annual.

As though my involvement with the NUTS wasn't enough (I was its first secretary), 1958 saw another major development in my life. I had always yearned to fly and, as mentioned earlier, I was obsessed with all things American, and in February 1958 I combined the two by spending two fabulous weeks in New York. My pen-pal Elliott Denman, at the time serving a two-year stint in the US Army, saved up his leave to be available as my host and I would be staying with him and his parents in Manhattan.

For as long as I could remember, my imagination fired by watching such films as *On The Town*, I had wanted to "discover" the New World, but I had dismissed the thought as absurd. How could I, a financially strapped young journalist, possibly afford the fare?

What initially sparked things off was the visit back to England in December 1956 of an old friend and training partner, Chris McKenzie (née Slemon), a member of a world record breaking 3x880 yards relay team in 1953 and whose career I had documented in AW. Her accounts of New York, Elliott and his family, and the New York track scene sent my imagination racing. Chris invited me to stay with her and her husband Gordon (US Olympic marathoner) any time, and that gesture really did it. I just had to get to New York.

I narrowed my enquiries to the British airline BOAC and Pan-American Airways. The cheapest air fare was £151 for a 17-day tourist return. That equates to around £1250 in today's prices. I was about to call the whole ridiculous idea off when I picked up a brochure explaining Pan-Am's "Fly Now – Pay Later" scheme. Theoretically, at least, I could buy my ticket with a £15 deposit and pay the balance monthly over two years. With what I was earning, around £6 per week plus a pound or two freelancing, it would be quite a stretch.

It was in October 1957 that Elliott informed me that he had booked two weeks Army leave for February 1958, a particularly apt time as the US indoor season would be at its height. It was all systems go. I paid £52 deposit on the fare (my paternal grandfather Jack loaning me £50, which made all the difference) with the remaining £100 to be paid in 18 monthly instalments. My parents, who at first thought the whole idea was crazy, rallied round when I arranged to visit cousins over in Long Island at the end of the trip.

I kept a diary of my first American adventure and here is an abridged version of my account. I still get out of breath just reading it! Oh to have the boundless energy of a 19 year-old again.

I left my Stoke Newington home at 8.15 pm on Sunday, February 9 and was driven to Victoria Air Terminal by my brother-in-law Charlie in his Isetta bubble car. A BOAC coach carried me to what was then London Airport's ramshackle North Section for long distance destinations – a far cry from the gleaming terminals of today's Heathrow. At 10.50 pm I boarded "Clipper Ganges", a magnificent white Pan-Am DC-7C airliner, the last word in piston engined aircraft. The air hostesses, all of whom looked a million dollars, made the passengers comfortable and as I was seated adjacent to the rear of the starboard wing I had an uninterrupted view of the two engines that side, their flaming exhausts illuminating the wing. At 11.05 pm we thundered down the runway, taking off at a speed I later learned was 140 mph. A few minutes later, dinner was served – my first experience of dining in the clouds. I was just beginning to doze off despite the monotonous drone of the engines when the captain announced while we were over the Irish Sea that owing to a fire warning he was going to "feather" the outer starboard engine, the one I had the best view of, and return to London. The crew told us everything was perfectly safe but as the dreadful Munich air disaster, killing 23 including several Manchester United players, had occurred only three days earlier it was an anxious time. However, my reaction was more frustration than fear. Here I was, with just 15 days to spend in the USA, wasting time before I even arrived!

The flight back to London was extremely uncomfortable. A DC-7C can fly perfectly safely on three engines but the wind tends to shake it unmercifully. The general effect was that of a rough English Channel boat crossing, most of our fuel having been jettisoned over the Irish Sea or Bristol Channel, but we made a perfect landing at 12.45 am. The technical fault took the mechanics over three hours to sort out and it was at 4.30 am that we were aloft again. I managed to sleep intermittently during the next six hours, finally awaking at around 7 am EST (noon GMT) on what was now Monday, February 10. We flew over the ice floes and barren tundra of Newfoundland, Labrador and New Brunswick before breakfast was served over Cape Cod. We passed low over Boston and at 11.25 am (4.25 pm GMT) we touched down at Idlewild (now JFK) Airport, just under 12 hours after leaving London at the second attempt. It was pretty nifty going for a 3500 mile trip in that pre-jet age.

Full of anticipation and perhaps a few qualms, I walked up to the visitors' gallery where I had arranged to meet Elliott. No one there was waiting for me. I knew Elliott would have phoned to check the arrival time so would have known of the delay. I hung around, not quite sure what to do next, when at around 12.30 pm someone tapped me on the shoulder. I whirled around – and there was Chris McKenzie with Elliott and his mother, Theresa. Were we glad to see each other! It transpired that the Denman family car had broken down *en route* to the airport.

Mrs Denman drove us back home by way of a circuitous sightseeing route. In between innumerable questions and reminiscences, we stopped off at the United Nations HQ, Rockefeller Plaza and Broadway. We finally arrived at the Denmans' home, 900 W 190 Street, at around 3 pm and talked incessantly. Elliott and I got on like a house on fire and Mrs D treated me like a long lost son. I got on well also with Elliott's dad, Jack, a dentist with a pronounced Bronx accent. Gordon McKenzie called round and after supper Chris, Gordon, Elliott and I left at 7 pm for an indoor training session. This was certainly going to be an unorthodox holiday!

Gordon drove us to the 369th AAA Armory in Harlem where I did a little training on the 220 yards unbanked track and Elliott introduced me to several members of the New York Pioneer Club, notably head coach Joe

Yancey (who had coached Jamaica's victorious Olympic 4x400m relay team in 1952), walker Ronnie Laird (who in years to come would amass more US national titles than any other athlete) and legendary 440/880 yards runner Reggie Pearman, a member of two world record relay teams in 1952. Everyone was so friendly and much to my surprise I was called upon to make a speech and made an honorary member of the NYPC. I was honoured to be associated with the club, which welcomed the black and Jewish athletes denied membership of the WASP-dominated New York Athletic Club with its ritzy headquarters overlooking Central Park. It wasn't until 1989 that any black athlete competed for NYAC. Some 32 hours after leaving home, I finally turned in at 11.15 pm.

I was up at 6.30 next morning. Elliott's sports journalist friend Marty Lader (who later became a noted tennis writer) called for us in his flashy 1958 Plymouth and at 7.20 we were off ... destination Washington DC. We reached the capital at 1 pm, took in many of the sights, checked in at a motel ($3 a night – those were the days!) and in the evening went to a cinema to see *Bonjour Tristesse* starring David Niven and Deborah Kerr. Next morning we visited the White House, the Smithsonian, the Zoo and Arlington National Cemetery before driving towards Baltimore where for "brunch" I tasted my first (and certainly not last) hamburger and on to Philadelphia, making brief stops at Franklin Field, home of the famed Penn Relays, and Independence Square where the cracked Liberty Bell is housed. We arrived back at 900 W 190 at 10.40 pm and it was 2 am before I finished writing postcards in bed.

Next day would be my first full day in New York City and it started with the first of numerous subway rides, costing 15 cents a time. Elliott and I travelled to downtown Manhattan, walked along Wall Street and toured historic Fraunces Tavern. We then took a trip on the Staten Island Ferry, passing quite close to the Statue of Liberty, and on Broadway we attended an afternoon performance of a fascinating Cinerama travelogue. Next came a tour of the Rockefeller Centre, followed by a visit to St Patrick's Cathedral. Highlights of the following day (other than a huge and delicious slice of cherry pie and an introduction to Grant's Hot Dog Emporium in Times Square) included meeting up again with the ever delightful Chris McKenzie and tours of the *New York Times* building and Radio City.

The schedule for Saturday (February 15) included a family shopping expedition to the local supermarket, which was light years ahead of anything comparable in Britain at that time, and in the evening we made for Madison Square Garden. I got in on a competitor's ticket kindly supplied by the NYPC and after changing in the club's dressing room I was thrilled to jog a mile with Elliott and Ronnie Laird on the famous banked 160 yards wooden track in front of about 12,000 spectators for the NYAC Games. The track was terrifically springy and a joy to run on. During the meeting I sat in "Pioneer Corner", just a couple of feet from the edge of the track. Exhilarating. Ron Delany won his 20th consecutive indoor mile race but boos greeted the Irish Olympic champion as he snapped the tape for the time was merely 4:10.0. Other winners included Dave

Sime in the 60 yards, Charlie Jenkins in the 500 yards, Don Bragg in the pole vault and Parry O'Brien in the shot. There were no women's events.

The vault ended after midnight and I had quite a shock on leaving the Garden for a blizzard had been raging and the snow lay several inches thick. The great freeze-up was underway and next day the temperature reached an all-time low for New York of 2°F (-16°C). The icy weather conditions forced us to cancel a proposed trip to Niagara Falls but otherwise our hectic schedule continued apace: an ice hockey match at the Garden ... a memorable performance in Greenwich Village of *The Threepenny Opera* ... the Mario Lanza movie *Seven Hills of Rome* at Radio City Music Hall followed by a stage show featuring the famous Rockettes ... through Central Park to the Hayden Planetarium and Natural History Museum ... up to the top of the Empire State Building ... a New York Track Writers' lunch with the great Hungarian runner István Rózsavölgyi as guest of honour ... shopping at Macey's ... lunch at an automat ... a concert at Carnegie Hall by the Philadelphia Philharmonic ... a tour of the fabulous United Nations building ... a matinée performance of a stage musical, *Jamaica*, starring the wonderful Lena Horne. We also fitted in two more training sessions at the Armory, although by then I wasn't feeling too fit because of so many very late nights not to mention a diet consisting largely of hot dogs!

On Thursday (February 20), after helping Elliott dig out the car which was well and truly buried by snow, we drove into New Jersey to call for Elliott's cousin Judy Cohen and her friend Maxine, and the four of us took in a basketball double-header at the Garden. It was a fun evening and 2 am before we dropped the girls home. Next day I renewed acquaintance with one of my closest school pals: Jeff Gelfand, the fastest sprinter of my year and fellow Arsenal supporter, who had emigrated with his mother to Toronto. It was good to meet up with him again after nearly four years and we quickly involved him in our whirlwind schedule. That evening we returned to the Radio City Music Hall to see the Yul Brynner film *The Brothers Karamazov* and Saturday, my last full day as Elliott's guest, provided a suitably hectic climax to this mad, wonderful holiday – the memories of which would last a lifetime.

While Elliott rested at home as he was to compete in the mile walk at the US Indoor Championships that evening, Jeff and I visited the Statue of Liberty, climbing 168 steps up a spiral staircase to the top. The statue was far bigger than I had expected, the rim of the torch alone can accommodate several people. That evening we left with Elliott for the Garden and again I squatted at Pioneer Corner for the meeting, cheering Elliott to second place in the walk just ahead of Ronnie Laird, and Gordon McKenzie in the 3 miles in which he placed third. Ron Delany was voted the meet's outstanding performer by the 15,000 spectators for his 4:03.7 mile win over Rózsavölgyi, just 0.1 sec outside the world indoor record. There were 15 men's events on the programme, with just a 4x160 yards relay put on for the women. American track and field was still in the dark ages in that respect, although Chris McKenzie would be a leader in the ultimately successful fight for the rights and opportunities of women athletes in the USA.

Following a snack after the meet with several NYPC members, at around 1 am Elliott, Jeff, Judy, Maxine and myself travelled out to Battery Park and took a crazy ride there and back on the Staten Island Ferry in freezing conditions. The girls phoned home that they would not be back that night and, with Ronnie Laird waiting up for us, we all trooped back to 900 West 190, eventually turning in at 5 am – eight of us (plus the cat) in an apartment normally occupied by three!

Bleary-eyed, I got up at 9.30 on Sunday. Maxine made us a breakfast of scrambled eggs and after some frantic packing on my part all eight of us squeezed into the Denmans' car for a ride up to Yankee Stadium in the Bronx for a well named Polar Bear walk handicap, with Ron posting the fastest time. Chris and Gordon McKenzie drove up as arranged to take me on to Levittown, Long Island to visit my cousins and I knew the time for goodbyes had arrived. It was a sad moment, particularly as I had developed quite a "crush" on Judy (we corresponded for a while but never met again) as well as cementing so many other friendships. I have never forgotten all the hospitality and goodwill I received.

My last night in the New World was spent with the Slade family. Although technically they were my cousins, one generation removed, I regarded Manny and Yetta as my uncle and aunt, for until they emigrated to the USA in 1949 they lived in the Camden Town area of London and we would frequently visit them on a Sunday, often taking a trolley bus to Parliament Hill Fields. They had two daughters a little younger than me, and I was able to renew acquaintance with Margaret although her older sister Sheila was away at college. On my final morning Manny drove me to a deserted Jones Beach, a popular resort in the summer, and onward to Idlewild for my long flight home.

We took off at 1.10 pm EST (6.10 pm GMT) and after a brief stop in Boston I got talking to a Scottish steward, who kindly took me to the flight deck to meet the captain (no chance of that amid today's tight security). The cockpit was fascinating and bewildering, and I learned that we were flying at 330 mph at 23,000 feet. There was one more stop, at Shannon, and we touched down in London at 7.10 am on February 25, and two hours later I arrived home safe and sound, bursting to tell everyone about my experiences. It had been the most wonderful time of my young life and I certainly had no regrets about having to fork out £6 and 10 shillings (£6.50) every month for the next 18 months. It had been worth every last penny.

After all that excitement it took me a while to settle back into my job at the *Gazette* but I was soon immersed in another stimulating project. Because of Derek Ibbotson's immense popularity, Jimmy Green suggested I write a booklet about him, to be published by AW. I gladly seized the opportunity and although the 47-page publication *The Ibbotson Story* was very much an apprentice work I was very proud to have become a published author just after my 20th birthday. The booklet was first advertised in the July 12 1958 issue of AW, and the following week AW devoted nine pages to my preview of the 6th Empire Games to be staged in Cardiff later that month. Never before had the magazine run such an in-depth guide to any meeting.

I broke new ground again with the extent of the coverage from Cardiff, filling 19 of the 24 pages of the August 2 issue. These were the first major Games I had attended and, as the youngest accredited journalist, I was indebted particularly to Neil Allen of *The Times* and Stan Tomlin for showing me the ropes in terms of getting quotes etc. In my intro I summed up the Games as "the greatest track and field festival ever held in the British Isles. Brilliant performances, keen friendly competition, triumphs and failures, comedy and tragedy ... all the 'Olympic' ingredients were here." World records were broken by Gert Potgieter of South Africa in the 440 yards hurdles (49.73), Polish-born Australian Anna Pazera in the javelin (57.41m) and the England team of Madeleine Weston, Dorothy Hyman, June Paul and Heather Young in the 4x110 yards relay (45.37). The athlete who impressed me most was 20 year-old Herb Elliott. First came the 880 yards. Brian Hewson and Mike Rawson may have beaten him at the AAA Championships ten days earlier but the Australian never gave the English pair a chance, following a ridiculously slow first lap of 58.8, for he covered the second quarter in an unheard of 50.5. Four days later Elliott ran away from his team-mates Merv Lincoln and Albert Thomas to take the mile title in 3:59.0, his last two laps taking 58.9 and 56.7. That here was a very special athlete was underlined ten days later in Dublin when Elliott massacred a top class field with a world record smashing 3:54.5, and he went on to set another world record, 3:36.0 for 1500m in Gothenburg.

I wasn't present at the 1958 European Championships in Stockholm but gloried from afar at the scale of British success. On day one Stan Vickers in the 20 kilometres walk started the ball rolling; on day three Heather Young won the 100m, John Wrighton the 400m and Mike Rawson the 800m; day five saw victory in the shot by Arthur Rowe; while on the sixth and final day Brian Hewson triumphed in the 1500m and the men's 4x400m team took that title. Seven gold medals was a great return, not to mention five silver and five bronze, and it would have been even more impressive but for the injuries sustained during the 200m by Heather Young and June Paul, either of whom would have been favoured to win, and their absence from the 4x100m relay probably cost the team another gold.

Early in 1959 I became unemployable. The *Hatfield & Potters Bar Gazette* ceased publication and although I was now a fully qualified journalist there was no likelihood of securing a regular job as in November I was due to be called up for two years' National Service in the Royal Air Force.

As one door closed, so another opened, for I plunged into the world of freelancing. NUTS president Harold Abrahams was kind enough to pay me for spending time updating his collection of statistics but my main sources of income, other than an ever increasing amount of work for AW, were from such news agencies as Exchange Telegraph (Extel), Press Association (PA) and Dixon's Sports Agency, and from newspapers – particularly *The Times* and *The*

(Manchester) Guardian when I would deputise for their highly respected athletics correspondents Neil Allen and John Rodda when they were unavailable. During the spring and summer of 1959 I reported on no fewer than 28 meetings, mostly in the London area. How different from today when usually the only top calibre meeting in London is the annual IAAF Diamond League fixture in the Olympic Stadium.

Although I felt privileged to report on so many meetings, I never enjoyed the routine of phoning in copy and results to agencies and newspapers. There were some copy-takers familiar with athletics for whom you didn't have to spell out each letter of a name, but all too often it would be a long tortuous process. It wasn't too bad if I was calling from an enclosed press box, as at the White City, but at Motspur Park for instance the press phone was situated in the middle of the stand and I would have to dictate my deathless prose within earshot of hundreds of spectators who must have wondered who the hell was this lunatic shouting into a phone. So embarrassing.

Naïve as I was, I remember being shocked on one occasion at the White City when a well-regarded athletics writer, sitting next to me, began dictating his copy – "Sprinter Ron Jones told me ..." – when I knew that he hadn't left his seat all afternoon! Whatever my limitations as a journalist, I **never** made up a quote.

Another project which kept me busy that year was the very first NUTS Annual, *British Athletics 1959*. As I was the new organisation's inaugural secretary and I was not in full-time employment it was left to me to do much of the spadework for this pioneering publication although it was essentially a team effort. The booklet ran to 106 pages and incorporated the 1958 lists. Among the 11 athletes pictured on the front cover was teenage sprint sensation Peter Radford ... who in 2009 would become the NUTS' fourth president after Harold Abrahams, Norris McWhirter and Sir Eddie Kulukundis. The compilers of the book included the eight founder members mentioned earlier plus the other 23 members of the NUTS at that time, who included John Bale (later Professor Bale, a sports scientist and prolific author of academic books), Roger Breese (who still faithfully attends the AGM each year), Pat Brian (secretary 1960-62), Les Crouch (chairman 1965-66, 1985-90 & 1992-2000), Andrew Huxtable (secretary 1968-79), Tom McNab (National Coach and later technical adviser for *Chariots of Fire* and best selling author), nationally ranked steeplechaser Paddy Montague, Keith Morbey (our relays specialist) and Enid Vivian (née Harding), who set world bests at 880y in 1952 and mile in 1953. At the time of publication, Alf Wilkins was chairman and Peter May treasurer.

The junior lists (boys under 19 on April 1 1958) threw up numerous names of athletes who would go on to win major honours. Apart from Radford (9.6 100y, 10.3 100m, 20.8 200m) there was Robbie Brightwell (9.7 100y, 21.3 220y), David Jones (10.1/22.4), Tim Graham (50.8 440y), Alan Simpson (1:57.6 880y, 4:22.5 mile), Maurice Herriott (4:22.5 mile, 8:59.2 3000m steeplechase), Mel Batty (4:26.0 mile, 4:38.2 1500m steeplechase) and future 400m hurdler John Cooper (13.80m triple jump), while the third ranked triple jumper at

14.01m was future coaching great Malcolm Arnold. The youths (under 17 on April 1) lists included Adrian Metcalfe (himself later a NUTS member; 23.2 220y) and John Whetton (1:58.6 880y). Ranked equal 25th in the senior women's 880y list was future marathon star Joyce Byatt (Smith) with 2:22.2, while 12th in the long jump (5.43m) was Ann Packer and another Olympic champion, all of 14 years ahead, Mary Peters, appeared in equal 34th place (5.19m) but 8th in the shot (11.89m) and 3rd in the pentathlon (3720).

The big event for me in 1959 was being invited to be *The Times'* special correspondent at the World Student Games in Turin in September. Normally Neil Allen would have covered such an event but he was unavailable, as was Reg Kerslake, the paper's university sport correspondent. This was a glorious opportunity for me to have by-lined reports in the country's most prestigious newspaper and to widen my experience. I was nervous at the responsibility but it went well and I phoned over my copy after each of four daily sessions. Britain's sole winner was Kevin Gilligan in the 5000m and I lavished particular praise also on John Holt, his Oxford University colleague, who smashed his personal best when finishing a very close runner-up in the 800m. Several years later he would become a universally respected executive director of the then London-based International Amateur Athletic Federation. The IAAF moved its headquarters to Monaco in 1993, and would become a frequent destination for me from that time but my very first visit there was on the train journey home from Turin. I stopped off to write up my AW report at a harbour-side café. Ah, this was the life!

5. RAF & MY FIRST OLYMPICS (1959-1961)

Unhappily for me, that high life ended two months later when I became very much a low life in the Royal Air Force. My two years of compulsory National Service, which had been deferred for three years while I completed my journalistic apprenticeship, began on November 24 1959. Apart from the culture shock I was so frustrated at having to put my career on hold and somewhat resentful that of all my circle of school friends only one – Arnold Rosenbaum – had been "called up", the rest staying at university or college long enough to outlast the termination of conscription. The six weeks of basic training at RAF Bridgnorth constituted, by a long way, the worst period of my life. As Aircraftman Watman I found myself bawled at by coarse drill corporals younger than myself and plunged into a parallel universe in which seemingly the most important things in life were to polish your boots and badges incessantly, make your bed with your kit laid out in accordance with a strictly enforced code, march in step and never drop your rifle.

My one saving grace was athletics, yet another reason for my love of the sport. Fortunately I had made sure, by my standards at least, that I was pretty fit when Her Majesty invited me to become part of her armed forces. As a consequence, within a day or two of arriving at Bridgnorth, I finished third in a recruits' cross country trial, winning me a place on the station's cross country team. That led to a couple of races away from the camp, enabling me to miss one or two particularly unpleasant activities, like bayonet practice.

I found I was quite adept at the actual square-bashing (marching and rifle drill) but actually firing weapons (with live ammunition, we were told) proved very nearly a disaster. Towards the end of the six weeks came the Bren gun test. The Bren is a light machine gun and it was loaded with a 20-round magazine. I really had very little idea of what I was supposed to do with this lethal weapon, and being short sighted didn't help, so somehow or other I managed to fire off all the rounds in one burst without any of the bullets hitting the target! This was considered rather freakish and the sergeant in charge warned me that unless, the next day, I did much better with the Lee Enfield rifle I would be back-flighted … in other words I would have to start the whole ghastly basic training from the beginning again. I have never felt more depressed or anxious.

I'm not a religious person but perhaps somebody up there was taking pity on me, for by some miracle I not only hit the target with all my rifle rounds but several of them were bulls-eyes. From zero to hero … I was designated a "marksman" and for the rest of my service I wore a special insignia on my sleeve denoting I was a crack shot!

Mightily relieved to be moving from Bridgnorth I was next posted to RAF Kirton in Lindsey, near Lincoln, for trade training. I was assigned to be a 'clerk equipment accounts' for the rest of my service – a rather tedious desk job. At some point the recruits were asked to nominate the three places they would most like to be posted to. I thought that if I was to have to spend the best part of two years doing boring work then let it be in some interesting place, so I chose Hong Kong, Singapore and Germany. In fact, as I later discovered, national servicemen were no longer being posted abroad so that was a completely fatuous exercise. Instead my home for the next 21 months or so would be RAF Wyton, a Bomber Command base which at the time was in Huntingdonshire but is now, due to boundary changes rather than a landslide, situated in Cambridgeshire.

RAF Wyton was an incredibly noisy place with V-Bombers and Canberra reconnaissance aircraft taking off and landing in close proximity to our sleeping quarters. Although at the time I deeply resented being used in effect as cheap labour (I worked alongside properly paid civilians doing much the same job), looking back I realise it was not all a waste of time. I made some good friends, mixed with blokes from all backgrounds and reached my highest ever state of fitness. The station had one of the strongest athletics teams in the RAF and it was my good fortune that I became a regular member of that team, competing in cross country, road and track events. We had three star runners: Corporal Brian Jeffs of Essex Beagles, a Welsh international cross country runner and steeplechaser who clocked 8:57.2 to rank fifth in Britain in 1963; SAC Johnny Lindsell of Portsmouth AC, a 4:10.0 miler in 1961; and Warrant Officer George Scutts, also of Portsmouth, an outstanding veteran distance runner who was among Britain's best at 20 miles earlier in his career. On several occasions the four of us would drive down to watch big meetings at the White City.

Training with them raised my own modest standards, and I also moved up in distance. In 1960 I ran 63 minutes for 10 miles, while in 1961 I clocked 41:58 for 7 miles, representing around 37 minute pace for 10km. In those years such times were exceedingly mediocre but today they don't look quite so bad! My crowning moment was at the RAF Wyton Sports in August 1961 when (thanks to Brian Jeffs opting out) LAC Watman won the "3000m steeplechase" by over half a lap. Something went wrong with the officiating as I actually covered a lap too many (shades of the 1932 Olympics). My time? Well, I did have to sign up to the Official Secrets Act for my RAF service, so I cannot possibly divulge such sensitive information. That was my first and only steeplechase, so unlike every Olympic champion and world record breaker I retired with a 100% win record!

Apart from the occasional parade and guard duty (protecting the armoury from a potential IRA raid) life carried on fairly smoothly. I got home on a 48-hour pass most weekends, when I would meet up with friends and family, catch up on the latest films and frequent such favourite haunts as Ronnie Scott's Jazz Club. Family ties were renewed and in March 1960 I became an uncle second time round when my sister gave birth to Lionel. It was always a wrench to board the coach near Marble Arch on a Sunday evening to whisk me back to Wyton but there were compensations. Servicemen were encouraged to pursue educational courses and I signed up for French lessons. My tutor turned out to be an attractive French girl who was working as an *au pair* for one of the officers and his family, and my stock rose among my room-mates when they saw me escort her to the camp's cinema! Our lessons mainly consisted of me bringing copies of the great sports newspaper *L'Equipe* to translate.

From the time I arrived at Wyton in March 1960 my preoccupation was to ensure I could get sufficient time off to attend the Rome Olympics. I put in my application for two weeks' leave, knowing it could be rescinded at any time if there was an emergency situation, but fortunately I was able to join the 200-strong *Athletics Weekly* tour party, led by Jimmy Green and former marathon champion Squire Yarrow.

I should add that I was still keeping my hand in with reports in AW. Just after the ordeal of basic training had ended in January 1960 I attended one of the earliest indoor meetings at RAF Stanmore – little knowing that 26 years later this London suburb would become my home. However, I was unable to continue sending in overseas news on a regular basis, and my great American friend Elliott Denman deputised for me during the US indoor season. I was at Hurlingham in April to report on Basil Heatley's British record of 48:18.4 for 10 miles, only just outside Emil Zátopek's world record. Fifth in 51:54.2 was one Harry Wilson, much later to find fame as Steve Ovett's coach.

The White City attracted an aggregate crowd of 60,000 for the two-day match between Britain and France and the fans went home happy as the men's home side beat their opponents for the ninth time running and the women's team won their encounter by a very wide margin. It's a pity that these dual internationals have long since been discontinued. The fans really cared about which team won and the matches provided a wonderful opportunity for two or three British athletes in every event to have the honour of representing their country – a rare occurrence these days in such events as the men's shot or women's javelin. Their points were just as valuable as those earned by the runners. The traditional and ever popular annual Finland v Sweden encounter proves the formula is still valid and a match between, say, Britain and France and/or Germany or Poland could be stimulating.

In the last two issues of August I put together the most detailed Olympic preview yet, including sticking my neck out by predicting the first three in each event. I was well off the mark when predicting in the women's 100m that Dorothy Hyman "seems to lack the blazing speed necessary to reach the final" when in fact she finished a brilliant second to the fabulous Wilma Rudolph. I also under-estimated Dorothy Shirley, who I thought at her best might make the top six in the high jump whereas she tied for second place behind the hottest of all favourites, Iolanda Balas. I was four years too soon in predicting Mary Bignal (later Rand) would win the long jump. However, I did foresee Peter Radford finishing third in the 100m.

As the youngest accredited journalist in Rome I was perpetually thrilled and overawed by my first experience of an Olympic Games. It was like entering a dream world. Although Don Thompson in the 50km walk was Britain's sole winner and potential gold medallists like Gordon Pirie, Arthur Rowe and Mary Bignal disappointed, the British team performed creditably with silver medals going to Dorothy Hyman (100m, plus bronze in the 200m), Carole Quinton in the 80m hurdles and Dorothy Shirley, and bronze medals won by Stan Vickers in the 20km walk and the 4x100m team of Radford, David Jones, Dave Segal and Nick Whitehead.

My report constituted by far the most extensive Olympic coverage in the magazine's history: some 40 pages in total. Reflecting on the Games, which I described as "the most eventful athletics meeting in history", I relived some special memories.

To me, Rome 1960 will always evoke the sight of Wilma Rudolph dwarfing her rivals physically and speed-wise. Life has not been easy for her. She was unable to walk until the age of seven because of rheumatic fever. One hopes that her athletic success will pave the way to a kinder future. [The mother of four, Wilma died of cancer in 1994 at age 54]. *The men's events were dominated, of course, by Herb Elliott* [who ran away with the 1500m in a world record 3:35.6]. *If ever there was a complete runner, then Herb's the man. Oozing power and self-confidence with every stride* [although he later revealed that in fact he was extremely nervous], *Herb made a great 1500m field look almost mediocre. Elliott's fellow Australasian, Murray Halberg, won the hearts and admiration of all not only for his courageous running in the 5000m but for his gesture of seeking from the crowd his coach and embracing him. This same coach, Arthur Lydiard, was responsible also for enabling Peter Snell to develop into the massively strong athlete who bulldozed past an agonised Roger Moens in the 800m to score the most unexpected triumph in the track events. Otis Davis, with no regrets but two gold medals and two world records to his credit, carved his name indelibly into the Olympic hall of fame. That look of incredulity when his 400m time of 44.9 was announced will never be forgotten by those who glimpsed it.*

More than anyone, though, the tragic figure of the Games was the man one had hoped would be the shining star – Gordon Pirie. In that fateful 5000m heat Pirie covered his final lap in 77.4. As he lumbered slowly towards the finish one could almost hear and see his world crumbling into little pieces. That heat was to have been just one step away from the culmination of Gordon's brilliant 20-year running career. Instead it marked the end of a dream which only a few weeks earlier seemed almost certain to come true – a gold medal. The Games of surprises ended with the most unexpected victory of all – that of an unknown Ethiopian in the marathon. Abebe Bikila, a 28 year-old member of Emperor Haile Selassie's Household Guard, not only won but clipped Sergey Popov's best on record time by 0.8 sec with 2:15:16.2. And all in bare feet!

His victory was of huge significance. It was the first Olympic success in any event by a black African and the world of middle and long distance running was about to change for ever. In 1964 not only did Bikila retain his title with another world record but Kenya claimed their first medallist when Wilson Kiprugut finished third in the 800m. Ethiopian and Kenyan runners have between them now collected the staggering total of 144 Olympic medals, 52 of them gold.

An update here on the NUTS. The organisation's main function was the compilation of deep and accurate UK lists, which it continued to do, but individually too our youthful members made a valuable contribution to the debates which were a feature of AW's letters to the editor page. Colin Young, at 17, had his first letter published in 1952, closely followed by Les Crouch (21). Len Gebbett was 31 when he entered the fray in 1954, Bob Sparks was 18 and Stan Greenberg 25 in 1956. Stan may have been a late starter but has made up for it ever since and must surely rank as AW's most prolific letter writer. Although Stan was a founder member and has been a leading light of the NUTS for 60 years, he should have been drummed out in 1960. Where were his priorities? Instead of being in Rome on September 4 he was in London for his wedding to the delightful Carole! Thanks to Charles Elliott, the NUTS were also promoting open track and field meetings at Hurlingham with its track incorporating a straight 220 yards and among new members were 800m runner Mike Fleet and high jumper Pat Mackenzie, both future internationals. In 1961 Oxford University AC secretary Adrian Metcalfe, who that summer set world junior and UK 400m records of 45.8 and 45.7, joined our ranks to keep the NUTS fully informed of performances by the Dark Blues.

After the intoxicating experience of my first Olympics it was even more difficult to readjust to the humdrum routine of my RAF service. I still had almost 15 months yet to serve. In the spring of 1961, Jimmy Green and AW owner Albert Anderson approached me to consider editing a monthly magazine, *World Athletics*, to complement AW. I jumped at the idea, particularly as they would contact the RAF authorities to persuade them to release me in order to concentrate on work "of national importance". They got nowhere with that but I was still happy to accept this new challenge. How on earth I managed to bring out single handed the first six issues, starting with the July 1961 edition, while still serving in the RAF (working from 8 am to 5 pm each day) and continuing my regular contributions to AW is a mystery to me now! Still, at the age of 23 one feels one can tackle anything. However, the project would never have got off the ground without the understanding and encouragement of my military superiors. They agreed to give me an extra 48-hour pass once a month to tie up each issue with the printers and in return I would extend my work hours.

The inaugural issue, with sprinter David Jones gracing the cover, was a joy to put together. Goodness knows when I was able to sleep but somehow I crammed into 28 A5 pages such features as an interview with Martin Hyman, British top ten lists for 1961 as at June 19, the reasons why US high jump favourite John Thomas lost in Rome, a book review quoting Herb Elliott on his rivals, a who's who of the world's top sprinters, a quiz, a forecast contest and news and results from 20 countries. I also included a piece in my off-beat track notes column about athletes who made it in Hollywood. Just recently I had watched the film *South Pacific*, a member of the cast being 1948 Olympic decathlon bronze medallist Floyd Simmons. I went on to mention even more distinguished fellow multi-eventers Bob Mathias, Rafer Johnson and Glenn "Tarzan" Morris, and wrote that the only athlete I could think of to appear in a film truly worthy of the Seventh Art was Adhemar Ferreira da Silva, Brazil's double Olympic triple jump champion, who played Death in Marcel Camus' poetic, prize-winning *Orfeu Negro*. In a later column I went on to mention the serious actor Roscoe Lee Browne, who ran the world's fastest 800m of 1:49.3 in 1951, another Tarzan in 1928 Olympic shot silver medallist Herman Brix (later known as Bruce Bennett), and Finland's 1948 Olympic javelin champion Tapio Rautavaara. Even William S Hart, one of the silent screen's first cowboy heroes, was entered for the AAU 3 miles walk in 1883.

From the second issue I introduced editorials, and in the October issue I sounded off against amateurism. The outstanding Swedish middle distance runner Dan Waern had just been banned by the IAAF for admitting he received substantial payments for competing at Swedish meetings – just like his compatriots Gunder Hägg and Arne Andersson from a previous era. I favoured scrapping the Victorian concept of an amateur.

Under-the-counter payments have been made by grateful promoters to star names for years and this practice (is it so wicked?) is unlikely to cease. The law of supply and demand operates in athletics as in everything else. Where is the harm in legalising payments to those athletes who, by sheer hard work and perseverance in most cases, have risen to the status of crowd-pullers? Without star performers the amount of gate money which can be ploughed back into the sport will dwindle away. Let's get rid of the outdated hypocritical amateur code and accept an athlete for what he is, not for what amateur purists would have him be.

6. THE FORMATIVE 'AW' YEARS (1961-1963)

As my demob date of November 23 1961 finally came into view I was faced with a choice. I had two job offers: to join AW as assistant to Jimmy Green or to accept editor Phil Pilley's invitation to join the staff of *World Sports*. The latter option had its attractions but to be honest there was only one direction I could take. Ever since my schooldays I felt my professional destiny lay with AW – and it was a decision I never regretted. I started in December 1961 very soon after rejoining civvy street and for the next 26 years, although often working crazily long hours, I could not have been happier in my work. The three days a week commute from North London to Rochester was tiresome and my salary was pitiful compared to what my Fleet Street colleagues were earning but that was more than compensated by the job satisfaction and the opportunity to travel around the world.

Although, or perhaps because, we came from opposite ends of the athletics spectrum Jimmy and I made a formidable team. Jimmy, nearly 30 years older than me, had been a classy runner with Surrey AC and Belgrave Harriers, representing the AAA at 880y, mile and 2 miles and had run the marathon in 3 hours dead. He was also an international category starter, senior coach of repute, meeting organiser and a county and club president. Shortly after his release from wartime service in the RAF he came up with the idea of launching a monthly athletics magazine. Forget it, he was told when he sought expert advice; there was no way such a venture could pay for itself. "I thanked them for their advice, and completely ignored it," Jimmy reflected. He skirted round a government prohibition of starting up new publications so soon after the war because of the paper shortage by making out that the magazine had a previous existence. In the first issue of *Athletics*, dated December 1945, Jimmy referred to "the resumption of this paper", numbered it Vol 2 No 1 and stated "this is the first issue of *Athletics*, revived after a lapse of nearly six years." Fortunately he got away with these economical with the truth statements and we in the athletics community were rewarded for Jimmy's initiative, hard work and financial struggle with a magazine (which went weekly in 1950) that has served us well and – rare for any publication – has never missed an issue in over 70 years.

What I brought to the table were the skills of a trained journalist, a love for statistics and the cock-eyed optimism and enthusiasm of youth. We were very different in many ways, not least politically, but we always respected the other's opinions and in a working relationship which lasted some 30 years we never exchanged a cross word. We agreed on the fundamentals … that AW should always be regarded as the club athlete's magazine above all else, that we would print every significant result we could obtain, publish training and technique articles by leading coaches, and enable anyone to express their viewpoint as long as it wasn't libellous.

As I settled in to my dream job in 1962 Jimmy encouraged me to expand my own specialist areas such as overseas news, interviews, profiles, historical features and stats, and I was allowed to provide increasingly comprehensive coverage of the major events. We disagreed only on tug-of-war (Jimmy wanted to continue including results, I didn't think they were relevant to an athletics publication) and metric measurements. Jimmy felt most readers would not relate to these, so we compromised. From September 1962 I started including metres in overseas field event results, but it wasn't until April 1969 that AW began printing all field event results in both systems of measurement … in the hope that by 1971 readers would be able to 'think' in metres and we would be able to dispense with those clumsy feet and inches and fractions altogether. It entailed a lot of time consuming extra work, wearing out several copies of the conversion tables, and I was being wildly optimistic, for it wasn't until 1977 that I felt the time had arrived to go purely metric. Only the Americans, insular as ever, still post results in feet and inches.

Another hobbyhorse of mine was racial prejudice and in the July 1962 issue of *World Athletics* I wrote:

The South Africans will be out of the Olympic Games unless, within the next year, the South African Government changes its policy of racial discrimination in sport. That is the gist of a reasonable and welcome decision taken by the International Olympic Committee at its recent Moscow congress. As is widely known, sport in South Africa is – by Government decree – conducted on the basis of apartheid. This means that no "non-white" athlete may compete against a "white" athlete. One of the functions of sport is to bring human beings together in conditions of complete equality and, by so doing, cut through the artificial barriers of class, colour and creed. Sport can lead the way in destroying prejudice. There is only one race – the human race – and the sooner South Africa is made to realise it the happier that nation, and the world, will be.

It was a case of later rather than sooner; South Africa was banned from the Olympics from 1964 to 1988 inclusive, the last remaining *apartheid* laws being repealed in 1991.

The September issue was the magazine's last. It had fulfilled a need, with subscribers in 46 countries, but a monthly cannot be as topical as readers would like and so it was decided to incorporate the features and international results service into AW, with four or eight pages of each issue devoted exclusively to the material that readers had been enjoying in *World Athletics*. It was a logical step forward and a marketing success as AW inherited hundreds of new subscribers.

I was proud of what had been achieved. In addition to the unprecedented volume of worldwide results, the 15 issues had included interviews with Martin Hyman, David Jones, Adrian Metcalfe, Derek Ibbotson, Robbie Brightwell, Buddy Edelen, Bruce Tulloh and Jim Beatty; profiles of Frank Budd, John Thomas, Valeriy Brumel, Gordon Pirie, Vladimir Kuts, Peter Snell, Dixie Willis, Paavo Nurmi and Michel Jazy; training articles featuring Otis Davis, Jay Silvester, Bruce Kidd, Bobby Morrow, Kuts, Sin Kim Dan, Budd and Hal Connolly; and a multi-part short history of athletics which drew valuable corrections from 25 year-old Peter Lovesey, THE expert on 19th century athletics who at the time was a college lecturer in English, many years before he became an award-winning crime novelist. Adorning the issues were photos primarily by Ed Lacey, Gerry Cranham and H W Neale but also including a nice action shot of high jumper Dorothy Shirley by my brother-in-law Charles Sharon. Speaking of photographers, a teenage Mark Shearman made the front cover of AW in May 1962 with an action shot of pole vaulter Trevor Burton. It was his very first photo to be published anywhere ... and, astonishingly, Mark continues to this day to grace the magazine with his work and estimates he has provided over a thousand AW cover photos. He deservedly received an MBE for services to sports photography in the 2014 New Year's Honours List.

In March 1962 I attended the English National Cross Country Championships for the first time. They were staged at Blackpool and the winner was the local club's Gerry North. What a prestigious event it was in those days with such star names as Bruce Tulloh finishing 2nd, Mel Batty 5th, Ron Hill 7th, Jim Alder 9th, Basil Heatley 13th, Alan Simpson 14th, Maurice Herriott 24th, Herb Elliott (up at Cambridge University) 35th and Derek Ibbotson 42nd. The 'National' was always the most challenging fixture for AW as, long before computerised results, Jimmy and I together with our secretary José Green had to collect all of the recorders' boards, time sheets and club scoring envelopes and laboriously put together every runner's placing the next day (Sunday) in order to meet our printing deadline.

Blackpool was cold and bleak but later in the month I was able to indulge in the comfort and warmth of Wembley's Empire Pool for Britain's first full-scale indoor athletics meeting since 1939.

What a welcome and successful return it proved to be. Clearly, indoor athletics is here to stay. Everyone seemed to enjoy themselves: the runners rose enthusiastically to the challenge of mastering the steeply banked pine track; the field event performers, for once, attracted as much attention as their more glamorous colleagues; the officials no doubt took pleasure in strutting about in dinner jackets; while the spectators, almost within whispering distance of the athletes, were treated to a new, exciting and intimate view of athletics. The overall presentation was satisfactory even if much of the showmanship so typical of New York indoor meets was absent. On the credit side, though, we were spared such transatlantic excesses as a band playing during races!

Who could have predicted then the continuous din (some might call it music) which is now considered obligatory at all major meetings.

The following week I witnessed my first International Cross Country Championships in Sheffield. The great Belgian steeplechaser Gaston Roelants won the title, with England (three in the first five home) comfortable winners of the team race. Another week later it was back to Wembley for the first post-war National Indoor Championships and my first glimpse of one Lynn Davies (19), second in the long jump with a personal best of 7.16m. I certainly didn't notice the 18 year-old who placed fourth and last in the junior 440y in 58.4 ... Andy

Norman, who would in time become just about the most powerful figure in British athletics.

I opened the track season on a melancholy note. The occasion was the Cambridge University v AAA match. I had the privilege of seeing Herb Elliott at his peak, at the Rome Olympics, and here I watched what I described as "a poignant finale to one of the most glittering careers in athletics history." The Australian, still only 24 and undefeated as a senior at 1500m and mile, trailed in fifth and last in the 880y in 2:00.3.

One of the most charismatic figures in British athletics was Robbie Brightwell and what proved to be the finest 440y race of his career came at the AAA Championships.

Without straining, he romped home an easy winner. It did not look unduly fast and Brightwell himself said afterwards he thought it was about 47 seconds. But in fact the time was a superlative 45.9, which was 0.2 sec outside the world record. One wonders what Brightwell might have achieved in better conditions, for his lane was pretty muddy around the final turn.

The highlight of 1962 was the European Championships in Belgrade, capital of what was then Yugoslavia and now is Serbia, and there was a treat for the British fans with a gold medal to savour on each of the five days: Ken Matthews in the 20km walk, Dorothy Hyman in the 100m, Brightwell in the 400m, barefoot Bruce Tulloh in the 5000m and Brian Kilby in the marathon. Dorothy's victory over German rival Jutta Heine in a wind assisted 11.3 was particularly sweet.

No two athletes could be less alike. Their differences extend far beyond the contrast in physique, colouring or even nationality. Jutta has enjoyed an easy life as the daughter of a wealthy industrialist; she has no need to work and has few worries outside of keeping fit for racing. Dorothy, on the other hand, has had to struggle all her life and in that respect is similar to the only girl who could have beaten her on this form: Wilma Rudolph. Dorothy, whose father – a coal miner – died some months ago, is a tracer for the National Coal Board at Cudworth, near Barnsley, helping to support the rest of her family. Fame has not spoiled the simple charm of the Yorkshire girl who has sacrificed so much in her efforts to become a great sprinter. Modest and reserved off the track, a "killer" on it, Dorothy is a wonderful example to the young hopefuls who idolise her.

In addition to my reporting duties I was also appointed an AW tour leader. It was through such tours organised for readers that Jimmy, his wife Pam and myself were able to qualify for free places to the big international events. I could have done without the responsibility for ensuring that my group of 25 were always in the right place at the right time. I was faced with an acute dilemma as the group minus one sat in the coach to take them to the airport for the flight home. Charles Elliott, always a free spirit, had stayed privately and a special pick-up *en route* was arranged. There was no sign of him at the appointed time. We waited ten minutes, 20 minutes … and I was growing increasingly anxious that we would miss our flight if we delayed any longer.

Just as I was about to signal to our guide and driver that we must leave, apprehensive about how Charles was going to make his way home, along he trotted as though nothing was untoward. I don't often swear but I might have on that occasion!

The last four days of our trip had been spent in the lovely Adriatic coastal resort of Opatija, which is now in Croatia. I reminisced in AW: *I shall never forget that early morning road relay, an event which amply confirms the foreigner's suspicion that the English are a race of madmen. Perhaps even more bizarre was the spectacle of Maeve Kyle, her husband Sean and yours truly running up and down the roads abreast of Colin Young, who happened to be walking!* A few weeks later I penned a lengthy profile of Maeve under the title "The Girl Who Never Gave Up." Hers was a remarkable story.

Few athletes have had to battle – as has Maeve – not only against physiological adversity but also against such prejudice and apathy. Yet, against all the odds, Maeve has won through to such effect that this year, at the age of 33, she set magnificent new Irish records for 440y and 880y and reached the final of the European 400m. Her first competition was as a high jumper back in 1944, aged 15, but she did not return to athletics for five years. Meanwhile she made her name in hockey, eventually being capped a record 58 times. In 1949 she won the all-Ireland high jump title and the future looked bright. Then the blow fell – certain interests disapproved. No actual written word, but references deploring athletic women and the lack of modesty in dress, etc. She took to other fields.

Encouraged by husband Sean she came back to the sport as a sprinter, aged 25, although later that year she had such a bad time giving birth to daughter Shauna (who would develop into a fine athlete herself) that doctors told her she would have to forget about sport. Maeve thought otherwise and in 1955, in addition to posting her best sprint times, she – all 1.59m and 55kg of her – even beat her protegée, a young Mary Peters, for second place in the Northern Ireland shot put championship! Maeve made history by becoming the first female athlete to represent Ireland in the Olympics (1956) and yet someone wrote to the Press in shock at seeing a married woman selected! Tragedy overtook the Kyles in 1957 when their son Michael, born in June, died in infancy. The following year she underwent a major abdominal operation, again being told she could never run again. However, that motivated her even more and she began to blossom as a one-lap runner, winning the 1961 WAAA 440y title, while in 1962 she set a UK all-comers record of 54.9 in a heat of the WAAA Championships. The inspirational Maeve went on to run 55.3 for 400m in 1970, aged 41, and also served for many years as a prominent official. Astonishingly, in 1973 both she and her 18 year-old daughter clocked a wind-aided 12.1 for 100m.

As the British Empire & Commonwealth Games in Perth, Western Australia drew near I published an open letter to the England team selectors, drawing attention to the omission of Mel Batty.

47

His coach [Colin Young] *believes he is, after Bruce Kidd, the greatest young distance running prospect in the world. I for one agree: Batty's exploits this year, at the age of 22, are really staggering. Batty is a puzzled young man. He has had a momentous season but has been consistently overlooked by yourselves. Throughout the year on track, road and country he has shown that he believes only in 100% effort. There is a vacancy for a 6 miler/marathoner in the team. I do hope you choose Mel Batty. He deserves a break, and he won't let you down.*

I don't know whether that plea influenced the selectors but he was a late addition to the team and performed creditably to finish sixth in the 6 miles (run in 29°C heat) and fifth in the marathon.

Bernie Cecins, who now shared duties with the long-serving Joe Galli as our Australian correspondent, provided fine coverage of the Games. England's winners were Brian Kilby in the marathon, Martyn Lucking in the shot, Howard Payne in the hammer, the men's 4x110y relay team, Dorothy Hyman, whose modest 100y time of 11.2 is explained by a 5.8m/sec headwind and a temperature of 37°C and who went on to take the 220y in 23.8, and Sue Platt in the javelin. Welshman Lynn Davies, still only 20, long jumped a UK record of 7.72m and was in bronze medal position until the final round. Two years later that frustration would be swept away at his first Olympics. Also 20 and two years before her Olympic triumph, Ann Packer went out in the semis of the 100y and 220y prior to placing sixth in the 80m hurdles final run into a 7m/sec wind (!) and picking up a silver medal in the 4x110y relay. At this stage of her career she had never raced at 400m never mind 800m. Sadly, Joe Galli – a valued correspondent since 1947 – died in October 1963 of a kidney infection aged only 48. He was the man who had alerted AW readers from very early in their careers of the richly fulfilled promise of the likes of John Landy, Herb Elliott and Ron Clarke.

New ground was broken in the first AW issues of 1963. I felt that although the magazine's primary function was the provision of results and news it also needed a more personal touch, exploring the background of top athletes and their thoughts and hopes. Jimmy approved and just before Christmas I taped two hours of conversation with Dorothy Hyman at her home in the Yorkshire mining village of Cudworth and the outcome was the fullest verbatim interview thus far in an athletics magazine. Next up on the interview front were Joy Jordan, the former world record holder for 880y who ran her final race at the Commonwealth Games; European and Commonwealth marathon champion Brian Kilby, voted Britain's sportsman of the year for 1962; and Buddy Edelen, the Essex-based American teacher who set a world marathon record of 2:14:28 in the 1963 "Poly".

It wasn't just me going around talking to athletes on behalf of AW. Alastair Aitken, who is still active in that role, kicked off with a conversation with cross country star Tim Johnston, while we had a real scoop when my good American friend Dick Bank quizzed world high jump record holder (2.27m in 1962) Valeriy Brumel, who used the straddle technique, with the USSR's chief coach Gavriil Korobkov acting as interpreter. Asked what he thought was the greatest achievable height under the current rules he replied: "I would say now that 2.40m is not possible." But of course Dick Fosbury and his revolutionary Flop were still in the future. Dick Bank followed up with exclusive interviews with the Soviet Union's long jump world record holder at 8.31m, Igor Ter-Ovanesyan (an Armenian born in Ukraine who considered the ultimate jump would be 8.60m), former decathlete Korobkov and New Zealand's Olympic 800m champion Peter Snell, who revealed that at 15 his best times were merely 2:16 for 880y and 5:21 for the mile. What an asset Dick was to AW. At the time he was 33, a real estate developer in his native Los Angeles, ATFS member and a TV commentator for the ABC network. He also had a wicked sense of humour and was a marvellous mimic, his speciality being W C Fields, but he also did a great impression of Jack Crump, then the most influential official in British athletics.

I also took great pleasure in researching and writing profiles of three of my favourite American athletes: Mal Whitfield, Harrison Dillard, the only man to win Olympic titles at 100m and 110m hurdles, and two-time Olympic 400m hurdles champion Glenn Davis. I tried to describe the "poetry in motion" running style of Whitfield, the 1948 and 1952 Olympic 800m champion (I had forgiven him for beating my boyhood hero Arthur Wint both times!), with his long and seemingly effortless stride giving the impression of his perpetually running downhill, but I could not compete with Red Smith's imagery in the *New York Herald-Tribune*. "He is the smoothest, most glossily graceful and most intelligently conditioned athlete in the world. Seeing him is like peering over Rembrandt's shoulder while he paints; hearing Toscanini drain music from a string section; watching the almost evil grace of Ray Robinson in the ring … the guy flows over a track as a mountain brook bubbles across a meadow."

In November I started one of the longest running series in AW's history: "Who's Who in British Athletics". It was part of my remit to tap into the hopes and thoughts of leading athletes as well as providing a statistical profile. I sent out a printed questionnaire to pretty well all of our internationals and the response was most gratifying. The first batch of replies to be printed came from Ron Hill, Linda Knowles, Mike Bullivant, Lynn Davies (aim: 8.03m in 1964 "which should place me in the final six in Tokyo") and Dorothy Hyman. The next group included Thelma Hopkins (33 hockey caps for Ireland as well as a world high jump record and Olympic silver medal), Fred Alsop (UK triple jump record holder with 16.03m; his target was 16.46m, precisely the distance he achieved when placing fourth in the 1964 Olympics), NUTS member and 1962 Commonwealth Games 880y fifth placer Mike Fleet, Derek Ibbotson (whose view of the UK administration was: "Could be better. Too many little tin gods") and his wife Madeline. Others featured before the end of the year included Mel Batty, Ken Matthews, 18 year-old schoolgirl Sheila Parkin (later Sherwood), Bruce Tulloh, Adrian Metcalfe, Ann Packer (yet to run 800m), David Jones ("would like to see BAAB abolished and a UK AAA body formed"), Mary Rand, Martin Hyman ("it is a shame that such a great sport which has so much to offer to both athlete and official should be bogged down by squabbles and inadequacy amongst many top officials"), Maurice Herriott, Robbie Brightwell and John Cooper.

As can be gleaned from the above, there was much dissatisfaction among athletes with British officialdom. In February 1963 a full page ad in AW signed by the executive committee of the newly formed British Athletics Union (Brightwell, John Salisbury, Ken Brookman and Harry Wilson with Bill Giddings as honorary secretary) called for the reform of British athletics' administration. Among the BAU's aims was the formation of a single controlling body for the sport in the UK, directly responsible to all clubs and organisations. The establishment closed ranks. At the 1963 AGM of the AAA it was announced that the AAA General Committee had decided it was not practicable at that time to explore the possibility of forming a UK AAA as the Women's AAA, Scottish AAA and Northern Irish AAA had stated they were fully satisfied with the present BAAB (British Amateur Athletic Board) constitution. The BAU's proposal for a British AAA was defeated by 297 votes to 111. A similar motion by the BAU and IAC (International Athletes' Club) the following year went down by 289 votes to 186. In fact it wasn't until 1991 that a single governing body for men and women came into being.

It was worrying that a pathetically small crowd of 8000 turned up at the White City for the second day (Saturday) of the AAA Championships but the match between Britain and the USA restored faith in the public's interest in the sport. On the first day (Saturday) a narrow victory for the British squad of Peter Radford, Ron Jones, David Jones and Berwyn Jones in a world record equalling time of 40.0 for 4x110y over a US squad anchored by the world's fastest human, Bob Hayes, received massive media coverage, and a crowd of 35,000 – the largest for years – swarmed into the stadium for the second day on the Bank Holiday Monday. No meetings in Britain where an admission charge was involved could be held on a Sunday until the 1970s and it wasn't until 1982 that the AAA Championships began to be held on a Saturday/Sunday. The British men lost their match but the women won theirs and the fans were thrilled to witness world records in the pole vault (5.13m by John Pennel with one of the new-fangled fibre glass poles which were to revolutionise the event) and women's 4x110y relay by Madeleine Cobb, Mary Rand, Daphne Arden and Dorothy Hyman who combined to clock 45.2.

My report of the meeting was uncontroversial but that couldn't be said of a piece in the same issue which faithfully reported the comments made to me by several disillusioned African-American members of the visiting team.

Bob Hayes: "Man, it's worse here than in Alabama. They turn round and stare at you like you were a wild animal or something. I've had people call me on the phone here. They've sworn at me and called me a dirty nigger. I'm glad I'm leaving. I don't ever want to come to London again." Hurdler Rosie Bonds: "You know, we were better off in Moscow. At least they treat you as humans. Why do your papers keep on referring to so and so as coloured? We are here to represent the United States of America; we're all Americans." Ralph

Boston: "To be frank a few things have happened in London that weren't exactly for the best. A woman refused to serve us in a store just around the corner from this hotel, in Oxford Street, because we were coloured."

There was criticism also of some meeting officials.

Rosie Bonds: "Did you know that one of the high jump officials swore at one of our girls [16 year-old Eleanor Montgomery] because she took rather a long time preparing to jump?" Willye White, the long jump runner-up: "My concentration was ruined by all the noise. I asked if I could please have some quiet but the officials took no notice at all."

One prominent official, Vic Sealy, wrote a long letter for publication which started "I was shocked and incensed to read such irresponsible, inaccurate and misleading reporting by Melvyn Watman. I have always looked upon AW as an **athletics** magazine; free from politics, racial questions, "kite-flying" and sensation-seeking. Your readers will know that there is no colour bar in British athletics and there has never been any race discrimination on the part of officials." He continued: "The accusation that an official at the women's high jump swore at a 16 year-old coloured athlete was absolutely untrue. In point of fact we officials had no occasion to speak to the coloured girl at all because there was no delay on her part at any time. The girl who *did* delay the competition was the white girl – Daniels. Her delaying antics were worse than anything I have ever experienced. We did speak to her politely, but firmly, and reminded her that she could be disqualified for unduly delaying the competition."

In response, I wrote: *I am glad and relieved that Mr Sealy is able to refute the allegation that one of the girl high jumpers was sworn at by an official, but in no way does this invalidate the various other complaints put to me. The treatment received by Bob Hayes and Ralph Boston was particularly distressing and, I would have thought, the concern of the whole athletics community. Yet Mr Sealy implies that these incidents were of no public interest. I must apologise to readers for inadvertently misleading them in one detail: the identity of the high jumper. From the context of the conversation generally I assumed – wrongly it appears – that the jumper concerned was Eleanor Montgomery. I should make it clear that the reference in brackets to 16 year-old Eleanor Montgomery in the article was inserted by me for purposes of clarification and was not a part of Miss Bonds' actual words to me.*

Following a further exchange of views by Mr Sealy and myself in the letters column the issue was – to my intense relief – settled by another of the high jump officials that day, Arthur Selwyn. He confirmed that the athlete concerned was Billee Pat Daniels and stated that: "Before her last jump, over which she took some four minutes, the three judges being by now in complete agreement that she had throughout the competition been taking longer than was reasonable and that she really ought not to have kept the other competitors waiting to such an extent, I spoke to her in these terms. Her retort was that she knew the rules and 'could take as long as she liked'. Apart from being rude, this happens also to be selfish as well as inaccurate, and my answer was sharpish –

that unless she hurried up she would be disqualified – though I hope and believe that I did not swear at her." That marked the end of an unsettling episode, one which brought home to me the importance of making no assumptions when reporting other people's words.

That letter was published the same weekend as when I was with a 50-strong AW tour party in Paris to watch an exciting men's match between France and the Russian Federal Republic which ended in a tie. I then travelled on by train to Naples to report on the Mediterranean Games where I was greatly impressed by the immaculate stride and remarkable finishing powers of a 22 year-old Tunisian soldier, Mohamed Gammoudi, who won both the 10,000m and 5000m (next day) with national records of 14:07.4 and 29:34.2 – good but not exceptional times. Just a year later he came within 0.4 sec of winning the Olympic 10,000m in 28:24.8 and in 1968 he became Olympic 5000m champion.

At the same time, in Volgograd (formerly Stalingrad), the British men's team – captained by the inspirational Robbie Brightwell – brought off an outstanding victory over the Russian Federal Republic by 112 points to 99. The British women lost 62-56 but overall the visitors won 168-161 for one of the most notable moments in British athletics history. There were so many heroic victories. The men's track events were almost embarrassingly one-sided with wins by Berwyn Jones (100m), David Jones (200m), Brightwell of course (400m), Mike Fleet (800m), Stan Taylor (1500m), John Anderson (5000m), Maurice Herriott (steeplechase, UK record), Mike Parker (110m hurdles, UK record), John Cooper (400m hurdles, UK record) and both relay teams, the one field event winner being Rex Porter in the pole vault. On the women's side there were successes by the ever dependable Dorothy Hyman (100m & 200m, both UK records), Ann Packer (400m), Linda Knowles (high jump), Mary Rand (long jump) and the 4x100m relay team.

Before leaving events in 1963 I must mention three other highly significant developments. In April I received a letter from Bert Nelson, publisher of the prestigious American monthly magazine *Track & Field News* inviting me to apply for the post of editor as Hal Bateman was leaving. I discovered that Elliott Denman had been offered the job but had declined and suggested I might be a suitable candidate. What a dilemma! If accepted, this would be a once in a lifetime opportunity to live and work in America, and an attractive part of it too as the TFN offices were located in Los Altos, near San Francisco. The salary on offer was two or three times what I was making at AW and another plus would be that I would travel to Tokyo for the 1964 Olympics, which did not seem to be the case with AW. Although I never doubted my ability to make a success of editing the publication, to which I had been subscribing for more than ten years and which had occasionally printed my articles, I really didn't know if I could adjust quickly to the American way of life and after all I was perfectly content working at AW and continuing to live at home with such perks as my mum's cooking!

I was torn both ways and decided to leave it to fate. I concluded my letter of application: "This job is probably the only one in the whole world that could lure me away from AW, where I am very happy. I owe a lot to Jimmy Green and I would not do anything to create difficulties for him. He told me he would not stand in my way, so that's why I'm applying. If you reject me, I shall not be heartbroken – just disappointed. At least I made the effort. If you accept me, I shall be a mixture of delighted, apprehensive and sad but ready and willing to rise to the challenge."

Fate, or rather US immigration policy, decreed I would be staying at home … to my relief. I felt I would be left wondering for the rest of my life if I hadn't made the effort, but I really didn't want to leave my family, friends and work colleagues for an unknown future. It all boiled down to dates. Bert Nelson needed someone to start right away whereas I had been told by the American Embassy that it would normally take seven weeks to be granted an immigrant's visa and green card work permit. Bert couldn't wait that long and instead the job went to Dick Drake. I never regretted the way things turned out.

Despite my more than adequate workload with AW and various freelance activities, I felt the need to try to add to the rather sparse collection of athletics reference books and in May I wrote to Eric Major, a fine distance runner for Woodford Green AC who happened to be the publicity manager of the publishers Robert Hale Ltd. They had produced three admirable encyclopaedias covering cricket, boxing and football and I suggested a book on athletics would be a welcome addition to the series. The following month I received a letter from Gordon Chesterfield, one of the company's directors, inviting me to meet him with a view to producing such a book and so was born *The Encyclopaedia of Athletics*. Its compilation required an enormous amount of research and typing and the book was not published until October 1964, so more about it in the next chapter.

The other event of note that summer was the formation of the British Athletics Writers' Association. A group of Fleet Street's finest, plus this young upstart at AW, wandered over from the White City to a nearby pub (naturally) to establish the BAWA. We had two main objectives: to honour the year's top athletes and to press for improved working facilities at the main athletics venues. Vernon Morgan, a 1928 Olympic steeplechaser who was a legendary Reuters sports editor, was elected our first chairman with Bob Trevor of the *Evening News* (three London evening newspapers in those days and no give-aways) appointed secretary and Jim Coote of the *Daily Telegraph* treasurer. Others I recall from the inaugural meeting include Neil Allen of *The Times*, Terry O'Connor and Roy Moor of the *Daily Mail*, John Rodda of *The Guardian*, Peter Wilson of the *Daily Mirror* and Desmond Hackett of the *Daily Express*. Later that year we held our first Awards Dinner with Maurice Herriott and Dorothy Hyman voted the top British athletes of 1963.

7. GREYHOUNDS & TOKYO OLYMPICS (1964)

The year of 1964 was a truly memorable one for me. I loved to travel and I had the good fortune to "go west, young man" as well as a journey to the Far East. In addition, my first real book was published and I gloried in the successes of several athletes who had become friends. As a journalist I am supposed to be totally objective and neutral but of course throughout my long career I have had personal favourites and become emotionally involved in their ups and downs.

In a typical week I would travel from North-East London to the office by bus and/or Tube to Victoria and then by train to Chatham or Rochester on Monday, Tuesday (when we went to press) and Thursday (when I would pick up a newly printed copy of the latest issue). The office was part of Kent Art Printers, effectively the owners of AW, and our staff numbered just three: Jimmy, myself and our lovely, ever smiling secretary José Green (no relation to Jimmy), a Kent county champion half miler who since 1961 had been in charge of subscriptions and distribution as well as dispensing countless mugs of coffee.

As the magazine grew in size and with Jimmy and me working anything between 50 and 70 hours most weeks, the bulk of my workload being research and writing at home and reporting on meetings, the staff increased to four during the summer of 1964 as 18 year-old John Lusardi joined us as an editorial assistant with coverage of teenage athletics his speciality. We all mucked in on typing out results, the bread and butter of the magazine, although the clatter of our typewriters was as nothing compared to the incessant din of the printing plant next door. These were still the days of hot metal printing, which would continue until well into the 1980s, and all our copy had to be passed on to linotype operators who would re-type everything into metallic lines which compositors would then fit into pages ready for the presses. Jimmy and I would design the layout of the pages in a "dummy", complete with headlines and spaces allocated for photos and ads, but union rules dictated that we could never touch the metal, only indicate. When the pages were made up we would proof read them and make any corrections.

It wasn't just the printing process that was so slow and cumbersome. There were, of course, no computers or faxes or emails then and almost all the results arrived by post and only a relatively small percentage could be processed in time to make the first available issue. Even the telephone was used sparingly to cut costs as AW was very much a shoestring operation in those days as the circulation was only a few thousand and advertising revenue was low. Albert Anderson, the owner of Kent Art Printers, would seek to justify the economy measures, including low salaries and contributors' fees, because AW ran at a loss from a publishing point of view although he must have profited from it as a week-in week-out printing job.

AW could never have appeared without the input provided by a dedicated corps of correspondents, and with the incorporation of *Modern Athletics* in February we also now benefited from the services of that excellent

54

writer and historian Jack Barlow with his long running "Barrier Breakers" series, while the incomparable Dick Bank contributed stimulating interviews with Gaston Roelants and one of my great heroes, Ron Clarke.

Almost every issue contained entries for the "Who's Who" series, among them one 'Ming' Campbell. The future leader of the Liberal Democrats was at the time a 22 year-old apprentice solicitor with personal bests of 9.8 100y and 21.4 220y who in 1963 had emulated Eric Liddell by winning the 100, 220 and 440y titles at the Scottish Championships. He set his all-time goals at 9.6 and 21.0, but did better than that for in 1967, as a student in the USA, he clocked 9.5, set a far superior UK 100m record of 10.2 and ran 20.8 for 220y. Asked for his dislikes about the sport, he replied: "The attitude that suggests there is no solution to problems except by an athletes v officials contest. Both should have the intelligence to appreciate that they require each other and that co-operation and understanding will go a long way." There spoke a future politician.

I was involved in two groundbreaking multi-part statistical compilations: the evolution of UK men's records in collaboration with Peter Lovesey and the women's equivalent with Peter Pozzoli, a man who had researched UK women's history to an unparalleled degree although his brilliant published work in a later series of books was flawed by his insistence that any printed performance should be listed, even if it was an obvious typing error.

Before the main outdoor track season started I was delighted, in April, to report on the deeds of two of the athletes I admired most: Mel Batty and Lynn Davies. The first came at Hurlingham, the occasion being the AAA 10 miles track championship, which was being held in conjunction with a NUTS-organised open meeting.

It has been my privilege and pleasure to witness dozens of world records over the years but none has afforded me quite so much private satisfaction as Mel Batty's glorious performance. I have followed Mel's career very closely in recent seasons, for his robust action, uncompromising aggressiveness on the track and unquenchable enthusiasm for hard racing and training – coupled with a young coach (the ubiquitous long distance walking star Colin Young) whose knowledge of distance running performances and tactics is second to none – struck me as an irresistible combination. No one can accuse Mel and his coach of faint heartedness. Together they hatched a schedule geared to covering the 40 laps in 47:30 – 17 seconds inside Basil Heatley's world record, which in turn had been 25 seconds faster than Emil Zátopek's celebrated 1951 performance.

Mel's time was 47:26.8 … and it took a rather good runner to beat it in Ron Clarke. I interviewed Mel at his home a week or two later. Who was his athletics idol? Not surprisingly it was Gordon Pirie. "The first big meeting I went to at the White City was the AAA Championships in 1953 and I saw Gordon win the 3 miles the day after breaking the 6 miles world record. Zátopek was also an idol of mine after his three wins at Helsinki, but Gordon was my number one."

My first sight of Lynn in Olympic year was at Wembley for an indoor match against Finland. My report started: *Lynn Davies stands on the threshold of greatness. That is apparent after his wonderful display of long jumping prowess.* He produced the four longest ever jumps, indoors or out, by a Briton with a best of 7.78m. *Davies looked almost indecently fit* [Lynn and his coach Ron Pickering always loved that quote]. *Following a winter of intensive weight training he is clearly much stronger than before and the controlled power of his run-up was quite an eye-opener. If Lynn can keep clear of injury he will surely exceed his target for the year of 26ft 4in (8.02m).*

On May 6 I attended the traditional first major outdoor meeting of the season, the Leyton Floodlit at Eton Manor, the main talking point being Ann Packer's commendable 800m debut – winning in 2:11.1 (with our José Green fourth). It was known that she had trained very hard alongside her fiancé Robbie Brightwell but no one, least of all Ann herself, could have dreamt of what would happen later that year in Tokyo.

Talking of Tokyo, I had been so disappointed at the lack of a free place for me on the AW Olympic tour that earlier in the year I decided to plan an ambitious coast to coast journey across America. The world's best travel bargain was Greyhound's 99 days unlimited bus pass for 99 dollars and although I could take off only 21 days it was still a marvellous deal. It was great fun just planning the itinerary, although the southern states were out as, disgustingly, there was still racial segregation in place. As a jazz fan I would have loved to visit New Orleans but not at that time (I did get there in 1992). I also tailored my route so that I could meet various friends and relatives and, of course, a strong athletics element had to be built in. A potential stumbling block was the transatlantic air fare, but as in 1958 I was able to take advantage of a fly now pay later scheme, this time with BOAC, and Harold Abrahams kindly agreed to stand as my guarantor should I default on payments.

Less than 12 hours after returning home from the Leyton Floodlit I took off from Heathrow (still known until 1966 as London Airport) bound for Montreal, the cheapest North American destination. From there I took an overnight Greyhound to Toronto where I met up briefly with my old school pal Jeff Gelfand. Then it was off to Chicago, over 500 miles away, with meal stops including one at Kalamazoo. Yes, I couldn't stop singing (in my head) the old Glenn Miller and Andrews Sisters' hit, "I've Got a Gal in Kalamazoo" After an overnight stay in Chicago came the longest single stretch of my tour: over 1400 miles and 34 hours aboard all the way to Salt Lake City. Through a bus window was a wonderful way to observe this vast country in close up detail, besides which it was so illuminating to chat with so many passengers on the bus and at refreshment stops. Incidentally, this was just after the Beatles had made it big in the States and as soon as anyone realised I was English I would be asked if I knew them personally. So many young Americans believed England was so small that everyone would know everyone else! Actually, one Briton who did get to know them well was a former schoolmate (and 440y rival) Ivor Davis, who was the West Coast correspondent for the *Daily Express*, and travelled all over America with them during the group's 1964 tour.

The West as I had always imagined it from countless John Ford and John Wayne movies really began once we reached Cheyenne with a climb up to almost 9000 feet and plenty of snow still around. Another legendary place name we stopped at was Laramie (cue another popular song: "The Man from Laramie"). I was living out a fantasy. I stayed overnight in Salt Lake City, with the following night on the bus. At one stop, in Reno, most of the passengers still awake made a dash for the one-armed bandits. I lost all of $1.50 … and 23 years would pass before I encountered American slot machines again. I've made up for that long interval ever since. With Al Jolson's "California, Here I Come" now playing in my mental jukebox we passed through the capital, Sacramento, and I finally caught my first sight of the Pacific Ocean shortly before that marathon bus journey terminated in San Francisco at midday on May 12. I had covered over 3000 miles since Montreal.

Now came the hectic part. I travelled out to Mountain View, where *Track & Field News'* 23 year-old managing editor Dick Drake collected me in his car, and we drove to the magazine's office in Los Altos. After spending the night at Dick's apartment it was back to San Francisco for a wondrous sightseeing tour of the city and bay (yes, "I Left my Heart ...") and a couple of cable car rides. That night was spent on the bus as it sped southwards to the Hollywood bus terminal, from where Dick Bank took me for a tour around Los Angeles in his beloved E-type Jaguar. In the evening we went to a star-studded track and field barbecue, Dick introducing me to such legends as Randy Matson, Bill Nieder, Payton Jordan and New Zealand's Bill Baillie. After a night spent at the Bank residence in Beverly Hills it was along to the 1932 Olympic Stadium that evening for the Coliseum Relays. The highlight was a world record in the 4x880y relay by Villanova University, anchored by Irishman Noel Carroll. There were 26 men's events plus a solitary women's 100y.

I hit the road again next day, catching a bus to San Diego, from where – just to say I had visited Mexico – I crossed the border to the hell-hole called Tijuana. Back to Los Angeles for the 12 hour overnight journey to Flagstaff, Arizona. I wrote up my Coliseum Relays report at the hotel that evening and next morning travelled to the Grand Canyon. Two English girls and an Australian guy teamed up with me and we walked about five miles around the rim of this truly spectacular natural wonder in sizzling heat. Back in Flagstaff I caught the overnight service for the 900 miles stretch to Oklahoma City. I was now getting my kicks on route sixty-six. As I didn't get much sleep aboard, I booked into a hotel there and left for the 500 miles ride to ("meet me in") St Louis next morning. Another overnight stop there before a 1000 miles stint to New York, where I stayed with the ever hospitable Theresa and Jack Denman for three days. Joined by Elliott and his English wife Jo, we made two visits to the World's Fair. On May 24 we drove over to Yonkers for the American AAU marathon championship. Our good friend Buddy Edelen had a fantastic run to win by almost 20 minutes in 2:24:26, the race being run in 91°F heat and high humidity, and intrinsically was probably at least on a par with his world record. On my final day in the Big Apple I took a three hour boat cruise around Manhattan, visited Coney Island and saw the marvellously droll Dick Shawn in the Broadway production of *A Funny Thing Happened On The Way To The Forum*.

After an overnight bus journey through upstate New York I reached Toronto where I stayed on my 26th birthday with Jeff Gelfand, his new wife Linda and his mother. Next day I took my final Greyhound bus ride, to Montreal, where my great North American adventure had started 8000 road miles earlier. I arrived home on the morning of May 28 – weary but full of joyful memories.

It was soon after I got back that Jimmy told me that a third free place with the AW tour was now available and I would be going to Tokyo after all! To say I was thrilled to bits would be an understatement.

After covering the London v New York match which was the inaugural fixture at the new Crystal Palace stadium (the track not yet all-weather), and the WAAA and AAA Championships, my next assignment was the English Schools Championships at Hendon's Copthall Stadium – the first time I had attended that remarkable meeting which is run on military lines and has been the first step to international stardom for so many. At this edition, winners who went on to achieve international status included David Cropper in the 880y, Mike Tagg in the mile, Dave Travis in the javelin, Paul Dickenson in the hammer, Sheila Parkin in the long jump and 14 year-old Ann Wilson in the junior girls high jump … as well as a Hungarian-born discus thrower, also 14, by the name of Joe Bugner, who became European heavyweight boxing champion in 1971 and fought Muhammad Ali for the world title in 1975. Two big names of the future who both placed fifth in their age group events were Alan Pascoe (16) in the 110y hurdles and Lillian Board (15) in the 100y.

With the domestic track season at an end I arranged an interview with Mary Rand, the delightful pin-up girl of British athletics, at her Henley-on-Thames home in late September. It didn't appear until the October 17 issue, by which time she had already won the first of her three Olympic medals. Asked about her long jump prospects, she had replied: "Of course, the greatest thing of all would be to do a world record at the Olympics – like Herb Elliott, for instance. That would be wonderful. Needless to say, that's what I would like to do in Tokyo!" Hopes were translated into deeds in her case, for not only did she become Britain's first ever female Olympic champion but she produced the greatest ever series of jumps, topped by a world record of 6.76m. Even today that's a very respectable distance and bear in mind that it was achieved into a 1.6m wind and the clay runway was rain-soaked. It was a performance ahead of its time. Off a synthetic surface and with that amount of wind in her favour it's possible she would have jumped very close to seven metres – the sort of distance that would not be attained for another dozen years. Her coach, John Le Masurier, was to write of that jump: "Technically it was superb – a fast approach, with the body becoming vertical as she crouched into a powerful take-off. A perfect hitchkick with the feet stretched forward together for landing and just sufficient forward speed remaining to allow her to stand up in the sand." With the previous world record holder, the USSR's Tatyana Shchelkanova suffering an off-day, the unexpected silver medallist with a world junior record of 6.60m was the lanky 18 year-old Polish sprinter Irena Kirszenstein, who had only taken up long jumping the previous season with a best of 5.84m. Under her married name of Szewinska she would develop into one of the all-time great 200m and 400m runners.

In the pentathlon, which started two days later, Mary again competed brilliantly to become only the second woman ever to exceed 5000 points. She totalled 5035 (10.9 80m hurdles, 11.05m shot, 1.72m high jump, 6.55m long jump, 24.2 200m) and finished ahead of Irina Press in three of the events. However, she lost so many points to Press in the shot – no fewer than 384 – that the muscular Soviet athlete ran out a clear winner with a world record breaking score of 5246. Mary Peters, whose own golden moments were still eight years away, placed fourth. Still Mrs Rand hadn't finished, for there was the 4x100m relay to come and she, along with Janet Simpson, Daphne Arden and Dorothy Hyman, finished a superb third behind Poland and the USA.

That Mary won her long jump competition was predictable, as in her final pre-Olympic outing she cleared the strongly wind-assisted distance of 6.86m from take-off to landing (official measurement was 6.70m), but in my AW preview I forecast third place for Lynn Davies. His UK record stood at 8.04m whereas Ralph Boston had recently set a world record of 8.34m while his main challenger was expected to be Igor Ter-Ovanesyan, European record holder with 8.31m. I was so happy to be proved wrong, although Lynn had been on the brink of disaster in the qualifying round when a poor first jump was followed by a foul. Fortunately he nailed it with his final attempt. Conditions for the final later that day were deplorable; the runway was covered with puddles, the wind blew against the jumpers and the temperature was a chilly 13°C. After four rounds, with everyone understandably jumping far below their best, Boston led with 7.88m from Ter-Ovanesyan (7.80m) and Davies (7.78m).

At that point Lynn sensed he could win the coveted gold medal. All too accustomed to such weather in his native Wales, he knew he was being unsettled by the damp and dismal conditions to a lesser degree than his opponents. With his fifth jump he cut the sand at the British record distance of 8.07m! "I was at the same time tremendously delighted and numb; I couldn't take it all in", he reflected. "Boston reassured me that that that jump would be the winner although he had one to go. The suspense was agony." He could barely dare to look as his rivals took their remaining attempts. Ter-Ovanesyan replied with a fifth-round 7.99m to move into second place, but in the final round Boston – landing heart-stoppingly close to Lynn's mark – recaptured second position with 8.03m. Typically, in his moment of triumph, Lynn was quick to share the credit with the man who had coached him for the past three years, Ron Pickering.

That was Britain's third gold medal as three days earlier Ken Matthews, judging his pace to perfection, had won the 20 kilometres walk by a huge margin in 1:29:34. That walkers were still unfairly regarded as second class citizens in the world of athletics became apparent when Britain's other Tokyo winners very quickly featured in the Queen's Honours List but it wasn't until 13 years later that, following a campaign organised by the Race Walking Association, Ken at last received his richly deserved MBE.

Ann Packer went through the full range of emotions during her Olympic campaign. Tipped to win the 400m, an event she had only taken up the previous year, she made an immediate impression by winning her heat in the British record time of 53.1 and in her semi-final she ran 52.7 for a European record and second place on the world all-time list with Australia's Betty Cuthbert, the 1956 Olympic 100m and 200m champion, a distant second in 53.8. Ann ran even faster in the final with 52.2 but was devastated to finish runner-up to Cuthbert's 52.0. "I suppose a lot of people would be very happy with a silver medal," she was quoted in Neil Duncanson's book *Tales of Gold*. "But I had hoped for the gold and I was favourite for the gold. I just wasn't good enough on the day, and I shall always be disappointed about it."

Next day, weary after her three 400m races, Ann lined up for the 800m, a distance she had moved up to as recently as May and had qualified for only in September. She was fortunate enough to be able to amble through her heat in 2:12.6, in fifth place some eight seconds behind the winner, conserving vital energy. Later that day she was thrilled to watch her fiancé, Robbie Brightwell, win his 400m semi-final in a UK record equalling 45.7, easing up, to boost his prospects of taking the gold medal. The following day she qualified comfortably for the 800m final in 2:06.0 but was mortified that Robbie's 45.7 left him just outside the medals in the 400m final.

In his 2011 autobiography, *Robbie Brightwell and his Golden Girl*, he graphically explained his demise. "Like a fool, I ran the first 200m in 21.8, over half a second faster than I should have done. I had committed myself and there was no way I could replace the energy expended. As I swept around the last turn, I knew I was in deep trouble. My legs felt wobbly and my strides started to shorten. A wave of despair and hopelessness swept over me. I knew I was going to lose. I gave up. If I could not win a gold medal it was the end of the dream. I let Andrzej Badenski ease past me on the last three strides." He continued: "Ann met me. We sat on a bench and cried together. The tears rolled down our cheeks as we consoled each other. She knew how much the dream had meant to me; just as I knew how distraught she felt on my behalf."

Having followed Robbie throughout his career I too shared a fraction of his dismay ... but there were still two races to come to attempt to salvage the couple's joint disappointment. Next day was the women's 800m final.

Love conquers all ... even the fairest field of female half-milers ever assembled. At least in Ann Packer's case it provided the motivation behind one of the most sublime racing performances I have ever witnessed. It was a rare privilege to watch Ann in this race, for here was a girl – inspired by her love for

Robbie – prepared to endure any amount of pain in her desire to present her man with a gold medal as compensation for his own personal disappointment. Prior to the men's 400m final, Ann had entertained no hopes of winning and was sceptical even of her ability to gain a medal.

Maryvonne Dupureur led at 400m in a fast 58.6 with Ann in sixth place (59.1). Dupureur reached 600m in 1:29.8 with Ann some six metres down in third (1:30.7). The French champion had five metres in hand over Ann entering the finishing straight but it proved grossly insufficient for as the crowd of nearly 70,000 roared with excitement and the British supporters went almost berserk Ann lengthened her stride and rushed past her defenceless rival to snap the tape five metres clear in the staggering world record time of 2:01.1. In two brief years, thanks to prodigiously hard work and determination on her part coupled with the expert advice of Denis Watts and the constant encouragement and inspiration of Robbie, she had developed from a promising sprinter – hurdler - high jumper - long jumper – pentathlete into Britain's first ever female Olympic champion on the track. All the media hailed Ann's victory as a complete shock, and continue to do so to this day, but in AW's Tokyo preview issue I did forecast Australia's Dixie Willis to win with Ann second – and so, as Dixie was injured and couldn't compete, Ann was actually my tip.

There was one more drama to play out. Robbie, over the moon by Ann's success, was anchorman for the 4x400m relay, and determined to win a medal of his own. Tim Graham, Adrian Metcalfe and 400m hurdles silver medallist John Cooper (Robbie's best friend) handed the baton to Robbie in fourth place behind the USA, Trinidad and Jamaica.

Entering the final straight, Henry Carr (USA) was out of any possible danger, but Wendell Mottley (Trinidad) and George Kerr (Jamaica) were beginning to buckle. Now was Brightwell's chance ... and he took it. Striding out to textbook perfection – chest held high, knees well up, arms working powerfully – Robbie edged up on his two adversaries. He caught Kerr 60 yards from the tape and took Mottley just 10 yards from the line in as stirring a finish as one can remember. The crowd rose to Robbie in admiration for one of the guttiest performances of the Games. From 4th to 2nd in 50 yards – the British fighting spirit, so much in evidence in Tokyo, had won through again. The times were sensational as the first three teams all broke the old world record, Robbie's anchor leg timed at 44.8. "I was happy," he wrote. "I had atoned, in part."

The British team's performance at the London Olympics of 2012 has often been described as the best ever but I rate the 1964 showing as superior. In London there were four gold medals, a silver and a bronze plus three fourth places, a splendid achievement, but in Tokyo not only were there four golds also but no fewer than seven silvers (Basil Heatley marathon, Maurice Herriott steeplechase, John Cooper 400m hurdles, 4x400m team, Paul Nihill 50km walk, Ann Packer 400m and Mary Rand pentathlon), a bronze for the women's 4x100m team, and fourth places by Brightwell 400m, Alan Simpson 1500m, Brian Kilby marathon, Fred Alsop triple jump and Mary Peters pentathlon. In all of British athletics history, collectively this was the highest point.

Knowing most of the British team personally and being of a similar age added to the wonderful experience of reporting on their accomplishments, although I was fortunate to have been able to witness all the great moments as, suffering from the effects of "Delhi Belly" acquired during a flight stopover in Bombay, I spent an inordinate amount of time in the press box toilet! One of my fellow passengers on that chartered British Eagle flight was my old hero Gordon Pirie, who was due to be part of ITV's commentary team. He asked if I could assist him but, mindful of the fact that I was going to be reporting for AW single handed, regretfully I had to decline. My behind-the-scenes television career could have started there and then; instead it began some 20 years later.

Although the British successes remain among my fondest memories, there was so much else to savour at those great Games. Apart from showcasing the enormous strides Japan had made as an economic power, in retrospect they were probably the last relatively innocent Olympic celebration. Subsequent Games would be clouded by repression, terrorism, boycotts, drug abuse and over commercialisation. Individual star of the Games was Bob Hayes, who on a soft cinder track won the 'blue riband' event, the 100m, by fully two metres in a world record 10.06 after an incredible wind-aided 9.91 semi-final – while on the last leg of the relay he went from fifth to first, from three metres down to three metres up! He was the forerunner of Usain Bolt. Other images to treasure include the sensational 10,000m victory of Billy Mills (though my heart went out to third placed Ron Clarke), Abebe Bikila's second Olympic marathon win in world record time, wearing shoes on this occasion, Peter Snell's majestic 800m/1500m double, and the bravery of Al Oerter. A cervical disc injury had necessitated his wearing a neck harness in competition for most of the year and in Tokyo, six days before the competition, he tore cartilages in his lower rib cage. With his ribs heavily taped and his right side packed in ice as a safeguard against internal haemorrhaging he was advised by doctors not to throw, but he went ahead anyway, hoping he could unleash a winning effort with his first throw, realising it could also be his last. It went only 57.65m and he noted "it felt like somebody was trying to tear out my ribs." He wasn't going to give in despite the pain and in the fifth round he threw an Olympic record of 61.00m for his third successive Olympic victory ... and he wasn't finished yet.

While in Japan I took two trips outside of Tokyo. Together with NUTS colleague Martin James, a fellow railway enthusiast, I travelled on a high speed 'bullet train' to Hakone, passing by snow-capped Mount Fuji. It must have been a wonderful sight ... only it was so misty we never saw the mountain. The other journey was of a melancholy nature. My Uncle Cyril's brother died as a prisoner-of-war in Japan in December 1942, aged 32, and my uncle knew that a memorial bearing his name, Gunner Nathan Lipman of the Royal Artillery, was located in the Imperial War Graves cemetery in Yokohama. It was the most beautiful place, meticulously maintained, and as I didn't have precise details of the location I walked up and down the rows of flat white stones (there were over 1600 of them), narrowing the search for a Star of David rather than a cross. I eventually found what I was looking for and took photos for my uncle.

While I was away in Tokyo my first full-scale book was published. The *Encyclopaedia of Athletics* filled a gap in athletics reference works in that it included not only complete lists of Olympic, European, Commonwealth and British champions, as well as the evolution over the past century of world and British records, but other features in this 228-page hardback included brief, fact-filled biographies of 140 all-time greats. Harold Abrahams, who had been so helpful in boosting my career and was something of a father figure to me, did me the honour of contributing a most complimentary foreword.

Modesty forbids that I should mention some of the gratifyingly enthusiastic reviews ... but to hell with modesty! *Athletics Weekly* (Andrew Huxtable): "There has long existed a need for a standard work of reference on athletics; Melvyn Watman has now filled the gap with this very sound piece of research. Quite clearly this volume will find its way onto every track and field enthusiast's bookshelf." *The Guardian* (John Rodda): "Its compiler is Melvyn Watman and no one in Britain is better fitted for the task. Watman, whose reporting of the last Olympic Games was a masterpiece of its kind, has been typically painstaking in his search for accurate information and, equally typically, he has unearthed much lively off-beat material in doing so. In short, this is both a valuable reference and an absorbing bedside book." *World Sports* (Bob Phillips): "He has managed to strike a remarkably even balance between cold statistics and revealing biographies ... the sketches of leading athletes are excellent."

8. "RON CLARKE: THE GREATEST" (1965-1966)

What with the victory over the Russians in 1963 and the brilliant showing in Tokyo, British athletics was on a high at the start of 1965, but that season proved to be a disaster. The big event was the inaugural edition of the European Cup, the men and women competing in separate venues. What happened was that the women's team failed even to reach the final, while the men's side suffered one setback after another in their final to finish last.

The popular Who's Who series was revived in February and numerous big names were featured throughout the year. Among them was Joyce Smith who stated she intended competing "at the most two more track seasons". Little did she or we guess what an amazing, protracted career lay ahead. My longest biographical article so far was headlined "Robbie Brightwell – Captain Extraordinary". It ran over three issues and some seven pages as I tried to do justice to a man who was not just an outstanding 400m runner but an inspirational team captain and campaigner for a better deal for his fellow athletes.

The amalgamation of *World Athletics* and *Modern Athletics* paid off in terms of enlarging the readership of AW and for the first time, in February, our certified circulation figure was published in the magazine. Between June and December 1964 the average number of copies sold was a barrier-breaking 10,019.

The first major event of 1965 was the International Cross Country Championships in Ostend, and the result remains controversial to this day. Only a photo finish could have decided for certain who won, but there was no such equipment to help the judges who gave the race to France's Jean-Claude Fayolle over Mel Batty. Jimmy Green and myself in the grandstand thought our man had got his chest over the line first but would have settled gladly for a dead-heat.

The following weekend I visited RAF Cosford for the first time … and for several years to come my fond recollections of indoor competition in that vast hangar would be somewhat overshadowed by the memory of all those times I would find myself standing shivering at Cosford's tiny station waiting for the connecting train to the main line at Wolverhampton and back to London. The occasion was the AAA and WAAA Indoor Championships. How odd that indoors the two governing bodies co-existed quite happily but outdoors the men's and women's championships remained completely separate until as late as 1988. Nearing his 33rd birthday, Derek Ibbotson showed there was life in the old boy yet by taking the 2 miles in the British indoor record time of 8:42.6. The next big indoor event was a GB v USA match at Wembley, the highlight being Lynn Davies setting a UK indoor record of 7.85m to beat Ralph Boston by just two centimetres.

The one race from 1965 that I will never forget was the 3 miles at the AAA Championships on a rain-soaked White City track. The Australian, Ron Clarke, came to this meeting having recently broken his own world records for 3 miles (13:00.4), 5000m (13:25.8) and 10,000m (28:14.0), and was up against young Gerry Lindgren, who at the American Championships had run Olympic 10,000m champion Billy Mills to inches in the 6 miles with both men credited with a world record time of 27:11.6.

Under the heading "RON CLARKE: THE GREATEST" I began my report with this quote from Clarke: "The only time I really felt all right was two yards past the tape! I was very tired indeed, as tired as I've ever been in my life."

So spoke Ron Clarke a few minutes after his stupendous new record. It was a relief to hear this, for it proved that Clarke is just flesh and blood like the rest of us and not an indefatigable running machine. One had one's doubts as he reeled off lap after lap at unheard of speeds – head and trunk erect, arms held low and relaxed, his magnificently fluent stride never faltering. Clarke's achievement in covering 3 miles in 12:52.4 is, I submit, the most prodigious in the long history of track running. Perhaps the full enormity of Clarke's feat can best be brought home by noting that his 2 miles time of 8:36.4 on the way would have constituted a world record prior to May 1955, and yet he went on to cover another mile at even faster speed."

I recall looking down at my stopwatch with incredulity. Astonishing too was the 19 year-old Lindgren, who I described as "looking like a scraggy little duckling beside the swan-like nobility of Clarke." He stayed with the Australian for 2 miles, setting a personal best for the distance, before dropping back but still hung on well enough to shatter the American record with 13:04.2.

Just four days later, in Oslo, Clarke produced a run that superseded that AAA performance as what was then considered the ultimate in athletic excellence. Few doubted that he was capable of breaking the twin peaks of 27 and 28 minutes for 6 miles and 10,000m, but his times of 26:47.0 and 27:39.4 were just mind-boggling. It meant that he maintained a faster speed than Chris Chataway and Vladimir Kuts in their immortal 5000m duel in 1954 ... for twice the distance! It made a nonsense of the widely held theory that records would inevitably be bettered by ever decreasing margins. More than half a century later, with the world 10,000m record standing at 26:17.53, it's imperative that we remember Ron Clarke and the manner in which he revolutionised what seemed to be humanly possible in distance running. He never did win any major titles but he most certainly ranks among the all-time greats.

During the summer we ran a survey, inviting readers to comment on and rate the various components of AW. Hundreds participated and it became clear that by far the most popular aspect of the magazine was the provision of results and reports of major British meetings (80% like, 20% satisfied). Among the least popular features were race walking notes and schools results, but Jimmy and I felt a duty to continue our coverage of those special interest areas of the sport. Among the readers' views we published was this: "There is too big an emphasis on road racing and cross country. All track and field marks above a certain standard should be given – AW is the only source of information." That came from a 20 year-old Peter Matthews, who would develop into the outstanding athletics statistician of my generation; a future editor of the

Guinness Book of Records, announcer, radio and TV commentator, club president, author and for these past many years my partner in producing the newsletter *Athletics International*.

Having studied Greek as well as Latin at school, I had long wanted to visit Athens and I made that my first destination in my summer holiday. I fell in love with the city and its antiquities, although the highlight of my week's stay was an excursion to Delphi, surely one of the loveliest places on earth. From Athens I flew on to Tel Aviv for my first and only visit to Israel. Athletics had to come into the equation and the occasion was the Maccabiah Games, often referred to as the Jewish Olympics. I was one of the British team selectors and knew most of the squad personally, so it was particularly gratifying to share in their delight when medals came their way. My NUTS colleague Alf Wilkins did a fine job as team coach. The only downside was that I foolishly dozed off on the beach at Herzlia, where I was staying, and suffered sunstroke. I covered up after that experience but it didn't stop me taking excursions to the Dead Sea and to Jerusalem in the amiable company of the celebrated (non-Jewish) US team coach Payton Jordan, a man who in 1938 was a member of a University of Southern California team which broke the world record for the 4x110y relay and who in 1941 ran 100y in 9.5 and 100m in 10.3 when the world records stood at 9.4 and 10.2. In 1997 he set a world age-80 100m record of 14.65 and he lived to 91.

My next trip abroad was to Stuttgart for the inaugural men's European Cup Final. Basically, everything that could go wrong did go wrong.

Britain's European Cup humiliation, which began with the elimination in the semi-final round of the women's side, was completed last weekend when the men's team finished a dispiriting and dispirited last. What made the rout so disturbing was the general absence of the fighting spirit that has animated the team on previous big occasions. Javelin thrower Dave Travis, the one member of the team to surpass himself [fifth with a personal best of 76.18m], displayed that quality in abundance, but precious few of the others followed suit. Just eleven months after Tokyo, our finest hour, we have plumbed the depths.

Among the catalogue of disasters: David Jones in the 100m remained motionless in his blocks while his five rivals streaked tapewards, the sprint relay team was disqualified, and in the 4x400m, won in a modest 3:08.3, the GB team finished last. In spite of Dick Bank's tongue-in-cheek observation – "I've already seen two European Cup Finals: the first and the last" – the match was undoubtedly a great success, and the tournament's future assured. A total of about 80,000 spectators watched the proceedings over the two days and witnessed a gripping battle for honours between the Soviet Union and West Germany, the USSR prevailing by a single point. The USSR also won the women's final in Kassel, well clear of East Germany, with world records by both of the controversial Press sisters: 10.4 80m hurdles by Irina and 18.59m shot put by Tamara.

In October we started another series which would continue for many a year. Entitled "Spotlight on Youth", John Lusardi's first subject was 15 year-old all-rounder Ann Wilson. It proved a good choice as Ann would develop into a world class pentathlete, a silver medallist in that event as well as the high jump and long jump at the 1970 Commonwealth Games. Others featured before the end of the year included 16 year-olds Ian Stewart, Della James (later Mrs Alan Pascoe) and Lillian Board (primarily a sprinter/long jumper then) and a 15 year-old hammer thrower by the name of Paul Dickenson.

Although semi-retired as an athlete, I took part with a conspicuous lack of success in the inaugural NUTS members' pentathlon at Hurlingham Park which saw 800m international Mike Fleet win ahead of 400m star Adrian Metcalfe, who scored a lot more points for his 10.0 100 yards than his painful 5:15.8 mile. Lowlight of the meeting was a 9ft long jump (about the length of an Arthur Wint stride) by our esteemed chairman Les Crouch, a decent 800m runner who admitted to suffering from inertia and vertigo when jumping!

Besides a wealth of athletics activity, 1966 was notable for England winning football's World Cup (my old school friend Stan Posner and I watched it on his TV, the pair of us getting progressively more excited, hysterical even) and, largely thanks to royalties from my *Encyclopaedia*, I bought my first car.

Early in the year the death occurred of one of my role models, Joe Binks, at the grand old age of 91. The crowning achievement of his days as an active athlete was winning the 1902 AAA mile title in the British amateur record time of 4:16.8 – a mark that remained unbroken until Olympic champion Albert Hill clocked 4:13.8 at the 1921 AAA Championships. That was the famous occasion when, knowing that Joe was reporting the race for the *News of the World*, a section of the crowd chanted: "It's going, it's going; His head is falling low; I hear those unkind voices calling; Poor Old Joe". Joe was athletics correspondent of that newspaper, which for so many years was the main, in fact only, sponsor of British athletics, for an amazing 54 years and attended every Olympics between 1908 and 1956. I was an avid reader of his reports from 1950 onwards and had the pleasure of sitting with him in the White City press box on a number of occasions.

Another major loss was that of Jack Crump, of lung cancer, aged only 60. A former road walker, he held high office as an administrator for 30 years. While honorary secretary of the Surrey AAA, he was appointed British team manager following the 1936 Olympics, served as honorary secretary of the BAAB from 1946 to 1964 and was in charge of the British teams at the 1948, 1952 and 1956 Olympics. He and Harold Abrahams were the most powerful officials in British athletics during that era; the most controversial too as both men wrote and broadcast on athletics for payment at a time when the athletes themselves had to be strictly amateur, and other journalists resented the fact that the pair obviously were privy to inside information about selection etc. Jack wrote regularly and authoritatively for both *World Sports* and the *Sporting Record* and was for a time the athletics correspondent of the *Daily Telegraph*. Jimmy Green considered him his best friend and although Jack was suspicious of me and the other young "nuts" at first, fearing we would be yet another group of agitators gunning for him, I did warm to him in later years.

The big event of the winter season was the inaugural European Indoor Games in Dortmund. The meeting proved a success and paved the way for full-scale European Indoor Championships in 1967 and every year until 1990 and usually every other year since. There were two British winners. One, John Whetton in the 1500m, was expected; the other, Barrie Kelly in the 60m, was certainly not. Previously a run-of-the-mill 10.5 100m man, he missed the world best of 6.5 by just a tenth. Two years later he would run 10.3. I wrote of Whetton: *He may play second fiddle to Alan Simpson as an outdoor miler but he is a different proposition altogether on the boards. That low slung action of his may not look attractive or even impressive, but it is ideally suited to the peculiarities of indoor racing – as borne out by his tally of 25 victories in 27 indoor events.* His time of 3:43.8 smashed the UK best. Whetton went on to win the title for the next two years and would become European outdoor champion in 1969.

A big talking point during the summer was the world relay record that wasn't. A 4x880y event was put on at the Oxford & Cambridge v Cornell and Pennsylvania match at Crystal Palace and, as I wrote: *I, one of nearly 10,000 deliriously happy fans, rose to the four British half-milers who knocked spots off the world record. The prolonged roar of approval by the crowd, so rarely encountered these days at the White City, produced that tingling sensation of actually participating in a little bit of history.* Graeme Grant opened with a leg timed in 1:49.5, Mike Varah clocked 1:48.9 and Chris Carter 1:48.0. John Boulter, who had, four days earlier, bettered Carter's UK 800m record of 1:46.6 by a tenth, took the baton some six metres ahead of his Russian opponent. *Boulter raced away like a quarter-miler. Literally ... for he covered the first lap in a sensational 49.8, perilously close to his best flat-out 440 time of 48.8! Coach John Le Masurier acted quickly and shrewdly: "Fifty-two" he called out to Boulter, who a little later was to reflect on the fact that a 52 lap had never before felt quite so bad.* The second lap was a struggle but Boulter managed an heroic 1:48.2 and the British quartet came home some 10 metres clear in 7:14.6.

However, and surely this could only happen in Britain where strict adherence to the rules over-rode common sense, the BAAB decided it would not recognise the time as a British record and therefore could not forward Britain's time to the IAAF for ratification as a world record. Why? Because John Le Mas had infringed the rule which forbids the unauthorised calling of intermediate times. As Jimmy Green rightly commented: "Many may feel that this is ludicrous and that the Board are not just bending over backwards to stick rigidly to the rules, but falling head over heels in the process." The official world record was awarded instead to the Soviet team (7:16.0), depriving the four British runners of the distinction of receiving world record plaques for their honest but ultimately unrewarded efforts. These days anything goes in terms of information given to runners during a race by the public address announcers but continued attempts to have the record recognised retrospectively have failed.

Mike Varah, who died in 2007 aged 62, was among those featured in the Who's Who series during 1966, others including one Jeffrey Archer, then aged 26 with best marks of 9.8 and 9.6w for 100y and 21.5 for 220y and with one appearance as a British international to his name when he placed third over 200m against Sweden. He would later find fame, fortune and notoriety in other fields of endeavour. John Lusardi's "Spotlight on Youth" column just before the start of the season focused on two very promising 16 year-old throwers in Geoff Capes and Joe Bugner. Capes was already almost 1.98m (6ft 6in) tall and weighed 105kg (230 pounds), but unbelievably was the smallest of five brothers and in his early days as an athlete ran a 4:48 mile and raced cross country! He had just come under the coaching influence of future Olympic high hurdler and TV commentator Stuart Storey, himself only 23. Filling out later to a massive 140kg (308 pounds) Police Constable Capes would go on to win the Commonwealth Games title in 1974 and 1978, become European Indoor champion in 1974 and 1976 and set his first British record in 1972 when he matched Arthur Rowe's figures of 19.56m. He ended up with 21.68m in 1980 and that remained the record until 2003. What with his two televised World's Strongest Man titles he became one of Britain's most famous sporting celebrities. Bugner, who had expressed a wish to compete in the Mexico City Olympics in two years' time, never threw the senior discus as in 1967 he turned professional boxer. During a very long career in the ring, finally retiring at age 49, he won 69 of his 83 fights, 43 by a knockout.

The highlight of 1966 for me was flying to Kingston, Jamaica for the British Empire & Commonwealth Games. The trip didn't start too auspiciously as the travel agency responsible had booked me into a hotel very high up in the Blue Mountains. The scenery was beautiful but staying there would have been totally impracticable for someone needing to be at the stadium from early morning to late at night. It didn't help, either, that my room was full of creepy-crawlies, many of frighteningly large dimensions. After one sleepless night I demanded a transfer to the Myrtle Bank Hotel (as mentioned in the James Bond novel, "Doctor No"), the official Press hotel down near the harbour, and from then on everything was just wonderful. All the facilities I needed were on hand, transfers to the stadium were laid on, my Fleet Street colleagues were staying there too and in addition to enjoying some great athletics I revelled in the whole pulsating experience of life in Jamaica.

It's a small world. One of the delightful young ladies who acted as Press officers was a graduate of the University of the West Indies where one of my school friends, Harold Heller, had been a tutor in Latin and Greek, and she remembered him. Dawn's sport was netball rather than athletics, but we found plenty to talk about and in my spare time she introduced me to the sights and sounds of Kingston, even teaching me a Reggae dance that was all the craze at that time. I should add that although Fred Astaire and Gene Kelly are in my pantheon of heroes, the description that I have two left feet is altogether too complimentary. Still, I got by and for a few moments I found myself gyrating opposite an enthusiastic 15 year-old Princess Anne, whose dance partner appeared to be the pole vault gold medallist Trevor Bickle from Australia. Another memorable, somewhat surreal, event was interviewing long jump winner Lynn Davies and Ron Pickering at a *Track & Field News* dinner before a largely American audience. Ron was the Welsh team coach and this was before he became one of TV's most recognisable faces and voices. It was my first public interview and I was a little nervous but chatting on stage to two of the most likeable personalities in our sport proved a pleasure, and the fans seemed happy too.

It was an inspiring experience to enter the stadium each day, for just outside is a superb statue of a runner driving out of his blocks which is a composite of 1948 and 1952 Olympic legends Arthur Wint and Herb McKenley. Disappointingly for the large and animated crowds, there were no Jamaican winners but one of the stars of the Games was from the Caribbean: Trinidad's (and Cambridge University's) Wendell Mottley. He set a Commonwealth 440y record of 45.8 in his heat, and in the final he clocked 45.0 and would surely have broken the world record of 44.9 had he not run a semi-final (46.3) only two hours previously. What poor scheduling, the athletes being the last to be considered. He never received official credit for it, but Wendell's electronic time of 45.08 (worth 44.82 for 400m) was a world best. However, he did achieve a ratified world record in the final event, the 4x440y relay, when he anchored his team to a time of 3:02.8 with a glorious 44.5 leg.

The Games were notable for the emergence of Kenyan middle and long distance runners. At Perth in 1962 the highest Kenyan placing in these events was fourth in the 880y, but in Kingston Kip Keino brought off a great 3 miles (12:57.4) and mile (3:55.34) double, Naftali Temu trounced Ron Clarke in the 6 miles (27:14.6) and there were medals also in the 880y and steeplechase. Clarke was also second in the 3 miles, becoming the first man to break 13 minutes and lose. He even led up to 15 miles in the marathon before dropping out two miles later.

What a dramatic race that was. It started at the unearthly time of 5.30 am when it was already 27°C with 75% humidity and Scotland's Jim Alder, who had placed third in the 6 miles, approached the finish some 50 yards ahead of England's Bill Adcocks.

Suddenly: panic ... confusion. The officials who should have been at the stadium entrance to direct the runners were absent – apparently lured from their posts in order to catch sight of the royal party who were just arriving – and the bewildered athletes were left to fend for themselves. Alder chose what was probably the correct route but Adcocks unwittingly took a short cut in the meantime so that he and not Alder was first on the track. Fortunately, however, Alder was able to pass his man and win by 20 yards. The times by both of just outside 2:22 were quite remarkable in the conditions, the mercury registering 30°C by the end. There was high drama too in the women's 880y.

With 50 yards to go it looked to be between Marise Stephen (New Zealand) and Abby Hoffman (Canada) but Judy Pollock (Australia) was weaving in and out in a desperate attempt to make up lost ground. Thirty yards left and the race was surely Stephen's for Hoffman had tried all she knew and could not get in front. Then, with barely a dozen strides between her and the first major title in over a decade of world-class running, Stephen stumbled to a halt – victim of her own fatigue for she appeared to trip over her own feet. Thus former infant prodigy Hoffman – who had finished dead last in this event four years ago as a 15 year-old – found herself out in front and in sweet ecstasy crossed the line a yard ahead of the swift-finishing Pollock in a great 2:04.3, nearly 3 sec inside her previous fastest. All these years later Abby remains a prominent name in the sport as a long serving IAAF Council member.

Athletes from the UK won seven titles in Kingston through England's David Hemery in the 120y hurdles, Howard Payne in the hammer, John FitzSimons in the javelin, Ron Wallwork in the 20 miles walk and Mary Rand in the long jump, Wales' Lynn Davies and Scotland's Jim Alder, together with 11 silver and 7 bronze medals. That level of success was not maintained at the European Championships in Budapest, which started just 17 days after the Commonwealth Games ended. At Stockholm in 1958 there were seven British winners and a total of 17 medals; at Belgrade in 1962 there were five golds out of 14 medals. The tally from Budapest was just two medals, albeit of the gold variety thanks to Lynn Davies and marathoner Jim Hogan.

The absence of any British track medallists created an unwanted record. That has never happened before in the European Championships – or in an Olympics for that matter (excluding 1904 when Britain was not represented). The close proximity of Kingston was obviously a key factor in the disappointing form of the team as a whole.

Just how disappointing can be gauged not just from the medal count but by awarding points for the top six places in each event. The British men achieved their lowest ever score and position (7th), as did the women (equal 9th). Significantly, these were the first European Championships at which East Germany competed as a separate entity. Victories were gained in the men's 800m, 10,000m, pole vault, discus and 20km walk; women's 80m hurdles, discus and javelin. The GDR had arrived. Non-arrivals in Budapest included four of the USSR's foremost female performers. As I noted in my report on the women's shot: *The main talking point about this event was the absence of Tamara Press, the all-time great of women's shot putting. Officially, Tamara and sister Irina stayed at home because their mother was seriously ill. Unofficially, though, it is believed that they – together with Maria Itkina and Tatyana Shchelkanova – were removed from the Soviet team in view of the strict medical examination demanded of women competitors in these Championships.* All four later announced their retirement.

Reporting on the second day's action, I wrote: *It was October 18 1964 all over again – rain, more rain and Lynn Davies defeating all comers. Only this time there can be no possible justification for those "lucky" jibes that Lynn had to endure two years ago. In Davies, Britain is fortunate enough to possess one of the greatest championship competitors in living memory and his dramatic victory here over Igor Ter-Ovanesyan completed the coveted hat-trick of successes ... Olympic, Commonwealth and European. Even Fleet Street cynics who claim to have seen it all stamped and yelled like pop fans when Lynn pulled out his show stopper in the final act."* He jumped 7.98m to his great rival's 7.88m.

Mary Rand, also hoping to complete the gold medal hat-trick, fell well short. After placing fourth in the pentathlon (two points away from bronze) she finished 11th in the long jump, won by Poland's Irena Kirszenstein, who had already taken silver in the 100m and gold in the 200m, and would gain another gold in the 4x100m relay. That relay featured an astonishing run by a team-mate of Irena's, who had won the 100m and placed second at 200m.

Ewa Klobukowska's anchor leg can be compared only to Bob Hayes' stint in Tokyo. One would not have believed it had one not seen it with one's own eyes. When Irena Kirszenstein passed the baton to Eva, Poland were way down the field some eight yards behind the leaders, West Germany. It seemed hopeless ... until Ewa was seen galloping past one girl after another. She caught Jutta Stöck (an 11.5 performer this year) a stride or two from the tape. It was the greatest sprint I have ever seen by a woman – and this reporter was simply mesmerised by Wilma Rudolph in Rome.

The following year, at the European Cup Final in Kiev, Ewa failed a gender test ("one chromosome too many" we were told), was banned and had her three world records (an 11.1 100m in 1965 and two relay records from 1964) annulled by the IAAF. That test was subsequently found to be flawed and in 1968 she gave birth to a son.

Mary Peters, who competed in the shot in Budapest, provided a graphic account of the humiliating sex test procedure in her 1974 autobiography *Mary P.* "I went into a bare room which contained two women doctors, one examination couch and one large enamel bowl containing some white, cloudy antiseptic in which the doctors apparently washed their hands after each examination. What occurred next I can only describe as the most crude and degrading experience I have ever known in my life. I was ordered to lie on the couch and pull my knees up. The doctors then proceeded to undertake an examination which, in modern parlance, amounted to a grope. Presumably they were searching for hidden testes. They found none and I left. Like everyone else who had fled that detestable room I said nothing to anyone still waiting in the corridor and made my way, shaken, back to my room." By the time of the 1968 Olympics that procedure had been supplanted by a saliva test and prior to the 1972 Olympics a hair follicle from the head was examined instead. Tests have since been abolished, except where there are exceptional circumstances.

For those who had followed his career closely, knowing how good a runner he was but sharing so many of his disappointments, Jim Hogan's marathon victory was an absolute delight.

Jim Hogan, Britain's most maligned athlete, showed his detractors a thing or two by winning the European title in only his third attempt at the marathon distance. Victory can never have been so sweet, for Jim has been regarded by many (unjustly so) as a quitter. Jim has had more than his fair share of misfortune in the past and, on the face of it, four retirements out of four in the Olympics and European Championships is hardly a proud record, but there was a good reason for each one and Jim has shown on many other occasions just how fine a runner he is.

Running with masterly judgement, he won by over a minute and a half in 2:20:05, a personal best. I interviewed the former Irishman shortly after his return to London where he worked as a groundsman and among his ambitions was to break the world record for 30,000m. That he did, just a few weeks later.

The other big interview I did for AW in 1966 was with Lynn Davies at his home near Cardiff and this appeared in the December 3 edition, a very special issue as it marked the magazine's 21st anniversary. With Lynn gracing the cover in colour (a first), the issue ran to a record 44 pages. Jimmy Green recounted how it all started, as a monthly in December 1945. The magazine went weekly in 1950. "From then on we have never looked back. There were difficult times when we wondered how we were going to keep pace with rising costs, but somehow we weathered the storms and hard work, long hours and at times much self-sacrifice by a dedicated staff." From its small beginnings, he wrote proudly, "AW is today recognised, respected and quoted as a leading authority on athletics in countries all over the world."

9. MY DREAM JOB: 'AW' EDITOR (1967-1968)

The first edition having sold out, I was commissioned by the publishers to bring out a second edition of the *Encyclopaedia of Athletics* in 1967, and one review which gave me particular pride was by Norris and Ross McWhirter, founders of the *Guinness Book of Records*. "As people who have to live with reference books every day of their working lives, we unreservedly commend the *Encyclopaedia of Athletics* as an exceptional work, even to the extent that if marooned on a cinder island in a steeplechase water jump and rationed to just one book of athletics, it would have to be Melvyn Watman's *Encyclopaedia* – at least, that is, until we have studied his forthcoming *History of British Athletics* which we so impatiently await."

A contract for that volume of history had been signed as long ago as June 1965 for completion by October 1966 but my workload had been so heavy that I was unable to deliver the completed manuscript before 1968. Looking back, I did commit myself to too many projects: AW was taking up an increasing amount of my time as Jimmy was concentrating more on the advertising and business aspects and leaving the bulk of editorial work to me and my capable assistant John Lusardi; I was still freelancing for various newspapers and agencies; I was researching and writing those two books; and I had also started the *International Athletics Press Service*, which provided regular world lists and other material for the media and which continued for the next 25 years.

Our sport was developing and in May I reported on a significant meeting in Leicester. *Fabulous ... terrific ... marvellous ... great. These were the sort of adjectives being bandied about by athletes like Lynn Davies, John Boulter, Tim Graham, Colin Campbell and Alan Pascoe after competing on the new En-Tout-Cas all-weather track. In fact the eight-lane porous rubber surfaced track, a delight to the eye as well as the foot, proved to be the hero of an excellent afternoon's athletics. The rain poured down almost without stop but the track presented a firm, springy surface throughout.*

It was, however, the cinder track at White City which continued (but for the last time) as the venue for the Women's AAA Championships. *A good meeting athletically but quite abysmal in terms of presentation. For how much longer will Bovril, the sponsors, spend money on a meeting that is run seemingly in contempt for the few members of the public [Saturday's attendance was a mere 1500] still willing to pay to see women's athletics? The time is long overdue for a combined men's and women's championships.* We had to wait another 21 years before that became a reality. As for Bovril, they terminated their sponsorship after the 1969 meeting.

In contrast, a crowd of 20,000 turned up at the White City for the AAA Championships. UK records were posted by John Boulter in the 880y and John Sherwood in the 440y hurdles, while that most popular of visitors, Ron Clarke, made his final appearance on this track, the fans rising to him as he came storming home in the 3 miles in 12:59.6. The junior 2 miles was won by Tony

Simmons in 8:50.4 but he would have been strongly challenged by Ian Stewart (4th) had he not fallen heavily during the race, while Dave Bedford finished 7th. They had placed 1-2-3 in that order in the Youths race at the English National Cross Country Championships in March and would go on to glittering careers as seniors. Later that month Simmons and Stewart competed in the first full junior international match, Britain beating France in Portsmouth. Over a period of several years such matches were of enormous benefit in offering future senior stars early experience of international competition and team spirit but the powers that be unwisely decided to discontinue them after 2003.

With no major international championships in 1967 the big event was the second edition of the European Cup. The British men's team, who had finished last two years earlier, this time failed even to reach the final but the girls made it through. The final was staged in Kiev, now the capital of Ukraine but then part of the Soviet Union. I was in an AW tour party of supporters who flew by Aeroflot first to Leningrad (now St Petersburg) where we spent two nights and visited that city's stunning buildings and museums including the Hermitage and the Summer Palace. Then it was off to Moscow for another couple of days during which we toured the Kremlin, filed past Lenin's Tomb in Red Square and marvelled at their Metro stations. Incidentally, while chatting to our Intourist guide she showed me her passport. In the section stating nationality, which would normally be Russian, Ukrainian, Georgian, Latvian, whatever, it was marked simply Jewish. She shrugged her shoulders; that was how she was defined in the Soviet Union – someone uniquely classified by her religion. It was probably like that in Nazi Germany too, and it was that sinister singling out of one segment of the Soviet population that was among the reasons I boycotted the Moscow Olympics 13 years later.

I was one of only three from the British media to be in Kiev for the match, the others being John Rodda of *The Guardian* and Adrian Metcalfe, by then a commentator for ITV. The British team performed pretty well as expected to finish fifth of six, the USSR winning ahead of East Germany. Our solitary winner was Lillian Board, clocking her second fastest 400m time of 53.7 in unfavourable weather conditions. The AW party was due to fly on to complete their Soviet Union tour in Yalta but I had arranged to return to London next morning on a charter flight carrying the British and West German athletes. Team manager Marea Hartman told me to be at the team's hotel at a certain time, which I was … only to discover the party had already left for the airport. Okay, no problem, I would take a taxi. Only there *was* a problem. The taxi driver explained as best he could in his limited English that there were two airports; which one did I want? I chose the one he seemed to think was for international flights and, with the minutes slipping by, it was an anxious ride. If it was the wrong airport I wouldn't have time to get to the other before the flight's departure and I would be stranded in Kiev without sufficient money to buy myself an air ticket home. Imagine my relief as I entered the terminal to see Jimmy and his tour members. I quickly explained my predicament. Had he seen the British team? Yes, they were over that way. I was in time. Phew! The flight back, with a stop in Germany, was blissfully stress-free and made all the more pleasant by enjoying the congenial company of that most consistent and durable of high jumpers, the 1960 Olympic silver medallist Dorothy Shirley.

The major event at home that summer was the Britain v USA men's match which attracted 35,000 spectators to the White City, the largest crowd since 1958. Although the much heralded Emsley Carr Mile failed to live up to expectations, Jim Ryun easily outkicking Kip Keino in an unexceptional 3:56.0, the young American having set a world record of 3:51.1 earlier in the season, those who stayed on to see the later stages of the long jump were privileged to see a blood and thunder contest of the highest level, a real test of muscle, skill and nerve between two of the most uncompromising competitors in the sport. In the first round Lynn Davies jumped 7.97m, followed a minute or two later by a 7.99m effort from Ralph Boston. Bob Beamon, who had defeated both in an Americas v Europe match in Montreal three days earlier, reached a windy 7.94m with his second jump but never improved after that. Boston increased his lead with a fifth round 8.01m.

The final round. Lynn, inspired rather than burdened by the knowledge that he required at least 8.02m to stand a chance of winning, powered along the runway, smacked the board and drove into his gravity defying act ... and came to earth far beyond the 26-foot (7.92m) mark. Thirty seconds of suspense, then a roar of approval as the feet and inches equivalent of 8.11m was announced. Lynn had raised his game [Ron Pickering's favourite expression] once again. But Boston, like Davies, is at his best when the chips are down. A hush descended as he set off on his swift, fluid run ... gasps of admiration as he soared like a bird ... unstinting acclaim. Boston, the supreme, had jumped a wind aided 8.20m. Who says field events lack spectator appeal?

Later in August the AAA International Meeting saw Keino return to the White City and this time he delivered the goods. He failed in his bid to break Ryun's world mile record but it was a brave try. Both his half mile splits were 1:56.9 for a time of 3:53.8 but it was far from being an even paced race. His first lap was around 56 sec (the pacemaker much too fast at 54.9), the second about 61, the third was 59.2 and the fourth 57.7. There was a world record, though, in the women's 3x800m relay when the British team of 19 year-old Rosemary Stirling (2:06.2), Pat Lowe (2:07.2) and Pam Piercy (2:06.6) clocked 6:20.0. I wrote a lengthy article on Rose, who I regarded as a potential world record breaker at 800m.

Rosemary is quite a paradox. For a start she is a miniature Commonwealth of Nations rolled into one: born in New Zealand [of a Scottish father and English mother], she lives in England and runs for Scotland. At 5ft 1in (1.55m) and 112lb (51kg) she must be the smallest quarter and half miler of international class. Off the track this charming girl is shy and retiring; on it she is transformed into a regular tigress oozing aggression.

In 1966 her target was to win the English Schools 880y, which she did, but never dreamed of running in the Commonwealth Games. However, after winning the Scottish 440y title she was selected for Kingston and there she finished fourth in both that event and the 880y, setting personal bests of 54.4 and 2:05.4. Her most impressive performances, though, were in 660y training time trials. The world records for 800m and 880y at that time were 2:01.0 and 2:02.0. Rose would eventually improve to a tantalising 2:00.15 for 800m but that was in 1972 and the record had moved on to 1:58.5 by then.

Having got to know Rose and her parents, I would often stay over at their home near Wolverhampton when reporting on RAF Cosford indoor meetings and on one occasion foolishly tried to join in one of her fearsome interval training sessions at Aldersley Stadium. I didn't last long! Incidentally, although long retired from track racing I attempted to keep reasonably fit by running alone around my local streets in North London. Nothing remarkable about that these days. Since the advent of mass marathons and half marathons it's a common enough sight but back in the 1960s one would almost inevitably attract comments, sometimes jeers, from passers-by. It was a different world then for road runners.

The world's most talked about athlete in 1967, as was also the case in 1966, was Jim Ryun and in addition to AW documenting his racing achievements and training log in some detail I penned a review of Cordner Nelson's newly published book, *The Jim Ryun Story*. There cannot be many 20 year-olds worthy of a hardback biography but Ryun's story was astonishing and inspiring. Not fast enough to make his junior high school track team at 440y, he decided to try his luck at the mile. His first attempt was in a Wichita East High School race in Kansas on September 7 1962. He was 15 and described as "a frail-looking boy, a gangling 6ft 1in in height and as awkward as a colt". His time was 5:38 and he finished 14th. A 2:22 half mile four days later was no more impressive but his great good fortune was that the track coach at his school was Bob Timmons, who had guided Archie San Romani Jnr to an American high school record of 4:08.9 in 1959. Jim's progress was astounding: before his 16th birthday he ran 4:19.7 and later in 1963 he was down to 4:07.8. Running more than 110 miles a week in training in February, much of it over ice and snow, he created a sensation in 1964 by becoming the first schoolboy to break four minutes and winning selection for the Olympic 1500m.

In 1965 Ryun took the scalp of New Zealand's Olympic champion Peter Snell at the US Championships, producing a 53.9 last quarter to beat the New Zealander by a tenth in 3:55.3, an American record which placed him fourth on the world all-time list behind France's Michel Jazy (3:53.6), Snell (3:54.1) and Herb Elliott (3:54.5). True greatness was achieved in 1966. A 46.9 440y relay leg indicated new levels of speed and an American 2 miles record of 8:25.1 was a measure of his stamina, but few were prepared for his first serious 880y race. With a previous best of merely 1:50.3 he put together laps of 53.3 and 51.6 to break Snell's world record of 1:45.1 with 1:44.9! That was the equivalent of 1:44.2 for 800m. The climax of his season was the mile at Berkeley where he demolished Jazy's world record with the dazzling time of 3:51.3, at 19 the youngest man ever to hold that prestigious record. He clipped that to 3:51.1 at the 1967 US Championships in Bakersfield, covering the second half in 1:52.2, and he finished even faster in the USA v Commonwealth match in Los Angeles when he smashed Elliott's 1500m world record of 3:35.6 with 3:33.1, the biggest single improvement for over 50 years. This time his last 880y took just 1:51.3 and he left Kip Keino four seconds behind. As mentioned earlier, Ryun beat Keino again at the White City and ended his momentous season in a Germany v USA match where he ran a slowish 3:38.2 but it was a race remarkable for his 24.8 last 200m and 50.6 400m.

Fast forward to October and news that, in training in high altitude Mexico City – the controversial choice of venue for the 1968 Olympics – Lynn bettered the world record with a leap of 8.42m (8.48m from take-off to landing). That couldn't count, of course, and in a competition there six days later Lynn (8.13m) was well beaten by Igor Ter-Ovanesyan, whose 8.35m equalled Boston's world record. Who could have guessed then what the Olympic long jump a year on would produce.

As the year drew to a close there came news of a startling marathon run in Fukuoka, Japan by Derek Clayton, who was born in Barrow-in-Furness, moved to Belfast when he was eight and emigrated to Australia in 1963. The world best stood at 2:12:00 by Japan's Morio Shigematsu in the 1965 Polytechnic Marathon ... but Clayton was timed in 2:09:37, the first time anyone had averaged sub-5 minute miles all the way. Even Abebe Bikila, operating at his Tokyo Olympic pace, would have been left over half a mile behind. In 1969 Clayton would go even faster with 2:08:34 in Antwerp but there has always been some doubt expressed about the measurement of that course and to this day Ron Hill believes that his own 2:09:28 when winning the Commonwealth Games title in Edinburgh in 1970 should have been regarded as the completely authentic world record.

Bearing in mind what was to occur at the 1968 Games, a report in our issue of December 16 of a possible boycott by black American athletes, including world 200m and 400m record holder Tommie Smith and fellow 400m star Lee Evans, was of some significance. Interviewed by our US correspondent, Dick Drake of *Track & Field News*, Smith stated: "There have been a lot of marches, protests and sit-ins on the situation of Negro ostracism in the US. And I don't think that this boycott of the Olympics would stop the problem, but I think that people will see that we will not sit on our haunches and take this sort of stuff. We are a race of proud people and want to be treated as such. Our goal would not be to just improve conditions for ourselves and team-mates, but to improve things for the entire Negro community. I have worked for a long time for the Olympics, and I would hate to lose that. But I think that boycotting the Olympics for a good cause is strong enough reason not to compete." Evans commented: "To the extent that I think things would be different for the American Negro by 1972, I am willing to consider boycotting. We are men first and athletes second."

On an altogether lighter note, our Christmas issue contained the first seasonal contribution by a 20 year-old Cliff Temple, entitled "All-Weather-Ella: An Athletics Pantomime". Both he and Peter Matthews, whose first long profile

– on Belgium's Olympic steeplechase champion Gaston Roelants – appeared in the final edition of the year, would become among my closest of professional colleagues. Meanwhile, one of my oldest friends, Colin Young, succeeded "Timber" Woodcock as AW's walking correspondent and provided, for many years, superb coverage of that side of our sport with the insight of a prominent competitor.

That December 30 1967 issue featured Jimmy Green's final editorial after 22 years at the helm. "For some time now, as the magazine has developed its coverage of events, its circulation and readership, with consequent increase of correspondence and work generally, it has become more and more difficult for me to write on topical matters, coaching, and manage reports of current events, never mind advertising and taking photographs! It has been obvious to us for some time that a reorganisation was becoming more and more necessary. While continuing to hold the reins as managing editor, I am handing over as editor of AW to Melvyn Watman, who has served you so well in recent years and will, I know, continue to do so in the years ahead."

Under the heading "Dream Comes True After 17 Years", I began my first contribution in January 1968 as AW editor:

All youngsters dream of what they would like to do when they grow up, and I was no exception. At about the age of five I wanted to become a naturalist, at seven a bus conductor and at ten I would have settled for being either left-half for the Arsenal or else a train driver. I was 12 when I first began to see myself as a future editor of Athletics Weekly. The year was 1950 and I had just become crazy over athletics.

I don't recall the exact date but it was some time in August 1950 that AW entered my life. From then on, Friday morning could never come swiftly enough for me and I'm sure I never did much work whenever the latest AW lay hidden in my school desk. Strange the number of times I found it necessary to open my desk-lid on Fridays! Gradually I became more and more keen to contribute in some way to the magazine and in March 1954 I received my first printed acknowledgement for acting as "middle man" for a questionnaire answered by the great American javelin thrower Bud Held. More questionnaires followed and then in July 1954 – a few weeks before I left school – I was thrilled to bits to find a full-page article of mine on Bob Mathias had been published.

In 1961 – after five years in journalism and two on National Service in the RAF – I joined the AW staff on a full-time basis. Now begins a new phase in my 17-year relationship with this magazine which has become so important a part of my life. I have a high standard to maintain but I shall do my best, never losing sight of Jimmy's maxim that this is essentially the ATHLETE'S magazine.

The first change I made was to abolish the separate long-standing "With The Ladies" section and integrate women's results with the men's. I had always regarded women's athletics as being as important, enjoyable and significant as the men's and saw no reason for any segregation. The commitment to documenting and celebrating the female side of the sport was augmented by the birth in April of *Women's Athletics*, Britain's first ever magazine devoted solely to that subject. A lively offshoot of AW, it was lovingly edited by the brilliant Cliff Temple – only 21 but already a skilled journalist and deeply knowledgeable. The monthly existed for only a year but it served its purpose: by catering for a specialist audience it built up a body of readers who had not all been AW subscribers and when it folded the content and goodwill were transferred, to the benefit of AW.

The other major alteration was to drop the traditional page three editorial column. I felt that there wasn't always an important topic to discuss, and often trivial items would fill out that rigid space, so I redesigned the page to feature the contents and a fixture list for the week ahead while an editorial – its length no longer restricted – would appear elsewhere in the magazine on an *ad hoc* basis.

In February I gave due prominence and the heading "Olympic Movement In Jeopardy" to a leader which began: *The International Olympic Committee has, one fears, dealt a death blow to the Olympic movement as we know it by its astonishing decision to allow South Africa to compete in the Mexico City Games, even though apartheid continues unabated in that country.*

In March I wrote in my "Trackwise" column: *There is hope yet for this year's Olympics. The Mexicans, in particular, are applying all possible pressure in an attempt to get the IOC to change its mind over re-admitting South Africa. At the latest count those nations who will boycott the Games should South Africa be represented include 32 from Africa (among them Kenya, Ethiopia, Nigeria, Ghana and Tunisia), plus several from Asia (notably India, Pakistan and Malaysia) and Cuba.*

In April I was able to write: *Good sense has prevailed after all, and the Mexico City Olympics will go ahead as originally conceived. Meeting in Lausanne last weekend, the nine-man executive board of the IOC came to the unanimous decision that a telegram be sent to all 71 members of the IOC strongly recommending that the invitation to South Africa to compete in this year's Games be withdrawn.*

I added: *The Olympic bosses had, sooner or later, to face up to reality. Had they refused to withdraw South Africa's invitation the Games would have declined into a farce, with most of Africa, Asia, East Europe and the Caribbean absent, not to mention a weakened USA contingent. There would, in fact, have been no guarantee that Mexico would have gone ahead with the staging of such a depleted Games. A word of sympathy, though, for those South African sportsmen and women whose hopes had been raised, only to be dashed again. I would liked to have seen athletes like Paul Nash and Humphrey Khosi in Mexico City but because of their government's inflexible attitude they will be deprived of the opportunity.* It wasn't until 1992, the year after *apartheid* was officially abolished, that South Africa was welcomed back to the Olympics.

The Olympics dominated AW's agenda throughout 1968. Quite apart from the South African issue there was the question of Mexico City's suitability as venue. The IOC had made a bad decision, for the high altitude would inevitably destroy the hopes of lowland athletes in the endurance events, thus nullifying the concept of fair competition for all. I felt particularly for Ron Clarke, whose scintillating form that summer would count for nothing in the rarefied air of Mexico's capital.

A big event for me that summer was the publication of *History of British Athletics*, the first book on the subject since the McWhirter Twins' classic *Get To Your Marks!* in 1951. Researching and writing this book had been a pleasurable but time-consuming task, so mindful that publication had already been delayed considerably because of my other commitments I was regrettably unable to provide the coverage that the history of British women's athletics deserved: a scant 14 pages compared to over 200 for the men. As someone who always sought to treat women's athletics on a par with men's that situation troubled me greatly, and I had to wait 44 years before I was able to make amends by writing the *Official History of the Women's AAA*.

Lynn Davies did me the honour of contributing a foreword and I was gratified to receive several favourable reviews. Harold Abrahams in AW wrote: "I am full of appreciation and admiration for all the intelligent research which has been so successfully undertaken. This is a fine book for reference and in addition a most happy chronicle in which to dip again and again, particularly to re-live so many events which one was lucky enough to see over the last 50 years." Cliff Temple in *Women's Athletics* obviously regretted the sparse amount of space devoted to that side of the sport but noted: "The book took two years of preparation, and anyone who ever saw Mel Watman at his desk surrounded by printers' proofs, newspaper cuttings, results, photographs, letters, press handouts and so forth, would wonder how he found the time to read them all, edit a weekly 36-page magazine, travel all over the place to report meetings for AW and run a press statistical service, let alone write this book. Yet he has managed it admirably and produced a book which is certainly destined to become the standard work on the subject – and most deservedly so."

One of the brightest developments of the season was the return to competition of Britain's greatest ever female sprinter Dorothy Hyman. She retired after the 1964 Olympics to concentrate on coaching and published an autobiography *Sprint To Fame* which, because payment was involved, caused her to be barred from competition under the strict amateur laws of that era. Having made a success of coaching and the Dorothy Hyman Track Club she felt the urge to return to the track and in April 1968 applied to the WAAA to be reinstated. She was permitted to run at club and county level but, absurdly, not at any meeting held under IAAF laws. After four years out and with only a few weeks of training she clocked 10.8 for 100y, finishing fourth in a race won by protégée Val Peat in a UK record equalling 10.6. By the following year, aged 28, she was again Britain's top sprinter but was ruled ineligible for the European Championships in Athens where Anita Neil in the 100m and Val Peat in the 200m – both well behind Dorothy in the WAAA Championships – gained bronze medals. In Val's opinion Dorothy "would definitely have been first in both sprints."

The archaic amateur rules still bedevilled the sport, as did the reluctance of the Establishment to implement an integrated British Athletic Federation as recommended by the Byers Report published in May 1968. This was a Committee of Inquiry, commissioned by the AAA and BAAB and chaired by Lord (Frank) Byers, the Liberal Party leader in the House of Lords and a former British Universities 440y hurdles record holder. Its terms of reference were "to examine the problems of development of athletics under the jurisdiction of the AAA and BAAB, including matters of organisation, administration, finance, coaching services and competition, and to make recommendations thereon." The Report found the case for one governing body for athletics in the UK to be proved beyond doubt, but the traditional conglomeration of autonomous male and female national and regional associations, keen to protect their own interests, prevaricated for year after year and it wasn't until 1991 that a unified governing body, the British Athletic Federation, finally came into existence.

The White City might have been the home of British athletics since 1932 but the stadium was owned by the Greyhound Racing Association, a 500-yard dog track encircling the cinder running track. The two sports usually co-existed well enough but that wasn't the case at the 1968 AAA Championships, which was attended by the Queen (Patron of the AAA) for the first time since 1952. It was the pole vault that was the problem. It started at 2 pm and dragged on far beyond the 5.30 finishing time which had been contracted with the stadium authorities.

As the minutes ticked by, and the competition neared its climax, high ranking officials of the GRA grew steadily more irate for "the dogs" were due to start at 7.45. A plea over the loudspeakers for spectators to leave the stadium was deservedly jeered and disregarded and efforts were even made to postpone the event until next day! Happily, this move also was ignored and the vaulters continued although Bob Sparks found his microphone cut off. Eventually with the bar at 16ft 11in (5.15m) Italy's Renato Dionisi was obliged to call it a day after one abortive attempt; it was after seven o'clock. They say these might have been the last AAA Championships to be held at the White City; the pole vault incident adds weight to the argument that it is time to move to a stadium that puts athletics first. In fact, the Championships transferred to the far more suitable Crystal Palace with its synthetic track in 1971.

As I was ill, John Lusardi ably covered the WAAA Championships, which had stolen a march on the men by already relocating to Crystal Palace and the crowd of 4000, the largest recorded at this meeting, was treated to a world record of 2:00.5 in the 800m by Yugoslavia's European champion Vera Nikolic with Lillian Board runner-up in 2:02.0, second only to Ann Packer on the UK all-time list.

The International Athletes' Club's Coca-Cola Invitational at the increasingly popular Crystal Palace produced two world records. Ron Clarke, who felt he was running better than at any time in his momentous career, bettered his own 2 miles figures with 8:19.6 (his 17th world record), out on his own after two and a half laps and winning by over 20 seconds. Watching that unfaltering stride of his it was hard to realise that this man was privately suffering; the external image was one of unruffled serenity. The other record came in the women's 4x200m relay where Maureen Tranter, Della James (later Pascoe), Janet Simpson and Val Peat managed, in spite of some pretty lethargic passing, to break the USSR's mark with 1:33.8. Lillian Board, Britain's number one, was out injured. Bearing in mind what would happen in the Olympic final, Colette Besson (53.8) was well beaten in the 400m by Holland's Lia Louer (53.2). Who could possibly have predicted the Frenchwoman's success in Mexico City?

Five days later, again at the Palace, the IAC put on another meeting to give Clarke the chance of attempting to break his world 10,000m record of 27:39.4. Before a few hundred spectators, he fell exactly 10 seconds short, but he commented afterwards, "this was my best ever run." He was hoping for a time of around 27:20 but a strong headwind gusting along the unsheltered back straight put paid to that. Finishing 20th and last in 32:16, sacrificing his own opportunity for a fast time by pacing Clarke whenever he was lapped, was an 18 year-old Dave Bedford, destined to hold that 10,000m record himself five years later. Still in London and again in windy conditions, but this time at the White City, Clarke clocked the fastest 5000m of the year with 13:27.8. If only those Olympics weren't 7000 feet up.

Shortly before the British Olympic team flew out, the squad competed in a match in Portsmouth and two athletes, both destined to win Olympic medals, stood out. Lillian Board not only won the 220y in a windy 23.6 but anchored a 4x110y relay team comprising Anita Neil, Maureen Tranter and Janet Simpson to a world record of 45.0; while David Hemery clocked an outstanding 35.2 over seven flights of hurdles in a race whose distance, oddly, measured 325 ¼ yards although listed on the programme as 330y. His time probably equated to 35.7 for 330 yards, equalling the unofficial world best. Meanwhile, the final US Olympic Trials, held over 7000 feet above sea level at South Lake Tahoe, served notice of the sensational marks to be expected in the explosive events at the Games as world records were set by John Carlos (19.7 200m), Lee Evans (44.0 400m) and Geoff Vanderstock (48.8 400m hurdles), tied by Jim Hines when winning the 100m in 10.0 and bettered (but ruled out by wind assistance) by Bob Beamon with a long jump distance of 8.39m. I liked the quote from a somewhat disappointed Evans: "I was hoping to run 43 today." "43-what?" asked the interviewer. "Just 43."

I went to town with the Olympic Preview, easily the most detailed ever, and even stuck my neck out by predicting the top eight in order in each event with a prediction of the winning mark. Forget the many ones I got wrong! I did correctly forecast Tommie Smith in 200m (predicted time of 19.8/19.9; actual time of 19.83 – world record), Evans in 400m (43.9-44.1; 43.86 – world record), Kip Keino in 1500m (3:39-3:40; an amazing 3:34.91 at altitude), Willie Davenport in 110m hurdles (13.3/13.4; 13.33), Hemery in 400m hurdles (48.7-49.0; incredible world record 48.12), Bob Seagren in pole vault (5.30-5.35m; 5.40m), Bob Beamon in long jump (8.35-8.48m; who could have foreseen

8.90m!), Randy Matson in shot (20.88-21.18m; 20.54m), Janis Lusis in javelin (88.40-89.62m; 90.10m), Bill Toomey in decathlon (8300-8400; 8193), USA in 4x100m (38.2-38.4; 38.24 – world record) & 4x400m (2:56.5-2:57.5; 2:56.16 – world record), Wyomia Tyus in 100m (11.0/11.1; 11.08 – world record), Irena Szewinska (née Kirszenstein) in 200m (22.5-22.7; 22.58 – world record). The other world records came from Hines (9.95 100m), Ralph Doubell (1:44.40 800m), Viktor Saneyev (17.39m triple jump), Viorica Viscopoleanu (6.82m long jump), Margitta Gummel (19.61m shot) and USA in women's 4x100m (42.88). Between us, John Lusardi and I filled 52 pages over two issues with our reports and results.

In terms of athletic performance and competition they were the greatest Olympics yet ... but the altitude made such an impact – helping many competitors to undreamt of achievements in the explosive events and depriving lowland dwellers of any sporting chance of success in the long distance races – that I shall remember Mexico as the scene of the Schizophrenic Olympics. So, plenty of delight and incredulity; but, alas, all too much despair also. Memories of Beamon and Hemery will linger for ever but so, too, will the haunting images of an ashen Ron Clarke sprawled out gasping for oxygen. My sympathy for the stricken often escalated into a helpless feeling of outrage. Well, Mr Brundage, I would fume, are you satisfied now that there is something in this business of altitude. Fundamental Principle One of the Olympic Rules preaches about assembling amateurs of all nations "in fair and equal competition". Humbug. In considering a list of the outstanding athletes of the Games one ought not to lose sight of men like Clarke, Ron Hill, Rex Maddaford, George Young and Kerry O'Brien, all of whom fought so valiantly against impossible odds. Medals are not the only criteria when assessing the worth of an athlete.

The two superstars of Mexico City, though, must surely be Bob Beamon and Al Oerter. With one jump Beamon transformed all ideas of what is humanly possible in his event and, by implication, in all others. An athlete must be judged by his competitive record against his contemporaries – and on that basis there has never been an athlete like "Big Al". I can safely predict that his achievement in winning four Olympics running will never be beaten.

That's still true, although Carl Lewis did equal Oerter's four straight gold medals and in an event, the long jump, which is less noted for longevity of career than the discus.

Beamon's long jump was the most incredible of so many startling performances, but he gave his supporters a worrying time in the qualifying round by fouling twice before advancing with 8.19m, second longest behind Ralph Boston's Olympic record of 8.27m. Lynn Davies also caused missed heartbeats for he too had two no jumps before qualifying in third place with 7.94m. The final was just three jumps old when Beamon took to the runway. I had my binoculars trained on him and here's how I described what happened next.

Here was the man to be feared, the one who could wrap up the title with an initial jump of 28 feet (8.53m). Fast on the runway (he's a 9.5 100 yards sprinter) the lanky, loose limbed American took off amid gasps of astonishment. Never had such elevation been seen in a long jumper. What mattered though was where he landed, and as he touched down after what was to prove the longest unaided flight by man, the crowd by the pit exploded with excitement. The officials in charge of measurement seemed to be taking an awfully long time so it seemed a pretty good bet that the world record of 8.35m had been bettered, but was it as far as the magical 28 feet? Still no figure flashed on the electrical indicator board, then suddenly everything was happening. Beamon was dancing around, kissing the track even, and fellow competitors dashed over to congratulate him. At last the board flickered into life. The figure 8 flashed up, then a 9 ... momentary confusion then the stupefying realisation that the jump was 8.90 metres. A frantic check of the tables ... 29 feet 2 inches! Those among the 60,000-odd spectators present who had witnessed the actual jump knew they had been privileged to see perhaps the greatest single achievement in the entire history of athletics. It could well survive as world record into the 21st century; after all Jesse Owens' 8.13m in 1935 stood for 25 years and that was only six inches better than the previous record. All Beamon had done was to add more than 1 ¾ feet to the mark shared by Ralph Boston and Igor Ter-Ovanesyan. If I hadn't seen it myself I would never have believed it. Several generations are going to have to live with it ... the unattainable record.

In fact it survived for 22 years, until Mike Powell's current record of 8.95m in 1991. Beamon himself would never jump beyond 8.20m again.

The knock-on effect of such a jump was profound. Boston, Ter-Ovanesyan and Davies had all been keyed up to bid for the title but as any chance of winning had vanished before any of them had set foot on the runway the inspiration had gone and all failed to do themselves justice. Lynn in particular lost all interest in the proceedings and finished a devastated ninth. Significantly, the silver medal, at 8.19m, went to an athlete who had never dreamt of making the podium and therefore was unscathed by Beamon's bombshell ... the GDR's Klaus Beer. I was obliged to print a number of letters critical of Lynn's attitude but I understood his mindset. Here was the reigning champion, the most competitive of athletes, pumped up to hold on to that coveted title and suddenly it was all over. In effect he was shell-shocked. He had been ready to jump 28 feet but 29 was out of the question. Lynn later wrote to me: "I made it clear before going to Mexico that a silver medal would mean nothing and this I sincerely meant. Whether it is acceptable to people or not does not matter. It was my own philosophy."

Despite the glut of world records, or maybe because of them as so many were made possible only because of the altitude factor which made a mockery of the longer distance races so dear to me, I still feel the awarding of the Olympics to a city perched 2248 metres up was a mistake. I had personal experience of the effect of high altitude. Before the athletics programme started I went out for a run of a mile or two ... and returned in such a state of collapse that my flatmates John Lusardi and Alf Wilkins feared for my life. The altitude folly was compounded by the ruthless slaughter by government forces of as many as 300 protesting students ten days before the Games opened (my friend John Rodda of *The Guardian* was a witness and lucky to escape with his life). There was huge controversy also over the "Black Power" or simply human rights demonstrations by some of the USA's greatest athletes. Tommie Smith and John Carlos, first and third in the 200m, each wore one black glove, bowed their heads and thrust out a clenched fist as "The Star-Spangled Banner" was played at the medal ceremony. The IOC, led by the obnoxious Avery Brundage (a white supremacist and anti-Semite), accused the pair of contravening one of the basic Olympic principles by using the ceremony "to advertise domestic political views" and the US Olympic Committee swiftly sent them home. Lee Evans, who considered withdrawing from the 400m final in a show of solidarity, chose instead to wear long black socks as a gesture of support for the cause.

The British team fell well short of the medal haul achieved four years earlier in Tokyo, but in David Hemery we had a champion of quite exceptional ability.

It wasn't just the time – a staggering 48.1 – that made one reach for every superlative in the dictionary ... even more it was the manner and margin of his victory. Here was the greatest field ever assembled for this event ...which Hemery beat by a good seven yards! He was off like a bullet and the huge crowd gasped in astonishment as Hemery whizzed along the back straight at unheard of speed for this event, his blond head barely rising as he took each barrier like a 220-hurdler. At 200m, which he reached in a phenomenal 23.0, he was yards clear of the field. Into the straight and Hemery's lead had grown still longer. Would he come unstuck in the closing stages? No fear. Hemery, one of the world's greatest indoor 600-yard runners, is not short of stamina and he maintained his form superbly. He had run the sort of race every athlete dreams of ... sheer perfection.

Team-mate John Sherwood closed with a tremendous rush that carried him from fifth to third (causing TV commentator David Coleman's famous *faux pas*), adding a bronze medal to the silver won the previous day in the long jump by his wife Sheila.

In a lengthy interview just after the Games, David Hemery attributed his success partly to the serious hamstring injury which caused him to miss practically the whole of the 1967 season. "I think in the long run the fact that I had a complete rest during the summer of 1967 probably was the best possible thing for these 60 weeks non-stop when I got back again. I just tried to rebuild the muscle by doing some weights in the winter of 1967 as well as running number three on the Boston University cross country team. There was no sprint work until I got to Mexico." Astonishingly, in view of his margin of victory, he didn't know if he was first over the line! "My coach had told me to go at the tenth hurdle as if it was the first in a high hurdles ... really attack the tenth and you get the carry-over for the run-in. I remember landing over the tenth hurdle and realising I had forgotten to go at it like the first. I tried to sprint but all I could do was stride and wait for the crowd reaction when someone is catching you. I had only looked right after the line, so I didn't know how close the others were. As I hadn't looked over my left shoulder I wasn't really sure I had won!"

Britain's other medallist was Lillian Board in the 400m. *Seven-hundredths of a second ... or about two feet. That's all that separated Lillian Board from the gold medal in this most emotional of races. It was the sort of finish that leaves the onlooker's pulse racing and his nerves shredded. At least that was my experience! Lillian carried the burden of being favourite on account not only of her best time (52.5) but of training runs the previous week in which she ran 200m in 23.2 and 300m in an incredible 36.3 (48.4 400m speed).*

Lillian takes up the story. "I felt good down the back straight [she passed 200m on schedule in 24.5] and really pushed it round the final bend. Then, going into the final straight, I found myself in the lead. I couldn't believe it. I thought it couldn't last ... and it didn't!" Ten yards to go and still Lillian was in front but in those last fateful strides France's relative outsider Colette Besson (pre-Mexico best of 53.8) inched past to win in a European record of 52.0. I was incensed when I read Chris Brasher's report in *The Observer* criticising Lillian for failing to win, for her performance was utterly praiseworthy.

As I wrote: *For a start, her time of 52.1 was inside Ann Packer's European record – and no one can ask more of an athlete than a personal best. Secondly, she ran uncompromisingly for victory – again no one can ask for more. Thirdly, let it be remembered that Lillian is still only 19 and this has been only her third season in the event. Finally, a silver medal is a tremendous achievement. So, in the words of the famous song, let's accentuate the positive aspects of Lillian's splendid run and not dwell too much on the negative.*

A big influence on Lillian was her London Olympiades clubmate Mary Rand who was present in Mexico City not as an athlete, having just announced her retirement, but as a TV commentator. Shortly before the Games we published a long and statistically detailed review of her glittering career.

Mary Rand will always occupy a very special place in the history of British athletics, and not simply because of her medals and records. It has been Mary, through her talent, good looks and pleasant personality, who has personified women's athletics in this country for the last decade; and the image she has projected has brought the sport a good deal of attention and made it a "glamorous" pursuit for the sports-minded young schoolgirl. Many members of the Olympic team in Mexico City right now were first attracted to the sport through watching and reading about Mary.

Attracted was the operative word. I wonder why so many of the young "nuts", myself included, used to install themselves close to the long jump pit at places like Chiswick whenever Mary was competing!

In September 1968 I wrote a full page editorial entitled "This Drug Menace Has To Stop". Of course, it hasn't, but that mustn't stop those with the good of the sport at heart from trying to end the cheating. As I wrote then, and it still holds true, the biggest problem confronting our sport is, without doubt, the menace of drug-taking by athletes. Referring in particular to anabolic steroids, Professor Arnold Beckett, a member of the Olympic Games Medical

Commission, was quoted as saying : "We would like to stop these drugs, but at this stage we have not got the tests to make it effective. If the competitors stop using the drug a week before the event, the result of any test will be negative. I simply hope the fact we are testing will act as a deterrent."

In a revealing interview with a London Weekend TV programme for which I provided some damning statistics, Swedish discus star Ricky Bruch told interviewer Adrian Metcalfe that after he started taking the anabolic agent known as Dianabol the previous winter, given to him by an American coach, his weight shot up by over 50 pounds (23kg) in the space of five months and he improved in the shot from 18.06m in 1967 to 19.30m in 1968 and in the discus from 59.34m to 61.98m. In 1969 he would move to second on the world all-time list with 68.06m and in 1972 he set a ratified world record of 68.40m. However, he said on the programme that he had given up anabolic steroids since learning all too painfully of the dangers ("I got too strong and my muscles developed too fast, and the tendons and cartilage inside my knee were completely destroyed") and recommended they should be banned. Dr Martyn Lucking, the 1962 Commonwealth shot champion, said there was "pretty conclusive evidence" that at least the first six in the 1964 Olympic shot competition had been using anabolic steroids.

How dispiriting that half a century later, despite all the sophisticated testing procedures, the willingness to take an illegal short cut to possible success remains so widespread. As a consequence, countless honest athletes have been denied medals, records and material rewards because of these cheats. It makes my blood boil!

On a lighter note, our last issue of the year contained Cliff Temple's humorous take on BBC television's Mexico City Olympic coverage, featuring David Coalman and Ron Puckering. A sample … *Puckering*: Over at the hammer circle, Howard Payne is trying to raise his game. He looks nervous and has been taking bites out of his hammer – but after all, the Olympics is only for 'ammer-chewers. *Coalman*: Our sprint relay team did tremendously well to be eliminated in the first round. They had a very tough draw against crack squads from the Channel Islands, British West Hartlepools, Umboland and Honduras, with four to qualify. Do you feel they were unlucky, Ron? *Puckering*: Yes, certainly. They tried to raise their game, and it didn't quite come off. Dropping the baton three times didn't help, though – and it was even worse on the SECOND leg!

10. SAD START TO THE SEVENTIES (1969-1971)

Early in 1969 I had the sad task of writing an obituary about a man who had been of great assistance in my journalistic career. Over the years I have written dozens, maybe hundreds, of tributes to famous athletes and others who have made a major contribution to the sport, but it's a particularly melancholy task when it concerns someone you knew personally. Stan Tomlin, who died at 63, was the 1930 Empire Games 3 miles champion, a vastly experienced official, athletics correspondent of the Sunday newspaper *The People* and editor of *Modern Athletics* before it was incorporated into AW. He was a friend and colleague for over a decade.

I first got to know him when I was working on a local newspaper in Hertfordshire; he was exceedingly helpful to me then and always remained so. The last time I spent any appreciable period of time in his company was at the Ovaltine Young Athletes' Course, of which he was director, at Lilleshall last April. He went out of his way to show me everything and introduce me to everyone, and I shall always recall his infectious enthusiasm for the project. This, clearly, is what he liked best in athletics – helping youngsters – and this is what he will be best remembered for. The courses he organised have made a tremendous contribution to British athletics over the years, as such Olympic medallists as Derek Johnson, Peter Radford, Robbie and Ann Brightwell, Dorothy Hyman, Mary Rand, Lillian Board and Sheila Sherwood can testify. They all have cause to look back with gratitude at those days spent at Lilleshall and the man who planned them, for it was there that so many of our greatest athletes first came to grips with athletics and what was required to reach the top.

We ran an unusual ad in February, inviting runners to appear as extras in Michael Winner's film, *The Games*. Gordon Pirie had been engaged as athletics advisor and coach to the star of the film, Michael Crawford, who trained so assiduously that it was claimed he could run a 4:20 mile. One of the sequences was shot at the Southern Cross Country Championships at Reading with Crawford (Harry Hayes in the film) racing Tim Johnston to the finish line.

The completed movie was released (escaped?) in 1970 with an American, played by Ryan O'Neal, a Czech (with a singularly unathletic Charles Aznavour trying to run like Emil Zátopek) and an Aborigine vying with Crawford to win the 1960 Olympic marathon in Rome. The screenplay was by Erich ("Love Story") Segal, himself an enthusiastic marathon runner, but the film was so unintentionally hilarious that a party of "nuts", including Stan Greenberg, Bob Sparks and myself disgraced ourselves at a showing by our persistent giggling and whispering, causing the cinema manager to threaten to eject us if we didn't behave! At a later date the AAA held a sale of the running kit used in the film and I purchased a USA singlet (possibly as worn by O'Neal) but I never had the nerve to be seen in it!

Innovations at the magazine in 1969 included British Merit Rankings for the previous year by Andrew Huxtable and Peter Matthews, the latter still compiling them all these years later, and the transfer from the now defunct *Women's Athletics* of Cliff Temple's "Cliffhangers" miscellany of news and gossip. We also had a new member of staff in 21 year-old Herne Hill Harrier and NUTS member Dave Cocksedge, who succeeded John Lusardi as my assistant editor and who, like John, was in charge of the young athletes' section as well as reporting senior meetings and sharing in the typing of results sent in to us. Welcoming new readers, I took the opportunity to explain the mechanics behind the production of AW.

What many people do not realise is that in order to bring you your mag on a Friday it has to be completed, so far as the editorial staff is concerned, by lunch time on Tuesday. In fact the inner 16-page section (pages 11-26) is finished before the previous weekend in order to be on the presses first thing Monday morning. Results of weekend events that do not arrive on Monday have little chance of being included.

In the April 26 issue I enthused: *Was there ever such a start to a British athletics season? Prior to last weekend we were already basking in the glow of such achievements as Bill Adcocks' superb marathon running, England's showing in the International Cross Country Championships [easy team winners in both senior and junior races, Dave Bedford first in the latter], a successful indoor campaign climaxed by nine medals in the European Games [victories for Ian Stewart at 3000m and Alan Pascoe at 50m hurdles], a succession of world class walks by Paul Nihill, a national javelin record by John FitzSimons and a superb AAA 10 miles duel [Ron Hill v Ron Grove]. But look what happened last Saturday: Dave Bedford, at the age of 19, became UK 10,000m record holder. Having seen him training prodigiously at Crystal Palace the previous weekend I knew he was remarkably fit but, I must confess, his time [28:24.4] came as a shock (a most pleasant one) when I heard about it at the IAC get-together at Loughborough. Stunned even more were the distance running internationals gathered there!*

That wasn't the only momentous race at Crystal Palace that month. *A prestigious record of 3:47.4 for 1200m (yes, 1200 not 1500) was set by Cliff Temple in winning the "Athletics Weekly/Women's Athletics" championship. A record? Well, as a founder member of the NUTS, I cannot recall another 22 year-old journalist from Folkestone belonging to Thames Valley Harriers who has registered such a time running barefoot on a Tartan track on a Sunday in April. The race was supposed to have been held behind locked doors as none of us wanted to show up the various international athletes who use that track but, somehow or other, there was a vast horde of athletes, coaches (talent spotting, no doubt) and officials around the start as Cliff, Dave Cocksedge and AW's 30 year-old editor rocketed away. The veteran of the field, racing (NUTS pentathlon apart) for the first time in eight years, tried to burn off the opposition with a vicious first lap of 75 sec but such foolhardy speed took its toll and the race resulted in an emphatic victory for Cliff over Dave. Yours truly occupied the bronze medal position but is not disheartened: he is building up gradually for the 1972 Olympic marathon in Munich ... where he plans to pace Bill Adcocks over the final 385 yards.*

Meanwhile, my former colleague John Lusardi was enjoying himself as a free spirit out in the USA while at the same time maintaining his links with AW. He covered the American AAU Championships in Miami, sent in articles on such legendary athletes as Bob Seagren, Lee Evans, Willie Davenport and Dick Fosbury ... and, astonishingly, became an AAU champion himself. The occasion was the 35km walk championship in Pittsburgh and in finishing 17th he clinched the 'junior' (i.e. novice not age related) team title for New Jersey's Shore Athletic Club, which he had joined courtesy of my great friend Elliott Denman. He was awarded a badge proclaiming 'AAU Junior Champion'. During his two years in the USA John worked at some 20 diverse jobs, ranging from journalist with a New Jersey newspaper to drilling water wells in Texas, driving film stars around in Hollywood and acting as a lifesaver (by day) and soda jerk (by night) at Miami Beach.

Unhappily, he later became seduced by the 'hippie' culture of Southern California and took up recreational drugs, and was very fortunate on one occasion when highway patrol officers failed to discover drugs secreted in his car. Had they done so, he would have served a long term in prison. As it was, he did eventually land up in an unspeakable Texan jail as he was not in possession of a labour permit, after which he was deported. John was never able to settle down back in England and went on to work as a roughneck in the Libyan oilfields, live on a kibbutz in Israel (a probably unique combination) and be employed on US Army bases in Germany. He wrote a largely autobiographical novel which was never published and eventually returned to England a deeply troubled young man. As a friend and former colleague, I hoped he could rebuild his life but in September 1977, in circumstances that will never be fully explained (the coroner brought in an open verdict), he fell 500 feet to his death from Beachy Head in Sussex. He was just 31.

The late 1960s was a significant period in marathon racing. In December 1967 Derek Clayton had shattered the world best of 2:12:00 with 2:09:37, while in the same Fukuoka event a year later Adcocks, despite two attacks of stitch, had run the second quickest ever time with his European record of 2:10:48. Now, in April 1969, Adcocks posted the third fastest ever time of 2:11:08 when winning the notoriously tough Marathon to Athens race for a course record which stood until the 2004 Olympics! The following month Clayton lowered the world best to 2:08:54 in Antwerp, just 11 days after clocking 2:17:26 in Turkey, but on a hot day in Manchester in July Clayton finished almost two minutes behind Ron Hill's 2:13:42 in the Maxol Marathon with Adcocks a distant fifth. Hill went on to claim the European title on the Marathon to Athens course in September in 2:16:48 with an injured Adcocks a non-finisher. There has always been some controversy surrounding Clayton's run in Antwerp as to whether the course was the full distance. The IAAF acknowledged it as a world best but the Association of Road Racing

Statisticians has not and instead lists Hill's 2:09:28 at the 1970 Commonwealth Games in Edinburgh as the successor to Clayton's 2:09:37.

The day before Hill's Maxol victory I was at Crystal Palace for the WAAA Championships to appreciate once more the sight of Dorothy Hyman in action.

It is difficult to believe that it was way back in 1964 when we last saw Dorothy in the "big time". Watching that dark, trim figure driving purposefully for the tape just like the old days played havoc with one's sense of time, not to mention feelings. I cannot recall a more emotional occasion since Derek Johnson's one-race comeback in 1963. It was too much to hope that Dorothy could defeat such an opponent as Chi Cheng, who last year clocked 11.2 for 100m and this season has been credited with a 10.3 100y, but she came close, with both clocking 11.9 into the 2.6m/sec wind. Dorothy went on to win the 200m but, remaining ineligible for international competition due to outmoded amateur rules (at a time when 'shamateurism' was rife), she could not be selected for the upcoming European Championships in Athens.

My next stop was Stuttgart for a wonderful match between Europe (but without any Soviet competitors) and the Western Hemisphere, a team of American athletes augmented by two Jamaicans, two Canadians and a Mexican. There was much to enthuse over, and most particularly Lynn Davies' long jump victory.

He was sick on the day and nervous as a kitten as the competition approached. This was the one that mattered very deeply to Lynn Davies. He had already beaten Olympic silver medallist Klaus Beer in East Berlin this summer, but now was the opportunity he had been waiting for: his chance to erase or at least soften the bitter memories of Mexico City by defeating Bob Beamon. For months Lynn had been thirsting for retribution, for his understandably sub-standard performance at the Olympics had cast a dark shadow over his career. The 27 year-old Welshman was anxious to prove the old magic is still there. It was. He opened with a marginal foul of 8.30m and in the fifth round he jumped 8.11m, while Beamon finished last with 7.75m.

Back to London's almost deserted White City for the first AAA Championships to be staged over metric distances, the star performers being Ian Stewart (13:39.8 5000m) and Dick Taylor (28:27.6 10,000m). On the same track, later in August, Taylor was seen to even greater advantage in a match against the USA. Not since Ron Clarke smashed through the 13 minute barrier in the 1965 AAA Championships had I witnessed such an exhilarating display of aggressive distance running as Dick Taylor's 5000m. He didn't just win races, he trampled the opposition into the dust. Throwing in a mid-race 60 sec lap and 4:16 mile, Taylor cruised past 3 miles in 13:04.6 and finished in 13:29.0, both UK records. Only four men had ever run faster over 5000m: Clarke, Kip Keino, Harald Norpoth and Michel Jazy. Runner-up Stewart, aged 20, clocked 13:36.4 for third behind Taylor and Mike Wiggs on the UK all-time list. Far, far behind was a man who would later become an American track icon – 18 year-old Steve Prefontaine – who was lapped with his 14:38.4.

It was a hectic month as next stop was Middlesbrough for a women's match against France, the British girls winning 11 of the 13 events. Like Lynn Davies in Stuttgart, Lillian Board was able to avenge Olympic defeat by beating Colette Besson in the 400m, 53.7 to 54.1 in very windy conditions. Another outstanding winner was high jumper Dorothy Shirley, nine years after her Olympic silver medal. On paper she should have placed fourth out of four, and arriving only 20 minutes before the start of her event due to traffic delays wouldn't have helped, but she not only won but, using her well-honed Western roll technique, cleared a personal best of 1.74m. That was 7cm above her own physical height, a British "record".

And so to Athens for the climax of the season, the European Championships. With Stan Greenberg typing out all the results in return for a free trip I was able to concentrate on the reports and interviews. It was a great meeting for the British team, winning 17 medals, although it has to be remembered that there were no West Germans competing (other than in the relays), the team voting to boycott as a protest against the IAAF ruling that Jürgen May, a former East German world record holder for 1000m, was ineligible to represent West Germany. Paul Nihill in the 20km walk was Britain's first gold medallist and he was followed by Lillian Board in the 800m in her best time of 2:01.4, Ian Stewart in the 5000m, John Whetton in the 1500m, the women's 4x400m relay team and Ron Hill in the marathon. My most vivid memory is that of the women's 4x400m.

*In the entire history of track and field athletics there has never been a race that was **more** exciting than this one. From my own point of view, even the Chataway v Kuts epic will now have to take second place. On paper France couldn't lose [two days earlier Nicole Duclos and Colette Besson had finished 1-2 in the 400m, both credited with a world record 51.7] but, luckily, races are fought out by people on tracks and not by mathematicians or computers. Rosemary Stirling, her troublesome foot feeling the strain of five races in as many days, led off to the utmost of her current ability. She handed over with a few girls ahead but her time was 54.2 (0.1 outside her best ever) and Britain was in touch. On the second leg Duclos rushed from third to first along the back straight and continued to pile on the pace. It was an awe-inspiring run, timed at 50.6, and at the end of it France were nicely set up some ten yards ahead. But only some ten yards up, for Pat Lowe – who has never run faster than 54.6 off blocks – covered her lap in an heroic 52.1. Britain's chances had been kept alive. Now it was Janet Simpson's turn. She gradually cut down her French rival and, though she could have forged ahead in the final strides to hand Lillian a lead, she deliberately held back ... and still ran a superb 52.1!*

The advantage in the anchor leg of a relay rests with the runner who takes over just behind and that was the position in which Lillian found herself. Would Besson destroy herself? As she pulled away from Lillian with every stride it looked for a while as though it would be no race but then came the realisation that the French girl was travelling too fast for her own safety – a situation borne out by the splits that became known later. Besson covered her first 200m, during which she opened up a lead of 6-8 metres, in a suicidal 23.6! Worse still, at 300m – when some 10 metres up – her time was an almost unbelievable 36.1 ... 48.1 speed for 400m! No woman – and not all that many men – could get away with it. Inevitably Besson began to crumble in the straight and Lillian – who had sensibly run her own controlled race – started to close. There was no question of a response from Besson, who was thrashing about wildly, the question was could Lillian pass her in time. With 40 yards to go Besson looked round, the ultimate sign of anxiety, and that gave Lillian renewed hope. It was still touch and go but in the last stride or two Lillian forced herself ahead for a famous victory. She had run her lap in 52.4 and the team's total time, shared by France, was a world record 3:30.8. Truly a glorious performance, one in which all four girls gave of their very best and from which no individual should be singled out.

I didn't produce any books in 1969 but I was heavily involved in an ambitious and brilliant publishing project. *The Game*, the Marshall Cavendish Encyclopaedia of World Sports, began life in October 1969 and consisted of 112 weekly parts available every Friday through to the end of 1971. It was a colossal undertaking, running to over 3000 large pages and 7000 photos. The editorial advisory board consisted of five legendary sporting figures in Harold Abrahams, Sir Donald Bradman, Henry Cotton, Dr Danie Craven and Sir Alf Ramsey, while athletics historian and prize winning crime novelist Peter Lovesey and myself constituted the athletics advisory panel. Editor Norman Barrett commissioned the contributions with Harold, Peter and myself responsible for most of the numerous athletics entries. Over the two years I wrote a total of 88 biographies plus several general entries. I was very proud indeed to be associated with this unique sporting part-work.

It was on Boxing Day of 1970 that Lillian Board died of cancer. The downside of my job is writing obituaries and in Lillian's case it was a more poignant task than usual. Apart from being British athletics' "golden girl", whose glittering career I had documented in detail, she was also a personal friend. Many a time, after training at Crystal Palace on a Sunday morning, she, Cliff Temple and I would adjourn to the stadium bar for a convivial chat. She was a lovely young woman, whose joyful personality endeared her to everyone, and after her exploits at the 1969 European Championships we looked forward to her succeeding at the 1970 Commonwealth Games in Edinburgh and ultimately at the 1972 Olympics in Munich. How ironic, then, that it was in a clinic in Munich that Lillian passed away.

Previously a sprinter and long jumper, it was in 1966, aged 17, that she was permitted under the rules then in force to tackle the 440y for the first time. Early that year her clubmate Mary Rand had said of her "she's going to develop into a great quarter-miler" and was quickly proved right. That opinion was endorsed by Denis Watts, who had coached Ann Packer and was now assisting George Board in his daughter's preparation. Her breakthrough came in Los Angeles in 1967 when she, the outsider, beat an all-star field to clock 52.8 for 400m to rank second to Ann on the European all-time list. In 1968, at the

Mexico City Olympics, she came so tantalisingly close to becoming Olympic 400m champion with her UK record time of 52.12 but the following year she proved herself a big-time winner by lifting the European 800m title in 2:01.50, quite close to the world record of 2:00.5.

One of her goals was to be the first woman to break two minutes officially and early in the 1970 season it all looked so promising as, having cut out weight training as a precaution against the back injury which had affected her in 1969, she built up her stamina instead, running a highly creditable 4:44.6 mile. Her quickest ever early season 400m time of 53.6 was another indicator that a sub-2 could be imminent, but then news trickled out that she was suffering from what appeared to be a stomach ailment. Pale and underweight, she finished third in the WAAA Championships in 2:05.1. It proved to be her last race. She was in and out of hospital all summer but few outside her immediate family circle realised just how seriously ill she was. Hers was a hopeless case, said top British cancer specialists, and so as a last resort she was transported to a German clinic, but after further intensive treatment the merciful end came just 13 days after her 22nd birthday.

It has been my sad duty to write many obituary notices for this magazine but none has caused me so much distress as this one. It still seems unbelievable that Lillian Board, who should have had at least 50 years of life ahead of her, is no longer among us and I feel a sense of deep personal loss that I know will be shared by all readers, whether or not they had the good fortune to have met Lillian. Lillian's fame will endure as a result of her wonderful athletics career and her incredibly courageous fight against the illness that was eventually to cut her life so tragically short. Certainly I shall always treasure such magic moments as her thrilling triumphs in Athens and ponder on the bravery of this young woman as she struggled against the unimaginable pain and debilitating effects of her illness. Most of all I shall remember with gratitude Lillian, the friendly and vivacious 'girl next door'.

Her stunning successes on the track, allied to her very attractive looks and bubbling personality, led to acclaim and publicity of film star proportions to be thrust on Lillian while still a teenager. It could have turned her head, but it most certainly did not. She remained a thoroughly delightful girl: charming, sincere, gracious. A credit to her parents. To say that athletics will never be the same again may sound like a cliché, but I mean it. The thought that not only shall we never see that familiar blonde figure pounding round the track again but that she should have been snatched from her family and friends in such a tragic manner leaves me with feelings of indescribable sadness. May her memory and shining example live on for ever.

Prior to Lillian's illness casting a dark shadow over the athletics scene, there were two brilliant performances by British team members at the first official European Indoor Championships in Vienna. Ricky Wilde astonished everyone by winning the 3000m in a world indoor best of 7:47.0, prompting me to write: *The Continentals must be scratching their heads as to how this man, who had never previously won an important international race, could destroy*

even the great Harald Norpoth with one of the most impressive displays of
sustained pace over the second half of the race ever witnessed. He covered the
last kilometre in 2:26.0 and 1500m in 3:44.6 – good enough to have won the
1500m title by four seconds!

A great future for him at 5000m was predicted but although in 1972 he ranked fifth in Britain with 13:30.8 he was content to be a good club runner rather than aspiring to international glory. In 1979 he ran a 2:14:14 marathon to rank fifth in the country. The other British winner did go on to further glory ... but not in a British or English vest. In Vienna, Marilyn Neufville – a 17 year-old London schoolgirl – won the 400m in a startling world indoor best of 53.0, a big step forward from her outdoor best of 54.2, but in a highly controversial move she opted to represent her native island of Jamaica at that summer's Commonwealth Games. There she became the first and to date only Jamaican woman to set a world outdoor record by taking the 400m title in 51.02. The following year she struck gold at the Pan American Games.

The Edinburgh Commonwealth Games were covered for AW by Cliff Temple, Dave Cocksedge and myself. I wrote that the ninth edition of the Games was without doubt the most successful yet to be staged. It wasn't just the competition that was so outstanding. I singled out for praise the highly informative announcing team led by Peter Matthews, the excellent electronic scoreboard, high quality printed programmes and the best Press facilities I had encountered in 15 years of international athletics reporting. Athletes representing Scotland rose to the occasion with rapturously acclaimed victories by Lachie Stewart in the 10,000m (with Ron Clarke second), Rosemary Payne in the discus, Rosemary Stirling in the 800m and Ian Stewart in the 5000m (with team-mate Ian McCafferty runner-up). English winners were Howard Payne (Rosemary Payne's husband at the time) in the hammer, David Hemery in the 110m hurdles, John (400m hurdles) and Sheila (long jump) Sherwood, Dave Travis in the javelin, Ron Hill in the marathon and Rita Ridley in the 1500m. Lynn Davies retained the long jump title for Wales, while for Northern Ireland Mary Peters completed a pentathlon and shot double and Mike Bull took the pole vault.

Marilyn Neufville's exploit was clearly THE performance of the Games, but running it close in my view was Ron Hill's marathon. Inspired in his early days as an athlete by Alf Tupper, 'The Tough of the Track' in *The Rover* boys' magazine, Ron had certainly experienced highs and lows during his career. He may have flopped at the 1964 Olympics and 1966 Commonwealth Games and European Championships but on the plus side he had smashed Emil Zátopek's world records for 15 miles and 25km in 1965 and broken Ron Clarke's world 10 miles record in April 1968. Much to his annoyance the selectors did not pick him for the Mexico City Olympic marathon but he did finish an overlooked but heroic seventh in the 10,000m – the first man home who had not either lived or trained extensively at high altitude. Then began his purple patch. Shortly after the Games he reduced his world 10 miles record to 46:44.0, while in 1969 he became the European marathon champion. In April 1970 he became the first

Briton to win the iconic Boston Marathon, and in the European record time of 2:10:30, and three months later in Edinburgh he ran the race of his life. Pulling away after 8 miles, he destroyed a world class field as he zipped through 10 miles in 47:45, halfway in 62:36 and 20 miles in 1:37:30. He was on course for a time in the 2:08 region but in the closing stages he played safe by easing off a little. He won by half a mile from defending champion Jim Alder in 2:09:28, at the time a European record, the second fastest performance of all time and easily the best ever in a championship race. Among the non-finishers was Derek Clayton, whose world best of 2:08:34 has long been disputed by Hill among others. World best or not, it was a fabulous piece of running by Hill. Alder, by the way, reclaimed the world record for 30,000m a few weeks later at Crystal Palace (75 laps of the Tartan track) with a time of 1:31:30.4 with Tim Johnston and Hill also inside Jim Hogan's old figures.

While on the subject of world record breaking distance runners, only Paavo Nurmi and Emil Zátopek were more prolific than Ron Clarke and to mark his retirement we ran a retrospective of some of the AW reports of his achievements, starting with Joe Galli's despatch in the January 22 1955 issue that this 17 year-old had run a 4:27.2 mile. The following year we reported on his world junior mile record of 4:06.8 on a five-lap grass track. Quoted after the 1964 Olympic 10,000m where, as strong favourite, he wound up third behind Billy Mills and Mohamed Gammoudi, the Australian remarked: "I thought I would win with three laps to go." Asked if he had worried about Mills, he replied: "Worry about him? I never heard of him." Four years later in Mexico City, having dominated distance running in the meantime, Ron was not only cruelly denied the opportunity for Olympic glory but was fortunate to escape with his life.

The arena [after the 10,000m] resembled a battlefield, with bodies sprawled all over the place. One in particular attracted the profound sympathy of all who care anything about athletics. The man on the stretcher, gasping for air until oxygen was administered, was Ron Clarke – his hopes shattered not so much by the opposition as by the folly of the men who, five years ago, glibly agreed to award these Games to an oxygen-starved city. He deserved a better fate.

Reporting on his final appearance at the White City for a lap of honour at the AAA Championships, I described Clarke as *a man who shares with Emil Zátopek the distinction of generating not simply respect and admiration from the fans, but also deep affection. We may regret that Ron never won a major gold medal, but does it really matter? What is important is that this man set such a fine example on and off the track wherever he travelled throughout the world. His modesty, sportsmanship and friendliness are as renowned as his running ability and now that he has retired from competition it is to be hoped that his values will be perpetuated by those in whom he kindled the flame of athletic ambition. Because of his human qualities, 'Clarkey' will live on in the memory long after all his records have fallen. That is worth any number of Olympic titles.*

Clarke was a front runner *par excellence* and one of his most fervent admirers was Colin Young, coach to Mel Batty, AW's hugely respected walking correspondent, one of the world's foremost ultra distance walkers, NUTS founder member with an encyclopaedic knowledge of all sports as well as jazz ... and one of my oldest friends. I was happy to publish in April 1970 a tribute to him by another legendary walker, Paul Nihill, the only Briton to win major international medals at both 20km (1969 European champion) and 50km (2nd 1964 Olympics). Paul wrote that Colin was preparing "to attempt a fantastic endurance double": a 24 hour walk in Rouen followed less than a month later by the Strasbourg to Paris event, a mere 512km (318 miles)! Colin didn't win either race but walked with his customary grit to finish second in Rouen with a distance of 204.5km (over 127 miles) and fifth in the Strasbourg to Paris in 74 hours 24 minutes. The latter was tough going indeed as daytime temperatures hit 90°F in the shade (but there was no shade), the road surface included long stretches of cobbles, and there were at least four climbs of 8-10km in length. "However," Colin wrote, "the worst suffering was from a severely wrenched calf muscle over the last 50 hours necessitating frequent short stops for massage. This was caused by the collapse of my heels on both pairs of my shoes." He ended his report thus: "To anyone thinking of competing in a future Strasbourg to Paris I would advise a long spell of serious thinking, a sit down, and a decision to forget the whole thing!" Colin didn't heed his own advice, for the following year he followed up victory in the Rouen race, covering a record 215.835km, with a close third place in the Strasbourg to Paris in 73 hours 37 minutes.

Another remarkable NUTS member, who like Colin still attends committee meetings, is Liz Sissons and in my "Trackwise" column I reckoned she was the only female athlete to have competed in all of what were then the standard events. Her best marks (as at 1970) were 13.1 100m, 26.7 200m, 58.2 400m, 2:17.6 800m, 5:06.3 1500m, 19.6 100m hurdles (but a far superior 12.7 for 80m), 32.2 200m hurdles, 1.50m high jump, 4.95m long jump, 11.37m shot, 30.92m discus, 32.92m javelin, 3518 pentathlon ... and even a mile walk in 10:56! She later improved to 2:14.8 for 800m and 4:49.1 for 1500m. Now in her seventies, she is still an active athlete, winning countless national throwing event titles in her age group.

The European Cup proved a disappointment again for the British teams. I travelled to Zürich to see the men eliminated from their semi-final (it was too soon after the Commonwealth Games) although Dave Travis shone by not only winning the javelin with a UK record of 83.44m but defeating the great Janis Lusis, Olympic champion and world record breaker. The women did make it through to the final but finished fifth of six, Cliff Temple (now the athletics correspondent of *The Sunday Times*) providing AW's coverage. Significantly, the GDR ran out the winners for the first time, as did their men's team for their final in Stockholm the following weekend. It was the climax to five years of unremitting effort by the GDR to establish themselves as Europe's strongest athletics power. Now both trophies were theirs ... a remarkable achievement by a nation of fewer than 20 million people. Of course there were always suspicions that drugs might have played a part in the GDR's success, particularly on the women's side as their athletes just never seemed to suffer a bad day in the stadium, but it was only after the fall of the Wall at the end of 1989 that documentation revealed the full deplorable extent of the state's doping programme.

It was Dave Cocksedge who first drew attention to Steve Ovett. In the June 27 edition he mentioned Steve's win in the Sussex Schools junior 400m in 51.6 – 0.2 away from the UK age-14 best – and an 800m time of two minutes flat. Seb Coe first got his name in AW in the March 13 1971 issue, winning the colts race at the Yorkshire Cross Country Championships. In the years to follow I would write more words about this pair than any other athletes before or since.

Although the AAA Championships were staged at the White City, the new home of athletics in London was now Crystal Palace and the IAC's Coca-Cola Invitational proved a rousing finale to the season. The British team of Rosemary Stirling, Georgena Craig, Pat Lowe and Sheila Carey set a world 4x800m relay record of 8:25.0 (although only after West Germany had harshly been disqualified for a take-over infringement), while in the men's 4x880y Kenya set new world figures of 7:11.6 highlighted by a remarkable anchor leg by Robert Ouko who held on to clock 1:45.4 after racing through his first 440y in 48.6!

Confirmation that athletics' days at the White City were over came with the announcement by BAAB honorary secretary Arthur Gold that with the intention of the owners, the Greyhound Racing Association Property Trust Ltd, to redevelop the site, a move would be necessary. Having spent a fair portion of the last twenty years watching athletics at the White City I would miss the old place. Nonetheless, I welcomed the more modern facilities of Crystal Palace with its synthetic track even if as a North Londoner it was a pain to travel to.

The December 5 1970 edition was a very special one as it marked 25 years since Jimmy Green produced that first ground-breaking issue of *Athletics*, the monthly forerunner of AW. The 25th Anniversary Issue at a record 48 pages was our most elaborate yet. With circulation now over 12,000 and with readers in 59 countries from Australia to Zambia the magazine was continually expanding although still run on a very tight budget. My own salary remained modest in the extreme and I was embarrassed at how meagre were the payments we made to outside contributors but at least the exposure guaranteed by their articles being published in the sport's "trade paper" was some compensation. It was a source of great satisfaction to me that so many writers and photographers got their first public recognition through AW.

We received a telegram from the ***Duke of Edinburgh***, president of the BAAB, conveying his "congratulations and best wishes to you all on the occasion of your Silver Jubilee." Among other messages were these: ***Harold Abrahams*** (BAAB chairman): "The undoubted success of AW is largely due to the courage, enthusiasm and hard work of Jimmy Green." ***Chris Chataway, MP*** (Minister of Posts & Telecommunications): "I have spent many happy hours

reading AW. It has always been unique in the services it gives to athletics."
Arthur Gold: "Congratulations on achieving your Silver Jubilee. May your typing fingers grow *citius*, your circulation grow *altius*, your output *fortius*."
Andrew Huxtable (NUTS secretary): "Members have long regarded it as the most reliable source for results in the UK. Even more importantly, perhaps, it provides a vital forum for the expression of views and ideas on all aspects of the sport." *John Le Masurier* (Senior National Coach): "Thank you for the tremendous contribution which you have made to our sport." *Mary Toomey (formerly Rand)*: "I never thought AW would become so important in my life. There is always a race between Bill and me as to who should read it first and I nearly always win! Now, living so far away in California, I read it from cover to cover."

Dick Bank, whose well informed and often provocative contributions were always welcome, wrote: "I find the publication indispensable, and with a warm quality that just cannot be matched." That remark about the magazine's warmth was particularly gratifying to the editorial staff as in addition to cramming in all the news, results, articles, opinions and photos we could, we also endeavoured to create an informal family atmosphere. The magazine was there to serve, inform and entertain the entire athletics community with everyone welcome to participate.

Dave Bedford was the personality who dominated 1971. Whether you were a fan or not (and I certainly was), you couldn't ignore his huge impact on the athletics scene that year. It started with the "National" at Norwich in March. The third fastest 10,000m runner of all time with his UK record of 28:06.2 the previous summer, and still only 21, he won the prestigious English cross country title by a whopping 40 sec margin. His training mileage was legendary, 200 miles a week, mostly on the road, until tapering off with merely 140 and 100 miles in the two weeks before the race. Weight training? "Lifting pints is the nearest I get to this." Two weeks later, on a muddy and windy course in San Sebastian, he front ran his way to a 22 sec victory over team-mate Trevor Wright in the International Cross Country Championship.

His first big track race of the season was in Edinburgh in June when, but for the vicious wind blowing in the Meadowbank Stadium, he might well have bettered Ron Clarke's 5000m world record of 13:16.6. He clocked 13:22.2, not only breaking Ian Stewart's European record set on the same track but moving to no 2 on the world all-time list. Dave estimated the wind, gusting up to 6m/sec, cost him at least half a second a lap. "No two ways about it," he emphasised. "If conditions were right today I would have got the world record."

After 20 years of watching top-class athletics I suppose I ought not to be surprised by anything now – but fortunately this is not the case and I gladly confess to being astounded by Bedford's run. A world reverberating exploit just was not on, or so it seemed as one sat shivering. For the last eight laps it was Bedford alone against time. Cheered on by an excited crowd of 9000, and most loudly of all by the local schoolchildren let in free to whom this dashing young man with the Mexican bandit's moustache became a new hero, Bedford maintained his hellish pace.

The following month I had cause to write: *There are no half measures with Dave Bedford. As in the British Games 5000m so again in last Saturday's 10,000m [in the Britain v France match] he refused to allow unfavourable weather conditions to deter him in his quest for records. At Meadowbank he had to contend with a vicious wind; at Portsmouth the temperature was up in the eighties. A first 5000m in 13:45.2 was followed by another in 14:01.8 for a final time of 27:47.0. Ron Clarke alone, with 27:39.4, has run faster. Consider how much faster Dave might have run in more benevolent circumstances. It was too hot, the track was of cinders and dusty at that, and blisters resulting from wearing long spikes to suit the track caused him agony during much of the race. Bedford was surely not over-stating the case when he proclaimed afterwards that "on a Tartan track in perfect conditions I could have broken the world record by ten seconds". To win such a class race by 52.6 sec might be considered unusual, not to mention lapping European silver medallist Mike Tagg and practically double lapping Commonwealth champion Lachie Stewart. But what about that outrageous second lap of **59 seconds**? He followed that with a 63.6 for an 800m stretch of 2:02.6 – only a couple of seconds outside his personal best!*

It was all too good to last. Later that month, reporting on the first AAA Championships to be staged at Crystal Palace, I was saddened to write: *If there is one thing that is certain in life, and therefore athletics, it is that nothing is certain. Thus the well publicised plans of Dave Bedford to break Ron Clarke's world record in the AAA 5000m came to a melodramatic end when cramp forced him out of the race shortly after the 3000m mark. One moment Bedford was striding resolutely towards another great performance, the next he was on the ground – sick with disappointment. How one felt for Dave at this time. On his name alone, the meeting was a sell-out with some 14,000 fans – many of them new to big time athletics – cheering him lustily as he completed his warm-up prior to the race. For eight minutes Bedford had thrilled the crowd as he battled against a phantom Ron Clarke; now there was an embarrassed silence.*

Dave's nightmare continued at the European Championships in Helsinki. On paper he was almost 26 sec faster over 10,000m than the second ranked entrant, Finland's Juha Vaatainen, but – fittingly in the land of legendary distance runners like Hannes Kolehmainen and Paavo Nurmi – it was Vaatainen who triumphed in 27:52.8 thanks to a 53.9 last lap by a man who was once a 10.9 100m sprinter. Bedford gave it his all. He led at halfway in 13:54.4, a time only he and Clarke had ever surpassed during a 10,000m, but there were seven men in contact. With six laps to go there were still six runners capable of winning.

It was easy enough from the stands to urge Bedford to make the big break, but Dave was trying all he knew to do so. The spirit was willing but the body was not up to it. He was, as he later reflected, suffering an 'off day' and yet he was still in there fighting. Bedford's extrovert personality may not win him the unqualified approval of everyone, but nobody can deny he has guts. Bedford plays his last ace, a penultimate lap in 65.2. It's a fantastic effort by a man clearly dying on his feet but his pursuers are not going to give up now after all they have suffered.

Dave completed his last lap in 65.5 for sixth place in 28:04.4, a time which would have equalled the European record just a month earlier. It was such a disappointment, but Bedford was not going to end an otherwise momentous season on a low note.

The ultimate in athletics entertainment was reached in the steeplechase, finale of a memorable Coca-Cola Invitation Meeting at Crystal Palace. Dave Bedford [in only his second serious try at the event] kept his promise of breaking the UK record, and yet his glorious time of 8:28.6 was a secondary factor. What gripped the capacity crowd was the swashbuckling manner of Bedford's running. They gasped at his audacious start (he was 30m clear after two laps), chuckled at his step-on-hurdle technique, roared with delight as he flung up both arms as he took the water jump, and cheered proudly as he outsprinted Andy Holden in a desperate finish. There was an almost tangible feeling of emotion as Bedford embarked upon a lap of honour, blowing kisses to the crowd. I cannot recall a similar bond between athlete and spectators in this country. Bannister, Chataway and Pirie often had huge White City crowds on their feet but they were detached figures, not easy for the man in the stand to identify with. The crowds warmed more to Derek Ibbotson, with his cheery good humour on and off the track, but Derek – as a Yorkshireman – was a visitor, albeit a welcome one, Dave Bedford, though, is very much a Londoner and his fellow citizens are revelling in the opportunity of watching a local lad – the boy next door – taking on all-comers.

Back to those European Championships. Because Britain had only one winner, many considered the British team had failed. I disagreed.

Measuring the success or otherwise of a national team in an event like the European Championships is difficult. What criterion does one use? Surely, not by gold medals alone – for there is much more to athletics than simply winning and losing. Of course we should hail the victory of David Jenkins [aged 19 he won the 400m in a UK record of 45.45] for all it is worth; but are we to regard Pat Lowe and Barbara Inkpen as failures because they were beaten? That would be utterly absurd, and yet to hear some people talk and to read certain press reports is to gain the impression that because we won only one gold medal the Championships were a disaster for the British team. What nonsense! In spite of the "knockers" the fact remains that only three nations gained more medals than Britain: East Germany, the USSR and West Germany.

Silver medals were gained by Trevor Wright (marathon), Alan Pascoe (110m hurdles), Lowe (800m) and Inkpen (high jump); bronze by Andy Carter (800m), Brendan Foster (1500m), Ron Hill (marathon), Paul Nihill (20km walk) and Rosemary Stirling (800m); and five British records were broken.

I enjoyed the action but for me the biggest thrill was to set foot in the historic Helsinki Olympic Stadium, scene of Zátopek's unique triple, Jamaica's epic 4x400m victory over the USA and so much else at the 1952 Games and with the iconic statue of Paavo Nurmi outside. Because of Finland's great distance running tradition, together with my love of Sibelius's music, I had long yearned to visit that fascinating country.

Much space in the year's first few issues was allocated to the aftermath of Lillian Board's passing. There was news of the Lillian Board Trust Fund, with more than 20,000 contributing to cancer research, I wrote a heartfelt obituary and a review of her all too brief career, there were tributes galore, and I described the Memorial Service at St Paul's Cathedral, packed with some 2000 people.

It was a solemn and poignant occasion as her family, friends, sporting colleagues and members of the general public who had shared her struggles on and off the track, joined together to pay a final tribute. Among the many British internationals present were several of the girls most closely associated with Lillian: her former rivals and relay team-mates.

I added a footnote that the arrangements for the service were largely organised by Marea Hartman – *and this may be an appropriate moment to record the appreciation of all in athletics for the part played by the WAAA secretary during these last unhappy months. Organising the Lillian Board Fund, visiting the Ringberg Clinic, comforting and helping the family ... Marea has been a tower of strength throughout, and I would like her to know that her selfless devotion and compassion has not gone unnoticed.*

On a happier note, Cliff Temple introduced Emily Lustbody to the world (her adventures becoming a fixture in his popular Christmas "funnies"), while AW's long serving subscriptions and distribution secretary José Green got married to fellow runner Ted Kimber, the downside being that she left the magazine to move to London.

I also moved in 1971, getting my foot on the first rung of the property ladder by buying a newly built one-bedroom flat in Bromley, Kent. The cost was £5,600 – an enormous amount to me at that time although it would now appear to be a ludicrously low figure. That converts to around £56,000 in today's money although that particular flat is now valued by Zoopla at over £240,000! Having lived happily in North London since the age of seven, going south of the Thames was a difficult decision but it made sense as Bromley was just a short train ride from Chatham and Rochester, where the AW office was situated, and it was in close proximity to Crystal Palace. As events turned out, to be related in the next chapter, I would be moving back across the river only two years later.

11. MUNICH AND MARRIAGE (1972-1973)

My life changed, immeasurably for the better, in 1972. That was due to a young lady by the name of Patricia Master. Most couples in those days met at dance halls, clubs, work or through mutual friends. We met via the *London Weekly Advertiser*! The chances of finding the ideal partner through a newspaper ad and going on to be happily married for decades must be fairly remote, but it happened to Pat and me.

Both of us had recently ended a relationship (in my case with an international athlete) and at the age of 33 I was becoming increasingly anxious to find the right woman and settle down. I remembered a conversation I had overheard between my dad and his brother-in-law discussing the *London Weekly Advertiser*, a publication that dealt mainly with the sale of goods but which also featured a 'lonely hearts' section, a new departure in those days outside of magazines aimed mainly at women. With nothing to lose, I bought a copy for the first time and inserted a classified ad outlining what I was looking for in a prospective partner. On April 27 I received a letter from Pat, whose interests and Jewish background were similar to mine. By chance, she had just moved into a flat she had found from the *London Weekly Advertiser* and saw a copy of that issue. Having just returned from a holiday in Israel she didn't have a recent photo ready to enclose as in those days you took your roll of film to be developed at, say, Boots, and it took a week before you could collect the prints. So it was literally a blind date when, after a preliminary phone conversation, I turned up at her flat in Temple Fortune in North West London on May 3. It was love at first sight, for me at least. She was very attractive, intelligent (she had a BA in modern languages from Southampton University) and easy to talk to. I was hooked!

As I left that evening, Pat said she had a spare ticket for a Nana Mouskouri concert just up the road at Golders Green in ten days' time and would I like to join her. Would I! Not wanting to wait that long to see her again I arranged for tickets to a Yehudi Menuhin recital at the Royal Albert Hall on May 7 and from then on we met at every opportunity, visiting cinemas, theatres, Woburn Safari Park and an open air concert at glorious Ken Wood on Hampstead Heath in the space of the first few weeks. On July 8 she accompanied me to the Women's AAA Championships at Crystal Palace, her first experience of big-time athletics. Until then, the only athletes she had been particularly aware of were Bruce Tulloh (she was in the process of reading his book about his epic run across America) and Martin Hyman at Southampton University, and she admitted that she had been "useless" at athletics at school and therefore hated it and dropped it like a hot cake as soon as she was able to. Little did she know ...! Now she was being plunged into a whole new world. On July 29 I met Pat's parents for the first time and on September 20, a week after I returned from the Munich Olympics, we announced our engagement.

My memories of those Games are so confusing. I remember the suspense and ultimate joy of watching Mary Peters winning the pentathlon by a very narrow margin with a world record score, only to be shocked by the murder of several Israeli team members by Palestinian terrorists, followed by anger at the seemingly indifferent reaction of the IOC's president Avery Brundage.

I reported for AW with the assistance of Dave Cocksedge and here is an extract from an overview of the Games for my book *Olympic Track & Field History*.

The organisers of the first Olympics to be staged in Germany since the Nazi-influenced festival of 1936 were hoping for a Games free of political influences. Their hopes were dashed. Pressurised by threats of a boycott by African nations, the IOC expelled the Rhodesian team, but that was of little consequence (except, it would seem, to the IOC president Avery Brundage) by comparison to the tragedy which befell the Israeli team on the eleventh day (September 5) of the Munich Games. A squad of eight Palestinian terrorists burst into the Israeli quarters in the supposedly security-tight Olympic Village and killed two members of the team and held nine others as hostages. That night helicopters lifted the terrorists and their captives to Fuerstenfeldbruck airport as the first step to being flown to an Arab country, but after police opened fire on the gang all of the Israeli hostages were murdered. It was the grimmest day in Olympic history.

While the terrifying drama was played out, the Games were put on hold. Officials agonised over whether they should be cancelled as a mark of respect to the slain; eventually – with the approval of what was left of the Israeli delegation – it was decided that the Games would resume following a memorial service in the main stadium. Alas, Avery Brundage managed to demean what was otherwise a sombre and moving occasion by using his address as an excuse for condemning what he termed the 'naked political blackmail' of those countries which had been strongly opposed to Rhodesian participation. It was a disgraceful speech, and all too characteristic of a man of so little sensitivity.

Until the massacre, the Games had been setting new standards of excellence. Enthusiastic crowds packed the stadium each day (there were even 70,000-plus fans in place to watch the morning sessions of heats and qualifying rounds) and they were treated to world records by John Akii-Bua of Uganda in the 400m hurdles, Britain's Mary Peters in the pentathlon, Lasse Viren of Finland in the 10,000m and Ulrike Meyfarth – who at 16 years and 123 days became the youngest ever individual champion – in the women's high jump.

There was a magical atmosphere in the stadium on that evening of September 4 as the West German schoolgirl flopped over 1.92m to equal the record and bring the first half of the athletics programme to a close. The terrible events of the next day would also bring to an end any last vestiges of the hope and belief that the Olympic Games were a refuge from the problems of the outside world. Other great performances did follow, with further world records in the 110m hurdles, decathlon, 4x100m relay, women's 200m, 1500m, shot and both relays, but the Olympic spell – the feeling that what was happening in the stadium was absolutely the most important thing going on in the world that moment – had forever been broken.

105

German athletes, from both the ill-named Democratic Republic (GDR) and the Federal Republic (FRG), performed magnificently to accumulate almost as many gold medals as the USA and USSR combined. The East Germans, subsequently discredited by evidence of systematic drug taking programmes, took eight titles and the West Germans six, as against nine by the Soviet athletes and just six by the Americans, who experienced their worst ever Games.

Few reports have given me more personal pleasure than my account of Mary P's glorious victory.

After 17 years of pentathlon competition and countless thousands of hours spent training, Mary Peters 'overnight' became one of the world's great sports stars, and a household name throughout the British Isles. She had joined the immortals of athletics by winning an Olympic title with a world record performance – in the tradition established by Britain's only previous female Olympic champions, Mary Rand and Ann Packer. Mary Peters' story is one of perseverance and determination to overcome all obstacles. Mary's career might well have ended four years ago after a disappointing showing at the Mexico Olympics where she placed ninth. Had she quit then, she would have been remembered as a very good and big hearted athlete, fourth in the Tokyo Olympics, but not a truly great one. Instead she took off 1969 in order to regain her zest and prepare all the more thoroughly for her next big target, the Edinburgh Commonwealth Games. She succeeded admirably, winning gold medals in both the shot and pentathlon. Her Olympic rivals may have been lulled into a false sense of security by the fact that Mary passed up competition in 1971. They probably thought that, at the age of 32, she had decided to retire. Not a chance!

The key factor in her improvement in 1972 was the high jump. Previously capable on a very good day of 1.65m, she was now a flopper who cleared 1.78m in her final pre-Olympic competition and that progress was worth over 150 points to her. She went to Munich ranked fifth among the pentathlon contenders with her UK record score of 4630 but straight away demonstrated her cracking form by clocking her quickest ever 100m hurdles time of 13.29. She followed with her best shot put in a pentathlon of 16.20m and then came her stupendous high jump display. After untroubled clearances at 1.55m, 1.60m, 1.65m and 1.68m she mucked up her approach run on her first two attempts at 1.71m but kept her gold medal hopes alive by clearing at the final attempt. She took 1.74m first time and survived another crisis with a third attempt success at 1.76m. At 1.78m, equal to her best, she went over first time and was now the only jumper left in. Her main rival, West Germany's newly crowned long jump champion Heide Rosendahl, had got no higher than 1.65m, and she could only watch aghast but admiringly as Mary slipped faultlessly over 1.80m and 1.82m.

It was like a dream, a wonderful dream as one shared with Mary the delight of soaring to new heights. It was an emotional experience not only for friends of Mary eager for her to succeed but equally for complete strangers who recognised they were watching a very rare athlete reaching for and attaining a new dimension in her performance. Or perhaps they simply, and understandably, warmed to the bouncy blonde with the flashing smile and cheery wave. Anyway, there was a sort of communal love affair going on between Mary and her thousands of anonymous admirers in the stands. The atmosphere was such that she all but cleared 1.84m, and so the first day ended with Mary out in the lead with a world's best on record of 2969, 97 points clear of East Germany's world record holder Burglinde Pollak, with Rosendahl fifth 301 points in arrears – but still full of menace on account of her brilliant long jumping and sprinting ability.

On the second day Rosendahl jumped a superb 6.83m, 1cm below her world record but wind assisted, wile Pollak registered 6.21m and Mary a near personal best of 5.98m. With just the 200m to come, Mary had 3871 points to 3824 by Pollak and 3750 by Rosendahl. Armed with various facts and figures, I greeted Mary during the interval. Steeling herself for the worst, she asked what was required of her in the 200. Fortunately I was able to reassure her that the position, although desperately tight, was slightly in her favour. If all three girls were to duplicate their personal bests then Mary (24.2) would win with 4790 points from Pollak (23.8) 4781 and Rosendahl (23.1) 4776. Basically, Mary had to finish not more than 1.2 sec behind Heide or 0.4 sec behind Burglinde to win the gold. She was going to have to run the race of her life.

Into the straight Rosendahl was about 3m clear of Pollak, with Mary close behind her, and while Heide continued to pull away steadily along the straight Mary guttily stayed within a metre of Burglinde. Clearly, at the finish, she was within the necessary 0.4 of the East German – but was Heide's winning margin too great? The latter's time of 22.96, a terrific effort into a 0.6m/sec wind, flashed up on the board but it seemed like eternity before the other times came through. Hasty mathematics showed that Mary needed 24.18 to win. Then, at last, her time went up ... 24.08! By a tenth of a second, ten points, Mary had won the Olympic pentathlon title – and with a world record score of 4801 points as a bonus. How pleasant that one of the nicest people in the sport should capture the ultimate prize.

Mary was quick to point out that "at least 50 per cent of this medal is due to Buster McShane for his coaching; he has coached me regularly since 1962 and he helped me with weight training before that." Alas, Buster died in a car accident in April 1973, aged 42. As I wrote: *He was always one of my favourite people in athletics. Friendly and down to earth, he bubbled with enthusiasm, eager to tell of Mary's latest achievements and hear the latest news of her rivals. He will be honoured in the history of athletics for his role in one of the greatest coaching partnerships of all time.*

A few weeks after the Games, prior to the British Athletics Writers' Association awards dinner in London, I taped a lengthy interview with Mary. As she was now a formidable high jumper herself, I asked whether she had witnessed Thelma Hopkins' world record of 1.74m in Belfast in 1956. She had indeed. "I actually competed against Thelma that day, although I was well out of it before she even started. I think I jumped only 4ft 8in (1.42m) on that occasion. But I was there and saw it ... it was tremendous! Thelma was always a very quiet athlete and I think that was the first time I ever saw her really happy and joyful about something she'd done. Of course I was only a little schoolgirl [aged 16] and I was very inspired to see somebody breaking a world record there in front of my eyes." Incidentally, her first pentathlon was when she finished third in the 1955 Northern Ireland championship behind Thelma and Maeve Kyle with 3253 points. "I'd never heard of a pentathlon when I was invited to do it. I had to ask Kenny [coach Kenny McClelland] what the events were. He told me about the shot and the hurdles, two events I had never done."

While Mary P was performing so admirably on the first day of the pentathlon, David Hemery was attempting to retain his 400m hurdles title. The bid ended in gallant failure.

Only he, among Europeans, has run faster than his 48.52 – but it was only good enough for the bronze medal this time. Who can disagree with the statement immediately made that John Akii-Bua's 47.82 is one of the greatest achievements in the history of athletics? It is possibly the finest single track performance of all time. Coached [in Uganda] by AW correspondent Malcolm Arnold, his previous best was 49.0. A right leg lead hurdler should be at a disadvantage in an inside lane, and Akii was in lane 1 – but great athletes cancel out unlucky breaks like that.

Next day came another world record. *Lasse Viren was rather like John Akii-Bua in that no one could have beaten him on this day. Dave Bedford tried the only way he knew how – by setting a blistering pace from the gun – and he ran himself into the ground [finishing sixth]. Viren himself tripped approaching 4600m and lost maybe five precious seconds, yet still pulled himself back into the race and won it from Emiel Puttemans with a blistering last kilometre. To cap it all, he broke Ron Clarke's world record by a second with 27:38.4. The new hero of Finland covered his last lap in 56.6 and the final 800m in 1:56.6!*

Viren went on to claim the 5000m title also, in the Olympic record time of 13:26.4, with Ian Stewart finishing a disappointed third, but this was after the massacre and by then the heart and soul of the Games had been extinguished for me and countless others. Britain's other medal came in the 4x400m relay, the team of Martin Reynolds, Alan Pascoe, Hemery and David Jenkins equalling the European record of 3:00.5 behind Kenya.

Another disturbing feature of the Games was the showing of the East German women's team with victories in the 100m, 200m, 400m, 100m hurdles, javelin and 4x400m plus another seven silver or bronze medals. Shortly before the Games we printed a letter from women's athletics expert Peter Pozzoli, drawing attention to the marked increase in weight of several female GDR athletes and posing the question: "Are all throwers and all-rounders in the GDR now on steroids?" The answer would eventually prove to be yes, and not just in those events. Chilling in another sense was the National Cross Country at the appropriately named Sutton Coldfield in March.

As the senior race progressed the rain turned first to sleet and then to snow as the temperature plummeted. Conditions underfoot were treacherous, all the more so as visibility worsened and few of the thousand runners escaped falling over at some stage of the three-lap nine mile race. Even the winner, Malcolm Thomas, took a tumble at the last ford about a mile from home. But it was the biting cold, and particularly the icy wind blowing into the faces of the runners as they headed towards the finish of each lap, that caused the most suffering. The scene in the officials' marquee after the race was gruesome as runners staggered in seeking shelter from the raging snowstorm outside. With icicles in their hair they shivered uncontrollably and speechless as helpers tried to massage their frozen bodies. These were the 'lucky' ones; others were whisked off to hospital or were left to make their own way back to the changing rooms about 1½ miles away.

Even trying to watch and report on the race was an ordeal, my numb fingers trying to write in a saturated notebook. No wonder I preferred covering indoor athletics to cross country! I always thought a special Sutton Coldfield 1972 medal should have been awarded to all 887 finishers, distinguished names including Allan Rushmer, Tony Simmons, Brendan Foster, Trevor Wright, Roy Fowler, Bill Adcocks, Andy Holden, Ricky Wilde, Lachie Stewart and Martin Hyman. This was a race they would never forget.

Sharing an ordeal like that strengthens the bonds between people and I have always enjoyed the friendships and camaraderie that the sport has brought me. However, there was one individual I simply could not get on with, and that was Frank Horwill. He was an influential if controversial coach and he made an important contribution to athletics with his passionate involvement with the British Milers' Club, but that good was negated by his muckraking writing. He always denied it but there is no doubt in my mind that he was largely responsible for the scurillous and ironically named *Athletics Truth*. This publication consistently peddled lies and its principal targets were Arthur Gold, Harold Abrahams, Marea Hartman and myself. In the second AW issue of 1972 I felt obliged to defend myself.

For those readers who may have seen a copy of Britain's first self-styled 'underground athletics news-sheet', I would like to set the record straight as it affects AW, which is accused of being 'biased in favour of the governing bodies'. The following astonishing statement is made in the introductory paragraph: 'We know that the editor of Athletics Weekly visits the secretary of the BAAB at his North London home almost every weekend.' Oh, really? I assume the anonymous producers of this sheet must maintain a permanent look-out at Arthur Gold's home, or perhaps they employ a detective to record my every movement. However, someone's imagination is working overtime, for I have visited Mr Gold's home exactly once in my life – following the 1971 European Indoor Championships when he was good enough to loan me a copy of the complete results sheets.

In March I published a letter from Horwill which stated in part: "I am greatly disturbed to find that more and more people are assuming that I am one of the driving powers behind the illegal, libellous and anonymous news-sheet called *Athletics Truth*. I wish to make it quite clear that I am far too busy … to engage in what virtually is an exercise in poison-pen writing." I didn't believe him, and the sniping went on for years. Despite the personal abuse I chose not to publicise the fact that Horwill, a London market inspector, was sent to prison in 1981 for tax evasion. In 2011 he went to Buckingham Palace to receive the MBE for services to sport, causing his most celebrated pupil, Tim Hutchings, to remark: "It was a more fitting way for him to be the guest of Her Majesty." Horwill died in 2012, aged 84.

On a brighter note, although he would be frustrated at the Olympics, it should be recalled that Dave Bedford was responsible for what Ron Clarke described as the finest ever distance double. His stunning running was the highlight of what I dubbed the greatest ever AAA Championships. Making a last minute decision to race in the 5000m, he charged into the lead after 200m and led throughout to reach 3 miles in 12:52.0, shattering his own European record, and at the finish he was just 0.6 sec outside Clarke's world record with 13:17.2, obviously also a European record. Barely 19 hours later, in hot weather, Dave produced a 10,000m time (27:52.8) which he and Clarke alone had ever bettered. That earned a thunderous reception from the crowd of nearly 20,000 as Bedford cruised the last circuit in 67.4, seemingly incorporating his victory lap as he veered over into the fifth lane along the finishing straight. What a showman he was, and the fans loved it.

Also loved by most AW readers were the contributions of Cliff Temple and in issue no 14 we printed a feature under the headline "Mike Bull Enthuses Over New Pole" in which Cliff revealed that the Rola-Pole, invented by the Italian Dr Looflirpa Naruo, promised to see an end to the days when vaulters have to lug their rigid 16 foot poles around on buses, trains, planes and taxis. The pole, constructed of a finely woven mixture of nylon and glass fibre, could be rolled up and carried around like a garden hose but when a specially developed 'core' is added it acts like a normal pole. UK record holder Mike Bull, who co-operated in the writing of the article, was one of its keenest supporters. Cliff's piece was the talk of the pole vaulting world, at least until in the following issue (dated April 8) it was revealed that Looflirpa Naruo spelt backwards reads 'o...u...r...an april fool'.

Cliff's much anticipated Christmas special took the form of an agony column, 'Dear Uncle Cliff'. Some examples: "In reply to my last letter, you suggested that I should wear heavy shoes and thick socks when training on the road. Last night I was arrested while running down the High Street. What did I do wrong?" *Uncle Cliff writes*: "I think you misunderstood my reply. I didn't mean **only** heavy shoes and thick socks ..." "I have got problems with my right leg. I pulled a calf muscle, injured my knee, tore a hamstring and the foot tendons are strained, all on the same leg. What should I do?" *Uncle Cliff writes*: "Try limping." "Could you please tell me the stride pattern used by David Hemery in the Munich 400m hurdles final?" *Uncle Cliff writes*: "Yes, all three medallists used the same stride pattern: left, right, left, right, left, right." Cliff's humour was not confined to AW; he sent gags to various BBC radio and TV shows including *The Two Ronnies*.

On a personal note, Pat and I travelled abroad together for the first time as members of the AW party which supported the British men's team at Stade Colombes in Paris. It proved a one-sided match as Britain triumphed 123-89, the winners including David Hemery in his fastest non-Olympic time of 49.30 in what was his final 400m hurdles race. I was watching his stride pattern closely … yes it was left, right, left, right. The following month Pat and I, together with Stan and Carole Greenberg, flew to Athens for a four-day stay, during which Stan and I raced over 100m at the 1896 Olympic Stadium. Stan, then 41, won but never sprinted again; obviously any further races would prove such an anti-climax.

Onward to 1973, a year of great achievements by Brendan Foster and Dave Bedford among others, but by far the most important event for me was marriage to my beloved Pat. The wedding was on April 8, eight days after my nephew Lionel's barmitzvah. The ceremony was at Wembley Synagogue, followed by a reception and dinner-dance at the Grosvenor Rooms in nearby Willesden. Happily, all four of our parents were there to share in the joyful occasion, as well as numerous other family members. Telegrams from Mary Peters, Ron Pickering and Harold Abrahams were read out, while in attendance from the world of athletics were Stan Greenberg (my best man), Arthur Gold (who delivered a flattering speech), Alf Wilkins, Cliff Temple, Jimmy Green and Dave Cocksedge. A warm glow prevailed over the entire proceedings … even if it was snowing by the end of the evening.

It was a year of change in many aspects. Pat and I started married life in Bromley but at the end of August we moved to a bigger flat in North Finchley, near neighbours including the Greenbergs, Jim Coote of the *Daily Telegraph* and Dave Bedford. The prices remain comical by today's standards: we sold for £10,500 and bought for £13,000. Zoopla estimates the North Finchley flat's value today as over £340,000! Change too at AW. Dave Cocksedge (who would die while on holiday in Thailand in 2016, aged 69) left for a job with IPC Magazines, although continuing to contribute to AW as a freelance, and the post of assistant editor was filled in August by 22 year-old Jon Wigley, a formidable distance runner who in 1975 would run 5000m in 13:49.47 and 10,000m in 28:35.84. A new position was created to cope with the magazine's continual expansion, with Tim Green (a promising runner until injury ended his active career) being appointed as his father's assistant business and advertisement manager.

The eternal debate over amateurism and professionalism intensified with the inauguration of the International Track Association, an American professional circuit created, in the words of its founder Mike O'Hara, to "provide track athletes with a chance to continue competing after college and in a few years they could perhaps be earning more than $50,000 a year. The circuit will offer a minimum of $600,000 in prize money. We have sufficient financial security to be able to hold out for a decade." Many big names did sign contracts and competed in the USA and Canada in 1973, including Bob Hayes, Jim Hines, John Carlos, Lee Evans, Jim Ryun, Kip Keino, Gerry Lindgren, Dick Fosbury,

Bob Seagren, Bob Beamon, Randy Matson, Brian Oldfield and Wyomia Tyus, but it was significant that certain world famous runners indicated that they could not afford to turn pro as they would be earning less than they did as "shamateurs"!

It seems doubtful whether many of the really top stars from Europe will be tempted. Men like Valeriy Borzov (USSR) and Wolfgang Nordwig (GDR), obviously, are unobtainable, while certain West Europeans who at present receive substantial appearance money (tax-free by implication) yet preserve their freedom as 'amateurs' to compete where they please – and bid for prestigious European and Olympic titles – have little to gain and much to lose unless they feel their best days are behind them. One might hope that the IAAF, which has set up a committee to investigate the current amateur eligibility rules, will in the not too distant future be more liberal in its attitude. Appearance money is a fact of life in the present structure of invitation meets and it might as well be recognised and accepted by the authorities – and thereby controlled. Athletes should also be allowed to capitalise on their fame through advertising and sponsorship. There is nothing 'dirty' about athletes earning money if they wish; it's the present hypocritical system that is at fault – one that makes apparent liars and cheats out of perfectly respectable people.

Those comments were not at all to the liking of Harold Abrahams. In a long letter published in the January 20 issue, he wrote: "I am not one of those who thinks that the present amateur rules are in any way sacrosanct, and therefore should not be amended; on the contrary for very many years I have argued (on occasions successfully) for changes. But what Mr Watman suggests can scarcely claim to be an 'amendment'. It strikes at the very fundamentals of amateurism, and in effect would abolish it. Practically speaking, the IAAF is most unlikely to entertain the passing of rules which would in effect mean the deleting of the word 'Amateur' from their title." [Unlikely or not, 'Amateur' was eventually dropped from the IAAF's title in 2001 to reflect the worldwide acceptance of athletes being paid openly, in many cases by the IAAF itself].

Harold added: "It is right to endeavour to secure that a successful athlete is not being paid solely for the use of his name as a successful performer. It is quite right that that he should not be able, while claiming to remain eligible to compete in amateur competitions, to receive payment for advertising some commodity or for signing some 'ghosted' article. But he should be allowed to write, broadcast or televise for payment. It would not be difficult to control such activities and see that the contributions were genuine, by making prior permission of the Governing Body essential."

In my editorial the following week I wrote: *Athletics will, I hope, always be a joyful recreation for 99.9 per cent of its practitioners, who are never likely to fall foul of the amateur rules. They are in athletics for the thrill of competition, the satisfaction of being fit and the comradeship of club life. This is the essence of this wonderful sport of ours, and athletics will thrive as long as youngsters enter the sport for the fun and challenge. It's a great adventure.*

However, largely through television there is a small body of star athletes who have become in effect public entertainers, whose presence at a meeting will probably help swell attendances and who, in their own countries at least, are household names. Reaching such a level of achievement carries its own inner satisfactions and some are content with that and such perks as travel. Others feel they are entitled to more material benefits as a reward for their fame and the hard work that has led to their reaching the top. These are the athletes, few in number but important as they represent a significant section of the sport's 'shop window', about whom there is so much soul-searching. Of course, if they don't like the amateur rules they can leave the sport, or now in some instances, try their luck as professionals – but that is to the detriment of athletics as we know it. What sometimes happens is that the athlete, while technically remaining an amateur, flouts the rules by accepting under-the-counter payments and inducements. We can maintain the present hypocritical situation of 'shamateurism'; or we can enforce the rules more rigidly and cast out the offenders; or we can move towards an 'open' sport more in keeping with the times.

In March, Britain's International Athletes' Club distributed a questionnaire to its members to find out what their opinion was as regards receiving appearance money, cash prizes etc. The results were published in July. Signed on behalf of the IAC by chairman John Whetton, the preamble stated: "The enquiry arose from a strong feeling of discontent among IAC members with the present amateur laws and from a desire to find out whether this dissatisfaction is shared by the athletes in general. On the whole the replies showed an unexpected degree of awareness of the inadequacies of the present set-up and of the urgent need for reform."

Among the figures presented (replies by all athletes with IAC members in brackets): Should athletes be able to receive payment for writing or broadcasting? Yes-243, No-14 (53/0); receive payment for advertising? Yes-193, No-53 (46/6); receive cash as distinct from goods as prizes? Yes-201, No-58 (47/5); appearance money for star athletes from promoters? Yes-79, No-169 (20/30); harmful for an athlete if allowed to be paid for competing? Yes-59, No-191 (9/44); in favour of completely 'open' athletics? Yes-197, No-57 (49/3). The document states: "In any democracy it is the duty of the governing body to legislate for the effective fulfilment of the wishes of the people they represent, rather than to insist on trying to perpetuate what they believed to be right in the good old days. Is it too much to hope that they [national governing bodies which collectively form the IAAF] will see the need and desire for a change in the amateur laws so as to enable all athletes to compete openly and honourably at all levels without being inhibited by the prejudices of the 19th century?"

My comment was that *this document is of great importance and significance to the future of our sport. Eventually there will be open athletics; of that I have no doubt. But let's make it sooner rather than later. The response to the IAC's poll makes it clear what athletes feel about the situation and the administrators would do well to remember that they are in office to run athletics for the benefit of the athletes.* Open athletics did come into being ... but not until the early eighties.

The big news in Britain during the early part of the year was 19 year-old Verona Bernard's terrific breakthrough at the European Indoor Championships in Rotterdam. Ranked sixth on paper for the 400m on 1973 form with 54.0, she won her heat in 53.98 and semi in 53.35 before seizing the gold medal in 53.04, the official hand time of 53.0 equalling Marilyn Neufville's world indoor best. Her target that summer was to break Lillian Board's UK record of 52.1; in fact she equalled it but did better it in 1974 with 51.94. She went on to win two more European indoor titles and following a long and distinguished active career as Verona Elder, representing Britain a record 72 times, she was appointed British team manager at the 1996 Olympics.

Dave Bedford, gloriously unpredictable as ever, had hardly raced that summer because of a persistent hamstring injury and much missed training but the enforced rest must have done him good for at the AAA Championships in July he stunned everyone except himself by breaking Lasse Viren's world 10,000m record with 27:30.8. He had promised himself that record ever since his demise in Munich.

The Crystal Palace stand fairly shook as it was announced that Dave Bedford had smashed the world record. These were magical moments with Dave blowing kisses to the crowd as he was pursued, Pied Piper fashion, by a line of young autograph hunters. It is a long time since a British athlete set a world record on home soil in one of the classic Olympic events; one has to go back to Peter Radford's 20.5 200m at Wolverhampton in 1960, while London fans have not witnessed such a feat since the Chataway-Kuts epic back in 1954. It's staggering to realise that Bedford's second 5000 in this race was covered in 13:51.4 (a fifth of a second faster than Chataway's winning time) – following a first 5000 in 13:39.4, which is faster than the Olympic record as it stood before Munich!

There was another sparkling performance at the Palace a few weeks later when Brendan Foster became the first Briton to set a world record for 2 miles since Alf Shrubb nearly 70 years earlier by covering the distance in 8:13.8.

It was an exhausting, emotional, bewildering but ultimately fulfilling day for the 25 year-old Gateshead Harrier, a chemistry teacher by profession. He learned that he had failed to equal Lasse Viren's world record of 8:14.0 by the galling margin of 0.2 sec; it was not until half an hour later that I was able to break the news that he had, in fact, clipped the record by the same tantalising amount. Although the manual clockings were 8:13.8, 8:14.2 and 8:14.2 and thus 8:14.2 was announced as the winning time, it was found that the photo finish equipment registered 8:13.68 which is 8:13.8 when rounded off to fifths of a second. Before the race Brendan had announced his intention of attacking Ian Stewart's UK record of 8:22.0 but secretly he and his coach Stan Long were aiming for 8:12. Brendan went through the mile in 4:05.4 some 40m clear. *The stress and pain as he continued with laps of 61.9, 63.5 and 63.2 can hardly be imagined, and still he was faced with the agonising task of running the last lap all alone in under a minute to break the record. A lesser man would have flinched, but Brendan – head wagging with the strain – strove hard all the way and thoroughly deserved his splendid record.*

Brendan was one of five home winners in the European Cup Final in Edinburgh, in which the British men's team finished fourth. A ridiculous opening 200m of close to 40 sec put paid to any fast time in the 5000m but Brendan, who threw in a vicious 60.2 lap between 2800m and 3200m, sprinted to victory in 13:54.8, a remarkable time after all the early nonsense. The women's team placed fifth in a match notable for the GDR scoring 72 points out of a possible maximum of 78. It was the most devastating all-round display of national strength ever witnessed in an athletics stadium. Individual highlights were world records by the GDR's Ruth Fuchs in the javelin (66.10m) and the USSR's Faina Melnik in the discus (69.48m). The latter added almost two metres to her own record, which for the first time was longer than the men's equivalent although of course the implement used is only half the weight.

Fuchs was the Olympic champion, and would retain that title in 1976, but who could have predicted that an athlete featured in Dave Cocksedge's "Spotlight on Youth" column would one day also win an Olympic javelin gold medal? Under the heading "Meet Miss Versatility", the article on 16 year-old Theresa (as she was known then) Sanderson predicted "a girl who may end up as a world class 400m runner just as possibly as she may become a top high jumper. Or hurdler. Or javelin thrower." Jamaican-born Tessa was such a talented all-rounder with best marks at that early stage of her career including 25.6 200m, 57.3 400m, 15.6 100m hurdles, 1.69m high jump, 5.64m long jump and 43.06m javelin. "Maybe I can make it to the Olympics", she ventured. Well, Tessa made it to SIX Olympics between 1976 and 1996, triumphing in 1984, while she improved her personal bests to 24.89, 13.46, 5.98m and a Commonwealth record 73.58m, not to mention 60.46 for 400m hurdles and a Commonwealth record heptathlon score of 6125. Another prodigy to feature in our columns in 1973 was 14 year-old Mary Decker, all 1.52m (5ft) and 39kg (86lb) of her at that time ... and all arms, legs and forward lean. What a competitor. She not only ran 800m in 2:02.4 in a West Germany v USA encounter in Munich but beat Olympic silver medallist Niole Sabaite in 2:02.9 in a match against the USSR in Minsk.

It was good to welcome new talent but sad to bid farewell to giants of the past. Among the obituaries I penned were two of the all-time greats in Paavo Nurmi and Abebe Bikila.

Of Paavo Nurmi, who died in Helsinki on October 2, aged 76, it can truthfully be said we shall never see his like again. The man, famous and respected throughout the world to a degree previously unheard of for an athlete, was – and will continue to be – a legend. His achievements will for ever be recalled with awe. Only one athlete in a million can hope to win an Olympic title or break a world record ... Nurmi won nine gold medals and set over twenty world records. He accomplished the unbelievable at the 1924 Olympics by winning the 1500m and 5000m with just 42 minutes between races. His range has never been surpassed: the fastest 1500m and mile runner of his or any previous age, he was also a world record smasher at 20,000m and the hour, an Olympic silver medallist in the steeplechase and, but for his untimely disqualification from amateur athletics in 1932, he would have been favourite for the marathon crown in Los Angeles.

Bikila was only 41 when, on October 25, he died of a brain haemorrhage in Addis Ababa. Shortly before Bikila's death Emperor Haile Selassie visited him and made arrangements for his most famous subject to be flown to England for treatment at Stoke Mandeville ... but it was too late. Bikila – the only man to have won the Olympic marathon twice – had been paralysed from the waist down ever since a car crash in March 1969. So ends the inspiring but tragic story of a very remarkable man, one whose memory will for ever be cherished by those who had the privilege to see him run. No athlete ever exuded such dignity and serenity as Abebe Bikila.

Sad too was the news that the outstanding ultra-distance runner John Tarrant underwent surgery to have his stomach removed a few days after it was diagnosed that he had cancer of the stomach. *John is renowned as a grand fighter, both as a runner and against what many consider was a personal injustice when he was barred from international competition. Now comes the most vital battle of his life and I know I speak for all AW readers when I wish John the very best of luck at this anxious time.* More about John later in this book.

And talking of books, the third edition of my *Encyclopaedia of Athletics* was published in November, updating everything until the early part of the 1973 season. As Cliff Temple correctly surmised, "I can well imagine the heart-searching that must have gone on when he had to eliminate some of the biographies from the earlier editions to allow room for today's biggest names." Harold Abrahams, in his foreword, pointed out the necessity for a new edition as since the previous version in 1967 close to 250 world records had been passed by the IAAF.

12. FOSTER & STEWART THE STARS (1974-1975)

The athlete I wrote about more than any other in 1974 was Brendan Foster. To younger generations of runners and fans his is the familiar Geordie voice commentating on long distance track races, cross country and road events for BBC television, but older followers of the sport remember with affection his belligerent style of racing. His particular weapon of choice was to throw in a very fast lap mid-race, more often than not killing off the unprepared or disheartened opposition. It was a brave way to win races.

His great 1974 season started early with the Commonwealth Games in Christchurch, New Zealand, in January. In the 5000m he was level at the bell with Ben Jipcho, who had already won the steeplechase, and after a 55.3 last lap the Kenyan won by a narrow margin in a Commonwealth record of 13:14.4 with Brendan smashing Dave Bedford's UK record with 13:14.6. Only Belgium's Emiel Puttemans with 13:13.0 had ever run faster. Four days later Brendan broke another UK record with 3:37.6 for 1500m but such was the standard of that race that he placed only a distant seventh as 20 year-old Filbert Bayi of Tanzania front ran through laps of 54.4, 1:51.8 and 2:50.3. Thirty metres clear at one stage, he just held on from a fast finishing John Walker of New Zealand, 3:32.2 (world record) to 3:32.5, with the seemingly indefatigable Jipcho third in 3:33.2. Spectating Roger Bannister said: "This was the greatest piece of front running I have ever seen."

That Foster was heading for an exceptional summer campaign became apparent when at the National Road Relay at Sutton Coldfield he smashed the hilly long lap (5 miles 900 yards) record with 24:28, equating to around 27:40 pace for 10,000m. In the AAA Championships 5000m he employed his trademark tactic by covering the lap between 2800m and 3200m in 59.21 and went on to win by a very big margin over Jos Hermens, the Dutchman who would set a world one hour record the following season and has for many years been one of the most successful of all athletes' agents. That was just the prelude to his dream race at his home track in Gateshead.

Regardless of whatever else he might go on to achieve, including the possibility of European and Olympic titles, Brendan Foster is in the happy position of having already fulfilled his life's ambition in athletics. The fulfilment came when, at a meeting he helped organise on the brand new Tartan track at Gateshead [he was the newly appointed Sports & Recreation Manager for Gateshead], Brendan rewarded his devoted Tyneside fans – at least ten thousand of them – with a world record. A great world record it was too, one that is three or four seconds superior to the 2 miles mark of 8:13.8 he set last year. By covering 3000m in 7:35.2, he cut 2.4 sec off Emiel Puttemans' figures. Old timers who still glow, and rightly so, at the memory of Jack Lovelock's world record breaking 1500m victory at the Berlin Olympics (3:47.8) might pause to reflect that Brendan maintained a slightly faster pace for twice the distance!

There was more to come at the European Championships the following month, but back to those Commonwealth Games and the bad luck that befell another of Britain's outstanding runners, Dave Bedford. He was in the form of his life as he put the finishing touches to his preparation for the 10,000m, believing he was ready to clock around 27:10, some 20 seconds faster than his own world record. However, he wound up a distant, badly spiked fourth in 28:14.8 after suffering from the roughhouse tactics of all three of his Kenyan opponents. "I lost my cool – and it lost me the race," he admitted. He fared even worse in the 5000m, finishing a listless 11th. Sadly, that was to prove to be his final major track championship race as leg injuries brought his international career to a premature end at the age of 24. He would go on to make an important contribution to the sport as an administrator and London Marathon race director, and "Bootsie" remains one of British athletics' favourite sons.

It was a melancholy year. At least Fred Housden, a First World War hero who taught David Hemery how to hurdle well and helped guide him to Olympic gold and world record, was 81 when he died in February, but three very distinguished British athletes passed away at much too young an age.

John Cooper, silver medallist in the 400m hurdles and 4x400m at the 1964 Olympics, was 33 and married for only four months when in March he perished in an air disaster while on his way home after a France v England rugby union match in Paris. In my tribute I wrote: *John Cooper was one of the most tenacious competitors I have ever seen and an inspiration to all around him; a man who by hard work, perseverance and grit rose to the heights of Olympic silver medallist. His rugged determination to succeed and his basically serious yet jokey personality made him a valued member of the British team from 1961 to 1969.*

His modest flat speed (48.6 for 440y) held him back until the winter of 1963-64 when he worked very hard training alongside his great friend Robbie Brightwell. By August 1964 he had lowered his best 440y time to 47.9, but that was no accurate indication of his ability. In a 400m relay leg at the White City he was timed at 45.9, while in Tokyo he contributed an even faster stage, having set a UK record of 50.1 in the 400m hurdles. That perceptive American observer, Dick Bank, paid tribute to his friend. "'Coop' went farther with less ability than any athlete I have ever witnessed. As I saw him, he was 75% desire and only 25% ability. He had no business being in the Olympic 400 hurdles final let alone winning a silver medal. His legs simply were not made to carry a baton around the track in 45.4 but that totally unexpected run made it possible for Robbie Brightwell to have a fighting chance to bring Britain a silver with an absolutely super effort of his own."

May saw the death from leukaemia of Phil Embleton, just 25. He had beaten Paul Nihill in the 1971 national 10 miles walk championship and early in 1972 he set a world's best for the 10,000m walk. He was rated a medal prospect at 20km in that year's Munich Olympics but placed a seemingly disappointing 14th. As Colin Young wrote: "The spirit and strength that characterised his training and racing had been sorely put to the test during the past 18 months when fighting the leukaemia which must have been affecting him even as he was competing in the Olympics. Those close to Phil who have seen him battle in and out of hospital can only be amazed at the fortitude and will power that sustained him." Among the letters we printed was one from John Tarrant, himself fighting for his life. He wrote: "Among the many letters I received while I was in hospital was one from Phil, and he had great difficulty in writing it because he was suffering from double vision. I had no idea he was so ill, because he made light of his own problem."

In September we lost Maureen Dyson, who as 19 year-old Maureen Gardner was beaten by inches for the 1948 Olympic 80m hurdles title by Fanny Blankers-Koen. The wife of former AAA Chief National Coach Geoff Dyson, she died after a long illness, aged 45.

Maureen, one of the most charming and attractive of women to grace the sport, was a good sprinter before her future husband made her into a great hurdler. She cherished an ambition of becoming a professional ballet dancer but after contracting bronchial pneumonia and pleurisy in 1945 she was told by doctors to put that out of her mind (she was later to run a ballet school, though). During her convalescence, her father happened to take her to the Oxford University track at a time when the newly founded Oxford Ladies AC were holding a training session and that evening Maureen decided to join the club. She won the WAAA 100m title in 1946 and became 80m hurdles champion in 1947. She married Geoff six weeks after the Wembley Olympics, retired to start a family but made a successful return in 1950, winning another silver medal behind Fanny Blankers-Koen, this time at the European Championships.

There was a tragedy also closer to home. In the June 15 issue there was a note which stated "owing to a serious illness in the family, Mel Watman has been unable to devote the usual amount of time to the production of AW". The reason was that my mother-in-law, Bella Master, had suffered a severe stroke on the way to a holiday in Bournemouth. Although she lived for another 11 years she never fully recovered her faculties and looking after her eventually proved too much for her husband, Sam, who died in 1980. In 1979 Pat and I sold our flat in North Finchley to move in to her parents' house in Wembley and for a while Pat was caring not only for her mum and dad but also giving support to her Auntie Betty who lived with them … at huge cost to my selfless wife's own health.

NUTS member Colin Shields took over as AW's Scottish correspondent in May, a position he filled diligently for many years, while the same month NUTS chairman Bob Sparks began as the magazine's overseas news editor as after 17 years in that role I was standing down, temporarily, to find more time to write other features. I was also freelancing widely and Ron Pickering as editor and myself as compiler produced *Athletics 74*, a 320 page book published by Queen Anne Press and with a foreword by Roger Bannister (who was knighted in the 1975 New Year Honours). These fact-filled yearbooks continued until 1980 and it was always a joy to work with Ron, the most enthusiastic and encouraging of collaborators.

The major event of the year for Britain's athletes was the European Championships in Rome and the team secured four gold medals. The first came in the 400m hurdles where Alan Pascoe added this title to his Commonwealth Games success. Despite a troubled summer when first he was unable to train because of bursitis and then developed a hamstring problem he triumphed with a personal best of 48.82 and later ran third leg for the victorious 4x400m relay team.

Brendan Foster said before his 5000m that it wasn't so much that he wanted to win as that he wanted to win memorably.

He did precisely that. Short of breaking the world record (and but for the sticky conditions he might well have run inside Puttemans' 13:13.0) it is difficult to perceive how he could have dominated the race to a greater degree. He won a major distance championship like Zátopek and Kuts used to. It was probably the greatest victory ever achieved by a British distance runner at this level of competition, for he made runners of the calibre of Lasse Viren look practically second rate. He darted to the front from the gun and at no time was he headed! It was front running at its best: positive, unflinching, challenging. The unspoken message to his opponents was – 'who's going to try and stay with me at world record pace, and in weather like this?' The temperature was 25°C with an 85% humidity reading.

He was 13 seconds clear at the bell and won by just under 7 seconds in 13:17.2, remarkable running in the conditions. *What an inspiration Brendan Foster is. Bren is an ordinary looking runner who through much hard work and intelligent application has become extraordinary. There's more to it than that, though; the character and temperament which are uniquely his have played a vital part in the making of Brendan Foster, champion.*

My colleague Jon Wigley reported on the marathon. It was Ian Thompson's fourth marathon and his fourth win. Previously an obscure 5000m runner who had never raced further than 10 miles, he had created a sensation by winning the AAA title in October 1973 in 2:12:40; in January 1974 he not only won at the Commonwealth Games but his time of 2:09:12 was a European record; in April he won the Marathon to Athens race in 2:13:51; and in September he clocked 2:13:19 to become champion of Europe. It was a fantastic start to his career as a marathon runner … but the magic wouldn't last. He never ran faster than 2:12:30 again.

No British man ever won a European 10,000m title until Mo Farah in 2010 but Tony Simmons came so very close in Rome, sharing the winning time of East Germany's Manfred Kuschmann but having to settle for silver. Runners-up also were David Jenkins, the defending 400 champion from 1971, and a prodigious 18 year-old 800m talent by the name of Steve Ovett. Yugoslavia's Luciano Susanj won by a big margin in the fine time of 1:44.1 but, as I reported, *Ovett was phenomenal, too, clocking 1:45.8 for a European junior record. He is the greatest young middle distance talent I have laid eyes on since the Jim Ryun of a decade ago.* Bronze medals went to Geoff Capes in the shot, Roger Mills in the 20km walk (as a result of a subsequent drugs disqualification of a Russian, a recurring theme over the years), Andrea Lynch in the 100m and Joyce Smith in the 3000m.

Okay, there was no one who matched the stunning global championship successes of Mo Farah but during the 1960s and at least the first half of the 1970s there was a seemingly unending conveyor belt of world class British distance runners. Gordon Pirie, Bruce Tulloh, Martin Hyman, John Merriman, Basil Heatley, Roy Fowler, Mike Bullivant, Derek Ibbotson, Mel Batty, Ron Hill, Don Taylor, Mike Wiggs, Ian McCafferty, Dick Taylor, Ian Stewart, Dave Bedford, Allan Rushmer, Lachie Stewart, Brendan Foster, Dave Black and Tony Simmons all ranked among the top six in the world at 5000m or 10,000m in one year or another, taking into account conversions from 3 and 6 miles. Then there were such marathon and long distance track runners, in addition to Heatley and Hill, as Brian Kilby, Bill Adcocks, Jim Alder, Jim Hogan, Tim Johnston and Ian Thompson.

These were golden days and, remember, nearly all of these men were holding down proper jobs, received no official financial assistance within the sport and did not have the medical support taken for granted these days by professional athletes. They were sturdy, competitive characters who simply trained damned hard and relished frequent races against each other whether on track, country or road.

Foster was the star turn in 1974 but the early part of 1975 belonged to Ian Stewart. He was outstanding from a young age. In 1965 he set a UK age-16 best for 2 miles, although he always maintained that records meant nothing to him; winning was the only thing that counted. As he said famously, "First's first and second is nowhere as far as I'm concerned." Win he did, his first major title being the National Junior cross country in 1968 on that notorious day in Sutton Coldfield. Just a year later he was European indoor champion at 3000m with a UK indoor record of 7:55.4. Outdoors in 1969 he improved at the mile from 4:06.3 to 3:57.3, becoming at 20 Britain's youngest sub-four minute miler, and went on to capture the European 5000m title. Better still was his victory at the 1970 Commonwealth Games in Edinburgh. Wearing the Scottish vest (his father was Scottish), although he had represented England as a junior in the International Cross Country Championships, Birmingham-born Ian unleashed a 26.4 final 200m to win from team-mate Ian McCafferty in a European record of 13:22.8, second only to Ron Clarke on the world all-time list. Defeated in that race were Clarke and Kip Keino. As no less an authority than Derek Ibbotson enthused: "He's the complete 5000m runner, the greatest Britain has ever produced."

True to his philosophy, Ian was mightily dissatisfied with his bronze medal in the 1972 Olympic 5000m. Uncompromising as ever, he stated: "I was terribly disappointed. If you've ever been in a position where all you've ever wanted was a gold medal and you come out with a bronze, it's choking. I'm not a very good sportsman; all I want to do is win races. This country's full of good losers. It's bloody good winners that we want."

Following a below par showing in 1973 and well beaten over 5000m and 10,000m at the Christchurch Commonwealth Games, Ian became disillusioned with athletics and switched to cycle racing in the summer of 1974. Batteries recharged, he returned to foot racing and in March 1975 he completed a momentous and unique double as on successive weekends he lifted the European Indoor 3000m title and, representing Scotland in the World Cross Country Championships in Rabat, Morocco, he won that 12km race too despite an attack of stitch early on. The last Briton to win that title, his defeated rivals included such names as Bill Rodgers, John Walker, Gaston Roelants, Waldemar Cierpinski, Emiel Puttemans and Frank Shorter. Surprisingly, those were the last major international medals of his career although he continued to produce high quality runs for several more seasons. The year before he retired in 1978 he was credited with a world best 10 miles road time of 45:13 and improved at 10,000m to 27:43.0. He later coached and for several years from 1994 he was promotions officer for the UK governing body, successfully putting together high class fields for the televised international meetings in Britain. And what a family! Elder brother Peter set UK records at 1500m, mile and 2 miles, while younger sister Mary (now Mrs Cotton) set a world indoor 1500m record in 1977 and was 1978 Commonwealth champion. Remarkably, all three siblings won European Indoor titles, while Mary's son Adam Cotton was European Junior 1500m champion in 2011.

AW kicked off 1975 with a special anniversary edition. *A milestone in the history of AW is reached with this issue, for it marks 25 years of unbroken publication. For Jimmy Green (editor for the first 18 years) and myself it has been a labour of love. Between us we have produced more than 1,300 consecutive issues – overcoming such potential disasters as strikes, power cuts, newsprint shortage and mechanical breakdowns. Yet only briefly, during transitional periods, has the full-time editorial staff numbered more than two! Looking back through that first volume of AW [1950] has been so illuminating. The sport was so different then in so many ways: huge crowds were the norm at White City, and yet international competition outside of the major Games seemed to be confined to matches against France; handicap racing and grass tracks were still widespread; champion distance runners tended to train three times a week; women athletes were over-protected; no one in the world had ever run 10,000m in under 29 minutes, or thrown the hammer 200 feet (60.96m) or broken 2:12 for the women's 800m.*

I recreated the flavour of athletics in 1950 by profiling four of the biggest stars – McDonald Bailey, Arthur Wint, John Parlett and Jack Holden – and reprinting snippets from that year's coverage in AW, which included Jimmy Green's prediction that Roger Bannister [whose best at that time was 4:11.1] was "the most likely athlete in the world to eventually approach that 4 minute mile".

In 1975 Sir Roger Bannister envisaged the mile record being down to 3:40 by the turn of the century. That never happened but the 3:50 barrier was cracked by John Walker in the same Gothenburg stadium that had seen world record miles by Gunder Hägg in 1942 and Arne Andersson in 1943. The strongly built New Zealander ran 3:49.4 ... and who would have thought that the man who would break that record, four years later, would be someone who hadn't yet ever raced at a mile. At the time of Walker's record in August, Sebastian Coe was aged 18, and had best times of 1:53.8 for 800m and 3:47.1 for 1500m, which he improved later that month to 3:45.2 when finishing third in the European Junior Championships.

At this stage of their careers, Steve Ovett was well ahead of his future arch-rival, having set a European junior record of 1:45.76 in taking the silver medal at the senior European Championships in 1974 and run 3:39.5 for 1500m and 3:57.00 for the mile in 1975. Ovett, with a 47.5 400m at age 18, had shown his versatility in March 1975 by winning the National Junior cross country title over 6 miles by a 35 sec margin.

Steve Ovett may have little in common with Sydney Wooderson on the physical plane, but the diminutive Blackheath Harrier is the only British athlete I can think of with such a wide-ranging talent. Wooderson could run the quarter in 49.3, was a world record holder for 800m, 880y and the mile, won the European 5000m title and ended his career at 33 as National 10 miles cross country champion. Ovett (19) can so far point to 47.5 for 400m, the European Junior 800m title and the silver medal in Rome (he is Britain's second fastest ever at the distance), a sub-four minute mile ... and he is thinking of trying the 5000m in two years time.

The only other Briton with such a phenomenal range was Derek Johnson, the 1956 Olympic 800m silver medallist, whose personal bests included 10.0 for 100y, 47.7 for 440y (but 45.9 in a relay), 1:46.6 for 800m, 3:42.9 for 1500m, 9:16.8 for the steeplechase, 53.7 for 440y hurdles ... and even a 2:55:47 marathon at age 50.

One of the delights of working for AW was giving young athletes their first national exposure in print, some of whom would develop into supreme champions. Ovett's first mention came in May 1970 when, aged 14, he won an inter-club Boys 800m in 2:07.0, while Coe's name first appeared in March 1971 as winner of the Colts race at the Yorkshire Cross Country Association Championships when he too was 14. Daley Thompson's first published result was his victory in the 1974 Sussex Schools Intermediate 200m (22.4) at 15. That Daley was more than just a promising sprinter became apparent during 1975. After winning the National Junior indoor 60m title in March, he – still only 16 – entered and won his first decathlon, scoring 6523 points using the present tables. He returned to Cwmbran twice more that season: in August, now 17, he won the AAA Junior championship and in October he broke the UK junior record with 6941 points in a senior international match against France.

A necessary aspect of my job was publishing obituaries and several notables passed on that year, including John Tarrant in January, Avery Brundage and Steve Prefontaine in May, Percy Cerutty and Vladimir Kuts in August.

It was particularly poignant that we published a letter from John's wife, Edie Tarrant, in the January 18 issue, thanking everyone who had written to him in hospital and giving details of his ward for future correspondence. The very next day he died in that Birmingham hospital after his long and courageous battle against cancer.

We reprinted Chris Brasher's appreciation from *The Observer*. It started: "The ghost is dead. John Tarrant, the most indomitable runner and the most honest man that I have ever met, died of cancer last week. He was only 42 years old. There are many famous names in British athletics, names that are known throughout the world, but among the vast body of athletes – the club runners who train and run because they love the sport – the name of John Tarrant is mentioned with as much honour as that of Ron Clarke." He went on to explain that because as a teenager John won £17 during a brief boxing career, and admitted it when switching to athletics, the AAA declared him a professional and he was barred from running officially in any amateur race. "That money was to haunt him throughout his short life," wrote Brasher. "From the age of 20 to 26 he was not allowed to compete even in the humblest race. Instead, he developed a technique of merging into the crowd, dressed in his running kit with a pair of ordinary trousers and an overcoat over the top, and when the starter's gun went he would shed his top layer and join in." The Ghost Runner was born, and over the years AW supported his bid for reinstatement, which eventually was granted in 1958. His ambition was to represent Britain in the marathon at the 1960 Olympics but, in Brasher's words, "John was never able to compete in the Olympic Games because of the petti-fogging, bureaucratic and unjust rules of the sport." He was told by the BAAB that under IAAF rules he could never compete abroad for his country. John went on to break world track records at 40 miles and 100 miles and in 1979, at Brasher's urging, I edited John's moving autobiography in the form of a book, entitled naturally *The Ghost Runner*.

I mourned John's untimely death and for many years kept in touch with his widow Edie, but I shed no tears for Avery Brundage (87), the autocratic president of the International Olympic Committee from 1952. During his 20 years in that office he waged an unceasing war against professionalism but his uncompromising attitude became increasingly far removed from the realities of modern international sport. I never met the man, an American millionaire who competed in the pentathlon and decathlon at the 1912 Olympics, but from all I've observed he was a despicable character. For a start he was implacably opposed to reinstating Jim Thorpe as the rightful winner of those two events in 1912 (like John Tarrant, Thorpe had earned a little money from another sport), while as a Nazi apologist and anti-semite he was largely responsible for persuading the American Olympic Committee, of which he was president, to send a team to the 1936 Berlin Games when there were strong calls for a boycott. In later years he was among those who was so appalled by the 1968 Olympic medal ceremony protest by Tommie Smith and John Carlos that they were summarily expelled from the Olympic Village and, as previously related, he appeared to be less dismayed by the massacre of Israeli team members in Munich than the absence from the Games, because of African pressure, of Rhodesia.

As with Lillian Board a few years earlier, the terribly premature death at 24 of Steve Prefontaine shook the entire world of athletics. Just four hours before the car crash that would end his life he had run what was then the fastest 5000m time (13:23.8) in the world that year before his adoring fans in Eugene. He was by far the USA's most popular runner, and his name resonates to this day.

No athlete in modern times had developed such a fanatical personal following. 'Go Pre' became the most famous slogan in athletics and the mass worship he attracted in his native state of Oregon was akin to that bestowed upon pop idols. Americans, particularly on the West Coast, identified with and responded to Steve's breezy image. He was cocky all right, self assured and ambitious to the extreme, but he was likeable too. Steve was an athlete's athlete, like Dave Bedford and Brendan Foster, universally admired for the way he would liven up any race he contested.

We printed this tribute from Bedford: "Steve always generated a great sense of youth, vitality and fun wherever he went and this, mixed with his dedication and enthusiasm for athletics, made him a man never to be forgotten by those who met him. I think I knew him better than most in Britain, having raced against 'the man' on the track and having joined him in a few drinks afterwards. After the Olympic 5000m he came up to me and said 'forget the results, we both lost; now let's go have us a few beers. That's what it's about after all.' We did, God bless you, Steve."

I described Percy Cerutty (80) as the larger than life Australian who guided John Landy and Herb Elliott to world records in the mile and whose unorthodox methods made him the most talked about coach in the world during his heyday. Cerutty advocated lots of weight training for his middle and long distance runners, and such resistance work as repetition runs up the famous 80-foot 1 in 1½ sandhill at his Portsea (Victoria) training camp. Interval training sessions on the track were anathema to him.

Elliott wrote of him: "Percy helped me to world records not so much by improving my technique but by releasing in my mind and soul a power that I only vaguely thought existed. He is an emotional person who is able to harness his emotion and transfer it to another person. He can inspire most of his athletes to run until they drop by his words and deeds." He was indeed a remarkable if controversial coach and motivator, but previously an admirer of his, I became disenchanted when in my one and only encounter with him in the 1960s he made some highly personal and derogatory remarks about John Landy, the man who made his reputation in the first place.

Under the headline "The Front Runner Supreme" I wrote a long appreciation of Vladimir Kuts, the 1956 Olympic 5000m and 10,000m champion and a world record breaker at both distances, who died aged 48. A stocky 72kg (159lb) in his prime, he had grown obese and become an alcoholic. He suffered a stroke in 1972 and there were reports that his death three years later may have been suicide. Both Zátopek and Gordon Pirie thought Kuts might have been on drugs during his racing career but there was no proof.

Kuts was the greatest distance running competitor of the mid-fifties, the successor to Emil Zátopek. Chris Chataway may have beaten him in the most talked-about 5000 duel in history, but that was one of only two significant defeats Kuts ever sustained during his epic seasons of 1954-57. His only other important loss was to Gordon Pirie, also over 5000, in Bergen in 1956. On both occasions it took a world record to conquer him, with Kuts himself finishing inside the previous mark.

On a more personal level two deaths that affected me were those of Sally Allen, who died at far too young an age, leaving heartbroken journalist husband Neil, a special friend of mine, to bring up two young sons (both of whom have made their mark in sports media), and Ross McWhirter – co-founder of the *Guinness Book of Records* and a noted athletics journalist and statistician along with twin brother Norris – who was assassinated outside his home by Provisional IRA terrorists.

Next to 'Pre', the USA's most acclaimed and influential runner was Frank Shorter and it was he who sounded the death knell of amateurism as preached by the likes of Avery Brundage.

In September I wrote: *The public 'admission' by Olympic marathon champion Frank Shorter that he has received money for racing in Europe could prove to be a most important landmark in the development of our sport. The fact that some top athletes are paid for appearing in invitational meetings will come as no surprise to most people involved in athletics; but it is unheard of for such a distinguished athlete – while at the peak of his career – to announce it to the world. The vital question now is whether the authorities will make an example of Shorter by branding him a professional and banning him from future international competition, as happened to such predecessors as Paavo Nurmi, Gunder Hägg, Arne Andersson and Dan Waern.*

Shorter, a lawyer, added: "I have probably violated nearly all of the rules of the IOC on amateurism." Fortunately for the sport, entering a more enlightened era, no action was taken against him. Indeed it was just the impetus required to hasten the introduction of officially sanctioned trust funds, itself a step towards full-blown open athletics.

Meanwhile, athletes who were already openly professional as members of the International Track Association came to Britain for two meetings, at Edinburgh's Meadowbank before a decent crowd of over 12,000 and London's Crystal Palace two days later when barely 4000 turned up. *They came, we saw ... and were not conquered. The ITA troupe boasted a few particular crowd pleasers and produced several outstanding performances, but they broke no records in terms of entertainment. Apart from the welcome opportunity to see again some of the glittering names of athletics there was nothing in the ITA format which cannot be matched, or bettered, by any orthodox high-class invitational meet.* The star turn in Edinburgh was Brian Oldfield ("have shot, will travel"), Garth personified, who threw 22.27m – well beyond the amateur world record although eclipsed by his own staggering 22.86m earlier in the season. In all the years since, only three men have tossed the shot further.

How much longer can the women hold out for their own separate championships? That was the question I posed at the start of my report on the WAAA Championships.

Each year the chorus demanding combined national championships grows louder, and at last weekend's poorly supported meeting (watched by fewer than 1500 spectators on the Saturday) it reached deafening proportions. We at AW have been campaigning for combined championships since 1967. Our referendum of late 1971, in which 800 readers participated, came out 81%-19% in favour of mixed national championships. The athletes themselves – who ought to be the first to be considered – are overwhelmingly in favour. So why the obstinate refusal? Surely it is not beyond the capabilities of British administrative expertise to organise a Friday to Sunday meeting for men and women, as has long been the case in practically ever other European nation. It did happen, but not for another 13 long years!

The big event of the season was the European Cup Final in Nice. Following a spate of hijacks Pat was reluctant to fly, so we travelled by train, the journey in those pre-Eurostar days taking over 18 hours. The British men's team finished fourth, including six event wins. The sequence was Alan Pascoe in the 400m hurdles, David Jenkins the flat 400m, Geoff Capes the shot, Steve Ovett the 800m, Brendan Foster the 5000m (with a 58.2 breakaway lap after 3000m) and 4x400m relay. The British women struggled to fill seventh place as the GDR (winner also of the men's cup) scored 97 points out of a possible maximum of 104.

I wrote – cautiously – *the ability of practically the entire East German women's team to attain peak form at just the right moment every time is a testimony to periodisation, unless the sports boffins in Leipzig have come up with something unknown elsewhere. The East German supremacy is* **so** *overwhelming one doesn't know whether to be full of admiration or suspicion.* Of course, I suspected widespread doping was the reason, but that couldn't be proved at that time ... or indeed until the vile GDR regime thankfully was dissolved after the Berlin Wall came down in 1989 and incriminating documentation was revealed.

Highlight of the season's finale, the IAC/Coca Cola floodlit meeting before a capacity crowd at Crystal Palace, was Brendan Foster's 10,000m debut. Not only did he win a loaded race but his time of 27:45.4 was the world's fastest ever by a first-timer. Despite his blisters, he uncorked a 27.9 final 200m to outkick Frank Shorter, Jos Hermens and Dave Black, all of whom clocked personal bests. "It wasn't that good, only a second ahead of three blokes," said Foster self-deprecatingly after the race. But he must have been alone in that view. His was simply a fabulous run at a distance he had never tackled before, a performance which would cause alarm and despondency among his Olympic rivals at 5000 and/or 10,000m.

13. A FAMILY IN MOURNING (1976-1977)

It was Olympic year, with all the anticipation and excitement that creates, but for me 1976 was a year which will always be remembered in sorrow. My mum, Flora, died in the Royal Northern Hospital, Holloway on August 27 of bronchopneumonia following a heart attack. She was only 65. My dad Alf, sister Benita, brother-in-law Charlie, their children Sandra and Lionel, my wife Pat, I and the rest of the family were devastated. Mum had been in a coma in that hospital for several days during the hottest summer for many years, and we all hoped and prayed she would revive. It was such a shock that she didn't. Everyone loved mum. She was a gentle, uncomplaining soul who would go out of her way to help anyone. As a mother, wife, grandmother and mother-in-law she could not have been bettered. Benita and I not only inherited her placid nature but also her heart problems as we have both undergone coronary artery bypass surgery. We have been lucky as that procedure was not available in mum's case.

Our loss was made even more poignant because after 30 years of renting council housing in Finsbury Park and Stoke Newington in North East London she and dad were in the initial stages of a move to sheltered accommodation in Stanmore, North West London, just around the corner from dad's sister Jean and her husband Cyril. It would have been a very cosy arrangement. However, dad did move in early in October and lived there until his death ten years later, aged 79.

Already seriously damaged by the terrorist outrage in Munich, the Olympic movement experienced further problems at the Montreal Games as 22 African countries boycotted the event on the grounds that New Zealand, whose rugby team had toured South Africa, should have been expelled from the Games. The IOC justifiably refused, insisting that the actions of rugby teams were outside its jurisdiction. There were emotional scenes as African teams, who had travelled to Montreal hoping for a last minute change of heart by the IOC, had to return home shortly before the opening ceremony. Among those who missed their big chance of Olympic glory were world 1500m record holder Filbert Bayi of Tanzania (the nation which led the protest) and Kenyan 800m star Mike Boit, while Uganda's John Akii-Bua was unable to defend his 400m hurdles title.

Nevertheless, the Games were a tremendous success with world records being set in the men's 800m, steeplechase, 400m hurdles, javelin and decathlon, and women's 100m, 400m, 800m and 4x400m relay. Finland's Lasse Viren made history by winning a second 5000m/10,000m double and Viktor Saneyev (USSR) chalked up his third Olympic triple jump title. Suspicions of what lay behind the success of the East German women were heightened by the fact that they won nine of the 14 titles available and in only one event (fourth place in the shot) did they fail to gain a medal.

The British team, which had travelled with high hopes, returned deflated with just one medal, a bronze by Brendan Foster in the 10,000m. He had expected better but wasn't at his fittest because of an upset stomach. The elegant Viren, who covered the second half of the race in a then unheard of 13:31.4, won by 30m from Portugal's Carlos Lopes in 27:40.38 to join Paavo Nurmi and Emil Zátopek as the only runners at that time to win a second Olympic 10,000m crown. "Viren is simply the greatest runner there has ever been," was Foster's opinion. Viren, who never beat Foster outside of the Olympics, outwitted and outran his opponents in the 5000m also. Knowing he was up against men who, in a last lap sprint, might be faster than himself, he began his drive for the finish from a full kilometre out. Commandeering the inside lane throughout, while his rivals ran wide in increasingly desperate attempts to wrest the lead, Viren was never headed and covered the last 400m in 55.0 to win in 13:24.76. Foster, who had won his heat with an Olympic record of 13:20.34, placed fifth although barely ten metres behind the winner. In a bid to emulate Zátopek's 1952 triple, Viren lined up the very next day for his marathon debut and did well to finish fifth in 2:13:11. Accusations that he used blood doping have always been refuted by the man who later became a Member of the Finnish Parliament; in any case the practice was not outlawed until 1986.

There were two other double winners in Montreal. Cuba's massively built Alberto Juantorena, known as *El Caballo* (The Horse), and until just before the Games regarded as a 400m specialist, made a late decision to contest the 800m. The American favourite Rick Wohlhuter, the world record holder for 880y, would live to regret his statement that "Juantorena will not be a factor because he is basically a 400m runner who will have trouble running three 800m races in as many days." Talk about famous last words! 'The Horse' trotted through his heat in 1:47.2, cantered through his semi in 1:45.9 and in the final his long, pounding stride never faltered as he galloped across the line in a world record 1:43.50. Wohlhuter had to settle for third place, overtaken in the closing stages by the inspired 22 year-old Belgian, Ivo Van Damme. Younger still at 20, Steve Ovett was disappointed with his fifth place after too slow a start but with 1:45.44 he had run faster than ever before. His turn would come four years later.

Ivo also finished a close second, to John Walker, in the 1500m but alas this tremendously talented athlete was destined to die in a car crash before the year was out. Like Steve Prefontaine in Eugene, his name is commemorated in the form of a great annual athletics meeting, in Brussels. A shocked Ovett contributed a moving letter to AW. "To win two silver medals in any Olympics is a fabulous performance; to win them in only your first Games and at the age of 22 marks the greatness of the man, who surely must have gone on to greater honours. As a friend I will miss him at the beginning of races when we used to worry and joke together, during them when we both raced hard, and then finally afterwards – the sharing of the joy and disappointment we both recognised in each other. Now all I feel is a certain numbness at the loss of a friend and the emptiness that will be left when it goes. My sympathy goes to his parents and friends."

Juantorena completed a momentous double by winning the 400m final, his seventh race of the Games, in 44.26 – fastest ever time other than at high altitude. Still he wasn't finished, clocking a 44.2 anchor leg in the 4x400m heats and 44.5 in the final, reportedly sprinting through the first flying 200m in 20.1! Two gold medals went also to the USSR's small, skinny and pale Tatyana Kazankina. The world record holder at 1500m first won the 800m in a scorching world record of 1:54.94 and then returned to take the 1500m in 4:05.48 with a last lap covered in 56.9! She went on to set a world record of 3:52.47 and retain her 1500m title at the 1980 Olympics but her achievements became questionable when in 1984 she refused to take a drugs test and was suspended for 18 months.

Another world record breaker was Poland's Irena Szewinska. What a remarkable athlete she was. As 18 year-old Irena Kirszenstein she gained an Olympic gold medal in the 4x100m relay at the 1964 Games following silvers in the 200m and long jump; in 1968 she won the 200m in world record time and was third in the 100m; in 1972 she placed third at 200m. Having become the first woman to break 50 sec for 400m in 1974, that was her event in Montreal, winning by a ten metre margin in what was then considered the phenomenal time of 49.29. One of her team-mates, discus thrower Danuta Rosani, made less welcome history by becoming the first of all too many athletes to be disqualified at an Olympic Games for testing positive for drugs.

The revelation of the year was surely Ed Moses. In May I wrote: *It won't take long to document the 400m hurdling career of Edwin Moses (20). His first ever race at the distance (actually 440y) occurred last year and he clocked 52.0. The second was on March 27 this year when he ran 50.1; the third was a 50.6 effort on April 19; the fourth a 49.8 win on April 23; the fifth a 49.5 heat on May 8. In the final he sped to a 48.9 clocking – running thirteens all the way! His coach Lloyd Jackson says of him: 'He's very strong, very tough, and he's conscientious. He is in shape right now to run 48'.*

He did better than that, for in Montreal he broke John Akii-Bua's world record with 47.64 and his winning margin of over a second was the widest ever at an Olympics – bigger even than David Hemery's in Mexico City. That was just the start for Moses, who went on to chalk up the greatest ever winning streak by a track athlete: 122 successive 400m hurdles races (107 finals) between 1977 and 1987!

Meanwhile, 19 year-old Seb Coe was starting to close the gap between himself and Steve Ovett. In very windy conditions at Gateshead, Coe dashed ahead in the mile and must have been 40m clear of Olympic champion John Walker at one stage. Walker caught him but Coe's 4:01.7 was a personal best and a week later in the Emsley Carr Mile at Crystal Palace he again held a big lead at halfway. He was reeled in as Dave Moorcroft beat Filbert Bayi and Brendan Foster in 3:57.06 but battled all the way to the line, his reward being a time of 3:58.35.

Adriaan Paulen (73), who represented Holland at 400m and 800m at the Olympics of 1920, 1924 and 1928, succeeded the Marquess of Exeter (71), who as Lord Burghley was Olympic 400m hurdles champion in 1928, as president of the IAAF. However, the nonsense of upholding a strict amateur code persisted.

The Alice in Wonderland situation concerning amateurism in international athletics has reached new levels of absurdity. In the space of a few days: (1) Guy Drut [France's Olympic 110m hurdles champion] was disqualified for life by the IAAF because he had admitted receiving appearance money; (2) the American professional group, ITA, was wound up – mainly because it was unable to sign up the big names who, alleged president Mike O'Hara, could make more money as amateurs than he could offer. As Drut had already bade farewell to athletics that was rather like locking the proverbial stable door. What is surely more to the point is that many other famous names, who remain officially amateurs, are equally 'guilty' of accepting under-the-counter payments from eager promoters. What is the IAAF going to do about them? Presumably nothing, because transactions are in cash and proof would be difficult to obtain – but also because the top IAAF officials must realise that a witch hunt would serve only to decimate the sport and deprive it of many of its greatest crowd-pullers. A fall in attendances would be ruinous to athletics at all levels, for governing bodies derive much of their income from crowd receipts.

Drut, by the way, was reinstated by the French Athletics Federation three years later and served as the French government's Minister of Youth Affairs & Sports between 1995 and 1997.

A word about Ed Lacey, who in November died in a car accident aged 55. He was acknowledged as one of the very best of all sports photographers and over a period of more than 20 years AW published thousands of his pictures. As Jon Hendershott, features editor of *Track & Field News* wrote: "Ed was an artist. He had that incredible knack of being able to capture the decisive moment. To me his greatest shot was fittingly of track's greatest moment – Bob Beamon straining for extra inches at the height of his 8.90m jump in Mexico City."

That AW was fulfilling a need as the sport's forum as well as its function of disseminating news and results was made clear by the latest audited circulation figure of 16,591– an increase of over a third since the start of the decade. The following year it reached 17,360; in 1978 18,340.

It was the year, 1977, that we began to realise that British athletics had not just one potential global superstar in Steve Ovett but three as Sebastian Coe and Daley Thompson made stupendous progress too. Seb established himself as an 800m runner of distinction by lifting the European indoor title in, appropriately, San Sebastián – just missing the world indoor record with 1:46.54. Fears that because of his light build he would be at risk in the hurly-burly of indoor racing proved groundless as he sped away from any possible trouble from the start and led all the way. An achilles tendon injury delayed the start of his outdoor season but he came on strongly during the late summer. In the Emsley Carr Mile at Crystal Palace he bided his time on this occasion and demonstrated he had a kick to be respected, edging ahead of Filbert Bayi to win in a personal best of 3:57.67, and he ended the season by clocking 1:44.95 for a

UK 800m record. Steve, meanwhile, was adding to his reputation by setting UK records of 3:54.69 for the mile and a considerably superior 3:34.45 for 1500m, the latter when destroying a glittering field at the World Cup in Düsseldorf in a race which proved that he could deliver a deadly kick even off a fast pace. That wasn't all, for he clocked a world class 5000m time of 13:25.0 in only his second race at the distance, became the second fastest ever British 3000m runner with 7:41.3 and even ("sheer madness" he admitted) won a half marathon in 65:38 a fortnight before his World Cup race!

As for Daley, he just kept on breaking all records for a decathlete of his age. Having impressed the USA's gold medallist and world record breaker Bruce Jenner [who in 2015 as a TV personality attracted worldwide media attention by changing gender to become Caitlyn Marie Jenner] as a likely successor to himself while celebrating his 18th birthday during the 1976 Olympics, Daley set world junior and UK senior records of 8056 and 8082 in 1977.

How encouraging too at the start of what would prove to be a golden era for British athletics following the disappointments of Montreal that several other ultimately famous names should now be drawing attention to themselves. I attended the English Schools Championships at Copthall and enthused over youngsters like Mike McFarlane (17), Steve Cram (16), Joanne Gardner (14), Kathy Smallwood (17) and Sue Hearnshaw (16). Gratifyingly, most of the above did go on to reach international level as seniors, with Cram who had earlier set a UK 1500m age record of 3:47.7, on his way to becoming a world champion and record holder, McFarlane a Commonwealth Games 200m champion, Smallwood (later Cook) a UK record holder at 100m, 200m and 400m, and Hearnshaw an Olympic long jump bronze medallist. Joanne Gardner later became Trinidadian champion at 200m and is the mother of American 400m star Natasha Hastings (personal best of 49.84), twice an Olympic 4x400m relay gold medallist. Other winners at Copthall included Gary Oakes (18; future Olympic 400m hurdles bronze medallist), Peter Elliott (14; Olympic 1500m silver medallist) and Fatima Whitbread (16; javelin world champion and record holder).

The year was notable for the inauguration of two important competitions: UK National Championships and the IAAF World Cup. Both proved a great success. The meeting in Cwmbran, organised by the BAAB, brought together at last men and women battling for national outdoor titles (the AAA and WAAA were still going their separate ways) and the athletes loved it. Versatile Tessa Sanderson, who threw the javelin a barrier-breaking UK record of 60.24m the day after finishing third in the 400m hurdles, said: "It's worked well. What's made it, is it being mixed. An all-male or all-female meeting or meetings like that held separately as trials would be a flop." So, for the first time, athletes could proclaim themselves British champions.

Staged at Düsseldorf's magnificent Rheinstadion, the World Cup brought together teams representing the USA, GDR, West Germany (men only), USSR (women only), Europe Select, Americas Select, Africa, Asia and Oceania

Steve Ovett was one of eight British athletes who competed with distinction for Europe. Sonia Lannaman finished 2nd in the 100 and later teamed up with Andrea Lynch and West Germans Annegret Richter and Elvira Possekel for victory over the seemingly invincible East Germans in the 4x100 relay, Tessa Sanderson placed 3rd in the javelin, Alan Pascoe and Nick Rose (with a personal best) 4th in their specialities, while David Jenkins and Donna Hartley ran useful legs in the 4x400 relays. This inaugural competition, organised by the IAAF to promote worldwide interest in the sport and raise funds for athletics coaching and equipment in the developing countries, proved to be a resounding success. There was a total 'gate' of some 130,000 for the three days of competition which saw the men's cup won by the GDR and the women's by the Europe Select team. Great performances abounded, among which was a world record by the USA of 38.03 for the 4x100 relay, fabulous duels in the 800 (Alberto Juantorena 1:44.0 v Mike Boit 1:44.1 with a 51.5 second lap) and women's 400 (Irena Szewinska 49.52 v Marita Koch 49.76), a distance double by Miruts Yifter (28:32.3 & 13:13.8), a masterly 400 hurdles display by Edwin Moses (47.58), and world record attempts in the pole vault (at 5.71m by Mike Tully) and both high jumps (at 2.01m by Rosi Ackermann and 2.34m by fellow straddler Rolf Beilschmidt). The presentation left much room for improvement, but the World Cup is certainly here to stay – and welcome.

It was East Germany all the way in the European Cup in Helsinki, but the British team fared better than previously as the men equalled their highest placing of fourth and the women excelled themselves by finishing third, two places better than ever before. My travels for the year weren't over.

It all began at the 'AW' office one morning in September. The phone rang; hold the line, instructed the operator, for an overseas call. "Hello, Mel. It's Derrick Marcus. How would you like an all expenses paid trip to Brazil?" I had only been waiting all my life for such a phone call! Derrick, a member of Ealing & Southall AC who has been 'our man' in Brazil for several years, filled in the details. Colgate-Palmolive were sponsoring, and the daily sports newspaper "A Gazeta Esportiva" were organising, a massive schools meeting in Sao Paulo and they wanted me to fly out to see and comment on it.

Operacao Juventude was the brainchild of Henrique Nicolini, the newspaper's genial head of promotions, and it was he and his team of young, enthusiastic assistants who directed the event's organisation. Between May and September 600,000 boys and girls, aged between 11 and 18, competed in preliminary meetings staged in 150 cities and towns throughout the vast country. There were just three disciplines contested: a sprint (50m, 75m or 100m depending on the age group), long jump and shot. The best 100 in each event, a total of 1600 taking into account the various age groups, were to assemble in Sao Paulo on October 8 for the finals.

Somewhat to my bewilderment, instead of being on the sidelines as usual to observe and report on a meeting, I was treated as a VIP. I was interviewed by the written media, numerous photos were taken, I appeared on television, presented trophies to the winners and even judged Colgate's "Miss

Smile" contest! It was all so exhilarating and another highlight was meeting Brazil's athletics superstar Joao Carlos de Oliveira, the triple jump world record holder with 17.89m. He was such an exciting talent but fate was not kind to him. He was possibly cheated out of the Olympic gold medal at the Moscow Olympics of 1980, lost a leg in a car accident the following year and was only 45 when he died of alcoholism in 1999.

Following wonderful hospitality provided by Derrick Marcus and his Rio-born wife Jo, and by Henrique Nicolini and his wife Lilian at their country estate, I took a 250 mile bus trip from Sao Paulo to Rio and checked into a hotel facing the celebrated Copacabana beach. During my three days there I took in all the fabulous "sights", watched a Brazil v Milan soccer match at the Maracana where a crowd of around 60,000 was lost in a stadium which could then hold 200,000, and took several runs along the mosaic pavement alongside the fabulous beach. I might not have been much of a runner but I always took my kit with me on my travels and over the years I was fortunate enough to stride out in such running meccas as New York's Central Park, Miami Beach, Waikiki (Hawaii) and the Promenade des Anglais (Nice).

In addition to my AW duties and ongoing International Athletics Press Service, I was involved in the publication of two books that year: *Athletics 1977* edited by Ron Pickering and dedicated to the memory of Ed Lacey, and the fourth edition of the *Encyclopaedia of Athletics*, the first to be published by St Martin's Press in New York as well as by Robert Hale Ltd in London. There was also a new dimension to my work as I stood in for Stan Greenberg as statistician for the BBC TV commentary team at the WAAA Championships and assisted again at the IAC-Coca Cola Meeting. Providing relevant facts and figures on information cards for David Coleman, Ron Pickering and Stuart Storey was not a problem but coping with the tension of live broadcasting was more of a test. I did deputise for Stan, the pioneer in this line of work, a few more times over the years, while in 1989 I became a TV statistician in my own right for Eurosport and later Sky Sports.

I have always been a supporter of race walking as a perfectly legitimate area of athletic endeavour and know how hard the top exponents train, and so I was delighted that at long last Ken Matthews received a richly deserved MBE, albeit over 12 years after his fellow Tokyo gold medallists Lynn Davies, Mary Rand and Ann Packer had featured in the Honours List. All credit to the Race Walking Association for their campaigning. More good news followed with the IOC's decision to reinstate the 50km walk as an Olympic event. Of course it was a colossal blunder that it was removed from the 1976 programme in the first place. The IOC, however, remained ultra-conservative in the matter of women's events. When determining the schedule for the 1980 Games in Moscow, the 400m hurdles (an official IAAF world record event since 1974) was turned down and 1500m would continue to be the longest running event.

On the domestic administrative front, things were changing. At the BAAB's AGM former hurdler Robert Stinson succeeded former high jumper Arthur Gold as honorary secretary. Arthur, who held the post from 1965, was presented with a silver salver inscribed "for outstanding services to British athletics". Unfailingly courteous and with a profound knowledge of the sport as a competitor, coach, official and administrator, and possessed of a very sharp brain, he did a commendable job in my opinion – even if that wasn't a view shared by all in the sport. Arthur, with all his experience, might have been appointed the Board's first full-time paid general secretary but he preferred to concentrate on his duties as president of the European Athletic Association, a prestigious post which suited him perfectly as a born diplomat. How he, a Renault dealer, managed to run a successful garage business at the same time was testimony to his multi-tasking abilities.

Arthur Gold will be remembered largely for his relentless battle against doping. He was a hard-liner when too many of his international colleagues seemed to lack the will to tackle the growing problem effectively. He was much too optimistic, though, when he told a press conference in London in November 1977 that he believed the war against the use of anabolic steroids could, at least in Europe, be won by 1980. "If we can make our testing as effective and widespread as we can, and make the risk of being caught much higher than it is, we may largely eradicate the use of anabolic steroids and make the sport healthier and more honest. I believe this will be achieved by 1980, because in Europe there is a change of climate."

A few weeks earlier the European AA had announced that three Finnish men and an East German woman had been disqualified from the European Cup Final after having failed tests for anabolic steroids. The woman was 21 year-old shot putter Ilona Slupianek whose longest throw of 21.79m ranked her third on the world all-time list. She was suspended for one derisory year and returned stronger than ever, setting world records of 22.36m and 22.45m in 1980, the year she won the Olympic title. The GDR coaches and their medical support teams went to great lengths to hide their widespread doping and this one lapse did not deter them; the state-sponsored drugs programme which ruined so many lives continued unabated until the Berlin Wall fell late in 1989.

The year's AWs ended with the return – despite public demand – of Cliff Temple's New Year Special. It took the form of an interview with top athlete Spike Marx. Asked which was his greatest performance in 1977, Spike replied: "I suppose it was improving my personal best from 2 hours 16 minutes to 2 hours 7 minutes 13.6 seconds." "Was that for the marathon?" "No, for getting out of the car park at Crystal Palace. Mind you, it was four o'clock in the morning." His tip for a star of the future was, predictably, Emily Lustbody. "We'll be seeing a lot more of her?" "We will, unless she gets over this unfortunate reaction every time a starter asks her to strip off."

14. ABRAHAMS, COE & OVETT (1978-1979)

There was a sad start to 1978 as Harold Abrahams died on January 14, at the age of 78.

He bestrode our sport like a Colossus. It is no exaggeration to suggest that he alone contributed more to athletics during the past half century or so than any other five men put together. He was unsurpassed as an athlete, administrator, writer, statistician and broadcaster, and right up to the time of his fatal stroke he retained an unquenchable enthusiasm – whether carrying out his duties as president of the AAA, formulating new technical rules for the IAAF, or taking a boyish delight in showing off his latest electronic stopwatch.

On a personal note: I was privileged to have been a friend of Harold's for all my adult life. From the time that I helped found the NUTS (an organisation which Harold presided over from its inception almost 20 years ago) he took a keen interest in my journalistic and statistical work, and I learned much from his unrivalled experience in these fields. I shall always appreciate the help and encouragement he offered me, and remember with pleasure the hours we spent together chatting about the sport as we sifted through his archives – a treasure trove of books, magazines, clippings, documents and photographs. We may have been poles apart on certain aspects of the sport and its administration, but there was always a mutual respect which enabled us to disagree without rancour. He was a courteous, good humoured man who, though he had his detractors, will be remembered by generations of athletes for his kindliness and sense of fair play.

In the following issue of AW I published a lengthy profile of the man who travelled to Paris in 1924 with no thought of capturing the Olympic 100m title but realised after winning his semi-final despite an appalling start that "I just could not lose the final" and consequently for the next 3 ¾ hours he "felt like a condemned man feels just before going to the scaffold." He went to his holes (starting blocks were not patented until 1927) with his professional coach Sam Mussabini's parting words installed in his sub-conscious: "Only think of two things – the report of the pistol and the tape. When you hear the one, just run like hell till you break the other." Off to a great start this time, he soared through the tape in that famous drop-finish of his two feet clear of his nearest rival. Those ten seconds or so would change his life. He may have become the first European and first Briton (until Allan Wells in 1980) to win the blue riband event of sprinting but there was no victory ceremony, no national anthem, no presentation of medals. Harold's gold medal arrived by post two or three weeks later!

A serious leg injury sustained while long jumping brought his active career to a painful and premature end in May 1925 but that enabled him to concentrate on other facets of athletics. A barrister by profession, he brought to the councils of the sport a clear, probing, analytical mind which quickly took him into high office. He remained in the public eye as a prolific writer (athletics correspondent of *The Sunday Times* from 1925 to 1967) and as one of the BBC's first broadcasters. His distinctive voice became one of the most familiar on radio and his disarmingly partisan commentary on Lovelock's 1936 Olympic 1500m victory ("Come on Jack ...") must be well known to many who weren't even born at the time it was recorded.

In his later years Harold was regarded as an establishment figure but back in the 1920s he was considered quite a rebel. He criticised the AAA's strict definition of an amateur and advocated the then heretical concept of permitting 'broken time' payments for athletes who could not afford to lose wages in order to compete internationally. He was less progressive in some other areas, notably women's athletics. "I do not consider that women are built for really violent exercise, " he wrote in 1928. "One has only to see them practising to realise how awkward they are on the running track." He did eventually see the light and for many years served as the Women's AAA's legal adviser.

From 1948 to 1968 he was treasurer of the BAAB, with Jack Crump secretary for most of that period, and both attracted criticism for writing and broadcasting on athletics at the same time as holding the highest official posts. I saw both sides of Harold. His love of the sport was immense and he could be charming and thoughtful. On the other hand he could be ruthless, using his legal skills to humiliate those who had the nerve to challenge him at annual general meetings. He was like a father figure to me but that didn't stop him on one occasion dismissing me as "just like the rest of your colleagues" because I had written something critical about one of the BAAB training camps. He was a complex character, and I can unreservedly recommend Mark Ryan's biography *Running With Fire* (2011) for the full, true story of the *Chariots of Fire* hero.

Colin Welland, who wrote the Oscar-winning screenplay for the 1981 film, did actually meet Harold in 1977 to discuss the project and Harold was delighted at the prospect that the general public would "know that this bald old bugger had won a gold medal." He might have been less delighted with the screenplay for, being a stickler for accuracy, he would not have approved of all the liberties that were taken with the historical facts. Colin met up with me, Peter Lovesey, Tom McNab and John Keddie at a Soho coffee bar in June 1978 to discuss his idea of making a film about two British Olympic champion sprinters of more than half a century earlier: one fighting against anti-semitism to make his mark, the other a committed Christian who gave up his chance of glory at 100m because he would not race on a Sunday. I warmed to Colin's enthusiasm but couldn't see how such a film, if it was ever made, could appeal to a wide public who had never heard of Harold Abrahams and Eric Liddell. How pleased I was to be proved so wrong!

It was a year full of surprises. The cover photo of issue no 1 was of Norwegian cross country star Grete Waitz, the former world record holder for 3000m. She had certainly never expected to make her marathon debut that year, but in October – a week before the race – she decided to have a go in New York, which with over 11,000 entrants was easily the biggest marathon yet staged. Not only did she win but her time of 2:32:30 took over two minutes from the world best. She would go on to win that race eight more times and become a running legend.

THE runner of the year was without doubt Kenya's Henry Rono, who set four world records. He began with 13:08.4 for 5000m at Berkeley in April. Whereas it had taken 11 years for the world record to improve from Ron Clarke's 13:16.6 to Dick Quax's 13:12.9, Rono had now chopped a whopping 4.5 sec from that mark. Aged 26, a member of the remarkable Nandi tribe from the Rift Valley, he was 20 before he began training seriously. His transformation into a world beater began with his enrolment in September 1976 at Washington State University where he came under the influence of his first ever coach, John Chaplin. In May he turned his attention to the steeplechase, reducing the world record from 8:08.02 to 8:05.4 (it would stand for 11 years) in a cool and windy Seattle. Over to Europe for a barnstorming tour where the Bionic Man of distance running opened with a 7:43.8 3000m win over Steve Ovett at Crystal Palace and went on to set further world records at 10,000m (27:22.4 in Vienna) and 3000m (7:32.1 in Oslo) in June.

Had Rono not got in first on June 11 then Brendan Foster's time of 27:30.30 when winning the AAA title 12 days later would have been a world record. With the rain lashing down on a chilly evening, puddles to be splashed through and countless lapped runners to negotiate, Bren's achievement in clocking the European record was indeed stunning – and all the more so as it was a solo performance throughout the last 21 laps. Unfortunately, Rono and Foster never did clash over 10,000m. At the Commonwealth Games in Edmonton, Canada, Foster won in 28:13.7 (his sixth victory in seven 10,000m races), while Rono took the steeplechase (8:26.5) and 5000m (13:23.0) titles with Foster third in the latter.

The Games in Edmonton were immensely enjoyable, as was the whole visit – organised with his customary efficiency by David Barnett of Track & Field Tours. During my stay I managed to fit in an excursion featuring some of the grandest Rockies scenery, including Lake Louise – surely one of the most beautiful places on earth – and the Columbia Icefields where I took a snowmobile ride, which was like something out of a James Bond movie. For me the star of the Games was Daley Thompson. He got his decathlon off to a dream start with windy marks of 10.50 for 100m and 8.11m for the long jump, although unfortunately the strength of the wind for that jump was over the 4m/sec strength permitted for records in the multi-events. The incredibly blustery conditions (one gust was measured at 11.76m/sec) cost him an estimated eight-tenths in the 400m but nonetheless his massive first day total of 4550 points was a world best with electronic timing. On the second day only a disappointing javelin prevented him becoming only the second man ever to top 8500 points and he had to settle for a score of 8467 (8470 on the current tables), winning by over 900 points. It was a nice touch when the decathletes took a communal lap of honour, arms linked, with the ever competitive Daley of course dipping as they approached the photo finish!

The English team fared exceptionally well. Winners in addition to Daley and Brendan were Dave Moorcroft (1500m), Roy Mitchell (long jump), Keith Connor (triple jump), Geoff Capes (shot), Olly Flynn (30km walk), Sonia Lannaman (100m), Donna Hartley (400m), Mary Stewart (1500m), Paula Fudge (3000m), Lorna Boothe (100m hurdles), Sue Reeve (long jump), Tessa Sanderson (javelin) and both women's relay teams. Scottish gold medallists were Allan Wells (200m) and the 4x100m relay team; while Berwyn Price (110m hurdles) took home a title to Wales.

Just 17 days after the Edmonton Games ended, the European Championships kicked off in Prague, and it proved too short an interval for many in the British team. Apart from the long journey home across so many time zones, several competed in an international meeting at Crystal Palace just before flying to the Czechoslovak capital. Another factor was that it was very warm in Edmonton and almost unbelievably chilly in Prague.

At first glance Britain's medal haul from the European Championships – 1 gold, 4 silver, 2 bronze – might not look very impressive, but taking into account all the circumstances it wasn't such a bad showing either. The unknown factor was whether the athletes would be able to prime themselves psychologically as well as physically for another supreme effort so soon after their triumphs in Canada. The answer, in many cases, was no. A classic example was Allan Wells, who performed so brilliantly in Edmonton [200m winner in 20.12w after placing second in the 100m in 10.07w]. A repetition of that dynamic sprinting would surely have gained him a couple of medals in Prague, but he was so bodily fatigued and emotionally drained by the time he got to the European – and he didn't really want to go at all – that he was reduced to sixth place in the 100 and decided to scratch from the 200 as he felt he would be unable to do himself justice.

The one winner, in the 1500m, was Steve Ovett , who did not compete in Edmonton. The race could not have been run in a more ideal manner for Steve had he stage-managed the whole affair. It was as though his opponents had no advance warning that he was likely to wing away with 200m to go … or maybe, as in Thomas Wessinghage's case, they were already reconciled to fighting for the other medals. The inevitable outcome was that Steve romped to victory in 3:35.6, his final 200m covered in just 24.8. Three days earlier Steve had broken Seb Coe's UK 800m record of 1:44.25 with 1:44.09. The 800m in Prague, their first ever track confrontation, was a race everyone had assumed would be a private British duel with the other finalists scrapping for the bronze. Here at last we would see what no meeting promoter had ever been able to arrange: a clash between the front runner *par excellence* and the most feared kicker of them all; between the frail-looking Seb and the powerfully built Steve. What a sensational race it turned out to be.

It was fairly obvious that Coe would blast away out in front, but few could have been fully prepared for the devilish tempo he was to set for even Seb himself admitted he got slightly carried away in the excitement of the occasion. Coe's 100m splits were 12.2, 24.3, 36.7 and 49.32! It was a fantastic, throbbing, thrilling pace, yet far from ploughing a lonely furrow, with the others waiting for him to crack, Coe was being closely tracked by the East German pair of Olaf Beyer and Andreas Busse as well as by Ovett. At the 400 mark Beyer was 2m behind (49.5-49.6) with Ovett on 49.9-50.0. Seb reached 600m in 76.2 (1:41.6 800 pace). He had truly flung down the gauntlet, and the challenge had been accepted. Entering the final straight Coe was just 1m up on Ovett and 3m ahead of Beyer, and within 30m Ovett had taken the lead for the first time. As Coe fell back, Steve must have thought the gold was his ... but Beyer was not done yet. The East German, running in inspired fashion to put it mildly, came storming past Ovett to snatch victory in the resounding time of 1:43.84 – an improvement of almost 2 sec over his previous best. Ovett ran 1:44.09, while Coe hung on gamely for 1:44.76 in third place. One could argue that Coe's 49.3 first lap was much too fast, and had he run the 50.5 which he had planned the result might have been different, but it was a daring attempt which could have succeeded – and I, for one, applaud Seb for trying. Next year, stronger and more experienced, he could be ready to take the world record.

I recall chatting to Seb after the race. He was rather crestfallen and I tried to reassure him that his had been one hell of a run and that one day he wouldn't fade after such a fast start. As for Beyer, his handlers must have done a very good job in preparing him for this one race as he never reached such heights again, failing to reach the 1980 Olympic final and placing seventh at the 1982 European Championships.

Daley Thompson raised his UK decathlon record to 8289 points (8258 on the current tables) but derived no satisfaction from that. He had finished second to Aleksandr Grebenyuk (USSR) and defeat had never entered his mind, particularly after his main rival, European record holder Guido Kratschmer of West Germany, had injured himself in the first event and took no further part. Nearly 300 points up on Grebenyuk after the first day the title appeared to be in the bag but a mini-disaster in the hurdles cost him many points and by vaulting only 4.20m as against his then personal best of 4.90m he opened the door to his Soviet opponent. It was the kick up the backside he needed; he vowed he would never lose another decathlon and between 1980 and 1986 he did indeed reign supreme.

Although, tantalisingly, they would not clash again until the 1980 Olympics, Coe and Ovett continued to make the headlines. Later in September, at the sold-out IAC/Coca-Cola Meeting at Crystal Palace, Coe put together laps of 51.0 and 53.0 (the perfect two second differential) to deprive Ovett of his short-lived UK 800m record with 1:43.97, but Steve was not to be overshadowed as he not only defeated Henry Rono in the featured 2 miles event but his time of 8:13.51 (4:04.4 second mile) beat Brendan Foster's world outdoor best of 8:13.7. He hadn't finished yet, for on a bitterly cold, wet and windy Oslo evening Steve managed to run 3:52.8 for a UK mile record and five days later won the "Dubai Golden Mile" in Tokyo in 3:55.5.

Excelling himself by finishing third in that Tokyo race in 3:59.2 was Graham Williamson, who together with Steve Cram represented the future for

British miling in a post-Coe/Ovett era. Both had smashed Ovett's UK age-17 record for 1500m with Williamson clocking 3:42.1 in the Scottish Championships and Cram running a solo 3:42.7 at the Durham Schools Championships. Later, now aged 18, Williamson finished second in the Emsley Carr Mile in 3:56.39, a UK junior record, with Cram (in his mile debut) fourth in 3:57.43, smashing Jim Ryun's world age-17 best. To the credit of the England selectors, Cram was picked for the Commonwealth Games and although eliminated in his heat he always regarded it as invaluable experience. The Scottish selectors thought otherwise and, to my consternation, they refused to add Williamson to their team for Edmonton. One of my most important functions as editor of AW was to fight injustice for the athletes and this was a classic instance.

There are times when the actions (or, in this particular case, inaction) of officialdom are beyond comprehension. In Graham Williamson, Scottish athletics has been blessed with a rare and exciting talent. In the eyes of any discerning follower of the sport, Graham's fantastic run in the Emsley Carr Mile must have clinched his selection. Any country would be proud to welcome into its team an athlete of his standard and potential ... any country, it would appear, other than his native land. I have, on occasions, over the years, felt sufficiently incensed to take selectors to task in print, but I cannot recall such an appalling decision. Several 'reasons' have been quoted by Scottish officials to justify their refusal to select Graham; all seem to me to betray a lack of judgement, flexibility and feeling for the athlete.

The selectors never did rectify their error and Graham continued to embarrass them by front running to a UK junior 1500m record of 3:39.7 in the AAA Junior Championships, a time he improved to 3:37.7 in Warsaw, and he followed with a 3:55.82 mile close behind Dave Moorcroft and ahead of Scottish record holder Frank Clement and Filbert Bayi in the Coke Meeting.

Although I hadn't raced in years, I still loved to run and would cover 2 or 3 miles around suburban streets at least a couple of times a week. In years gone by such an activity would have been deemed eccentric if not downright crazy but the jogging boom was just about to happen. As I wrote in March: *Jogging in Britain has a long way to go to reach the epidemic proportions the movement has attained in the USA but its popularity is growing fast. Helped by the Government's Health Council campaign and the worthy pioneering work being undertaken by "The Sunday Times" (who are organising the first National Fun Run on October 1), jogging is gradually becoming accepted by the general (read, unfit) public.*

Just a week after I wrote those words I happened to be in Milan for the European Indoor Championships (dominated by a world high jump record of 2.35m by Ukrainian straddler Vladimir Yashchenko) and Cliff Temple and I decided to go out for a run from our hotel. "A couple of miles or so?" Cliff, then training twice a day in preparation for his marathon debut, nodded. However, we managed to get completely lost and it took 43 minutes of running before we found our way back to base. We must have covered five or six miles, my longest non-stop run since my RAF days 17 years earlier. Suddenly, a long cherished but long dismissed notion of running a marathon came back to haunt me. Maybe it was possible? I was only a couple of months short of my 40th birthday and needed a new challenge. Part of that challenge was contesting the 40-49 age division of the National Fun Run over the flat 4km course in London's Hyde Park. Little did I think that one day I would be lining up alongside such familiar figures and heroes of mine as Bruce Tulloh, Stan Eldon and John Disley! Bruce, still ferociously fit, was a runaway winner in a time of around 11 minutes. I came in 347th out of 824 some five minutes later. A few weeks after that I ran a 6:00 mile at the Haringey track, but my 18 year-old nephew Lionel finished 2 sec ahead, the first time he had ever outrun me. About a decade later he would become the second marathon runner in the family, completing the Glasgow race, and in 2004 he succeeded in entering the London Marathon – clocking around the same time (4:20-ish) as his uncle in 1981. A sub-4 hour time remains his goal.

There was a changing of the guard also at AW. After five years of sterling service as my assistant editor, Jon Wigley left in November to take up an appointment with the IAAF at its London headquarters as assistant to general secretary John Holt. Jon, a great fan of J.R.R. Tolkien, presented me with a boxed set of *The Lord of the Rings*, and I was moved by his inscription: "For all that you have taught me", followed by this quotation from Lebanese-American poet, Kahlil Gibran: "When you part from your friend, you grieve not; For that which you love most in him may be clearer in his absence, as the mountain to the climber is clearer from the plain." Jon went on to enjoy a highly successful career at the IAAF and his move helped me financially as I was able to point out to the owner of AW that Jon's salary at the IAAF was far in excess of what I was being paid. A few months later my salary was raised by 50% and for the first time I was given a company car. Thanks Jon!

There were more than 30 applications to succeed Jon and after much deliberation Jimmy Green and I offered the job to Barry Trowbridge, who had limited journalistic experience but impressed us with his enthusiasm and knowledge. It proved a good choice as Barry settled well into a demanding job and when I stepped down as editor in 1984 he took over the reins. Barry started in January 1979 as did Tim Green as advertisement manager in his own right with Jimmy continuing as business manager.

It's not that Steve Ovett had a bad season in 1979, but the year belonged to Seb Coe. Although he was averaging only 50 miles a week in training (but high quality miles), Seb displayed impressive stamina by winning the national indoor 3000m title in 7:59.8 while his quest for more leg speed proved successful as in May he was timed at 46.3 for a 400m relay stint. He was never reluctant to experiment. He knew he could survive a 50 sec first lap in an 800m and in one slow race he covered the second lap in 50.3. The remarkable change of pace he achieved along the finishing straight when winning the 800m in the European Cup semi-final in Malmö hinted at great things to come, but no one –

not even Seb himself – was prepared for what happened in Oslo just four days later.

When Alberto Juantorena, in his first year at the event, won the Olympic 800 in Montreal with a world record of 1:43.5 everyone thought that here was the man to revolutionise two-lap running. And yet, for all his speed and power, the Cuban succeeded only in clipping another tenth off the record. Instead it is the slight figure of Britain's Sebastian Coe who will go down in history as the athlete who, like Rudolf Harbig in 1939 and Peter Snell in 1962, pushed back the frontiers of 800m performance. In the 17 years since Snell ran 1:44.3 the world record had advanced just nine-tenths of a second ... until, at Oslo's Bislett Stadium on July 5, Seb Coe chopped a complete second off Juantorena's mark with a phenomenal 1:42.4 [actually 1:42.33].

His splits were 24.6 at 200m, 50.6 at 400m, 1:15.4 at 600m. "I think I could have run even faster," he said. "I wasn't exhausted at all at the end." John Walker, who watched the race, enthused: "The way he ran was just unbelievable. He looked like he could run under 1:40; he never tied up at all."

Coe's next appearance was at the AAA Championships, where on July 13 he won his 400m heat easing up in a personal best of 46.95 and next day finished second, but first Briton home, in the final in 46.87. Three days later, back in Oslo, came the second world record breaking bombshell. Soundly defeating a field so loaded that Graham Williamson smashed the European junior record with 3:53.15 in seventh place and Dave Moorcroft wound up ninth despite his best time of 3:54.35, Seb won the IAAF's Dubai Golden Mile in 3:48.95. His 440y splits were 57.8, 57.5, 58.1 and 55.6. He thus became the first man since Snell to own simultaneously the world records for 800m and mile, while en route he set a European 1500m record of 3:32.8. Ovett held the previous UK records with 3:34.45 and 3:52.8, while Seb's own personal bests had stood merely at 3:42.67 and 3:57.67!

The figures were impressive, but it was the way in which Coe dominated the race which will be remembered by those who saw the run live or on TV. For a man who entered the race with a question mark hovering over his ability to handle a tough third lap, and who had run only two mile and no 1500m races in almost three years, he acquitted himself rather well! Seb commented: "As an 800m runner the early pace did not disturb me, but all day I had been worrying about how I would feel on the third lap. I was mentally prepared to be hurt on that lap and to go through a pain barrier but it didn't happen. It was not all that hard. When I looked back twice in the final straight it was fear, it was panic, not pain, that I was feeling. I certainly wasn't in the slightest distress at the finish. I was astonished when told I had broken the world record."

Analysing his sudden rise to becoming the most exciting runner in the world, I wrote: *The pattern of Sebastian Coe's career makes one wonder how many middle-distance runners of comparable talent never realise their potential due to an over-emphasis on training mileage and neglect in the vital area of leg speed. For it has been unremitting work in this department that has largely been responsible for Seb's dazzling world record double in recent weeks.*

Although Seb's early successes came at cross country and 3000m, he and his father-coach Peter Coe realised that speed was the key to his future development at 1500m. When Seb was 13 with a best 1500m time of 4:31.8 and the world record stood at 3:35.6, Peter projected that by 1980 his son could be running 3:30. His faith would be justified.

Seb's next international race, in the European Cup Final in Turin on August 5, resulted in a routine 800m victory in 1:47.3 although his final 200m in 24.4 was anything but ordinary, as was a 45.5 anchor leg in the relay. Ten days later came another world record, his third in the space of 41 days. By running 1500m in 3:32.1 (3:32.03) in Zürich he shaved a tenth of a second from Filbert Bayi's mark and became the first Briton to hold that world record since the IAAF began recognising records in 1913 although Roger Bannister unofficially equalled the record of 3:43.0 on the way to his 3:59.4 mile in 1954. It said much for Seb's endurance that he succeeded in spite of the energy-squandering early pace. Kenya's Kip Koskei set too fast a tempo for the first lap but Seb felt bound to stay with him and his time was a potentially suicidal 54.3. The second lap took 58.9 with Seb in front at around 760m and leading by nearly 20m at 800m in 1:53.2. Most runners would have permitted themselves a slight respite on the third lap; not Seb. He zipped through that circuit in 56.3 (2:49.5) and covered the final 300m in 42.6. Craig Masback, who would serve as chief executive officer for USA Track & Field from 1997 to 2008, was runner-up fully 35m behind. "As a piece of pace running it was pretty diabolical, but I suppose the final time is all that counts," said Seb, who also found time that summer to take his final exams and graduate from Loughborough University with a B.Sc honours degree in economics and social history.

In October I interviewed Seb at Loughborough, where he was doing post-grad work. I asked him for his views on drugs. "I would never take drugs," he replied. "I'm well aware that I may have run against in the past, and probably will in the future, people who have some kind of artificial stimulant. In terms of drugs you have three options in athletics. One is you join them; you take the drugs if you feel that only that way can you compete on an equal footing – you have to settle that with yourself morally. Or you can go on competing, possibly knowing that all sorts of things are going on, but forgetting about it and just worrying about what you are doing and what *you* want from the sport. The third option is to get out completely if it becomes too offensive. At the moment I'm taking the middle option. I'm competing fairly successfully against people that may or may not … I don't really want to know. Drug abuse or taking should never be associated in the same breath with success at athletics. I suppose as contemporary athletes we have a duty to make sure that the sport is kept clean. I think we have to fight to keep our sport clean and nice and wholesome, because it won't stay of its own volition."

Back in March I had interviewed Steve Ovett, which was something of a scoop as Steve basically did not talk to the press. It was he who contacted me to say he was available and I was only too happy to drive down with Pat to his

144

home in Brighton. He was very open, nothing was off limits. He emphasised that he was not obsessed by world class athletics, was not concerned with image-building and had no specific goals, not even the 1980 Olympics in Moscow.

What does emerge is a refreshingly free spirit, a young man who does not take himself or his sport too seriously, who values his independence and privacy, and who runs because he LOVES to run. In many ways he is the ultimate fun runner, although instead of being an anonymous jogger he happens to be the finest middle distance runner in the world today. Forget the surly, vaguely hostile image fostered by certain sections of the press; don't be misled either into dismissing Steve as cocky or arrogant because of all that waving to the crowd. I hope, as you read through this interview, that you will draw your own conclusions as to the true nature and character of Steve Ovett.

Of course Steve was the world's number one at the time of the interview, and winning races rather than chasing after records was what motivated him. However, Coe's fantastic summer season forced Steve to reassess. He suddenly found he was no longer the king of the middle distances in Britain never mind the world. After Seb's 3:49.0 mile Steve offered his congratulations but commented "For me it doesn't change anything. I don't get caught up in times. I never run against the clock. I run against men on the day."

In keeping his unbeaten record at 1500m and mile intact (his most recent defeat was by Steve Scott in May 1977 and he would chalk up a record sequence of 45 consecutive victories until his third place in the 1980 Olympics), Steve clocked his fastest times after Seb had ended his season. At Crystal Palace he ran 3:49.57 and in Brussels 3:32.11, respectively third and second on the world all-time lists. Despite his earlier statements, the Brussels run was effectively a world record attempt, being paced until the final 250m. Steve was so very close to the record, which officially (in tenths) stood at 3:32.1. Had he run just $1/100^{th}$ of a second quicker he too would have been awarded a time of 3:32.1. He ended his season with a 3:55.29 mile at the IAC/Coca-Cola Meeting. It was too cold and windy for a very fast time, plus the pacemaking went awry and Steve himself was tired after a surfeit of racing in previous weeks (his seventh in 18 days) but the most significant feature of the race was that 18 year-old Steve Cram was runner-up in his fastest time of 3:57.03. However, Graham Williamson (19) remained the top teenager with his European junior records of 3:36.6 and 3:53.15. The European Junior Championships in Bydgoszcz produced gold medals for both, Williamson at 1500m and Cram at 3000m, while Fatima Whitbread smashed her own UK junior record for victory in the javelin with 58.20m. East Germans won ten of the 14 women's events but had to settle for second place in that one. Much earlier in the year I had again drawn attention to the likelihood of wholesale doping in the GDR.

What price have East Germans athletes had to pay in terms of their own health and self-respect to create the GDR athletics miracle? Mass participation, good facilities, sophisticated training methods, advanced sports medicine, and high incentives in the form of state-accorded privileges have all contributed to the dramatic rise of the GDR (population of less than 20 million) to the status of an athletics super-power alongside the USA and the USSR, each with a population more than ten times greater. However, admiration for the achievements of East German athletes has long been tinged with doubts in the minds of those – like myself – who feel their success is altogether too remarkable, particularly in the case of their women athletes, who almost without exception summon peak form on just the day it is needed most ... at a major championship. The East Germans' strenuous denials that drugs play any part in their methods were seen to be false when shot putter Ilona Slupianek was caught out in the steroid tests at the 1977 European Cup Final. It's hardly likely that in such a well-ordered society Frau Slupianek would have been taking drugs purely on her own initiative.

All, eventually, would be revealed but – unlike the similar Russian situation decades later – the numerous East German medals and world records gained by cheating have never been rescinded.

Slupianek, by the way, was back to win at the next edition of the European Cup, in Turin, but I remember the meeting mainly for the empty press seat reserved for Jim Coote. The effervescent, ever helpful 42 year-old athletics correspondent of the *Daily Telegraph* since 1961 was killed when the aircraft he was piloting from Elstree to Turin crashed in the Alps.

Jim would have been the first to admit he was not the greatest of writers in terms of literary style [me neither] but his despatches from all over the world reflected a lively and enquiring mind, a love of the sport and an understanding of athletes' needs. He was a good and honest reporter, and in our trade I can pay no higher tribute than that. I shall greatly miss his breezy personality, and remember with affection our times together – whether sunning ourselves by a pool in Jamaica or munching NAAFI sausage rolls at Cosford.

It was another significant year for AW. The cover photos were now always in colour, nearly all taken by Mark Shearman; the audited circulation figure rose to 19,539 with an estimated readership of 50,000; and we celebrated Jimmy Green's special birthday. Jimmy wrote: "On April 20, at the ripe old age of 70, I am retiring and handing over the reins [as business and advertisement director] to my son, Tim, and this seems an opportune time to thank all those readers who have given us such wonderful support over the years. Without their loyal support we could not have made *Athletics Weekly* what it is today. I will still be around, working part-time and helping out at holiday times or when the others are away at major events, and I hope to continue as a tracksuit coach and starter for many years to come, but this semi-retirement will enable me to take a few hours off without feeling guilty!"

It was an eventful year for me too. The exclusive interviews with Steve Ovett and Seb Coe created quite a stir; my travels included trips to Malmö for a European Cup Semi-Final (filling in for BBC TV again), Turin for the Final, Montreal for the World Cup (incorporating a visit to Niagara Falls) and Brussels; and AW published *The Ghost Runner*, which I edited from John Tarrant's manuscript. This was a labour of love. All proceeds went to John's widow Edie and the book has become a collector's item. As Chris Brasher wrote in his moving foreword: "It is the story of a proud and honest man who, because he could not tell a lie, was banned from the sport he loved. He wrote it in pain while dying of cancer. And yet you will find no self pity here, just the simple story of a brave and generous man who, after having had half his stomach removed, ran for 10 miles to raise money for the hospital that was looking after him. Was there ever such a man? Was there ever such a book as this? I believe that it is destined to become a classic of sporting literature." Several attempts have been made to turn John's inspiring, poignant and ultimately tragic story into a film or TV drama but none yet has come to fruition.

John Tarrant was a victim of a strict and outdated amateur code but slowly but surely the sport was beginning to move with the times. A new breed of athlete emerged as the amateur rules were made more liberal to allow substantial sponsorship and broken-time payments, although closely scrutinised and administered by the governing bodies. Thanks to organisations like the Sports Aid Foundation, the BAAB was able to channel four-figure sums annually to several top athletes to enable them to compete on equal terms with heavily state-sponsored or athletic scholarship supported opponents from abroad. For an Olympic medal contender it was possible to be – quite legally – a full time athlete. For example, Brendan Foster took a year's leave of absence from his post as recreation officer for Gateshead, while Daley Thompson spent so many hours training and recuperating it would have been impossible for him to hold down a job as well. At the AGM of the AAA in November 1979 a resolution urging the General Committee "to make an urgent revision of the amateur rules" was approved by an overwhelming majority. Over in the USA, the Athletics Congress (governing body for American track & field) voted 150-3 to recommend that the IAAF drops its definition of an amateur as "one who competes for the love of sport and as a means of recreation, without any motive of securing any material gain from such competition."

There were other changes in the British athletics set-up. In 1978 former steeplechaser David Shaw had been appointed the BAAB's first professional general secretary and the 1938 European marathon silver medallist Squire Yarrow was elected AAA president in succession to the late Harold Abrahams. In 1979 both of the two principal national coaches, John Le Masurier and Denis Watts, retired after some 30 years of outstanding service. That led to Frank Dick, the 38 year-old national coach for Scotland who was AAA Junior 200y hurdles champion in 1960 and a GB indoor 440y international, to be appointed the BAAB's first director of coaching. He remained in charge until resigning in 1994 and those years proved to be halcyon days for British athletics. Olympic and/or world titles were won by Allan Wells, Linford Christie, Steve Ovett, Seb Coe, Steve Cram, Colin Jackson, Daley Thompson, the men's 4x400m team, Liz McColgan, Zola Budd, Sally Gunnell, Tessa Sanderson and Fatima Whitbread, while several of the above set world records indoors or out, together with the likes of Peter Elliott, Dave Moorcroft, Steve Jones, Keith Connor and Steve

Backley. A distinguished band of personal coaches were involved but all credit to Frank for putting into place such a successful preparation programme.

The fast developing world of women's marathon running received deserved attention, with Cliff Temple providing a fascinating interview early in the year with Grete Waitz, who had set a world marathon best of 2:32:30 in New York despite never having run further than 19km beforehand. She described the difficulties of training in snowbound Oslo during the winter. "I get up at about 5.30 and start running at 5.45 or 6 o'clock. At this time of the year it's dark and very, very cold – usually 10 or 15 degrees below freezing! I run for about 50 minutes, and then I go to work [she taught PE and Norwegian] at about 8 o'clock. I'm home again about 2 or 2.30 in the afternoon, do some shopping and some preparation for next day, and about 5 o'clock I do my second training session of the day. By 9 o'clock I'm ready to go to bed, so that it can start all over again next morning." All that work paid off, for in October she ran her second marathon, again in New York, and knocked nearly five minutes off her world best with 2:27:33. At this stage no other woman had bettered 2:34. Meanwhile, Joyce Smith was also making marathon history. She made her debut in June, aged 41, in 2:41:37 ... over nine minutes inside the previous UK best. She improved to 2:36:27 when winning a German race in September and finished first also in Tokyo in November in 2:37:48.

Marathon running, at an infinitely lower level, was also on my mind. In May I had my longest continuous run yet, timewise, from North Finchley to Wembley and back in 1 hour 11 minutes, and I decided that if, by the end of the year, I could run a half marathon then I would devote 1980 to a serious crack at the marathon. In December, Pat and I having moved to her parents' house in Wembley so she could look after her ill father, I ran 13.1 miles around the streets of Wembley and Harrow in 1 hour 58 minutes. "Operation Big Apple" was on ... the aim being to complete the New York Marathon ten months later.

15. MARATHON DREAM COMES TRUE (1980)

First, the sad news in 1980. Pat's beloved father, Sam Master, passed away in London's Charing Cross Hospital in March; and in the same month two athletes of renown died. One was Sam Ferris (79), who served in the RAF for 32 years and was not only one of Britain's greatest marathon runners, a close second in the 1932 Olympics and eight-time winner of the Polytechnic race, but was loved by AW readers for his knowledgeable and humorous road race reports. The other was perhaps the most famous athlete who ever lived (at least until the era of Usain Bolt): Jesse Owens.

At a time when the future of the Olympic Games is in the balance, should President Carter's will prevail and the USA boycott Moscow this summer, the world mourns the passing of one of the supreme American Olympic heroes. Jesse Owens, star of the 1936 Games with his four gold medals, died of lung cancer in Tucson, Arizona. He was 66. James Cleveland Owens was a classic example of the great American success story. Born on a farm in Alabama, the second youngest of 11 children of a poverty-stricken sharecropper, Jesse developed into one of the world's most celebrated sporting personalities, worked his way through college, became a presidential representative at the Olympic Games, and earned big money as a public speaker and PR consultant. At a time when segregation in the Southern States was still rigidly enforced, he broke down some of the barriers and helped pave the way for full acceptance of later generations of black American sports stars.

It was on May 25 1935, at Ann Arbor, Michigan that he entered the world of sporting legend.

What he achieved that day is, 45 years later [over 80 now], *still spoken about in awed tones. At 3.15 pm he equalled the world 100y record of 9.4. Ten minutes later he took his one and only long jump of the day, landing at the prodigious distance of 8.13m – smashing the previous world record of 7.98m, and a mark destined to survive a full quarter of a century. Back he went to the track at 3.45 for the straight 220y event ... and obliged with two more world records. His time of 20.3 was the fastest ever both for 220y and the slightly shorter 200m event. At 4 pm he lined up for his final event, the 220y low hurdles, again run over a straight course. His time of 22.6 constituted world records at both 220y and 200m. Six world records in well under an hour! Nothing like it had been seen before – or has been since. And to think this stunning demonstration of versatility came about while Jesse was nursing an injury! He had hurt his back a week earlier and it was still so painful on the big day that, as he recalled, "I had to be helped to the automobile that took us to the field, and my team-mates practically dressed me into my track outfit." He wasn't able to warm up or exercise before the meeting, but refused to withdraw. "I could hardly go to my mark at the start* [of the 100y], *but when the starter said 'get set' my pain left. When the meet was over the pain returned to my back and I had to be practically carried to the dressing room."*

Just over a year later, at the Berlin Olympics, Owens set the seal on a fabulous career by winning the 100m in 10.3, the long jump with a wind aided 8.06m, the 200m in 20.7 (a world best around a turn) and the 4x100m relay in a world record 39.8. Four events, four gold medals – and all achieved in that relaxed, graceful, light-footed style which was such a delight to behold. Who knows? Had he not been forced to forfeit his amateur status shortly after the Games he might well have turned to other events in 1937. He might have broken the world record of 46.1 for 400m, bearing in mind he ran an effortless 29.5 300y time trial in 1936, or even the high jump mark of 2.08m considering he once cleared 1.98m in training without any preparation.

Overshadowing all else in 1980, of course, were the Moscow Olympics. As a protest against the Soviet invasion of Afghanistan, President Jimmy Carter (shame on him, a former cross country runner) decreed that if Soviet troops were not withdrawn by February 20 the US would boycott the Games. It was a cheap political gesture, for the Americans could have exerted real pressure had they threatened to stop trading with the USSR, a move which might have caused the Kremlin to reconsider, but no such action was forthcoming, the troops remained and the boycott went ahead. Several other countries, in deference to American aid and influence, followed suit – including West Germany, Kenya, Japan, Canada and New Zealand. Instead of the 125-130 teams expected, only 81 turned up (69 in athletics). Had Prime Minister Margaret Thatcher got her way, Britain would have stayed away too, but to its credit the British Olympic Association refused to bow to political pressure and a large team was sent to Moscow.

The US "Olympic Trials" meeting in Eugene was a melancholy affair ... trials to pick a team that would not be competing in the Games. Those who missed their chance of glory in Moscow included world record holders Renaldo Nehemiah in the 110m hurdles and Ed Moses (the title holder) in the 400m hurdles, along with such luminaries as long jumper Larry Myricks, triple jumper Willie Banks, discus thrower Mac Wilkins, 800m runner Madeline Manning and 1500m runner Mary Decker. Matt Centrowitz, who won the 5000m, would have to make do by seeing his son of the same name triumph in the 2016 Olympic 1500m, while 18 year-old Carl Lewis – four years before he emulated Jesse Owens – qualified for "the team" in the long jump and 4x100m relay. The loudest cheers were reserved for a man who finished fourth in his event. The astounding Al Oerter, four times Olympic discus champion (1956-1968), received a standing ovation of three minutes after his final throw. Aged 43, Oerter threw 65.56m in the second round, much further than anything he achieved in his four previous Olympic Trials. His best ever distance while he was reigning Olympic champion was 64.78m in 1968 but earlier in 1980 he threw the colossal distance of 69.46m, albeit in very favourable wind conditions.

The most eagerly awaited confrontation in Moscow was that between Seb Coe and Steve Ovett, the conventional wisdom being that Coe would win the 800m, Ovett the 1500m. Indeed both did emerge as gold medallists – but the other way around!

The pair reached the Olympic arena in tip-top form. After setting personal bests at 3000m (7:57.4) and 5000m (14:06.2 in his debut) early in the season, Seb clocked 800m times of 1:47.5, 1:45.5, 1:45.0 (and 46.4 400m relay split) and a world leading 1:44.7 in quick succession. Steve meanwhile beat Filbert Bayi in a 3:38.7 1500m in Jamaica and went for a fast time at Crystal Palace, posting a world leading 3:35.3 with Steve Cram breathing down his neck in 3:35.6, breaking Jim Ryun's world teenage best of 3:36.1. It was in Oslo on July 1 that the two most exciting runners in the world threw off the wraps. Within the space of an hour both men set world records. Conditions were perfect and a capacity crowd of over 22,000 provided marvellous encouragement.

Seb was first up in the 1000m. He had never raced at this event before but it was a perfect distance for him and the world record of 2:13.9 achieved on this track in 1974 by the USA's Rick Wohlhuter looked distinctly vulnerable. However, Seb had been on antibiotics for a throat infection which caused him to withdraw from a Swedish 1500m race he had planned for a few days earlier … and the early pacemaking was almost suicidally fast. Stan Greenberg, the BBC statistician, timed Seb at 25.5 at 200m and 51.0 at 400m. Seb was 30m clear at 600m in 1:17.8, flashed past 800m in a spectacular 1:45.2 and held on grimly for a final time of 2:13.40. He now held four world records (800m, 1000m, 1500m, mile), but not for long as Steve was about to make history in the mile.

He had changed his philosophy since the interview the previous year when he remarked: "I don't think I've got the appetite for world records. I don't think I ever will have. It seems pointless to me." His outlook altered as a result of Seb's record breaking spree and he felt that it was now important tactically to outshine his rival at his own game. He was anxious, in the pre-Olympic war of nerves, to wrest the limelight from Seb and the only way was to break the world mile record. Dave Warren set a good pace with Steve passing the quarter in 55.7 and halfway in 1:53.8. On his own for the last lap and a half, Steve ran a very fast third quarter for a split of 2:51.0 as against Seb's 2:53.4 in his 3:49.0. Wearing his favourite USSR national team vest, Steve just managed to clip the record with 3:48.8, commenting: "One of the big goals this season was to take this world record from Seb … it tasted terrific." Another miling barrier had been broken: the first sub-4:00 occurred in 1954, the first sub-3:55 in 1958, 3:54 in 1965, 3:53 & 3:52 in 1966, 3:51 & 3:50 in 1975, 3:49 in 1980. Looking to the future, Seb would lead the way under 3:48 in 1981, Steve Cram under 3:47 in 1985, 3:46 & 3:45 by Nourredine Morceli in 1993 and 3:44 by Hicham El Guerrouj in 1999. The runner-up in Oslo was Cram in his best time of 3:53.8. The apprentice was learning his trade.

Ovett's prospects of winning that Olympic 1500m were enhanced further when in his last race before Moscow, back in Oslo on July 15, he not only chalked up his 43rd consecutive 1500m or mile victory in three years but equalled Coe's 1500m world record of 3:32.1. The situation was complicated as the IAAF at that time ratified hand timed records at that distance to 1/10th of a second. Thus Coe's 1979 mark in Zürich was officially 3:32.1 although his electronic time was 3:32.03. Ovett in Oslo ran 3:32.09 but the hand time of 3:32.1 sufficed for a world record plaque. Had he not waved to his fans 50m from the finish he would have become sole holder of that record. In fifth place Graham Williamson, despite his career being beset by injuries, clocked his best time of 3:35.72.

Like every athletics fan in the world, I couldn't wait for the Coe v Ovett clashes. As was the case in Rome, Tokyo, Mexico City, Munich and Montreal, I would normally have watched the action from the Olympic press area, but this time I opted to view the BBC's television coverage from home. As I wrote in March: *Long before Afghanistan hit the headlines I had made my decision. The Soviet authorities' treatment of dissidents and various minority groups* [notably Jews] *is so repugnant to me that I did not wish to be a guest – albeit indirectly – of that same regime as an accredited journalist in Moscow. It was relatively easy for me to take that course of action ... it would be much, much tougher for an athlete for whom the Games is probably a once-in-a-lifetime challenge. What is important, if we value our individual liberty, is that our athletes should be free to choose whether or not to go to Moscow.*

So AW covered the Games in two ways: from home I wrote a day-by-day commentary on the highlights spread over two issues, while Barry Trowbridge – who was in Moscow – provided his report plus complete results in a third issue. Here are excerpts from my commentary:

July 24: *A disturbing feature of the day's proceedings in the Lenin Stadium was that both of the new women's champions [Nadyezhda Tkachenko, USSR, pentathlon and Ilona Slupianek, GDR, shot] have in the past been suspended by the IAAF for taking anabolic steroids. There are many who feel that whatever the disqualification period no athlete banned for drug taking should ever be allowed to compete in the Olympics – and, in view of the controversy still raging over the clemency shown to five women athletes who were reinstated by the IAAF in time for the Games, there is a strong chance that the IOC will take a tough stand on this issue in future* [we are still waiting]. *Much too late in the day, IAAF president Adriaan Paulen – who had cast the decisive vote in favour of reinstating the athletes – admitted in Moscow that he had been wrong.*

July 25: *Who would have thought when Harold Abrahams died at the beginning of 1978 that at the very next Olympics a Briton would emulate his achievement of winning the 100m title. British sprinting was at its lowest ebb for years; we hadn't even sent any men for the 100m in Montreal in 1976. Powerfully built Allan Wells was quite the most unorthodox as well as the fleetest sprinter Britain has ever produced* [he set a UK record of 10.11 in the heats the day before]. *A product of the Scottish professional running school of training with great importance attached to speedball work, Wells was remarkable also for the fact that he scorned the use of starting blocks ... until the IAAF ruled them compulsory at Moscow. With the two favourites, Silvio*

Leonard (best of 9.98) and Wells, drawn the width of the track apart it was difficult to gauge their position against each other but Leonard, in the inside lane, was ahead at 95m. He was just a split second away from the gold medal when it was plucked from his grasp. While the Cuban maintained his upright form, the Scot lunged forward to win by such a narrow margin that their times could not be separated by even 1/100th of a second at 10.25. At 28 Wells had become the oldest man ever to win this Olympic crown.

What a day it was for British athletics, for in addition to Wells' golden success, Daley Thompson was well on his way to winning the decathlon – and with a possible world record. He enjoyed a superb first day for a halfway score of 4542 points. He won his 100m heat by a six-metre margin in 10.62 but it paled by comparison with his long jump performance ... a mighty leap of exactly 8 metres, his best ever legal distance. Another fine result followed: a shot put of 15.18m, easily his best in decathlon competition. Daley pulled further ahead of world record schedule with a high jump of 2.08m, but hoping to run close to 47 sec for 400m he had to settle for 48.01, hampered by the swirling wind. His halfway lead was a yawning 264 points.

July 26: *Some people are never satisfied! British runners fill first and second places in the Olympic 800m, which for all our glorious tradition in the event has never happened before, and yet I'm left with a feeling of anti-climax. Steve Ovett ran so physical a race that he can consider himself lucky not to have been disqualified; while Seb Coe chose an Olympic final of all occasions to run the most abysmal tactical race of his career. Instead of the full-blooded battle we had been anticipating so excitedly, the race turned out to be an untidy, ill mannered affair won in the modest time of 1:45.4. We didn't see the best of either Ovett or Coe. Having got that off my chest, I must congratulate Steve on his victory. After much frenzied pushing and shoving earlier in the race, Steve – the supreme racer – got himself in the right place at the right time and when he struck for home early in the finishing straight there was never any doubt as to the outcome. Whereas Coe was left floundering in the cut and thrust of an Olympic final, Ovett was absolutely in his element. He has taken time out to break world records recently, but it's man against man that really motivates Steve. Watched by over 100,000 spectators, the leaders reached the bell in a pedestrian 54.55. Coe was dead last and remained in last place until it was too late. Ovett went on to complete the second lap in about 50.5. Coe remarked: "I went into the race feeling I was capable of coping with anything that might be thrown at me, but when they broke I didn't have the speed of thought or movement necessary. Don't ask me why. Some days you perform well, others you don't."*

Later another British athlete struck gold when Daley Thompson fulfilled his destiny: to be Bruce Jenner's successor as Olympic decathlon champion. It was a shame that world record holder Guido Kratschmer was unable to compete but Daley was in such cracking form that there is little to suggest that the German would have been any more successful against Thompson than was the case when they clashed at Götzis earlier in the summer. He enjoyed a solid, disaster-free day which gave no hope at all to his opponents. His final winning margin of 164 points would have been appreciably larger had he wished to push himself to the limit in the 1500m. Instead he took it relatively easy, savouring the delight of an ambition achieved. Hopes of a world record fizzled out due to the weather. It was pouring in the morning and Daley ran the hurdles (14.47) somewhat cautiously. He fell behind world record pace after the discus (42.24m), the throwers doubly handicapped by a slippery circle as well as greasy implements. He vaulted 4.70m and threw the javelin 64.16m. A world record was still a possibility, but it would need a formidable personal best of 4:17.2. He settled for a steady run at the back, taking 4:39.9 for a score of 8495 (8522 on the current tables).

August 1: *"I've got to come back and climb the mountain again. The 1500 was going to be a hard event, anyway, but now it's going to be the big race of my life. I must win it." That was Seb Coe talking prior to the climax of the Games, the 1500 final. Instead of Coe* [had he won the 800] *regarding the 1500 almost an optional extra, it became a dire necessity for his own self-esteem as a runner – never mind the public's expectations – that he make speedy amends for that disastrous showing (by his standards) in the 800. Not that Ovett wasn't anxious to complete the prestigious double, but with a gold medal already tucked away the race was not so much a matter of athletic life and death for him as it was to Coe. Seb stressed in all his interviews that the cardinal sin he had committed in the 800 final was failing at a crucial moment to stay in touch with the leaders That was an error which would not be repeated. Indeed, at no point in the race, from the shuffling beginning to the flat-out sprint finish was Coe ever outside the first two places and he was at all times well poised either to launch his own strike or cover anyone else's. Instead of the hesitant near-novice of the 800 final here was a man in complete control – the answer to critics pigeon-holing him as merely a record breaker and not a racer.*

The early pace was disappointingly slow: 61.6 at 400m, 2:04.9 at 800m. The warm up phase ended abruptly at this point and the Olympic 700m championship began as the GDR's Jürgen Straub, in effect, began his run for home! Fearfully slow as the race had been, it now became fearsomely fast. Just subtract the 800m time of 2:04.9 from the winning 1500m time of 3:38.4 and you will find that the last 700m took just 1:33.5 ... that's 1:46.9 800 speed! Straub's initiative was a godsend to Coe in particular. Seb was happy to tuck in three metres behind, the times at 1200m being Straub 2:59.1 (54.2 for that lap), Coe 2:59.5, Ovett 2:59.7.

Faster and yet faster went Straub along the back straight; he was running the race of his life and both Coe and Ovett were having to work hard to stay in contact. With 200 to go the East German held a 4m lead over Coe, 6m over Ovett. Turning into the straight Coe drew level and then with another burst of acceleration 80m out, the 'double kick' we had heard whispers of, he was away and winging to everlasting glory. Just for once Ovett's explosive acceleration was missing. Indeed, the determined Straub refused to give an inch and Steve was unable to pass him. Coe covered the last 400 in 52.2. It took a lot of character, as well as physical talent, for him to climb and conquer that particular mountain. Seb's father and coach Peter commented: "You've seen an athlete come back from the grave. He's got all the guts in the world." Steve commented: "It looks as though Seb buckled in the 800 and I did the same in the 1500. I was a man with tired legs. I'm proud of my bronze as I am of my gold because I did my best."

In addition to those four glorious victories, Wells came so very close to completing a sprint double, finishing just 2/100ths behind Italy's Pietro Mennea (20.19) in the 200m; and there were bronze medals for Gary Oakes in the 400m hurdles and both the women's relay teams although the absence of the Americans certainly helped.

The boycott apart, the most disheartening feature of the Moscow Games was the blatant cheating by Russian officials. This extract comes from my account of the Games in *Olympic Track & Field History.*

Five champions from Montreal did manage to hang on to their crowns, the most resounding defence being put up by Yuriy Sedykh, whose opening hammer throw of 81.80m was a world record. A later throw of 81.46m by Sedykh was shown in a TV replay to be clearly a foul, and although the Soviet athletes did not need any help in this event it was a major talking point at the Games that judging decisions tended to favour the home team.

The result of the triple jump shows that Estonian Jaak Uudmae won with 17.35m ahead of Soviet colleague Viktor Saneyev (17.24m) with Brazil's Joao Carlos de Oliveira, Britain's Keith Connor and Australia's Ian Campbell next. However, both Campbell and de Oliveira were, in the view of expert observers, robbed of possible victory. In the third round Campbell landed beyond the Olympic record marker set at 17.39m only to find the red flag raised. The jump was ruled a foul on the grounds that his left foot had dragged along the runway during the step phase, which was against the rule then in force, but Campbell denied that was the case – as borne out by scrutiny of videotape. But his demand for the referee to be summoned was ignored and the sandpit raked over before any further protest could be made. Similarly, two huge jumps by de Oliveira of beyond 17.50m were inexplicably ruled out.

There was controversy also in the discus and javelin, won respectively by Viktor Rashchupkin (66.64m) and Dainis Kula (91.20m), both of the USSR. With his final effort in the discus, Cuba's Luis Delis threw what might have been a winning distance but an official was seen to place the marker some way short of where the discus landed. The official measurement was 66.32m and Delis had to settle for the bronze. Kula was another to benefit from questionable judging. After two fouls he had to land a decent throw in the third round to stay in the competition, but although he did get off a long throw the spear landed tail first and should have been ruled out. Not so; up went the white flag, the throw was measured at 88.88m and the Latvian lived to fight another day. Curiously, that particular throw was never replayed on TV. In the next round Kula threw the winning distance of 91.20m.

The rules were bent also in the men's and women's 4x400m relay. At that time, substitutions were permitted only on production of a medical certificate and yet individual 400m champion Viktor Markin plus two of their best women runners in Nina Zyuskova and Irina Nazarova were all somehow too ill to run in the heats but, miraculously recovered (not to mention rested), were able to play their part in the final. As the victory margin over the GDR was just 0.2 sec in each race the Soviets' manipulation of the rules was probably crucial.

Who said cheats never prosper? It's well documented now that elite GDR athletes underwent a strictly monitored doping regime and East Germans accounted for 11 titles in Moscow. As for the home competitors, they won no fewer than 15 gold medals and in view of the current scandal concerning widespread doping of Russian athletes, said to be a legacy of the Soviet era, one wonders how many of those triumphs were also chemically assisted. Apart from Britain's victorious quartet and Mennea, the only non-GDR/USSR winners were Ethiopia's Miruts Yifter in the 5000m and 10,000m, Poland's Bronislaw Malinowski (steeplechase) and Wladyslaw Kozakiewicz (world pole vault record of 5.78m), Italy's Maurizio Damilano in the 20km walk and the divine Sara Simeoni in the high jump, and Cuba's Maria Colon in the javelin.

Both Coe and Ovett continued to chase world records after the Games. Seb just missed out at 1500m with his time of 3:32.2 (3:32.19) in Zürich but, two weeks later in Koblenz, Steve became the first to crack 3:32 with 3:31.36. It was a sensational race as two Germans, Thomas Wessinghage (3:31.58) and Harald Hudak (3:31.96), also finished inside the old world record.

Two days after the close of the Olympics a most significant race was held through the streets of central London. It was the Avon Cosmetics International Marathon Championship for women, the intention being to demonstrate that women's marathon running had now gained such international acceptance that it was worthy of Olympic recognition. More than 200 entries were drawn from 27 countries and the race did indeed help pave the way for the women's marathon to be added to the 1984 Olympic schedule. Lorraine Moller of New Zealand won on a hot and humid day in 2:35:11; Joan Benoit (USA), who would become the inaugural Olympic champion, finished fourth while Joyce Smith placed a brave seventh. Joyce shouldn't really have been running at all, having caught chickenpox from her daughter a month earlier and then sustaining a torn calf muscle. In November, aged 43, she won again in Tokyo, setting a Commonwealth record of 2:30:27, a world best in a women-only race.

The big marathon news of the year was Grete Waitz's stunning new world best of 2:25:42 in New York, Alberto Salazar taking the men's race in 2:09:41. Among the 14,012 starters on October 26 was one star-struck editor of AW, lining up with (well, in the same race as) those two plus such other greats as Bill Rodgers, Lasse Viren, Filbert Bayi and Ingrid Kristiansen. My once seemingly impossible dream of completing a marathon ("Operation Big Apple") was about to become a reality.

A combination of long working hours and a series of injuries had severely limited my training mileage and my longest single run prior to August was 14 miles in just over two hours in the inaugural Peoples Marathon staged near Birmingham in May. It was the first time I had ever dropped out of a race but I knew that at that stage I wasn't ready for a full marathon and it didn't help that I suffered from dehydration after 10 miles on an exceedingly hot and windy day. In August I ran 15 miles non-stop on grass and in September I took part in the Burnham Beeches Half Marathon, finishing 15 minutes behind former AW secretary José Kimber but, astonishingly, 50 seconds ahead of former UK 10,000m record holder Stan Eldon who must have been jogging, if not walking, around! In the week of October 13-19 I covered 40 miles, my previous best being 26 miles. However, my weekly average for the year thus far was only 14 miles or about half of what I had planned, and I realised it would be a struggle to get round in New York. Incidentally, by an extraordinary coincidence, the turnaround point in the training run I did most often – eight miles from Wembley to Stanmore and back – was at a block of maisonettes which in 1986 became the home in which Pat and I have lived ever since.

Although the start time on Staten Island was 10.30 am there were already thousands of runners at the staging area by the time I arrived shortly before 8 am. It was bitterly cold and much of the waiting time was spent queuing (standing in line as the Americans say) for coffee, doughnuts and toilets. I spent time chatting and limbering up, and there was plenty of lively banter. As the runners flowed towards the starting area at the Verrazano Bridge, the longest single span bridge in the world, someone tripped over a brick barrier. "Gee, I've hit the wall already", he cracked to laughter all round. Lining up in the group designated to finish in a time between 4:15 and 4:30 it took three and a half minutes of slow walking even to reach the start line. As we trundled up towards the highest point of the bridge the views were stupendous: New York Harbor and the celebrated skyline of lower Manhattan to the left, the Atlantic Ocean to the right. After 2 miles we entered Brooklyn. I was knocked out by the crowd's warmth and enthusiasm, and I basked in the cheers and cries of encouragement. I felt terrific as I ran along the dead straight Fourth Avenue, all six miles of it, and had to restrain myself, opting for caution as I reminded myself that finishing the race was all that mattered.

Pulaski Bridge over into the next borough of Queens marked the halfway point and I was thrilled to reach it 2 hours 3 minutes after crossing the start line. I felt so fresh that I even toyed with the idea of speeding up in an attempt to break 4 hours. Caution prevailed again, and just as well for within two miles I was starting to suffer from aching thighs. With more than 10 miles to go my earlier elation was turning to concern. Would I make it? The rather melancholy trek over the Queensboro Bridge was a low point, but another high awaited as I descended into Manhattan's First Avenue. Huge crowds were waiting to cheer us stragglers along, and as my spirits soared so the pain in my legs subsided. Passing through Spanish and East Harlem (18-19 miles) my right hand was becoming sore as I "slapped five" with kids along the route. The rapport with the spectators was terrific.

They say the marathon really starts at 20 miles. I wish 'they' hadn't, because at that stage (in The Bronx) my knees had by now struck in sympathy with my thighs on the grounds of having been worked too hard and too long. I could handle that; what worried me more was that my right hip was playing up and I was scared it might cramp up altogether. I was maintaining 10 minute miles but it was confirmation that 26 miles is a long, long way to run when you haven't prepared adequately. To make matters worse, the final 5 miles back in Manhattan were into the strong wind that had been such a boon earlier in the race. Amid the usual cries of "looking great" only the guy in Harlem who called out "man, you're looking *terrible*" was being quite candid! From 23 miles I was reduced to walking long stretches in hilly Central Park but the adrenalin started pumping again as the end drew near and I finished in pretty good style. It was an emotional moment as I crossed the line in 10,779[th] position in an official time of 4:26:41 (around 4:23 actual), was warmly congratulated by one young woman and had a medal draped round my neck by another. I had done it. I had proved to myself that dreams can sometimes be made to come true given a modicum of work, determination and luck. Within half an hour of crossing the line I was on the transatlantic phone to the person whose constant encouragement and understanding ever since I started jogging was such a vital factor ... my wife Pat. Unfortunately, she couldn't be with me in New York as she was at home looking after her mother. After giving her the glad tidings, I added, "That's my first marathon, and my last". Famous last words?

AW continued to thrive. Circulation broke through the 20,000 barrier and thanks to an increased amount of advertising we produced several issues of 56 pages and one of 64. It also enabled us in September to augment our staff by engaging 18 year-old Brian Smyth of Herne Hill Harriers as editorial assistant. We welcomed a new freelance contributor in Pat Butcher, who had spent four years teaching and running in France and was now starting a career in journalism. He went on to become the athletics correspondent of *The Times*, a Eurosport commentator and the author of acclaimed books on Coe & Ovett and Emil Zátopek. Another highly valued contributor was Hungarian emigré Ivan Berenyi. Most published information on Eastern European athletes came from strictly controlled Communist government sources but Ivan had excellent contacts which enabled him to produce profiles of far greater human interest. The most prolific interviewer, though, continued to be Alastair Aitken and I kept my hand in with lengthy profiles of Mary Decker, Joyce Smith and Alberto Salazar.

The AAA, the world's oldest national athletics governing body, had reason to celebrate. As I reported in September: *It was a proud occasion: the Nationwide Building Society AAA Centenary Championships. They came too late in the season for the best turn-out of athletes or a really large crowd, but for the AAA – currently playing a more influential role in national and international affairs than for many a year – the proceedings at Crystal Palace were more than a track and field meeting. They were a celebration of 100 years of history. Tom McNab presented a reconstruction of what the sport was like at the time of the first championships in 1880. Brian Hooper, complete with twirly moustache, even re-enacted a famous little piece of AAA championship history. He played the part of Irving Baxter (USA), the Olympic champion, who in 1901 arrived at the stadium minus his pole. None of his fellow competitors would lend him one, and to quote Peter Lovesey in his splendid "Centenary History of the AAA", 'undaunted, he took a look round the ground, uprooted a flagpole and vaulted with that, sharing the Championship at 2.99m.' Hooper, who completed his flagpole vault to the manner born, then took part in an extraordinary competition. First Keith Stock cleared 5.52m to add 1cm to Hooper's UK record before passing at the Commonwealth record height of 5.54m, which Hooper cleared. At 5.55m Stock went clear while Hooper chalked up two failures before flying over 5.56m on his remaining attempt. It was the most astonishing cat and mouse game. Stock, who had never jumped higher than 5.40m before this meeting, seized back the initiative by sliding over 5.57m. Now it was Hooper who was fighting for his life but his resolve was matched by his technical skill and he was successful at 5.58m. The contest was in effect decided at 5.59m, a height cleared by Hooper for his fourth record of the afternoon. Stock could still retrieve the situation if he made 5.60m but failed. What a contest ... there's nothing in athletics to beat a really gripping field event competition.*

Tom McNab was involved also that year as technical consultant for the film *Chariots of Fire*, and an item appeared in AW inviting applications as extras. "The AAA and the Scottish AAA have granted permission for the use of amateur athletes in the film, with expenses paid and an *ex gratia* payment being given to the athletes' clubs. Tom McNab requires athletes in the 18-39 age range for sequences which involve a Highland Games, a Scotland v France international meet and the 1924 Paris Olympics. Filming will take place in May and June in Liverpool/Birkenhead and Glasgow/Edinburgh." Scenes purporting to take place at the Stade Colombes in Paris were actually filmed at the Oval Sports Centre in Bebington, Merseyside; Eton College stood in for Cambridge University which had refused filming rights; while the famous beach running scene to the haunting music of Vangelis took place at St Andrews in Scotland. Who could have predicted that a film about Harold Abrahams and Eric Liddell would win four Oscars, including best picture (producer, David Puttnam) and best original screenplay (Colin Welland), and – made on a budget of $5.5 million – would earn $59 million at the box office?

Such was the amateur ethos, not to mention snobbery, in 1924 that there was criticism of Abrahams, a product of Cambridge University, paying for the services of a professional coach, the great Sam Mussabini, whose portrayal in the film won Ian Holm a BAFTA Award and Oscar nomination for best supporting actor. In 1980 there were further significant moves towards openly rewarding athletes. The BAAB Council favoured a change to the IAAF rule which limited the value of prizes to $250 to permit the payment of actual prize money at certain international meetings and also allow athletes (and their governing body) to benefit from advertising contracts. The IAAF postponed a planned debate on the issue but over in America road race promoters jumped the gun and the male and female winners of the Atlantic City Marathon received $15,000 each. Shortly afterwards the IAAF consented to the trial staging of a grand prix series of road races proposed by the US governing body (TAC). The first of these races offered a total of $50,000 in prize money to the top 20 men and 10 women. Officially the money would be paid to the athlete's club but, as I commented, it's entirely possible that some of the clubs would quietly reimburse the athletes concerned or invest the money on their behalf.

The IAAF, under the presidency of Adriaan Paulen (himself a 400m opponent of Liddell at the 1924 Games), was beginning to come to terms with the end of amateurism but the world governing body made a calamitous decision in relation to doping. As mentioned earlier, instead of being unyielding in its opposition to the use of drugs and issuing long bans on athletes whose urine samples tested positive, five Bulgarian and Romanian women athletes found guilty in 1979 of taking anabolic steroids were reinstated with indecent haste. Representatives of the athletes had requested clemency in view of the fact that the bans would rule them out of the 1980 Olympics ... and the IAAF Council, with Paulen casting the decisive vote, agreed. Particularly incensed, justifiably so, was UK 1500m record holder Chris Benning who, as president of the British Milers' Club, signed a letter in June addressed to the IAAF protesting about the reinstatement. Expressing "feelings of shock and dismay", the letter stated "in our opinion this inability to compete in the Olympics is the only effective punishment for athletes who have blatantly cheated and brought the sport into disrepute." Chris had previously announced she would not be seeking Olympic selection in view of the fact that three of those athletes were likely to be in her event in Moscow. "I am completely disillusioned. These girls have cheated and yet they've been banned for only nine months and can compete in the Olympic Games. The International Federation has let down the athletes in a complete abrogation of their responsibility."

All credit to IAAF Council member Professor Arne Ljungqvist, a former Swedish Olympic high jumper, who would devote his life to fighting the drugs menace and serve as a vice-president of the IAAF from 1981 to 2007. In strongly opposing the Council's majority decision, he made this statement: "Misuse of drugs is one of the most serious and difficult problems in our sport today. It is my decided conviction that the acceptance by Council of the request put forward by the two Federations will have disastrous effects on the fight against drugs in our sport. Their acceptance will be a slap in the face to all those sporting and scientific experts who are now making a common effort to solve the problem of doping."

16. COE & OVETT RECORD FRENZY (1981)

The 1981 season was dominated by the rivalry of Coe and Ovett. It was too bad that they never actually raced against each other (that wouldn't happen again until the 1984 Olympics) but they continued to thrill the world of athletics and beyond as further global records came their way. It was reminiscent of Gunder Hägg and Arne Andersson in the 1940s, only the Swedes' records usually came in competition against one another. Seb kicked off the proceedings with 1:46.0 for 800m at RAF Cosford, a world indoor best, but that was small beer in comparison to his astonishing new outdoor world record of 1:41.73 in Florence on June 10.

Conditions were perfect when the race got under way at 11 pm. Kenya's Billy Konchellah strode briskly through 200m in 24.4 with Seb at 24.5 and completed the first lap in 49.6 (Seb 49.7). Sensing the pacemaker was starting to flag, Seb took the lead after another 50m and, out on his own, reached 600m in 75.0. Because of a fault with the electronic timing equipment it took ten minutes before the record time was confirmed. "It's getting under 1:42 that is the great thing for me," he said. "It was as hard a race as I have run for a long time. In the last 30m I was beginning to tie up but apart from that there was no problem." That time stood as the world record for 16 years.

Both men turned up in Oslo on July 11, frustratingly in separate races. Richard Hymans was there in the Bislett Stadium to report for AW that Seb was ahead from just after halfway in the 1000m, reached 800m in 1:44.6 and finished in 2:12.18 to chop more than a second off his own world record despite a blister on his foot bursting during the race. It was a time which would remain unbeaten for 18 years. Later, Steve won what Richard described as "the finest mile race ever seen". Three men dipped under 3:50 and a total of seven broke 3:51 in this "Dream Mile" with Steve recording the third fastest ever time of 3:49.25. Steve Cram, now a world class miler in his own right, clocked 3:50.38 in sixth place. "It was a super race," said Ovett. John Walker, fourth in 3:50.26, went further: "That has to be the greatest mile race of all. At my age I should know. I seem to have run in most of them." Earlier that week, both had astoundingly clocked the very same 1500m time of 3:31.95: Coe in Stockholm (the pacemaker's ridiculous opening lap of 52.43 effectively ruining chances of a world record) and Ovett in Milan.

Steve continued to go so tantalisingly close with a 3:49.66 mile in Lausanne, which meant he owned four of the six fastest miles ever run, and a 3:31.57 1500m in Budapest, his and the world's second quickest ever time. While Steve was out recovering from a leg injury, Seb stole his thunder in Zürich on August 19. Aiming for a time in the region of 3:46/3:47, he had to settle for 'only' 3:48.53. With splits of 56.2 at 400m, 1:53.6 at 800m and 2:51.68 at 1200m he was behind Steve's corresponding time of 2:51.0 in his 3:48.8 record but Seb's final lap proved sufficient. Steve's priority, once recovered to full fitness, was to regain that record and opportunity knocked just one week later in Koblenz. He was originally due to run 1500m but the promoter was happy enough to add a mile race to the programme. Steve was paced through the first two laps in 56.6 and 1:54.5 before hitting the 1200m mark in 2:51.5 and finishing in 3:48.40. However, Steve's triumph was short-lived for in Brussels just two days later (August 28) Seb struck back ... and how! I was fortunate enough to be in the Heysel Stadium, as was my nephew Lionel who was on holiday in nearby Bruges, to witness a mind-blowing run at the Ivo Van Damme Memorial meeting.

The atmosphere was electric as the runners were presented to the crowd of nearly 50,000. What a field it was: Seb Coe and John Robson (UK), Steve Scott, Sydney Maree, Craig Masback and Tom Byers (USA), Eamonn Coghlan and Ray Flynn (Ireland), John Walker (New Zealand), Thomas Wessinghage (W Germany), Mike Boit (Kenya) and Omer Khalifa (Sudan). Byers [who had scored a sensational 1500m victory over Ovett in Oslo in June] acted as hare and went off at a merry clip, towing Coe in his wake. The pace was perfect: 54.92 at 400m by Byers, with Coe passing the 440y mark in 55.3. The second lap was made to measure too for Coe as he continued to track Byers whose 800m time was 1:52.67. Seb's probable 880y clocking was 1:53.3. At the start of the back straight on the third lap Coe was seen to stumble but he recovered quickly and with some 130m to go before the bell Coe slipped ahead. Seb reached the 1200m mark in 2:51.0 and three-quarters in 2:51.9, with the ever astonishing Mike Boit continuing to lurk menacingly some 3 or 4m down. To break the record Seb needed inside 56.5 for the final quarter. He raced past the 1500m point in 3:32.93 and then really opened up along the finishing straight. Boit maintained his magnificent cadence to the end, running an African record of 3:49.45, and yet he still finished 15m down as Coe stopped the clock at 3:47.33. Seb had covered the last quarter in 55.5, the ultimate 100m in 13.2. Seb was full of praise for Byers and Boit. "I knew Mike was there all the way and it was tremendous. I knew I couldn't even subconsciously relax. I had to work all the way to the tape."

I was responsible for Seb Coe's next record ... the slowest 1500m of his career at 8:46! The occasion was a mass participation 17.4km road race in Rome, two days after Seb had completed his season with a comfortable 800m victory in the IAAF's World Cup.

No, he wasn't walking backwards, but that's how long it took him, Brendan Foster and the editor of AW to reach the first checkpoint in the "Marathon of History and Peace" from St Peter's Square. Instead of starting with the other stars (Australia's Rob de Castella won in 51:02) Seb and Bren joined in at the back of the massed ranks of scrubbers for what was intended to be a gentle training run. After your editor decided to let the pair move away from him, for reasons not entirely unconnected with the fact that the heat together with constant surging through the tightly packed field had left him knackered already, Seb and Bren threaded their way past thousands of runners and eventually finished somewhere in the first 20 or 30.

That wasn't my longest race that year. Despite my "never again" assertion following the New York Marathon, I couldn't resist the chance of taking part in the inaugural London Marathon at the end of March. This was the brainchild of Chris Brasher and John Disley, track rivals of the 1950s, who had been so impressed by the New York Marathon that they set about organising a similar event in London. There were so many problems but like the great steeplechasers they were they negotiated every obstacle in their way and set up a race which has become part of the capital's very fabric – a challenging but joyful annual festival. It was a success from the outset. Brasher had expected no more than 3000 or 4000 runners in the first year, but there were almost 22,000 applications and as it wasn't possible to accommodate that number of runners at that time the field was limited to 7000-plus, still by far the biggest race ever staged in Britain. The predominantly flat course and refreshing rain made for fast running and the overall depth was superior to New York's with 143 finishing inside 2:30 (119 in New York) and 406 below 2:40 (as against 294). There was no prize money on offer for the joint winners, who finishing hand in hand in 2:11:48 were Dick Beardsley of the USA and Norway's Inge Simonsen, while an inspired Joyce Smith (2:29:57) became the first British woman, and the world's third, to better two and a half hours. The 1971 European silver medallist Trevor Wright was the first British man home, in third place (2:12:53), while his wife Rosemary (née Stirling), the 1970 Commonwealth 800m champion, ran 2:54:10 … unprecedented surely for a woman who had a 53.2 400m to her credit. She later improved to 2:43:29.

As with New York, my experience of running in the London Marathon was a mixture of elation and pain. Again, my training mileage was wholly inadequate, averaging 18 miles a week from the start of the year, although I did log a record 41 miles between March 15 and 21. Similar to New York, I felt marvellous for the first half of the race (2:01), accompanied for much of the way by an old Grafton clubmate, Henry Martin. I was astonished to see him running a marathon as he had been a classy sprinter who would usually "die" in his quarter mile races. On this occasion I was the one who struggled to complete the distance, my aching thighs reducing me to a walk for stretches from 18 miles onwards. Amusingly, at around 20 miles I overtook – while walking – my distinguished fellow journalist John Goodbody, who was determined to run, however slowly, the entire distance. John, a remarkable all-round sportsman, was a shot putter at Cambridge University, became one of Britain's top judo fighters and in 1991, aged 48, swam the English Channel in 15 hours 40 minutes! Knowing my wife would be watching at a particular point on The Embankment I managed to put on a show of strong running for her benefit but my finishing time was a few minutes slower than in New York. Nonetheless, it was an experience I shall always treasure, as was running in the inaugural Great North Run half marathon from Newcastle to South Shields in June, clocking around 1:56. This race, the brainchild of Brendan Foster, superseded the London Marathon as Britain's biggest race with a field of some 12,000.

Another highlight that year was attending a preview showing of *Chariots of Fire*. From the moment that Vangelis' iconic theme accompanied images of Britain's 1924 Olympic team running through the water I was hooked and transported to another era.

Thanks to Colin Welland's admirable screenplay, the vision of producer David Puttnam, the directing talents of Hugh Hudson, the splendid acting of the entire cast and the brilliantly realised period flavour created by the production team and technicians, the film is an absolute delight. I came away not only thrilled, but deeply moved, by this story of two of our greatest ever athletes as they prepare for and meet the supreme sporting challenge of the Olympic Games. It could be argued that many of the incidents in the film didn't happen that way in real life. For instance the film makes out that Liddell only discovered on the journey to Paris that the heats of the 100m would be held on a Sunday, whereas in truth he knew – and made known his decision – the previous winter. In Harold's case, he didn't meet his beloved wife Sybil until some years after the period in question. These and other fabrications don't matter. The film was, in fact, extremely well researched and what liberties have been taken are fully justified for dramatic effect. The film was never intended to be a documentary account; it is drama, based on fact, and faithful to the character, circumstances and driving forces relating to Abrahams and Liddell. I came out of the cinema with a lump in my throat, proud that Harold Abrahams had been a friend, and sorry that I had never known Eric Liddell. They were both, in their differing ways, remarkable men as well as superb athletes and "Chariots of Fire" is a worthy testament to their memory.

During the year, three celebrated athletes who were team-mates at those 1924 Games passed away. Guy Butler (81) was at that time Britain's most bemedalled Olympic athlete with four awards as a 400m and 4x400m runner in the Games of 1920 and 1924, including gold in the 1920 relay. He set an unofficial European 400m record of 48.0 in his Paris semi-final and in 1926 he equalled the world 300y record of 30.6. In later years as a coach he helped guide Alastair McCorquodale to a totally unexpected fourth place in the 1948 Olympic 100m, lectured and wrote widely on the sport, and became Britain's foremost producer of coaching films and loops. On the very day that *Chariots of Fire* was being celebrated at a Royal Premiere attended by the Queen Mother, Douglas Lowe, QC, died at 78. He was Olympic 800m champion in 1924 and 1928 (in British record time on both occasions), the first man to win the title twice and until Seb Coe in 1984 the only Briton to have struck gold at two Olympics. At the age of 29 he became honorary secretary of the AAA and helped draft the constitution of the body which eventually became the BAAB. Professionally, he was called to the Bar in 1928 and from 1972 until his retirement in 1977 he was a Recorder of the Crown Court. He could have featured prominently in *Chariots* but withheld permission to be portrayed. Likewise, Lord Burghley (the Marquess of Exeter), who died at 76, did not consent to be represented in the film, so a character named Lord Andrew Lindsay, who happened to be a hurdler, was invented and played by Nigel Havers. Lord Burghley was only 19 when he competed in the 110m hurdles in Paris and it was he, not Harold Abrahams as in the movie, who dashed round the 370 yard flagstone path at the

Great Court of Trinity College in less than the 44.9 seconds it took the clock to strike 12. At the 1928 Games he won the 400m hurdles and was a triple gold medallist at the inaugural British Empire Games in 1930. He was elected president of the AAA in 1936, aged 31, was president of the IAAF for 30 years from 1946, and was chairman of the organising committee for the 1948 Olympics in London.

The death occurred also of Geoff Dyson (66), who had been appointed chief national coach to the AAA in 1946, soon after being demobbed from the Army with the rank of major. It was an inspired choice, for Dyson was just the man for the job. Imaginative, talented, energetic and charismatic, he made a tremendous impact. However, his strong personality and forceful views led to bitter squabbles with leading officials like Harold Abrahams and Jack Crump. Mostly it was a question of status. Dyson was a professional, paid to do a certain job, and he felt his authority was being constantly undermined by certain highly placed administrators. A dispute over salary and terms of service resulted in his resignation in 1961, a grievous loss for British athletics. His book, *The Mechanics of Athletics*, was hailed as the definitive work on the subject and proof of his varied coaching expertise was that his personal group of pupils reached the top in the hurdles (Maureen Gardner, whom he later married), steeplechase (John Disley), pole vault (Geoff Elliott), long jump (Shirley Cawley) and shot (Arthur Rowe).

The march towards open athletics continued, albeit cautiously. *The IAAF Congress tackled the thorny problem of eligibility and made some progress towards a situation where athletes can openly receive monetary rewards for their prowess. The day of officially sanctioned cash prizes and/or appearance money has not yet dawned but there is a possibility that from 1983 a new rule permitting national federations to set up Trust Funds for athletes could be in effect. Congress agreed in principle that such a rule should be adopted. The IAAF's new definition of an amateur is 'one who abides by the eligibility rules of the IAAF.' Financial assistance to athletes, properly channelled through the appropriate national federation, can now include accommodation, food, transport, education and professional training.*

Some American road race promoters continued to defy the authorities, with the Nike Marathon in Eugene, part of the Association of Road Racing Athletes circuit, paying the male and female winners $20,000 each. However, the Virginia 10-Miler two weeks later became the first race in which amateurs and professionals were allowed to compete together without jeopardy to the amateurs' status due to the change in the IAAF's eligibility requirements for US domestic competition.

The other perennial issue was that of drugs. In July a statement from the IAAF announced that gigantic American discus thrower Ben Plucknett, who had recently reached world record distances of 71.20m and 72.34m, and Australia's Commonwealth shot champion Gael Mulhall had been banned after tests in New Zealand in February had revealed traces of anabolic steroids in their samples. Plucknett's case made history as he became the first athlete to have set world records which would not be ratified due to disqualification for a doping offence as the IAAF annulled all of his results from the date of the positive test ... but, perversely, the AAU recognised his marks as American records. Both athletes were banned for 18 months from the time of the test, which meant they would be eligible to compete again from August 1982; in Mulhall's case just in time to prepare for the late season Commonwealth Games. I was unhappy with these lenient sanctions.

My own feeling is that both athletes, and any more who may be caught subsequently, should be banned internationally for life. Harsh? Yes, but if those who believe in free and fair competition are to save the sport from developing into a pharmaceutical contest (and we're perilously close to that now) then severe deterrent measures are vital. Athletes should be left in no doubt as to what will happen to them if their doping tests prove positive. For the sake of the sport – and its own credibility – the IAAF must stand firm this time. That warning, echoed by so many in the sport, went unheeded and consequently cheating has continued on an industrial scale ever since.

I tackled that issue also in my introduction to the fifth and final edition of *Encyclopaedia of Athletics*, dedicated "to the memory of Harold Abrahams (1899-1978), who so kindly contributed a foreword to the four previous editions, and who helped and encouraged me so much during their compilation; and to my wife Pat for her unfailing support and understanding." The first edition had appeared in 1964 and back then, I wrote, "the use of drugs by athletes was practically unknown; now it is depressingly widespread and apparently growing all the time. The IAAF must accept some of the blame, for despite instituting dope control tests which have caught out many offenders the penalties meted out have been so mild as to have been no real deterrent at all."

The updated book contained 150 biographies including all the 1980 Olympic champions and current world record holders in the standard international events but the 'greats' of earlier eras – athletes like Walter George, Jim Thorpe, Paavo Nurmi, Jesse Owens, Cornelius Warmerdam, Emil Zátopek, Fanny Blankers-Koen and Roger Bannister – were not neglected. A new and unique feature provided details of prominent athletes who went on to make a name for themselves in other fields of endeavour and of other famous figures who achieved some athletic distinction in their younger days.

Politicians included Philip Noel-Baker, 1920 Olympic 1500m silver medallist, who served as Minister of Fuel & Power in the Labour Government 1950/51 and was awarded the Nobel Peace Prize in 1959; Chris Chataway, 5000m world record breaker, who was Minister of Posts & Telecommunications in the Conservative Government 1970-72; and Jeffrey Archer, British 200m international, an MP from 1969 to 1974 and later a best-selling author. Urho Kekkonen, the longest serving president of Finland, was national high jump champion in 1925; Norman Manley, Prime Minister of Jamaica, set a national junior 100y record of 10.0 in 1911; Habib Thiam, Senegal's Prime Minister, had been a French 200m champion. Among distinguished lawyers were Richard E Webster (later Viscount Alverstone), who set a world amateur best for 2 miles in 1865 and became Lord Chief Justice of England and presided as judge in the Dr Crippen case, and Sir Montague Shearman, the AAA 440y champion of 1880 and one of the founders of the AAA, who became a judge and member of the Privy Council. Field Marshal Earl Alexander of Tunis, who led the Allied invasion of Italy in the Second World War, was the 1914 Irish mile champion; Arnold Strode-Jackson, the 1912 Olympic 1500m champion, won a quadruple DSO in the First World War in which, at 26, he was the youngest brigadier-general in the British Army. On the medical front, Arthur (Lord) Porritt, bronze medallist in the *Chariots of Fire* Olympic 100m for New Zealand, was surgeon to King George VI and his Queen, while 1948 Olympic 400m champion Arthur Wint was not only a London-trained surgeon but served as Jamaican High Commissioner in the UK from 1974 to 1978.

Many athletes moved on to careers as cinema actors, including two Tarzans in Herman Brix (later known as Bruce Bennett), the 1928 Olympic shot silver medallist, and 1936 Olympic decathlon champion Glenn Morris. Three more Olympic decathlon winners in Bob Mathias (1948 & 1952), Rafer Johnson (1960) and Bruce Jenner (1976) appeared on the screen, as did O.J. Simpson, whose CV included a world record plaque for the 4x110y relay as a member of the University of Southern California team in 1967 and a best 100m time of 10.3 in 1968. Among established actors were Roscoe Lee Browne, the world's fastest 800m runner in 1951, and Dennis Weaver (*Gunsmoke* and *McCloud* on TV), who placed sixth in the 1948 US Olympic decathlon trial. Oscar winner Jack Lemmon was a New England high school record holder as a distance runner. Singers Paul Robeson and Johnny Mathis were good high jumpers (1.93m and 1.96m respectively), while Anne Pashley – a British Olympic silver medallist in the 1956 4x100m relay – became a noted operatic soprano.

The best news for the IAAF was the great success of the third edition of the World Cup. Staged in that most inspiring of settings, Rome's Stadio Olimpico, the Italians took the shrewd step of adding a ninth lane in order to accommodate their own national squad. With Italians to root for in every event, plus the presence of such superstars as Coe, Ovett, Ed Moses, Carl Lewis and Evelyn Ashford, the public came in enormous numbers – a total of 185,000 over the three days. As a result of the splendid ticket sales, together with TV rights and other lucrative sources of income, money poured into the IAAF's coffers and its new president, Primo Nebiolo, started his term of office with his prestige sky-high. The World Cup was, after all, instituted in 1977 with the prime objective of raising money which could be ploughed back into developing the sport, particularly in the Third World. It was the most successful World Cup yet for British athletes. The only previous individual winner was Ovett (1500m in 1977), but in Rome there were three: Allan Wells (100m), Coe (800m) and Ovett again, while Wells (200m) and Kathy Smallwood (100m) finished second, the future Kathy Cook setting a UK record of 11.10 which would survive until 2008. An injured Carl Lewis – who set world low altitude bests that year with 10.00 for 100m and 8.62m long jump – took only two jumps, winning with a modest 8.15m, and jogged in a distant last in the 100m where UK resident

Ernest Obeng, representing Ghana and Africa, finished just 1/100th behind Wells. Obeng was later, for many years, in charge of TV operations for the IAAF.

I had the honour of being elected chairman of the British Athletics Writers' Association for 1981-82, following in the footsteps of Vernon Morgan, John Rodda, Bob Trevor, Jim Coote, Roy Moor, Colin Hart, Cliff Temple, Pat Collins and Terry O'Connor, and at the awards dinner at the Café Royal in October it was my privilege to make a speech and presentation to our athletes of the year, Seb Coe and Kathy Smallwood. I was nervous enough as it was but only the previous day, having just flown in jet-lagged from the USA, I was informed that the ceremony would be televised, adding considerably to my anxiety. Fortunately, it all went off smoothly.

That trip to America had been pretty special. Since my mum died five years earlier, I had got much closer than previously to my dad and I hit upon the idea of taking him to the USA so he could meet up with family who lived in Florida and New York. Aged 74, he had never before set foot outside the UK so it was all a great adventure for him. We flew by Laker Skytrain from Gatwick and stayed for seven nights in Miami Beach, during which time we met up with my "Uncle" Manny and "Auntie" Yetta (Yetta was actually my dad's cousin), who we used to visit in London before they emigrated in 1949. I also managed to squeeze in a 15km race from Miami Beach's famous Fontainebleau Hilton hotel which started in the dark before 7 am but it was already so hot and humid that I had to drink seemingly gallons of water at the finish.

We then travelled by minibus to Orlando, our three nights there highlighted by trips to the fabulous Disney World, and then a flight to New York. There we met up with my cousin Margaret (Manny and Yetta's younger daughter) and her two daughters. My dad had never looked so happy as he was on this American trip; he would talk about it for the rest of his life. Athletics, of course, had to come into it and I was able to report on a great New York Marathon in which both Alberto Salazar (2:08:13) and New Zealand's Allison Roe (2:25:29) set world bests, although as the course was later found to be 170 yards (roughly 28 sec of running) short those times were not officially accepted.

On the subject of marathons, I'll close this chapter with the heartfelt "Lament of a Marathon Runner's Spouse" by one Pat Watman as published in the August 22 issue of AW:

Sisters! (and/or brothers?)

When he first mentioned running a marathon, did you think "relax, he'll never really do it" and then, when you realised he would, think "I'll leave him!"?

Have you heard all the jargon till it comes out of your ears? – achilles tendons, hamstrings, carbohydrate loading, target runs, marathon runners nipple …

Do you sometimes wish that Phidippides – or whatever his name was – had dropped dead 20 miles earlier and saved everybody all this fuss?

Does he sometimes want supper at 10.30 at night after a training run and then go straight to bed?

Do you cringe in embarrassment when he sticks a "Marathon runners keep it up longer" sticker on the back of the car?

Do you find jars of vaseline keep disappearing as he ladles on dollops all over till he's oiled like a channel swimmer?

How often have you answered telephone calls with "Well, he's in, but he's out …?"

Does he burst in after a run and collapse into your arms dripping from head to toe saying "only 10 more miles and it'll be my best week's mileage ever?"

Does he come back from a run groaning about his achilles and do you have to play coach and remind him to do his warming-up exercises next time?

Do you find myriad items of training gear flung over the radiator in the bedroom to dry them quickly, thus lending the nightly atmosphere a certain "*je ne sais quoi?*"

Do your carpets show signs of dried earth (not to mention leaves and various unfortunate livestock) just when they've had their weekly clean?

Do you sometimes think if you hear another word about THE MARATHON you'll dive out the nearest window?

And then, when it's all over, does he cry "It was fantastic, darling, but I'll **never** do it again!"?

Well, pack your bags, girls, he doesn't mean it!

17. AROUND THE WORLD IN 28 DAYS (1982)

It was too good to be true ... and so it proved. Coe and Ovett, it was proclaimed in January 1982, would clash over 3000m in the England v Kenya v Japan v Spain match scheduled for Crystal Palace on July 17. England team manager Andy Norman, fast becoming the Mr Fixit of British athletics, played a significant role in bringing off this coup for the AAA who as promoters of the match stood to make a profit of at least £100,000 from the event in sponsorship, gate receipts (tickets would be like gold dust) and worldwide TV rights. There was a problem, though. While out on a training run near his home in Hove on December 7 Steve had momentarily lost concentration and had run into some church railings. He punctured a muscle above the right knee and tore the inside of his leg, necessitating surgery 12 days later. "It's a massive setback and my big achievement of the season will be to get back." In May the pair appeared together at a press conference to confirm that the duel was still on.

In June Steve was back in world class form with a 7:43.87 3000m, while Seb ran 4:58.84 for 2000m, but early in July Seb had to pull out of the much anticipated encounter due to what turned out to be a stress fracture of the lower right shin and wasn't able to resume training until the end of the month. Steve meanwhile lowered his UK 2000m record to 4:57.71 but just as things seemed to be going well for him he was forced to drop out of a race for the first time in his career. It happened in Paris, just after the bell in the 1500m when he was a distant fourth. Suffering from a stomach ailment, he collapsed and was taken to hospital. He wasn't fully recovered for that once so significant July 17 3000m race and was merely an also-ran, finishing tenth in 7:48.07 in a race won by Dave Moorcroft in a European record of 7:32.79.

It was Dave in fact who would prove to be Britain's track star of the year. He never possessed the blazing speed of Seb and Steve but back in 1976 he had displayed impressive stamina by finishing runner-up in the English National cross country championship over nine miles just a month after winning the AAA indoor 1500m title. In 1978 he beat Tanzania's world record holder Filbert Bayi for the Commonwealth Games 1500m gold medal in 3:35.48, the world's fastest time that year. The following season he reduced his best mile time to 3:54.35 but that sufficed only for ninth place as Coe won that race in a world record 3:48.95. He opted for the 5000m at the 1980 Olympics but injury restricted his training and a stomach bug in Moscow resulted in his failing to reach the final. It was only in 1981, when he clocked 13:20.51, that he began to consider himself a true 5000m runner.

Free at last from the injuries which had constantly plagued his career and thanks to a great winter's training in New Zealand, Dave experienced his *annus mirabilis* in 1982. In just his second track race of the summer, in Oslo, he knocked five seconds off his best mile time with 3:49.34, moving to fifth on the world all-time list. Eleven days later, on July 7, he set foot again on the famed Bislett track, aiming for Brendan Foster's UK 5000m record of 13:14.6. In a classic example of British understatement, the entry in his training diary relating to that race includes the words "quite pleased". In fact, Dave shocked everyone, himself included, with a phenomenal run as he ripped almost six seconds from Henry Rono's world record with the sensational if tantalising time of 13:00.41. What's more this wasn't the result of the usual choreographed pacemaking job so common in the big invitational races; he was out on his own for the final four kilometres and ended up 20 seconds ahead of the next finisher, Ralph King (USA), who thought he had won not realising Dave was still in the race, so far ahead was he!

Four days later I drove up to Coventry to interview Dave whose modesty, good humour and sporting demeanour had long endeared him to the fans. I asked if he had been nervous approaching the race. "Just the usual: panic stricken, wobbly knees ... my usual approach to races," he smiled. Reflecting on the race, he said: "When I got to the bell and it had just turned to 12:01 I knew I had got the world record. For the whole of that last lap, although I was absolutely shattered, I was savouring the fact that I was going to be world record holder." He confessed that front running was "so totally out of character for me ... but I felt good, I felt strong, and I enjoyed it. I guess it's an added satisfaction knowing that I did it all on my own."

He was now on a roll. Next came that European 3000m record, falling only just short of Rono's world record of 7:32.1, and further personal bests followed at 800m (1:46.64), 1500m (3:33.79) and 2 miles (8:16.75). However, the pressure was taking its toll; he developed an eye infection and swollen glands, and was far below his best when finishing a forlorn third in the European Championships 5000m. He did, however, bounce back with victory in the late season Commonwealth Games.

Attempting to simulate what would be required at the European Championships, Seb ran three fast 800s in the space of four days in August with 1:44.48, 1:45.85 and 1:45.10, and then a week later ran a sensational solo anchor leg of 1:44.01 (passing 400m in 49.1!) at Crystal Palace to seal a world record for himself and colleagues Peter Elliott, Garry Cook and Steve Cram in a 4x800m relay. Ovett too was rounding into promising form but following his fastest 800m time (1:46.08) since the Moscow Olympics he tore a hamstring during training and that was the end of a most frustrating season. As for Seb, everyone must have assumed he would clinch his first major 800m title at the European Championships in Athens but in a stunning upset he was overhauled in the finishing straight by the previously unheralded West German, Hans-Peter Ferner, 1:46.63 to 1:46.68. It transpired that he was suffering from glandular fever and his season too ground to a premature and distressing halt. "I just didn't have the legs when it mattered. I've taken too much out of a shallow well."

Every cloud has a silver lining and in 1982 it took shape in the tall, long striding figure of Steve Cram, still only 21 but now a master in his own right after several years of serving his apprenticeship under the world's two foremost milers. The race which demonstrated he had entered the world elite was when he front ran to the world's fastest 800m time that year with 1:44.45, a huge advance on his previous best, and the belief that he could now take on anybody at 1500m was reinforced when he won in Zürich in a personal best of 3:33.66. His last race before Athens was that world record breaking relay in which he clocked 1:44.54 on the third leg, his 50.5 first lap being perilously close to his quickest 400m time of 49.1!

His victory in Athens was achieved the hard way: after a long run for home 600m out. He might have preferred to have gone at the bell but, with his keen racing brain, he took advantage of the momentary confusion by accelerating hard when the luckless Graham Williamson was tripped. Covering the third lap in a stunning 55.4, he opened up a 20m advantage. A man of lesser nerve might have crumbled as he saw (on the giant TV screens at the end of each straight) his lead dwindling but he raised enough of a gallop in the finishing straight to win by four metres in 3:36.49.

Despite Coe's shock defeat, Athens proved a memorable meeting for the British team as, in addition to Cram's success, European record holder Keith Connor won the triple jump with 17.29m and Daley Thompson broke the world decathlon record in emphatically beating his West German rival, Jürgen Hingsen. In addition to Coe, there were silver medals by Cameron Sharp in the 200m (the father of current 800m star Lynsey Sharp lost by 1/100th), the men's 4x400m relay team, Kathy Smallwood (who set a Commonwealth 200m record of 22.13 and later in the year married Garry Cook) and the women's 4x100m relay team, plus the previously mentioned bronze for Dave Moorcroft in the 5000m.

The decathlon was expected to be the event of the meeting. In May, in Götzis, Daley had not only comfortably disposed of Hingsen (8529) but seized the world record with 8704 points, re-scored on the current (1984) tables as 8730. However, in August the record passed to Hingsen at 8723 (re-scored as 8741) while to add to Daley's woes, after badly injuring himself when a pole broke in a club match, the Briton was struggling to regain peak fitness for the big showdown in September.

The first five events in Athens showed why Daley was the world's greatest all-round competitor. Right from the start he imposed both a points and a psychological advantage over Hingsen. It was expected that Daley would show up better in the 100m but hardly to the tune of 128 points (10.51 to 11.01), but even more significant was that Daley easily surpassed Hingsen in the latter's specialist event, the long jump, with 7.80m. Daley then produced an outdoor personal best in the shot (15.44m) for an enormous three-event lead of 167 points. The decathlon consists of ten potential disasters, however, and although the result was not calamitous the high jump checked Daley's headlong progress. He managed only 2.03m, while Hingsen cleared 2.15m to narrow the gap to only 66 points. That was just the stimulus Daley needed and he reasserted himself by blazing round 400m in 47.11 to sleep on a 114 point lead.

Although well pleased with the day's work, Daley remarked that although "any chance of a world record is out of the question, I'm confident that I can keep it up and win the gold." Happily, he was right about winning the title … and equally happily he was quite wrong about the world record being out of reach. His first day score of 4549 might have been 83 points fewer than in Götzis but he hadn't bargained on a flawless second day. He didn't put a foot wrong as he ran 14.39 in the hurdles, spun the discus 45.48m, vaulted 5.00m and tossed the javelin 63.56m. His lead was now 237 points and he needed only to trot round the 1500m to make sure of the gold medal. He wanted that world record back, though, but he needed to run no slower than 4:26.5, a formidable target. He was up to the challenge and a gutsy 63.5 last lap stopped the clock at 4:23.71 for the grand total of 8743 points (8774 on the 1984 tables) to Hingsen's 8517. Daley thus became the first man in any event ever to hold Olympic, Commonwealth and European titles plus being world record holder.

For the first time in twenty years I didn't attend the European Championships. My niece Sandra Sharon married Ian Hardman just before the meeting (sons Michael and Daniel would be born in 1984 and 1986) and I left it to Barry Trowbridge and Brian Smyth to report in detail from Athens although I did provide a day-by-day summary of the main action for AW. Instead I spent the week assisting the ever genial Dickie Davies in the London Weekend TV studios, my fee approximating to a month's AW salary! To be fair to AW, though, I did receive a decent Christmas bonus in recognition of the circulation topping 22,000 for the first time and my Commonwealth Games trip to Brisbane was a very expensive undertaking, with my air tickets costing more than £1000 (something over £3000 in today's money) together with four weeks of hotel accommodation.

Jules Verne's immortal creation, Phileas Fogg, used a hot air balloon, trains and ships to circumnavigate the globe in 80 days in order to win a wager. My trip, solely by air, took 28 days and may have been less hazardous but to me was equally exciting. I had already been lucky enough to have travelled all over Europe plus forays into Asia and North, Central and South America, but this trip fulfilled a lifelong ambition to journey clean around the world. Flying Qantas, the first leg was from Heathrow to Singapore (24 hour stopover) via Bahrain, followed by another long flight to Brisbane, which would be my home for the next 12 nights. Following the Games, I flew on to the magical city of Sydney for two days, highlights of which included enjoying the hospitality of journalist and former sprint ace Mike Agostini, touring Sydney Opera House and taking a cruise around the harbour, bumping into newly crowned 1500m champion Chris Boxer on board. Having by then airmailed the last segment of my AW report, I was now free to treat the rest of the trip as a holiday.

I spent five idyllic days in Honolulu, one of those places I had always wanted to visit but never thought it would be possible, and then I renewed acquaintance with delightful San Francisco where I was captivated by the newly released *ET* and vowed to take Pat to see the film as soon as it reached British screens. From there I was due to move on to Los Angeles for three days but by then I was beginning to feel homesick and so I rescheduled my flight to travel direct from San Francisco to my final American destination, Miami, and another family reunion. I had left Heathrow at 9.30 pm on September 25 and landed back there at 6.45 am on October 23. It was my longest ever trip abroad and it had been a fabulous experience.

The Commonwealth Games have a special warm, homely atmosphere not always apparent at other major championships, and Brisbane was no exception. The "Friendly Games" lived up to their name. They were conducted in a marvellous spirit before spectators who, though they understandably cheered everything that moved in the green and gold of Australia, were always sporting and enthusiastic towards competitors of all nations. I forged new long lasting friendships with knowledgeable Aussie journalists Mike Hurst and Len Johnson, as well as Mike Agostini, himself a Commonwealth Games 100y champion in 1954 representing Trinidad.

Although athletes from the British Isles did not match the record gold medal tally (19) of Edmonton, their total of 46 medals topped the 1978 haul by six. Steve Cram (3:42.37 1500m with a 50.9 last lap to beat John Walker and Mike Boit), Keith Connor (a heavily wind assisted triple jump of 17.81m compared to the world low altitude best of 17.56m) and Daley Thompson (8410 decathlon, 8424 on current tables) completed magnificent European and Commonwealth doubles, while other UK winners were Dave Moorcroft (5000m), Bob Weir (hammer), the men's 4x400m team, Chris Boxer (1500m), Shirley Strong (100m hurdles), Judy Oakes (shot) and the women's 4x100m team for England; Steve Barry (30km walk) and Kirsty McDermott, later Wade (800m) for Wales; Meg Ritchie (discus) for Scotland; while the 200m resulted in a dead heat between Mike McFarlane of England and Scotland's Allan Wells who had previously won the 100m ahead of a 20 year-old Canadian by the name of Ben Johnson.

Some weeks later, as BAWA chairman, I had the pleasure for a second time of presenting Kathy Smallwood, who finished a very close second to Jamaican superstar Merlene Ottey over 200m and was in the victorious relay team, with the female athlete of the year award. Kathy now held the UK records in all three sprints (11.10, 22.13 and 50.46). Daley was the men's winner but predictably he was unavailable to collect his trophy (his relations with certain journalists were none too cordial) and so his 'Aunt' Doreen (Doreen Rayment) stood in for him.

The overwhelming success of the first London Marathon led to the second edition leap-frogging over New York to become the world's biggest marathon with 16,350 official starters from the staggering total of 90,000 hopeful applicants. The race would continue to grow: there were more than 20,000 starters in 1987, 30,000 in 1998 and a record 39,406 finishers in 2017 ... when almost 254,000 applied for entry. There were British winners in both races in 1982: Hugh Jones came home in 2:09:24, the fastest ever time in Britain, while Joyce Smith set her sixth UK marathon record with 2:29:43, finishing well over a mile clear of her nearest opponent. One of the aims of the London Marathon was to improve the standard of British marathoners, and that was the case initially. In 1981 51 Britons dipped under 2:20; in 1983 the figure was a staggering 102. But in recent years, for all the mass participation, the standard has dropped alarmingly. Just 12 managed to break 2:20 in 2017.

We produced a record 72 page issue of AW to preview the 1982 London, including – fortuitously – details of Hugh Jones' performances and training in our long running "Who's Who" series. In my report I tried to convey the atmosphere of the race. *There can be few events as universally appealing as the London Marathon. For the spectator it offers not only a genuine sporting contest but also the most fascinating of processions – far more enthralling, amusing, moving and essentially **human** a spectacle than any Lord Mayor's Show, Easter Parade or State ceremonial. The purists might object, but I'm all for the rich and stimulating mixture which is the London Marathon. The leading finishers were marvellous ... but so too were the unsung thousands who strove so valiantly to achieve their own less exalted but no less worthy goals.*

At Boston on a hot day in April, Alberto Salazar was involved in one of the greatest duels in marathon history, finishing just two seconds ahead of Dick Beardsley in 2:08:51 – the first time two men had broken 2:09 in the same race.

Salazar literally ran himself into the ground to defeat Beardsley. He was rushed away for medical treatment, suffering from hypothermia. Instead of the average 98.6°F temperature, Salazar's was down to an abnormal 88°, and he was suffering from acute dehydration. It was the second time Salazar had finished a race in a serious state: four years ago he collapsed at the end of a 7 mile road race with a temperature of 105° (that was hyperthermia) and received the Last Rites.

At a London press conference in May, Salazar explained that the problem in Boston was because he didn't drink enough during the race. Asked how fast he could run, he replied: "I think I could run 2:05." In fact, he would never break 2:08. Is 2 hours possible? "No one has yet run that fast for the half marathon. I don't see it in the next 100 years." Salazar, who was born in Cuba but taken by his family to the USA as an infant, began coaching in the 1990s and two of his athletes, Mo Farah and Galen Rupp, finished first and second in the 2012 Olympic 10,000m. He remains a highly successful but controversial figure.

Salazar admitted in 1981 that he made his living from running, and the first British athlete to take advantage of the new international rules which permitted athletes to advertise and endorse products without prejudicing their eligibility was Seb Coe, who appeared in TV commercials. The arrangement was that Seb would be able to draw expenses against the fee, after 15% had been retained by the BAAB to plough back into the sport, and the rest would be held in a trust fund awaiting his retirement from active athletics. In fact, Seb continued in competition until 1990, by which time there were no restrictions on athletes' earnings. Steve Ovett quickly followed Seb in benefiting from the new rules.

News of Seb's TV commercials deal was the final item in my 160-page book, published in April by AW, entitled *The Coe & Ovett File*. This was literally a scissors and paste job, reprinting the various AW reports, articles and interviews relating to the pair from 1972 onwards. As I wrote in the introduction: "You can trace – step by step, as it happened – just how these remarkable young men developed from promising schoolboys into the great runners we know today." Like *The Ghost Runner* the book generated gratifying reviews but as only a limited number of copies were printed it too has become a collector's item.

I was sorry to say goodbye to two of my favourite athletes, Rosemary and Trevor Wright, who emigrated to New Zealand, the land of Rose's birth, with their two young daughters, Emma and Jessica. The latter became a New Zealand international as Jessica Ruthe; she did not inherit her mum's track speed but was faster at the marathon with 2:39:12 in 2007. Her husband, Ben Ruthe, was himself a 2:22:11 marathoner, a year after running 4:00.17 for the mile in 2006. Before they left I visited Rose and Trevor at their Wolverhampton home and the interview appeared in March. Although she set an age-13 440y best of 60.3 Rose said "I don't think I ever had a lot of talent really; I used to train very hard." Some of her training time trials were sensational. " I think I did about 84 seconds for 600m," she recalled. "I went through 400 in 54 and then slowed and ran the last 200 in 30." Although she had the potential to go well under two minutes for 800m, her best was 2:00.15 at the 1972 Olympics, which broke Ann Packer's UK (and former world) record of 2:01.1. She still resented the late Jim Coote's remark after she ran 2:05.4 for 880y at the 1966 Commonwealth Games that she would never improve because she was too small (1.57m or 5ft 2in). "After Munich I went up to him and said 'See, I've done it.' It stuck in my mind all those years."

Jonathan Edwards' achievements were so overwhelming that it is largely forgotten that Britain had another world-beating triple jumper several years before him. He was Keith Connor, born in Anguilla but who was brought over to Britain aged six. The 1978 Commonwealth Games champion, he set a world indoor record of 17.31m off a shortened run-up in 1981 while in June 1982, competing at high altitude in Provo, Utah he broke every record in the book except for the world mark of 17.89m with a jump of 17.57m in windless conditions. Four days later and some 5000 miles away, Connor thrilled the fans at an international meeting at Crystal Palace.

The technically and physically demanding discipline known as the triple jump has always been a fascinating event to watch but, until the advent of the 'Willie Banks Road Show', it rarely attracted the attention due to it. The extrovert American law student has changed all that and Willie's showmanship and infectious enthusiasm, allied to his formidable talent (he has, at 17.56m, jumped further than anyone else in history at or near sea level), has caused otherwise track-orientated fans to discover the subtle delights of the triple. He personally involves the spectators – inviting them to clap in rhythm as he prepares and takes his run up – and they simply love it. Banks came to Crystal Palace and won over another adoring public. He may not have won, and he

HATES to lose, but he paved the way for the greatest, noisiest and friendliest triple jump competition ever staged in Britain.

In the second round Banks touched down at 17.00m to break the UK all-comers' record, but Connor's immediate response, despite only just getting his foot on the board, was a winning jump of 17.30m. Keith went on that season to capture the European championship with 17.29m and retain his Commonwealth Games title with two monster, if wind assisted, jumps of 17.72m and 17.81m.

Connor and Banks weren't the only horizontal jumpers to excel. Stan Eales, a great friend of Dick Bank's and an equally good W. C. Fields mimic, was now our US correspondent (all too briefly as he died in 1984 aged 63) and reported: "Fabulous Carl Lewis is closing in on the record of Bob Beamon. At Indianapolis on July 24 he had a great jump of 8.76m (second longest in history) with virtually no wind. Carl started out with two very long fouls – both, he claims, farther than Beamon's world record of 8.90m. His third trial was a run through. On his fourth jump he thought he had a 30ft (9.14m) jump but was called for a foul. Lewis claimed that he did not put a mark on the plasticine but the official ruled that his toe had gone past the board and waved the red flag. His fifth jump was the 8.76m and his final jump was an 8.55m."

Two significant developments at the end of the year. The IAAF Congress approved by 366 votes to 16 (only the USSR and Romania with eight votes apiece opposed the motion) the establishment of trust funds, a system which was already in operation in certain countries like Britain and the USA. Rather more revolutionary was the decision to allow appearance money in designated international spectaculars. The vote was 386 to 24, the dissenters being the USSR and Romania again, together with Poland – all communist countries pursuing their own agenda. In Britain the AGM of the AAA voted overwhelmingly in favour of Cardiff AAC's motion "that athletics in the UK be administered by a single governing body". Only four out of more than 100 delegates voted against, but we had to wait until 1991 before that intention became a reality.

18. WORLD CHAMPIONSHIPS ARE A HIT (1983)

Both Seb Coe, with world indoor bests at 800m (1:44.91) and 1000m (2:18.58), and Steve Ovett, who reclaimed the world 1500m record with 3:30.77, had their moments in 1983 but were outshone by Steve Cram, who added the world 1500m title in Helsinki to his European and Commonwealth golds and for a second year topped the world 800m list.

Little went right for Coe during the outdoor season. In June he suffered his first defeat at 1500m since 1976 when Spain's José-Luis González beat him in Paris (3:34.84 to 3:35.17). "To lose a race at this stage of the season isn't a catastrophe," Seb remarked, and indeed it did appear to be just a hiccup for in Oslo he won the 800m in 1:43.80, the world's fastest time for two years. With Ovett taking the 1500m in a brisk 3:33.81, ahead of González, at the same meeting, the 'old firm' was back in business.

However, both encountered problems in July. Seb experienced another shock defeat at 1500m, this time at Crystal Palace at the hands of Dragan Zdravkovic of what was then Yugoslavia. As in Paris, Seb crumbled in the finishing straight to lose 3:35.28 to 3:36.03 although he was running with a swollen ankle. The AAA Championships saw both in trouble. Coe was well beaten by the USA's Steve Scott, 3:51.56 to 3:52.93, in a special mile race (his first loss at the distance for seven years), while Ovett – for the second time that summer – pulled up with cramp in the 800m, costing him a place in Britain's team in that event at the World Championships. A disastrous month for Seb ended with yet another defeat, this time at 800m, as he wound up fourth (1:45.31) in a race at Gateshead won by Cram (his first ever victory over Coe) in 1:45.03. Next day he withdrew from the team for Helsinki on medical advice. Suffering from a lymph gland infection he was told by a medical specialist that he must stop all exercise until he had undergone full hospital tests. It turned out that he was suffering from a rare infection, glandular toxoplasmosis, and his consultant said Seb was "quite debilitated" by the infection, adding "I'm surprised that anyone in his condition could have done as well as he did."

Rather like Coe in the Moscow Olympic 800m, Ovett made a mess of one of the supreme tests of his career: in his case the world 1500m championship. Whether Ovett would have beaten Cram had he positioned himself better can be argued, but Ovett ("it was the worst race of my life ... I ran like a goon") was eighth and boxed in at the bell and despite a 51.9 last lap he could finish no higher than fourth (3:42.34) while Cram took the gold in 3:41.59. However, all was not lost. With the major prize lost, he set his sights on breaking his world 1500m record of 3:31.36. As preparation he won a 3:50.49 mile, defeating the USA's former South African Sydney Maree by 25 metres in Oslo, while in Brussels he clocked his fastest 800m time (1:45.25) for four years. Spurred on by the news that Maree had broken his world record with 3:31.24, Steve announced he was confident of regaining his property in Koblenz, but the first lap was much too slow and he ended up with a 3:32.95 timing. It was at Rieti on September 4 that he emerged successful. Paced through 400m in 54.17 and 800m in 1:51.67, he took over at the kilometre to pass 1200m in 2:49.14 and stopped the timer at 3:30.77. He declared that if it hadn't been so windy he might have broken the 3:30 barrier. His season ended five days later at Crystal Palace at the sold out IAC/Coca-Cola Meeting.

Here was the world 1500m champion Steve Cram against the world 1500m record holder Steve Ovett, two men at the peak of their powers prepared to race it out. Enormous credit must go to both the Steves, firstly for rewarding the faithful British public with the opportunity to witness the mile race of the year, and secondly for the pulse-quickening spectacle they put on. After all the manufactured paced record attempts and mutual non-aggression pacts that have tended to distort the point of top class athletics, this was a refreshing return to the basics of the sport.

Agreeing to ignore the pacemakers, Cram – his every stride shadowed by Ovett – reached halfway in a shade under 1:59 more than 15m behind the leader. At the three-quarters Jack Buckner was a metre ahead of Cram (2:59.0) with Ovett another couple of metres behind. It was Cram who launched his strike first, from as far out as 350m. Ovett responded immediately but that initial two-metre advantage was to prove all important.

With both men running flat out that gap remained constant ... along the back straight and around the final turns. With the 17,000 enthralled spectators screaming their heads off, Ovett strove mightily to catch his man, but Cram is not world champion for nothing. He kept his head and his stride and still Ovett could make no impression as they sped down the finishing straight. Only in the last ten metres did Cram slacken ever so slightly and Ovett, with a desperate lunge at the line, reduced the deficit to a metre. The times were academic, but at 3:52.56 and 3:52.71 they were remarkable in view of the slow early pace. Cram covered the last 400m in 53.4; Ovett was perhaps a tenth of a second faster.

"I can die a happy man now," beamed Ken Finding, the hard working, long suffering but ever patient press officer at all the big Crystal Palace meetings. After eight years of politely asking Steve Ovett if he would care to come up to the Press Box and being equally courteously turned down, he succeeded at last at the Coke meeting. The two Steves faced the Press together, Ovett making the point "that Great Britain has got the world record holder, the Olympic champion and the world champion – and they are three different blokes!" Could a clean sweep for Britain in the 1984 Olympic 1500m be envisaged? Ovett: "No, I can't visualise anything like that at all." Cram: "Athletics is such an up and down thing that to ask all three of us to arrive on August 3 or whatever it is in Los Angeles – all three of us in top condition so that we can finish first, second and third – is a bit ridiculous." In fact, as we shall see in the next chapter, it wasn't that ridiculous as Britain did fill first and second places, and had Ovett not been ill a clean sweep might have been possible.

Cram could look back on a fabulous season, despite having lost six weeks of training through first a groin injury and then a twisted ankle. Over a two month period starting on July 18 he went unbeaten over all distances from

179

800m to 2 miles, picking up personal bests at 800m (1:43.61 with Peter Elliott second in his best time of 1:43.98), 1500m (3:31.66), 3000m (7:43.1) and 2 miles (8:14.93). The icing on the cake was that world title victory in Helsinki, proving to any remaining doubters that he was indeed one hell of a racer. It was funereal in the early stages with a first lap of 64.98 (slower than Mary Decker in the women's final!) and an 800m time of 2:07.73.

It was Brendan Foster who provided the key to Cram's ultimate success. Bren had heard that the speedy Moroccan, Said Aouita, intended to make a break 500m from home and passed on the message. Right on schedule, Aouita bolted ahead, and Cram was ready and able to respond. At the bell, reached in 2:49.4, Aouita led Cram by a stride. Aouita was operating at a furious pace as he tried all he knew to drop his opponent. His third 400 took just 54.78 and he continued to increase the pace along the final back straight, but Cram was not at all troubled and with a little less than 200 to go his giant strides carried him past the gallant North African. Steve Scott had his work cut out overtaking Aouita in the final few metres of the race, never mind catching Cram. Forget the winning time of 3:41.59; the significant figures related to the end of the race ... 1:49.0 last 800, 52.0 400, 26.0 200. John Walker, ninth in the final, proved a good prophet. Before the race, he had said: "The man with the best head out of all of us is Cram. He's a tough young guy who just goes out and does his own thing, supremely confident and unconcerned about others. If he's in front on Sunday with 100m to go, God help the rest of us."

Britain's other Helsinki hero was Daley Thompson.

The man cannot countenance defeat (it's five years since he last lost a decathlon), yet he put himself on the line in Helsinki in facing up to a gruelling contest with a superbly trained and in-form world record holder Jürgen Hingsen while he himself could not possibly have been at his very best after struggling to recover in time from injury. Actually, it was touch and go right up to the last moment whether Daley would take part but, after being snubbed by Hingsen and Siggy Wentz in the athletes' village, he couldn't wait to take them on! Having made the decision to compete, Daley knew he had to strike a psychological blow by piling up the points in his strong early events. That he did, and the opposition never quite recovered.

A 10.60 100m and 7.88m long jump gave him a 114 point advantage over Hingsen, who narrowed it to 96 after the shot but it grew again to 121 after the high jump. There was little in it at 400m and the first day scores were 4486 for Daley, 4366 for Hingsen. After finishing just inches behind his German rival in the hurdles, Daley picked up unexpected bonus points in the discus and by vaulting 5.10m, equalling his best ever in a decathlon, his lead stretched to 188 points. Following the javelin the scores were 8075 to 7913. Hingsen's world record score of 8779 was safe – but so too was Daley's gold medal as Hingsen would have needed to finish some 22 sec ahead in the 1500m. With a final score of 8666 (8714 on the 1984 tables) Daley won by 105 points. "It went better than expected," he reflected. "I thought it would be won with 8500. The 100m decided the whole event. If one event had gone badly I would have stopped. I wasn't fully fit and my concentration was bad because of my groin injury. The pain became especially bad during the last two events. That must be the best yet; the awful weather was worth another 150 to 200 points."

Fatima Whitbread went so agonisingly close to being crowned world javelin champion. Having been suffering from tonsillitis, climbing out of her sickbed only six days earlier, Fatima made heavy weather of the qualifying round, squeezing into the final in 12th and last place with 60.96m whereas Finland's world record holder Tiina Lillak threw 69.16m. However, Fatima let rip with her opening throw in the final.

It was a beauty, the 50,000 spectators watching mesmerised as it sailed on and on, finally dipping earthwards just short of the 70m line. A roar of approval erupted from the stands, repeated when the distance of 69.14m flashed on the indicator board. As for Fatima, she was in seventh heaven. Maybe not quite the best throw of her life, but what a time to unload a potential winner! Everyone had assumed Lillak, whose world record stood at 74.76m, would clear the 70m line but after five rounds her best was 67.46m.

And so we came to the point where the hopes and aspirations of a whole nation, it seemed, rested on the result of one final throw. The tension was unbearable if you were Finnish, or if you were British. Lillak had used up five attempts without ever coming dangerously close. And yet ... there was something in the atmosphere that pervaded the stadium that spelt doom to Fatima's aspirations. The collective bated breath as Lillak picked up her javelin, the wave of sound that accompanied her as she made her approach run, building into a crescendo as the spear left her hand. The crowd willed a winning throw, and they got it ... 70.82m! It was an emotional moment, one's joy at sharing the Finns' elation tempered by the realisation of how shattering a blow that must have been to Fatima. Of course, second place in the World Championships is a fantastic performance, one of which she can be so very proud, but it's a tough way to lose.

Those IAAF World Championships proved a huge success. The 1980 Olympics in Moscow had been devalued because of the boycott led by the USA, and it was widely anticipated that the Soviet bloc would retaliate by shunning the 1984 Games in Los Angeles, so this was a welcome competitive opportunity for all of the world's top athletes. The standard was higher than at any Olympics, the number of countries represented (153) easily outstripping any previous international gathering. The total paid attendance was over 320,000, while an immense number of televiewers throughout the world caught the athletics bug as the dramas of the week were played out on their screens.

What a feast of athletics was provided! For my money, it was better than any Olympic Games – for we had all the advantages of the Olympics in terms of seeing the greatest athletes in the world but without the distractions and hassles of the Games. Great athletics, centre stage, for an entire week. Who could ask for more?

The stars? These inaugural Championships will forever be associated with the names of Carl Lewis, a triple gold medallist who could probably have won a fourth title had he gone also for the 200m, and Jarmila Kratochvilová, the iron woman of the track who attempted – and achieved – a double that on paper looked impossible. We shall also remember Ed Moses, Daley Thompson and Mary Decker as among the supreme champions, while Helsinki '83 and Tiina Lillak will always be inextricably linked. There were so many happy moments to savour, but there was sadness too. Alberto Juantorena [800m], Sara Simeoni [high jump], Evelyn Ashford [100m] and Krzsysztof Wesolowski [steeplechase] were among the athletes carried off on a stretcher, and injuries generally appeared to be more prevalent than at other major championships. The British team acquitted itself with honour. Seven medals were gained and five UK records were broken, four of them in the women's events.

Actually, Britain had another world champion that year, for in San Diego in December Wendy Sly won the IAAF's inaugural women's 10km road championship.

Lewis's first victory came in the 100m where the USA completed a clean sweep of the medals, something that hadn't been accomplished at the Olympics since 1912. After trailing Emmit King for nearly 70m he unleashed all that awesome power at his command. It's probably an optical illusion the way Lewis appears to accelerate towards the end of a race, for he must actually be *decelerating less* than his opponents at that stage after hitting peak speed of 40km/25 mph between 50 and 60m. Whatever, by the finishing line he was fully a metre and a half clear of runner-up Calvin Smith, the world record holder with 9.93 at altitude, in 10.07. Two days later, minutes after anchoring the US to a 4x100m relay semi-final win in 38.50, he produced a winning long jump of 8.55m at his first attempt. Following a pass in the second round and 8.42m in the third he decided he was safe enough and retired from the contest in order to rest for a momentous relay final just over an hour later.

The team of King, Willie Gault, Smith (who went on to win the 200m title) and Lewis smashed through the 38 sec barrier with a world record time of 37.86. Gault, who had placed third in the 110m hurdles, later became more famous – and much richer – as an American football wide receiver and was a member of the Chicago Bears team which won the Super Bowl in 1985. A contemporary football star was Renaldo "Skeets" Nehemiah, who in 1981 became the first man to break 13 seconds for the high hurdles. The following year he signed a contract with the San Francisco 49ers as a wide receiver and was part of the team which won the Super Bowl in 1984. What a talent he was: a 10.24/20.37 sprinter, without specialised training he ran 44.3 for a 400m relay leg. Even Ed Moses might have been troubled had he ever tried the 400m hurdles.

Talking of Moses, he continued to reign supreme. He had to wait seven long years for a second global title as politics cost him the chance defending his Olympic laurels in 1980. Undefeated for six years and owner of 17 of the 20 fastest ever times, he won by over a second in 47.50.

Impressive as the statistics are, they don't compare to the thrill of seeing the master practising his art. Still the only man to have perfected the technique of striding thirteens all the way, and with no obvious signs of straining, he was as ever a joy to watch. It was a devastating display, yet he might have been only a hairsbreadth away from disaster, for he finished the race with the laces of his left shoe flapping loose. His crushing victory reinforced his status as one of the greatest athletes (in any event) who has ever lived – and what an inspiration he is. An outspoken critic of the use of drugs in sport, Ed is living proof that it is still possible to reach the dizziest heights without recourse to cheating. Long may he prosper.

He was certainly prospering financially as according to figures published in *USA Today* he earned $457,500 in 1983. He did better still in 1984 with $617,000, but Carl Lewis topped that with an estimated $783,000. These sums had to be channelled through trust funds, but the days of what passed for amateurism among elite athletes had gone at last.

Kratochvilová, the immensely strong Czech of peasant stock who after all these years still holds the world record for 800m and ranks second of all time at 400m behind Marita Koch, has long been the centre of controversy. What she achieved in Helsinki was deemed 'impossible'. With Koch opting to go for the short sprints, winning the 200m after finishing second in the 100m, Kratochvilová had decided to concentrate just on the 400m ... until in her final tune-up meeting she set a world 800m record of 1:53.28. The timetable made it impractical to double up, but that didn't deter her. On August 7 she eased through the heats of both events. Next day she ran a 52.40 400m quarter-final and 1:59.58 semi. Crunch day was the day after that when she won her 400m semi in 51.08 and the World 800m title in 1:54.68, the third quickest ever time ... within the space of 35 minutes! In fact, the highly respected Czech journalist Jan Popper revealed that her recovery interval from the time she left the track after her 400m until her return for the 800m final was 24¼ minutes, during which time she received a massage. Her 800m time would have been faster still but as a near novice at the distance she covered many metres extra by running much of the race in lanes 2 and 3 to avoid the risk of a collision. The question then was would her performance in the 400m final next day (August 10) be affected. The answer proved to be 'not at all'. Utilising all her considerable strength, she reached the finish in the stupendous time of 47.99 to smash Koch's world record of 48.16. Still she hadn't finished, for on August 13 she ran in the heats of the 4x400m relay and next day anchored the Czech team to second place behind the GDR with a leg timed at 47.75!

Another double winner was Mary Decker. *Nothing in this marvellous week's athletics gave this observer more pleasure than the success of Mary Decker. It seems a lifetime ago (ten years actually) that little 14 year-old Mary, pigtails flying, was astonishing the world with her performances at 800m. What, we wondered, would she be doing as an adult? Happily, and what a tribute it is to her determination, courage and enthusiasm, Mary has come through innumerable setbacks over the years to emerge as the world's outstanding female middle distance runner. We all knew before Helsinki she could run terrific times at a variety of distances against little or no opposition; what we didn't know was how she was going to cope against the previously all-conquering Eastern Europeans.*

The 3000m proved it was still possible in a major championship to run the legs off your rivals from the front. Mary threw down the gauntlet, leading from the very start and challenging others in the star-studded field to keep up with her. The last lap was a thriller as the American held off every challenge to win in 8:34.62, with Wendy Sly excelling herself by finishing fifth in the Commonwealth record time of 8:37.06. Four days later Mary showed that although a natural front runner she also possessed a formidable kick. It looked all over in the 1500m when the USSR's Zamira Zaitseva opened up a five metre lead around the final turn. For about 100m the gap remained constant, then slowly but inexorably Zaitseva's lead began to shrink. Zaitseva was now the prey, Decker the hunter. Less than 10m from the end Mary passed her rival, a 60.2 last lap carrying her to victory in 4:00.90. Wendy Sly picked up another meritorious fifth place, her 4:04.14 ranking her second on the UK all-time list behind Chris Benning.

Of all the meetings I have been privileged to attend, Helsinki 1983 rates among the very best. There was so much else to write about, including Ireland's Eamonn Coghlan's win in the 5000m, the unexpected pole vault triumph by a 19 year-old Sergey Bubka, the long jump gold medal won by the even younger Heike Daute (later Drechsler), and appropriately the great Grete Waitz becoming the first global champion in the women's marathon. Looking back at the results now, one notices that Ben Johnson failed to reach the 100m final, Alberto Salazar was the 17th and last finisher in the 10,000m final, Trevor Wright represented New Zealand in the marathon, one George Barber of Canada no-heighted in the pole vault (his son Shawnacy would win the 2015 world title), Florence Griffith (in her pre-Flo Jo days) placed fourth in the 200m behind Marita Koch, Merlene Ottey and Kathy Cook, and the future all-time great of heptathlon, Jackie Joyner, had to pull out injured after the first day.

The boom in marathon running was such that AW's issue of April 16, incorporating the London Marathon preview, ran to 120 pages or 40 pages more than our previous biggest edition. It included a report on a classic Rotterdam Marathon in which Rob de Castella prevailed by just two seconds over Carlos Lopes in 2:08:37 with the previously undefeated Alberto Salazar fifth, and a profile of Grete Waitz, who would go on to win in London in a world best of 2:25:29. The feature reminded readers that when interviewed at the end of 1974, the year she became European 1500m bronze medallist, Grete was asked whether she would be moving up to 3000m. "No," she replied. "I've raced the distance once and thought it far too long." Ironic, considering she was to develop into the world's greatest marathon and cross country runner! The very next day after London, Joan Benoit demolished the world best with 2:22:43 in Boston although that point to point course falls outside the criteria demanded of official records.

My first full-length interview that year was with Kathy and Garry Cook at their home near Cannock in March. The tall (1.80m or 5ft 11in), leggy Kathy had her best seasons still to come but had already made history by becoming the first in over half a century to hold UK records at 100m, 200m and 400m, and had won medals at the 1980 Olympics and the Commonwealth Games and European Championships of 1978 and 1982. But for the East Germans her medal haul would have been even more impressive. Asked if she had a complex about running against them, she replied: "They are a bit daunting when you see them warming up; they seem so in control and professional, and no sign of nerves. But once you're on the track they are opponents the same as anyone else although you always know they are going to be in top form for the big occasion." Garry, with his 46.0 400m speed (45.0 in a relay), was the fastest of Britain's leading 800m runners and was a member of England's winning 4x400m team at the 1982 Commonwealth Games. Kathy may have more medals but Garry still had bragging rights as the only world record holder (4x800m) in the marriage!

The other interview was with Fatima Whitbread, whose intense rivalry with Tessa Sanderson to determine who was Britain's (or possibly even the world's) number one javelin thrower was bubbling along nicely. It was a bit like Coe v Ovett with the difference that they actually competed against each other. Tessa, five years the elder, held sway until 1982. Early that year she fell heavily during an indoor relay, rupturing her achilles tendon and breaking the bone in her throwing elbow. She was on crutches for four months and for the first time since 1973 she did not top the UK list, Fatima improving to 66.98m. Fatima beat Tessa for the first time in 19 meetings since 1977 at the 1983 UK Championships, and that was just the spur Tessa needed as the following weekend she produced her first throw of over 70m. Later she improved the Commonwealth record to 73.58m for third place on the world all-time list, but at the World Championships it was of course Fatima who went so close to victory. Tessa placed fourth with 64.76m, "a good result" in her estimation as she was still suffering the effects of that indoor injury and a few days later she underwent further surgery on both legs.

Fatima, the adopted daughter of national javelin coach and former British international Margaret Whitbread, became the first British thrower to win a European Junior title (1979) and it was in 1981 that, after both she and Tessa had experienced a disastrous Olympics, she broke into world class with a throw of 65.82m. When Tessa returned to the fray in 1983 Fatima was in no mood to revert to being the British second string and although she could not match Tessa's 70m-plus throws she herself improved to 69.54m prior to Helsinki and completed a remarkable season with victory in the European Cup at Crystal Palace with 69.04m. The only other home winners were Allan Wells in the 200m, Steve Cram in the 1500m and the men's 4x400m team.

Fast (11.9 100m in training) as well as strong, Fatima reflected: "It's been a marvellous season and I can't have asked for much more, especially as I had so many problems before Helsinki with tonsillitis." Margaret elaborated: "Fatima still had a high temperature when we arrived [in Helsinki], her throat was very swollen and she had a persistent headache. On that basis she needed to be kept in a quiet environment, and we were very grateful to Eddie Kulukundis for making it possible for her to stay in a very quiet hotel." Sir Eddie, as he became, was a wonderful benefactor, financially assisting dozens of athletes to help realise their potential. I first met him, a very large man in a very small plane from Copenhagen to Malmö prior to the 1979 European Cup semi-final, and he was to become a major influence in my career, of which more anon. How important, I asked Fatima, was throwing over 70m? "It's got to be just a stepping stone now, although this year it was a target. Having four times thrown over 69, next year 70 is no longer a barrier. Next year there's a chance of going through 72, 73 ... the sky's the limit. What I want to do is step on that rostrum in Los Angeles for the gold medal with a notice proclaiming 'DONE WITHOUT DRUGS'. That would be an inspiration for all those who haven't stooped to taking drugs."

The drugs problem was an issue I returned to time and again in print ... and continue to do so well over 30 years later. Following completion of drug testing procedures in Helsinki the IAAF announced there had been no positive findings. In an editorial I wrote that the press release might create the impression that the drugs problem in athletics has been solved.

Unfortunately, all the Helsinki doping tests prove is that certain athletes (and their coaches and/or medical advisers) from countries where drug-taking is rife are becoming more careful and sophisticated. Ed Moses reckons that half the athletes taking part in this year's USA Championships were using some form of drugs and he criticised the US governing body (TAC) for not establishing doping control at the meeting. John Walker told a New Zealand newspaper that many competitors in Helsinki were taking drugs. "It scares me to know what is going on in athletics. Once it used to be the hulking heavyweights in the field events who pumped themselves with anabolic steroids and ephedrine stimulants. Now drug taking is widespread ... sprinters, middle distance runners and high and long jumpers are living dangerously on a life of drugs. Many believe drug taking is the easy way to the top."

Another issue that troubled me was that in too many events the current world record was achieved at high altitude.

I must confess to being less than thrilled at the news of the world 100m records set by Calvin Smith (9.93) and Evelyn Ashford (10.79) at the 7000ft-plus altitude of Colorado Springs. It is apparent that the time has come for the IAAF to reappraise its policy regarding the ratification of world records. With timing now recorded to $1/100^{th}$ of a second and scrupulous regard taken of wind readings (anything over 2.00m/sec disqualifies a record) it is anomalous that a blind eye is turned by the IAAF towards the huge advantage incurred by competing at altitude in certain events. To be fair, two sets of records should be created for those events. The twin records where applicable would thus read: 100m: 9.93A Calvin Smith; 9.97 Carl Lewis; 200m: 19.72A Pietro Mennea; 19.75 Lewis; 400m: 43.86A Lee Evans; 44.26 Alberto Juantorena; Long Jump: 8.90mA Bob Beamon; 8.79m Lewis; Triple Jump: 17.89mA Joao Carlos de Oliveira; 17.56m Willie Banks; 4x400m: 2:56.16A USA; 2:58.65 USA; women's

100m: 10.79A Evelyn Ashford; 10.81 Marlies Göhr. I thought it was a sound argument but the IAAF never have recognised separate altitude (1000m elevation and upwards) and 'sea level' records.

On the home front it was a particularly difficult year for Pat as early in the year her mum, who had suffered a stroke in 1974, contracted pneumonia and nearly died. She recovered, but looking after her was becoming increasingly stressful and physically exhausting for Pat and an arrangement was made for a local hospital to accommodate Bella on a regular basis. Pat was interviewed by presenter Pamela Armstrong on a Channel 4 programme, *Well Being*, on the difficulties of caring for an elderly mentally infirm relative, broadcast on BBC radio and contributed a most moving account ("A Carer's Eye View") of her experiences in a book, *Caring*, edited by Anna Briggs and Judith Oliver. We did manage to snatch a holiday in May, driving to Bournemouth and catching a plane for the short flight to Jersey for a week's recuperation. Plucking up her courage, this was Pat's first flight since our honeymoon in Tenerife ten years earlier. Little did she know that her next would be all the way to Florida!

19. OLYMPICS IN LA LA LAND (1984)

It was the best job in the world as far as I was concerned, but I had decided that at the end of the 1984 season I would step down after 16 years in the hot seat as editor of AW. I gave my reasons in the September 15 issue.

From next month I shall leave the day-to-day editing and responsibility for AW in other, capable, hands and instead devote myself to the writing side. In addition to continuing to report on major events I intend to broaden the scope of overseas coverage in these pages and contribute more feature material than has hitherto proved possible. I am excited by this fresh challenge and am confident that the new arrangements will improve the range, quality and topicality of the magazine.

As from October 1 I would be succeeded as editor by Barry Trowbridge, who had been a tower of strength as my right hand man for the past five years, while the equally industrious Brian Smyth would become the new assistant editor. I would continue as consultant editor, working more from home instead of commuting from North London to Kent three times a week as had been my custom for many years.

As athletics has grown and flourished over the years, so too has AW ... and that has posed a personal dilemma. For, as the magazine has expanded from 32 pages weekly when I took over to today's 64-80 pages, while the circulation has nearly trebled [the audited circulation for 1984 was 24,850], *so too the volume of work has grown correspondingly. Being responsible not only for producing so many more pages each week (even with the excellent support afforded me by Barry and Brian) but also for contributing so much of the material published in AW has – to be realistic – become too much for one man. Therefore, in fairness to my own health (and sanity?), and that of my patiently-suffering wife Pat, I have decided to rationalise my work schedule. My stint as editor has been incredibly fulfilling and enjoyable for me, and it has been an honour to serve the wonderful community of athletics in some small way. I would venture to suggest that no periodical in Britain has a more loyal and stimulating circle of readers than AW, and it has been a privilege to have edited the past 870-odd issues for you. I look forward to maintaining that happy association for many more years to come.*

The big event of course was the Olympics in Los Angeles, although unfortunately the Games, like Moscow in 1980, would suffer grievously from a politically inspired boycott. In May I wrote:

The decision of the Soviet Union and its followers not to attend the Los Angeles Games represents a crushing, and possibly fatal, blow to the Olympic movement, for this summer's Games will be diminished to an even greater degree than were the Moscow Olympics. Within a week of the announcement that the USSR would be boycotting, the GDR, Bulgaria and Czechoslovakia followed suit, with every likelihood of the rest of Eastern Europe (except for Romania) joining them. The probability of withdrawal by such countries within the Soviet sphere of influence as Cuba and Ethiopia will be a further blow. For the first time, there will be as many potential medallists absent as will be present. Take the 1983 World Championships results as a guide. Athletes from the Eastern bloc collected 28 medals out of the 72 available in the men's events (16 out of 24 in the field events) and no fewer than 34 – if we don't count Romania – out of 51 in the women's events.

In my book *Olympic Track & Field History* I summed up the 1984 edition in these terms.

On the positive side, the Games attracted the greatest number of countries (121) ever to be represented in the Olympic athletics events, the crowds in the Memorial Coliseum were huge (well over a million in aggregate), the organisation was generally commendable and a handsome profit was made. Many scintillating performances were recorded and there was much stimulating competition. Nevertheless, there was no getting away from the fact that the communist bloc boycott did cast a giant shadow over the proceedings. Stars like Carl Lewis, Joaquim Cruz, Seb Coe, Said Aouita, Carlos Lopes, Ed Moses and Daley Thompson would have won their titles regardless, but the absence of Soviet and East German athletes in particular did devalue the worth of several events, including practically the whole of the women's programme.

Lewis was the individual star of the Games, emulating Jesse Owens' 1936 achievement by winning the 100m, 200m, long jump and 4x100m relay. He was most nervous about his first event, the 100m, but he need not have worried as with a time of 9.99 he won by over two metres, the widest margin in Olympic 100m history, with future arch-rival Ben Johnson placing third. It made good sense to him that after running a pair of 200m heats in the morning and not wishing to take chances with a slightly sore leg, he did not take the full complement of long jumps. He settled for two, an opener of 8.54m and a foul, but when it became evident that he was sitting out the rest of the contest many fans gave vent to their feelings by booing him as he walked up to receive the second of his gold medals. In winning his third, Lewis produced what was probably the finest ever 200m up until that time. When Pietro Mennea set his world record of 19.72 he enjoyed the twin advantages of high altitude and a following wind close to the allowable limit. In clocking 19.80 Lewis encountered a headwind in the straight. He completed his momentous Games by anchoring the US relay team to a world record 37.83. Competing in his 13th event in eight days, he was timed at 8.94 from a flying start.

There were three gold medals for Britain and it was Tessa Sanderson who led the way.

Was there ever such a contrast in one athlete's fortunes at successive Olympic Games? In Moscow four years ago Tessa was considered a good bet for either gold or silver. She had a rare victory over Ruth Fuchs to her credit and a month before the Games had fallen only 26cm short of the East German's world record with a throw of 69.70m. Apparently paralysed by some form of stage fright, unable to withstand the pressure, she was unable to do anything else than go through the motions during the qualifying rounds. Reduced to a best throw of 49.74m, she was tearfully eliminated – along with Fatima

Whitbread and Tiina Lillak amongst others. The plan [in LA] was the same as Fatima's in Helsinki ... get a great throw in the first round and let the others sweat it out. Tessa unleashed a beauty: an Olympic record of 69.56m. The rest of the competition could not have been more tense, particularly as Tiina went uncomfortably close in the second round with 69.00m. As round succeeded round, it became evident that the Finnish world champion had had to retire injured after that second throw and so it was down just to Fatima.

Her best proved to be 67.14m, so Britain finished first and third – a brilliant achievement. Tessa, Britain's first Olympic women's champion since Mary Peters (her team manager) in 1972, became the first Briton – male or female – to win an Olympic throwing title.

Back in those pre-computer and email days, I had to type out my copy and as AW couldn't afford telex or fax facilities I needed to airmail my reports and results at the end of each day. Aware that from the moment the javelin event ended I had only about an hour before the last mail could be posted, and it was vital that the report arrive at the printers in time to be fitted into our first results issue, I was under immense pressure to write a 600+ word account before the deadline. I managed it but with only a minute or two to spare!

An entry worthy of inclusion in any collection of famous last words. Back in June, the 2.00m (almost 6ft 7in), 100kg (220lb) Jürgen Hingsen broke his own world decathlon record with 8798 points and boasted: "Daley can't affect me any more. I'm immune to his tricks now and strong as never before." That was just the sort of talk to motivate the Briton even more, and Daley started as he intended to continue by speeding to a 10.44 100m into the wind, leaving his German rival nearly five metres and 122 points behind. Daley increased that margin to 164 points after long jumping a legal lifetime best of 8.01m. The shot saw another nail being driven into Hingsen's coffin as in one of his strongest events he gained only a derisory nine points as Daley came up with his longest put (15.72m) in a decathlon. Hingsen made up some substantial ground in the high jump where Daley cleared 2.03m but the latter ran a storming 400m in 46.97 for a world best first day score of 4633, 114 points ahead of Hingsen.

Hingsen lost a good chance to narrow that deficit significantly in the hurdles but finished only 0.05 ahead of his rival who clocked 14.34 despite hitting nine of the hurdles. It was in the discus that Daley displayed the full extent of his competitiveness. After two rounds Hingsen had thrown a personal best of 50.82m while Daley had reached no more than 41.24m. If Daley didn't come up with a decent last throw, Hingsen would move into a lead of 68 points. The sign of a supreme champion, Daley got his act together when the chips were down ... and the discus sailed out to 46.56m, barely a metre below his best ever. He, and we, could breathe again. After seven events Daley held a 32 point lead, but it could still go either way as the pair were fairly evenly matched as pole vaulters and Hingsen was on paper the better javelin thrower and 1500m runner. The vault proved decisive as Hingsen, bothered by stomach trouble, cleared only 4.50m (his best was 5.10m), whereas Daley made 5.00m. He was now 152 points clear and unless he failed to record a javelin mark or collapsed during the 1500m a second Olympic title was assured. With his morale now at rock bottom, Hingsen threw some seven metres below his best, while a relaxed Daley boosted his lead to 209 points with a massive score of 8241. He needed to clock 4:34.8 to break the world record, well within his capabilities, but he was content to enjoy his victory without killing himself in the process and was timed at 4:35.00. With a final score of 8797, 124 points clear, he appeared to have fallen one point short of the world record. However, later close re-examination by Bob Sparks of the photo finish showed he had run 14.33, not 14.34. That was worth an extra point so he equalled the record. No he didn't, because when the IAAF's new scoring tables came into effect on April 1 1985, Hingsen's 8798 was converted to 8832 while Daley's 8798 turned into 8847. Trust Daley to get the upper hand over his rival yet again!

While Daley performed in ten events on August 8 and 9, his great friend Seb Coe raced seven times between August 3 and 11. He opened with a 1:45.71 800m heat, which was faster than his silver medal winning time in Moscow, and survived a near fall in the second round to finish third in 1:46.75. Peter Elliott and Steve Ovett also qualified in 1:45.49 and 1:45.72, season's bests for both, but unhappily it transpired that Elliott was suffering from a foot injury and was unable to line up for the semis. Joaquim Cruz won the first semi in a South American record of 1:43.82 with Ovett just making it through in fourth place in 1:44.81, his fastest for six years. Coe took the other semi with a controlled run in 1:45.51.

There are silver medals and silver medals. When Coe was beaten by Ovett in Moscow his silver medal was of no value to him for he – and almost everyone else – had assumed he would take the gold. This time, he said, "I'm happy to get the silver medal in what was a great field. I was beaten by a guy who was younger and stronger. He is a supreme champion worthy of an Olympic crown." He was referring to 21 year-old Cruz, whose winning time was 1:43.00, the third fastest ever time behind Coe's world records of 1:41.73 and 1:42.33. The tall, powerfully built Brazilian struck hard at the start of the finishing straight and before Coe could respond he had built a five metre lead which he maintained to the finish. Coe's time was 1:43.64. Saddest sight of the race was Ovett walking in. He was taken away on a stretcher and admitted to hospital where he was given intravenous feeding to increase his fluid supply. It was diagnosed that he was suffering from dehydration, broncho-spasms and hyperventilation. "My respiratory system wasn't working," he explained, "so what happened was it was like taking the fuel away from an engine. I just gave out. Coming around the last 200 it was difficult for me to just keep upright."

Coe had two days rest before lining up for the 1500m heats, happy to cruise round in 3:45.30. Steve Cram won his heat in 3:40.33 and Ovett showed up, producing a 51.5 last lap to take his heat in much the slowest time of 3:49.23. In the semis next day Coe qualified in third place in 3:35.81 after easing up a little too drastically. In the other semi, Cram won in his season's best of 3:36.30. Ovett, obviously a sick man yet determined to give his all after two days in hospital, got through in fourth place in 3:36.55. Again he was in some distress at the finish and was taken to the Olympic medical centre. His actions may have been unwise from a medical standpoint, but they won him the admiration of all. And so to the final a day later.

Coe's run at the Coliseum, jam packed with over 90,000 spectators, was an absolute gem. He was always in control of the situation and his final kick was of such power that no matter what Said Aouita may say ("If I'd run in the 1500 I'd have won that") I would seriously doubt that any man on earth could have beaten him. Seb was followed in by Steve Cram, clearly not yet at his very best following injury, and for a moment on the last lap the vision of a British clean-sweep loomed large – until poor, brave Steve Ovett was forced to drop out with 350 to go while in fourth place. Steve Scott ensured the race would be a good, honest one with victory going to the strongest. That Seb should emerge as the most durable and inspired as well as the fleetest should come as no surprise to those who recall the events of Moscow; he may look frail but he has immense physical resources at his command. Seb's final time of 3:32.53 was barely half a second outside his fastest ever. Seb made his move with 200 to go, neatly slipping between Cram (whose own strike he pre-empted at that moment) and Spain's José Abascal. He kicked hard around the turn, opening up a 3-4m margin over Cram, and then drew away so smoothly along the straight. While Cram's head rolled wildly as he toiled in pursuit, Coe never lost form for an instant as he completed the final lap of 53.25, although he felt that "the last 20 paces seemed to take a lifetime." Cram, too, was magnificent. Despite all his problems this season he beat everyone else out of sight to record 3:33.40.

Seb rated this victory as even more satisfying than the one in Moscow. There had been controversy surrounding his selection ahead of Peter Elliott, who had beaten him at the AAA Championships, and some of the Press had written him off. "This year has been as much a mental comeback as anything, and it's a bit of a dream come true. This time last year I had just come out of hospital and didn't run from July to Christmas. This took me back to 1981. It's the best I've felt over 1500m since then." Both he and Cram paid tribute to Ovett's bravery. Ovett said he had felt well through the first 900m, but then he began experiencing acute pains in his chest and down one of his arms. "It's a long way to go before the finish and if I were to push it any harder I could be in very serious problems, so I decided to bale out as it were." He was carried away on a stretcher although he did not need to be taken to hospital this time.

In terms of medals won, the British team with 16 (three gold, seven silver, six bronze) surpassed Tokyo's 12 from 1964, although that total was influenced by the communist bloc boycott. In addition to those gained by Coe and Cram, there were silver medals for Mike McLeod in the 10,000m (originally placed third he was promoted when runner-up Martti Vainio of Finland was disqualified after a positive drugs test), Dave Ottley in the javelin, the 4x400m relay team of Kriss Akabusi, Garry Cook, Todd Bennett and Phil Brown whose time of 2:59.13 was a European and Commonwealth record, Shirley Strong in the 100m hurdles and Wendy Sly in that still talked about

3000m featuring Mary Decker and Zola Budd, of which more later. The bronze medallists in addition to Fatima were Charlie Spedding in the marathon, Keith Connor in the triple jump, Kathy Cook in the 400m with a Commonwealth record of 49.43, Sue Hearnshaw in the long jump and the women's 4x100m relay team of Simmone Jacobs, Cook, Bev Callender and Heather Oakes. Kathy's 400m time stood as the UK record until 2013, while her 22.10 for fourth in the 200m survived until 2015!

There was no getting away from Zola Budd, who must have generated a record amount of media attention. AW readers were alerted in January that a tiny barefoot 17 year-old had smashed Mary Decker's world record for 5000m with 15:01.83 in very windy conditions but it wouldn't be ratified as she was South African and her country was not affiliated to the IAAF. Someone at the *Daily Mail* came up with the supposedly bright idea of bringing her over to Britain, arrange for her to receive UK citizenship (which, thanks to the newspaper's influence, was granted in just ten days rather than the normal year or two), and render her eligible to compete in the Olympics where she would stand a chance of winning a gold medal wearing a British vest. It was a cynical, commercial project aimed at boosting the paper's circulation.

Zola's ties with the UK were tenuous, the link being that, as she had a British-born grandfather, her father was able to take up British nationality. English was not her first language, she was painfully shy and whatever her private thoughts might have been at the time (a political science student, she said she had never heard of Nelson Mandela) she would not speak out against apartheid, provoking demonstrations wherever she raced in Britain. She was a lost, unhappy young woman from the time she arrived, the only positive being she now had the opportunity to develop as a phenomenal runner. In view of the *Daily Mail*'s ceaseless campaign in recent years against certain athletes from the USA and Caribbean becoming eligible to compete for Britain, usually on the basis of parentage, it was ironic that they were responsible for the first of what they would describe disparagingly as 'plastic Brits'.

In my first editorial on the subject, in mid-April, I wrote that Zola, 'British' or not, *remains a symbol and product of South African society and athletics, and as such wider political considerations come into play. There is a danger that the Union Jack might be used merely as a flag of convenience, and so until such time as it can be seen that Zola intends to make this country her real home and not just a base, and that will take more than just the couple of months from now until Olympic selection date, the British Board ought not to consider her for international competition. Unfair? Maybe. But not as unfair as it would be to the genuine British athletes who have been working so hard for what may be their one and only chance of Olympic selection.*

I quoted Jane Furniss, who had placed fifth in the recent World Cross Country Championships. "I feel very strongly that Budd should serve a year qualification period. That is the period laid down in the rules if you change clubs in Britain, so I think it should be the same if you change countries. Before Budd came here I thought I had a good chance of going to the Olympics. I will be upset if my plans are wrecked. I don't think it is fair that she is being considered." Wendy Sly, whose own place in the Olympic team was pretty secure, told Neil Allen of *The Evening Standard* that she would consider boycotting the Olympic Trials in protest. "It's got to be unfair and so discouraging if Zola Budd can come in at such a late juncture, get a British passport at incredibly short notice and take a place in our team." Later in April I traced her career to date.

There is no doubt that she is the most phenomenally gifted teenage middle/long distance runner in women's athletics history. Zola doesn't turn 18 until May 26, yet she has already run 5000m faster than any other woman (15:01.83), set world junior bests at 1500m (4:01.83) and 3000m (8:37.5), and also displayed enviable speed (2:00.9 800m) and endurance (32:20 10km at altitude). Why is she so good so young? The seeming frailty of her physique is one of the most important reasons. Inside that tiny frame (1.58m or 5ft 2in, 39kg or 86lb) are remarkably well developed heart and lungs – the consequence perhaps of being born and raised in Bloemfontein, which stands at an altitude of 1392m – and her power/weight ratio must be formidable.

Zola didn't set any personal bests on the track during the summer of 1984 but she did clock 31:43 for 10km on the road in Oslo not too far behind Ingrid Kristiansen and Grete Waitz. Kristiansen, who would win the London Marathon a week later in a European record of 2:24:26, described Budd as "unbelievable. She looks like a 12 year-old, runs like a 25 year-old and is only 17." The same day, over in Eugene, Mary Decker won a race at the same distance in 31:38. The Budd v Decker hype was about to begin in earnest. The American, though, held the upper hand in times as well as experience. Prior to the Olympics, Mary ran 3:59.19 for 1500m and 8:34.91 for 3000m, while Zola's bests were 4:04.39 (winning the UK title) and 8:40.22 for victory in the Olympic Trials.

A world pole vault record of 5.90m by Sergey Bubka was clearly the highlight of the Peugeot/Talbot Games at Crystal Palace but much more media attention was centred on Zola whose time of 5:33.15 for the rarely contested 2000m event broke the world best held by Maricica Puica. Three weeks later, in Eugene, Decker ran 5:32.7, although that paled in comparison to the race next day in Moscow when Tatyana Kazankina – who, of course, would be absent from LA – clocked 5:28.72. The Russian made bigger headlines later in the year when she was banned for 18 months for refusing to submit to doping control at a meeting in Paris a week after setting a world 3000m record of 8:22.62 in what was then Leningrad.

I set the scene for the eagerly awaited 3000m final.

Mary Decker had waited a long time for her Olympic chance. The 1972 Games came too soon for her; in 1976 she was out of the sport injured; in 1980 she was ready to do battle in Moscow but her government wasn't. Now as double world champion and America's sporting sweetheart, she was geared up for the climactic moment of her brilliant yet chequered running career ... Olympic victory before her adoring fans, leading to a commercial bonanza of

Navratilova-like proportions. There was only one threat to the realisation of that dream, she and coach Dick Brown figured: Romania's world cross country champion Maricica Puica. The consensus of informed opinion agreed that despite all the hype surrounding her, Zola Budd could not realistically be expected to vie with Decker and Puica at this early stage of her international career. She was rated a bronze medal contender along with Wendy Sly and Germany's Brigitte Kraus.

Mary's race plan, as revealed by Dick Brown, was based on a final time of 8:29. In the event, Mary allowed the pace to drop quite considerably – she reached 1500 in 4:18.6 – and yet reacted somewhat truculently when Zola ('the barefoot contestant', as she was dubbed in the States) moved in front early on in the fifth lap. There was a slight brush between them as they came out of the bend, but by the time the straight had been reached there was no disputing that Zola was established in front and although running very close to the outer edge of the inside lane, the pole position was hers. With only half the lane unoccupied, and bearing in mind also Zola's natural wide arm carriage, there was no room for anyone to creep up with impunity on the inside. But Mary insisted on attempting to come through on Zola's nearside. At around the 1730m point, the inevitable happened: there was a collision.

Mary was out of the race. She fell onto the grass infield, sobbing from an accumulation of pain (she pulled a hip muscle), shock, anger and frustration. It was she who was responsible for her downfall but thousands of partisan spectators jumped to the conclusion that Zola was the athlete at fault and booed her as the race progressed. By 2000m the first three were 20m clear of their nearest pursuers: Zola, running in tears, led from Sly and Puica. With just under 600m to go Wendy took the lead and with a totally disheartened Zola slipping back approaching the bell (she would finish seventh) the race for gold was between the Briton and the Romanian.

Running a brilliant race and confounding those who had so little faith in her – and that includes those officials who failed to pre-select her for the Games months ago – Wendy pulled out all the stops in her quest for victory. But Puica, always a tough customer, could not be shaken. She ripped past Wendy along the final back straight to win by 20m in 8:35.96. Wendy's terrific run for the silver medal in 8:39.47, the second fastest time of her career, will have come as a shock only to those who have failed to take stock of her previous achievements.

Regrettably, because of all the publicity devoted to the Budd and Decker incident, Wendy's Olympic medal – the first by a female British middle distance runner since Ann Packer in 1964 – was largely overlooked.

I spent two weeks in Los Angeles and, before the Games opened, Stan Greenberg and I accompanied Eddie Kulukundis on a trip to Point Loma, near San Diego, where the British team was training. I also visited the iconic Hollywood Bowl, with which I was so familiar from old Hollywood musicals, while Stan and I relived other movie memories at Universal Studios.

My Life in Athletics

With the Olympics being staged in the Coliseum, it was rather appropriate that a British hero of the 1932 Games in that same stadium should be remembered and honoured. Early in the year I arranged to visit Winnie Hampson, who was keen to show and lend me the meticulously detailed diary kept by her late husband, Tom, from 52 years earlier. As I wrote in my introductory paragraph to the feature, whatever the result in the 1984 Olympic 800m no one could surpass Tom Hampson's achievement as he not only won the gold medal but in so doing he set a world record with the barrier-breaking time of 1:49.7. An advocate of even pace running, he judged his race perfectly by covering the laps in 54.8 (nearly 20m behind the impetuous leader) and 54.9!

The journey to LA was hardly ideal preparation for the race of his life. It took 12 days ... sailing the Atlantic and then travelling over 3000 miles by train, mainly in stifling hot conditions. It was during that journey and in the days leading up to the big race that Tom kept the diary, from which I published numerous excerpts. It was a simply fascinating, informative and deeply moving document. "Just sit back," I implored readers, "imagine the year is 1932 and you are a young, somewhat impoverished schoolteacher – head over heels in love [with his then fiancée Winnie] and on his way to meet his athletic destiny."

His entry for July 26, the day after arriving in LA, mentions the bad rate when changing £2 for $7.06 [those were the days!]. Next day, while writing to Winnie suggesting they get married early in September, he pauses to meet Hollywood stars Douglas Fairbanks, Snr and Jnr. On July 30 he takes part in an "awe inspiring" opening ceremony and writes emotionally of his love for Winnie. "Oh God, if she were here! Would her heart swell with pride, almost to bursting, as mine did. A knight of olden time could not be more keen to fight for his lady than I am." August 2 (the day of the final): "I ate only a moderate lunch – boiled fish, dry toast, egg custard and a cup of tea – and kept to my usual practice of smoking a cigarette after the meal. Briefly, I calculated that 1:50 could make certain of the race. Therefore, believing as I do in level pace running, I wanted to run 55 over the first 400m and hope for the same over the last lap." That he did and more, running two whole seconds faster than he had ever done before. "That I, of all people, should be the first to accomplish what has hitherto been regarded as a physical impossibility – lowering 1:50 for 800m. Small credit to me, too. I have had 'the breaks' all along the line, my greatest being my association with Winnie. I can truly say that but for her I would never have got where I am. A world beater must, like a great artist, be inspired – and what greater inspiration can anyone have than the love of such a beautiful, kind, gentle, sweet, good creature."

Tom and Winnie did marry that year, just, on December 31 and they had two sons. He gave up teaching to serve in the RAF from 1935 to 1945, rising to the rank of Squadron Leader (acting Wing Commander). After the War he worked in social welfare, was among the first ten honorary AAA coaches to be appointed and was a press steward at the 1948 Olympics. Sadly, he died when only 57 in 1965.

196

Financial considerations won out in negotiations over who would be awarded the contract to televise the major AAA and BAAB meetings. The BBC offered £9 million for exclusive rights for the next five years but ITV and Channel 4's bid of £10.5 million, a four-fold increase over the previous BBC payment, won the day. The decision provoked a torrent of readers' letters and Jimmy Green, still the consultant director of AW, wrote: "May I pay a tribute to David Coleman and Ron Pickering for the great work they have done over the years and the great pleasure they have given athletics followers when reporting major events at home and abroad." In a footnote, I agreed with Jimmy and gave some insight into what's required of a commentator.

As someone who has sat beside commentators of both BBC and ITV, feeding them information, I can testify to the astonishing expertise and professionalism of the top men. The commentator has a very difficult, nerve-wracking job, requiring him to listen (to the producer's instructions over headphones), watch (both what is happening in front of him and what is appearing on the TV monitor) and talk intelligibly and authoritatively – simultaneously and usually in a live situation with no possibility of correcting himself. I salute them.

As I wrote when he was posthumously inducted into the England Athletics Hall of Fame in 2009, *Ron Pickering was the renaissance man of British athletics. He was a coach, broadcaster, writer, motivator, visionary, administrator ... a force of nature, a communicator par excellence, an inspiration. Perhaps even more important than anything else was his role as the conscience and guardian of the sport. An insightful and independent thinker, his was considered by many to be the authoritative voice of athletics.*

Believing it to be a document which merited wider dissemination, I reprinted Ron's view of athletics which had first been published in the NUTS Annual, *British Athletics 1984*. He praised many aspects of the sport but was particularly damning in his criticism of doping and how it was being tackled. He wrote: "Our sport flounders on a wide range of moral issues. Serious political intrusion, addiction to drugs, violence, total disregard of existing rules, cheating, cant, hypocrisy and total acceptance of double standards is merely an abbreviated list of our ailments. We ban the use of substances to enhance performances yet allow the practice of 'blood boosting' which is far more effective to that performance. We test for anabolic steroids yet we cannot test for the far more effective growth hormone or even natural testosterone where the side effects are far more serious. We failed to ban anabolic steroids for more than a decade, during which time dependence grew and the record books were re-written. When we catch the offenders we ban them not for life but for a period of 18 months, during which time they simply fortify themselves awaiting their return."

Another long-time friend and prominent crusader in the fight against performance enhancing drugs, Arthur Gold, was knighted in the New Year Honours for his services to athletics. The pre-war high jump international and highly qualified coach was serving his third term as president of the European

Athletic Association since 1976, having been honorary secretary of the BAAB from 1963 to 1977. The British athletics team leader at the 1968, 1972 and 1976 Olympics, he listed his recreations in *Who's Who* as "walking, talking, reading, weeding."

There was plenty of great action before and after the Olympics. Intrinsically superior even to Bob Beamon's altitude-assisted 8.90m with a friendly 2m/sec wind behind him was Carl Lewis's world indoor long jump best of 8.79m in New York's Madison Square Garden. Not only was that mark achieved at sea level and obviously wind free, but a short run-up (5 metres less than his normal 51m) and a couple of loose boards were distinctly unhelpful. He said afterwards "I think I can jump 30 feet (9.14m) and I think I have a great chance of winning four Olympic gold medals." Well, he was half right.

Richard Hymans, a British statistician whose knowledge of American track and field history is unsurpassed, had a wonderful time covering the US Olympic Trials in the Coliseum for AW. In his opinion, Lewis's 10.06 into a 2.2m/sec wind was "probably the finest 100m ever run". He also saw Lewis win the 200m in 19.86 after clocking 19.84 in a heat and the long jump with 8.71m, while his younger sister Carol was also a long jump winner with 6.89m. Mary Decker took the 3000m in 8:34.91 ("and looked capable of 8:25") but was narrowly beaten in the 1500m next day by Ruth Wysocki in 4:00.18. That prompted her to go for just one event at the Olympics, that fateful 3000m.

The always outstanding Weltklasse meeting in Zürich soon after the Games produced a great women's 100m in which gold medallist Evelyn Ashford not only defeated Marlies Göhr, who as an East German could not compete in LA, but lowered her world record to 10.76. Another Olympic champion, Joaquim Cruz, became the second man to break 1:43 for 800m with 1:42.34, a time surpassed only by Coe with 1:41.73 and 1:42.33. As for Coe, he ran his swiftest 1500m (3:32.39) for three years. Two days later, in Brussels, Cruz went close again with 1:42.41, and another two days after that, in Cologne, the Brazilian missed the record by a whisker with 1:41.77. Seb had intended running 2 miles at the IAC/Coca Cola meeting but a foot injury after Zürich forced him to end his season prematurely, and the race went to Tim Hutchings, fourth in the Olympic 5000m and destined to become one of the most experienced of all TV athletics commentators (primarily for Eurosport), in 8:19.46. Among all the world stars in action at this Crystal Palace meeting, who could possibly have predicted that the girl who finished ninth in the junior girls 800m in 2:22.56 would, 20 years later, become a double Olympic champion? It was Kelly Holmes.

Following the success of the *Coe & Ovett File*, Norman Barrett – who I had worked with on the multi-part *The Games* several years earlier – contacted me about collaborating on booklets reviewing the careers of Cram and Daley Thompson. Norman provided the narrative, linking it with reprints of reports from AW, plus statistics (by decathlon guru Alan Lindop in Daley's case), and the two booklets were published as part of a Virgin Profile series prior to the Olympics.

Before the year was out, there was an astonishing and unexpected development in the world of marathon running.

The eagerly awaited rematch between the Olympic champion and the world champion in the Chicago Marathon proved to be a close-run affair with Carlos Lopes finishing in 2:09:06 and Rob de Castella 2:09:09 ... but those two great runners were totally eclipsed by Britain's Steve Jones. The 29 year-old Welshman, contesting the second marathon of his career (and the first he has completed) ran out a sensational winner in a world's best of 2:08:05. He reportedly covered the final 10km in a staggering 29:39. Steve's previous main claim to fame was finishing third in this year's World Cross Country Championships. For several seasons he has been an international class track runner, but has fallen just short of the very highest level.

The marathon was the culmination of a six-week road racing tour of the USA during which he won three of his five races, netting something in excess of $100,000 – which is more than Corporal Jones had earned during his 11 years of service in the RAF.

Pat and I were also in America in October. Just six days after my final day as AW editor we flew off to Florida – a big and anxious leap of faith for Pat, whose only flight in more than a decade had been that short hop across to Jersey. This journey from Heathrow to Orlando, with a brief stop in Miami, covered over 4000 miles. All went well and we spent four idyllic days exploring enchanting Walt Disney World and futuristic Epcot. Having rented a car, and driving in the States for the first time, I allowed bags of time for the 230-odd mile journey to Miami as we had a cruise ship to catch. Only it proved to be more like 250-plus miles, for although we had made good time when we actually caught a distant sight of our ship in the Port of Miami we simply couldn't find the one road that led to the embarkation point at Dodge Island. With time slipping by, I found myself driving frantically in and out of downtown Miami. Eventually, aware by now that we could be too late, I pulled up in a park and asked another motorist if he could point us in the right direction. He did more than that. "Follow me", he said, and he guided us to our destination. After offering our profuse thanks we grabbed our luggage and, glowing and sweating respectively, Pat and I were the last people to board the magnificent S/S Emerald Seas.

The cruise was for four nights, bound for Nassau and Freeport in The Bahamas. All was fine as we stood on deck in the port for lifeboat drill, but once we moved into the swell of the ocean Pat realised she was not a natural-born sailor. Admittedly, it was the hurricane season and the captain had to cancel a scheduled stop at Little Stirrup Cay, one of the small islands en route, but we haven't cruised again. However, we enjoyed our brief visit to The Bahamas – and would return for a proper holiday some years later, but flying there – and when we returned to Miami we relaxed for almost a week in the Sunny Isles. We both loved Florida and its climate, and would spend many more vacations there.

20. STEVE CRAM'S RECORD SPREE (1985)

By the time of his 24th birthday in October 1984, Steve Cram had been crowned world, European and Commonwealth Games 1500m champion and Olympic silver medallist as runner-up to Seb Coe. That was impressive enough, but in 1985 he outshone the rest of the planet's athletes by setting three world records in the space of 19 days, becoming the first man to break through the 3:30 1500m barrier in the process. Having developed a useful turn of speed late in 1984 with a 47.6 400m relay leg, he displayed his stamina by winning the Northern cross country title over seven and a half miles in February 1985. If he could only keep free of injury it was clear that something special was on the cards that summer. There were no titles to be won, so fast times – and possibly world records – were the targets. In fact he wasn't free from injury, as he suffered from continuing calf problems, but he still managed to put together one of the greatest series of races in middle distance history. Here is how I summarised his season in *All-Time Greats of British Athletics*, a book of mine which was published in 2006:

On June 27 in Oslo he ran the third quickest ever 1500m with 3:31.34 and 19 days later in Nice he achieved immortality by becoming the first to duck under 3:30. Following splits of 55.5, 1:53.9 and 2:36.3 at the bell a last lap of under 54.5 was needed by Cram for the record. "I knew we were on a fast time and I just decided to go for it from the bell," he said. That early strike won him the race for as he strode past the 1200m mark in 2:49.66 he was at least six metres clear of Spain's José Luis González and Said Aouita, the Olympic 5000m champion. Realising his mistake, the Moroccan tore into second place and set about reducing the deficit. However, as Cram was winging along the back straight at 13.13 100m pace he gained nothing. Cram was still 5-6 metres up entering the final straight, but from then on Aouita closed with every stride. Unaware, until the last few metres, of what was happening behind him Cram sailed on serenely as Aouita pulled out all the stops in frenzied pursuit. At the line just 4/100ths separated them. Cram had run his last lap in 53.4 for a time of 3:29.67, Aouita around 52.7 for an African record of 3:29.71. Cram had broken the world record by the biggest margin since Jim Ryun in 1967.

That was just the start of a record blitz. In Oslo on July 27 Aouita opted for the 5000m, clipping 1/100th from Dave Moorcroft's world mark with 13:00.40, and barely had the excitement subsided than the runners were out for the Dream Mile. After a cautious start (57.5/1:54.9) Cram was always in a good position but Seb Coe ran with alarming lethargy in the early stages and had to run a very swift second quarter to get up to fifth place at halfway. However, the third quarter was so slow at 59.32 (2:53.14) that Coe was able to close up behind Cram (2:53.3), who at that stage thought the chance of a world record had gone. Cram accelerated at the bell, with Coe in pursuit, but when Cram fairly exploded around the final bends even Coe had no answer – not surprising since Cram covered that last 200m in 25.39! The final quarter took him 53.0 and his time of 3:46.32 (1:54.9 plus 1:51.5) took 1.01 sec from Coe's record.

Coe himself was passed just before the 1500m mark by González, who went on to finish in a Spanish record of 3:47.79 with Coe (3:49.22) next.

When Coe broke three world records in the space of 41 days in 1979 we doubted whether we would ever see the like again. Well, Cram surpassed that by setting three world records in just 19 days. In Budapest on August 4 he broke John Walker's 2000m mark (hand timed 4:51.4) with 4:51.39. Cram passed 400m in around 59.0 and 800m in 1:56.1 before running the second half of the race solo. He reached 1200m in 2:54.58 and 1600m in 3:53.95 (estimated 3:55.4 at the mile) prior to a last lap of 57.47. But for cold, windy weather back in Gateshead on August 9 he might have made it four world records in 24 days. Although Coe's greatly admired 1000m record of 2:12.18 (set in near perfect conditions in Oslo) survived – indeed, right through to 1999 – Cram's 2:12.85 was probably intrinsically the greater performance. A capacity crowd cheered on the local hero and if human warmth could only have cancelled out the cold and wind the 'Jarrow Arrow' would surely have scored another bullseye. Cram went for it, reaching 800m in 1:44.94. He now required a final 200m of 27.23, but it was too much to ask with the wind in his face along what must have seemed like an endless finishing straight. His final time was the second fastest ever. He completed a momentous season with a slow European Cup 1500m win notable only for the speed of his last 200m (24.7) and a scintillating 800m victory over Brazil's Olympic champion Joaquim Cruz in Zürich in a personal best of 1:42.88, making him the fourth fastest ever at the distance – not bad for someone who never considered himself to be an 800m runner!

At the end of August I travelled to Newcastle to interview Cram for AW and *Runner's World (USA)*. What, I asked him, was the key factor which enabled him to set those world records. "It's a combination of a lot of things. Because of the problems I had in 1984 with my calf, and because I felt that last year I'd run far too many miles in training and got very sluggish, I decided I would change that this year. I used to run 100 miles a week at times but I decided I would get back to running a lot more cross country and road races, kept the mileage down but run it at a good pace. The highest week's mileage I had all winter was 74, but most of the time I was running between 50 and 60 miles a week. However, I was running very, very hard. Much of it was done at five minutes mile pace." Did Aouita make a mistake in letting him get too far ahead on the last lap in the Nice 1500m? "I think he probably didn't expect me to go off so fast at the start of the last lap. Indeed, I was hoping that he was going to be in front of me as he was the one who was supposed to be going for the world record and I was pretty disappointed he wasn't there. Coming into the home straight I wasn't feeling all that relaxed but I wasn't tying up and as I could hear the crowd roaring I assumed it was for me against the clock. I didn't know they were roaring because Aouita was coming up! I knew I'd won, but it was close."

What gave him more satisfaction when winning the Dream Mile: breaking the record or beating Seb Coe for the first time at 1500m or mile? "Beating Seb, without question. In Nice I always had the record at the back of my mind, whereas in Oslo I couldn't have given it two hoots. The main thing was to win the race. I usually discuss my races beforehand with Bren [Brendan Foster] and he had to curb the little bit inside me which wanted to go out and try to run 3:44 or 3:45. I thought I was capable of that after Nice. But Bren is a little more cautious, and he advised me just to win the race because that's the most important thing. It was particularly pleasing to beat Seb more than anything, and the world record was an added bonus." How fast could he run a mile? "I reckon both Aouita and myself are capable of running about 3:44 and within a couple of years a time of 3:42 (1:50 plus 1:52) is feasible." In fact, Cram's record stood until 1993 when Noureddine Morceli of Algeria ran 3:44.39 (1:52.6 plus 1:51.8), while Morocco's Hicham El Guerrouj clocked 3:43.13 (1:51.6 plus 1:51.6) in 1999. The only other man to have bettered Steve's time is Noah Ngeny of Kenya, who ran 3:43.40 behind El Guerrouj. Would he willingly trade his records for an Olympic gold medal? "Definitely! If someone said to me 'You're guaranteed to win the gold medal in 1988 but you'll not win another race between now and then', that would be good enough for me. I would settle for that. The Olympics are the measure of anyone's career."

Steve's mile, run at 11.26 pm, was just one of three world records at a fabulous Bislett Games, my first visit to Oslo's famous stadium. The congenial strawberry party the day before the meeting provided one delicious feast; events in the stadium proved even more tasty. Like so many record breakers before him, Steve was inspired by Bislett. "You know you're going to run fast whenever you come to Oslo. The atmosphere is fantastic. It lifts you." The first world record, a particular delight for the capacity crowd of almost 20,000, came from Norway's own Ingrid Kristiansen. Already the world's fastest at 5000m (14:58.89) and marathon (2:21:06), she had set her sights on breaking 31 minutes for 10,000m and that she did, just, with 30:59.42. With her tortured facial expressions, she was the closest female version yet of Emil Zátopek, and like the Czech she had no need for pacemakers. The other record, Dave Moorcroft's 13:00.41 5000m, fell to Aouita, who cut it rather fine by clocking 13:00.40. It looked as though Dave's time would survive when the bell was reached by Sydney Maree in 12:05.96 but, pressed hard by the American, Aouita produced a remarkable last lap of 54.2 to achieve his goal although he had been contemplating a time of around 12:55. Cram, by the way, wasn't the only UK record breaker on this memorable evening as Derek Redmond, aged 19, ran a 44.93 400m and in the women's mile Kirsty McDermott (later Wade) pressed Mary Slaney (née Decker) all the way to register 4:19.41 behind the American's 4:19.18.

Mary, who married British discus thrower Richard Slaney in Eugene on New Year's Day, raced in Los Angeles 17 days after her wedding, her first track appearance since that dramatic Olympic 3000m. Her reaction to the Olympic incident and failure to make a public apology to Zola Budd had severely dented her previous popularity with the American public and she was greeted with some boos when introduced at the indoor meeting ... although she finished the race amidst ecstatic cheering as she smashed the world best for the rarely contested 2000m event. The following weekend, in New York, she failed in her bid to break her own world indoor mile record of 4:20.5 but her time of 4:22.01 was praiseworthy indeed as a few days earlier she had been knocked down on a training run by a man attempting to steal her jewellery, bruising her hip as well as the emotional trauma involved.

There were problems too for Zola. She made a successful indoor debut at the National Indoor Championships at RAF Cosford, having never even seen an indoor track until two days before the meeting. She won the 1500m by a distance and in her next race there she broke the UK 3000m record in a match against West Germany with the crowd stamping and cheering in appreciation. It was different the following weekend at the National Cross Country Championships in Birkenhead. My colleague Brian Smyth reported: "It was inevitable really. Pampered and protected since her appearance in Britain almost a year ago, Zola Budd's decision to race cross country this winter provided new opportunities for her political opponents to make themselves heard. Miss Budd was obstructed after three-quarters of the first lap, to the extent that she found herself unable to continue." Zola did not compete in the European Indoor Championships in Athens, where Todd Bennett won the 400m in a world indoor best of 45.56, opting instead to represent England at the World Cross Country Championships in Lisbon. Revelling in the grassland course and warm weather, barefoot Zola raced to victory by the huge margin of 23 seconds.

Covering the event for AW, *The Times* athletics correspondent Pat Butcher wrote: "The ambivalence towards Budd as a British athlete will still remain. Because, after her first major international title, she stopped over in England for two days before going back home to South Africa for at least 10 weeks. She is due to return to England in mid-June, which means that she has spent about five weeks in the country of her adoption since leaving for the Olympic Games last July. Considering the furore over her suspect translation from a South African to a British citizen, that is hardly the wisest of moves."

A major innovation that winter was the inaugural IAAF World Indoor Games, forerunner of the fully fledged World Indoor Championships. I reported from the magnificent Palais Omnisports de Paris-Bercy that on the credit side there was much keen competition among the athletes from 69 of the IAAF's member federations but the drawback was that the entry was embarrassingly thin in all too many events – just five runners in the women's 400m for example.

The meeting simply didn't justify four separate sessions, although one advantage accruing from the paucity of track races was that there was more time to appreciate the field events. One black mark in the presentation of the meeting, though, was the almost incessant playing of pop music over the loudspeakers. Whose bright idea was this? It was insulting to the athletes, as though they constituted merely a sideshow, and I wasn't alone among spectators in feeling growing irritation at this unwarranted distraction.

As I tap in those comments more than 30 years later, when very loud sounds purporting to be music are the norm at all major meetings, my views remain unchanged.

He wasn't selected for the World Indoors and was eliminated in his 200m heat at the European Indoors but as the AAA Indoor 200m champion in 1982 and 1983 we featured 25 year-old Linford Christie in the long-running "Who's Who" series. At that time his fastest marks were 10.44 and 21.0, and he may have wondered whether his best event might be the 400m, which he claimed to have run in 47.3 in 1980 when his best sprint times were merely 10.73 and 21.89. He stated his all-time goal was to win a medal in the 1988 Olympic 100m and intended competing until about 1990. He was emphatic in his views on doping: "Drugs is the main thing now, because more and more athletes are being caught and what they don't realise is that not only are they damaging their sport but their own health. So many people have made the top on natural ability and hard work before steroids; why not now? Can those athletes who are not caught ever feel good knowing that they are cheating themselves?"

Marathons continued to become bigger and faster.

The news of Carlos Lopes' sensational 2:07:12 the previous day [in Rotterdam, breaking Steve Jones' world best of 2:08:05] could have had a dampening effect on the London Marathon had not the two principals, Steve Jones and Charlie Spedding, not made it perfectly clear beforehand that the $50,000 bonus payable for a world best was not a motivating factor. Paramount was the competitive challenge to decide which of them could be considered the king of British marathon running. Would it be Jones, winner in Chicago last October in his only completed race at the distance in 2:08:05 ... or would it be the more experienced Spedding, winner of his first two marathons (Houston and London) and bronze medallist at the Olympics – all in the space of seven months? "It is fair to say that Steve must be the favourite and will be a hard man to beat," said Charlie the week before the race. "But I have to say that he will need to be at his best to win." Prophetic words, for in one of the greatest duels in British marathon history, Jones came out on top, but had to run at tremendous speed (1:03:32 for the second half!) to drop Spedding. Jones' winning margin was a little less than 100m as he registered the superb time of 2:08:16, easily the fastest ever recorded in Britain. Spedding set an 'English record' of 2:08:33.

The women's race in London was even more eventful as Ingrid Kristiansen clocked 2:21:06 to smash Joan Benoit's world best and earn $75,000 in prize and time bonus awards for her morning's work, not to mention undisclosed appearance money.

Steve Jones missed out on a $50,000 world record bonus by a second in Chicago in October but was still handsomely rewarded for winning in 2:07:13, which remains the British record to this day. He went out too fast, his halfway time being an unprecedented 61:43. I drove out to his home in South Wales the following month to interview him. At the time he was an air frame technician, with the rank of corporal, servicing Phantom jets at RAF St Athan, near Cardiff.

He was no teenage athletic prodigy; indeed from the age of 12 to 19 he was a heavy smoker and something of a drifter. It wasn't until he joined the RAF [at 18] that running seriously entered his life. At 29, after years of dedicated but less than world-beating international competition on the track, he completed his first marathon ... and set a world best. During the next 12 months he ran and won two more classic marathons. Despite his marathon triumphs, Steve refuses to consider himself a superstar; he sees himself as a club runner who has made good and who, one day, will be equally content to return to a less exalted level of competition. "I run with my head, my heart and my guts, because physically I don't think I've got a great deal of talent or ability," he says. What he does have in abundance is mental toughness, a balanced attitude to sport and life, and genuine modesty. He's a runner's runner if ever there was, and his success – and the way he has handled it – is an inspiration to all.

The other big interview I arranged that year was with Tessa Sanderson, who was living in Leeds at the time to be near her coach, Wilf Paish. Her Olympic gold medal had brought her fame but not so much in the way of fortune. Was she able to make ends meet? "At the moment the answer is just about. I'm out there grafting, doing the odd 150 quid TV job to pay for my mortgage and stuff like that. I've not had an endorsement so I have to run here and there. I would say I'm just about surviving, but my trust fund is going down drastically. I'm going to Hungary to train with Miklós Németh [the 1976 Olympic javelin champion], who played a vital part for me at the Olympic Games. Last year I went there five times for two weeks at a time, and I hope to do the same again this year, but all this has to be financed myself."

Her attitude to the drugs problem? "I've always said that I would never take stimulants or anabolic steroids or whatever these athletes are taking. I'm a woman first and one day I would like to have a baby and I'm not going to jeopardise my chances. I'm totally against drugs. I have accepted the majority of throwers in my event are on anabolic steroids although I can't really prove it. What really annoys me is that I don't think the tests are as random as they should be. If there is going to be testing they should do it to everybody. At every competition *the first three* should get done, otherwise they will never lick it." Was she upset that her UK record throws of 70.82m and 73.58m in 1983 received so little media attention? "I've never been so disappointed. I had been out of competition for something like 20 months, came back and threw a British record – and yet nobody wanted to know ... it was just Coe and Ovett, Coe and Ovett. It's the same thing that happened when Geoff Capes was on the scene. He never had the recognition I thought he should have had. I'd say it was Geoff and myself who really put British field events on the map."

Steve Cram didn't quite monopolise the headlines in Britain, for Zola Budd too was constantly in the news. Andy Norman, British Athletics' promotions officer, was instrumental in organising a 3000m re-match between Zola and Mary Slaney at the Crystal Palace but I was not impressed by the requirements of American television influencing not just the race but the whole meeting.

The Peugeot Talbot Games, Britain's first Grand Prix meeting, was to provide a glimpse of the shape of international athletics spectaculars of the future. It did ... and gave cause for deep concern. For all the publicity hype and astronomical sums of money involved, the end result fell far below what the public had the right to expect. There were many reasons why this meeting left the fans feeling short-changed, the principal one being that what could have been a first-rate one day fixture was stretched to two days primarily because of the lure of lots of American television money. The condition for that was that the women's 3000m, featuring Mary Slaney and Zola Budd, should be staged late on the Saturday night in order to be beamed live into American sports programmes. That request should have been politely rejected by the British Athletics Promotion Unit, but it wasn't, and at indecently short notice the Games, advertised and practically sold out as a Friday evening meeting, became a two day fixture with one of the main events switched to the second day. Scrutiny of Saturday's events shows the programme to have been decidedly on the thin side, and the public voted with their feet. The first evening was a 17,000 sell-out, the second attracted only a modest crowd – which just goes to show that you can't fool all the people all the time.

*That brings us neatly to the women's 3000. "This is the re-match the world has been waiting for", proclaimed Mr Norman. It wasn't; it was the re-match **television** was waiting for – and they were prepared to pay preposterous sums of money to stage manage the event. [Zola was paid $125,000, equivalent to about $340,000 today, and Mary $75,000!]. It's significant that the Romanian Federation was offered a derisory $2000 for the participation of Maricica Puica. No wonder the Romanians turned it down, although the Olympic champion had expressed a keen desire to compete. It had become increasingly obvious in recent weeks that Zola, who is not running as well as she was last year, was going to be out of her depth against Mary, who is rounding into probably the greatest form of her distinguished career – and so it turned out on the night. Slaney v Puica ... now that would be a **real** race.*

The race proved no contest. Mary led from the outset and her fierce pace gradually disposed of the opposition. She won in a brisk 8:32.91 with Zola trailing in fourth place (8:45.43) some 70m behind. "It's a relief this is all over," said Mary. Zola shared that sentiment: "I'm glad the race is all over. It has taken the pressure off and now we can enjoy the rest of the season like normal athletes." Except that Zola was not a 'normal athlete' because of her background. Three days later she was due to race in Edinburgh. Sensitive to the Scottish capital's image as host to the following year's Commonwealth Games, the Labour controlled Edinburgh City Council insisted on displaying banners proclaiming *Edinburgh – Against Apartheid* above and below the electronic scoreboard at Meadowbank Stadium. That led to Channel 4 cancelling their TV coverage on the grounds of being prohibited to show political advertising, and then in the mile race itself an anti-apartheid demonstrator ran across the track and sat in the path of the runners. He was dragged away by stewards but not before Zola neatly side-stepped the obstruction and went on to win in a personal best of 4:23.14. She was now on a roll, improving to 4:22.96 in Gateshead and her 3000m victory in 8:35.32 in Moscow helped the British women's team to its highest placing of third in the European Cup Final. She and Mary Slaney clashed over a mile in Zürich in a notable race which saw the American win in the world record time of 4:16.71 with Puica second in a European record of 4:17.33 and Zola third in a Commonwealth and UK record of 4:17.57. Five days later, at Crystal Palace on August 26, Zola achieved something really special.

A women's 5000m event was specially arranged to enable Ingrid Kristiansen to break her world record of 14:58.89. She duly obliged with a time of 14:57.43 ... although unfortunately from her point of view Zola Budd finished some 50m ahead! Zola produced her third scintillating run in nine days as she pulverised the world record with 14:48.07. Although Ingrid knew three days beforehand that Zola was likely to be running, there was no advance notice for the public – on security grounds. At 3000m Zola was timed at 8:50.44 – the sort of time she was struggling to achieve earlier in the season ... and there were still five laps to go. Ingrid, suffering from stitch, fell back and from here on it was a battle against the clock. Zola, running with marvellous fluidity, never flagged for a moment.

Four days after that, in Brussels, Zola broke through the 4 minute 1500m barrier with a Commonwealth record of 3:59.96 – although well beaten by Slaney (3:57.24) and Puica (3:57.73) – and she brought her season to an end at the IAAF Mobil Grand Prix final in Rome with yet another Commonwealth record of 8:28.83 for 3000m ... but again beaten by Slaney and Puica with their US and Romanian records of 8:25.83 and 8:27.83. That was Mary's tenth and final race of her European tour; she went undefeated and registered very fast times in all of them.

It had been quite a year for Slaney, who would give birth to a daughter in May 1986, but the female athlete of the year was Marita Koch, an East German with all that implied. She won the 200m at the World Indoor Games and European Indoor Championships as well as setting a world indoor 60m record of 7.04. Outdoors, she ran 10.97 for 100m, 21.78 for 200m and 48.97 in her only 400m of the season prior to the World Cup in Canberra in October. There she won the 200m in 21.90 into a headwind, anchored the successful GDR 4x400m relay team with a leg timed in 47.9 and chalked up the 16th world record of her career as she ran an incredible 47.60 400m, timed by her coach and future husband Wolfgang Meier as passing 200m in 22.4 and 300m in 34.1. Just how remarkable a time that is can be gauged from the fact that the quickest mark in the 21st century is 48.70 by US record holder Sanya Richards, while the world list in 2017 was headed by Olympic champion Shaunae Miller-Uibo with 49.46. On the men's side, apart from Cram, the major stars were Said Aouita with world records at 1500m (3:29.46) and 5000m (13:00.40) plus the second fastest ever mile of 3:46.92 and the third best ever 3000m of 7:32.94, and Sergey Bubka who opened the six metre era of pole vaulting with a clearance of exactly that height.

I was flattered to be invited by book publisher Peter Cowie, a distinguished film critic and historian who is also a massive athletics enthusiast, to assemble the third (1985) edition of the *International Running Guide*, previously edited by Cliff Temple. This was the sort of book I loved to compile and edit – primarily a comprehensive review of international athletics (not just running) in 1984, full of facts and figures, but with lots of stimulating reading elsewhere. Among the articles were an appreciation of Carl Lewis by Richard Hymans, Seb Coe's new challenge by David Miller, the African emergence by Pat Butcher, the history of women's marathon running by Cliff Temple and, appropriately in a book published by a cinema expert, a survey ("Hooray for Hollywood!") by Stan Greenberg of athletes who later made it to the silver screen. The indispensable Mark Shearman provided the photos, over 170 of them.

It was a notable year for AW. The circulation crept up to a record 24,873 – a figure in the realms of fantasy for any present day track and field magazine – and in December we produced a 40th anniversary edition with a new, more modern design. Seb Coe graced the cover and I contributed an overview of the career of the man I rated as Britain's greatest ever runner. Only Daley Thompson, I ventured, could compare as the country's greatest athlete. The article included quotes from an interview I conducted for *Runner's World* (USA) in August, and included Seb's opinion of his three main rivals at 1500m. On Steve Ovett: "I'll stick my neck out and say Steve is probably the most talented middle distance runner I've ever seen. Steve is a great runner and arguably the best stylist around. For courage there's nothing to compare with his comeback in the Olympic 1500 in Los Angeles." On Steve Cram: "Mentally he is as tough as anybody I've run against, he has a good running brain and has a nice ability to put things in perspective. I have to say he's as gracious in victory as he is in defeat, and I've a lot of time for Steve." On Said Aouita: "On balance he's got a greater range than anybody at the moment. He's a phenomenally talented athlete, and I enjoy watching someone who moves so well."

We received stacks of congratulatory messages, including one from *Prince Philip*, the BAAB president since 1952. A selection of other kind comments: *Daley Thompson*: "The only morning I get up before the crack of noon is on a Friday when the postman pops my AW through the door around 10 am." *John Holt* (IAAF general secretary): "The IAAF particularly values its objective and fair evaluation of meetings and championships, and its thoroughly lively and modern 'letters to the editor' section which over the years accurately reflects trends and opinions. On behalf of all our 174 member federations, may we express our gratitude to AW for their sterling work in the past and wish them continued success in the years to come." *Seb Coe*: "I remember at Loughborough the biggest queue in the library was always for AW. It was the bible. Also, at home, there was always a race on Friday morning to get to AW first!" *Sir Roger Bannister*: "I am glad to send my good wishes for the 40th anniversary of AW. Long may it continue." *Mary Peters*: "Sincere congratulations to AW on reaching its Ruby Anniversary. May you continue to flourish and serve the sport, which is so dear to my heart, for many years to come." *Ron Pickering*: "For much of my life you were my quiet private read but for the past 20 years or so you have been my life-line, my dictionary, Thesaurus and bible. Without AW or Stan Greenberg's accurate précis of it, I wouldn't even attempt to broadcast, or at least not for long." *David Coleman*: "Thanks, AW, for years of pleasure, education and essential information. And an affectionate 'thank you' to Jimmy Green, whose vision began it all and whose personal sacrifices kept it going, and to Mel Watman, who followed as editor sharing Jimmy's beliefs, enthusiasm and knowledge." *Chris Brasher*: "You, dear AW, are the historian of our sport – that is the greatest of all your valuable roles." *Joyce Smith*: "Congratulations to Jimmy Green for starting what has become part of British athletics. Ever since our involvement in athletics we have relied on AW for news and information and have never been disappointed."

Jimmy and I were singled out in several of the tributes but the success of AW was due also to our editorial colleagues over the years – John Lusardi, Dave Cocksedge, Jon Wigley, Barry Trowbridge, Brian Smyth and Cliff Temple, together with Tim Green, José Kimber and her secretarial successors, a roster of superb correspondents and contributors, and a loyal and appreciative readership.

On a personal note … Pat's mum – victim of a stroke 11 years earlier – finally passed away in August. She had long been in a nursing home and in and out of hospital, and it was probably a blessing that her ordeal was over. Pat always felt she could and should have done more but I can testify that she did all that was humanly possible, and her own health suffered in consequence. With her Auntie Betty, another who had depended on Pat's support for many years, also now in a care home, we were at liberty to sell Pat's parents' house in Wembley and we started the process of moving four miles north to Stanmore.

21. "SHORT, SQUAT" DALEY THE TOPS (1986)

There was no doubt in my mind as to the male athlete of the year for 1986 and this is what I wrote in the *International Athletics Guide*, which broke new ground by reviewing that year's activities and yet was published as early as November.

He didn't break any world records but Daley Thompson achieved enough last summer to warrant the title of Male Athlete of 1986. He contested three decathlons, won them all with great scores and added two more gold medals to his already fabulous collection. His last defeat in a decathlon was as long ago as August 1978, when just turned 20. An 8667 point victory in Arles in May marked a successful return to decathlon competition after an absence of 21 months. Daley scored four points fewer in winning his third Commonwealth title, in Edinburgh in July, but he was content to amble around in the 1500m when victory (by 490 points!) was secure. But that was just the warm-up for THE contest of the year: the European championship in Stuttgart with Daley up against the West German trio of Jürgen Hingsen, Guido Kratschmer and Siggy Wentz. Some sections of the crowd did attempt to wreck Daley's concentration, behaviour for which his German rivals apologised, but ultimately the jeers turned to cheers of appreciation as Daley fought as he had never had to fight before and emerged a brilliant champion with a score (8811) which, despite difficult weather conditions and the disadvantage of throwing the new-style javelin, fell only 36 points short of his world record. The way he handled the pressure from Hingsen and Wentz (Kratschmer, alas, pulled up injured in the second event), bouncing back after each mini-disaster with a superlative performance to seize the initiative once more, added to his legend as the toughest competitor in athletics. This was his stiffest examination yet, and he passed with flying colours – as he always knew he would, although there were some heart-fluttering moments on the way.

In a two-part interview, published in May, Daley told me "I don't really think I've yet achieved enough to justify the talent I've got." How important a goal was scoring 9000 points? "It's a big deal to me. Barriers are nice to break through. To be honest, I **should** have done it in '84 because when I went to Los Angeles I was in the best shape so far. But we had a headwind in the 100. If the wind had been the other way round I may have run a tenth or maybe two-tenths faster and that 40 or 50 points would have taken me to 8850 or 8900, and I could have run the 1500 faster." Asked for his opinion of Hingsen he replied: "I have the highest regard for him, despite the way I carry on. He really is a great athlete and I don't know if I would have the perseverance that he's got. I'd be really browned off by now. Just look at him. How could anyone who's 6ft 7in and looks as good as him get beaten all the time by a little, short, squat, ugly guy!" Drug taking? "I don't think the IAAF does enough to safeguard the sport. Take blood doping, for instance. They tell me that's not illegal, but I think it should be banned on the grounds that it is **morally** wrong … that it's cheating.

I'm really worried for the sport. The governing bodies have got to be much tougher. They should be the guardians of our sport."

British athletes fared well in all the major international championships. First up were the European Indoor Championships in Madrid and the emergence of a new star.

What a difference a year can make in the life of an athlete. Take a look at the results of the 1985 European Indoor Championships: eliminated in the first round of the 200m was Linford Christie. Who could have imagined that 12 months later that same athlete would win the title? Not Christie himself, for one. Prior to racing on the tight, steeply banked 164m track in Madrid, Christie would have gladly settled for a place in the final. Even when he reached the final he had no thoughts of winning. Always strong in the closing stages, even though he regards the 200 as "too far", the powerfully built Thames Valley Harrier pulled out all the stops to win by a clear-cut margin in 21.10, the fastest 200 of his life.

Next came the World Cross Country Championships in Neuchatel, Switzerland, and despite slithering on the muddy and hilly terrain barefoot Zola Budd not only retained her title by an 18 second margin but led England to team victory. The medals were presented by Lamine Diack, then a vice-president of the IAAF … only he refused to hand Zola her gold medal. "As far as I am concerned she is a South African," he stated. "I have nothing against Miss Budd but I cannot give a prize which will be seen as propaganda for South Africa." That Diack, president of the Supreme Council for Sport in Africa, should have been asked to make that particular presentation in the first place was either mischievous or naïve on the part of those making the arrangements. Still, it was a great start to the year for Zola, still only 19, who the previous month had set a world indoor 3000m best of 8:39.79 at RAF Cosford.

The question being asked was would she be deemed eligible to run for England at 1500m in that summer's Commonwealth Games in Edinburgh. She said she would like to, but her main objective was to win the European 3000m title in Stuttgart. Her chances of racing in Edinburgh were slim as there was a Commonwealth Games Federation stipulation that athletes representing a country in which they or their parents were not born must have resided in that country for at least six months in the 12 months preceding the team declaration date in July. But because of her lengthy spells of training back in South Africa it would not be possible for her to fulfil that requirement.

Zola went on to win the WAAA 1500m title in 4:01.93, a remarkable time in very windy conditions, but was beaten once more by Maricica Puica when they clashed at Crystal Palace. The Romanian won the 2000m in a world record 5:28.69 with Zola clocking 5:30.19 – the shock being that they were split by the fast improving Scot, Yvonne Murray, with a Commonwealth record of 5:29.58. Yvonne's target had merely been 5:40 and she gasped afterwards: "I've always dreamed of beating Zola but never thought it would come true." More importantly, she beat her again at the European Championships as they finished third (8:37.15) and fourth (8:38.20) in the 3000m. Zola, whose summer season was increasingly hampered by a hamstring injury, led at the bell before fading.

Zola never did compete in Edinburgh. She was selected for the 1500m but the Commonwealth Games Federation ruled her ineligible. The Federation had other, more pressing problems for because Prime Minister Margaret Thatcher refused to apply sanctions against South Africa there was a mass boycott (led by Nigeria and Ghana) of the Games by African, Caribbean and Asian nations.

No boycott of a sporting event has ever led to the fulfilment of its political aims (for example, the Soviets are still in Afghanistan six years after the American-led withdrawal from the Moscow Olympics); all that happens, apart from the political posturing involved, is the shattering of the dreams of the athletes affected. Ultimately 32 countries stayed away as against the 26 who did participate. It was a melancholy state of affairs, for that marvellous racial, cultural and social mix that is the Commonwealth Games' special contribution to international sport was seriously diminished. They continued as 'The Friendly Games' but as a gathering mainly of representatives from the UK, Canada, Australia and New Zealand it wasn't the same. The mass boycott cast a dark shadow over the celebrations (as did the abysmal weather which prevailed for practically the entire week), and the consequent paucity of entries in many of the events led to many preliminary rounds being cancelled. Many an athlete came away with a medal he or she could hardly have aspired to had all the leading contenders been present.

Yet, despite all the negative aspects, the Games did produce many great performances and contests. Ben Johnson [10.07] confirmed his status as the world's foremost 100m specialist ... Steve Cram [1:43.22/3:50.87] was magnificent in completing the 800m/1500m double (but how unfortunate that Seb Coe was laid low by illness just as fans all over the world were licking their lips in anticipation of two momentous clashes) ... Daley Thompson was, well, Daley Thompson ... Rob de Castella [2:10:15] and Lisa Martin [2:26:07] triumphed brilliantly in the marathon ... Tessa Sanderson [69.80m] upset Fatima Whitbread [68.54m] in every sense in the most dramatic of javelin competitions ... the heptathlon was a nail-biter, and so it went on. The Games were badly damaged but the talent and competitive qualities of those who did take part ensured all was not lost.

Apart from the English athletes among those mentioned above there were gold medals also for Roger Black (400m), Steve Ovett (5000m), Jon Solly (10,000m), Andy Ashurst (pole vault), John Herbert (triple jump), Billy Cole (shot), Dave Smith (hammer), Dave Ottley (javelin), the men's 4x400m team, Heather Oakes (100m), Sally Gunnell (100m hurdles), Joyce Oladapo (long jump), Judy Simpson (heptathlon) and the women's 4x100m team, while Phil Beattie won the 400m hurdles for Northern Ireland, Kirsty Wade notched up an 800m/1500m double for Wales and Liz Lynch (later McColgan) took the 10,000m on home ground. The European Championships, which started 24 days later, were of a much higher standard overall but the British team performed magnificently.

National coaching director Frank Dick summed it all up. "This is the greatest team I've ever been with, and we should all be proud of them." Absolutely. The team has returned from Stuttgart with the astonishing total of eight gold medals, two silver and five bronze, won the admiration of everyone and provided Europe with a reassuring image of talented and dedicated British youth to offset the dreadful reputation established by football hooligans. It was the finest ever performance by a British team at the European Championships. The medal table shows Britain is the third ranking power in European athletics behind the USSR and GDR (and therefore fourth in the world taking into account the USA), which is the highest we could reasonably aspire to.

It might be invidious to place the British gold medals in any sort of ranking order but we'll start with an athlete who hauled herself up from the depths by her (javelin) bootstraps to win her first major gold medal as a senior ... and achieving a phenomenal world record into the bargain. It's difficult in words to express the enormity of Fatima Whitbread's achievement. Take first of all, her world record in the qualifying round. With hardly a soul in the stadium at nine in the morning, she proceeded to throw 77.44m! That didn't simply break Petra Felke's highly regarded record of 75.40m ... it pulverised it. Further history was made for it was the first time a British thrower (male or female) had broken a world record. In the final, despite the pain in her shoulder, she was simply brilliant. In the fourth round she took the lead with 72.68m. Felke improved in the final round, but at 72.52m she fell just short. The gold was Fatima's. She still had one more attempt. With the pressure off she was able to relax, as she had in the qualifying round, and the spear sailed out to 76.32m – the second longest throw in history!

Fatima's gold medal came on August 29, but Britain's gold rush started two days earlier when Linford Christie won the 100m in glorious style. What a year it has been for him: internationally unknown prior to his European Indoor 200 triumph, he has since broken Allan Wells' UK record with 10.04, won a silver medal in the Commonwealth Games and now is champion of Europe – Britain's first at this distance for 40 years. He powered through to win in a cracking 10.15. Illness prevented Seb Coe's Commonwealth 800/1500 showdown against Steve Cram but in the month since he had managed to make a complete recovery to top form and high spirits. In previous attempts to land the 'big one' at 800m he had: (a) set too fast a pace in the 1978 European and finished third; (2) gone to the other extreme and hung too far off the pace in the 1980 Olympics and failed to catch Ovett; (3) been overhauled in the closing stages of the 1982 European but later found to be suffering from a debilitating illness; (4) been forced to withdraw from the 1983 World Championships because of ill health; (5) run a faultless race at the 1984 Olympics only to find Joaquim Cruz even more brilliant on the day. Coe's 800 in Stuttgart was his final attempt. What a race it was, with – for the first time in European Championship history – British athletes gaining a clean sweep of the medals.

This was no cosy private duel between Coe and Cram, for it was Tom McKean who led into the final straight and it was only by reaching to the very limit of his powers that Coe edged past to win by less than a metre in 1:44.50, covering the final 200m in a sizzling 24.7.

August 28 was, one could argue, the most notable single day in British athletics history. Fatima broke a world record, Britain scored a 1-2-3 in the 800 ... and Daley Thompson prevailed in the most thrilling three-way decathlon battle there has ever been. He normally builds up such a huge lead on the first day that the opposition is demoralised. On this occasion the scenario was somewhat different. For the first time since he became the world's undisputed number one Daley was forced to fight a rearguard action. That he still emerged as a clearcut winner is testimony indeed to his qualities. For the first time since David Jenkins in 1971 a Briton is European 400m champion. Roger Black's progress to date has been astonishingly quick; it wasn't until 1984 that he raced 400 for the first time. After winning the Commonwealth title he reduced his personal best to 45.00 in Zürich and in Stuttgart on August 29 he succeeded Derek Redmond as UK record holder with 44.59, the second fastest ever by a European. Two days later he would become the first British athlete since Alan Pascoe in 1974 to win two gold medals in one European Championships [anchoring the 4x400m team of Redmond 45.4, Kriss Akabusi 45.4, Brian Whittle 45.1 despite losing a shoe soon after the start, with a 43.9 leg for victory in 2:59.84].

It was rather like Seb Coe in Moscow when, after a comparative disaster in the 800, he just had to win the 1500 in order to restore his self-esteem. The spike was on the other foot this time, so to speak, because it was Coe who stood between Cram and the successful defence of his 1500 title. Not that Coe was lacking in motivation himself, for having fallen at the first hurdle in two Olympic bids for the double he was finally in contention this time. Of the two, though, it was significant that Cram was the hungrier. "I was just so disappointed that I couldn't run at my best on Thursday [800m final]; it wasn't the real Steve Cram out there." The genuine article was to be seen in the 1500 on August 31. It was a slow race which might have been made for Coe had he not made a tactical error in falling too far behind before the race really hotted up on the last lap. He closed to within four metres along the back straight but the lead Cram had stolen proved decisive. With both men running flat out the margin remained constant with Cram having covered the last 300 in an amazing 37.9 (50.9 final 400) for a time of 3:41.09. The cheers for a British one-two in the 1500 had barely died away when it was the turn of the 5000m runners. Had he been well, Steve Ovett, as Commonwealth champion, would have been the great British hope but Steve was visibly unwell and wisely decided to drop out after 3000m when well behind the leaders. It was now up to Jack Buckner and Tim Hutchings, second and third to Ovett in Edinburgh, and how they did us proud. Buckner came in a superb if not totally expected winner in 13:10.15 and now ranks second to Dave Moorcroft on the UK all-time list. Hutchings' reward for a typically forceful run was a bronze medal.

But an even more aggressive piece of running, by Steve Jones in the marathon in humid conditions, led to disaster.

In this his first marathon race for ten months his strategy against a relatively modest field was to run at world record pace for the first half of the race (aiming for 63:00-63:30), break the opposition and then coast home. The Welshman did indeed run away from his rivals, striking out on his own after 5km and covering the next 5km stretch in an amazing (but imprudent) 14:27. By 20km he was not only two minutes clear but operating at well inside 2:07 pace. Unhappily for him, a misunderstanding about his drinks contributed to his subsequent downfall. Instead of plain water he was handed fizzy water, which he found he couldn't swallow. As a result he became dehydrated and he had to slow drastically. Still a minute up at 30km he was caught during the 34th kilometre. "I got to halfway feeling fairly comfortable, but it was a struggle from 29km. My hips and knees got sore, I felt dehydrated and I was just running on the spot. I've never felt so bad." He could have been forgiven for dropping out but pride and raw courage kept him going to the end, finishing one from last of the 21 who completed the course [in 2:22:12] and receiving an ovation from the sporting crowd.

Elsewhere at the Championships, surely the best yet staged, there were world records by Yuriy Sedykh of the USSR in the hammer, his throw of 86.74m still unsurpassed more than 30 years later; team-mate Marina Styepanova with 53.32 in the 400m hurdles (which she improved to 52.94 two weeks later); and Heike Drechsler of the GDR whose 200m time of 21.71 equalled the world record she shared with Marita Koch, who in Stuttgart won the 400m in 48.22. There was another great run by Ingrid Kristiansen, who had already won the Boston Marathon in 2:24:55 and set world records of 30:13.74 for 10,000m and 14:37.33 for 5000m. On this occasion she won the 10,000m by half a lap in 30:23.25. Ingrid's Norwegian compatriot, Grete Waitz, was one second quicker when winning the London Marathon the day before Boston by almost six minutes in a personal best of 2:24:54. This race was the biggest yet with 19,261 starters, but that distinction passed to New York later in the year with 20,502 starters, Grete notching up her eighth victory in that race.

Having finally won a major 800m title, Seb Coe went in search of a fast 1500m time in Italy. Seb Coe was only 13 and had a best 1500m time of 4:31.8 when his father drew up a projection of progress for him up to 1980 with an optimum time of 3:30 – over five seconds inside the world record of the day. Some 17 years, two Olympic titles and numerous world records later, Peter Coe's prediction was at last fulfilled! Racing in Rieti on September 7, Seb not only smashed his 1981 personal best of 3:31.95. but came within two strides of breaking the world record with a time of 3:29.77. That ranked him equal third on the world all-time list behind Said Aouita (3:29.46 and 3:29.71) and Steve Cram (3:29.67), level with Sydney Maree. "'I am taking nothing away from Cram, but that makes up for the way I ran in Stuttgart." Cram went for the 800m and improved his 1986 world leading time from 1:43.22 to 1:43.19, the second fastest of his career.

My Life in Athletics

Brian Smyth covered the inaugural IAAF World Junior Championships in Athens. It's fascinating now to scrutinise the results and see how subsequent Olympic champions fared in what would have been the most searching test at that stage of their careers. Peter Rono (1988 1500m) was 2nd in Athens; Brahim Boutayeb (1988 10,000m) 4th 5000m; Javier Sotomayor (1992 high jump) 1st; Lars Riedel (1996 discus) 4th; Robert Zmelik (1992 decathlon) 10th; Irina Privalova (2000 400m hurdles) 7th 100m semi-final; Hassiba Boulmerka (1992 1500m) 6th heat; Fernanda Ribeiro (1996 10,000m) 4th 3000m; Svetlana Krivelyova (1992 shot) 6th; Ilke Wyludda (1996 discus) 1st. British winners were David Sharpe in the 800m, Colin Jackson in the 110m hurdles in a European junior record time of 13.44 with Jon Ridgeon, who anchored the British team to victory in the 4x100m relay, second.

During a year in which AW's audited circulation reached an all-time high of 24,898 and I completed 25 years as variously assistant editor, editor and consultant editor, my regular contributions to the magazine included the compilation of overseas reports and results and a "Trackwise" column of news and views. In that pre-Internet era, details of what was happening abroad came from a dedicated corps of worldwide correspondents supplemented by what I could glean from the French sports daily *L'Equipe*, the West (*Leichtathletik*) and East (*Der Leichtathlet*) German weekly magazines and the American *Track & Field News* and its offshoot *Track Newsletter*. In addition, as I had been doing on a weekly basis for years, I would visit the City Library (and before that the Guildhall Library) to skim through the sports pages of the numerous foreign newspapers that were on display there. I continued with previewing and reporting major meetings at home and abroad, arranged the occasional in-depth interview and researched and wrote lengthy profiles. Obituaries and book reviews were other areas involved. I now only rarely visited the office and the usual way for me to get my copy to Barry Trowbridge in Rochester was to Red Star a package from Victoria Station on a Monday in the knowledge that it would be transported on the first available train. It was a challenging but fulfilling job, and I was proud of each issue of our little magazine. Little did I know then that this cosy routine would come to an end in 1987.

Family news: On May 6 (an auspicious date for any athletics enthusiast) Pat and I moved into our new home in Stanmore, which just happens to be on the 1948 Olympic marathon route. I could just imagine Delfo Cabrera, Etienne Gailly and Tom Richards passing by, gathering themselves for the final four miles to the finish at Wembley Stadium! My dad was living in sheltered accommodation five minutes' walk away but, alas, his health was failing and in November he died in University College Hospital, aged 79, from cancer of the oesophagus. A couple of weeks later, while I was in Monte Carlo for the World Athletics Gala, my niece Sandra's younger son Daniel was born, and his middle name of Alfred was in memory of my dad, the grandfather he never knew.

22. THE DEMISE OF 'AW' (1987)

All was normal at AW until the end of March 1987. The cross country, road racing and indoor seasons were covered in the usual thorough fashion; there were features on Evelyn Ashford (Olympic 100m champion and world record holder at 10.76), 50 year-old quadruple Olympic discus champion Al Oerter (still throwing beyond 62m!), triple jump star Keith Connor, fast-rising Yvonne Murray ("Zola has been a very big factor in my progress; she has provided a standard of excellence for me to aim at") and Liz Lynch, while Ron Pickering voiced his concerns about British athletics. The 1986 UK Intermediate Women's lists revealed that Kelly Holmes was ranked sixth at 800m (2:11.0) and third at 1500m (4:26.9) behind Bruce Tulloh's twin daughters Katherine and JoJo, and future world champion (but in Italy's colours) Fiona May topped the long jump list with a windy 6.47m. The Junior Women's lists placed Denise Lewis equal seventh at 75m hurdles (11.4) and equal fourth in the long jump (5.45m). Paula Radcliffe, aged 13, was mentioned in editorial assistant Martin Forder's report on the Women's National Girls cross country championship; she finished fourth – a giant advance on her 299th position in the previous year's race. I travelled to Liévin in Northern France for the European Indoor Championships, where Todd Bennett won the 400m and Yvonne Murray the 3000m, and two days after my return I flew off to New York.

Courtesy of Mobil, who were sponsoring both the US and World Indoor Championships, I was provided with an open air ticket which would take me to New York and Indianapolis, plus any other American destination during the interval between the two meetings. So on February 27 I found myself back in Madison Square Garden for the first time since I was 19. Not at trackside with the New York Pioneer Club this time but high up in the press box, I watched a great meeting highlighted by world indoor records of 17.76m in the triple jump by Mike Conley and 7.32m in the long jump by Heike Drechsler – one of many East European stars using the championships as preparation and acclimatisation for the Worlds. I took the opportunity during my four night stay at the Penta Hotel just across the street from "The Garden" to meet up with friends and my cousins Margaret and Naomi; it was great to be back in one of my favourite cities. The Penta, by the way, was previously known as the Hotel Pennsylvania and was immortalised in the Glenn Miller and Andrews Sisters classic *Pennsylvania 6-5000* (the hotel's phone number).

Taking advantage of that air ticket, I thought I would visit somewhere new … and headed out to Las Vegas. It proved to be an inspired choice, because I found the place so appealing that I have returned there on more than 30 occasions, most recently in November 2016. Many of the famous hotels which existed then have long since been imploded to make way for newer, even more extravagant properties, "The Strip" remaining one of the modern wonders of the world. Where else would you find replicas of the New York skyline, the Eiffel Tower, the Venetian Grand Canal, an Egyptian pyramid and a Roman Colosseum in one locality? You will either love Las Vegas (or "Lost Wages" as

Elliott Denman prefers to call it) or hate it for being so over-the-top and commercialised.

I must have inherited my dad's gambling gene (he was into horse and greyhound racing but with a conspicuous lack of success) for I instantly got hooked on what were then termed "one armed bandits". Back in 1987 you fed quarters (25 cents) into the slot machines and pulled a handle, hoping your spin would be rewarded by a torrent of coins which you than scooped up and poured into a large plastic cup. It's all much more sophisticated nowadays in this computer age. No coins, only banknotes will suffice, and although there is still a handle that you can pull almost everyone simply presses a button to start the spin. Any winnings come out of the machine in the form of a paper slip which will be converted into real money by inserting into an electronic cash dispenser. Of course it's a mug's game but I still get a kick playing slot machines (these days at a casino close to London's Olympic Stadium as I have now at last 'retired' from Vegas), for you never know what the next spin may yield. On one memorable day, in 2003, I won $2700 at Caesars Palace, crossed the road back to the Flamingo where I was staying and promptly won another $6000. Funny how I remember that and not the numerous occasions I lost!

Anyway, back to 1987 and after four nights in Vegas I flew to Indianapolis where I stayed in a Holiday Inn (now Crowne Plaza Hotel) situated within Union Station where some of the rooms were actually converted train carriages.

The first IAAF World Indoor Championships, held in the vast Hoosier Dome from March 6 to 8, must be adjudged a success from most points of view. Although indoor athletics competition has traditionally been staged only in North America, Europe and Japan, no fewer than 84 countries were represented at this pioneering event, many of the athletes having never before set eyes on an indoor track. The facilities were superb, and so was the standard of performance achieved. World indoor records were established in the 60m (Ben Johnson 6.41), 60m hurdles (Greg Foster 7.46 in a heat), women's 200m (Heike Drechsler 22.27), women's high jump (Stefka Kostadinova 2.05m) and, controversially, in both walks (Mikhail Shchennikov 18:27.79 5km and Olga Krishtop 12:05.49 3km). The attendance figures of 20,023 (Saturday) and 20,971 (Sunday) represented the largest crowds in indoor athletics history. Most of the spectators in the Dome had probably never seen a Russian or East German in person before, but they were unstinting in their appreciation of the athletes wherever they came from. The atmosphere throughout was friendly and as 400m champion Antonio McKay remarked: "It's a great meet and maybe will help promote world peace. It can't hurt."

The only medal for Britain's 18-strong team came from Nigel Walker, bronze in the 60m hurdles. He went on to become a Welsh rugby union international, winning 17 caps between 1993 and 1998 and scoring 12 tries.

The Hoosier Dome housed the USA's National Track & Field Hall of Fame with, at that time, 118 notable names in American athletics history enshrined: predominantly competitors, but including some coaches and officials and even a journalist. Each person so honoured had a framed photograph on display and there were various showcases containing such memorabilia as the first starting blocks (a couple of chunks of wood, basically) as used by sprint ace Hal Davis, the baton used by the 1936 Olympic 4x100m relay team and Dave Wottle's famous hat. There was even a photo of Greta Garbo in running gear poised 'on her marks' alongside the legendary coach Dean Cromwell.

It was on March 26 that I learned that AW had been sold to the giant publishing company, EMAP (East Midland Allied Press), based in Peterborough. The news came as a surprise and a shock. In view of my long connection with the magazine I felt I should have been informed about what was being proposed. On April 6 Norman Wright, publishing director of EMAP Pursuit Publishing Ltd, called at my home for a chat about my future with the company. I had the option of taking redundancy but if I remained with the magazine I would be given the title of associate editor and was assured that my wealth of experience would prove invaluable to the success of this transition.

The very next day I flew off to Seoul for the World Cup Marathon, a trip paid for by the IAAF. I had much to think about on the long flight and came to the conclusion that if my role continued as previously then it could be a golden opportunity. Backed by EMAP's vast resources the magazine could provide an even better service to its readers. I was unaware of the fundamental changes ahead as I arrived in the South Korean capital on the same day that back in Rochester the AW staff were informed that their employment was shortly to be terminated. Brian Smyth opted to move to Peterborough as news editor but Barry Trowbridge, who was to be ousted as editor and replaced by EMAP's own Keith Nelson, accepted redundancy and went on to enjoy a fulfilling career as a sub-editor on *The Times*.

My five days in Seoul were fascinating even though the actual marathon races, run in very windy conditions, were unexceptional. I wrote a lengthy report which, for the first time, I faxed back to the office. The technological revolution in terms of communication had begun.

During my stay, which included a visit to the border with North Korea only 40 miles away, I was shown round the impressive 100,000 capacity Olympic Stadium, the Olympic Village and other facilities, and I assumed I would be returning to cover the Games in September 1988.

Four days after I arrived home, the April 18 edition informed readers: "As from this issue, AW becomes a member of EMAP plc, the Peterborough-based company that publishes more than 30 consumer titles. EMAP has established a reputation for publishing top quality titles in the outdoor leisure market, and AW will be joining a company which launched *Today's Runner* last year and is committed to providing the best possible coverage for athletes and their sport." Barry Dennis, managing director of EMAP Pursuit Publications Ltd, added: "EMAP is delighted to have acquired the title and is determined to carry on all the good work which has been put in over so many years." The unsuspecting Jimmy Green, founder and consultant director, wrote: "This first issue of AW with its new publishers will ensure your own magazine will continue as the 'bible' of British athletics. I want readers to know that the change of publisher is in the best interest of AW, and will ensure it progresses from strength to strength."

I'm not sure of the exact figure but I believe EMAP paid around £800,000 (the equivalent of over £2 million today) to buy the title from World Athletics & Sporting Publications Ltd, the company headed by Albert Anderson. Jimmy, without whom there would be no AW, and his son Tim, as directors, were paid a token dividend when the magazine changed hands. As for me, who had been a full-time employee for 25 years during which time I had worked ridiculous hours for a modest salary, owed goodness knows how many weeks of untaken holiday entitlement and helped triple the magazine's circulation ... what was my *ex-gratia* payment for my role in making AW such an attractive commercial proposition? Zilch. Even now, just writing about it all these years later, makes me resentful ... as does my treatment under the EMAP regime.

Life carried on as normal for a few more weeks. On April 24 I met Keith Nelson, hopeful of a fruitful editorial relationship, and before confronting the new challenge I snatched some overdue holiday. Pat and I flew out to Orlando on May 1, spending a mainly Disney-themed week there, but including a mind-blowing trip to the Kennedy Space Center at Cape Canaveral, followed by a relaxing week at Clearwater Beach on the Gulf of Mexico.

On our return we received the devastating news that the young son of our close friends Lionel and Sigrid Peters had died. We attended the funeral on May 20 of Marcel, who had been knocked down while cycling.

Meanwhile, the May 16 issue was the last to be edited by Barry. In the May 23 edition, Keith Nelson introduced himself to readers. "Moving into the editor's chair on AW is something I could never have imagined doing when I bought my first issue in January 1975. In those days I would devour each weekly issue, thumbing my way through the results to see who'd done what in recent races. I think it took me a year or so before my name appeared in the 'bible' and it was probably for a lowly placing in the English Schools Cross Country Championships. Having been editor of *Today's Runner* since its launch in 1985, the move over to AW is a great challenge for me personally, and one I am looking forward to with a great deal of relish. AW is the magazine for the committed club athlete. It is the athlete's bible and, rest assured, it will stay that way. Both Brian Smyth and Mel Watman, whose worldwide respect as an athletics journalist is second to none, will continue to report each week in AW. AW will be moving with the times and we've got some pretty exciting plans for the weeks and months ahead."

This all sounded very encouraging and the following six issues were perfectly conventional, still produced by Kent Art Printers in the usual small A5 format. My first collaboration with Keith came at the UK Championships at Derby on May 24/25 where I wrote the introduction and event reports while Keith supplied the athletes' quotes. Star of the meeting was Fatima Whitbread, whose throw of 75.62m would have been a world record had she not reached

77.44m and 76.32m in Stuttgart the previous year. One of my last reporting assignments in June was a UK v Poland v Canada match at Gateshead on the 13th which featured Welsh and Scottish 1500m records of 4:02.13 and 4:04.55 respectively by Kirsty Wade (Scottish-born though) and Yvonne Murray despite the cold and windy conditions. Later in the season they improved to 4:00.73 and 4:01.20.

The first significant changes introduced by Keith were announced in the June 20 issue. Traditionally most British results had arrived by post but starting from Sunday, June 21 race organisers and club secretaries could fax or phone in their results to copytakers or a permanent answerphone service by 11 am on a Monday. That would enable a quicker turnaround and from the July 11 issue AW would be available a day earlier than previously, on a Thursday. It was in the July 4 issue that Keith revealed that "perhaps the biggest difference you'll notice in your next AW is not only that it has more colour, but we're also improving the format and, from next week, will be producing AW in a larger, A4 size."

On the rare occasion I was invited to express my views, I opposed the increase in size. The A5 format had served AW well over so many years; it was cosy and familiar, liked by the readers and when on display at the newsagent it stood out from the numerous other A4 sports magazines. It wasn't until the first issue appeared on July 9 that the full horror of what had been perpetrated became apparent. Printed on cheap paper, the confusing layout was a mess. Apparently it had been designed to appeal more to the youth market, but what was immediately apparent was that the trumpeted "great new look" alienated the majority of our long-standing subscribers. Over the next few weeks I heard so many refer to it as a "comic" and my esteemed fellow journalist Roy Moor, practically with tears in his eyes, whispered "what have they done to your lovely magazine?" To his credit, Keith did publish some letters critical of the format change.

I was as appalled as anyone but I had accepted the position of associate editor and had a job to do. Of course it wasn't all bad; for a start Dave Moorcroft was hired as a regular columnist and was always worth reading, and at least to begin with I continued to compile the overseas results and was given a free hand with "Watman's World", a weekly *potpourri* of news and analysis. My first reporting assignment was the Peugeot Talbot Games at Crystal Palace where UK all-comers' records were set by Butch Reynolds in the 400m with 44.15, close to his world low-altitude best of 44.10, and by Ed Moses, who may have recently had his fabulous win streak terminated after 122 races (107 finals) but was still the world's best 400m hurdler and his time of 47.94 was his 40th mark inside 48 seconds.

Over the next few weeks "Watman's World" covered such subjects as Kathy Cook's retirement, quotes by Ed Moses, Seb Coe (now vice-chairman of the Sports Council) being involved in a government investigation into the misuse of drugs in sport, Moroccan athletes (Said Aouita had run a 3:46.76 mile and broken world records at 2000m with 4:50.81 and 5000m with 12:58.39),

John Walker's rejuvenation, and a tribute to one of Walker's predecessors as holder of the world mile record.

"One of the most delightful experiences of my journalistic career occurred just the other day when, along with a number of colleagues, I had lunch with one of my all-time heroes, Sydney Wooderson. It was a marvellous idea of IAC chairman Dave Bedford to mark the forthcoming 50th anniversary of Sydney's world mile record by inviting the press to meet the great man.

Sydney's 4:06.4 in 1937 came in a handicap race and, to mark the golden jubilee, meeting director Bedford organised a handicap mile at the IAC Meeting at Crystal Palace. It proved a stunning success. Bedford and statistician Stan Greenberg allotted the starting distances, the objective being to provide the closest possible finish. It worked out beautifully, and had the crowd on their feet, as Steve Crabb (not to be confused with his near namesake), off scratch, won in 3:51.76 after being only tenth at the bell, finishing just ahead of Jack Buckner (off 22 yards) 3:51.88 and Chris McGeorge (off 52 yards) 3:52.03.

The big event of the year was the 2nd IAAF World Championships in Rome and to mark the 75th anniversary of the IAAF's foundation in 1912 the world governing body under the presidency of Primo Nebiolo published a weighty tome entitled *100 Golden Moments*. I was honoured to be appointed an honorary editor, along with Robert Parienté and Roberto Quercetani, our pleasurable but fiendishly difficult task being to agree on which 100 moments from so many worthy candidates to select. A brilliant team of writers was invited to assemble the material, including Jim Dunaway (USA), Matti Hannus (Finland), Richard Hymans (UK), Len Johnson (Australia), Kenny Moore (USA), Bert Nelson (USA) and Gustav Schwenk (Germany), and I was assigned to write accounts of the 1932 Olympic victories by Bob Tisdall (400m hurdles) and Tom Hampson (800m), Naoto Tajima in the 1936 Olympic triple jump, Rudolf Harbig's 1939 world 800m record, Roger Bannister's 1954 sub-4 min mile, Parry O'Brien's 1954 world shot record, David Hemery's 1968 Olympic 400m hurdles triumph, Grete Waitz's 1979 New York Marathon, Seb Coe's 1:41.73 800m in 1981, Dave Moorcroft's 1982 world 5000m record, Daley Thompson's 1984 Olympic decathlon, Steve Cram's first sub-3:30 1500m in 1985 and Ingrid Kristainsen's 1986 world 10,000m record. Reflecting on great deeds and athletes of the past continues to be the most enjoyable aspect of my coverage of the sport.

Reporting on the action in Rome, event by event, was shared among Brian Smyth, Dave Cocksedge and myself. No overview of the meeting appeared in AW but in a supplement to the *American Track & Field* magazine, published by Larry Eder, I wrote (in part):

With the Los Angeles Olympics of 1984 decimated by a Soviet-led boycott the world had to wait until Rome in 1987 for an opportunity for all the best athletes to assemble again. Another feast of track and field ensued, but unhappily the abiding memory is that of cheating. Certain elements in Italian officialdom were so determined that their nation's athletes should fare well on home ground that the long jump result was rigged in favour of Giovanni

Evangelisti – an innocent party in the deception, it should be stressed. As he prepared for his final jump, Evangelisti was in fourth place with 8.19m behind Carl Lewis (8.67m), Robert Emmiyan (8.53m) and Larry Myricks (8.33m). The Italian's final effort visibly fell short of 8m but, astonishingly, the electronic scoreboard flashed up 8.38m and the bronze medal was his. The media quickly sensed a scandal, and ultimately it was discovered that while Evangelisti was waiting for a victory ceremony to take place prior to his final jump – at a time when the long jump area was in virtual darkness – an official stuck a marker in the sandpit at 8.38m and the figures fed into the electronic measuring system. The following year Myricks received his medal and a number of Italian officials were suspended.

The memory of the meeting's highlight, the 100m final, has been equally soured. The duel between Lewis and his much more powerfully built Canadian rival Ben Johnson had been hyped as though it was for the world heavyweight boxing crown. Lewis looked much the sharper in the preliminary rounds but in the final he was blown away at the start as Johnson catapulted himself into a two-metre lead. Lewis finished more strongly but Johnson still won by a good metre in the phenomenal time of 9.83, a full tenth of a second inside the world record. The stadium erupted in excitement (and was only just starting to die down when Bulgaria's lithe and graceful Stefka Kostadinova high jumped a world record 2.09m) ... but a year later Johnson failed a drugs test after winning the Seoul Olympic title in 9.79, ultimately he admitted to long-term steroid use and was retroactively stripped of this world title also. The race was eventually awarded to Lewis in a world record equalling 9.93.

The most significant trend to be observed in Rome was the dominance of African men in the middle and long distances. In Helsinki four years earlier the African medal count in this area had been a modest two: silver in the marathon and bronze in the 1500m. This time gold medals were won by Billy Konchellah of Kenya in the 800m, Abdi Bile of Somalia in the 1500m, Said Aouita of Morocco in the 5000m, Paul Kipkoech of Kenya in the 10,000m and Douglas Wakiihuri of Kenya in the marathon ahead of Ahmed Salah from Djibouti. One element which did not change was the crushing supremacy of the East German women, a state of affairs which owed much to the GDR's state-approved use of a performance-enhancing drugs programme.

The British team fared well. Fatima Whitbread won the javelin by nearly five metres with another colossal throw of 76.64m, her and the world's third longest; following Ben Johnson's disqualification, Linford Christie (10.14) was promoted to third place in the 100m; John Regis was third in the 200m in a UK record of 20.18, Peter Elliott second in the 800m in a grand personal best of 1:43.41, Jack Buckner (13:27.74) third in the 5000m, Jon Ridgeon (equalling his UK record of 13.29) and Colin Jackson (13.38) second and third in the 110m hurdles, and the 4x400m team of Derek Redmond, Kriss Akabusi, Roger Black and Phil Brown finished second in a European and Commonwealth record of 2:58.86. Despite setting a Commonwealth record of 31:19.82 Liz Lynch could finish no higher than fifth in the 10,000m won by Ingrid Kristiansen, while there was acute disappointment for three of the sport's biggest names. Steve Cram's self assurance had been dented after being outkicked (despite a 50.2 last lap!) in the European Cup by José Luis González, his first defeat at 1500m since the 1984 Olympics, but appeared to be in top form after a 3:31.43 win in Zürich. In Rome he went with 450m to go but ("there was nothing there") faded drastically in the finishing straight and jogged over the line in eighth place. Steve Ovett wound up tenth in the 5000m and Daley Thompson, hampered by an injury which had curtailed his preparations, slipped from third to ninth on the second day of the decathlon, his first loss for nine years and his lowest score (8124) since 1977. He could have dropped out before the finish but won many new admirers for sticking it out as an also-ran and his graciousness in defeat. The meeting's most exciting race was the 400m hurdles, won by Ed Moses in 47.46, scrambling desperately at the finish to stay just ahead of Danny Harris (the man who had ended his win streak) 47.48 and Harald Schmid who equalled his European record, also with 47.48.

Two days after my return from Rome I was off to Brussels, along with Keith, for a relatively uneventful IAAF Grand Prix Final, and then Pat and I jetted off to Corfu for two weeks. I had one more trip abroad: to Monte Carlo to witness Ingrid Kristiansen win the world 15km road title by over a minute and a half and interview her coach, Johann Kaggerstad. Another marathon star was the subject of "Watman's World" in November: Priscilla Welch, winner in New York at the age of 42 and holder of the UK record and world veterans best of 2:26:51. In December I charted the numerous ups and downs in Mary Slaney's career. She had resumed running only six days after giving birth to her daughter in May 1986 and clocked a promising 4:32 road mile in September but then had to undergo arthroscopic surgery on her achilles tendon in November. She returned to clock 32:02 for a road 10km in February 1987 but never made it to the track season never mind the World Championships as the achilles problem resurfaced, requiring another operation in June. Currently back in full training, she stated her goal was to wipe out the disappointment of LA 1984 by winning the Olympic 3000m in Seoul.

Although I still disliked the appearance of the magazine, there was plenty of good material within its pages each week, and an important innovation appeared in the final issue for the year as Stan Greenberg, Peter Matthews and myself came up with world merit rankings for 1987. Our American colleagues at *Track & Field News* had been publishing such lists for decades but this was the first time a British publication had entered this controversial but stimulating arena. We went only six deep but added a fairly detailed account of the main action in each event, making the compilation a valuable review of the season.

It had been a game-changer of a year. The magazine I loved and nurtured was now virtually a stranger. My output was much the same as it had been since I stepped down as editor, but my sense of pride as each issue rolled off the press had gone. I missed too the camaraderie of my years at Rochester. Only once a week, if that, did I drive up to Peterborough, faxing being my usual means of delivering my copy although occasionally a courier would collect.

When I did visit the EMAP premises I usually felt uncomfortable, an outsider. There was no friendly discussion with Keith. I found him a cold, aloof figure, shut away in his own private office or ivory tower. On one occasion I mentioned to him that I would be happy to cover a particular meeting, to which his icy response was on the lines of 'it's not a question of you being happy; this is your job'. There was no attempt to tap into my experience, which I had been assured by Norman Wright would be the case.

I got on well of course with Brian Smyth, with whom I had worked since 1980. Always cheerful and industrious, he was doing an excellent job as features editor. The other member of the editorial team, hired first as editorial assistant and then promoted to reporter, was Richard Tuck whose enthusiasm for the job could not have been greater. A worrying trend, though, was that Richard was being requested by Keith to involve himself in overseas news coverage – previously my exclusive province – and so a confusing situation arose as to who did what. But the event that would ultimately hasten my departure from AW was the appearance on the scene in December 1987 of Julie Stott, who had been transferred from EMAP's *Match*, a weekly football magazine aimed at the teenage market and probably the model for the revamped AW. Now Julie may have been an expert on soccer but she had no in-depth knowledge of athletics and yet straight away she was appointed news editor! Every time I was at Peterborough she and Keith would be discussing something or other, while I was shut out, and the situation would only get worse.

23. YES, THERE WAS LIFE AFTER 'AW' (1988)

This was a year which started horrendously but ended well, proving there was life after AW. The first blow came from Albert Anderson, who in the first week of January 1988 responded to a letter I had sent to him in August 1987 setting out my case for some form of payment as a consequence of the sale to EMAP. Appearing to criticise me for stepping down as editor in 1984, he ended: "We therefore feel that we are unable to agree to your proposals. We do realise that you have 'missed out' this year on the Christmas bonus and therefore we would be happy to offer you a £100 in the spirit of goodwill. Please let me know."

In my reply, I wrote: " I'll remind you that had I not worked far beyond the reasonable call of duty for so many years at a salary other journalists considered demeaning for an editor of a national magazine, AW would not have developed into the commercially desirable publication it became. When I took over as editor the circulation was around 10,000; by the time I handed over the reins it was up around 25,000." I continued: "Do I have to remind you that the reason I stepped down as editor at the end of 1984, having given a full year's notice of that intention and agreeing to a pay cut, was precisely because after 16 years of editing the magazine and writing vast chunks of it, working all hours on a laughably low editorial budget, I knew I would eventually crack under the pressure if I didn't get off that treadmill. You could hardly complain when I decided enough was enough." I ended: "You then offered £100 'in the spirit of goodwill'. That is the ultimate insult, and if I wasn't such a polite fellow I might be tempted to tell you what to do with it. Instead, I suggest you donate it to a charity of your choice."

Pat was equally incensed and, writing independently at length, expressed her disgust and provided some insight into my dedication to the job. "I well remember his being ill once (from exhaustion?) and he still did his copy, lying in bed, and I took it to Victoria to Red Star it to the office. You never saw how hard he worked either, single handed, at the Los Angeles Olympics, not to mention countless other meetings over the years, including the Commonwealth Games in Edinburgh. I was in the room when he was typing frantically till the small hours almost every night, after being in the stadium working all day. His hours seemed to be endless, not to mention the freelance work he was forced to do as well to give us a living. ... What you in fact sold was what Mel built up and put his heart and soul into, at great cost to himself, both financially and health-wise – as I can testify, because I watched it happen! But I'm not saying these things because I'm his wife, Mr Anderson, but because they are the truth!"

Not surprisingly, we never heard any more from Mr Anderson but, with a wife like that to support me, I was reminded that nothing in life is as important as a loving partner. I was a lucky guy.

I was fortunate too that for practically the whole of my career I had adored my job. But that was no longer the case and as the weeks ticked by, and my own role steadily diminished, I realised that I had no future with AW. Keith was laying down guidelines which I found increasingly unacceptable. I had always regarded AW as a journal of record as well as being as topical as possible, and in the case of overseas results in those pre-Internet days many performances of note took quite a while to surface. My policy had always been to include any significant results, no matter how dated, but Keith laid down a rule that "we will only publish results that are a month or less old." However, the area which caused me most distress was that Julie was making changes to my column. When I protested to Keith, he replied: "I fully back her subbing judgements."

That was the same Julie who, presumably with Keith's approval, ran a by-lined story in May 1988 under the screaming headline "Zola's suicide bid" ... which turned out to be totally false. Two issues later came the follow-up. "Zola Budd has denied AW's story that she tried to commit suicide several days before she flew back to South Africa. The 21 year-old, who said she was quitting athletics for a year because she was suffering from nervous exhaustion, claims she is disgusted that she wasn't asked to confirm or deny the allegation. Possibly if Budd had chosen to answer numerous messages left on her telephone answer machine, three requests made via her mother for a comment, and a recorded-delivery letter, AW would have got her side of the story which we were given in good faith." Of course, without proper substantiation, that story should never have been published.

Earlier, on April 3, I wrote a very long letter to Keith outlining my grievances. I kept a copy, which I hadn't looked at for nearly 30 years until writing this book. Reading it again reminded me of how bitter I felt at that time. "The experience and knowledge for which I thought I was being employed are being increasingly ignored and my status has been so eroded that I feel I'm being treated as the office junior. I would remind you, without wishing to sound too pompous, that I have more journalistic experience than the rest of the editorial staff put together and am employed as a senior/executive member of staff. I fully accept your authority as editor, but in turn I expect the courtesy and consideration due to someone in my position."

I continued: "You and Julie should be concerning yourself less about my copy and more about the appalling waste of the biggest story to hit athletics in years. We were the first magazine to carry the Evangelisti story (remember, I wrote it from Brussels) and yet now, at the moment when it's been ascertained that several officials conspired to falsify a result at the World Champs, it's dismissed in a 15-line brief [in the March 31 issue] when it cried out for a lead story and editorial comment. But then, my opinion on these matters is never sought and probably of no account." Belatedly, in the April 21 issue, under the heading 'The Italian Job', I was given a full page to document the affair in detail.

Never, in the history of international athletics, has there been a scandal to compare with the rigging of the men's long jump at last September's IAAF World Championships in Rome. Athletes and coaches have been known to cheat, and even at Olympic level judging standards haven't always been beyond reproach, but that a group of officials would conspire to falsify a measurement in order to guarantee a medal for an athlete from their own country almost defies belief.

Following a further dispute with Keith over my freelance activities, I wrote him an even longer letter on June 3, drawing attention to the many factual errors I spotted in the May 27 issue (I wasn't involved in any proof reading) and stressing "the standard of punctuation and grammar throughout the mag is a disgrace. Doesn't anyone in the office understand where and when an apostrophe is used?" I ended my missive: "Together with mutual respect and a pooling of our talents and knowledge, we can achieve a great magazine. On the other hand, if you're going to persist with a 'you do this and no argument' attitude, then I'll have to give serious thought to my future with AW. I believe I have strong grounds for suing for breach of contract. I am deeply disillusioned and frustrated. That your persistent downgrading of my work and lack of consultation is leading me to consider leaving AW after 27 years is something which ought to concern you. If it doesn't, then there's not much to be discussed."

On June 20 I met Ian Beacham, the EMAP Pursuit publisher, to discuss my departure. He did not agree there had been any breach of contract and in a subsequent letter to me he wrote: "I see the situation as being one of resignation by you through your dissatisfaction over your current working position on AW. From the magazine's viewpoint, there has been no change to the job specification verbally offered to you when the publication was taken over by EMAP. In these circumstances, there is no legal entitlement to any financial compensation." He added: "In recognition of your long service, I am prepared to make an *ex-gratia* payment of £2000. This is a gesture on our part for the immense contribution you have made to AW and is not a legal obligation."

I formally tendered my resignation on July 5 in a letter to Ian Beacham, bringing up another bone of contention. "Another blow to my status was the way it was decided that I would not be covering the Olympic Games in Seoul. It was from incredulous national newspaper colleagues that I found out a few weeks ago that I was not even on the list of accreditations being considered by the British Olympic Association. Despite repeated requests to the editor since last autumn that we urgently needed to discuss Olympic coverage plans and the part I would be asked to play, no such discussion ever took place." I continued: "As the job I was contracted to do no longer exists in any meaningful sense, I am claiming constructive dismissal and will be making application to an industrial tribunal on those grounds." I sought backing from the National Union of Journalists, but in the end I didn't need to take the case to a tribunal as I reached a severance agreement with Ian Beacham. My employment ceased on July 30.

Incidentally, when it became obvious that I would not be covering the Olympics in September I assumed Keith or, better still, the more experienced and knowledgeable Brian Smyth would travel out to Seoul ... but no, it was Julie! Long after leaving AW she went on to forge a successful career as a rugby league reporter for the *Sun*, *News of the World* and *Daily Star*, but it really wasn't a bright idea to expect her to cover an Olympics single handed at that early stage of her career in athletics journalism. By then I didn't care. My freelance career was booming and I was involved in an exciting new project. Life was good again.

But back to the athletics action in 1988. The first major occasion was the European Indoor Championships in Budapest and I was able to report that British athletes matched their best ever tally of six medals. Wendy Sly finished third in the 3000m while Brian Whittle (400m) and Jon Ridgeon (60m hurdles) placed second. David Sharpe, the world junior champion and still only 20, ran the best planned and executed race of his career to win the 800m, but the star of the show was Linford Christie.

[He] didn't quite manage to bring off an unprecedented sprint double but his feat of winning the 60m and taking the bronze at 200m was still remarkable – particularly for a man who, at the start of the winter, vowed he wouldn't race at 200m indoors again and whose personal best for 60 stood at an exceedingly modest 6.85. His cracking form quickly became evident when in the semis he let rip after a sluggish get-away to win in a scintillating 6.55 to shave 3/100ths off his recent UK record. In the final, some four hours later, we saw the worst and best of Christie. His start was appalling. At halfway he appeared out of contention but produced one of the most devastating displays of sprinting ever seen. He tore through the opposition to score a famous victory in 6.57.

Although Zola Budd didn't compete on the track in 1988 that didn't mean she was out of the news. In the April 21 issue I was actually allowed a prominent comment piece.

The British Board has been plunged into the most severe crisis in its history. The IAAF Council has, in effect, pointed a gun at the Board's head: either suspend Zola Budd for at least a year, or risk Britain's total exclusion from international athletics. The IAAF's grounds for requesting the Board to suspend Budd remain spurious despite its assertion that she breached Rule 53(1). Budd, of course, has been as well aware of that rule as anybody and – knowing the consequences – has never raced in South Africa since being granted British nationality in 1984. What the IAAF Council decided last weekend is that a person can 'take part' in an athletics event without actually competing. No one is disputing that Budd was present at a cross country meeting in Brakpan, South Africa, last June. She was wearing running gear and took the opportunity to train. What remains in dispute is whether such action constitutes spectating or participation in the event itself. The IAAF Council says it "cannot accept that a 'mere spectator' is permitted to run on or close to the course while races at a meeting are in progress." That really is nonsense. At almost any cross country event there are more tracksuited figures jogging around the course or from point to point than there are actual competitors in the race. Is the IAAF seriously telling us those physically active bystanders are not spectators but are actual participants? Had Budd blatantly transgressed the rules, the IAAF's measures would have been justified. But there is an element of the 'kangaroo court' about the way in which this decision was reached, without 'the defendant' even being invited to speak up on her own behalf. Fair play and natural justice are indispensable in sport as in all other areas of life ... and they seem to have been conspicuously lacking in the IAAF's judgement.

The crisis was averted as on May 9 Zola flew back to South Africa, stating "my general medical practitioner and other medical advisers have told me that I am suffering from nervous exhaustion and that I need a substantial period of recuperation along with the support of my family and friends to regain my health. I am, therefore, on medical advice, withdrawing from international competition during this period of recovery." We didn't know it at the time but the Zola Budd saga was over. She married Mike Pieterse in April 1989 and two months later she announced that "after careful consideration of all the elements affecting my personal and professional life, I have decided not to return to the United Kingdom to pursue my running career."

That year, in *Zola*, her autobiography, she wrote: "You only have to study the Bible to recognise the injustice of *apartheid*. The Bible tells me all men are born equal and that we will all be equal before God. I can't reconcile segregation along racial lines with the teaching of the Bible and as a Christian I find *apartheid* intolerable." What a pity she did not make her views known earlier – although if she had she would have been targeted in South Africa by white supremacists. She was in a no-win situation. In April 1991, in Durban, Zola ran 8:35.72 for 3000m, second fastest in the world that year ... but in second place to South Africa's new superstar Elana Meyer (8:32.00). That was her last outstanding performance although she did make the team for the 1992 Olympics as post-*apartheid* South Africa was welcomed back into the fold, and she remains a runner to this day, competing in marathons and ultra-marathons.

As the Seoul Olympics drew closer, one of the events most eagerly awaited – particularly by British fans – was the 1500m. Steve Ovett was no longer a serious contender but Steve Cram, Seb Coe and Peter Elliott all had high hopes. The first big confrontation came in Oslo on July 2 when Cram posted the fastest mile time of the year (3:48.85) ahead of Elliott (personal best of 3:49.20), Jens-Peter Herold of the GDR (3:49.22) and Somalia's world champion Abdi Bile (3:49.40). No one took much notice of what was in effect a "B' race, at 1500m, won by Kenya's Peter Rono in a modest 3:36.71. At Crystal Palace on July 8 Coe won the 800m in 1:46.13 and declared "it is frightening to think I'm running better now than at the same time in 1984. Everything is going to plan." Bile (2:17.75) prevailed in a close finish to the 1000m over Cram and Elliott, while Said Aouita took the 1500m in 3:36.50 and two days later in Nice clocked 3:32.69. Aouita had made it known that he was vacating his Olympic 5000m crown in favour of doubling at 1500m and 800m, and put down a marker in Verona on July 27 by beating Elliott, 1:44.64 to 1:44.75. Coe won a 1500m in Switzerland on July 31 in 3:37.74, achieving the Olympic qualifying standard, but met with disaster at the Olympic Trials in Birmingham six days later when, suffering from a heavy cold ("I could barely breathe") he finished fourth in his heat (3:45.01) and failed to reach the final, won in slow time by Elliott from Steve Crabb, while Cram took the 800m in a speedy 1:44.16 ahead of Tom McKean.

What would the selectors do? The stated policy was for the first two in the Trials to be chosen automatically with the third place awarded at the selectors' discretion. Thus the invidious choice was between Coe and Elliott in the 800m, Coe and Cram in the 1500m! In his 2012 autobiography *Running My Life*, Coe claimed that he knew he had been the unanimous choice of the six selectors (Frank Dick, Andy Norman and four former team managers) for the 800m slot "and that two of the six thought I could do both distances and should be given time to prove my fitness for the 1500m. Their recommendation would now go through to the general council who were meeting a couple of days later. The council's job was to ratify the decision of the selectors. Everything duly went through on the nod – except mine."

By a 11-10 vote Elliott (800m) and Cram (1500m) were nominated. "My failure to be selected for either the 800m or 1500m marks the lowest point of my career on the track, and ranks among the lowest of my life," Seb wrote. He knew, as when he struck gold in Moscow and Los Angeles, that he would be in top form when it counted, and his acute frustration was shared by his army of admirers, myself included. IOC president Juan Antonio Samaranch even advocated a wild card entry for Coe in order to defend his 1500m title but that would have set a precedent and he withdrew the proposal. In later years the IAAF did bring in wild cards for defending world champions.

Still suffering from respiratory problems, Coe had to give the Zürich meeting on August 17 a miss. In a very fast 800m Cram finished third in 1:43.42, Elliott fifth in 1:44.51 and McKean seventh in 1:45.05, while Aouita won the mile in 3:50.82. Two days later in Brussels Aouita confirmed his Olympic ambitions at 800m by winning in 1:44.36 with McKean fourth in 1:46.38. Cram won the 1500m in a world leading 3:30.95, followed in by Elliott (3:32.94) but Crabb finished far behind, fifth in 3:37.49. Aouita set a personal best of 1:43.86 in Cologne on August 21. Coe returned to the scene in Berlin on August 26, beaten by McKean (1:47.60 to 1:47.87), but two days later in Koblenz, although losing to Brazil's José Luiz Barbosa (1:43.34), Seb displayed a return to good form by clocking 1:43.93. On the same day at Crystal Palace, Aouita won at 1000m in 2:15.16 and Cram (a world leading 4:55.20) beat Elliott (4:55.72) in a hard fought 2000m. The final pre-Olympic meeting, in Rieti on August 31, saw Elliott win the 800m in 1:44.19, Coe place third at 1500m in 3:35.72 with Crabb fifth in 3:36.24 and Cram worryingly fail to finish in the 1000m after reaching 800m in 1:46.09. A significant result from Kenya was that Peter Rono won his Olympic Trials race at high altitude in 3:36.5.

So who won at the Olympics? Two Kenyan outsiders! The November edition of the monthly magazine *Athletics Today*, of which more later, carried my detailed Olympic event by event reports and here are my (abridged) accounts of the 800m and 1500m.

You will look in vain for the name of Paul Ereng among any list of contenders prior to 1988, for the simple reason that the 20 year-old Kenyan – a 45.6 400m runner at altitude last year – had never raced at the distance! His transition from promising 400m runner to Olympic 800m champion had been extraordinarily quick. He first drew attention to himself in April when he broke 1:47 for the first time. Victory in the National Collegiate (NCAA) Championships followed, but it was in Sweden in June that he blossomed into international class – running Abdi Bile close in 1:44.82. Later European races were less productive ... and he only just scraped into the Kenyan Olympic team. There were a couple of major shocks even before the semi-final stage. Tom McKean was justly disqualified for blatant pushing and shoving, while in the next quarter-final Steve Cram faded from fourth to sixth in the closing stages. "I pressed the pedal but there was nothing there," he said. Britain's sole survivor, the ever dependable Peter Elliott, had a close call himself in the semis. He tied up in the closing stages and only narrowly salvaged a qualifying place as Ereng strode to victory in a personal best of 1:44.55.

The final was a cracker of a race. José Luiz Barbosa reached the bell in a pulsating 49.54. At that stage Ereng was seventh in about 51 sec. Joaquim Cruz, bidding to become the first man since Peter Snell in 1964 to retain an Olympic 800m crown, struck round the turn to lead into the finishing straight ahead of Elliott, Ereng and Aouita ... but he started to run out of steam in the last 30m. The unheralded Ereng, it was, who strode confidently past for a remarkable victory in a lifetime best of 1:43.45. Cruz clung on for second in his best time (1:43.90) for three years, while Aouita (1:44.06) outlegged the ever game Elliott (1:44.12) for the bronze. Aouita may have lost his first race, at any flat event between 800m and 10,000m, for three years but he did make history by becoming the first athlete to gain an Olympic medal in both 800m and 5000m. Elliott's performance was all the more laudable considering he had to have a pain-killing cortisone injection for a groin injury only 25 minutes before the race.

Paul Ereng wasn't the only virtually unknown Kenyan to strike gold. Peter Rono? Who he? Well, he's 21, his best time before this season was 3:39.2 in 1985, and in 1986 he placed second in the World Junior Championships and even now his fastest time stands at 3:35.59. A run of 3:35.96 sufficed for victory in Seoul. What with the non-selection of Seb Coe, the withdrawal before the Games of injured world champion Abdi Bile and the hamstring trouble which caused world record holder Said Aouita to pull out of the semis, the line-up for the final was less distinguished than is the norm at such spectaculars as Oslo and Zürich. It was a race which Steve Cram would normally have expected to win but alas the world mile record holder was not in the best of health and the supreme prize – the only honour to elude him – again slipped from his grasp.

Gritty is an adjective often used to describe Peter Elliott, and never was it more deserved than in Seoul. Suffering from a groin injury necessitating daily painkilling injections, he did well enough in the 800m but his second place in the 1500m was quite remarkable in the circumstances. The early pace was slow until Rono – who took the lead after 700m – began to stretch the field on the third lap which he covered in 56.38. With 200m to go, Rono held a two metre lead over Elliott with Cram and Jens-Peter Herold abreast, and that margin remained substantially unaltered until the line, the final 400m taking 52.8. In the finishing straight Herold (3:36.21) momentarily crept past Elliott on the inside, but Elliott (3:36.15) counter-attacked to make sure of the silver while Cram (3:36.24) strained unavailingly to catch the East German. Rono, though, was never headed throughout the last two laps to become the most unexpected Olympic 1500m champion since Luxembourg's Josy Barthel in 1952. Steve Crabb placed ninth in his semi in 3:39.55.

Of course, the event which overshadowed everything else in Seoul was the 100m.

Ben Johnson will go down in athletics history not, gloriously, as the fastest man the world has ever seen but, infamously, as the athlete who cheated his way to an Olympic 100m title and was found out. His reign as champion lasted less than three days, and that sensational time of 9.79 will never make the record books. The news of Johnson's disqualification, following a test which revealed the presence of an anabolic steroid, cast a shadow over the entire Olympic athletics programme and not least the 100m itself. But it would be unfair if the splendid achievements of Carl Lewis and Linford Christie were to be somehow devalued. Both ran faster than ever before, and Christie's time of 9.97 was the fulfilment of a dream – to become the first European to crack 10 seconds. Finishing nearly a metre and a half behind Johnson, Lewis trimmed the American record to 9.92 [later ratified as a world record when Johnson's 9.83 from 1987 was retrospectively annulled]. Thus, albeit in unhappy circumstances, Lewis also realised his dream: to become the first man to win the Olympic 100m crown for the second time.

Lewis also became the first man to retain an Olympic long jump title, leaping 8.72m for his 56th consecutive victory, but narrowly lost in the 200m to his friend Joe DeLoach (19.75 to 19.79) and never got to run in the 4x100m relay as the US squad was disqualified in the heats.

The most successful athlete of the Games was Flo-Jo with three gold medals and a silver. She never failed a drugs test but there have always been suspicions as, a very good sprinter before 1988 with best times of 10.96 and 21.96, she reappeared in 1988 as a much more muscular figure and proceeded to set a staggering world record of 10.49 (with a sceptically received zero wind reading on a breezy day) at the US Olympic Trials.

One of the enduring images of the Seoul Olympics is that of Florence Griffith Joyner sprinting to glory with a huge smile on her face. We're used to sprinters with agonised, distorted features ... but grins well before the finish line is reached? Truly, Flo-Jo is a one-off. There has never been a female sprinter like her. Not only does she run like the wind, but her grace, relaxation and muscular power set her apart from all others. She is the Jesse Owens of women's sprinting. She started off with an Olympic record of 10.88 and then improved to 10.62 in her quarter-final. In the semis she coasted to a windy 10.70, while in the final she sped to another Olympic record of 10.54 with the wind over the limit. Evelyn Ashford, running as well as ever, was fully three metres behind in second place, the widest victory margin since 1952.

233

"You ain't seen nothing yet!" is what Flo-Jo might have called out after the 100m, for it was over 200m that we saw the full flowering of her astonishing talent. She kicked off with a sedate 22.51 heat before stretching those muscular legs in the quarter-finals with an American and Olympic record of 21.76. In the first semi-final the next day, Merlene Ottey ran 22.07 and Silke Möller 22.15, good times by any standards, but some five metres in front of them was the peerless American in 21.56 and thus the world record of 21.71, established by Marita Koch and equalled by Heike Drechsler, had been shattered. One hundred minutes later the finalists settled into their blocks. Griffith Joyner held a narrow lead at the half distance in 11.11 but powered away in spectacular style along the straight to stop the timing device in an amazing 21.34!

She hadn't finished yet, for she ran third leg for the winning team in the 4x100m relay and then performed a near miracle in the 4x400m.

We had the intriguing situation of a last lap duel between the world's number one, Olga Bryzgina, and an athlete who had never before raced 400 at international level and whose pb of 50.94 dated back to 1983. With 200m to go Bryzgina had lengthened her lead to four metres but Flo-Jo came back a little in the finishing straight to end up a little more than a stride behind. The times were tremendous – Bryzgina 47.80, Griffith Joyner 48.08 – with the Soviet squad clocking a world record 3:15.17 and the USA 3:15.51.

This most enigmatic of athletes did not race again on the track. Unhappily, she was to hit the headlines again ten years later when she died in her sleep, aged just 38. Flo-Jo's world records still stand unchallenged, as does the heptathlon score in Seoul of 7291 points by her sister-in-law Jackie Joyner-Kersee. All she did was to clock 12.69 for the hurdles, high jump 1.86m, put the shot 15.80m, sprint 200m in 22.56, long jump 7.27m (she later won the individual title with 7.40m), toss the javelin 45.66m and run 800m in 2:08.51! In the corresponding men's event, Daley Thompson failed in his bid to become the first man to win a third Olympic decathlon title … but how heroically he tried.

Just as he won many new admirers last year for his graciousness in defeat in the World Championships, so in Seoul he won plaudits for his courage and tenacity in the face of mounting adversity. The Thompson of old would have destroyed this field, but he was handicapped before the competition even started. A thigh injury, sustained while training for the pole vault a week before the contest was a blow to his hopes, and it was clear from the first two events he was not going to be near his best. At the halfway mark it was the 2.01m (6ft 7in) tall East German, Christian Schenk, in the lead with 4470, with Thompson (4332) third. Thompson was still in third position after seven events. The pole vault was critical to his fast receding medal chances. The gods were not with Daley, though. His pole snapped at his first attempt at an opening height of 4.70m – a terrifying experience at the best of times. Yet, despite the shock and pain (he aggravated his leg injury and hurt his shoulder), Daley resisted any temptation to quit. He bounced back to clear 4.70m and 4.90m but effectively he lost further ground and after eight events he was fourth. The javelin proved to be Thompson's shining hour. Off a limp-up rather than a run-up, he threw a miraculous 64.04m for a pb with the new javelin! He was back in third place. The 1500m was a dramatic finale to a 13 hour day of competition. With his left thigh encased in a bandage, Thompson gave his all to run 4:45.11 but Canada's Dave Steen leapfrogged over him for third place with 8328 to Thompson's 8306. The title went to Schenk (8488) ahead of team-mate world champion Torsten Voss (8399).

No golds for Britain this time but in addition to Christie and Elliott there were silver medals for Colin Jackson in the 110m hurdles (13.28), the men's 4x100m relay team (38.28), Liz McColgan (née Lynch) in the 10,000m (31:08.44) and Fatima Whitbread in the javelin (70.32m), while bronze was won by Mark Rowland in the steeplechase with a time of 8:07.96 which remains the unthreatened UK record, and by Yvonne Murray at 3000m (8:29.02).

As mentioned, I wasn't in Seoul but I saw all the action close up as I was employed for 17 nights (midnight to 9.30 am) as a statistician/sub-editor by Thames Television at their London studios. Having left AW some weeks earlier, it was crucial that I made a success of my freelance work, and luckily it proved fruitful. In addition to my regular long-established press service, I worked with the ITV commentary team at the IAC international meeting in Edinburgh, contributed several items to *The Times*, wrote articles for the IAAF and a number of magazines, compiled an Olympic form guide for the *Racing Post* and acted as athletics betting consultant for Mecca. The most lucrative assignment, though, was being hired by Thames Television, largely thanks to Neil Duncanson – a major player in TV sports production and author of such outstanding athletics books as *Tales of Gold* and *The Fastest Men On Earth* and its updated version *100 Metre Men*. My first week in the studios was a little fraught as suddenly I needed to become an instant expert on every Olympic sport but once the athletics started I was in my element, compiling biographical notes and other background information for the presenters and caption writers. Roger Black, on crutches with his foot in plaster following surgery, was one of the regular guests.

However, the most significant development in my professional career began in late June, just before I escaped the clutches of EMAP. I met Eddie Kulukundis at his company's offices near Fleet Street to discuss a possible new publication. My idea was a modest little fortnightly magazine entitled *Athletics International* which would continue, but expand, the overseas results and news service that I had built up and compiled for AW for so many years. Eddie, a prominent theatre impresario as well as being chairman of the Sports Aid Foundation, was crazy about athletics and became the sport's most generous philanthropist. Among the athletes he has supported financially have been Olympic champions Steve Ovett, Linford Christie, Sally Gunnell and Denise Lewis, plus numerous other stars including Roger Black and Fatima Whitbread. He shared my enthusiasm for the idea and Tim Green, with his background in advertising and business, was brought into the discussions.

We were about to get quotes from the firm which printed Eddie's theatre programmes when a much more ambitious project was floated. *Athletics Today* was an attractively produced monthly edited by Randall Northam and on August 8 he, Eddie, Tim and myself began talking about converting *Athletics Today* into a weekly magazine to compete against AW. So many AW subscribers were unimpressed since its conversion a year earlier that we thought we could bring out a far superior weekly and win over their readers. It would be a gamble and we were realistic enough to acknowledge that in the long run the market could sustain only one such magazine.

I had mixed feelings at first. I had been greatly attracted by the prospect of bringing out a small-scale *Athletics International* and wasn't at all sure whether, after all those years on the AW treadmill, I was prepared to commit myself to another full-time editing job with all the pressure involved. I talked it over with Pat, who encouraged me to go for it if I wanted to, and after several more meetings the fateful decision was made, on September 5, that *Athletics Today* (hereafter referred to as AT) would go weekly from the beginning of January 1989. Eddie, as publisher, would finance the operation; Randall and I would be joint editors and Tim would be the publishing director.

Much planning would be necessary before we launched but, shortly after the Olympics ended and I had filed my Olympic report for the November edition of the monthly AT, Pat and I took off for the holiday of a lifetime. We had both turned 50 in 1988 and we were going to treat ourselves. On October 10 we flew from Gatwick to Los Angeles, spending two nights in Hollywood (a dream for a couple of dedicated film fans), and then on to Las Vegas for another two nights. Next it was back to LA for a flight to Honolulu. After a delightful week's stay there it was a short hop over to Maui for four nights, followed by three nights on Kauai. The weather throughout was perfect, the scenery stunning and I had to pinch myself that I wasn't dreaming as I drove around these exotic islands. It was a fantasy come true. Our final two night stopover was in San Francisco and we arrived home, jetlagged but full of pleasant memories, on October 31.

One week later Eddie, Randall, Stan Greenberg, Peter Matthews and I met to hammer out top ten world merit rankings for 1988 for insertion in the final monthly issue of AT. Controversially, perhaps, we ranked Peter Rono only fourth in the 1500m behind Aouita, Cram and Elliott on the basis that they could point to much more impressive records over the season, Aouita being unbeaten until injury forced him to scratch from his Olympic semi. After that it was full speed ahead with preparations for the first weekly edition and it was excellent news when Brian Smyth agreed to leave AW and work for us. This tumultuous year drew to a close with a weekend trip to Monte Carlo for the IAF Gala and an exclusive interview with Daley Thompson as the star feature of our launch issue.

24. AT v AW: LET BATTLE COMMENCE (1989)

After weeks of preparation the first weekly issue of *Athletics Today* was scheduled to appear on Thursday, January 5 1989. Published by the ever enthusiastic Eddie Kulukundis, the joint editors were *Daily Express* athletics correspondent Randall Northam and myself; pole vaulter Brian Smyth was appointed chief sub-editor, sprinter Nick Davies was production editor, Samantha Bull editorial assistant. The peerless Mark Shearman was our photographer; Tim Green publishing director and Lisa Thompson (now the London Marathon operations director) our office manager in Kingston-upon-Thames. And what a line-up of columnists we had: Seb Coe, Linford Christie, Peter Elliott, Hugh Jones, Alan Parry of ITV and John Rodda of *The Guardian* together with Neil Wilson of *The Independent* as a feature writer!

In a joint editorial, Randall and I welcomed readers to the first new weekly athletics magazine to be launched in Britain since 1950 and Jimmy Green wrote that "the editorial team is second to none in knowledge and experience, and I visualise the magazine setting new standards in athletics journalism, backed by one of the sport's greatest benefactors, Eddie Kulukundis."

Unfortunately, we got off to a false start. The launch issue was delayed by a printing machine breakdown and appeared a day late, but the magazine proved an instant hit with discerning readers. Not only the content, but also the layout was so superior to AW's, and when word got round many AW subscribers were persuaded to switch allegiance.

The big feature of that first issue was my exclusive interview with Daley Thompson, an athlete whose relationship with the rest of the Press was somewhat strained. Our chat was revealing. Having been unbeaten in the decathlon from 1979 to 1986 his defeats in Rome 1987 and Seoul 1988 indicated that even he was not invincible. How tough had it been to accept? "It's been worse than I could ever have imagined. It's a terrible feeling." Which loss hurt more? The answer was Rome.

"To be honest, I couldn't believe it and I still can't believe it. That wasn't me - it must have been some other bloke who looks like me! I lost three to four months of training before Rome because of abductor muscle trouble, but I thought I was going to win, no problem. It's just the way I am. Most of my life things have gone well for me, and so I always think there's no reason why it shouldn't happen again." Was he tempted to drop out? "Even if I had been on one leg I would have hung in. I wouldn't have been able to look at myself the next day if I had dropped out. I'm not a quitter."

Prior to Seoul all was going well, until he injured himself in pole vault training just five days before the competition. "It was the abductor muscle again and it never went away although I was having treatment every day. Nevertheless, I was happy to go out and give it a go." He thought Jürgen Hingsen had the best chance of winning but a score of 8500 might be enough. He was shocked when Hingsen was disqualified for three false starts in the

100m and with another top contender, Siggy Wentz, a non-starter "my chances looked really good. I didn't think anyone else was going to score much over 8400 points."

However, the injury severely affected his speed and he knew a big score was out of the question. "At halfway, when I was third, I still thought I could win. After the discus I didn't think I could win anymore, but I might still come in second. The pole vault, though, was a bastard. The pole broke and I hurt my leg again. I still thought I could get second even though I could barely walk." What was the worst thing about losing? "It hurts, not because I got beaten but because I like to perform better, that's all. I just wasn't able to do the kind of things I should have been able to do ... that's why it hurts, not because I was beaten."

On drugs? "I hope the authorities make sure that Ben Johnson can never run again because of the damage he has done to our sport. I can't believe he could be let back in two years. I think someone of his stature should be made an example of. It's so bad; you have no idea how abhorrent I find it. It's just so wrong. Until we ban people for life we're not taking the drugs problem seriously enough. We are supposed to be the moral guardians of the sport so that we can hand it on to the kids."

Would he want his year-old daughter Rachel to become an athlete? The reply was rather shocking and was quoted widely. "No, with the sport in its present state I wouldn't want my daughter to be an athlete. I would much rather she played tennis or something else. Athletics is not something I would push her into, even though there's so much good fun to be had from it. I feel the sport is tainted. Apart from the drugs, I look around and see kids talking about shoe contracts. There's a lot more talk about money than there used to be. It's all gone too serious."

Seb Coe, in his first column, was also unhappy. "We were the first country to try and set up an integrated coaching structure but we have not progressed very far from the now distant days of Geoff Dyson. We have no more national event coaches now than in the old days. We are no better off, well comparatively so, in the field of sports science and sports medicine. There is not a structure in which well qualified physicians and surgeons could practise sports medicine exclusively and obtain a proper financial reward and there are still no adequate indoor training facilities for Great Britain."

Another columnist, Linford Christie, expressed his annoyance over financial arrangements. Referring to Carl Lewis, he wrote: "The last time we met outside of the Olympic final was in Zürich when Carl and Ben Johnson got $250,000 each and the other six of us got chicken feed. I don't mind facing Carl if we both get nothing, but if they are offering Carl loads of money and me peanuts they can forget it."

We were all proud of the 52 page inaugural edition, and it had been worth working for 16 hours non-stop on the Monday to complete the issue. Helped by Randall and Tim, I had even graduated from using a manual typewriter (for the past 35 years) to tapping my copy into an Apple Mac computer! What a boon that has been.

I was particularly gratified by the comprehensive overseas news and results service, with no Keith Nelson strictures about what to include. The *Athletics International* section which I had originally envisaged as a stand-alone publication was now an integral part of the magazine and I could rely on an incomparable team of correspondents, including Yves Pinaud (Africa), Mike Hurst and Paul Jenes (Australia), Cecil Smith (Canada), Matti Hannus (Finland), Robert Parienté of *L'Equipe* (France), Heinz Vogel of *Leichtathletik* (W Germany), Richard Ashenheim (Jamaica), John Velzian (Kenya), Luis Vinker (South America) and Scott Davis and Walt Murphy (USA). During the first year our team of columnists expanded to include John Anderson and Judy Simpson.

One of our most popular series, continued from the monthly version of AT, was Tony Ward's nostalgic "Yesterday's Heroes". His subjects during 1989 were Bob Hayes, Jan Zelezny, Dave Bedford (who admitted "I was absolutely scared stiff – petrified" at the 1972 Olympics), Don Thompson, Igor Ter-Ovanesyan, Jay Silvester, Derek Ibbotson, Mike Boit, Sonia Lannaman and Geoff Dyson ... an eclectic mix indeed. Michael Butcher was also busy on our behalf with his revealing interviews with Roger Kingdom, Ana Quirot, Kriss Akabusi, Charlie Spedding and Wendy Sly among many others.

I followed up the Daley interview with one with Portugal's Olympic, world and European marathon champion Rosa Mota, who revealed that when she first started running round the streets "the men would call out 'go home, woman'. They were offended by the sight of a woman out training." Her coach, José Pedrosa, added: "Women were also antagonistic, but not as much as the men. Portugal is a male chauvinistic country!" But Rosa's fame had led to acceptance. Pedrosa: "Now athletics is a respectable sport, and many women are running, jogging and exercising."

My next interview, which like Rosa's had been conducted at the World Athletics Gala in Monaco, was with Butch Reynolds, 400m world record holder with 43.29 but a disappointed second at the Olympics. As he once remarked: "I have learned to love the 400 but I hate it still with a passion." That record would stand for 11 years until bettered by Michael Johnson but Butch would soon be embroiled in a long and bitterly fought doping case.

High jumper Dalton Grant was my next subject, at the time UK record holder with 2.31m although he would go on to clear 2.37m. He was the most entertaining of jumpers, adding to the suspense of a competition by daringly passing at considerable heights. Often, but not always, the tactical gamble paid off. He certainly was not lacking in self confidence. "I reckon I've got eight feet (2.44m) in my legs. I'm aggressive and I'm determined, and I'm not scared of the bar the way a lot of jumpers are." What I didn't realise at the time was that Dalton went to the same school (Hackney Downs) as myself, Stan Greenberg, Arthur Gold, hurdler Harry Kane and pre-war walking world record breaker Bert Cooper. The school high jump record when I was a pupil was 1.78m, which was considered quite outstanding. Dalton, a Fosbury flopper of course, cleared 2.10m as a 16 year-old.

The February 16 issue featured an interview with Flo-Jo, conducted in California by Neil Duncanson of London Weekend Television. She revealed: "I set goals for the Olympics and achieved more than I dreamed of. But now there's the 400m world record and I feel like a challenge again. I know I can go on to 1992 and maybe the Olympics after that." None of that happened. She announced her retirement from the track later that month, her career forever the subject of controversy. For the record, she strongly denied any involvement with drugs and stressed that any athlete found guilty should be banned for life. I would like to believe that her staggering performances in 1988 were achieved legitimately but I remember that at the age of 28 her body shape noticeably changed as she progressed from best times of 10.96 and 21.96 to 10.49 and 21.34. The jury remains out.

After my doleful year under the EMAP regime it was wonderful to be working again in a friendly office environment. With Eddie always a source of encouragement and happy to finance our efforts at producing the best athletics magazine the world had ever seen (his accountants were less content!) we all got on well together. Monday was the crucial day each week as we tapped away and Nick expertly made up the pages, juggling headlines, text, photos and ads. Monday nights were particularly stressful as we put the final touches to an issue, with just a brief respite when one of us would pop down the road to bring in pizzas or hamburgers for sustenance, along with bottomless mugs of coffee. Often we worked through to dawn and I have to confess that driving home bleary eyed some 20 hours after getting up is not to be recommended.

Our first major international event, covered by Randall and me, was the European Indoor Championships at The Hague when the British team excelled with its best ever haul of nine medals, including golds for Ade Mafe (200m), Steve Heard (800m), Colin Jackson (60m hurdles) and Sally Gunnell (400m), while Dalton Grant jumped 2.33m, a UK record, losing only on countback.

Randall and I took turns to provide the weekly editorial. In the March 9 issue I commented on coach Charlie Francis' testament on oath that Ben Johnson had been taking performance enhancing drugs since 1981, the year he improved as a 19 year-old from 10.62 to 10.25.

If that is correct it's not only the 1988 Olympic title he should have been stripped of. It calls into question his 1987 world title and listed world record of 9.83, his 1986 Commonwealth Games gold medal, 1984 Olympic bronze medal, 1987 world indoor 60m title and world record among other achievements. John Holt, general secretary of the IAAF, says the rules do not allow for retrospective action in terms of taking away medals or world records from athletes proven to have taken drugs, but surely consideration should be given to framing legislation to cover that issue. There were, long before femininity tests were instituted, examples of world records being rescinded when it was discovered that certain athletes weren't quite what they appeared to be.

The IAAF did eventually take action and Johnson forfeited most of those honours. In recent years, as retrospective testing has become more sophisticated, numerous athletes have been stripped of their drug-assisted medals and records. What a pity that when the Berlin Wall fell and masses of documentation revealed state sponsored doping of leading GDR athletes that no such action was taken and many of those illegitimate performances remain in the record books.

Randall and I teamed up again to report on the World Indoor Championships in Budapest, enthusing in particular over John Regis and Ade Mafe scoring a 1-2 in the 200m. There were world indoor records for Olympic champion Paul Ereng with 1:44.84 for 800m, Holland's Elly Van Hulst with 8:33.82 for 3000m, outkicking Liz McColgan whose 8:34.80 was also inside Zola Budd's previous record, and Cuba's Javier Sotomayor who soared over 2.43m. Dalton Grant improved the UK record again to 2.36m, the same height as the silver and bronze medallists, but placed a frustrated fourth on countback. There was a silver lining, though, for Colin Jackson in the 60m hurdles. Perhaps the most pleasing performance came in the women's 200m where, after so many near-misses, Merlene Ottey finally won a global title.

Just when you think you may have seen it all in athletics, someone like Liz McColgan pops up with a performance which sends you reeling. The ultimate in 'impossible' doubles may have been Paavo Nurmi's Olympic 1500m/5000m success in 1924 and Jarmila Kratochvílová's 400m/800m triumph at the 1983 World Championships with amazingly brief recovery intervals, but Liz's Budapest exploits will also long be talked about in awe. Straight after the 3000m, Liz made her way to an ambulance outside the stadium, breathed in pure oxygen while she changed her kit and jogged back in time for the start of the 1500m just 15 minutes after she finished the 3000! It was madness, surely. Or was it? She was less than 10m behind the leader at the bell, and although understandably outpaced in the closing stages she hung on astonishingly well to clock 4:10.16 in sixth place.

In March our editorial team was strengthened by the recruitment of Mark Butler, who some years later would succeed Stan Greenberg as the BBC's statistician and would compile numerous invaluable statistical books for the IAAF. Richard Liston joined as news editor in May and the following month Mark was designated results and fixtures editor as well as specialising in features on young athletes. Meanwhile, over at AW I noticed that Julie Stott was promoted from news editor to assistant editor … only to leave in July to edit the football mag, *Match*. Keith Nelson didn't last much longer; in October he moved to another position in the company. Referring to AW, Wikipedia stated "by late 1989 one-third of sales had been lost." Steven Downes, an experienced athletics writer, took over as editor, a post he held only until February 1991. AW would flounder for many more years. Ultimately they would outlast AT but only because of greater financial resources. In terms of quality there was no contest.

My Life in Athletics

One of the brightest memories from my year as an EMAP employee was working with Richard Tuck and I was devastated in May to hear of his tragic end. *It was with great sadness that I learned of the death of former colleague Richard Tuck, a reporter for AW. Richard, who was 30, went missing during a walking holiday in Austria and more than two weeks went by before his body was discovered by police. I last chatted with him at the National 12-Stage Road Relay on the eve of his ill-fated holiday. Although now on rival publications we remained friends, and I shall remember with affection Richard's infectious enthusiasm and his love for athletics history. He was a walking encyclopaedia of the sport's trivia.*

In June I interviewed Sally Gunnell who, at that time the previous year, had a best (and only) time for 400m hurdles of 59.9. Now she was UK record holder at 54.03 and on her way to greatness. Although she was Commonwealth Games champion and UK record holder for 100m hurdles with 12.82 she felt that she did not have the basic speed to go faster than around 12.78. "If I could have been the best 100m hurdler in the world I would have stuck with it. Now I would like to be the best in the world at 400m hurdles, and I think I have more opportunity in that event."

Prior to 1989 if you, as a British televiewer, wished to watch top class athletics you were served by the BBC, ITV and Channel 4. But that year a major new player appeared on the scene in the form of Eurosport, then a division of Sky, with former NUTS member, 400m star and Channel 4 head of sport Adrian Metcalfe in charge. Richard Russell, formerly with ITV, moved to the station as controller of production, Ian Darke – previously at BBC Radio – became head commentator and I was invited to join the team as statistician. It was the perfect job for me as it dovetailed nicely with my work for AT, enabling me to travel to and report on all the top meetings throughout Europe at no expense to the magazine. What a schedule it was! Our first assignment was to Lausanne on June 27 and between then and September 15 I travelled to Helsinki, Oslo, East Berlin, Nice, Barcelona, Pescara, Budapest, Zürich, West Berlin, Cologne, Koblenz, Brussels, Monaco and finally Barcelona again for the World Cup. There were also studio dubbing sessions at Sky HQ in London and in addition I reported for AT on meetings at Crystal Palace, the European Cup in Gateshead and the combined AAA/WAAA Championships in Birmingham. Once that hectic season was over, Pat and I flew off for two weeks in Florida and in December I was in Monaco again for the World Gala. Lucky I enjoyed travel!

On most of the Eurosport trips during the next couple of years or so there were five of us: commentators Ian Darke, Stuart Storey (long a mainstay of the BBC team) and newcomer Tim Hutchings, producer Tony Baines and myself. From close quarters I marvelled at the commentators' calm and expertise, my main contribution being to provide them with cards packed with statistical and biographical information. That was pretty stressful as I was totally dependent on obtaining the start lists before I could write out the cards (one for each commentator and for each heat or final) and the guys needed time to prepare for the transmission. During the live broadcast I would hold a stopwatch

242

to provide splits and scribble notes during races with guidance as to the likelihood of any records being broken plus any other items of information which might be of significance. We were worn out by the end of each meeting but there was satisfaction too over a job well done and altogether it was an experience I would not have missed for the world.

What great performances I was privileged to witness that hectic summer. Among them were world records by Paula Ivan (4:15.61 mile in Nice), Roger Kingdom (12.92 110m hurdles in Zürich), Said Aouita (7:29.45 3000m in Cologne), Arturo Barrios (27:08.23 10,000m in W Berlin) and Santa Monica Track Club anchored by Carl Lewis (1:19.38 4x200m in Koblenz).

The most intriguing if unsettling trip I undertook was to East Berlin. I was travelling alone, my mission being to fax back to the studios in London the start lists for the Olympischer Tag (Olympic Day) Grand Prix meeting and a report on the highlights, one of which was Merlene Ottey's 11.04 100m into a 2.5m/sec wind. The journey started conventionally enough, flying Pan-Am to West Berlin. East Berlin in July 1989 was cut off from West Berlin by the infamous Wall and my means of getting there, after much scrutiny of my travel documents, was to take the S-Bahn (subway train) from the west's Bahnhof Zoo station to the east's Friedrichstrasse. My first taste of GDR society came as I emerged from the station to take a taxi to the Palasthotel. I joined the back of a long queue, which only very slowly moved as every few minutes someone would walk up to the front of the line and grab the next taxi to arrive. No one objected, for these queue-jumpers were Communist party officials or others designated as more important citizens than the *hoi polloi*. To protest would have spelt big trouble. I eventually did get into a cab and found the hotel, open only to foreign visitors and the privileged, to be excellent.

Next morning, the day of the meeting, I requested a taxi to take me from the hotel to the Ludwig-Jahn Stadium. No problem. I got the start lists I needed and asked for a taxi to get me back to the hotel so I could fax them to London and work on my notes. Not possible, I was told. Somewhat mystified I walked out to the main road intending to flag down a cruising taxi. Several appeared but none would stop (I learned later they were allowed to pick up passengers only at specified locations). Aware that precious time was slipping by, I started walking and quickly found an apparently deserted S-Bahn station. I couldn't work out how one bought a ticket so I made my way to the platform, saw that the station close to my hotel was the next stop and boarded the train, full of apprehension that there could be trouble ahead trying to explain (I don't speak German) why I was travelling without a ticket. Fortunately, there was no barrier, no ticket collector and I exited the station breathing a sigh of relief. Back at the hotel I tried to find out why I couldn't get a taxi back from the stadium, only to be met with shrugged shoulders. Again, I had no problem getting there for the evening meeting but wondered about the return journey. Fortunately, I spotted a group of athletes, including Merlene, heading for a coach, and to my delight discovered it was bound for my hotel. I was more than happy to leave the GDR next morning for my flight back from West Berlin. I felt sorry for the imprisoned East

Berliners, cut off from the infinitely higher standard of living and personal freedom enjoyed by their western neighbours, and I was so happy – if astounded – when the dreaded Wall was demolished just four months later.

One of the most gratifying editorials I penned for AT appeared in the August 10 issue. *It isn't often that dreams come true, but what many people dismissed as sheer fantasy – the notion that the British men could win the European Cup, or at any rate qualify for the World Cup by defeating either the USSR or the GDR – actually became a reality in Gateshead. Kriss Akabusi's morale-boosting victory in the first event set the tone. From then on anything, it seemed, was possible and an unquenchable spirit – fuelled by the responsive crowd – raised the team to unprecedented heights of endeavour. Athletics is essentially an individual's sport; that is what attracts so many to it. But, on occasions, there is a bond which links the sprinter with the distance runner, the high jumper with the hammer thrower. Never was that seen to better advantage than last weekend.*

British athletics has enjoyed golden moments in the past. There was that famous victory over the Russians in Volgograd in 1963, various Olympic triumphs and the medal spree at the last European Championships. But the European Cup, the supreme test of a nation's all-round athletic strength, was – it appeared – beyond our grasp. We could always be relied upon to supply some of the winners but there were too many weak events for us to seriously challenge the mighty Soviet and East German teams. Well, we still have our weak spots, but so too does the opposition (not a single East European won a men's track event) and progress in several departments has been marked. We are no longer simply a nation of harriers. Of the nine victories achieved, only one, Tom McKean, came in the middle and long distance running department. The others were by sprinters Linford Christie, John Regis and the two relay teams, hurdlers Colin Jackson and Kriss Akabusi, and field events athletes Dalton Grant and Steve Backley.

The 100th AAA Championships in Birmingham the following weekend (the 39th I had attended) brought together Seb Coe and Steve Ovett for the first time on a British track. The clash wasn't what we had anticipated so eagerly. Coe chalked up his first AAA 1500m title, while a despondent Ovett trailed home in ninth place over 30m behind. Approaching the bell, Steve Crabb fell and Coe – who strained his left hamstring hurdling over the sprawled figure – lost some 20m to the leaders. Eighth at the bell, he moved through relentlessly to win in 3:41.38 thanks to a 51.8 last lap. In contrast, Ovett's heart was never in this race and he broke down later during an ITV interview with Jim Rosenthal. He felt he had been exploited and pressurised to take part in a race he didn't want to run. In what proved to be his last full season, Coe went on to run 800m in 1:43.38 (his fastest for four years) to rank third on the year's world list and 3:34.05 for seventh spot at 1500m. Ovett's best times were 1:48.16 and 3:37.40, Steve Cram ran 1:46.37 and 3:35.3 *en route* to a 3:51.58 mile, while Peter Elliott – with his best days still to come – clocked 1:47.10 and 3:37.6 on the way to a 3:52.93 mile.

Arguably the most spectacular of all the world records set that year was Javier Sotomayor's high jump of 2.44m (equalling 8 feet, the height of a football crossbar!) in Puerto Rico.

He might well spawn a new schoolboy riddle. What has two legs and eight feet? Answer: a Cuban high jumper. He high jumped precisely 8 feet to break one of the sport's most accessible but tantalising barriers. Sotomayor, amazingly still only 21 after six seasons as a world class high jumper, was always the man most likely to succeed. He did, after all, clear a phenomenal 2.33m at the age of 16 and has improved every single year of his career. The accelerating pace of athletic progress is demonstrated by the fact that it took 80 years to improve from 6 feet to 7 feet but only 33 years from 7 feet to 8 feet ... although all-weather take-off areas, weight training and the advent of the Fosbury Flop has had much to do with the event's development in the past decade or two.

One of the most fascinating interviews we published was one with Gordon Pirie, then aged 58, conducted by that prolific contributor Alastair Aitken. He gave examples of his legendary training sessions, which included covering 30 miles (120 laps) round and round the Tooting Bec track, striding out for 330 yards on each circuit and jogging the bend. Asked his score against Chris Chataway, Pirie replied: "Including cross country we are 13 all. But what annoyed me about Chataway was that I never ran a race with him where he did any work. I would say that if I had walked he would still have walked behind me." The athlete he admired most: "Zátopek. I beat him three times; he beat me three times. Herb Elliott was the epitome of a competitor. With him you could go home, throw your spikes in the corner and say forget it!" If he had his time over again? "I wish I knew when I was running what I know now. I did some terrible things in training and I got away with murder. I used to do enormous training and then go out and run a world record straight on top of it, whereas now I know I need ten days to freshen up. I would have done some really good times then!"

Their Olympic medals or world records lay many years ahead but it was interesting to look back at the results of the English Schools Championships. Darren Campbell (2004 Olympic 4x100m gold) won the Intermediate 200m in 21.9 and Steve Smith (1996 Olympic bronze) was second in the high jump with 1.99m. Fiona May (1996 & 2000 Olympic silver for Italy) won the Senior long jump with 6.65m with Denise Lewis (2000 Olympic heptathlon gold) sixth with 5.63m; Paula Radcliffe (marathon world record) placed fourth in the Intermediate 1500m in 4:35.0, while 14 year-old Katharine Merry (2000 400m bronze) won the Junior 100m by an extraordinary 0.9 sec margin in 11.8. One J Davis finished seventh in the Intermediate 800m in 2:16.4 ... we know her better today as Jo Pavey!

Staged in the unfinished stadium which would host the Barcelona Olympics of 1992, the IAAF World Cup was marred by torrential rain falling on two of the three nights. The final session started 90 minutes late because of the vicious downpour, making the result of the first event even more remarkable as for the first time two men broke 13 seconds in the 110m hurdles. There was a following wind over the limit at 2.6m/sec but the times of 12.87 for Roger Kingdom and 12.95 for Colin Jackson were sensational, particularly as a following wind is not always an advantage for hurdlers. As Spain's Javier Moracho, who placed fifth, explained: "I think Kingdom would have beaten the world record [12.92] just the same without the following wind, and might even have done a better time because under these conditions he has problems taking three strides between hurdles because his stride is too long as it is." The British men's team placed third (119 points) behind the USA (133) and Europe (127), and individual wins were posted by Tom McKean in the 800m, Linford Christie in the 100m and Steve Backley in the javelin, while in the women's match Yvonne Murray, representing Europe, won the 3000m. There might have been another British victory but in the 1500m Seb Coe was baulked by Abdi Bile as they fought for the lead entering the finishing straight. Covering the final 300m in a savage 37.7, Bile won by less than a stride in 3:35.56. A protest was lodged but the Jury of Appeal rejected it. Six days later, at Crystal Palace, Coe ran his last race on a British track.

The first time Seb Coe travelled to Crystal Palace for an 800m race was on May 13 1973. He was a skinny 16 year-old schoolboy from Sheffield, primarily a 3000m runner in those days. He came with a personal best of 1:56.6 and left with 1:56.0, having finished second in a BMC youths race. What a leap of imagination would have been required to envisage the scene in the same stadium 16 years later as Coe bade farewell to a doting public. Twice Olympic 1500m champion, holder after eight years of one of the greatest world records on the books with his 1:41.73 800m, a man who in 14 years of competing for Britain never came away from a major international occasion without a medal ... arguably (Daley Thompson being the only other claimant) the greatest British athlete of all time. Coe, accorded a standing ovation by the sell-out crowd, may have run nearly 40 faster races but he will always remember his final 800m in Britain. It was an emotional occasion, joyous yet sad, as he toured the two laps in 1:45.70.

A final word on Zola Budd. Under the heading 'Zola – J'Accuse', I reviewed Zola's newly published autobiography.

According to her account she was the victim of circumstances, unable or unwilling to influence events, and the accusations start on the very first page. Zola makes it clear that she was reluctant to leave South Africa in the first place, but was too naïve and too much under her father's influence to resist. She pours scorn on the statement made by Daily Mail editor Sir David English that it would be a tragedy if she couldn't run for Britain "when her heart lies here." As Zola writes, "It was news to me that my heart lay in Britain. At the time I was desperately unhappy in England and even telephoned my coach shortly after my arrival to tell him I didn't want to go to the Olympics." Critics might eventually have overlooked the way she was thrust on the British athletics scene had she made more of an effort to integrate but her constant trips back to South Africa and her refusal, until it was too late in the day, to speak out against apartheid provided plenty of ammunition for those who alleged she was using her British citizenship as a passport of convenience. At the same time it's impossible not to feel compassion for Zola. Never mind the trials and tribulations of her athletics career ... here was a girl whose beloved elder sister Jenny died at the age of 24, whose parents divorced when she was 20, and whose estranged father was murdered a couple of months ago. She deserves the happiness she has found at last in her native land as the wife of Mike Pieterse.

Richard Liston left the magazine in November but continued to freelance for us and he was succeeded as news and features editor by Duncan Mackay, who had previously reported for AT on the Chicago and New York Marathons, and would develop into the most prolific of all of our writers. His output, whether reporting or interviewing, was stupendous.

At the end of the year we presented our 1989 world merit rankings, only this time the panel was extended to include two of Europe's leading authorities in Lennart Julin from Sweden and Robert Parienté from France. The highest ranked UK athletes were Steve Backley (1st javelin), Tom McKean (2nd 800m), Colin Jackson (2nd 110m hurdles}, Yvonne Murray (2nd 3000m) and Veronique Marot (2nd marathon). We asked our readers to choose their leading athletes of the 1980s. The winners were Carl Lewis (world male), Marita Koch (world female), Seb Coe (UK male) and Fatima Whitbread (UK female).

25. MAN WITH THE GOLDEN ARM (1990)

Long before anyone had heard of Mo Farah, the most celebrated athlete to be born in Somalia was Abdi Bile, the 1987 world 1500m champion and (controversially) 1989 World Cup winner. I interviewed him at the Monaco World Gala and that was the main feature of the first 1990 edition of AT. He wasn't lacking in self confidence. He felt that but for illness and injury he would have broken the world records for 1500m (3:29.46) and mile (3:46.32) and claimed "it's not so much a case of whether I could break the world records but rather by how many seconds I could break them. This year (1989) I was thinking of 3:27, or maybe even faster. Certainly such a time, and 3:44 for the mile, is possible for me." Even more astonishing was his statement that he didn't train in the winter, never runs more than 50 miles in a week and trains only once a day in the summer, nearly all of it on grass. In 1989 Bile had run personal best times of 1:43.60 for 800m, 2:14.50 for 1000m and 3:30.55 for 1500m, just missing his mile best of 3:49.40 with 3:49.90, but he would not come close to those world record targets. Although he competed at a high level until 1996 he would never again break 3:32 or 3:50.

I undertook a somewhat bizarre task in January. As Marita Koch had been voted by our readers the leading female athlete of the eighties, the director of the Sindelfingen indoor meeting in Germany invited AT to make a presentation there to Marita. I was chosen to make the trip (Randall was about to travel out to Auckland for the Commonwealth Games) and, after shopping at Selfridges to find an appropriate piece of silverware, I took part in an award ceremony that was warmly applauded by the crowd and featured on German television. My feelings were mixed; Marita was indeed an outstanding athlete and her 47.60 400m remains unapproached to this day ... but, as with all of the GDR's elite athletes, one couldn't be sure that their performances were not chemically assisted. More on this topic later in this chapter.

The Commonwealth Games provided many grand moments for UK competitors. For England, Linford Christie won the 100m, Marcus Adam led a clean sweep in the 200m, Peter Elliott took the 1500m, Eamonn Martin the 10,000m, Kriss Akabusi the 400m hurdles, Simon Williams the shot, Steve Backley the javelin and the men's team the 4x100m relay; women's winners were Diane Edwards (later Modahl) in the 800m, Sally Gunnell in the 400m hurdles, Myrtle Augee in the shot, Tessa Sanderson (for the third time) in the javelin and the 4x400m team. Colin Jackson won the 110m hurdles and Kay Morley the 100m hurdles for Wales and Liz McColgan the 10,000m for Scotland. Seb Coe's final fling ended in frustration as a respiratory infection held him down to sixth place in the 800m final and he consequently withdrew from the 1500m.

With Coe retired, Steve Ovett's international career at an end and Steve Cram unable to regain his very best form, it was Peter Elliott who took over as Britain's foremost middle distance runner. In Seville in February he broke the world indoor 1500m record with 3:34.21 ... 12 years after he set his first UK age best of 1:52.1 for 800m at 15. He consolidated his reputation as a versatile teenage prodigy by winning the 1979 English Schools cross country title for his age group before clocking 1:50.7 for a UK age-16 best. He won the 1980 English National Youths cross country title and the following year placed fourth in the European Junior 800m in a big personal best of 1:47.35. In 1982 he improved to a UK teenage best of 1:45.61 and ran first leg for the British team which broke the world record for the 4x800m relay. He became an elite performer at 800m, clocking 1:43.98 in 1983 and 1:43.41 when winning the silver medal at the 1987 World Championships, while in 1988 he broke 3:50 for the mile for the first time (3:49.20), and at 1500m progressed to 3:32.94 and finished second in the Olympics. Another stress fracture held him back in 1989 but now he was Commonwealth Games champion and a world indoor record holder, and although he wasn't a thoroughbred type of runner like "the big three" his no-nonsense attitude to racing endeared him to the fans and fellow athletes. He was also among the last athletes to hold down a manual job (a joiner with British Steel until 1990) while training and racing at a world class level and was the nearest approach to the fictitious athletics hero Alf Tupper, the 'tough of the track'. After winning an 800m in 1:42.97 back in Seville in May, becoming only the sixth man in the world to break 1:43, anything seemed possible that summer – including even world records at 1500m and mile. But, again, injury ruined his plans. A damaged calf muscle interrupted his season and he did well to clock 3:49.76 in Oslo's Dream Mile. That was encouraging but then he lost further training time because of a chest infection and a knee injury. It was all so frustrating.

There were several changes at AT during the year. Tim Green stepped down as publishing director in March, with Andrew O'Kelly becoming the magazine's publisher and Eddie Kulukundis its chairman, and at the end of May Mark Butler left to take up a position with the IAAF. He was succeeded as results and fixtures editor by Steve Smythe, who in 2017 became the first marathoner to break 3 hours over a 40-year span, his first such time achieved in 1976 as an 18 year-old. In September, Olympic silver medallist Wendy Sly took up the post of events & classified sales executive, while in November steeplechase international Eddie Wedderburn was appointed promotions manager and Nick Davies was promoted to deputy editor.

Much as I enjoyed co-editing AT, I found myself in the same situation as with AW in 1984. The long hours and stress levels were beginning to take their toll and now that the magazine was fully staffed and Randall was happy to become sole editor I felt it was time to step off the treadmill once more. I would still be involved but as from the December 6 issue I became consultant editor while Peter Matthews presented the *Athletics International* section and was styled international editor. Among our freelance contributors I must single out Richard Hymans who in almost every issue supplied a "Star Profile" featuring all the essential facts and figures of one of the world's current top athletes. Between February and April, for example, he profiled world record breakers Petra Felke, Butch Reynolds, Javier Sotomayor, Randy Barnes and Renaldo

Nehemiah. On a more nostalgic note, Tony Ward's "Yesterday's Heroes" series continued with Ian Stewart, Jean Pickering, David Hemery and Kip Keino his subjects.

As in 1989, I was able to travel extensively throughout the Continent as Eurosport's statistician. We started in Bratislava and then on to Helsinki, Stockholm, Nice, Lausanne, Oslo, Brussels, Zürich and a now unified Berlin prior to the European Championships in Split. From a British perspective, the outstanding performance occurred in Stockholm.

Men like Arthur Rowe, Geoff Capes, Lynn Davies and Keith Connor came fairly close, but the distinction of becoming the first British male to set a world record in a field event has fallen to the man with the golden arm, Steve Backley. His moment of glory came in Stockholm's historic Olympic Stadium and there could have been no more fitting venue. Not only was the first ever officially ratified world javelin record set there in 1912 by Sweden's Eric Lemming (62.32m), but it is also the home patch of the pending record holder, Patrik Bodén. Everything clicked for the 21 year-old Cambridge Harrier on his first attempt. With 20,000 pairs of eyes trained on him, he launched the javelin some 50cm behind the scratch line. Flying high and true, into the wind, the implement touched down to an appreciative roar from the crowd at the momentous distance of 89.58m. Understandably, Backley decided to call it quits after the opening throw.

I took the opportunity to chat with the new record holder on the way to the airport next morning.

Steve Backley smiled as he reminisced about his early days as a javelin thrower. "I didn't show any great talent at first. I seem to recall that I threw only 22 metres." He was originally a cross country runner, attempting to follow in the footsteps of his policeman father John Backley, who ran 1:52.2 for 880y and a 4:10.8 mile in the mid-sixties. However, Steve – who was already well over six feet tall by the time he was 14 – soon realised that he was not cut out for a career on the track and looked around for another athletics event. Having always enjoyed throwing things, he decided to give the javelin a try and despite the modest start he was hooked. Within two years, when he was 16, he had become the second ranked youth in the country for 1985. It was the 1986 English Schools Championships which provided Backley with his first major success. John Trower, an 81.06m performer in 1980 who was beginning to make a name for himself in coaching circles, first met Backley in 1986. With Trower supplying the technical expertise and Backley senior continuing to coach his son in terms of overall fitness and conditioning, a fruitful partnership was established. In 1987 Steve won the European Junior title and set three UK junior records, culminating in 78.16m – a staggering improvement of over 13 metres from one season to the next. After winning the 1988 UK title with a world junior record of 79.50m he looked a clear favourite for the World Junior title but Backley came back disappointed with the silver.

He advanced at such a rate in 1989 that he became the world's undisputed number one. Two days after his European Cup victory in Gateshead he relieved Mick Hill of the Commonwealth and UK records with 85.86m in Budapest. By then he was in unbeatable form ... he reeled off seven consecutive Grand Prix victories, also triumphing in the World Student Games and the World Cup with his longest throw yet of 85.90m despite unhelpful conditions. The Commonwealth Games in Auckland showed Backley at his most commanding. He started with a daunting 84.90m but reserved his best to last: a Commonwealth record of 86.02m. Mentally attuned to a throw of 88m being good enough to break the world record, Backley received a rude shock in March when the previously unconsidered Swede, Patrik Bodén, threw 89.10m. But for that throw, Backley's own early season effort of 88.46m at the UK Championships would have earned him a world record plaque. No matter: "I am interested in breaking world records, of course, but I'm much more interested in the competition aspect of it. Bodén is now the man to beat." And beat him he did, in Stockholm to rub it in.

Randall covered the IAC Grand Prix in Edinburgh and was greatly impressed by an American by the name of Michael Johnson whose 200m time of 19.85 was the third fastest ever at sea level. He wrote: "Johnson runs bolt [who knew the significance of those four letters then?] upright, with no knee lift to speak of and a stride length which would not inconvenience an elderly jogger. 'He doesn't start very well either,' said national event coach John Isaacs. So, John, what would you do if you coached him? 'Leave him alone. He just runs very fast.'" In Lausanne I saw for myself just what a stunning performer Michael Johnson was.

Everything comes bigger and better in Texas, as any Texan will tell you, but there is no denying that in Dallas-born and bred Michael Johnson the lone star state has presented the world with an athlete of seemingly limitless possibilities. This year has seen Johnson take the world sprint scene by storm. A 19.90 TAC [US] title win and 44.58 400m, plus relay legs of 43.5, 43.7 and 43.9 were high points of his domestic campaign, while at Meadowbank he ran an astonishing 19.85. Clearly, in more advantageous conditions, Pietro Mennea's world record of 19.72 could fall to the 22 year-old. Nevertheless, many felt the 400m would prove to be his best event. The big test came in Lausanne, his first international race at the distance, and he passed with flying colours. Not only did he reduce his personal best to 44.27 but he soundly defeated two of the men who rank above him on the all-time list in Danny Everett and Roberto Hernández. That curiously upright stance of his proves just as effective over 400m as at half the distance.

Next stop was Oslo where the javelin was one of the most anticipated events. When Steve Backley opened with 87.24m and 87.94m it looked entirely possible that he would take his world record beyond 90 metres, whereas Jan Zelezny, the world record holder before Bodén, began with three fouls, which would have spelt the end of his competition had there been more than eight contestants. In the fifth round, though, Zelezny produced a lifetime best of 88.24m.

Suddenly Backley was confronted with the challenge of producing a near world record throw for any chance of winning. It was a situation which appealed to his competitive instincts, but it fell short of what was required at 87.32m. For the first time in a year he had lost an international competition. Zelezny could now relax and enjoy himself as he prepared to take his final throw. Knowing he was in the form of his life, and victory assured, he could afford to go for broke. Zelezny let rip and from the moment the javelin left his hand he knew it was something very special indeed. The capacity crowd collectively gasped as the spear (the controversial model designed by Miklós Németh) flew out to 89.66m. Backley's reign as world record holder was over – for the moment, anyway – after just 12 days. The race to 90 metres continues, though.

We didn't have to wait long for that particular contest to be decided.

It was like a dream come true for Steve Backley. Here he was at Crystal Palace, just a few miles away from his Kent home, the main attrraction at Britain's most prestigious athletics occasion of the year, the Parcelforce Games – London's Grand Prix meeting. On the most beautiful of evenings, the stadium was filled with 17,000 spectators, all of them willing him not only to beat Jan Zelezny but to break the world record into the bargain. And he did ... with the added bonus of crashing through the 90-metre barrier. It was an occasion that nobody who was privileged to be present will ever forget. For the first time in British athletics history a thrower has become the biggest attraction in the sport, a point that was underlined when the climax of a very good 1500m race went practically unnoticed in the excitement of Backley's record breaking throw. Backley was using – for the first time in competition – the controversial Németh javelin. Backley picked up the Hungarian model for his fourth throw. This time it travelled clearly beyond the 90m line ... and the stadium erupted. A further roar went up when the figures appeared on the results board: the fabulous distance of 90.98m. World record holder for 12 days, Backley was back in the books again after an interruption of just six days!

Under the heading 'Promoters Must Limit The Fields' my editorial in the August 16 issue drew attention to the practice of having too many runners in middle distance races at major invitational meetings.

After finishing second over 1500m in Monte Carlo last Sunday a battle-scarred Yvonne Murray declared: "It was just about the toughest race I've ever been in. It was like a boxing match out there with 18 people in the race." Her experience was all too typical of the international circuit these days, as promoters permit middle distance fields to reach unmanageable – indeed unsafe – numbers. It's no surprise that the incidence of runners falling or being pushed off the track or being spiked is so high. Among the worst offenders are some of the IAAF/Mobil Grand Prix meetings, The 800m races in Lausanne and Brussels had 12 runners apiece, the 1500m in Brussels no fewer than 20! There really should be more control by the IAAF to ensure that in meetings under their aegis no more than eight runners are allowed to contest an 800m race (nine if it's a nine-lane track) and that 1500m/mile races are limited to the dozen starters which is the norm for championship finals.

No such action has ever been taken and fields today remain just as unwieldy and perilous.

Continuing my tour of the Grand Prix circuit, the highlight in Zürich was the greatest one-day double in women's sprinting history by Merlene Ottey. Her 10.93 100m into a 1.2m/sec wind was impressive enough but the 30 year-old Jamaican surpassed that with a wondrous run in the 200m. Again the wind along the straight (-1.0m) did her no favours but such was the power and cadence of her stride that her time of 21.66 had only ever been beaten by Flo-Jo with her 21.56 (+ 1.7m) and 21.34 (+1.3m) at the Seoul Olympics. Her performance was all the more notable in comparison to the male sprinters with Leroy Burrell defeating Linford Christie in 10.13 (-0.7m) and Michael Johnson clocking 20.07 (-1.1m). Merlene followed up with a 10.82 100m, her second fastest time, in Berlin and a 21.81 200m in Cologne where Michael Johnson reduced his best 400m mark to 44.25 in beating Butch Reynolds. The stay in a reunified Berlin was particularly fascinating as Checkpoint Charlie was now just a tourist attraction and I, like so many others, purchased a fragment of the hated Wall.

AT went to town on the European Championships in Split, producing a 32-page supplement containing men's event reports by Randall, women's event reports by Steve Smythe, interviews by Michael Butcher, superb colour photography from Mark Shearman and an analysis of the British team's performance by myself, who during the week-long meeting was working practically around the clock preparing data for the Eurosport commentary team. Every preliminary round and final required a separate card (82 men's and 64 women's), each containing brief details of every competitor! The commentators were brilliant and seemingly tireless, on air throughout as distinct from the more selective treatment by the BBC. In my opinion, Ian Darke was right up there with the very best of commentators on our sport and it was a pity that with Sky Sports, his employers, dropping athletics after the early 1990s the rest of his TV career has been devoted to football and boxing.

By any reckoning it was Britain's best ever showing at the European Championships. The highly acclaimed team in 1986 garnered a record equalling eight golds but its tally of 15 medals overall fell two short of the number accumulated in Brussels (1950), Stockholm (1958) and Athens (1969). Happily, Split 1990 cleared up the problem of deciding Britain's most successful championships once and for all ... a total of 18 medals were gained, of which nine were gold. Only one nation fared better: the GDR, making its swansong on the international stage as a separate entity. The British men's collection of eight gold medals was equal to that of East Germany, West Germany and the USSR combined.

It may be invidious to select one performance above all others, but Kriss Akabusi's 400m hurdles triumph takes some beating. In Split he not only struck gold but – in true David Hemery style – he pulverised the opposition. It was an exhilarating display and his glorious time of 47.92 finally demolished Hemery's celebrated 22 year-old UK record. Among Europeans, only Harald Schmid has ever run faster. Not bad for a man who never managed to break 48 sec for 400m until he was 24! Ironically, Akabusi is now faster than ever on the flat and his contribution to a superlative relay victory was a supercharged 44.4 leg. Two golds for Akabusi, and two also for fellow relay heroes Roger Black and John Regis. Black maintained his perfect record in European Championships; he has contested four events, won four gold medals (the most by any British athlete), and he's still only 24 with his best surely still to come. Black was the first to admit he misjudged his pace and was struggling at the 400m finish in 45.08, but victory must have been sweeter the second time around after those bleak times when he wondered whether he would ever be able to run again.

Regis ended up with four medals – the most any man has ever won in a single edition of the European Championships. He took the bronze in the 100m final in a windy 10.07, won the 200m in his best time of 20.11 and contributed to Britain's astonishing 4x100m mark of 37.98 along with Darren Braithwaite, Marcus Adam and Linford Christie. His ninth race provided a golden finale when he simply ran out of his socks in the 4x400m. Paul Sanders did a good job on the first leg (45.9) and Akabusi followed. Regis blasted through the first 200m in 20.5 or faster and held on heroically to be electrically timed at 43.93! Black completed the job with a 43.96 stint, enabling Britain to win by a 20m margin in 2:58.22, a European record.

Christie came away with three medals, one of each colour. He remains a master at preparing for the big occasion and this time he ran ten flat with the wind only just over the limit and remain 100m champion for another four years. He was edged out of the silver medal position in the 200m, while in the 4x100m even Christie at full tilt could not catch his opponent on the anchor leg as the French team hurtled around the track in 37.79 for a totally unexpected world record. What we didn't know until shortly before he appeared for the 110m hurdles final was that Colin Jackson had been suffering from a knee injury for some time. It was a fingers-crossed situation as he settled into the blocks with his right leg strapped up, but luck was with him. The knee stood up to the test as he and Tony Jarrett duelled for the title three metres ahead of the rest. Both dipped so low for the finish line that they passed under the display clock's beam (the 13.52 shown relating to the third place finisher), and it was Jackson who came out on top in 13.18. Jarrett's reward was an English record of 13.21.

There was a British one-two also in the 800m. It was the turn of Tom McKean (pipped by Coe four years ago) to prove to himself and to the world that he is a great two-lap racer, and he ran the race to perfection. No one could live with him and he won by six metres from David Sharpe in 1:44.76 to become the first native Scot to lift a European individual title since high jumper Alan Paterson back in 1950. Little more than an hour later Yvonne Murray launched a fearsome run for home in the 3000m from 500m out. Murray (8:43.06) was never seriously troubled ... not surprising as she had just covered the last 800m inside 2:08. She made history by becoming the first Scottish-born woman to win a European title, while Steve Backley (87.30m) won the first men's throwing title by a Briton since Arthur Rowe won the shot 32 years ago. Of course, there were disappointments too, and none was felt more keenly than in the men's 1500m. For the first time since the 1976 Olympics there was no British medallist in this event at a major championship. Steve Cram, bidding for an unprecedented third European title but not quite ready yet, gave it his best shot and went down gallantly, just pipped for fourth place by another troubled man in Peter Elliott, who was at the centre of the championships' greatest controversy and understandably not at his best.

What happened was that in his heat Elliott failed to finish after he was pushed in the back by an East German runner, hitting the track so hard that he hurt his wrist and was badly shaken up. To his surprise, the Jury of Appeal advanced him to the final. In his AT column, Peter wrote: "While I was warming up for the final, Spanish athletes were going by and jeering at me. Then when I stood on the line the crowd were whistling and I began to think what would happen if I won. I mean it wasn't my fault that I got in because of a rule. So I was in a no win situation, on a hiding to nothing. There was no way mentally I was ready to run. I was even thinking that if I found myself in the lead with 100m to go I would step off the track." Jens-Peter Herold won the title in 3:38.25, with the two Spaniards finishing behind the two Britons. Herold was one of three East German men to strike gold, but the GDR women captured no fewer than nine of the 19 titles on offer. It was their last hurrah before an integrated German team took over.

Elliott and Cram went on to take part in the Grand Prix Final in Athens but had to settle for third and fourth in the mile, outkicked by Noureddine Morceli (3:53.28) and Herold. Much more would be heard of Morceli, a 20 year-old Algerian who had improved in 1990 from 3:37.87 to 3:32.60, the year's quickest 1500m time. He would become Olympic champion in 1996 and set world records at 1500m, mile, 2000m and 3000m. Both the Britons displayed better form in Sheffield, the final major UK meeting of the season, with local lad Elliott winning with a UK all-comers' record of 3:32.69 ahead of Cram's 3:33.03, and they shone also in New York's Fifth Avenue Mile with Elliott winning for the third time, clocking 3:47.83 for the slightly downhill course, and Cram second in 3:48.39.

Duncan Mackay, always so industrious and now making a name for himself as an investigative journalist, produced a revealing three-part series in September on how and why the GDR had succeeded so spectacularly in sport. He wrote: "In the five Olympics in which it competed as a separate nation, East Germany, with a population of only 17 million, won 519 medals – a total only just behind the Olympic superpowers, the United States and Soviet Union, and far more than anyone else. East Germany channeled a fifth of its gross national product into sport, winning the struggle for recognition from the rest of the world through sport. It was the Soviets who encouraged the East Germans to use sport as a vehicle to show the world that it was ideologically superior to its neighbour, West Germany, and the inherent worth of a socialist society. The successful athlete was reasonably well paid and was allowed to travel overseas regularly to compete and for holidays. Sporting success equalled privilege. But they were always closely monitored whenever they were abroad and the team always contained members of the Stasi (secret police) who kept a check to make sure that athletes did not speak to western journalists or coaches. Marlies Göhr, one of the world's greatest sprinters, told recently of how athletes were forced to toe the party line. 'All of us in the team knew that the Stasi were watching us. Every fourth or fifth person in athletics had contact with them. They were following us, bugging telephones ...'

"East Germany's success over the years has stemmed from a combination of scientific research and theory, medical knowledge and a careful selection programme that allowed a minority of competitors to concentrate on preparing for major championships. Much of their success was carefully planned by the almost legendary College of Sport and Physical Culture in Leipzig. It used to employ nearly 600 people when it was operating at full capacity. The College has recently admitted doping was used to help East German athletes prepare, although officials maintain that their use did not become widespread until 1972 – the year that East Germany made its major Olympic breakthrough at Munich. No athlete was allowed to compete outside the country without first being tested – and passed negative – by the IOC accredited drug control centre at Kreischa. Only once did this system fail. In 1977 Ilona Slupianek, a shot putter, was found positive. State control was total in East Germany – from the moment an athlete was selected as a promising youngster to attend one of the sports schools until allowed to end their careers. Heike Drechsler and Göhr were both prevented from starting families before the 1988 Olympics." At midnight on October 3 the GDR officially ceased to exist, becoming part of the Federal Republic of Germany.

In one of my final editorials I wrote: *Let us hope that, in athletics as in a wider context, the unification of Germany will prove to be for the good of all. Certainly few will mourn the passing of the inappropriately named German Democratic Republic. Politically it was repressive, athletically it was dubious. Although only one East German athlete was ever caught out in an external drug test it would be naïve to suppose that drugs did not play a significant role in making the GDR an athletics superpower ... and particularly on the women's side. Statements by various former East German sports stars and coaches make it pretty clear that the state's massive funding of major Olympic sports like athletics encouraged a win-at-all-costs policy to bring glory and international approval to an otherwise discredited regime. [Sound familiar?]*

The careful use of drugs played a part, as did scrupulous monitoring of athletes before they faced the possibility of doping control at international events. Time and again, athletes of medal winning potential would mysteriously fail to be selected when, invariably at the last possible moment, GDR teams were announced. In some cases they could have been ill or injured; more likely they had tested positive in domestic checks and no chances could be taken. In

Slupianek's case someone must have been uncharacteristically careless. Of course, plenty of athletes from western countries have been caught cheating, having made an individual decision to resort to drugs, but in certain Eastern European countries that decision was made for the athletes. One would like to believe that some of their most admired athletes may have made it to the top legitimately by talent, hard work and the advantages of a system which enabled the athletically gifted to realise their full potential. Young stars like Katrin Krabbe, Grit Breuer and Ilke Wyludda are among the last to come off that state-controlled production line. Now they must come to terms with the commercially-backed sports world of the Federal Republic. Some will thrive with the financial incentives now available, others – unable to adapt from the old system – will never regain their previous level. It will be fascinating to observe.

That drugs were not just an Eastern European problem was demonstrated in the first two issues in November. We reported that the USA's double world indoor long jump champion Larry Myricks faced a life ban after having tested positive for a banned substance at three different meetings, world record holders Butch Reynolds (400m) and Randy Barnes (shot) had been banned for two years, while Mike Hurst informed us that Australian 400m star Darren Clark (who he coached) had switched to rugby league because of his frustration over fighting a losing battle against Olympic opponents he described as "drug-fuelled robots".

My big exclusive interview for the year was with Carl Lewis, in London to promote his autobiography. I regarded Lewis as the greatest athlete of them all and in my introduction I listed his astonishing catalogue of achievements. In brief, at 100m he was the only man ever to have won two Olympic titles [Usain Bolt was aged four and 26 years away from topping that], he also won two world titles and set world records of 9.93 and 9.92 as well as clocking a heavily wind aided 9.78. At 200m his 19.75 easing up would have been a world record had there been a separate category for low altitude marks and he won Olympic gold and silver at the distance. But it was his long jumping which really set him apart from mere mortals. At the time of writing he had won 64 consecutive contests and had not lost outdoors for ten years, picking up two Olympic and two world titles. But for high altitude marks he would have been world record holder with 8.79m, the same distance as his world indoor record. That was the situation at the end of the 1990 season ... and there was much more still to come.

Carl was about ten when, at least in retrospect, a very significant meeting took place. He was introduced to the legendary Jesse Owens. I asked him what he recalled of the encounter. "I don't remember a lot," said Lewis, "but I remember him saying to have fun. You know, there were thousands of kids there and I was just another one of them. But he made an impression on me and then of course I dove in and tried to get more information." Never in his wildest dreams could Lewis have imagined that one day he would emulate Owens' crowning achievement and win four Olympic gold medals in one Games. At the time he and his sister [Carol, long jump bronze medallist at the

1983 World Championships], two years his junior, would compete against each other in their own improvised track meets at home ... with Carol invariably the winner. "Every family seems to have someone who is not talented, and I thought I was the one for our family," said Carl. However, encouraged by his parents [his mother ranked number four in the world at 80m hurdles in 1951, his father a 49 sec quarter miler] he persevered. In his sophomore year at high school, when he shot up in height so quickly that he had to walk with crutches for a while to ease the pain in his knees, he started to display something in the way of athletic talent.

In one year, between 1977 and 1978, aged 16-17, he improved his 100 yards time from 10.6 to a wind assisted 9.3 and in 1979 he set a world age-17 long jump best of 8.07m. He was on his way!

Goals? "I still feel that I can run faster than 9.90 for 100m and that I can long jump 29 feet. Those are the two things I'd like to do." Why 29 feet? That works out at 8.84m and Bob Beamon's record is 8.90m. "I first jumped over 28 feet in 1981, so the next barrier for me is 29 feet. If it's 29-3 (8.91m) that's great. I expect to jump farther than that anyway." What effect did being labelled the second Jesse Owens have on you? "I took it as a compliment – and still do. But I think that people started to take it too far. No matter what I did, I was always being compared to Jesse or someone else; they wouldn't just let me be me." Life bans rather than two years for drug offenders? "I think they should ban them for life but give them an opportunity to be reinstated. Right now you're off for two years and that's it; you have something big to come back to. That part should be taken away, I feel."

26. THE GREATEST DUEL OF THEM ALL (1991)

One of the reasons I stepped down as co-editor of AT was to spend more time preparing for and conducting interviews with many of the biggest names in athletics. In 1991 I quizzed Kriss Akabusi, Merlene Ottey, Dave Bedford, Roger Kingdom, Seb Coe, John Regis, Greg Foster, Peter Elliott, Mike Powell, Tessa Sanderson and Heike Henkel. It was a journalistic privilege to chat to them and pose the questions their fans would be interested in – and those fans included me!

Kriss Akabusi's determination on the track, his extrovert personality and that instantly recognisable laugh of his made him one of the most popular athletes ever to don a British vest. The sight of him celebrating wildly when he saw his time of 47.92 when winning the 400m hurdles title was one of the most memorable moments of the European Championships in Split. Just how important was that time? "The reason I acted so crazy after seeing my time in Split was that not only did I break David Hemery's record but I'm the first Briton to run under 48 seconds. I tried to do it in so many places all season. All of a sudden, the realisation was 'Look, guys, I've just done it!'. And that's why I was so crazy, because I made history. No doubt there will be a lot of other British guys who will run faster than I've done, but I was the first. And I realised then that when they talk about David Hemery they'll also talk about Kriss Akabusi."

Never mind "a lot of other British guys", all these years later no Briton has run quicker than Kriss, who went on to improve to 47.86 in 1991 and 47.82 in 1992, although Dai Greene did go very close with 47.88 in 2010 and 47.84 in 2012. Kriss was a better prophet when it came to assessing Britain's chances in the 4x400m relay at the 1991 World Championships. "At this moment in time I would put myself in the team along with Derek Redmond if he's in full flight by then, John Regis and Roger Black, and I reckon we could run 2:56 and beat any American team." They did indeed beat the Americans, in the European and Commonwealth record time of 2:57.53.

Kriss was an inspiration for athletes who by their late twenties may have felt their best days were behind them. "At 28 I changed over to the hurdles and began a new career in track and field, and others can do the same. I like to think I am a role model for people, and I take my profile in the sport very seriously. I want to be a role model in all areas … for black people, to say you can achieve in life; for children who have had a very bad start in life [Kriss was taken into child care when he was eight]; for people who are late starters; for Christians. I want people to know that you can be all these things and be successful and keep your feet on the ground."

Kriss was 32 when I interviewed him and he bowed out from racing in 1993. Merlene Ottey was 30 and the world's foremost female athlete. In 1990 she had won every one of her 31 races, mostly by huge margins, and established herself as second only to Flo-Jo on the combined world all-time lists for 100m and 200m [10.78 and 21.66]." Astonishingly, she continued to compete internationally (for Slovenia from 2002) until she was 52, her Olympic career spanning a record seven Games between 1980 and 2004.

The sight of the glamorous, sophisticated yellow-costumed Ottey outstripping all opponents has been one of the most stirring images of the Grand Prix circuit. Yet it's all a far cry from the start of her sprinting career when, because her family was unable to afford the cost of a pair of running shoes, she would race barefoot. Right from the earliest days it was clear that Merlene was a natural sprinter. Born and raised in Jamaica, an island as celebrated for its sprinting tradition as for its rum, she used to beat all the boys of her age. Reminiscing about her schooldays, she giggled as she recalled her starting technique at that time. "I didn't use starting blocks. I used to start with both knees on the ground, and then simply stood up and ran! At one time my best 200m was 24.2 but I ran only 12.8 for 100m, which is ridiculous." It was in 1978, aged 18, that she was given her first pair of spikes and the following year she made her international debut. In 1980 she went straight from being a promising youngster to one of the world's elite, lowering her personal best for 200m to a Commonwealth record of 22.20 for third place in the Moscow Olympics, becoming in the process the first Jamaican woman athlete ever to win an Olympic medal.

Although she went on to win the Commonwealth 200m title in 1982 and remain splendidly consistent throughout the eighties, when it came to the Olympics or World Championships she was always the bridesmaid, never the bride. Silver in the 200m at Helsinki 1983 ... bronze in both sprints at Los Angeles 1984 and Rome 1987. She did win the world indoor 200m title in 1989, but that's hardly the same as winning an outdoor championship against the world's best. But it was in 1990 that everything fell into place and Ottey was elevated to the status of world's number one female athlete. It was a year of tremendous change for her. She left California for a new life in Rome, where she is coached by her boyfriend Stefano Tilli (himself a 10.16/20.40 sprinter). At the age of 30 she feels she is starting again, receptive to new training methods designed to generate even more speed.

His great running days behind him, 41 year-old Dave Bedford was now an influential figure behind the scenes as president of the International Athletes' Club and organiser of the prestigious IAC international meeting. Other posts he held included being chairman of the Shaftesbury Barnet club and member of AAA General Committee and BAAB Council. Later in the year he would be appointed honorary secretary of the newly formed national governing body, the British Athletic Federation (BAF), which brought together at last all the clubs of the UK under a single umbrella organisation. Did he have any desire to become chief executive of BAF? "I have absolutely no ambitions in that direction. I am happy to continue to give service to athletics very much on the honorary basis that I always have done. The only difference is that I would earn my living outside of athletics. I've done a lot of things in life – I've been a schoolteacher, I've done some public relations work, run night clubs and been involved in athletics and sporting promotions. What I'll do for the next 20 years is unclear at the moment." [He would go on to make a massive contribution to the success of the London Marathon as a long-time race director].

Any regrets looking back on his racing career? "The only regret is that injury ultimately forced me out of competition while I was still young and that never gave me the opportunity to learn from my mistakes and then go on to win championships. What I do remember is that my period as an athlete was full of happiness. What a great way to spend your youth … absolutely brilliant! There were great characters in those days, like Dick Taylor and Ian Stewart, and it was still fun. The fact that you ran to win or achieve something, and you didn't run to earn your living, made it very much easier and more relaxed. That's not to say we never earned anything out of it but it was always seen as a bonus; it was never seen as the way to live and survive. I think we were the last generation which had the benefit of that approach.

"I was brought up as a youngster by Bob Parker to believe that breaking a world record was as important as winning a gold medal, and remember that my formative years were when Ron Clarke was breaking record after record. That had a major impact on me. I was always fascinated by how fast I could run and, in hindsight, I genuinely believe that without injuries and with luck I could have run 30 seconds faster than the world record of 27:30.8 I achieved in 1973. Actually the 27:47 I did at Portsmouth in 1971 was a far better run than the world record."

As someone closely involved with fighting drug abuse in athletics, what further measures should be taken? "Until we eradicate the mentality that believes it's worth cheating we've got a major problem. It's almost like drinking and driving. A lot of people drink and drive and they do it because the penalty is not so severe as to deter them. You could stop drink driving overnight with a life ban. Not being able to drive for a year is one thing; not being able to drive for ever is another. I believe in athletics too that only a life ban will be a sufficient deterrent."

Olympic 110m hurdles champion in 1984 and 1988, and world record holder with 12.92, Roger Kingdom had a dream: to become the first track athlete ever to win three consecutive Olympic gold medals in an individual event. "I think it would assure me of my real place in history; that would get me into the hall of fame. I would like to be remembered in the sport as a nice human being and one hell of an athlete." He certainly was that even though he never made the US Olympic team in 1992. His margin of victory in 1988, over Colin Jackson, was a stunning three metres and he reckoned he made numerous errors during his 12.92 race! "I stepped on the first hurdle and I hit about three other hurdles in that race. Also I started to cut back instead of running straight through after about the fifth hurdle, slowing down a little bit. Every time you hit a hurdle it adds a few hundredths or thousandths of a second to your time. In that perfect race you need to be very aggressive, attacking each hurdle but not hitting them – just clearing them in a good position so you can attack the next one." He under-rated one of his main opponents, Colin Jackson. "Colin is an excellent hurdler, and must be nearing his peak. He's probably going to run a couple more 13-zeros in his career and maybe 12.99 or something like that." In fact it would be Colin, at the 1993 World Championships, who would succeed Roger as world record holder with 12.91, a time that would remain unsurpassed until 2006.

I interviewed Seb Coe at his Surrey home a couple of weeks before he was due to fulfil a long-held ambition by running the London Marathon. Would he be satisfied to finish in three hours? "If I roll in at 3 hours 20 minutes I'm not going to panic; I just want to get round and be in a position to enjoy as much of it as I can." As it happened, Seb came home 1728th in 2:56:20.

As someone whose selection for the 1988 Olympics had been overturned, what were his views on the selection process? "I prefer any system that actually selects. I say that because selection is a mixture of a whole series of things: it's intuition, it's regard for previous performances … you have to take note of the fact that some people on the day do come back with medals. You have to take into consideration current form. You also have to consider athletes who will go away and can be trusted to prepare as well as they know in order to bring home the spoils on the day. You should have a system which actually demands some intellectual commitment and some serious consideration by selectors, as opposed to the American system of the first three regardless of previous form.

"I don't have any problems with the judgement of the selection committee; I never did. The problem is: what is the *role* of the selectors? The role of the selectors is basically to pick a team, and I don't see how any selector can operate in a system where that decision can be over-ruled by a committee of 25 people. You can't have five or six specialists being over–ruled by people who don't coach. There is one golden rule for me about selectors: they have to possess coaching experience and knowledge of how athletes prepare."

John Regis made history by becoming the first man to win four medals at a single European Championships. He won the 200m but the real eye-opener was being Britain's secret weapon in the 4x400m relay with a 43.93 leg. Was he surprised? "The Europeans to me were just a revelation. Track and field is not all about physical strength; it's about mental strength as well. If you believe, and if you have the talent, anything is possible. That's what got me through to the 100m final, and got me to a bronze medal. It was an amazing championships for me. The 4x400 in particular. In my wildest dreams if someone told me to run 20.5 for 200 [his halfway time in the relay] and keep going I would get to 250 and fall over! I just couldn't believe it." His target in 1991? "It's a BIG deal for me to break 20 seconds. I see that as a major landmark for British sprinting." He had to wait until 1993 to achieve that ambition, clocking 19.94. The following year he ran 19.87 at altitude, still the quickest ever time by a Briton.

He never broke the world record or won an Olympic title but Greg Foster rates as one of the all-time greats of sprint hurdling thanks to three successive world titles (1983, 1987 and 1991) and remaining a world class performer from 1977 to 1992. I interviewed him on the 42nd floor of the New York Hilton the day before he ran in the US Championships (which he won). I asked him whether he regarded a world title as equal in status to an Olympic gold medal. "The American public, which is not very knowledgeable, is only really aware of the Olympic Games. As a track and field athlete I would consider them equal. I would probably be a little more excited about winning an Olympic gold medal, but that's because I don't have one!"

Shortly after he won Oslo's Dream Mile in 3:49.46 I taped a discussion with Peter Elliott, who was now Britain's foremost middle distance runner ... "people talk about Coe and Ovett and Cram, and I just say to them that not until I've won an Olympic title or broken a world record at 1500m or mile can I be considered in their bracket." Was Coe a particular influence in Elliott's younger days? "I admired Seb in that he always turned out in the Yorkshire Championships, and to me he is the greatest athlete Britain has ever produced. But, if I go back to Moscow in 1980 when I was working in a Sheffield factory, I was more of a Steve Ovett fan. When Steve won the 800, which he wasn't supposed to win, I was delighted but all the Sheffield guys in the factory weren't too happy about the local man being beaten. Then on the day of the 1500 final I was working on a roof outside and when Seb won all the guys came out, took the ladder away and left me up there for the rest of the afternoon!"

Few athletes have achieved as much as Peter considering the seemingly endless setbacks he had endured. He reeled them off for me: "I had a stress fracture of the foot at the 1984 Olympics which kept me out of the 800m semi-finals. I was out most of 1985 with a stress fracture and torn calf muscle. In 1988 I went from January 1 to the Olympic 800m final at the end of September without missing a day's training but when I did get to the Olympics I got the bad groin injury. Then in 1989 I had the stress fracture and tried to get back too quickly, and last year I damaged a calf muscle after I had got really fit and run my fastest ever 800m. At the beginning of this year I missed seven weeks of training and the indoor season after falling down a pothole while running."

I had the pleasure of talking with Mike Powell at the World Championships in Tokyo, where he had just succeeded Bob Beamon as world record holder for the long jump. I have often been asked what has been the most exciting race I have ever witnessed ... but if I had to choose the most exciting athletic *contest* I would go for the Powell/Carl Lewis clash in Tokyo. Here (in a condensed version) is how I reported on it for AT:

Previewing the event, we wrote: "The Lewis-Powell duel promises to be one of the most dramatic confrontations of the entire Championships – and if the conditions are conducive even Bob Beamon's world record of 8.90m could be seriously threatened by the winner." Okay, we were wrong on two counts. Beamon's mark was finally eclipsed, not merely threatened, and it wasn't just the winner who came close to toppling the oldest world record on the books! Like the 100m it was a contest which exceeded all expectations, sky high as they were; but unlike the 100m it was not Carl Lewis who triumphed. That fantastic win streak of his was finally brought to an end. After 65 victories, stretching back to March 1981, Lewis was beaten ... although it took a world record to do it and Lewis himself produced the greatest ever series. The final will go down as one of the most extraordinary competitions in athletics history. It was a titanic struggle in which the result was in the balance until the very end.

Powell messed up his opening jump, measured at a mere 7.85m, but Lewis slipped easily into top gear from the start; he added a centimetre to his championship record with 8.68m. Powell's second round response was an 8.54m, while Lewis fouled. Powell (8.29m) still hadn't found his touch in the third round but when Lewis landed a windy 8.83m – the longest jump of his life – it looked as though victory number 66 was on its way. The first real inkling that Lewis could find himself under acute pressure came in the fourth round when Powell cut the sand in the area beyond 8.80m. The red flag was raised. The TV replay showed his toe was only just over the board, but the real fireworks started a few minutes later when Lewis kicked out to a colossal 8.91m. Beamon's figures had been surpassed after almost 23 years although Lewis's elation was dampened somewhat when the wind reading of 2.9m/sec flashed up, thus nullifying it as a world record.

It was a case of "you ain't seen nothing yet, folks", for Powell channneled all his aggression and frustration into his fifth jump ... and leapt into the history books. A flurry of sand around the 9 metres mark signified something rather special and Powell waited in suspense. First came the wind reading, a legal 0.3. Another long pause – and then pandemonium as the figures 8.95 flickered into life. The TV close-up showed he had about 5cm to spare on the board, so from take off to landing Powell had probably spanned nine metres! Arms outstretched, he set off on a celebratory run ... but even amid all the euphoria Powell realised that the gold medal was not necessarily his. Lewis still had two more tries, and Powell knew from bitter experience [15-0 in Lewis's favour] that you could never count him out in advance. Sure enough, Lewis continued to fire on all cylinders. Now 30, he hadn't experienced a long jump defeat since he was 19 and was in no mood to countenance it now. His fifth round effort of 8.87m was a legal personal best. Powell fouled his last try, and so all depended on Lewis's final attempt. Bathed in perspiration, willing himself to jump beyond anything he had yet achieved, Lewis executed yet another brilliant leap but at 8.84m it fell short and he went over to pat Powell on the back. He had averaged 8.86m for his last four jumps and lost; it was an unbelievable situation.

Powell gasped: "This is a dream come true. Honestly, I thought Carl would beat me in the last jump. I have conditioned myself for so long to see him come from behind and beat me. I thought he would jump nine metres. He's a great athlete and competitor and I've learned a lot from his mental toughness. But I've always been confident in my abilities. I'm hoping he lets me keep the world record for a while!"

At the time of writing, Mike Powell has held the record for 26 years – surpassing even Jesse Owens' span of 25 years and 2 months and Beamon's reign of just under 23 years.

I followed the long jump so intently that I was barely aware that at the same time Liz McColgan was on her way to winning the 10,000m title. The long jump was one of nine events that I reported on for AT's comprehensive 72 page results issue, the 10,000m being part of Duncan Mackay's quota. He wrote: "She won the world title she had desperately wanted for so long the hard way: from the front. To lead every step of the way in a World Championship final and grind the best 10,000m runners around today, including the defending champion and world record holder [Ingrid Kristiansen], into the ground in conditions [heat and humidity] totally alien to European runners must rank as one of the greatest ever performances by any British woman." Her time was 31:14.31 and she won by over 20 seconds. Brendan Foster, commentating for the BBC, called it the greatest performance ever by a British distance runner. Britain's other golden moment came in the 4x400m relay, another of "my" events.

There could not have been a more rousing finale to these magnificent World Championships. We sensed it was going to be awfully close between the British and American quartets, but this was ridiculous! British fans in the stadium couldn't have had a finger nail left among them. It was a mind-blowing, excruciating, joyous race for the British camp – for the Americans it was just mind-blowing and excruciating. No, that's not being fair. American journalists came over to congratulate their British colleagues, grateful to have watched such an enthralling battle and hopeful that the defeat – the first by a British team at this level since the 1936 Olympics in Berlin – would prompt changes in the US selection system. That Michael Johnson, clearly the world's number one 400m runner for the past two seasons, should not even have been considered for a spot on the relay team because he did not contest that event in the trials is a classic case of shooting yourself in the foot.

The first sensation of the race occurred when the first-leg runners came out to try the blocks ... for there was Roger Black, traditionally the anchorman for the British team. As Kriss Akabusi explained later, "the reason why Roger was on the lead-off leg is because we had to neutralise the American strength." It was a gamble, agreed upon by the athletes involved, the coaches and team management. Black, who ran 44.62 three days earlier and came so close to winning the world individual title, gave Britain the lead as expected, and ran a swift 44.7, but his lead over Andrew Valmon (44.9) was less substantial than hoped. On the second leg, despite an excellent 44.0 contribution by Derek Redmond, it looked as though the British plan had misfired. Quincy Watts came up with one of the fastest splits on record – 43.4 – to build up a lead of almost four metres.

Next to go was John Regis against Danny Everett. He needed a great run not only for the sake of the team but for his own self esteem, having failed to reach the 200m final. He produced a 44.22 split, gaining valuable ground on Everett, but even so Akabusi took over a daunting three metres behind world champion Antonio Pettigrew. Akabusi, whose bronze medal in the 400m hurdles was such an inspiration for the rest of the British team when things weren't going so well, has run some great races in the past – but this was his finest and proudest moment. He closed the gap, swung out to challenge the American and miraculously found the very last ounce of speed and strength to edge past some four strides from the line. His split was 44.59 and the British team had won a famous victory by 4/100ths in 2:57.53, a European and Commonwealth record. Chief Coach Frank Dick explained: "We worked out the best way to tackle the Americans and decided to pressurise them. They are not used to pressure because they are usually well in front. And didn't it work?"

My previous visit to Tokyo, 27 years earlier, provided many good memories and so too did these outstanding World Championships. Carl Lewis won the 100m in a world record 9.86 and anchored the US team to a world record 37.50 in the relay (Britain third), Michael Johnson took the 200m in 20.01, at 33 Greg Foster nailed his third 110m hurdles title in 13.06 with Tony Jarrett third, Akabusi lowered his UK 400m hurdles record to 47.86 for the bronze medal, while the ever adventurous Dalton Grant set new UK high jump figures of 2.36m, the same height as the silver and bronze medallists, but placed fourth on countback after entering the contest at the crazy height of 2.31m. Another British record fell in the women's 400m hurdles where Sally Gunnell's 53.16 was good for silver, just 5/100ths behind the winner. She also contributed a sizzling 49.46 leg for the team which finished fourth in the 4x400m relay. There was a downside too. Steve Cram failed to make the 1500m final, while Peter Elliott didn't even start in the heats because of an achilles tendon problem, and an injured Colin Jackson had to scratch from his 110m hurdles semi. Even the usually so consistent Steve Backley failed to make the javelin final, although he was in good company as his successor as world record holder, Jan Zelezny, messed up too.

Sergey Bubka, representing the Soviet Union but very much a Ukrainian, notched up his third world pole vault title (and there would be three more to follow!) ... but only after a suspenseful competition. Having set numerous world records during the year, climaxing in 6.12m indoors and 6.10m outdoors, it was practically taken for granted that he would win, but the event came close to ending in disaster for him. A troublesome heel injury necessitated one pain killing injection 90 minutes before the start of the competition and another during a vital stage of the contest. The inspired Hungarian, István Bagyula, cleared 5.90m at the first attempt, a height Bubka failed at his first try. Realising he would have to succeed at the next height for a chance of winning, Bubka reserved his two remaining attempts for 5.95m. He failed with his first, so the pressure must have been immense as he prepared for his final attempt. Having gone straight up from his 5.70m opener he would place just equal seventh if he failed again ... but, displaying the competitive flair which made him the world's greatest ever vaulter, he soared over.

Another of the undisputed all-time greats, Jackie Joyner-Kersee, experienced mixed fortunes. The long jump came first and her opening leap of 7.32m held up, just, against her German arch-rival Heike Drechsler, winner of this title in 1983 when aged 18 and competing then for the GDR. Next day she began her challenge to retain her heptathlon title. Undefeated in the seven-event test since finishing a close second at the 1984 Olympics and world record holder with the stunning (and still unapproached) score of 7291 points, she made a solid start with a 12.96 hurdles, 1.91m high jump and 15.30m shot for a 165 point lead ... but on the way to a probable sub-23 sec 200m she collapsed in agony after 80m with a hamstring injury. Merlene Ottey also had her ups and downs. She was a disappointing third in both sprints, won by former GDR star Katrin Krabbe, but joy awaited in the relay as on the anchor leg she took over a metre or two down but swept the Jamaican team to victory by a good two metres.

How Ron Pickering would have loved to commentate for the Beeb in Tokyo, particularly on that fabulous Lewis v Powell long jump, but sadly he passed away in February, aged merely 60. Mine was one of numerous tributes we printed in AT to a man who was the personification of all that was good in athletics and the fiercest opponent of those who would demean the sport by cheating.

Ron Pickering was a big man in every way. Physically he was imposing, but it was his character, his personality and his deeds which made him such a giant in our athletics community. He had done everything in the sport: PE teacher, national coach (guiding Lynn Davies to Olympic victory), BBC television commentator for more than 20 years, president of Haringey AC during its remarkable rise from obscurity to the most successful club in the land. Above all else, he was a communicator par excellence. He had passionately held views on the sport, considered it was his mission in life to fight for its soul and integrity (particularly in relation to drugs) and spent much of his time writing and speaking on the subject. Essentially anti-establishment in his views, his was considered by many to be the authoritative voice of British athletics.

I had the privilege and pleasure of being a friend and professional colleague of Ron's for some 30 years. Warm, compassionate and witty, he was a joy to travel and work with. He enjoyed his lifestyle and public recognition (he was awarded the OBE for services to the sport in 1986), but possessed a keen awareness of the plight of people less fortunate than himself and he was particularly concerned with race relations. The tragedy for athletics of Ron's death is that there was so much still to do to ensure the future well-being of the sport he cared so much about. As his son, Shaun, points out, who is going to replace him as sport's moral guardian?

Three other deaths that affected me personally were those of Peter Hopkins (63), a long serving club and county official who was a former secretary and chairman of the NUTS; Joe Yancey (80), of the New York Pioneer Club, of which I was proud to have been made an honorary member back in 1958; and my old hero Gordon Pirie (60).

It will be difficult for anyone much younger than fifty to appreciate the impact Gordon Pirie had on British athletics. He was a megastar of his time, a runner whose appearance in any race would produce a frisson of excitement and anticipation. Among later generations of distance runners perhaps only Dave Bedford came close to matching Pirie's effect on the public. You either loved him or hated him; you certainly couldn't ignore him. In a more conventional era before the term was coined, Pirie 'did his own thing'. Inspired by the example of Emil Zátopek he trained like a demon (often covering well over 200 miles a week), he bucked the system by being coached by a foreigner (the German, Waldemar Gerschler), he was continuously at odds with officialdom and the media. Such was the high regard for his achievements that in a magazine readers' poll, which I organised in 1965, Pirie came out an easy winner as the greatest British male athlete of all time.

One forward looking feature of AT was a "Junior of the Month" award which consisted of a pair of Asics training shoes and spikes, a clothing contract with that company, £100 paid into the athlete's trust fund by AT and a week's warm weather training courtesy of Eddie Kulukundis. The winner of this sought after package of goodies for January was 17 year-old Paula Radcliffe, whose best track times were 4:31.3 for 1500m and 9:41.4 for 3000m but was best known for her cross country exploits. Paula would develop into a world champion and world record holder but an Olympic medal eluded her. That wasn't the case with February's award winner, for high jumper Steve Smith, also 17 and UK junior indoor record holder with 2.27m, went on to gain a bronze medal in the 1996 Games. August's award went to David Grindley (18), the European Junior 400m champion in 45.41. A year later, at the Barcelona Olympics, he set a UK record of 44.47.

There was a nostalgic aspect to the indoor season as RAF Cosford bowed out with a star-studded international meeting. The first meeting staged there was in 1955 on a four-lane unbanked 160 yards track marked on the gymnasium's wooden floor. In 1961 a 250 yards concrete circuit was installed in the huge hangar that remained the home of British indoor athletics, and that was replaced in 1965 by a banked 220 yards wooden track and the AAA/WAAA Championships were held at Cosford for the first time ... and would continue there for the next 26 years. At the end of 1967 the track was converted to 400m, while from 1972 athletes could enjoy running on a synthetic surface. Writing in the programme for the last national championships to be staged there, Cliff Temple summed up what Cosford meant to so many of us: "Over the years I've cursed your remoteness, your January snow and your biting wind, your broken telephone boxes and your British Rail waiting shed. But although I never thought I'd ever say this: I think somehow we're all going to miss you."

Having negotiated a lucrative (by my standards) contract with Eurosport for 1991 I looked forward to another exhausting but exhilarating tour of Europe's top meetings with the commentary team and we started with an indoor match in Paris which featured the first unified German team since the 1964 Olympics. A few days later we were in Seville to see Noureddine Morceli become the first Algerian to set a world record as he shaved 0.04 of a second from Peter Elliott's indoor 1500m figures with 3:34.16. It was quickly back to Seville for the World Indoor Championships where the standout performance was Merlene Ottey's 22.24 200m, equalling her own world indoor record.

A nasty shock awaited me. Sky Television's legal people wrote to me on April 15 confirming my new contract and, in high spirits, Pat and I left on April 24 for a week's holiday in Miami Beach followed by a week in The Bahamas. We arrived home on May 9 to find a letter from Richard Russell informing me that Eurosport, as part of the Sky network, was no more, due apparently to a violation of fair competition regulations, and therefore my contract was cancelled. I did continue with occasional TV work, and I did receive a percentage of what I would have earned with Eurosport that summer, but that magical if hectic period in my life was over.

In May, AT's staff – already the fittest working for any magazine (the co-editors excepted, of course) – was strengthened further by the appointment as event and classified sales executive of Mary Kitson, who ran 2:02.83 for 800m that year and placed second in the UK Championships. However, she stayed for only three months, to be succeeded by international javelin thrower Peter Yates (pb of 77.84m). Also during the summer, Olympic 400m hurdler Martin Gillingham (pb of 49.82) transferred from AW to become our news editor, with Duncan Mackay taking over as features editor, while Wendy Sly rejoined the magazine as publishing manager.

Back home from the UK Championships in Cardiff on the Monday to file my report and pack, I was off to New York the following day for the American Championships. Serving as the sudden-death trials for the World Championships, it was a great meeting but ill served by the public and the media.

Gazing at row upon row of empty seats in the 22,000 capacity Downing Stadium on Randalls Island in New York was a salutary reminder that athletics in the USA continues to be a minor sport. Even the resounding highlight of these 116th national championships – a world record 9.90 100m by Leroy Burrell – failed to gain a mention in that night's CNN sports news summary. The New York public stayed away in droves, although it didn't help that the decrepit 55 year-old stadium is located in a practically inaccessible part of town up near Harlem. Held in scorching weather with the temperature in the nineties on the final day, the championships proved that the USA is still a powerhouse in the sport.

Taking advantage of the hot weather and a friendly 1.9m/sec tailwind, Burrell not only broke Carl Lewis's world record but beat the great man himself, who clocked 9.93 despite an appalling start which saw him two metres adrift at one stage. Next day Lewis came out on top in a thrilling long jump battle with Mike Powell. The latter's second round 8.63m led the way until Lewis produced a last gasp 8.64m. Another highlight was Dan O'Brien's decathlon. Watched by Daley Thompson, he scored 8844 points, just three digits shy of Daley's world record, but even if he had picked up another few points it wouldn't have counted for record purposes as, astonishingly, there was no wind gauge on hand for the 100m (where he set the fastest ever decathlon time of 10.23) and long jump.

Despite the end of the Eurosport connection, I wasn't doing badly in terms of attending major meetings abroad. New York was followed by Oslo, where Peter Elliott succeeded Seb Coe (1979), Steve Ovett (1980 & 1981), Dave Moorcroft (1984) and Steve Cram (1985-1988) by winning the Dream Mile, defeating a field which included the reigning Olympic, world, European and African 1500m champions in his second quickest time of 3:49.46. Later I would travel to Tokyo, New York again and Monaco, but next stop was Sheffield for the World Student Games. There were two British victories, both coming on the sixth and final day. Steve Backley's javelin triumph (87.42m), winning by nearly seven metres, was totally predictable but Yorkshire's own John Mayock, an occasional training partner of Peter Elliott's whose best 5000m time prior to the Games was merely 14:06.80 (he came into the team as a reserve), kicked home in 13:39.25 for the breakthrough of the meeting.

I returned to Sheffield's Don Valley Stadium following the World Championships to witness, along with a sell-out crowd of 25,000, Steve Backley throwing 91.36m for a Commonwealth record. Recovered from the adductor muscle injury which caused him to flop in Tokyo, Backley had another massive throw of 90.48m and defeated an all-star field. Another highlight was Peter Elliott's victory over Steve Cram in the Emsley Carr Mile (3:52.10 to 3:52.97), while it was also good to see a rejuvenated Mary Slaney (33) run away with the 3000m in 8:43.19. Zola Pieterse (née Budd) was in even better shape in 1991, clocking the second fastest time in the world that year with 8:35.72 in South Africa, but they would never clash again on the track.

I never needed an excuse to visit the ever exhilarating city of New York and in late October I flew out to kill two birds with one stone. *Runner's World* magazine invited me, a member of a panel to determine the best middle/long distance runners of the past quarter-century, to their glittering Silver Anniversary Gala. The awards went deservedly to Seb Coe and Grete Waitz ... and what a gathering there was, including Flo-Jo, Joan Samuelson (née Benoit), Ingrid Kristiansen, Mary Slaney, Rosa Mota, Carl Lewis, Billy Mills, Frank Shorter, Jim Ryun, Carlos Lopes, Kip Keino and Steve Jones. I was completely starstruck! After taking time out to meet up with my cousins Naomi and Margaret and a day trip to Atlantic City, I returned to Manhattan to report on the New York Marathon with Liz McColgan completing a truly memorable year by not only winning but recording the fastest ever time by a marathon debutante with 2:27:32. The London Marathon's record of 24,953 finishers in 1990 was eclipsed as 25,617 crossed the finish line in Central Park ... and both races would continue to grow dramatically over the next quarter-century.

27. AMERICAN TRIALS AND TRIBULATIONS (1992)

The Olympic year of 1992 started promisingly. In addition to my normal magazine and freelance work I was spending considerable time putting together a history of Olympic athletics which appeared as a six-part AT supplement. I thoroughly enjoyed the research and writing involved and Nick Davies did a great job arranging the text and photos. The history, suitably updated, would appear in book form in 1996. I was busy again with television work, acting primarily as statistician for Sky Sports although mostly that involved studio dubbing sessions.

All of us at AT were delighted when, in February, Cliff Temple joined our team of writers. The much respected athletics correspondent of *The Sunday Times* for 23 years, co-author of Brendan Foster's and Dave Moorcroft's highly readable biographies, successful coach and the most humorous of athletics writers, Cliff was one of my best friends and it was good to have him on board. We teamed up, along with Michael Butcher, to cover the European Indoor Championships in Genoa, at which Jason Livingston won the 60m and Matthew Yates the 1500m. Unhappily, the meeting was overshadowed by the sudden death in his hotel of the popular British team manager Les Jones at the age of 48.

The cover photo of our March 16 issue was of 18 year-old Paula Radcliffe winning the World Junior cross country title in Boston. Duncan Mackay was out on the snow covered course to report on her triumph. After recovering from anaemia (but still on iron tablets) she had won the English Schools title by over a minute and, Duncan wrote, "the signs were there that something special was on the cards for Boston but not even Radcliffe herself seriously believed that she would strike gold." Her target was to place in the top ten. Paula covered the 4km course in 13:30 to win by five seconds from China's Wang Junxia, aged 19. Paula, progressing steadily, would go on to clock 4:11.6 for 1500m and 8:40.40 for 3000m the following year ... whereas Wang strained credulity with her 1993 times of 3:51.92, 8:06.11 (still the world record), 29:31.78 for 10,000m (the world record until 2016) and even a 2:24:07 marathon! Paula would herself become a world record breaker, but not for another decade.

I had always wanted to attend the US Olympic Trials with its dramatic 'sudden death' format. No matter who you are or what you have achieved in the past, if you don't finish in the first three at the trials then your Olympic dream is over. The cost of my flight to New Orleans and hotel accommodation there was shared by AT (i.e. Eddie) and Sky Sports, for whom I would be transmitting information to their commentators in London.

I flew initially to Las Vegas for two nights at the Sahara Hotel before continuing to New Orleans. Although I lost a few dollars on the slot machines all went well until I checked out of the hotel to catch a cab for the airport. In order to settle my bill the clerk at reception asked for my credit card, which was in a travel wallet containing my passport, airline tickets and travellers cheques.

271

The transaction concluded, I stepped outside with my travel bag and suitcase to the taxi rank. During the short journey to the airport I rummaged through my bag to check my ticket for the 11.30 am flight to New Orleans. The wallet ... where was it? With increasing desperation I emptied the bag's contents on the seat. No wallet! I guessed I must have stupidly left it on the reception desk counter when settling my bill, so I asked the cab driver to turn round and take me back to the Sahara. My heart was beating much too rapidly as I marched up to the reception desk. Had I left my wallet there about 20 minutes earlier? No, sorry.

Now I was in deep trouble. I had no ID and, having paid the cab driver, no money but for about 30 dollars in my pocket. The hotel management sympathised with my plight and kindly allowed me free use of the room I had recently vacated while I tried to sort myself out. It was just about the lowest point in my life. First I phoned Pat back in London to tell her what had happened and could she alert the credit card company. Next I took a cab to police headquarters to report the loss, essential for insurance purposes. Thankfully, I can't recall the complete sequence of events after that, but I do remember the ghastly feeling of someone with no identity, stranded virtually penniless in a foreign land 5000 miles from home. I now knew what it's like to be stateless or a down-and-out.

Anyway, I struck lucky with Thomas Cook. I found the address in Vegas of their local agent and with a minimum of fuss they replaced their missing travellers cheques, but I got nowhere with American Express – big on advertising instant no quibble replacement but unable to do anything until I could prove my identity. Thanks to Pat's herculean efforts I was able to collect a temporary credit card from somewhere or other and was able to get out to the airport to pay for a 1 am flight to New Orleans. Bleary eyed, I made my way to my hotel, did some hasty preparation for the trials and got to the stadium in time for the start of the meeting. I never actually saw any of the action on the track itself as I was working from a trailer, mercifully air conditioned for outside it was incredibly hot and humid. I watched everything on a TV monitor, making notes and faxing information sheets to the London-based commentary team. There was no shortage of dramatic storylines. The first concerned Carl Lewis.

You expect shocks at the US Olympic Trials, but it was difficult to accept that Carl Lewis, only ten months after his greatest 100m triumph, would not be defending his title in Barcelona. He didn't need to win in New Orleans but he did have to place in the first three. However, for once he found himself unable to storm through in the later stages and finished fully two metres behind the winner [Dennis Mitchell 10.09] in sixth place ... his worst race since placing last in the World Cup in Rome way back in 1981.

Next came the long jump qualifying round. I had never seen him so flustered and diffident. Appearing to be suffering from a lack of self-confidence, he opened with 8.14m, one of his poorest jumps in years, and that proved to be his best of the night although he did go through as the third best qualifier. In the final he lost to Mike Powell for the second time running but he did produce a respectable distance of 8.53m to Powell's 8.62m. The 200m final saw him clock his fastest time (20.15) for four years but that was in fourth place as Michael Johnson pattered home in a personal best of 19.79, the fourth fastest ever time. That meant that Lewis would be confined to just one individual event at the Olympics. He at least made the team for Barcelona. Among the big names who failed to qualify the most sensational was surely Dan O'Brien.

American athletics shot itself in the foot on this eighth and penultimate day of the Olympic Trials. The absurdity of the selection system's inflexibility was accentuated by the demise of Dan O'Brien, world decathlon champion and by common consent the man most likely to take the world record beyond 9000 points in the near future. One moment he was on cloud nine, on course once again to seriously challenge Daley Thompson's world record ... the next, because of a stupid error of judgement, he found himself consigned to athletics history as the most celebrated victim of the sudden-death trial process since high hurdler Harrison Dillard in 1948. At least Dillard made the 100m team and won gold in that event instead. O'Brien is going to have to wait four long years for his next Olympic opportunity even though he is unquestionably the finest all-rounder in the world.

It was a sickening turn of events for O'Brien, who was riding high after a world's best first day total of 4698. After seven events his score was 6467, as against 6408 by Thompson when he set his world record of 8847 at the 1984 Olympics. The pole vault should have added to his margin, for Daley's LA mark was 5.00m and O'Brien (best of 5.25m) had cleared 5.20m at the World Championships. After soaring over 4.90m in warm-up O'Brien made a decision which will haunt him for the rest of his life. Disregarding the advice of 1976 Olympic champion Bruce Jenner to play safe by opening at a low height, say 4.40m, O'Brien elected to come in at 4.80m. It made no sense. This was no occasion to throw caution to the winds in a do-or-die world record attempt; all that mattered really was to place in the top three, for which a score of 8200-8300 would surely be adequate. Alas, everything went wrong on his first two attempts and, with the nerves getting to him as he stared over the precipice, the increasingly desperate Dan totally botched his final try. Instead of scoring anything between 700 and 1000 points he had scored nothing ... and he was out of the team.

In his absence, Robert Zmelik won the Olympic title with 8611 points but a month later, in Talence, O'Brien gained some consolation by breaking Daley's world record with 8891 points with Zmelik a distant second on 8344. Another star who missed out was 400m world record holder Butch Reynolds. It was hugely controversial that he was allowed to compete in New Orleans at all.

On what had been designated a rest day [June 23], the Butch Reynolds affair moved from the courts and committee rooms to the track as the first two rounds of the 400m, postponed three times while the legal issues were being argued, were finally contested with Reynolds allowed to compete. The IAAF had previously been implacable in its opposition to his being permitted to run in the Trials. As far as the world governing body was concerned, Reynolds remained ineligible for competition anywhere in the world until August 11. If Reynolds took part in a race, the IAAF would apply its 'contamination' rule and suspend the other competitors. However, an 11th hour order by a Supreme Court judge, preventing TAC [US governing body] and the IAAF "from impeding or interfering with Harry L Reynolds Jr's ability to compete in the 1992 US Olympic Trials" added a new dimension to the legal wrangle. The TAC could not defy a Supreme Court directive, and therefore Reynolds had to be permitted to compete.

IAAF president Primo Nebiolo, himself a lawyer, understood TAC's predicament and recommended to IAAF Council members that they should vote to waive the contamination rule on this occasion. Approval was granted, but although Reynolds was given the green light to compete in the Trials the signals were still firmly at red so far as the Olympics were concerned. The IAAF could certainly prevent an athlete under suspension from taking part in the Games as the Supreme Court's jurisdiction does not extend to Europe. With the exception of his brother Jeff Reynolds, none of the other 400m entrants had much sympathy for Butch's plight by the time they trooped to the stadium for the oft-delayed heats. They had warmed up unnecessarily too many times, expended too much nervous energy, to feel other than aggrieved by their rival's seeming indifference to the threat which had hung over them by the contamination rule until the IAAF's change of heart. Despite – or maybe because of – all the turmoil, Reynolds produced two excellent runs, clocking 44.58 in the first round and 44.68 in the second for the best ever one-day 400m double. "Seems like I went faster on guts and heart. I thrive on emotion and I think that made me run faster today," he said.

Next day Reynolds ran 44.14, his quickest since 1988, in his semi-final behind Quincy Watts, whose 43.97 was the fastest time in the world for four years. Two days after that came the final.

Courtesy of the US Supreme Court, Reynolds managed to get a lot further along the road to Olympic 400m selection than anyone had envisaged, but it was on the track that his dream was finally punctured. Had he placed in the first three his name would have gone forward for selection, the IAAF would have objected and the legal wrangling would continue. By finishing fifth (44.65) Reynolds lost whatever slim hope he might have entertained of chasing the title which narrowly eluded him in Seoul. "Too much pressure," Reynolds explained. "I didn't have it from the gun. I'm tired, real tired. Now I can take a minute to go cry." Tears of joy rather than anguish were in order for Danny Everett, whose time of 43.81 was the second fastest in history. The field Everett beat was the greatest ever assembled for a 400m race. Of the six men who have ever broken 44 sec, four are still active ... and all were in the line-up.

While all this drama was being played out, I was still striving to regain my identity and financial wellbeing. American Express finally came through and replaced my travellers cheques, and by an extraordinary coincidence I was in their New Orleans office at the same time as my Australian colleague Mike Hurst, who had his stolen from his hotel. There was still the vital task of obtaining a passport, or else I would be unable to get home. I phoned the British Embassy in Washington but they couldn't help other than advise me to travel to the nearest British consulate to New Orleans, over 300 miles away in the Texan city of Houston. After a complicated, deeply frustrating series of phone calls I finally got through to a human voice and arranged to fly out on June 25, a rest day at the Trials. After explaining all the circumstances I received an emergency passport and when I returned to New Orleans I set about organising my flight home as the original booking had been cancelled.

Despite all these trials and tribulations, I thoroughly enjoyed my ten days in the "Big Easy". I had wanted to visit New Orleans during my Greyhound bus tour way back in 1964 but racial segregation ruled that out for me. Now it was possible for me to soak up the unique laid-back atmosphere of the city, admire the distinct French and Spanish Creole architecture, attend a jazz brunch and take a trip along the Mississippi River on a paddle steamer which could have come straight out of "Showboat". But there was a potentially dark side too. Late one evening I was desperate to fax that day's report and results to AT but the business office at the Hilton where I was staying was closed. When I asked at reception whether there was a nearby bureau open I was given directions and began what I was told would be a ten minute walk. I had barely started when a taxi drew up and the black driver asked where I was headed. When I told him, he strongly advised me to ride with him as it wasn't safe for a white person to be walking along that street at that time of night. I thanked him, hopped in for the short ride and asked him to wait while I faxed over my copy. On my return to the hotel, I complained to reception that I should have been warned about the potential dangers of walking at night in that particular direction.

After arriving back in London I exchanged my emergency passport for a proper one and sorted out my travel insurance claim. I wasn't out of pocket as everything was refunded, including the cost of the various flights. There was, however, a blip. Unknown to me at the time, whoever stole my travel wallet in Las Vegas used the credit card to buy a large amount of jewellery that day, resulting in my account going over the permitted monthly limit. When I next used my credit card, checking out from a hotel in Lausanne where I was part of the Sky Sports team which covered that meeting, I was shocked to find it was rejected and our producer had to come to the rescue. I made my objections known to the bank, who must have been informed that the excess expenditure on my card was fraudulent. I learned a lesson the hard way from losing that wallet and ever since I have been quite obsessive about guarding my valuables when travelling abroad. I have never forgotten that empty and frightening feeling of when I was in effect a non-person.

Unheeded warning sign no 1: I was still training after a fashion, mainly around the playing fields at Copthall, and entering the occasional fun run. On July 15, at Battersea Park, as a member of the AT team, I took part in the Chemical Bank Corporate Challenge road race and recall running alongside our office manager Liz Sissons at no great speed when I suddenly felt totally breathless and had no option but to drop out for the first time in my running career, except for the special case of the Peoples Marathon in 1980. Feeling very stressed, I walked slowly back to the car where Pat was waiting. She thought we should call for an ambulance but I didn't want any fuss. I gradually recovered although it was quite a while before I felt well enough to drive home.

Unheeded warning sign no 2 came a little later in Barcelona. Randall, myself, Chris Brasher and Joe Lancaster were sharing a house rented out to the media for the period of the Games. The weather was exceedingly hot and humid and as there was no air conditioning we all went out to the local supermarket to buy electric fans but it was still pretty stifling. On the athletics rest day (August 4) Randall and I decided to go for a gentle run out but, as at Battersea, I had to stop when I suddenly felt quite ill. Maybe I just got dehydrated but with the benefit of hindsight I believe that on both occasions I suffered a very minor heart attack … because the following year I would experience the real thing.

Just prior to the Games I interviewed Linford Christie. The obvious opening question was how did he rate his chances in the Olympic 100m. He replied: "I think I've got as good a chance as anybody else. It's a wide open field and there's no outstanding favourite as such." How was his season going compared to the 9.92 in Tokyo the previous year? "This has been my most consistent year. I'm bigger, I'm stronger and I believe I'm faster. Because of the consistency of my running this year I feel that if I need to run faster than 9.92 to win in Barcelona I can do it." His reaction to Carl Lewis not being able to defend his 100m title? "The only regret I have about Carl not being there is that to some people it will detract a little bit from winning. What they don't realise is that the reason Carl isn't there is that the three Americans who have been selected were faster than him at the Trials. Carl's a great athlete but every dog has his day. When your time's up your time's up." Was Carl ever a particular hero? "No, I never had any heroes, but I love the way he runs because technically he's the best sprinter in the world." If he won in Barcelona, would it be of any significance that, at 32, he would be easily the oldest ever Olympic 100m champion? "The only significance it would have for me is that I'd be able to shut up half the British press. They were always saying I was too old. That would be the only pleasure, because then I could turn round and blow a raspberry!"

It was a day to remember and savour. It was the day that Linford Christie won the blue riband event of the Olympics and became one of the sport's immortals. As he had stressed in our interview last week, Christie considered he had "as good a chance as anybody else," a fair assessment, but even he could not have dreamt of winning the biggest race of his life by such a convincing margin. At the finish he had six-hundredths of a second – more than half a metre – to spare over Frank Fredericks, with Dennis Mitchell third.

The capacity crowd of 64,800 was hushed as the eight men settled in their blocks. At the third try they were away ... and Christie got a beauty of a start. For once, and on absolutely the right occasion, Christie found himself on level terms with his main rivals almost from the outset. By 60 metres he was clear and sprinting towards gold and glory. He crossed the line upright in 9.96, the second fastest time of his career. After so narrowly failing to win a medal in last year's World Championships Christie considered taking his leave of the sport but, as he said after his victory here, "I'm just glad I didn't retire then. That's the best decision I've ever made. This is something that Ron [coach Roddan] and I have been working for over the last 10 to 12 years."

Christie also earned the distinction of becoming the first Jamaican-born athlete (not counting Ben Johnson) to strike gold at 100m and Jamaica had high hopes of a first victory in the women's 100m the same day. The final proved to be an astonishing race, easily the greatest ever in depth, as Merlene Ottey ran 10.88 into a 1m/sec wind and yet finished fifth. In a stunning upset it was Gail Devers, better known as a hurdler, who succeeded Flo-Jo as champion, swooping over the finish line in 10.82, 13/100ths faster than her previous best. Devers it was who made a miraculous recovery last year from Graves' Disease, a life threatening condition, for which she would have to receive medical treatment for the rest of her life. "I don't feel there's any hurdle too high or any obstacle in my life I can't get over," she said earlier in the year. "This is why I say dreams come true." Unfortunately for her, the 100m hurdles final was more of a nightmare. Up until the final hurdle the race was hers by a wide margin but she hit the final barrier with the heel of her lead leg, almost fell and stumbled across the finish line in fifth place.

The other women's hurdles race, over 400m, saw Sally Gunnell emerge victorious in 53.23. The race she had visualised so often went completely to plan, striding fifteens to hurdle six, changing down at seven and then sixteens home – the first time she had managed that sequence. A few weeks later I interviewed Sally at her home in Sussex and asked her for her recollections of the race. "I remember going down the back straight thinking 'okay, I haven't lost too much on Sandra [Farmer-Patrick]. I'm in a good position.' Then my next thought was coming off the eighth hurdle, being level almost and realising that a lot of people had said to me that if I could be up there at the eighth hurdle it was mine on the way home. That gave me a lot of positive thought and I just concentrated so hard down the home straight. I ran very conservatively at the beginning just to keep my energy for the last part of the race. So many people went off so fast and that's why, apart from Sandra and I, the times were very slow. I really stretched for the last hurdle. I was so determined and had run it so often in my mind that I was going to get there. I was still running scared, waiting for Sandra to come up, but I was just as determined that she wasn't going to be able to."

Her first thought as she crossed the line was, she said, "just total disbelief." She paid tribute to her coach, Bruce Longden. "I've been with him for 12 years and for sure he has been a big influence. He knows what training works for me and it does take a long time, and it was nice to see that both Linford and I have been with our coaches for a long time." It was some year for Sally, as in October she was married in Florida to former junior international 800m runner Jon Bigg (1:48.40 in 1985), a successful coach these days. Their son Finley Bigg was the 2016 English Schools 800m champion and ran 1:49.24 at age 19 in 2017.

The men's 400m hurdles was perhaps the highlight of the Games, for Kevin Young – watched from the stands by Ed Moses – smashed the latter's world record of 47.02 with the stunning time of 46.78 despite bashing the last barrier and celebrating his victory before the finish. That time, which would have won the 1956 Olympic *flat* 400m title, has been unapproached ever since. The long-legged American was unique in that he was able to mix 12 and 13 stride intervals between the hurdles. In third place the ever dependable Kriss Akabusi lowered his own UK record to 47.82 and other British bronze medallists were Steve Backley in the javelin and the 4x400m squads of Roger Black, David Grindley, Akabusi and John Regis; Phylis Smith, Sandra Douglas, Jennifer Stoute and Gunnell. Particularly frustrating from a British point of view was the 110m hurdles, where Tony Jarrett placed fourth in the same time as the bronze medallist and Colin Jackson clocked the fastest time of the competition with 13.10 in his heat but picked up a hip muscle injury and was only seventh in the final, won in 13.12 by Canada's Mark McKoy – who was coached in Wales along with Jackson by Malcolm Arnold, the man who had guided John Akii-Bua to 400m hurdles gold 20 years earlier.

In winning his third Olympic long jump title Carl Lewis brought his total of individual Olympic golds to six (two at 100m, one at 200m), a new record if you count only those events currently on the Olympic programme and further evidence that the 31 year-old American is the greatest athlete who ever lived. Bouncing back after two successive defeats by Mike Powell, his only long jumping losses since 1981, Lewis made the score 16-2 in his favour against the world champion and record holder. Lewis, fully recovered from the sinus infection which affected his showing at the US Trials and claiming to be as fast as ever, had the chance to strike first. He opened his account with an 8.67m, a distance which only he, Powell and Larry Myricks have ever exceeded at sea level [Lewis jumped 8.68m in qualifying], but he realised it might prove insufficient with six jumps to come from Powell. As it turned out, it did prevail … although only by three centimetres. "This is my best gold medal of all," enthused Lewis. "I had a rough time earlier this summer and I was so down; to come back and win is so exciting."

There was further glory for Lewis in the 4x100m relay as he anchored his team to a world record shattering 37.40 for his eighth Olympic gold medal, while the US squad in the 4x400m relay also set a world record of 2:55.74 with 400m champion in 43.50, Quincy Watts, timed at 43.1 for his leg.

The Games were notable in that with Cuba and Ethiopia back in the Olympic fold for the first time since Moscow in 1980 every nation of consequence was present in Barcelona. The era of boycotts was over. Politically, many momentous events had occurred since the previous Games. Communist East Germany had ceased to exist and Germany was represented by one team; the dismembered Soviet Union competed under the title 'Unified Team' while the Baltic States previously under its control proudly participated

278

as Estonia, Latvia and Lithuania, and back from the sporting wilderness came a reconstituted South Africa, welcome at an Olympics for the first time since 1960. Perhaps the most indelible image of the Games was the sight of Derartu Tulu, a black Ethiopian, and Elana Meyer, a white South African, running a joint lap of honour following the 10,000m in which they finished first and second respectively. It was an emotional scene which proved that for all their shortcomings – as with every other human endeavour – the Olympic Games remain an important force for harmony and friendship transcending political and racial differences.

I arrived back from Barcelona on August 11. The following day, at a board meeting, Eddie announced that he could no longer financially support the magazine. In theatrical terms AT was a critical success but a box office failure, and the drain on Eddie's resources was proving too great, particularly as he had been hit by losses at Lloyd's. For more than three years we had outshone *Athletics Weekly* but EMAP's pockets were deeper than Eddie's and ultimately the market could support only one weekly title.

In the September 23 issue Randall announced that AT had been taken over by Burlington Publishing, a subsidiary of Harmsworth Magazines which was a part of Associated Newspapers, and that the editorial office would be moved to Windsor. At about that time Nick Davies, who had been with us from the start, left to take up a position with the IAAF, then still based in London (he moved to Monaco in January 1994), and my own involvement with the magazine as consultant editor was greatly reduced. Liz Sissons and former ultra distance star Don Turner took charge of results and fixtures, while Peta Bee – these days the most prominent and prolific of health and fitness journalists – joined as editorial assistant. Duncan Mackay was promoted to deputy editor in December.

I had the sad task in October of writing an appreciation of 1948 Olympic 400m champion Arthur Wint, who had died in his native Jamaica, aged 72.

He was Jamaica's renaissance man. To have become his nation's first Olympic champion would have been sufficient glory for one lifetime, but Arthur Wint achieved high distinction in other areas too ... as an RAF pilot, surgeon and High Commissioner to London. Although recognised as a strong contender for a medal, he was given little chance of beating his fellow Jamaican and former schoolmate Herb McKenley, a man who had set world record figures of 46.0 for 440 yards (worth 45.7 for 400m) two months earlier. Whatever hopes Wint might have entertained seemed to be dashed when he streaked to a brilliant but extravagant clocking of 46.3 in his semi-final ... with the final to follow less than two hours later. But McKenley, aware that his friend was in the greatest form of his life, attempted to run the legs off him – and committed a fatal error of pace judgement on the heavy cinder track. At the 200m mark McKenley was seven metres up in 21.4, only three-tenths slower than the winning 200m time at those Games, but began to tie up when the finishing straight was reached and the 28 year-old University of London medical student almost reluctantly overtook his desperately flailing opponent 20m from the tape to win in 46.2. He had fleetingly wondered whether to let McKenley win, knowing how much victory would mean to his rival, "but he was decelerating so fast I passed him." Together with McDonald Bailey, Arthur Wint became the greatest crowd-puller in British athletics. He was an awe-inspiring apparition when in full flight, his towering height and prodigious stride always drawing gasps of wonder and admiration from spectators, one of whom was this writer who – as a young schoolboy attending his first AAA Championships in 1950 – was so entranced by the sight of Wint that he became hooked on the sport for life.

Another 400m star hit the headlines again in December when Butch Reynolds, whose doping suspension by the IAAF was extended until December 31, was awarded $27.3 million damages against the IAAF by a court in Ohio. "No amount of money can justify the damage and harm done to me," he said. "The fight was to protect my name and my reputation. I just hope this proves my innocence." He had always maintained that the drug testing procedure was flawed. However, the IAAF, who did not contest the lawsuit, said that an American court had no jurisdiction over their affairs. Reynolds continued to compete at the highest level for several seasons, clocking 43.91 in 1996, but never received any damages as a federal appeals panel overturned the Ohio court's verdict.

In the final issue for 1992 I reviewed the year's activities. Among the items listed: Steve Backley's throw of 91.46m in New Zealand in January remained the official world javelin record as Jan Zelezny's 94.74m in July was with an implement which was ruled illegal by the IAAF; Fatima Whitbread retired due to a shoulder injury; Sergey Bubka vaulted 6.13m for the 16th world indoor record of his career and 6.13m again for his 16th outdoor mark – but no-heighted at the Olympics; Seb Coe was elected Conservative MP for Falmouth and Camborne in Cornwall; South African athletes returned to international competition after 17 years; Tessa Sanderson became the first British athlete to compete in five Olympics, placing fourth in Barcelona; Daley Thompson's career came to a poignant end when, just five seconds into his first ever decathlon on English soil, he pulled up in the 100m with a torn hamstring; the two longest ever jumps were recorded at Sestriere, helped by the 2050m altitude and illegal following winds: 8.99m by Mike Powell and 7.63m by Heike Drechsler; Mike Conley triple jumped 18.17m at the Olympics, way beyond the world record, but that too was wind assisted; Moses Kiptanui, who failed to make the Kenyan Olympic team, set world records for 3000m both on the flat (7:28.96) and over the barriers (8:02.08); Noureddine Morceli broke Said Aouita's world 1500m record with 3:28.86; Steve Smith's winning height at the World Junior Championships of 2.37m equalled the world junior record and broke the Commonwealth senior record.

28. ENTER 'ATHLETICS INTERNATIONAL' (1993)

There were three happenings which affected me profoundly during 1993. I suffered a heart attack … *Athletics Today* ceased publication … and *Athletics International* was born.

The heart attack seemingly came completely out of the blue. It was only in retrospect that the possible significance of those two unsettling episodes while running the previous year became apparent. To celebrate my 55th birthday Pat and I enjoyed a pleasant stay in Nice. We returned home on May 28 … and on June 1 it happened. I was just walking around the corner to the shops when I felt distinctly odd. There was no pain as I recall but a very uncomfortable feeling in my chest and a certain amount of giddiness. I decided to return home immediately but dismissed it as a bad case of indigestion. However, I still felt under the weather next day, and so the day after that Pat insisted I go to the surgery. My regular GP wasn't there that day but I was examined by a locum, Dr Rajani, who quickly realised there could be a serious problem. He took an ECG, which was transmitted over the phone line to the local (Edgware General) hospital, and was informed that I should go straight away to that hospital for further tests.

That's how I recall the attack, but Pat's recollections are more vivid.

"I knew there was something very wrong. Mel couldn't lie down comfortably and sat up in a chair in the lounge all night and he was very grey and sweaty. Being a typical male he wouldn't call a doctor (you could do that in those days) and wanted to see if the discomfort would just pass. Meanwhile, I was very worried and agonised about it with him all the next day and night as well. Fortunately our cleaner Helen was due the following morning – a very nice young woman with a car. By now Mel realised it wasn't just going to pass and I was able to persuade him to go to the doctor. I said to Helen 'forget the cleaning, please help me take my husband to the doctor', which thank goodness she did (I don't drive). The surgery was only a ten minute walk away but he couldn't have managed that … that's how ill he was. Even at the doctors, he still thought it wasn't anything important and nearly made for the door to go home instead of waiting for the result of the tests! Needless to say, Helen and I put our feet down about that and made him stay!"

For the next nine days I was under observation at Edgware General, although after the initial shock of this sudden turn of events I considered myself a fraud for occupying a valuable hospital bed while feeling quite normal again. On one occasion I was reprimanded for leaving the ward for a walk outside in the fresh air. What kept my spirits up were the constant visits by Pat, chuckling over Bill Bryson's recently published travel books and listening through headphones to the newly launched Classic FM radio channel. However, the tests confirmed that I had indeed suffered a heart attack. On June 12 a young female doctor came up to tell me that she had good news. My feeling of relief that the crisis was over was short-lived, though, for the 'good news' was that a stress test had shown me to be fit enough to undergo quadruple heart by-pass surgery!

An ambulance transported me to Harefield Hospital, near Uxbridge, where I spent the next three days undergoing further examination.

It was sod's law that just a few weeks earlier, because of ever escalating premiums, I had renewed our medical insurance policy at one level below the previous arrangement to stabilise the cost. Pat and I had never claimed anything over the years but on this one occasion when we needed help the company informed us that the new policy would not cover such an operation at Harefield, which was world renowned for its treatment of heart and lung conditions. There was the option to pay as a private patient but that would have cost in the region of £10,000 (equivalent to around £20,000 today), assuming there were no complications. Bearing in mind that I didn't know at that time whether I would be able to work again we ruled that out. As my operation was considered non-urgent I was instead placed on Harefield's NHS waiting list while several further stress tests were conducted. In November I was told that the earliest date for surgery would be in May 1994 but I could be admitted earlier if a vacancy occurred. My time on the waiting list proved longer than that ... 15 months.

Although I felt perfectly normal, the heart attack did have knock-on effects. Having taken only a handful of pills during the previous 55 years, I was now on a six a day regime that has continued ever since; I was ineligible to drive for some time; I had to cancel my trip with Eddie to the US Championships in Eugene and did not feel confident enough to fly to Kraków for the wedding of my nephew Lionel to his lovely Polish bride Bernadetta. My workload was much reduced and my only printed contribution to AT was a farewell message in the final edition, dated July 7.

The closure of a magazine is rather like a death in the family. It's a time of sadness and regret, of course, but it can also be the occasion for looking back with appreciation and affection. When, four and a half years ago, Randall Northam and I began co-editing the weekly version of "Athletics Today", with the financial and enthusiastic support of Eddie Kulukundis, it was the start of a great adventure. Our aim was to produce the best athletics magazine the world had ever known and to topple "Athletics Weekly" from its perch. Well, we succeeded in the first aim if not the second. Sufficient well respected people in the sport have assured us that the magazine has set new standards of excellence for us to believe them; unfortunately, in the current economic climate, we simply couldn't attract enough readers and advertisers to make the project financially viable. Still, we tried, and even after Eddie had to bow out last autumn we managed to maintain our standards under a new publisher. I can confidently predict that no other athletics publication will surpass AT for its breadth and quality of coverage.

Most of the credit for that must go to Randall Northam, an outstanding editor, and I would also pay special tribute to the indefatigable Duncan Mackay for his prodigious output, Mark Shearman for the consistent excellence of his photographs, Peter Matthews for making AT the world's best source for quick and detailed overseas results ... and Sir Eddie [who was knighted in June] for getting the whole show off the ground in the first place, against all the odds.

After leaving the revamped AW five years ago, totally disillusioned, I hadn't planned to get involved again in editing a magazine, but the challenge offered by AT was too exciting to pass up. I'm proud and grateful to have been part of this venture; my thanks to all my colleagues and to you, the loyal readers who supported us in our quest.

In his message, Randall explained the reasons for the magazine's demise. "Our publishers, Harmsworth Active, have decided there is no future for us. We have been losing money since we joined the group last September and that situation could not go on indefinitely. Yet, I believe, and I also know I am not alone in believing it, that we produced the best athletics magazine in the country if not the world. We could not have produced a magazine of such consistent excellence without the help of many people and I would like to thank some of them:

"*Burlington Publishing* (later to become *Harmsworth Active*) and *John Fletcher*, the publishing director, for rescuing us when the cold draught from Lloyds forced Eddie Kulukundis to withdraw his backing. Eddie, or *Sir Eddie* as he is now – deservedly so for his support for athletics and the theatre – was an untiring enthusiast and inspirational publisher. *Mel Watman*, the safest long-stop in the business, whose eminence as a statistician occasionally and unfairly obscured his excellence as a writer. It was a source of great glee if we caught out Mel on a fact. I suppose it happened two or three times in nearly five years. *Duncan Mackay*, my deputy, who went on a course recently and was almost called a liar when he described his workload. *Nick Davies*, my first deputy, who helped shape the philosophy of the magazine with a constant search for accuracy and the truth. *Wendy Sly*, who was thrown into the deep end but who learned to swim in the strange world of publishing far quicker than we had a right to expect. *Peter Matthews*, who produced the best international pages in the world. *Mark Shearman*, whose excellent photographs brought many admiring letters. *Cliff Temple*, whose crusade against falling standards will be cut off just as it was getting going. Other top athletics writers like *John Rodda*, whose 'Corridors of Power' column caused so many irritations within the establishment, *Neil Wilson* and *David Powell* graced these pages.

"There are many others, who helped, to thank. Star athletes like *Seb Coe, Linford Christie* and *Peter Elliott. Hugh Jones*, who goes back to the first monthly issue I edited, *Wendy Green, Alan Parry, Geoff Harrold, Louise Davis, Andrea Ford, Lizzie Benn, Martin Gillingham* and lately *Peta Bee* and *Konrad Manning*. And last but not least our results and fixtures team, headed recently by *Liz Sissons* and *Don Turner* and before them *Mark Butler, Steve Smythe* and *Steve Roe*. They and our regional correspondents produced without question the best service there has been in British athletics. So thanks and goodbye to everyone. Life won't be the same."

Peter Matthews wrote: "It was in November 1990 that Eddie, Randall and Mel persuaded me to compile the international pages for AT. A page, perhaps two, a week was the suggestion. As it transpired space was found to expand that a little, so that it has become two or three pages every week since then. It has been hard work, keeping in touch with the sport worldwide, and endeavouring to include every significant result. It has, however, been most gratifying to all of us to hear from many of our readers that AT has become regarded as the world's best athletics magazine, and in particular that it has the best coverage of international results. Sadly that now ends, but I would like to take this opportunity of thanking very sincerely all my correspondents."

As it happened, it wasn't the end for the *Athletics International* section but happily a new beginning. But first, let me recount the major events of the first half of the year.

While in Birmingham in February for an indoor international meeting at the National Indoor Arena I took the opportunity to interview Noureddine Morceli who had won the mile in what was then the third fastest ever indoor time of 3:50.70.

Although Morceli is a quiet and modest man who, unlike his early hero, Said Aouita, is not given to making outlandish claims, he expressed absolute conviction that he won't merely trim Steve Cram's 1985 world mile record of 3:46.32 but will smash it. "I think last year I was ready to run 3:44 or 3:45, but I didn't get another chance to race after my world record 1500m (3:28.86), which was a pity. This year I will do it for sure." It was Abderrahmane Morceli – one of his older brothers – who was the inspiration for Noureddine to become a runner and is today his coach. Steve Ovett's victory in the inaugural World Cup 1500m in Düsseldorf in 1977 was one of the supreme displays in middle distance running history. Unnoticed, but running the race of his life to finish fourth, was 19 year-old Abderrahmane Morceli, representing Africa. He ran 3:36.26 that year and clocked 3:54.63 for the mile in 1983. Noureddine was aged seven when his big brother took on the world's elite and, watching the race on TV, his imagination was fired. He too wanted to be a runner and fly away to far-away countries.

Impatient to become the first Algerian ever to set a world record, Morceli achieved his ambition over 1500m indoors in Seville on his 21st birthday in 1991 with 3:34.16. Ten days later, on the same track, a 52.0 last 400m carried him to the World Indoor title. That summer he would lower his 800m best from 1:48 to 1:44.79. Indeed, his leg speed is exceptional and he revealed to me that in a 400m time trial he had clocked 46.85. He was less forthcoming about precise details of his training. When I mentioned a workout of 15 x 400m in 54-55 sec he was somewhat taken aback. "How did you know about that?" he asked. Although the obvious favourite at the World Championships in Tokyo, few could have anticipated his margin of victory. A 51.55 last lap carried him over the line a full two seconds clear. He ran the final 800m of the 3:32.84 race in a prodigious 1:50.1, uncannily similar to Seb Coe's 1:50.0 when winning the 1984 Olympic crown in 3:32.53. Coe, along with Cram and Aouita, is Morceli's hero. "He was a great athlete. He could run 45 sec for 400m and his records for 800m and 1000m are very fast and have stood for many years. That is the test of a great runner."

The only event that mattered to Morceli in 1992 was the Olympic 1500m. Unfortunately for him, his carefully constructed plans were ruined when, while training at altitude near Mexico City, he injured a sciatic nerve. That problem with his right hip cost him 45 days of speedwork at a crucial time and was largely responsible for what proved to be a disastrous showing in Barcelona. He trailed in a disconsolate seventh. For his final race of the year, in Rieti, everything slipped into place and history was made. He flashed past 1200m in an awesome 2:47.30 and hung on grimly to register the sensational time of 3:28.86, a substantial improvement on Aouita's 3:29.46. Understandably changing his perspective, he commented: "This world record is worth as much as an Olympic title."

As a devout Muslim he reads the Koran and prays five times a day, abstains from alcohol and, although it's difficult to maintain hard training during that period, he observes Ramadan, the month-long fast between dawn and dusk. He is no fundamentalist, though, and has no objections to women running. He is proud of Hassiba Boulmerka's achievements [1991 World and 1992 Olympic 1500m titles], unlike some of his co-religionists who regard women appearing in public in scanty clothing as unacceptable behaviour. Following his Birmingham indoor mile, Morceli returned to Algeria for one of his occasional visits home. He has become a citizen of the world, ceaselessly moving from one high altitude training area to another – Mexico City, Colorado Springs, St Moritz, the Atlas Mountains of his own land. He is, in effect, a nomad, a bedouin. Where's home? "Anywhere."

My next interview was with Dan O'Brien and conducted while I was at the World Indoor Championships. I always enjoyed visiting Canada in the summer months but Toronto in March was something else … not since my first trip to New York in February 1958 had I experienced such cold. The massive (50,000 capacity) but sparsely populated Sky Dome was the venue for Britain's best performance yet at the World Indoors, largely thanks to the Scots. Tom McKean, sometimes brilliant, other times racing like a novice, was on song this time as he front ran to win the 800m in 1:47.29, while Yvonne Murray did likewise in the 3000m, finishing 12 seconds clear in 8:50.55. Raised in South Africa and based in the USA, Scottish-born David Strang unexpectedly snatched second place in the 1500m; there was silver too for Colin Jackson in the 60m hurdles and Steve Smith cleared the UK record height of 2.37m for bronze in an outstanding contest. Many thought Jackson was the rightful winner although he clocked 7.43 behind McKoy's 7.41. The Canadian controversially got away with what several observers felt was a "flier"; indeed the electronic starting device recorded a reaction time of 0.053 sec when anything faster than 0.100 sec is deemed to be a false start although subject to the starter's discretion. Jackson, always quickly away, found himself a metre down on McKoy at the first hurdle.

As for Dan O'Brien, he began the invitation heptathlon contest at 12.15 pm on day one with a 6.67 60m courtesy of a rocket start (0.104 reaction time) and followed with a 7.84m long jump and 16.02m shot before ending up at around midnight with a 2.13m high jump clearance. Next day he put together

7.85 for 60m hurdles, vaulted 5.20m and covered 1000m in 2:57.96 for a world record score of 6476 points.

As the supreme decathlete of the eighties, and probably of all-time, Daley Thompson became the role model for young all-rounders all over the world, and no one idolised him more than Dan O'Brien. Now it is the American who is inspiring new generations of decathlon hopefuls and who is getting ready for athletic immortality. O'Brien might have fluffed his Olympic opportunity last year but he did add the world record (8891 in Talence in September) to the world title he captured in 1991 and the target this year is to crack the 9000 point barrier. As he told me in Toronto shortly before smashing the world indoor heptathlon record, a 9000 score was no wild dream. He was quite matter-of-fact about it. He explained: "Overall fitness is the main key to the decathlon. I was fatigued after the first day in Talence and I'm always fatigued at the end of the second day. So I need overall fitness for the 400m and 1500m. I also need to throw a better discus in the decathlon and pole vault a lot better. I should be a consistent 5.20 pole vaulter. In the 400m I need to get into the 46s, throw the discus over 50m, high jump 2.12 or better ... and that's your 9000 right there."

Dan was born in Portland, Oregon. His father was an African-American, his mother half Finnish, but he never knew either of his natural parents and at the age of two he was adopted by an Irish-American couple who gave him their surname, O'Brien. "It seems like I had to screw up totally in order to grow up." He admits while at the University of Idaho that he would often drink upwards of 12 cans of beer a day, he smoked marijuana and ran up debts totalling $8000. He missed classes as well as training. He was lucky that his coach [Mike Keller] stood by him. It wasn't until the end of 1987 that O'Brien faced up to his problems and resolved to change his ways. O'Brien doesn't like to dwell on the New Orleans disaster. "Sure, I'll remember it for the rest of my life, but it's history now. Hopefully I can do some great things to lessen the pain when I do think about it."

O'Brien, who trained for up to nine hours a day, never did reach 9000 points but he did go on to win further world titles in 1993 and 1995, become Olympic champion in 1996 and between 1992 and 1998 went unbeaten in 11 consecutive decathlons.

As a great fan of Mel Batty in his racing days, it was a pleasure to watch him develop as a coach, no doubt influenced by his own mentor Colin Young, and so it was a delight to witness his star pupil's success in the London Marathon.

It was quite a week for Eamonn Martin. During the early hours of Thursday his wife Julie presented him with their third child, a first son named after him, and on Sunday morning he made a glorious marathon debut to become the first Englishman to win London since Charlie Spedding nine years ago. As his ecstatic coach Mel Batty put it, "they both delivered the goods." Any man who has run 10,000m on the track in 27:23.06 has to be seriously considered if his preparations have been thorough and, as Martin said last *week, "endurance wise, I've got what it takes to run a good marathon. I know I can run at least 2:10." Martin never put a foot wrong. He was always among the leaders, remained strong and focused while his rivals dropped away and eventually produced an unmatchable kick to destroy the final opponent standing between him and a famous victory in 2:10:50. It was a spectacular beginning to his marathon career at the age of 34. Martin, one of the few world class athletes still holding down a proper job (he was due back at work at Ford's next day, regardless of winning $59,500 in prize money), feels he has a few more good years ahead. Eamonn is proud of his longevity as a top-class runner ("it's 20 years since I won the English Schools junior cross country") and summed up his marathon exploit as "another step in my long career."*

Eamonn, the 1990 Commonwealth Games 10,000m champion and the last British male to win London, remained remarkably consistent. In 1994, when placing eighth in London, he was close to his debut time with 2:11:05. In 1995 he finished 13th in London (2:12:44) and won Chicago (2:11:18); in 1996 he was fourth in Chicago in 2:11:21 and in 1997 13th in London in 2:12:29. He ran 2:17:22 at age 40.

One of the most pleasing occurrences of the year was the announcement in June that Eddie Kulukundis had been awarded a knighthood for services to sport and the theatre. Born in London into a prominent Greek shipping family and educated in the USA, Eddie made his name as a theatre impresario but in the world of British athletics he was regarded fondly as the sport's leading philanthropist. He financially supported so many of the athletes who would go on to win Olympic and world titles, paid for numerous coaches to attend major events abroad, was the patron of Belgrave Harriers, and his generosity extended to having his solicitors help Mo Farah, early in his career, acquire British citizenship. As well as being my employer on AT, Eddie kindly invited Pat and me to several glittering functions in his role as chairman of the Sports Aid Foundation and it was always an added joy to be in the company of his gorgeous wife, acclaimed actress Susan Hampshire.

Although AT's final issue appeared on July 7, I was determined that part of its legacy should live on in the form of *Athletics International* (from here on referred to as AI). That idea of producing a modest magazine specialising in results worldwide, first mooted in 1988, could now become a reality although without any outside financial backing. On July 8 I called round to The Triumph Press in nearby Edgware to print off a sample copy of AI and faxed it to Peter Matthews for his comments. They were favourable and, wasting no time, we as joint editors and myself as publisher produced issue no 1, dated July 20. Peter at the time was editor of the *Guinness Book of Records*, a member of the ITV athletics commentary team since 1985 after ten years with BBC Radio, editor of the ATFS International Athletics Annual (from 1985 to the present day) and a leading announcer.

Under the heading 'Greetings!' I wrote: *Welcome to ATHLETICS INTERNATIONAL, no longer part of 'Athletics Today' magazine, which unfortunately has ceased publication, but now a self contained publication.*

Peter Matthews and I hope you will derive as much information and excitement from this newsletter as you did from the international pages of AT. Although produced in Britain, this newsletter intends to live up to its name and be truly international, bringing you results and news from around the world.

It was indeed a modest offering, just 12 A5 pages, but we crammed in coverage of all the major events thus far in July, including Grand Prix meetings in Stockholm, Lausanne and Oslo, the European Cup Final for Combined Events, AAA Championships and World Student Games. As a promotional exercise we posted the first five issues free to ATFS members and the response from them and dispossessed AT readers was most gratifying. We were off and running ... but I certainly could not have predicted that we would still be going strong, but now in an email format, more than 800 issues and nearly a quarter of a century later! What a loyal readership we built up and what a continuing source of satisfaction it has been for me to have a regular outlet over all those years for my writing on the sport I cherish.

The big meeting of 1993 was, of course, the World Championships in Stuttgart. I didn't attend but I had plenty of work previewing the event, including a statistical form guide for David Barnett of Track & Field Tours – a service for his clients which has continued until the present day. AI printed the leading results and various concise statistics but did not attempt a detailed report. However, in a World Championships historic supplement to *American Track & Field* magazine published in 1999 I provided an overview of the meeting.

Such was the popularity of the World Championships that the IAAF decided to stage them every two years, with effect from 1993. Of the 187 nations participating – a big improvement over the previous record of 164 in Tokyo – the Americans dominated to an unprecedented extent, capturing 13 gold medals as against four by the next best, China, three of which came from their sensational band of female middle and long distance runners. Far-reaching political changes were reflected in the teams present: post-apartheid South Africa were invited to the World Championships for the first time, while Sergey Bubka – winner of the pole vault at the first three editions representing the USSR – this time retained the title in the colours of his native Ukraine as the former Soviet Union split up into its component republics.

Once again the African runners displayed their might, and not only in the middle and long distance department as Frankie Fredericks took the 200m in the brilliant African record time of 19.85 (with third placed Carl Lewis picking up a record tenth World Championship medal) and the Kenyans placed second in the 4x400m relay. Africans retained the 800m (Paul Ruto), 1500m (Noureddine Morceli), 5000m (Ismael Kirui), 10,000m (20 year-old Haile Gebrselassie) and steeplechase (Moses Kiptanui) titles, South African-born Mark Plaatjes won the marathon although representing his new country, the USA, and Maria Mutola took the women's 800m.

Stuttgart proved to be a memorable venue for Britain's athletes. Of their three gold medals, two were won with world record performances while the other went mightily close. The near-miss was by Linford Christie in the 100m. At the age of 33 the Jamaican-born Olympic champion became the oldest man ever to win a global title at 100m and his time of 9.87 with just an 0.3m wind was clearly superior to Lewis's world record 9.86 with a 1.2m wind. Welshman Colin Jackson compensated for his Olympic disappointment of the previous year by becoming the first Briton to set a new world record in the men's sprint hurdles since his namesake Clement Jackson ran 16.0 back in 1865! The time on this occasion was a spectacular 12.91. In second place, for good measure, Tony Jarrett set an English record of 13.00 for Britain's first ever 1-2 in any World Championship event. The other British triumph came from Olympic champion Sally Gunnell; her 52.74 400m hurdles was the first women's track world record since the 1988 Olympics ... and she was pushed to it all the way by Sandra Farmer-Patrick of the USA, and formerly of Jamaica, whose 52.79 was also well inside the former mark.

Two other men's world records came in the relays. The US 4x100m team tied the global mark of 37.40 in their semi before taking the final in 37.48 while the 4x400m squad finished an unprecedented 50m clear in 2:54.29. Michael Johnson, whose solo 42.94 anchor leg remains the quickest ever relay split, had won the individual 400m in 43.65. There was one more world record, in the newly introduced women's triple jump where Anna Biryukova jumped the barrier-breaking distance of 15.09m. Perhaps the most popular victory was Merlene Ottey's in the women's 200m. Beaten by just 1/1000th of a second in the 100m by Gail Devers (10.811 to 10.812) the 33 year-old Jamaican finally triumphed after collecting two silvers and eight bronzes in individual events at the Olympics and World Championships since 1980. It was close, though, as Gwen Torrence finished 2/100ths behind Ottey's 21.98.

Among the statistical titbits in AI: John Regis, second in the 200m in 19.94, set a European best at or near sea level; Morceli covered the last lap of his 3:34.24 1500m in 50.62; Steve Smith's bronze medal with 2.37m, equalling his UK record, was the first by a male high jumper representing Britain at global level since Irishman Con Leahy at the 1908 Olympics (two other British bronze medallists in the field events were Jonathan Edwards in the triple jump and Mick Hill in the javelin); Bubka became the only athlete to win a fourth consecutive world title, vaulting 5.70m in 1983, 5.85m in 1987, 5.92m in 1991 and now 6.00m; never before has a 4x100m team run as fast as 37.77, a European record by Britain, and lost, the team being Jackson, Jarrett, Regis and Christie; Gunnell claimed another medal in the 4x400m relay, bronze, clocking 49.9 for her anchor leg; while the three female Chinese winners all ran what are termed negative splits, that is covering the second half of the race faster than the first. All produced spectacular finishes: Liu Dong (4:00.50 1500m) sped round the last lap in an unheard of 57.48, Qu Yunxia (8:28.71 3000m) ran the final kilometre in a phenomenal 2:39.26 with a 59.22 last lap and Wang Junxia (30:49.30 10,000m) ripped through the second 5000m in 15:05.89 and a 61.07 final lap. Much more startling news of these and other Chinese runners would emerge a few weeks later.

With all of the world's elite in Europe there were many great performances in meetings staged shortly after Stuttgart. First up was Berlin where Morceli went very close to Steve Cram's world mile record of 3:46.32 with 3:46.78 in a race in which a record equalling 14 men broke the once formidable four minute barrier. Two days later the javelin world record was broken in Sheffield. The evolution of this record was a complicated affair. When Uwe Hohn of the GDR threw 104.80m in July 1984 the IAAF realised the danger such a distance posed to others in the arena and as from April 1986 a new specification implement had to be used. The centre of gravity was moved forward and the surface area of the tail reduced so that distances thrown would be curtailed. The first officially ratified world record with the new spear was 85.74m by Klaus Tafelmeier in September 1986. Subsequently Jan Zelezny threw 87.66m in 1987, while in 1990 Patrik Bodén achieved 89.10m and Steve Backley 89.58m. Meanwhile, the 1976 Olympic champion from Hungary, Miklos Németh, had developed a new model with superior flight qualities and using that implement Zelezny threw 89.66m and Backley 90.98m later in 1990, and Seppo Räty 91.98m and 96.96m in 1991. All these were ratified by the IAAF but subsequently deleted when the Németh model was banned and Backley's 89.58m was reinstated as the record. The Briton improved that to 91.46m in New Zealand in January 1992 but the record passed back to Zelezny when he threw 95.54m in South Africa in April 1993. Here is how AI reported the Sheffield exploit on August 29 and subsequent international highlights.

Perhaps the hallmark of a great champion is to perform indifferently and yet still win. That was Jan Zelezny in Stuttgart [85.98m]. Just 11 days and no training later Zelezny thrilled the capacity crowd in Sheffield with a superlative display. He did not quite hit the first throw right, yet it soared out to 87.04m. That was followed by a huge throw, taking full advantage of favourable wind conditions, sailing high and handsome out to 95.34m, just 20cm short of his world record. The spear landed close to officials and the TV presentation crew, who moved respectfully back for Zelezny's next throw. This went, like the previous one, well into the right hand side of the sector, but even further – a world record 95.66m.

Interviewed for AT in February, Noureddine Morceli was in no doubt that some time this year he would smash Steve Cram's world mile record. His confidence was ultimately justified when, after three good but unsuccessful attempts this summer (3:47.78 in Oslo, 3:46.78 in Berlin, 3:47.30 in Brussels), he delivered the goods on September 5 in Rieti, the Italian track on which he had set his world 1500m figures of 3:28.86 last year. It was an astonishing run by the 23 year-old Algerian, for he took almost two seconds from the record with a time of 3:44.39, thus simultaneously breaking through the 3:46 and 3:45 barriers and improving the previous global mark by the biggest margin since Jim Ryun obliterated Michel Jazy's figures by 2.3 sec with 3:51.3 in 1966. On the way, Morceli passed 1500m in 3:29.57, itself the fourth quickest in history, and a time which, says Morceli, "proves I can run 3:26 for the distance."

My Life in Athletics

The 1993 edition of the IAAF Mobil Grand Prix Final, held before a record 23,000 crowd at London's Crystal Palace on September 10, was a statistician's dream. Six men and five women came to the final on maximum points and, assuming they won again, were in contention for the overall first prizes of $100,000 (plus $30,000 as an individual event winner). Just who would be crowned as the overall Grand Prix champions would depend on the Hungarian Scoring Tables which award decathlon-style points for all events.

On the men's side, the standard was set by Noureddine Morceli, but his final time in the 1500m was adversely affected by the relatively slow first couple of laps. His 3:31.60 was the fastest ever seen on a British track although only the ninth quickest of his career. Morceli's time was worth 1221 points, but any hopes he might have harboured of winning the big prize were dashed when Jan Zelezny threw 88.28m worth 1250 points. To surpass that score Sergey Bubka would need to vault 6.05m, a height only he has ever cleared, and not thus far outdoors this year. He succeeded. As cool as always he sat out 6.00m and made 6.05m at the second try for 1253 points. It was literally a gold vault, worth a total of $130,000.

The women's contest proved equally exciting, and was resolved only by the result of the final track event. Sonia O'Sullivan, who would have been a double world champion in Stuttgart but for the Chinese presence, staked her claim in the 3000m with 8:38.12 worth 1206 points. Maria Mutola with an 800m time of 1:57.35 (1190 points) and Stefka Kostadinova (1.98m high jump for 1195 points) fell just short and it was now all down to the 400m hurdles in which both Sally Gunnell and Sandra Farmer-Patrick had maximum points. The winner, as long as the time was 54.08 or faster, would outscore O'Sullivan. As it turned out, Gunnell ran 53.82 but instead of pocketing $130,000 she took away 'only' $35,000 ... because a metre ahead of her in 53.69 (1217 points) was Farmer-Patrick

Under the headline "Unease As Chinese Women Rewrite Record Books", I reported on the remarkable (and, I would submit, suspicious) happenings in Beijing between September 8 and 13.

An angry and tearful Lynn Jennings summed up the feelings of many when informed of Wang Junxia's world records at the Chinese National Games in Beijing. "I believe these performances are out of scale. I believe they are derived from something illicit. Here is a 20 year-old coming out of the blue. It goes against everything in athletics. You train to progress and get better. There is no progression with the Chinese. It doesn't make sense. My sport has been soiled." Wang, the world 10,000m champion, went on to complete the most extraordinary sequence of world record breaking races in middle and long distance history: three (plus another race in which she bettered the previous record) in five days.

Whatever reasons are put forward to explain the amazing advance by the Chinese women (and five of them broke the world 3000m record in the heats!) the gut reaction of most non-Chinese observers is that something unnatural is happening. As British Olympic team manager Joan Allison, herself

291

a former world class middle distance runner, commented: "I believe these girls are taking drugs. You just cannot go out and run those times, certainly not at the age of 20. I walked away from the sport once because I was so disillusioned about the drugs being taken by Eastern bloc competitors. I just throw my hands up and say: 'Here we go again'."

Wang kicked off on September 8 with a 10,000m time which practically defies belief. Ingrid Kristiansen's 1986 world record of 30:13.74 was itself an awesome achievement, yet Wang recorded 29:31.78! That would have constituted a men's world record until Emil Zátopek ran 29:28.2 in 1949. Isao Sugawara from Japan informs us that the first 5000m was covered in 15:05.69, the second in 14:26.09 with the final 3000m taking 8:17.47! This is science fiction material. It means that Wang ran the last 5000m over 12 sec inside Kristiansen's hitherto unapproached world record for the distance and the final 3000m some 5 sec faster than Tatyana Kazankina's world mark.

Three days after that exploit, Wang returned for the 1500m final. World champion Liu Dong acted as pacemaker, reaching 400m in 57.13 and 800m in a staggering 2:00.71 before dropping out. However, world 3000m champion Qu Yunxia and Wang survived that seemingly suicidal pace to finish in 3:50.46 and 3:51.92 respectively. The 1980 world record of 3:52.47 by Kazankina had gone at last. The very next day, Wang and Qu were among five athletes who broke Kazankina's 1984 world 3000m record of 8:22.62 in the heats! Wang came home in 8:12.19 just ahead of Qu (8:12.27). One day after that, on September 13, Wang took the final in 8:06.11 with Qu second in 8:12.18. Thus Wang put together two 4:03 1500m efforts with zero recovery.

Was there ever such a transformation? Wang's best times before this year were 4:17.18, 8:55.50 and 32:29.90 and now she has run 3:51.92, 8:06.11 and 29:31.78 to set alongside her world's fastest ever marathon debut of 2:24:07 (69:09 second half) in April. Qu, also 20, has improved this year from 3:57.08 to 3:50.46 and from 8:55.1 to 8:12.18 as well as running a 2:24:32 marathon. Both women are members of a group coached by Ma Junren, who has reacted angrily to allegations of drug taking. "The 'Ma Family Army' (as his group is known) has never used steroids. We rely on our own talents." They train for long periods at high altitude and cover up to 40km (25 miles) a day.

Another popular feature from AT that AI salvaged was the world merit rankings and, with backing from Sir Eddie, Peter and I held a discussion meeting in London with him, Stan Greenberg, Alfons Juck and Lennart Julin. In December we printed the 1993 rankings, together with world top 50 lists compiled by Peter and Richard Hymans, highlights of the year, drug bans (Ben Johnson was barred for life and 13 Russians were on the list) and obituary, which poignantly included Britain's Anne Smith, world record breaker for 1500m and the mile, who died at 52.

29. THANK YOU, HAREFIELD (1994)

What an upsetting start it was to 1994 … the death of one of my dearest friends. I paid this tribute in *Track Stats*, the admirable quarterly journal of the NUTS edited at that time by Tim Lynch-Staunton and, since 1995, by Bob Phillips.

The sudden, tragic death of Cliff Temple on January 8, at the age of 46, shocked the world of British athletics. His contribution to the sport was immense and diverse. A modest club runner whose proudest achievement was running 2:52:27 in his one and only marathon, Cliff was influential as a journalist, writer and coach. I had known Cliff since 1966 when, as a teenage member of staff at "World Sports", he joined the NUTS. Two years later, when I took over as editor of AW, he edited a monthly offshoot entitled "Women's Athletics". Cliff would later coach several women athletes to international level, among them Shireen Bailey, Hilary Hollick, Sarah Rowell and Gillian Horovitz, while his greatest success on the male side was [London Marathon winner] Mike Gratton.

Cliff was appointed athletics correspondent of "The Sunday Times" in 1969, and his insight, knowledge and humour made him the most authoritative and entertaining of sportswriters. For many years he also graced the columns of AW, his witty Christmas specials (featuring Emily Lustbody et al) being a particular treat, and he was such a good professional that, uniquely among the magazine's contributors, I could forward his reports and articles to the printer totally unscathed. He was a prolific writer and his output of books included two outstanding biographies written in collaboration with Brendan Foster and Dave Moorcroft, and a couple of coaching books which became classics in the early days of the British mass participation running boom. He was also involved in a number of TV programmes about running and for some years was coaching editor for "Running" magazine. He was a tireless campaigner for a better deal for women's athletics. He helped pave the way to the acceptance of girls and women being permitted to run longer distances and to the amalgamation of women's organisations with their male equivalents. I have lost not only a professional colleague of high standing and renown but a very special friend. How sad that a man who enriched so many lives should have ended his in such melancholy circumstances.

It was tragic that Cliff, such a life-enhancing person and the father of four, should have been driven to such depths of despair that he committed suicide by throwing himself under a train near his home in Kent. The inquest jury pointed to two main contributory factors: his divorce in 1992 and "the allegations made against him which we feel tipped the balance." Those groundless but hugely damaging allegations were made by Andy Norman, the British Athletic Federation's promotions officer. Cliff was already suffering from what was diagnosed as an acute psychotic illness before Norman phoned him in July 1993 threatening to expose him for sexual harassment. Cliff, who was guilty of no such behaviour, had been working on an article critical of Norman for *The Sunday Times*.

The affection and respect Cliff commanded within the British athletics community could be gauged by the attendance at his moving service of thanksgiving at St Bride's, Fleet Street in February. Officials and coaches included Sir Arthur Gold, John Anderson, Harry Wilson and Tom McNab; the media were represented by Andrew Neil (*The Sunday Times* editor), John Rodda, Peter Matthews, John Bryant, John Goodbody, David Powell, Colin Hart, Ian Darke, David Emery, Andy Etchells, Steve Smythe, Ian Chadband, Randall Northam, Tom Knight, Dave Cocksedge, Duncan Mackay, Peter Cowie, Ken Mays, Pat Butcher, Tim Hutchings, Jon Wigley, Steven Downes, Terry O'Connor, Sandy Sutherland and myself among many others; while international athletes present included Dave Bedford, Jean Pickering, Alan Pascoe, Dave Moorcroft, Steve Ovett, Chris Brasher, Bruce Tulloh, Eric Shirley, Mel Batty, Joan Allison, Hugh Jones, Steve Jones, Veronique Marot, Frank Sando and Wendy Sly.

Following an investigation into the affair, Norman – a powerful but ever controversial figure who managed several of Britain's most successful athletes – was sacked by the British Athletic Federation in April. BAF's executive chairman Professor Peter Radford, the former 200m world record holder, announced: "Mr Norman's conduct in certain matters was not appropriate for someone employed as director of promotions of BAF." Norman continued to deny he campaigned against Cliff. Meanwhile, Prof Radford publicly cleared Cliff of any impropriety. "There should be no slur whatsoever on his good name." Norman, who married Fatima Whitbread in 1997 (the couple split up in 2005), did not quit the sport. He was employed for some years organising meetings in South Africa and Eastern Europe before he died in 2007 aged 64.

Although, thanks to my six pills daily, I felt fine physically, the shadow of the impending by-pass surgery continued to hang over me for month after month. I phoned Harefield in February for any news of a vacancy ... call back in July, I was told. Eventually, early in August, I was notified that the hospital might be able to see me in about a month's time. On September 7 they ran tests on me and told me to be ready for admission on September 22. At short notice I was told that date was cancelled because of emergencies, so it was three days later that my Uncle Cyril drove Pat and myself to the hospital with the operation scheduled for next day. Another emergency occurred, and it was at 10 am on September 27 that I finally underwent the pre-med process and at noon was wheeled in to be anaesthetised. The next I knew was waking up in the Intensive Treatment Unit at five next morning. The coronary artery bypass operation was a success and after seven days of recuperation, with Pat (staying in the hospital's hostel) in constant morale-boosting attendance, I was allowed home on October 4 to start the rest of my life. It took a while before I was pain-free and able to walk a significant distance, and I still carry the scars, but I shall forever be indebted to the doctors and nurses at that wonderful hospital for their care and skill.

Back to the athletics scene in 1994. Peter and I produced 26 issues of AI, ranging from 8 to 16 pages, fulfilling the commitment to our 500 subscribers in more than 60 countries to print every result of international significance as well as meeting reports, news items and statistical compilations.

Our first in-depth coverage of a major event was of the European Indoor Championships and I was in Paris-Bercy to witness a remarkable performance by Colin Jackson. Colin had already created a sensation that winter by setting a world indoor 60m hurdles record of 7.30 at Sindelfingen, a record that stands to this day, and in Paris he had six races. On the Friday he won his 60m heat in 6.57, semi in 6.55 and final in 6.49, just 1/100th outside Linford Christie's European record; next day in the hurdles he clocked 7.48 in his heat to equal the championship record, 7.39 semi (giving him six of the eight sub-7.40 marks in history) and 7.41 in the final. Colin inspired the British team to its highest ever tally of gold medals, the others going to Du'aine Ladejo (400m), David Strang (1500m) and Dalton Grant whose leap of 2.37m was a personal best and just 1cm below Steve Smith's recently established UK record of 2.38m.

AI wasn't the only newsletter to etablish a foothold among close followers of the sport. Frustrated by the paucity of junior results in athletics magazines and newspapers, my good friend Lionel Peters sought to correct that deficiency by publishing *World Junior Athletics News*. Providing hugely detailed results, lists and other statistics relating to the junior age groups worldwide, the newsletter quickly attracted a loyal following. It continued until 2001, Lionel having meanwhile set up a dedicated website in 1999. He died in 2013 aged 76 but a WJAN website is still going strong thanks to New Zealander Tony Hunt (worldjuniorathleticsnewsnzl.co.nz).

May 6 marked the 40th anniversary of the first sub-four minute mile and I was lucky enough to be invited to a glittering gala in London which brought together 14 of the 16 world mile record breakers still alive. *Track & Field News* (USA) commissioned a report from me on this historic occasion, part of which appears below.

For a miling buff it was like dying and waking up in heaven. There they were, in the Great Room of the swanky Grosvenor House Hotel: no fewer than 14 of those legendary figures who have held the world mile record. From little, frail Sydney Wooderson, with 4:06.4 back in 1937, through to the equally diminutive but awesomely fit Noureddine Morceli, current holder of the all-time best with 3:44.39. Wooderson, representative of a vanished age of amateurism at the top level, and Morceli, the consummate professional athlete, may be worlds apart in age, attitude, background and track times, but they – along with the other record breakers gathered to commemorate the 40th anniversary of Sir Roger Bannister's pioneering sub-4:00 mile – are inextricably linked together as the highest achievers in the most glamorous track event of them all. The gala, organised by the BAF to celebrate world miling as well as Bannister's historic feat, was attended by some 700 people paying around $110 [£75] for the privilege. And a privilege it was, for never has there been such an array of miling talent in one place.

295

In descending order of age, the record breakers honoured were Wooderson (79), Arne Andersson (76), Bannister (65), John Landy (64), Derek Ibbotson (61), Michel Jazy (57), Herb Elliott (56), Peter Snell (55), Jim Ryun (47), John Walker (42), Filbert Bayi (40), Seb Coe (37), Steve Cram (33) and Morceli (24). What a pity that Gunder Hägg (75) had to miss the occasion because of illness. As for Steve Ovett (38), he says he does not believe in dwelling on the past and declined to interrupt a family vacation in Florida.

To date more than 700 runners have broken 4:00 since Bannister opened the floodgates with his 3:59.4 at Oxford on May 6 1954 [The figure now is over 1450!]. A significant representation of them were in the audience – among them Olympic 1500m champions Ron Delany, Kip Keino and Pekka Vasala. Also present were Jerry Cornes (84), 1500m silver medallist at the 1932 Olympics, and Diane Charles (née Leather), who in 1954 became the first woman to break 5:00. Of course, the party could not be complete without Bannister's two pacemakers, Chris Brasher and Chris Chataway, and the two other surviving runners from the historic race, Alan Gordon and American George Dole. Remarkably, after 40 years, the race result is still being disputed! The normally published version is: 1 Bannister 3:59.4; 2 Chataway 4:07.2; 3 the late Bill Hulatt 4:16.0; 4 Brasher ... dnf – Dole and Gordon. Gordon, however, insists that he finished 4th, Dole 5th and Brasher 6th. "Everybody finished, although the crowd was getting difficult towards the end."

The fun wasn't over, for next day a masters' handicap mile race was staged at Oxford's iconic Iffley Road track. The ten runners included four Olympic champions and it was one of them, Kip Keino (54), taking advantage of an over-generous 380 yards start, who won in 4:02.7 ahead of Bruce Tulloh (4:06.7 off 290y), Bayi (4:08.0 off 440y) and Ryun (4:19.3 off 330y). Eamonn Coghlan, who indoors in February had at 41 become the oldest sub-4 min miler with 3:58.15, ran off scratch but, troubled by a calf injury, could manage only 4:31.5.

"Ethiopia's First World Record" was our page one headline in the June 8 issue. That should have read World *Track* Record in view of earlier marathon exploits, but running at Hengelo in the Netherlands, world 10,000m champion Haile Gebrselassie (21) broke Said Aouita's 5000m record with 12:56.96. That was just the beginning for 'Geb' as he would go on to set 23 world records or bests indoors or out at distances ranging from 3000m to the marathon.

World records continued to tumble throughout the year. Leroy Burrell reclaimed the 100m mark with 9.85 (his son Cameron ran 9.93 in 2017), Morceli set new 3000m figures of 7:25.11, William Sigei ran 10,000m in 26:52.23, Sergey Bubka vaulted 6.14m (his 35th world record, 1cm below his indoor best from 1993), Sonia O'Sullivan clocked 5:25.36 for 2000m, while in two women's events still in their infancy Sun Cai Yun vaulted 4.12m and Svetlana Sudak threw the hammer 67.34m.

Birmingham was the venue for an enthralling European Cup competition and in both men's and women's contests the winners were Germany ahead of Britain and Russia. On the men's side the British heroes were

Linford Christie in both 100m (for a fifth time) and 200m, Roger Black in the 400m and both relay teams, anchored by Christie and Black. The women's match was so close with Germany finishing a single point ahead of Britain with Russia only another two points adrift. British winners were Diane Modahl (800m), Jackie Agyepong (100m hurdles), Sally Gunnell (400m hurdles) and the 4x400m team anchored by Gunnell, but valuable second place points were garnered by 19 year-old Katharine Merry in the 100, 200m and 4x100m, Melanie Neef (400m) and Kelly Holmes (1500m).

In July I made a fleeting visit to Nice where I saw a significant 1500m race in which Venuste Niyongabo, a 20 year-old from Burundi, clocked 3:30.95 to join Morceli, Aouita and Cram as the only men to have bettered 3:31 on more than one occasion. In third place, in 3:33.61, was a 19 year-old Moroccan by the name of Hicham El Guerrouj. He had been a 5000m bronze medallist at the 1992 World Junior Championships but had absolutely no previous form at 1500m! Niyongabo would go on to win the Olympic 5000m title two years later, while El Guerrouj would blossom into the world's fastest ever at 1500m, mile and 2000m. While in the area I took the wonderfully scenic bus ride on the coastal road to Monaco to visit the IAAF's new HQ and meet up with my old colleague Nick Davies.

For our coverage of the European Championships in Helsinki, Peter Matthews originated a novel way of presenting the results so that one can easily see how the athletes fared round by round. It's a format we have used ever since. Highlights included Christie's third successive 100m title, a British one-two in the 400m through Ladejo and Black, who also ran the last two legs of the victorious 4x400m team, and more gold medals for Jackson and Backley. Gunnell, the only British winner in the women's events, joined Daley Thompson and Christie as the only holders of Olympic, World, European and Commonwealth titles. Her time of 53.33 was the world's fastest that year and she also contributed a 49.45 anchor leg in the relay.

Those championships ended on August 14, and just eight days later the athletics events of the Commonwealth Games in Victoria, British Columbia began. It was a tall order for the British athletes, but most of the top stars responded magnificently to the challenge. Christie produced the second quickest legal time of his career, 9.91, to win the 100m, while Jackson, Backley and Gunnell added to their treasure trove. Other UK competitors to be crowned champion were Rob Denmark (5000m), Neil Winter (pole vault), Julian Golley (triple jump), Matt Simson (shot), the England men's 4x400m squad, Kelly Holmes (1500m), Yvonne Murray (10,000m), Judy Oakes (shot), Denise Lewis (heptathlon) and the England women's 4x400m team.

A big financial incentive that summer was to be successful in the "Golden Four" … the big international meetings in Oslo, Zürich, Brussels and Berlin. Any athlete who won their event at all four fixtures would be awarded, or share, 20 one-kilo gold bars worth about £160,000. Only two, Colin Jackson and Mike Powell, made it unscathed to Berlin and, as both won there, they split the spoils. Jackson's lucrative victory in 13.02 came just seven days after his 13.08 in Canada.

There was more big money on offer at the IAAF/Mobil Grand Prix Final in Paris and the main beneficiaries were Noureddine Morceli (1500m) and Jackie Joyner-Kersee (long jump). They accumulated the most points over the season and came away with $130,000 apiece. It was ironic that the IAAF, founded in 1912, still stood for International *Amateur* Athletic Federation when at the top level the sport was openly professional. Only in 2001 did the IAAF Congress vote unanimously to change the organisation's name, retaining the same acronym, to the more appropriate International Association of Athletics Federations.

The last meeting I attended before my operation was the IAAF World Cup at the Crystal Palace.

Thanks to their immensely powerful track team, the African men retained their grip on the World Cup although their winning margin over Britain was narrower than two years ago: 5 points as against 12 in Havana. British victories, cheered by a crowd totalling nearly 60,000 for the three days of competition, came in the 100m (Linford Christie), 200m (John Regis from lane 1), 110m hurdles (reserve Tony Jarrett), javelin (Steve Backley) and both relays – none of which was too surprising – plus the long jump which was totally unexpected [Fred Salle with a lifetime best of 8.10m]. The team foundered with no points in the pole vault, last in the shot and hammer, and seventh in the discus. However, the British men avenged their European Cup defeat by Germany and for the second successive World Cup were the top national team. In the women's match the Europe Select team were victorious for the first time since the inaugural meeting in 1977. The British women did compete after all, placing fifth and with wins for Yvonne Murray (3000m), Sally Gunnell (400m hurdles) and the 4x400m team. However, the IAAF has warned that the British women's results will be annulled if, subsequently, Diane Modahl's appeal against her doping ban proves unsuccessful.

Diane Modahl (née Edwards), the 1990 Commonwealth Games 800m champion, was sent home from Victoria BC after it was revealed that she had produced a positive sample in a drug test conducted in Lisbon in June. Following analysis of her 'B' sample, which confirmed the result of the 'A' test (excessive testosterone), she was suspended from competition. The eight points she won for Britain in the European Cup, if forfeited as a consequence, would result in Russia and not Britain finishing second to Germany and thus qualifying for the World Cup. The British women's team was given the go-ahead to compete in London but with that proviso.

A BAF Disciplinary Committee announced in December that it "was satisfied unanimously beyond reasonable doubt that a doping offence had been committed by Mrs Modahl." It was argued on behalf of the athlete that there was degradation of the urine sample, which had the effect of rendering it unrepresentative. "I am horrified at the decision," said Diane. "I will carry on fighting to clear my name because I know I am innocent. I have never taken any banned substance." As a result of the ban, the British team was demoted from second place to third in the European Cup and initially the team's results at the World Cup were annulled. However, following a successful appeal to an independent panel, the BAF lifted her ban in July 1995 and the following year Diane was cleared by the IAAF, Britain's Cup scores were reinstated, and she went on to compete in her third (1996) and fourth (2000) Olympics. She and her husband and coach Vicente Modahl spent several years at great expense to themselves pursuing the BAF for nearly £1 million in punitive damages, legal and medical costs but the High Court ruled against her in 2000 as did the Court of Appeal in 2001.

While the Commonwealth Games were taking place, Dame Marea Hartman died of cancer at the age of 74. She had her detractors and I didn't agree with all of her views but she worked tirelessly for what she believed would benefit the sport and I always found her helpful, efficient and courteous.

Marea was the most influential female administrator in British athletics history. She was involved in the sport for all her adult life, first as a runner and then, from soon after the war, as an official. She became honorary treasurer of the Women's AAA in 1950, later took over as honorary secretary and for over two decades was also the British women's team manager. Among the athletes she looked after ("my girls" as she fondly referred to them) were Olympic champions Mary Rand, Ann Packer and Mary Peters. Marea was for many years chairwoman of the IAAF Women's Commission and did much to broaden the programme of events available to women. Although she spent most of her long career in favour of a separate English women's governing body she finally came to terms with the new order and after her beloved WAAA merged with the AAA she was elected the first president of the AAA of England. She received the ultimate accolade for her distinguished services to athletics by being made a Dame earlier this year.

Among the countless thousands of athletes I have watched and reported on, there is a select band who I remember with particular pleasure and admiration. One of them was the female star of my first Olympics in 1960 and it was my sad duty to record her death at far too early an age.

How tragic that one of the world's greatest and most graceful athletes, Wilma Rudolph, should die so young (age 54) of brain cancer at Brentwood, Tennessee, on November 12. She deserved better, having battled so courageously against a variety of serious illnesses as a youngster. That Wilma ever became an athlete, never mind the fastest sprinter up to that time, was little short of a miracle. Born prematurely and with polio in Clarksville, Tennessee on June 23 1940 the 20th of 22 children, her impoverished childhood was one long list of medical problems. She suffered scarlet fever and double pneumonia when she was four, causing one of her legs to be crooked with the foot turned inward, and much else besides. There seemed little hope that she would ever walk normally. For two years members of the family took turns to massage the stricken leg, four times a day. From the age of five to ten, she wore a steel leg brace all the time, and for the next two years just when the leg ached.

Yet, astonishingly quickly after she was finally rid of that brace she was showing her aptitude for sport, first at basketball and then at running. As a 13 year-old, tall and slim, she won all her school races and just three years later she made the 1956 Olympic team. She was in over her head but performed with credit, with a bronze medal in the 4x100m relay. Little more was heard of her until in 1959, a year after the birth of her first child, she won the US 100m title.

In 1960, though, the 1.80m tall student at Tennessee State University was to rock the athletics world. At the US Championships she equalled the national 100m record of 11.5 and smashed Betty Cuthbert's world 200m mark with a barrier-breaking 22.9, but her Olympic dreams came close to being shattered when the day before the 100m heats in Rome she twisted an ankle while training. Immediate treatment did the trick, though, and she equalled the world record of 11.3 in her semi. Wilma was timed in what was then considered an almost unbelievable 11.0 (11.18 on electric timing) in the final with a 2.8m following wind and beat Britain's Dorothy Hyman by two and a half metres. After clocking an Olympic record 23.2 easing up in a heat, she won the 200m final against the wind in 24.0, four metres clear. With her third gold in anchoring the relay, the US team having set a new world record of 44.4 in the heats, Rudolph was the heroine of the Games. The rest of her track career was something of an anti-climax, although in 1961 she did set a new world record of 11.2. She retired in 1962 to become a schoolteacher, coach, goodwill ambassador and inspirational public speaker, and established the Wilma Rudolph Foundation to work with under-privileged children. Both her marriages ended in divorce and she is survived by four children.

30. PHENOMENAL JONATHAN EDWARDS (1995)

It was an encouraging start to 1995. In January I began what turned out to be two years of weekly rehabilitation classes at Harefield, teaming up with another heart surgery patient from Stanmore, retired policeman Steve Dennis. We took turns to call for the other every Tuesday afternoon and drive to the hospital where we underwent an hour of circuit training. Admittedly we were younger and fitter than most of the others in the class, so we turned out to be the star performers in our ability to run, jump and lift. Psychologically as well as physically these sessions were of enormous benefit – so, again, thanks Harefield. In March I felt ready to begin jogging again, for the first time in nearly two years, and by April I was running for half an hour at a time.

Although I had left school over 40 years earlier, I had remained in touch with Les Mitchell, the PE master who had introduced me to the joys of athletics, and Pat and I had the pleasure of attending a lunch near Newmarket to celebrate his 80th birthday. He was in good form and lived on until the year 2000.

Britain's star of the indoor season was Linford Christie, weeks away from his 35th birthday. At Liévin in France, an hour after setting a European 60m record of 6.47, he just held off Frankie Fredericks in the 200m in 20.25 for his first and only individual world record. He was present, as British team captain, but did not race at the World Indoor Championships in Barcelona, where Canada's Bruny Surin took the 60m title in 6.46 and proclaimed "If Christie had run, I would have run faster." Darren Braithwaite proved to be the most successful British athlete on show, finishing a clear second in 6.51 to rank as the third quickest ever European behind Christie and Colin Jackson. Virtually unnoticed in fifth place was an American who would develop into one of the all-time greats of sprinting … Maurice Greene. Britain's only other medallist was Tony Jarrett, third in the hurdles in 7.42, tying his English record

In March we reported that 16 members of Ma Junren's women's squad, including world record breaker Wang Junxia, had left his training camp following a dispute over money and excessive training demands. Wang was quoted as saying: "We simply could not take it any longer. We had absolutely no freedom. We were all on the brink of going crazy. The pressure was too intense. The Ma Family Army has been disbanded and will never be brought back together." Later in the year, though, Wang praised Ma although it was under a new coach that in 1996 she won Olympic gold (5000m) and silver (10,000m) in Atlanta. As for Ma, he would continue to be the centre of controversy for many years to come.

Meanwhile, middle and long distance runners from other parts of the world made 1995 a special year for world records. Noureddine Morceli smashed Said Aouita's 2000m figures with 4:47.88 in Paris on July 3 and lowered his own 1500m mark to 3:27.37 in Nice on July 12; Moses Kiptanui clocked 12:55.30 for 5000m in Rome on June 8, only for Haile Gebrselassie to reclaim the record with a startling 12:44.39 in Zürich on August 16, having earlier seized the 10,000m best with 26:43.53 in Hengelo on June 5, while Kiptanui ran a barrier-breaking (not literally) steeplechase in 7:59.18 at the Zürich meeting. On the women's side, Maria Mutola covered 1000m in 2:29.34 in Brussels on August 25 and Fernanda Ribeiro clocked 14:36.45 for 5000m in Hechtel on July 22. Gebrselassie, the first to have broken 13 minutes for 5000m and 27 minutes for 10,000m, said after his exploit in Hengelo: "In my country [Ethiopia] you are not judged by breaking world records. It is more important to be a champion. I will not be really famous until I win the Olympic crown." That was to be remedied the following year.

Thanks to Sir Eddie, I was present at the US Championships (and World Championships Trials) in Sacramento. We flew to San Francisco and travelled by stretch limo to the sumptuous Auberge du Soleil, a five star hotel in the celebrated wine-growing Napa Valley where rooms go today for around $1000 a night. To be honest, stretch limos and super-luxury hotels are not my style (even if I could afford them) ... but who's complaining!

Michael Johnson, already considered the finest combination 200/400 runner of all time, completed a fabulous double in the USA Championships. He took the 400m in 43.86 and the 200m in a windy 19.83 for the first such double in this meeting since Maxie Long (22.4/50.8) back in 1899. Carl Lewis, who won his first US senior titles in this stadium 14 years ago, described the 100m [6th in 10.32] as "my worst race; I don't think I've ever been more disappointed in my career." However, he bounced back to make the long jump team. Mike Powell's opener of 8.55m (+3.6m/sec wind) sufficed for his fifth US title. Lewis moved into second with a third round 8.45m (+6.0m) and vowed he would be in better shape for the World Champs. Conditions for the multi-events on the first two days were unexpectedly cold, wet and windy. Indeed the weather was among the worst, for the time of year, in Sacramento's history; normally it is dry and blisteringly hot. In the circumstances Dan O'Brien's world-leading 8682 decathlon was quite remarkable.

Even more astonishing, though, was the triple jump display by Jonathan Edwards at the European Cup later in June at Villeneuve d'Ascq, near Lille. He had opened the season with a splendid British record of 17.58m at Loughborough two weeks earlier and on this occasion he started with a leap of 17.90m with the allowable wind just over the limit at 2.5m/sec. That was nothing compared with his second attempt; again the assisting wind was too strong at 2.4m but the distance was a stupendous 18.43m (over 60 feet for our American friends), by far the longest triple jump ever. The previous best under any conditions was 18.20m (+5.2m) by Willie Banks. Jonathan's hop measured 6.50m, step 5.60m and jump 6.33m. He hadn't finished yet. His third effort, legal this time, was a UK record of 17.72m and in the fourth round he produced another amazing wind-aided jump of 18.39m (+3.7m). Feeling understandably "shattered", he passed his final two attempts. Thanks to other wins by Linford Christie in the 100m and 200m (plus 4x100m), Mark Richardson (400m and 4x400m) and Steve Smith (high jump), the British men placed second to Germany, while the women's team finished third to Russia and Germany with victories by Melanie Neef (400m), Kelly Holmes (1500m) and Ashia Hansen (with a UK triple jump record of 14.37m). Edwards' next appearance was in Gateshead, his home stadium. Again he exceeded the world record distance of 17.97m by Banks ten years earlier but once more there was too great an assisting wind (2.9m) as he landed at 18.03m. He did, however, improve his UK record to 17.74m. Watching Edwards in action was an aesthetic pleasure. Many leading triple jumpers crash and thump their way to the pit but Jonathan just simply seemed to flow; his technique was like a stone skimming over the water.

I reported on Kelly Holmes's storming 800m in Birmingham at what were known as the KP National Championships, incorporating the AAA Championships and World Championships Trials. Her Olympic triumphs were still nine years in the future but she was already showing potential world-beating form.

Although controversial actions involving Linford Christie and Colin Jackson attracted most media attention, there was plenty to cheer. First and foremost was the magnificent 800m display by Sergeant Kelly Holmes of the British Army. Taking the lead at the bell (58.4) she reached 600 in 87.2 and crossed the finish line in 1:57.56. It broke her own English record of 1:58.64 and fell just short of Kirsty Wade's UK record of 1:57.42. With her great strength, Holmes' first string event remains the 1500m but at the moment only Maria Mutola could be ranked ahead of her at 800. When Linford Christie finished 4th (10.93) in his 100m heat, easing off too drastically after feeling tightness in a tendon behind his right knee, it was assumed that was the end of his involvement in the meeting. However, Christie felt he could benefit from another race that day and asked if he could run as a guest in the final as there was a spare lane. Astonishingly for the oldest national championships in the world, he was granted permission "as a gesture to him and the crowd", although in fact some fans booed him when he appeared for the final. He won the race in 10.18 but the title went to Darren Braithwaite. Christie was later to be seen limping and seeking treatment in Germany. Colin Jackson, who reportedly aggravated an adductor muscle injury in his 100m heat, withdrew from the semis and a statement was made that he would not be competing for several days while he underwent treatment. Imagine the British Athletic Federation's dismay and anger when it was learned next day that the supposed invalid had just won a 110m hurdles race in Italy in 13.32! BAF's executive chairman, Peter Radford, said he was "very surprised and very disappointed" at Jackson's actions and would demand a full explanation from him.

That led to a very public dispute, one of the consequences being that Jackson was unable to defend his world title in Gothenburg.

The star turn in Gothenburg would prove to be Edwards, but before that he found ideal conditions at last to break the world record. Competing in Salamanca with its friendly 800m altitude, primarily to reassure British selectors that he had recovered from the ankle soreness which has caused him to miss the AAA Championships a few days earlier, Edwards bounced his way to 17.98m with the wind gauge registering 1.8m. Five days later, in Sheffield, Edwards jumped a windy 18.08m, while Holmes broke Wade's Commonwealth 1000m record with 2:32.82 and Christie, with a 3.9m wind behind him in the straight, clocked the fastest ever 150m time of 14.74.

Edwards' final competition before the World Championships was at the Italian ski resort of Sestriere, where a Ferrari sports car worth $132,000 was on offer to a world record breaker. He jumped 'only' a wind aided 17.58m, but there was a sensational result in the long jump.

Unless the IAAF decides to change the rules, Mike Powell's world record long jump of 8.95m will be replaced by a mark which, by any standard, is an inferior performance. True, Iván Pedroso did jump 8.96m with a legal 1.2m wind ... but with the immense advantage of the 2050m altitude. Of course it was a terrific jump, perhaps worth in excess of 8.70m at sea level, but by no stretch of the imagination did it measure up intrinsically to Powell's record figures or, for that matter, numerous leaps over the years by Carl Lewis. Despite long campaigning by statisticians and other interested parties (I first recommended the creation of separate altitude-assisted records in the wake of the 1968 Olympics), the IAAF has refused to recognise the unfairness of accepting high altitude performances in events such as the sprints, hurdles and horizontal jumps where the thin air is certainly as beneficial as following winds of way over the 2m/sec limit. Now, assuming Pedroso's leap is ratified (although the Italian newspaper "Tuttosport" has accused someone of deliberately obstructing the wind gauge whenever the Cuban jumped) we shall be back to the unsatisfactory situation when Bob Beamon's 8.90m in Mexico City was the record for so long. During the entire meeting in the fog-shrouded Alpine resort, only four readings below 2m/sec were registered – three of them for Pedroso. The Italian daily, "Corriere Della Sera", posed the question: "Are we talking sabotage, chance or programmed cheating?"

In fact, the Italian Federation (FIDAL) refused to submit the mark to the IAAF for ratification, a move which drew a sharp protest from Alberto Juantorena, president of the Cuban Federation, who demanded an explanation. The reason eventually emerged some months later, confirming those newspaper suspicions, when a FIDAL official was banned for life for obscuring the wind gauge as Pedroso jumped (the gauge registered +1.2m when readings of 3-4m were the norm) and two judges were suspended for three years. What is it about Italian officials falsifying long jump results (remember the Evangelisti affair in 1987?).

Having been unable to attend the 1993 World Championships I was thrilled at the prospect of being in Gothenburg and I flew out to Sweden on August 4, the day after my nephew Lionel and his wife Bernadetta became the proud parents of a daughter, Natalia Flora (named after my mum). Despite the continuing furore over Sestriere, Pedroso proved his worth at those Championships, winning the title by a 40cm margin with 8.70m. Powell placed third while Lewis was out with a hamstring injury.

My retrospective review of the meeting for *American Track & Field* included the following observations.

Stuttgart was a hard act to follow, but Gothenburg – which attracted athletes from 191 countries – continued in the world record breaking tradition. Both Kim Batten (52.61) and her American team-mate Tonja Buford (52.62) obliterated Sally Gunnell's 400m hurdles record, and Inessa Kravets from the Ukraine revolutionised women's triple jumping standards with a massive leap of 15.50m, an improvement of 41cm over the previous best. Such a distance would have won the Olympic men's title as recently as 1948. But the Gothenburg World Championships will be remembered first and foremost for the triple jumping display of Jonathan Edwards. He took the event into a new dimension.

The Englishman has been a world class performer for several years but nothing prepared him or anyone else for his transformation in 1995. Faster and stronger than previously and now using an arm action modelled after Mike Conley, he was certainly technically more accomplished but Edwards was still unable to explain how, at the age of 29, he managed to improve by nearly a metre. Perhaps it was due to a debilitating virus forcing him to miss much of the previous season and thus give his body a chance to recuperate from the punishing demands of the event ... possibly it was down to his new-found ability to maintain high velocity throughout the three phases. It was at the Championships that the 18m barrier was officially breached at last. At his first attempt he jumped 18.16m and one round later, with plenty of room on the board, he made further history with a spine-tingling distance of 18.29m [6.05m hop, 5.22m step, 7.02m jump]. He thus became the first triple jumper ever to set two world records back to back and his winning margin of 67cm was the longest in World Champs/Olympic history since the 1896 Games.

The American team dominated again, garnering a dozen gold medals whereas no other nation won more than two. A massive contribution was made by Michael Johnson in what proved to be a dress rehearsal for the following year's Atlanta Olympics. First he retained his 400m title in 43.39, the second fastest ever time, with a winning margin over Butch Reynolds of seven metres – the widest in a global championship at this distance since the 1896 Olympics. Track and field's own "Magic Johnson" took the 200m final (his eighth race in seven days) by another huge margin in 19.79, equalling his best, and as a finale he anchored the USA to 4x400m relay victory. Gwen Torrence, the 100m champion in 10.85 and anchor for the winning 4x100m team, might have collected three golds also but had to settle for two after being disqualified for stepping on the line during the 200m which she had "won" in 21.77, stunning time into a 2.2m wind. The title went instead to Merlene Ottey (22.12), who at 35 became the oldest ever female world champion. Her three medals in Gothenburg brought her total to 13, a World Championships record, as was Sergey Bubka's fifth straight pole vault title.

Probably the most dramatic event of all was the women's 800m, for which the favourite was defending champion Maria Mutola with her win streak standing at 42. However, she was disqualified for a lane infringement after winning her semi-final. That enhanced the chances of Ana Quirot and she seized *the opportunity to triumph in 1:56.11, her fastest run for six years. It marked an astonishing comeback, almost literally from the dead, for the 32 year-old Cuban. She came close to dying of burns after a kerosene cooker exploded at her home in Havana in January 1993 but, following numerous plastic surgery operations, she vowed to return. That she did, although terribly scarred, and the sport found its most courageous champion.*

In other action, Donovan Bailey won the 100m in 9.97 with Christie, suffering from a hamstring injury, sixth; Noureddine Morceli notched up his third 1500m title in 3:33.73, his 51.3 last lap leaving Hicham El Guerrouj a distant runner-up; Haile Gebrselassie produced a 25.1 final 200m to take the 10,000m in 27:12.95; Allen Johnson (13.00) was pressed hard by Tony Jarrett (13.04) in the 110m hurdles; Jan Zelezny (89.58m) and Steve Backley (86.30m) went 1-2 in the javelin; Dan O'Brien captured his third world decathlon title with a score of 8695; Marie-José Pérec clocked the fastest 400m time (49.28) for three years; Kelly Holmes broke Kirsty Wade's Commonwealth record with 1:56.95 in placing third in the 800m having earlier finished second to Hassiba Boulmerka over 1500m (4:02.42 to 4:03.04); Sonia O'Sullivan won the 5000m in 14:46.47; and UK-born Fiona May, competing for Italy, long jumped a windy 6.98m for the gold medal.

Just three days after the end of the Championships, many of the stars assembled in Zürich for another superb Weltklasse meeting with some $3 million up for grabs in appearance and prize money. As mentioned earlier, there were world records by Gebrselassie (12:44.39 5000m) and Kiptanui (7:59.18 steeplechase), but among a plethora of other great performances were a 3:45.19 mile by Morceli, a 1:55.93 800m win for Mutola over Quirot, and 52.90 400m hurdles by Buford with Pérec clocking 53.21 in only her second season at the event.

There were lucrative pickings also in the last two major European meetings of the season. In Berlin, as a reward for winning their event in all of the "Golden Four" fixtures, Michael Johnson (44.56 400m), Sonia O'Sullivan (Irish 5000m record of 14:41.40), Gwen Torrence (21.98 200m) and Natalya Shikolenko (67.72m javelin) received gold bars worth around $62,500 each, although the finest performance came from Gebrselassie, who not only left Kiptanui over 7 seconds behind in the 5000m but posted the second quickest ever time of 12:53.19 in cold and damp conditions.

Johnson wound up his campaign with a 19.93 200m win at the Grand Prix Final in Monaco. Thanks to bonus points awarded for world records achieved at earlier Grand Prix meetings, Kiptanui and Mutola held on to their advantage to clinch the overall GP awards worth $100,000 apiece. Kiptanui front-ran an 8:02.45 steeplechase, while Mutola clocked the world's fastest 800m of the year with 1:55.72, Holmes following her in with a Commonwealth record of 1:56.21. Not counting her disqualification in Gothenburg, that was Mutola's 51st successive win at 800m/1000m; her last defeat was three years earlier. However, the best performance came from Morceli, also undefeated at distances above 800m for three years. What a sequence of runs since the beginning of July: 4:47.88 2000m (world record) in Paris, 3:27.37 1500m (world record) in Nice, 3:27.52 1500m (2nd fastest ever) in Monaco, 3:33.73 to win world 1500m title in Gothenburg, 3:45.19 mile (2nd fastest ever) in Zürich, 7:27.50 3000m (3rd fastest ever) in Brussels, 3:48.26 mile in Berlin, 7:29.36 3000m in Rieti and now 3:28.37 1500m (3rd fastest ever) in the GP Final, his 42nd win on the trot at 1000m and upwards. Seventh in that last race in a Northern Irish record of 3:34.76 was Gary Lough, who would marry Paula Radcliffe five years later.

Finally, hats off to editor Nigel Walsh for a magnificent 50th anniversary issue of *Athletics Weekly* dated December 20. It was a glorious wallow in nostalgia. The 88 pages celebrating AW's history began with an interview with 86 year-old Jimmy Green. As Nigel explained in his introduction: "Among those recently demobbed [in 1945], 37 year-old P W 'Jimmy' Green had £150 in his pocket and was about to embark on a career which would ultimately consume the next 42 years of his life. After joining the RAF as a boy apprentice when he was 15, Jimmy had been in uniform for most of his life. He'd bought himself out of the RAF in 1936 to start his own business, but had barely got up and running before finding himself back in uniform at the start of the Second World War. So after the war, ignoring advice from friends and associates who felt there would be no demand, Jimmy persuaded John Langdon Ltd of Maida Vale to publish an athletics magazine with himself as editor. The first edition of *Athletics* hit the street in December 1945. It cost 6d and sold about 2000 copies. In 1950 the magazine went weekly, changed its name to *Athletics Weekly* and the rest, as they say, is history ... well almost. Jimmy explains: 'A year after becoming a weekly, Langdon Ltd folded with AW its only asset. Fortunately, Kent Art Printers, one of the creditors, took AW over, and continued to print it with me as editor. The magazine developed and every year the circulation increased, as did the workload and the staff required to produce it'."

Asked if there was a team, individual or single performance that really stood out, Jimmy replied: "One person stands out in my mind above anybody else ... Seb Coe. To me he was the man. Forget Morceli and the other top middle distance runners now. Okay, they break more records, but Seb Coe stands out as the best runner I've ever come across. He was the greatest. To me he was just like a 400m runner that ran for four laps." Jimmy was adamant about what was wrong with current middle distance running. "Pacemaking. I have no time for it. I think it's all wrong. If you didn't have that chap out in front you would probably get a different result. I don't think it is a true and fair race." Who was the best athlete he coached? "In 64 years – I only stopped coaching in 1994 – you see a lot of talent. I used to love getting hold of youngsters and giving them a good grounding. But the best was 'Roy' Beckett. I'll never forget his run in the 1951 AAA 3 miles championship, that was a real crunch race. I told Beckett to stick to Chataway and to go like hell when he got to the 200m marker, which he did. He tried to take Chataway but Chataway would not let him in. They fought it out, no more than the thickness of a vest between them the whole way and Beckett got it by inches on the tape. Wonderful race that."

Sydney Wooderson (81), Britain's biggest star just before and just after the war, was interviewed by Trevor Frecknall. He too named Coe as the athlete who has impressed him most, and when asked if but for the war years he might have become the first sub-four minute miler he modestly demurred. "Perhaps 4:01, something like that." He rated his greatest race as the 4:04.2 mile, his fastest ever, that he ran behind Arne Andersson in Gothenburg in 1945. "It was better than my world record [4:06.4 in 1937]. Remember, I hadn't been able to train during the war. It was a remarkable thing after one summer's training and only three real races." My contribution to an issue to treasure was a selection of highlights from the 12 post-war Olympics, 1948 to 1992, and reprints of my feature on Mary Rand (1968) and interview with Steve Ovett (1979).

31. GEORGIA ON MY MIND (1996)

It was Olympic year again, and 1996 was particularly special for me as I fulfilled another ambition by having published in book form a *History of Olympic Track and Field Athletics*. In my introduction to the 280-page paperback I wrote: "In this comprehensive history of Olympic athletics, an edited and updated version of the supplements which were published by *Athletics Today* in 1992, I have attempted to present the highlights and flavour of each of the Games since 1896." An added feature was a who's who, providing essential facts and figures as at April 1, of some 2000 athletes in contention for selection for the Atlanta Games that summer. I thought I had covered all possibilities but three subsequent Olympic champions eluded me ... there was no mention of South Africa's marathon winner Josia Thugwane, Ecuador's 20km walk victor Jefferson Pérez or Nigeria's long jump gold medallist Chioma Ajunwa. But that's part of the the fascination of the Olympics – the breakthroughs by previously unconsidered athletes. The book was published by myself in association with Shooting Star Media, Inc of Madison, Wisconsin and marked the start of a long and fruitful partnership with American publisher Larry Eder.

I made two trips to Atlanta, Georgia, on both occasions meeting up with my English-born cousin Sheila and her family who lived in that city. The first visit was particuarly hectic. From June 14 to 16 I was in Birmingham for the AAA Championships, the standout performances coming from Linford Christie (10.04 100m for his record eighth title in that event), Roger Black (UK 400m record of 44.39), Colin Jackson (13.13 110m hurdles), Jon Ridgeon (49.16 400m hurdles following four achilles tendon operations), Nick Buckfield (UK pole vault record of 5.71m), Kelly Holmes (1:57.84 800m and 4:08.14 1500m for the first such double since Diane Leather in 1957), Sally Gunnell (54.65 400m hurdles) and Tessa Sanderson (world veterans javelin record of 62.88m at age 40), qualifying for her *sixth* Olympics. That was Tessa's tenth AAA title but shot putter Judy Oakes surpassed that with her 14th victory.

I was back home that Sunday evening for frantic packing as next morning I flew off to Atlanta for the US Olympic Trials. They had already started on June 14 but there was no way I was going to miss the British selection meeting. In my absence Dennis Mitchell won the 100m in 9.92, Kenny Harrison triple jumped a heavily wind assisted 18.01m, Gwen Torrence beat Gail Devers in a 10.82 100m and Kim Batten took the 400m hurdles in 53.81. However, Sir Eddie and I, seated together in the press box from June 19, witnessed many wonderful performances with one particular athlete paramount.

Pietro Mennea's 19.72 200m, set 2300m up in Mexico City in 1979 and the oldest of all standard world records, was finally – and comprehensively – beaten when Michael Johnson ran a scorching 19.66 in the final event of a superb US Olympic Trials in Atlanta (300m altitude) on June 23. On June 19 he took the 400m in 43.44, third fastest in history, with Butch Reynolds clocking 43.93 for his best since 1988 and the quickest ever non-winning mark. Johnson reeled off 100m segments in 11.02, 10.25, 10.37 (note 20.62 for that middle 200m!) and 11.80. Just how much Johnson wanted a world record was evident in the 200m semis when he gave vent to his feelings after crossing the line, easing up, in 19.70. A 2.7m aiding wind brought him down to earth, but next day – with the temperature at 35°C – he fulfilled his destiny with that scintillating 19.66 (1.7m wind). Looking ahead to the Olympics, he says: "I feel capable of 19.58."

Another world record, Colin Jackson's 12.91 110m hurdles, only just survived as on Atlanta's super-fast track the other world champion Johnson – Allen – tied Roger Kingdom's US record of 12.92. Spare a thought, though, for Jack Pierce. The 33 year-old must have experienced every emotion known to man as, in the semis, he ran 12.94 to become briefly the fourth fastest ever ... only to have his Olympic aspirations shattered next day when he crashed into the first barrier. Carl Lewis finished last in the 100m final, placed fifth from lane one in the 200m, but in between those events he kept alive the prospect of a fourth Olympic long jump title. He qualified in third place with 8.30m but it was Mike Powell who suffered most from selection jitters. Going into his final jump he was only sixth with 8.15m, but he responded to the occasion by producing a winning 8.39m. Mary Slaney's spirited finish in the 5000m brought her selection 23 years after she first represented the USA. World leading marks included Dan O'Brien's 8726 decathlon in which his score after nine events of 8233 was the highest ever. He needed a 4:43.48 1500m to break the world record but in 34°C heat he settled for 5:12.01.

I was back in Atlanta on July 24 for the start of the Olympic athletics programme two days later. For the first time in this, my eighth Olympics, I was not viewing the action from the press seats but as part of the lovely and super-efficient Jayne Pearce's media information team which involved wearing the official Atlanta Olympic uniform. Peter Matthews was in charge of our group, which included Matthew Brown, Mark Butler, Jeff Hollobaugh, Dr David Martin and a young Finnish statistician, Mirko Jalava, who for many years since has run an absolutely invaluable results, lists and biographies internet database, *tilastopaja.eu*. Our task was to produce, very speedily, accounts of events, biographies and significant stats for the benefit of the written press, TV and radio. Despite spending an inordinate proportion of each day commuting from my hotel to the stadium and back (the media bus drivers were not from the area and frequently got lost!), I also found time to write reports for AI. The glossy IAAF Magazine had for some years been one of my main freelancing outlets and, as for the World Championships of 1991 and 1995, I was flattered to be asked to provide extensive event by event coverage. My report, completed a month after the Games, obviously was in English while Robert Parienté, who I would bracket with Neil Allen as the most stylish writer on the sport in that era, submitted the French version.

Although the sheer scale and over-commercialisation of the Games attracted press criticism, as did transportation arrangements and computer problems, the athletics programme of the Centennial Olympics in Atlanta was nothing short of superb. The competition was great, performances outstanding with many events being the best ever for depth. The weather was kinder than expected and the number of spectators was unprecedented; more than 80,000 turned up for the first morning session and the total attendance soared to over 1,170,000. That wasn't the only Olympic record. All 197 countries within the Olympic movement were represented at the Games, and far more nations than ever before came away with medals: 45 as against the previous highest of 35 in Barcelona four years ago. The number of countries claiming Olympic champions rose to 24. Not surprisingly, the USA was the most successful team with 23 medals, 13 of them gold.

There was no problem nominating the athlete of the Games. The timetable was altered for the benefit of Michael Johnson and his bid to become the first man to win both the 200m and 400m, and he grasped the opportunity to become an Olympic legend. After winning the 400m in an Olympic record of 43.49 he returned to take the 200m in the "sci-fi" time of 19.32. For nearly 17 years no one could beat Pietro Mennea's world record of 19.72 and yet now it is fully four tenths of a second faster ... that's over four metres measured on the track. Johnson's phenomenal exploit eclipsed the other world record: Donovan Bailey's 9.84 100m. The winner of the world title last year went on to share in another gold medal and add to the US sprinters' discomfiture by anchoring Canada to victory in the 4x100m relay. This was the only occasion in the event's Olympic history that the American team has lost other than through disqualification.

Many defending champions lost their laurels. Not so Carl Lewis. Only his most faithful supporters believed that at 35 he could win the long jump again but he twice delivered a big leap when it mattered most to join discus thrower Al Oerter as the only athlete to win the same event four times. Lewis brought his total of golds to nine, equal to Paavo Nurmi's record if one does not take into account Ray Ewry's victories in the Interim Games of 1906, while Merlene Ottey – who sadly will now never be crowned Olympic champion – expanded her collection of medals to seven (spread amazingly over 16 years!), matching the women's record.

Michael Johnson's 55th consecutive victory in a 400m final since 1989 was the one he had really been waiting for all those years – the Olympic title. It was widely anticipated that he would break Butch Reynolds' world record of 43.29 into the bargain but it mattered little to Johnson that he fell just short yet again. His 43.49 clocking was the fourth quickest ever and his 12th sub-44. His 0.92 margin was the widest in Olympic history if you ignore the one second gap in 1896 (54.2-55.2!). With Reynolds pulling up with a hamstring injury on the first bend of his semi the way was open for Roger Black to take the silver, and he duly obliged for the first British medal in this event for 60 years.

To a track fan the significance of the figures 1932 might have been as the year of the first LA Olympics, or maybe a shot measurement. But as a 200m time? Even Johnson was astonished at what he had done. He thought he might one day run 19.50 or even a little faster, but 19.32 was never envisaged. The

311

wind was only 0.4, yet Johnson took 0.34 – the biggest improvement ever on the 200m record – from his previous mark. Despite the incredible pressure of public expectation, he produced what could be argued to be the greatest performance in athletics history. Remember, he had already won the 400m in 43.49 and this was his eighth race of the Games. Johnson was just in front at 100m in 10.12, but covered his second flying 100m in a phenomenal 9.20. The winning margin of four metres over Frankie Fredericks, who was running faster than anyone else in history (19.68), was the widest in an Olympic 200m since 1936, dominated by the man Johnson with his upright stance and pitter-patter stride is most often compared to ... Jesse Owens. In the 100m itself, despite a sluggish start (he had the slowest reaction time of 0.174) it was the Jamaican-born Canadian Donovan Bailey who won the big prize. The final was marred by the disqualification for two false starts of Linford Christie, of all people. Christie refused at first to accept the decision and the race was delayed for several minutes, adding to the general nerviness of the contestants. Bailey, who generated a peak speed of 12.1m/sec (over 27 mph) at 60m, zipped to a time of 9.84, thus adding the world record to his world and Olympic titles for a grand slam of sprinting honours.

Black, whose time was 44.41, was absolutely delighted with his silver medal. As he wrote in his autobiography; "As I crossed the line, peace was what I found. After a career which had switchbacked between triumph and disaster for ten dizzying years, I had an Olympic medal. It was silver. It felt like gold – because it testified to a race which I had run to perfection, something I had been striving for since first setting foot on a track." There were individual silver medals also for Jonathan Edwards and Steve Backley. Kenny Harrison opened with an American record of 17.99m and was never headed, improving to 18.09m in the fourth round for history's third longest legal distance. Edwards, who alarmingly fouled his first two attempts, jumped 17.88m earlier in that fourth round to clinch second place. Backley, who only returned to competition on June 30 following achilles tendon surgery in April, knew that his best chance of beating Jan Zelezny was to get in a very long throw ahead of the Czech. Throwing first, he registered an impressive 87.44m. Would it suffice? The answer came in round two when, following an initial foul, Zelezny reached 88.16m to become the first man since 1924 to claim a second Olympic javelin title.

With Reynolds out injured and Johnson withdrawing to rest a slight hamstring injury sustained in the closing strides of his record 200m, the US 4x400m team was reduced to human proportions and both Britain and Jamaica could at least hope for an upset. The first leg saw Lamont Smith hand over nearly 3m ahead of Iwan Thomas (44.92) but Jamie Baulch (44.19), after a storming first 200m, lost further ground to Alvin Harrison's 43.84. Mark Richardson ran out of his skin to clock the quickest split of the race and the best ever by a Briton of 43.62 but Derek Mills was almost as fast with 43.66, and both Anthuan Maybank and Black clocked 43.87 on the anchor leg. The Americans won in 2:55.99 with Britain setting a European record of 2:56.60.

There were two British bronze medallists in Steve Smith with a 2.35m high jump, the first Olympic medal by a British representative since Irishman Con Leahy in 1908, and Denise Lewis – largely thanks to a javelin personal best of 54.82m – held on to third place in the heptathlon by five points with a score of 6489. With Jackie Joyner-Kersee dropping out with a hamstring injury following the hurdles, the winner by a big margin with 6780 points was Syria's world champion Ghada Shouaa. The meritorious but dreaded fourth place was filled by Colin Jackson in the 110m hurdles, Kelly Holmes in the 800m (despite the pain of a hairline fracture of the lower left leg) and Ashia Hansen in the triple jump.

Although he made the 800m final only as a fastest loser, Norway's Vebjørn Rodal ran a superb race to win in 1:42.58, breaking Joaquim Cruz's Olympic record of 1:43.00 ... but it was like Hamlet without the Prince of Denmark. The absence of world champion Wilson Kipketer cast a shadow over the proceedings. He had beaten Rodal in Oslo and Nice earlier that month, the latter race in 1:42.51 for the world's quickest time since 1985. But although granted dispensation by the IAAF to represent Denmark, his home since 1990, at the World Championships the Olympic eligibility rules are more stringent and Kipketer was unable to compete in Atlanta for his new country and unwilling to turn out for Kenya, the land of his birth. The 1500m did not live up to the promise of the preliminaries. Noureddine Morceli's 3:32.88 semi (with four others inside 3:34) was not only the swiftest ever non-final time but only 0.35 outside Seb Coe's 1984 Olympic record. The final, though, was a slow race until Morceli injected a 53.4 third lap, marred by Hicham El Guerrouj's falling with a lap to go and finishing last. Coming up to the bell he tucked in behind Morceli but got too close and tripped. Morceli was spiked in the process but went on to win in 3:35.78.

Better known as a 1500m runner, Venuste Niyongabo took a calculated gamble by opting for the 5000m, a distance he had contested only twice before in his life. Luck was with him: Salah Hissou, who topped the world list, restricted himself to the 10,000m; the next fastest, Daniel Komen, failed to make the Kenyan team, and Haile Gebrselassie scratched after badly damaging his feet when winning the 10,000m in 27:07.34 ahead of Paul Tergat, a race in which the second 5000m was covered in under 13:12. Niyongabo was only slightly faster with his winning time of 13:07.96, becoming the first athlete to earn an Olympic medal for his war-ravaged nation of Burundi. Another first was an Olympic victory by a black South African, which is what Josia Thugwane (2:12:36) achieved in the marathon.

Already widely acknowledged as the greatest athlete in history, Carl Lewis still had one more ambition ... to win a fourth Olympic long jump crown. His detractors may have scoffed; they felt he was yesterday's man and pointed to the US Trials at which Lewis only just scraped into the team with 3cm to spare. His final pre-Olympic competition had been profoundly disappointing as he jumped a mere 8.00m. At 35, his critics argued, the magic had gone. But Lewis continued to dream about matching discus thrower Al Oerter's unique

313

feat of four successive golds in the same event, convinced he could rise to the challenge one more time. First he had to reach the final by jumping 8.05m or placing in the top 12. It should have been merely a formality but Lewis was in deep trouble after two rounds. His first leap had been only 7.93m and on the second try he had run through. He was looking into a chasm as, languishing in 15th place, he prepared for his last attempt. What a fine dividing line there is between triumph and disaster. One moment Lewis is sinking into an abyss, the next he is scaling a mountain as a clearance of 8.29m propels him to top place among the qualifiers! After passing that test of nerve the final was practically a breeze for him. In the third round, following a foul and 8.14m, Lewis harnessed all his skill, determination and experience into a jump which, despite a 1.3m/sec headwind, dented the sand at 8.50m. The crowd roared. The master conjuror had pulled out one last rabbit from his hat and even those who had doubted him saluted the ultimate competitor. That was it; no one came close. "There were 80,000 people out there for me and I felt their support. This is my biggest thrill." The American public, cool to Lewis when he won four gold medals in LA, had come to love and appreciate him.

Judged by most criteria, Dan O'Brien – world record holder and three times world champion – is one of the all-time greats of the decathlon, but there has been one glaring omission from his otherwise impressive credentials. There was no Olympic title, no Olympic medal, no Olympic anything. He had famously failed to make the team for Barcelona. This time he qualified for the Games and in his eyes, to rank up there alongside the likes of Bob Mathias, Rafer Johnson, Bill Toomey, Bruce Jenner and Daley Thompson, he had to win. Normally, O'Brien would count on getting a great start in the 100m and long jump to demoralise the opposition from the outset. It didn't happen; he found himself third after those two events way behind Frank Busemann and Erki Nool. The shot came to O'Brien's rescue but his overnight lead over Busemann (4592-4468) was not as commanding as anticipated. The 21 year-old German was on a roll. In all he would establish personal bests in five events and go close in all the others. Busemann opened the second day with a world decathlon hurdles best of 13.47, leaving O'Brien four metres behind. Leading by 8180 to 7971 it meant that O'Brien had to stay within about 32 sec of Busemann in the 1500m to clinch the title. O'Brien never allowed himself to get too far behind and brought his score to 8824, sixth highest ever and his eleventh consecutive decathlon win since September 1992. Now he was certainly up there with the greatest. Busemann's dream competition ended with a score of 8706 (his highest before this year was 7938), amazing for someone with less than two years of decathlon experience.

It didn't attract the hype surrounding Michael Johnson's corresponding double, but France's own MJ (Marie-José Pérec) earned her place in Olympic history, 15 minutes before Johnson, when she followed up her great 400m (48.25 for third place on the world all-time list) by defeating the luckless Merlene Ottey for the 200m title in 22.12. She had become the first athlete, male or female, to retain an Olympic 400m title and had to run that fast to pull clear of Australia's Cathy Freeman whose 48.63 smashed the Commonwealth record. Earlier, Ottey had come so close to victory in the 100m. Just 5/1000ths of a second separated them as Gail Devers retained her title with both credited with a time of 10.94. Maria Mutola, whose country of Mozambique was now in the Commonwealth, ran the fastest time of 1:57.62 but that was in a semi and unexpectedly she was shunted to third in the final, her first defeat in an 800m final for four years. World champion Ana Quirot finished ahead of her but the Cuban had to settle for silver as Russia's Svetlana Masterkova brought off a front-running coup in 1:57.73, holding off her challengers with a look of disbelief on her face. Masterkova, in her first serious season at the event, went on to win the 1500m in 4:00.83, Kelly Holmes bravely leading for three laps before she fell apart to finish eleventh. She returned home from Atlanta on crutches. Also seeking a double was Wang Junxia. She won the 5000m all right in 14:59.88 but was overhauled in the final straight in the 10,000m by Portugal's Fernanda Ribeiro (31:01.63) to suffer her first ever defeat at the distance.

What with completing the Olympic book and various freelancing activities, the early part of the year was even more hectic than usual, particularly as I was invited by *The Sunday Times* sports editor John Lovesey to help compile the athletics entries in the highly informative part-work *1000 Makers of 20th Century Sport*.

My first trip abroad in 1996 was to Madrid for the European Cup, Germany winning both trophies with the British men finishing second. Linford Christie completed a record-breaking sequence of Cup victories by taking the 100m in 10.04 and 200m in a windy 20.25 but the only other British winners were Jonathan Edwards (windy 17.79m) and the 4x400m team. Sally Gunnell and Ashia Hansen won their events but the women's team placed only sixth. The big early season news was Jan Zelezny's still standing world javelin record of 98.48m. Talking of javelin throwers, Tessa Sanderson never set a world record in her prime but at Crystal Palace in July she threw 64.06m, a remarkable world age-40 best.

As soon as the Olympics were over, all of the world's elite flew across to Europe and the first of the post-Atlanta Grand Prix meetings was staged in Monaco. No fewer than 21 newly minted Olympic gold medallists were on display but it was two athletes who missed the Games who stole the show. Daniel Komen, fourth in the Kenyan Trials 5000m, came within a whisker of Morceli's world 3000m record with 7:25.16, while Wilson Kipketer ran another swift 800m in 1:42.59. Among the Olympic champions who continued on their winning ways was Masterkova who was again too strong over 800m for Quirot, clocking a personal best of 1:56.04. Four days later, in Zürich, Masterkova smashed the world record for the mile with 4:12.56, passing 1500m in 3:56.77. The Weltklasse meeting lived up to its reputation as virtually a one-day Olympics, other highlights including an emphatic victory by Kipketer over Rodal in 1:42.61, El Guerrouj beating Niyongabo over 1500m in 3:30.22, Komen getting the better of Gebrselassie at 5000m in a Kenyan record of 12:45.09, and Edwards turning the tables on Harrison, 17.79m to 17.23m. The circus then moved on to Cologne where Gabriela Szabo won the best ever in-depth women's 5000m in 14:44.42, with Paula Radcliffe, who had placed fifth in Atlanta, again finishing fifth but with a time (14:46.76) that was inside Zola Budd's UK and former world record. I joined the circuit in Brussels, travelling by Eurostar for the first time and, as an old railway buff, excited to be whisked along at up to 186 mph.

Many past world record setters who over the years have graced the Ivo Van Damme Memorial Meeting, founded in tribute to the outstanding Belgian middle distance runner who aged 22 was killed in a car crash in December 1976 , just a few months after winning Olympic silver medals at 800 and 1500m, were introduced to the big crowd assembled for the 20th edition. Among them were Don Quarrie, Seb Coe, Steve Cram, John Walker, Emiel Puttemans, Dwight Stones, Willie Banks, Irena Szewinska, Jarmila Kratochvilová and Fatima Whitbread. They, along with everyone else, were thrilled to witness two more world records which added further to this fixture's prestige. First Svetlana Masterkova's purple patch continued as she beat both Maria Mutola and the latter's 1000m mark with 2:28.98, and the final event produced a staggering 10,000m time of 26:38.08 for Salah Hissou. There was very nearly a third world record as Allen Johnson missed Colin Jackson's figures by 1/100th (with 12.92) and the quality across the board enabled this meeting to rival Zürich's. Wilson Kipketer took another crack at Coe's world 800m record but yet again fell short with 1:42.77. It was his fifth successive sub-1:43, an unprecedented sequence. More frustration for Daniel Komen. He may hold the world 2 miles best of 8:03.54 but for the third time in less than a fortnight he just failed to set his first official world record. He missed Morceli's 3000m figures of 7:25.11 by 5/100ths in Monte Carlo and in Zürich finished 0.7 outside Gebrselassie's 5000m record of 12:44.39. This time Komen ran 3000m in 7:25.87, the third fastest ever and an astonishing time in view of the cautious start (2:32.25 opening kilometre). Hicham El Guerrouj clocked the world's fastest 1500m of the year, breaking Said Aouita's Moroccan and former world record with 3:29.05, making him the second fastest ever performer behind Morceli.

Berlin was the next stop and five athletes – Frankie Fredericks, Wilson Kipketer, Jonathan Edwards, Lars Riedel and Stefka Kostadinova – shared the spoils for winning at each of the 'Golden Four' meetings: four gold bars apiece, worth around £32,000. The meeting commemorated the 60th anniversary of Jesse Owens' four Olympic victories in this stadium and five Olympic 100m champions – Harrison Dillard, Lindy Remigino, Armin Hary, Jim Hines and Allan Wells – were present to watch the multinational "dream team" of Donovan Bailey, Michael Johnson, Frankie Fredericks and Linford Christie win the 4x100m, but only just as a result of slack baton passing, in 38.87. Komen won the 5000m in a comparatively routine 13:02.62 but two days later, in Rieti, he struck … and how!

The 20 year-old Kenyan produced one of the most startling runs in history to claim his first official world record [one which stands to this day]. His target once again was Morceli's 7:25.11 3000m and this time he succeeded

316

with over four seconds to spare! His time of 7:20.67 was the biggest improvement on the record since Kip Keino opened the sub-7:40 era in 1965. The exceptional nature of this new record can be gauged from the fact that 40 years ago the world record for 1500m stood at 3:40.8 and now Komen has run twice as far at a rate of under 3:40.4 per 1500m. His en route time at 2000m of 4:53.4 would have been a world record until John Walker got to work on it in 1976 ... and yet Komen went on to cover another two and a half laps at about the same speed. His 400m splits [provided by Lennart Julin] were 57.6, 59.4, 57.9, 58.7, 59.8, 57.9, 59.9 and 29.5 last 200m. Earlier there had very nearly been another world record when Wilson Kipketer came up with the fastest 800m time since 1984, falling just 0.10 sec short of Seb Coe's 1981 record with 1:41.83. The 1500m was of brilliant quality too, Morceli clocking 3:29.99, his eighth time under 3:30 (no one else has run more than two). Martin Keino, in sixth place, ran 3:33.00 – well inside his father's best of 3:34.91 when winning the 1968 Olympic title.

Daniel Komen and Ludmila Engquist of Sweden were the biggest prize winners at the most lucrative IAAF Grand Prix Final yet. By respectively taking the 5000m and women's 100m hurdles in Milan each won $50,000, and as overall winners they picked up $200,000 apiece, double last year's jackpot. But the star of the show was ageless (36 actually) Merlene Ottey, who not only trounced Olympic champion Gail Devers but produced the fastest 100m time of her lengthy career! She breezed past her American rival at 70m to win by a metre in an astonishing 10.74, moving her into second place on the world all-time list. Olympic champion Engquist had to work hard for her success. After a tentative start she was well down in mid-race but came through strongly for victory in 12.61. [She was 1991 world champion as Lyudmila Narozhilenko of the USSR]. Thanks to the bonus points he received for his 3000m world record, Komen knew he had only to win the 5000m to ensure that he captured the overall Grand Prix title. However, with Salah Hissou in the field that was no certainty and they staged a great race. The final result: a win for Komen in 12:52.38. Hicham El Guerrouj ended Morceli's four-year 45 win streak at 1500m/mile, although it has to be noted that the Algerian was suffering from a heavy cold. He outkicked him in 3:38.80 after a very slow beginning. The third lap was covered in 52.99 and El Guerrouj completed the final 300m in 39.99. That final 700m of 1:32.98 represents 1:46.3 800m pace!

The final major international track and field meeting of the year, in Tokyo, yielded another superlative 800m performance by Kipketer. By clocking 1:42.17 he produced the fourth quickest time in history and brought his total of sub-1:43.00 marks to nine, seven of them in 1996. With a tumultuous season over, it was time for some sun and relaxation and in October Pat and I jetted over to Florida for four nights in Miami Beach and 13 nights in Clearwater Beach where we teamed up with Stan and Carole Greenberg.

32. HITTING THE JACKPOT (1997)

It could hardly have been a better start to 1997. I was staying at the celebrated Stardust Hotel (subsequently imploded) in Las Vegas in January when I hit the jackpot. A mass of sevens spun onto the screen, loud music blared from the machine and I found I had won $1300 for a spin that had cost me 75 cents. Fellow punters came up to congratulate me ("way to go"), as though I had exercised any skill other than pushing a button! Eventually a manager approached with the appropriate paperwork. That's when the thrill was diluted somewhat as he informed me that any single win in excess of $1200 was taxable by the IRS (USA's Internal Revenue Service) at a rate of 25%. Okay, a quarter of the excess $100 would cost me only $25, no big deal. But no, that's not how it worked. I was told it's 25% deducted from the whole amount ($325), so I would collect $975. I argued that was illogical as I would have been better off winning, say, a tax-free $1000 rather than $1300. No, that was the law, he insisted. I was still very happy with the win but that ridiculous tax system did bug me.

I was back home for the beginning of what turned out to be a remarkable indoor season. World records fell to Hicham El Guerrouj with 3:31.18 for 1500m in Stuttgart and 3:48.45 for the mile in Gent, Haile Gebrselassie with 12:59.05 for 5000m in Stockholm, and Cuba's Aliecer Urrutia with a 17.83m triple jump in Sindelfingen. Impressive also was Mary Slaney, who won the 1500m at the US Indoor Championships in Atlanta in a world leading 4:03.08 … at the age of 38. Her last appearance at that meeting had been when she won the 880y back in 1974!

Being present at the World Indoor Championships in Paris-Bercy was of particular significance as I was appointed the IAAF's official statistician for the meeting, working closely with former world long jump record holder Igor Ter-Ovanesyan on the seeding.

The sixth edition of the IAAF World Indoor Championships will be forever linked with the name of Wilson Kipketer. The Kenyan-born runner, who will officially become a Danish subject in December after seven years of residence, proved doubly sensational as he smashed the world indoor 800m record both in his heat and in the final two days later. Competing indoors for the first time since 1992, he made a brisk start to his heat and with 77.23 at 600m it was clear that Paul Ereng's world mark of 1:44.84 was under threat. Finishing over 30m clear, having hardly raised a sweat, he registered an astonishing 1:43.96 … to claim the $50,000 bonus on offer to world record breakers. Kipketer cruised through his semi the next day in 1:48.49 before launching another assault in the final. Stringing together four seemingly effortless laps of 24.22, 26.00, 26.27 and 26.18 he finished in a glorious 1:42.67. This is how a world record attempt should be executed: just the runner against the clock without the intrusion of pacemakers. The successful conclusion was immensely fulfilling for the spectators as well as the athlete.

With prize money ($50,000 for a win) on offer also for the first time at a World Championships, the meeting attracted the best entry yet. One other world record was broken, by the Russian women's 4x400m squad with 3:26.84, while Stacy Dragila tied Emma George's pending pole vault record of 4.40m for an auspicious start to the event's world championship status. El Guerrouj won the 1500m in 3:35.31 and Gebrselassie the 3000m in 7:34.71. Three British athletes finished second: Jamie Baulch in the 400m (45.62), Colin Jackson in the hurdles (losing by 0.01 in 7.49) and Ashia Hansen in the triple jump (Commonwealth record of 14.70m).

In some ways the most remarkable event was the women's 1500m. The last time Slaney and Yelena Podkopayeva met on the world stage was at the 1983 World Championships when the American won the 1500m with the Russian third. Who could have imagined that nearly 14 years later they would fight it out for another world title. It was Podkopayeva who possessed the stronger finish this time, passing the ever game Slaney literally with her final stride to win in 4:05.19 for an indoor personal best … at 44! However, in May it was revealed that a urine test at the 1996 Olympic Trials had indicated an unacceptably high testosterone level and Mary was suspended by the IAAF. She disputed the reliability of the test result and in October was cleared by the American governing body, USA Track & Field, whose doping hearing board concluded "Mary Slaney committed no doping violation last year." Nevertheless, she remained banned by the IAAF and in April 1999 she was stripped of that World Indoor silver medal as all of her performances for two years from June 17 1996 were declared null and void.

As part of my remit as statistician I was invited to offer suggestions for improvement. I pointed out the inherent unfairness of the 'preferred lane' system for the 200m and 400m. It was clear from the results that lanes 4, 5 and 6 were the most advantageous but 3, 4 and 5 were assigned to the athletes who produced the best results in the previous round. I was also critical of the totally random allocation of lanes in the first round of those events, effectively ending the chances of several contenders before they even started. For example, Britain's Doug Turner (20.61 that year) was reduced to 21.90 from lane 1 in his heat. Surely, I urged, seeds should be protected in the inititial stages. Alternatively, races at 200m and 400m should be restricted to a maximum of four runners with lanes 1 and 2 empty. It would lead to an extra round of heats but that would be more acceptable to the athletes than the current system. Nothing changed at the next World Indoors in 1999 but the 2001 edition allowed no more than four runners in the heats and semis of the 200m, and the event was dropped altogether from the schedule after 2004.

The year was memorable for a number of 'firsts'. The NUTS formed a group of historians who have continued to meet each year since to compare notes over new research and publications; I teamed up with a chartered accountant cum professional gambler, Tony Ansell, to advise him on current form prior to major international championships to help him take advantage of the bookmakers' odds; I began selling off newspaper and magazine clippings that I had accumulated over the years, with Ron Clarke (about to open an athletics exhibit at a resort in Australia) my best customer; and I took part in my first Harefield Hospital Fun Run, a 5km fund raising event which I have participated in most years ever since. The year was notable also for my compiling *Who's Who in World Athletics 1997*, published in association with Larry Eder's company and containing data as at April 1 on more than 2000 of the world's current leading athletes, and editing the sumptuously illustrated *IAAF World Championships Official Preview Guide*. I also began compiling the biographies of leading entrants for the London Marathon as well as continuing a long established statistical service for the IAAF and individual subscribers ... and, of course, there were 30 editions of AI to produce in collaboration with Peter Matthews. All in all it was another busy but fulfilling year, enhanced still further by the birth in December of Anthony (Lionel and Bernadetta's son), the youngest of my three great-nephews, and the landslide General Election victory by the Labour Party led by Tony Blair – although in later years I would become totally disillusioned by him and the party.

Sometimes there is a noticeable dip in performance levels in the year after an Olympics, but 1997 saw an amazing upsurge in the middle and long distance running department with several world records set between 800m and 10,000m.

May 31, Hengelo*:* Gebrselassie smashed Daniel Komen's world best for 2 miles of 8:03.54 but failed by just over one second to win the million dollars on offer for a winning time of inside 8 minutes. He finished in 8:01.08.

July 4, Oslo: Stringing together 5000m splits of 13:16.74 and 13:14.58 (which up to 1972 would have constituted a 5000m world record), Gebrselassie regained the 10,000m world record from Salah Hissou with 26:31.32, while El Guerrouj went so close to Noureddine Morceli's world mile record of 3:44.39 with 3:44.90, number two on the all-time list.

July 7, Stockholm: The trackside photo-cell displayed the frustrating figures of 1:41.74 but the photo-finish itself showed that Kipketer had equalled Seb Coe's iconic world record for 800m of 1:41.73. His laps were covered in 49.6 and 52.1, so similar to Coe's 49.7 and 52.0.

July 19, Hechtel*:* Unfortunately for him there was no million dollar bounty at this Belgian meeting, but Komen succeeded where Gebrselassie had so narrowly failed by breaking through the 8 minute barrier for 2 miles. Martin Keino, whose father Kip was himself a world record breaker at 3000m and 5000m in 1965, was the chief pacemaker up to 2000m. Forty three years after Roger Bannister ran his historic 3:59.4, here was a man who would clock exactly that time at halfway and then proceed to cover the second mile in 3:59.2 for a still standing world best of 7:58.61.

August 13, Zürich: Just three days after the conclusion of the World Championships in Athens the ever superb Weltklasse yielded world records by three newly crowned champions. First was Wilson Boit Kipketer, the Kenyan steeplechaser not to be confused with Denmark's two-lap marvel Wilson Kipketer. It was close, but by a margin of a tenth of a second he reduced Moses

Kiptanui's figures to 7:59.08. Next up was the great Dane. Following the pacemaker so closely through a screamingly fast first lap (48.3 for Kipketer!) should have spelt disaster but he managed to hold himself together sufficiently well to finish in 1:41.24 and Coe's reign as world record holder was over after 16 years. That was excitement enough for one evening, but the final event was the 5000m, pitting Gebrselassie against Komen: Ethiopia v Kenya. Could Komen, the front runner, shake off his rival? Try as he did, he couldn't and a 26.6 last 200m carried Gebrselassie to victory in 12:41.86 with Komen's 12:44.90 only just outside Geb's previous world record of 12:44.39. At the World Championships Kipketer (800m), El Guerrouj (1500m), Komen (5000m), Gebrselassie (10,000m) and Boit Kipketer (steeplechase) had emerged as gold medallists.

August 22, Brussels: Three days after setting a Kenyan 1500m record of 3:29.46 in Monaco, Komen lined up for a world record attempt at 5000m, and – on his own before 3000m – he succeeded with a time of 12:39.74. Even though he won the 3000m in an Ethiopian record of 7:26.02 it was not a good night for Gebrselassie. Komen had taken the 5000m record from him and at the end of the meeting Paul Tergat relieved him of the 10,000m record with a time of 26:27.85. The first half was covered in 13:17.6, the second in 13:10.3! On such an evening even a 1:42.20 800m by Kipketer and 3:28.92 1500m by El Guerrouj were totally overshadowed.

August 24, Cologne: Two more exceptional world records were created. Kipketer's first lap in the 800m was fast at 49.3, but relatively restrained compared to Zürich, and he finished in 1:41.11, a mark that would stand for 13 years. In the steeplechase Kiptanui ran the splendid time of 7:56.16, well inside the record of 7:59.08 … but three metres ahead of him in 7:55.72 was Bernard Barmasai whose kilometre splits were 2:38.2, 2:42.3 and 2:35.3.

Of course, much else was going on in other events. The most hyped but anti-climactic race of the year occurred indoors in Toronto's SkyDome. This was designated the "One To One" Challenge over 150m between the Olympic champions and world record holders at 100m (Canada's own Donovan Bailey) and 200m (Michael Johnson) and promoted as if it was a world heavyweight boxing showdown. This sort of artificial contest was not in the best interests of the sport (in fact the IAAF specifically banned match races the next year) and it proved a monumental flop. Johnson was nearly two metres down at the 80m mark when he sustained an injury to his left thigh, leaving Bailey to run on alone in 14.99 and scoop the million dollars for the winner – the biggest single prize yet paid to an athlete. Both men received half a million just for competing. Johnson's injury kept him off training for a while, and when he returned to competition, in Paris 24 days after the Toronto race, he was only a shadow of his usual self and I watched him "die" in the finishing straight of the 400m to finish fifth in 45.76. One of the great winning streaks had come to an end; it was his first defeat at the distance since February 1989 and, counting finals only, he had won 58 in a row.

Unlike Johnson, I was present at the US Championships in Indianapolis, in the ever genial company of Sir Eddie. I was now becoming quite a regular at the top American meetings (with a side-trip to Las Vegas added on of course!) and it was always a pleasure to meet up again with one of my oldest friends, Elliott Denman, together with Garry Hill and Jon Hendershott of *Track & Field News* among others.

Sprinters attracted most attention. Maurice Greene, who hadn't run faster than 10.08 legally before this meeting, won the 100m in 9.90 and proclaimed (accurately as it turned out): "I'm the person that's going to put American sprinting back where it's supposed to be." He was pressed hard, though, by former junior sensation Tim Montgomery, who improved in Indy from 10.06 to 9.92. Both would become world record breakers but in Montgomery's case he would eventually be stripped of his record (9.78 in 2002) after admitting the use of performance enhancing drugs and he later ended up in prison for fraud and drug dealing. His future partner, Marion Jones, would also end her highly successful athletics career in disgrace and she too would serve a jail sentence, in her case for lying under oath to federal agents. But in Indianapolis a glorious future beckoned for her.

Jones, a former prodigy whom many thought might never make it to the top in senior competition because of foot injuries and her involvement in college basketball, was a revelation from her opening heat in the 100m. She clocked 10.98 to destroy her previous legal best of 11.14 set in 1992 when she was 16, and improved later that day in the semis with 10.92 despite "shutting down" at 85m. Hopes of a momentous clash with Gail Devers were dashed when the Olympic champion scratched with a sore right calf muscle, leaving Jones to win by over 2m in 10.97 into a 1.1m wind. Jones, who only started training for athletics three months earlier following the basketball season, went on to defeat Jackie Joyner-Kersee in the long jump, improving on her pb from 6.75m to 6.93m.

Peter Matthews was in Munich to cover the European Cup and witnessed victory by the British men's team over Germany and Russia. Individual winners were Linford Christie in the 100m (for the eighth consecutive time) and 200m (in a rare dead-heat), Roger Black at 400m, Jonathan Edwards in the triple jump, Steve Backley in the javelin, the 4x400m team … and, this one totally unexpected, sixth ranked Robert Hough in the steeplechase. The women's team placed third behind Russia and Germany with Kelly Holmes (1500m) and Sally Gunnell (400m hurdles) scoring maximum points.

No sooner was I back from the Paris Grand Prix than I was off to Sheffield, where despite the cold and windy weather there were Commonwealth records for Holmes, whose 59.69 last lap carried her to a 1500m time of 3:58.07, and Hansen who triple jumped 14.92m and 14.94m. Had Iwan Thomas not begun his victory celebrations on the wrong side of the 400m finish line he might well have broken Roger Black's UK record of 44.37 – instead he had to settle for 44.49. Three days later, in Lausanne, Thomas improved to 44.46 and he finally nabbed the British record, which still stands, when he ran 44.36 at the UK Championships in Birmingham.

Those championships were organised by the British Athletic Federation but only a few months later that body went into administration. As I wrote in *The Official History of the AAA*, published in 2011:

During its six years of existence BAF, despite launching many useful initiatives, appeared to be constantly in a state of crisis, a situation not helped by various power struggles within the Federation. Malcolm Jones resigned as chief executive in 1993, to be replaced by Professor Peter Radford as executive chairman. At the 1994 AGM Dave Bedford was ousted as honorary secretary by Matt Frazer with Ken Rickhuss becoming chairman. Also that year Frank Dick resigned as director of coaching following a reduction in the development budget and Andy Norman was dismissed as director of promotions in the wake of the suicide of noted journalist Cliff Temple. Mary Peters succeeded Arthur McAllister as president at the 1996 AGM, where John Lister stood down as honorary treasurer.

With the AAA of England declining to bail out the financially ailing BAF its future looked bleak, the accounts showing a deficit of £324,000 in 1996, and there was a further shock when Prof Radford announced his resignation in January 1997. In July 1997 former world 5000m record holder Dave Moorcroft defeated 127 other applicants to be appointed the new chief executive ... but within days of his beginning work in October he had to announce the devastating news that BAF had been placed in the hands of the administrators after declaring a substantial cash shortfall which included payments of £860,000 yet to be made to athletes who had competed in BAF meetings. The pain was widespread as, in order to maximise the return to BAF's creditors, the administrators quickly made redundant several employees including nine national coaches or development officers.

It was always a pleasure to visit Athens and that was the venue for the be-all and end-all of the 1997 season: the IAAF World Championships. Accompanied by two of my closest friends in Stan Greenberg and Alf Wilkins, I attended the lavish but somewhat over-extended opening ceremony. A plaintive Alf asked when would it ever come to an end, to which I replied in time honoured fashion: "It ain't over until the fat lady sings" ... at which precise moment the generously proportioned Spanish soprano Montserrat Caballé appeared!

Two important innovations were that prize money was paid for the first time at the outdoor World Championships ($60,000 for a win) and wild cards were awarded to reigning champions who had failed to achieve national team selection in the normal manner. I reported for the *IAAF Magazine's* Athens Souvenir Edition:

Each of the five previous IAAF World Championships produced at least one magical moment which would for ever be associated with that celebration. In Athens, for the first time in the meeting's history, no world records were broken – but that did not prevent another of those truly memorable moments occurring. The athlete who stole the show and personified the excellence, challenge and drama of the World Championships was Sergey Bubka. Against all the odds he picked up his first world pole vault title at the inaugural meeting in 1983 as an obscure 19 year-old selected by Soviet officials primarily to get experience of world class competition. He won all the subsequent titles too (from 1993 representing his native Ukraine) but, with only a handful of mediocre competitive appearances and a few specific training sessions behind him since he hobbled out of the Atlanta Olympic arena with an achilles tendon injury a year earlier, few expected him to be a major factor this time. But Bubka is no ordinary superstar; he represents a galaxy of his own. Once more his special mixture of technical skill, bravado and a refusal even to contemplate defeat conspired to demoralise the opposition. What's more, in capturing his sixth world title he registered the greatest height (6.01m) ever seen in international championship competition. There are many other vivid memories of Athens 1997 to cherish, but nothing to compare with Bubka's almost frightening look of sheer determination as he gazed down the runway. Six title wins from six attempts over a 14-year period is a record that may well stand for all-time.

With three-time winners Noureddine Morceli (1500m) and Moses Kiptanui (steeplechase) being beaten and decathlete Dan O'Brien unable to defend, the only other athlete to make it four straight titles was discus thrower Lars Riedel. The next best streak is three by Michael Johnson in the 400m and Haile Gebrselassie in the 10,000m. When it comes to medals of all hues there is no one to rival Merlene Ottey. The stylish 37 year-old Jamaican, despite not being at her fittest following illness, collected a bronze in the 200m to raise her total to 14. She achieved another distinction by becoming the oldest of all female medallists in World Championships history, which is remarkable for a sprinter who won her first Olympic medal back in 1980.

Striking was how few Olympic gold medallists proved equally successful just a year later. The number of Atlanta winners to emerge victorious was a mere seven: Johnson, Gebrselassie, Allen Johnson (110m hurdles), Riedel, Robert Korzeniowski (50km walk), Ludmila Engquist (100m hurdles) and Astrid Kumbernuss (shot). But it was encouraging for the sport's future that there were so many new faces among the winners. Maurice Greene restored the USA's 100m fortunes with his emphatic victory in 9.86 and Marion Jones revived memories of Wilma Rudolph as she sped to her 100m triumph in 10.83. Perhaps the most stunning breakthrough was by South Africa's Marius Corbett in the javelin. Of the 40 entrants he ranked equal 19th on personal records with 83.90m, itself a vast improvement over his pre-1997 best of 77.98m when winning the 1994 world junior title, and yet he threw 88.40m to astound himself quite as much as his bemused rivals.

Britain's medal haul consisted of five silvers and a bronze, but one of those silvers turned to gold many years later. After a close 4x400m battle, the USA clocked 2:56.47 to defeat Britain (2:56.65) … but Antonio Pettigrew, who ran a super-fast 43.1 second leg for the Americans, admitted under oath in 2008 that he had been using human growth hormone and EPO between 1997 and 2003 and he, and consequently the team, was disqualified. Thus the British squad of Iwan Thomas 44.8, Roger Black 44.2, Jamie Baulch 44.08 and Mark Richardson 43.57 were promoted to champions. The silvers went to Colin Jackson (13.05), Jonathan Edwards (17.69m), Steve Backley (86.80m) and Denise Lewis (6654); bronze to the men's 4x100m team (38.14). Just missing out in fourth place were Richardson (44.47 for a personal best), Dalton Grant (2.32m; a "world record" opening height!), Mick Hill (86.54m) and Paula Radcliffe (15:01.74).

The IAAF Congress, meeting in Athens, made a deplorable decision to reduce the sanction for a first serious doping offence, such as the use of steroids and amphetamines, from four years to two years. The reason was to avert the possibility of legal action in certain countries but that threat should have been resisted. Instead the floodgates opened with all too many athletes prepared to take the risk that even if caught they would miss only a couple of seasons and then be welcomed back as if the fact that they had cheated fellow competitors out of medals, money and deserved recognition was of little account. Huge damage was caused to the sport and it wasn't until 2015 that four year bans were reintroduced. Hardliners like myself would prefer the most serious drug offenders, if guilt is beyond any doubt, to be kicked out of the sport altogether, along with any support staff who aided and abetted the athlete. Only harsh measures, like the IAAF's brave decision in 2016 to suspend Russian athletes from international competition, might improve the situation.

The international season concluded with the climax in Berlin of the Golden Four series with El Guerrouj (3:45.64 mile ahead of Komen's 3:46.38), Frankie Fredericks and Gabriela Szabo sharing the 20 gold bars, and the even more lucrative Grand Prix Final in Fukuoka where Wilson Kipketer (a front running 1:42.98 for his seventh sub-1:43 800m for the year) and shot putter Astrid Kumbernuss picked up a cool quarter of a million dollars each. The big news for British athletics was the terrific Commonwealth triple jump record of 15.15m by Ashia Hansen, who defeated all three Athens medallists when adding 21cm to her previous best to rank fifth on the world all-time list. Only 19 British men bettered that in 1997!

China had the last word, for in Shanghai in October there were echoes of the scarcely credible events of 1993. Chinese athletes won no medals in Athens but, as Peter Matthews explained in AI: "It must be realised, as in 1993, that these Chinese National Games are very, very important for them. Really the Chinese Olympics. Further, valuable prizes are on offer; no doubt essential targets for these athletes, who cannot travel the world for reward as Westerners do."

Peter reported: "On the first day [October 17] 12 women (five of them juniors) broke 4 minutes for 1500m – in the heats! These included two world junior records, and a third followed in the final [October 18] when Lang Yinglai ran 3:51.34 behind the winner Jiang Bo's 3:50.98. Then perhaps the most remarkable thing happened, in that the women who were 6th, 4th and 3rd in that

1500m returned the next day to take the first three places in the 10,000m, all breaking 30:40, with winner Dong Yanmei (19) clocking 30:38.09. Coach Ma Junren's new squad took the leading placings in that 1500m, yet his top athlete Qu Yunxia fell in the race (yet still ran 3:57.83 for 8th). Ma accused rival coaches of orchestrating the fall, saying "Without the accident, three of my disciples were sure to break the world record" [3:50.46].

I took up the story in the next issue, thanks to information supplied by Mirko Jalava. It was evident that the women's 5000m would produce something sensational ... and so it proved. Fernanda Ribeiro's world record of 14:36.45 did not even survive the heats! Dong Yanmei won the first heat in 14:31.27 ahead of Jiang Bo (14:31.30) and Liu Shixiang (14:32.33); two days later in the final on October 23 victory and the world record went to Jiang Bo in 14:28.09 while Dong Yanmei improved to 14:29.82. Jiang Bo (20) thus completed a momentous double, having earlier won the 1500m in the second fastest time in history. Her previous best at 1500m appears to have been 4:11.76 in 1995. Dong Yanmei, whose pre-97 bests were 4:18.41 in 1996 and 15:11.80/32:04.42 in 1995, reeled off this sequence of races: Oct 17 – 3:55.82 heat, Oct 18 – 3:55.07, Oct 19 – 30:38.09, Oct 21 – 14:31.27 heat; Oct 23 - 14:29.82 ... plus a 2:28:09 marathon on October 26.

There were also Chinese records for Han Chaoming (45.46 400m), Song Mingyou (3:36.54 1500m), Xia Fengyuan (13:25.14 5000m), Sun Ripeng (8:10.46 steeplechase) and Gao Yonghong (49.34 400m hurdles) on the men's side, while new women's marks were set by Li Xuemei (10.79 100m and 22.01 200m) and Jiang Limei (53.38 400m hurdles) with a terrific junior 400m record of 50.01 established by 17 year-old Li Jing. There was even an astonishing girls' age-13 800m best of 2:03.63 by Yu Junping.

My immediate suspicion that many if not all of these performances were either drug assisted or phoney in some other way was lent credence by the disqualification because of doping violations of the 53.38 hurdles and the 54.54 behind Jiang Limei of a world junior record by Peng Yinghua. Both served two year bans. An Asian women's long jump record of 7.03m by Qiong Xiying was also later removed from the Chinese lists on account of a doping control result. So did any of the others go on to make their mark internationally? None of the men listed above nor the 13 year-old prodigy were heard of again, while Li Xuemei subsequently never ran faster than 10.95 and 22.53 and Li Jing clocked only 52.19.

33. SILVER WEDDING CELEBRATIONS (1998)

It didn't seem possible that 25 years had flown by but on April 8 1998 Pat and I celebrated our silver wedding anniversary. Early in January, to mark the occasion, I booked an afternoon tea for two for that day at The Ritz. No sooner had I arranged it than Pat was diagnosed as being a coeliac, barred for the rest of her life from consuming food containing gluten – in other words the main components of The Ritz spread: bread and cakes! However, full marks to the hotel's staff who responded by providing Pat with a gluten free selection of fruit and specially made scones. It was the time when the coeliac condition was only just becoming widely known and there was little or no gluten-free food available in the shops. Following tea we wandered around the West End stores and in the evening we enjoyed a performance of the hit musical *Chicago*, starring Ruthie Henshall. Athletics connection warning! Also in the cast was the award winning actor Henry Goodman who, coached by Alf Wilkins, had been a decent runner in his youth in the 1960s.

On April 19 we hosted a family celebration for 15 at a restaurant in Barkingside, the area where my sister and her children and grandchildren lived, and on May 3 (the day Pat and I first met 26 years earlier) we welcomed 14 of our friends to a meal in Edgware. My oldest pal from schooldays, Stan Posner, and his wife Rhea were there and the rest of the guests were from the world of athletics: Stan and Carole Greenberg, Alf Wilkins and Paula (they were married later that year), Lionel and Sigrid Peters, Peter and Diana Matthews, and two knights of the realm in Sir Arthur Gold and Lady Marion, and Sir Eddie Kulukundis and Lady Susan (Hampshire).

There were other treats in this special year. Shortly after my 60th birthday we spent a week in Portugal and later on we were members of Shirley Bassey's adoring audience at the Royal Festival Hall, revelled in an open air concert of George Gershwin's music by the lake at Ken Wood and thrilled to watch the superb National Theatre production of *Oklahoma!* One of our favourite actresses (and authors), Maureen Lipman, played the spirited Aunt Eller … and Pat fell for the charms of a then little known Australian by the name of Hugh Jackman in the role of Curly.

It wasn't all joy that year, for the man who gave me my big chance in athletics journalism and with whom I worked contentedly for over a quarter of a century died in March at the age of 88. I wrote in AW:

Few people have made such a lasting and wide-ranging contribution to their chosen sport as Jimmy Green, the "Grand Old Man" of British athletics. His place in athletics history is secure as the man who had the vision, enthusiasm and courage to start AW. He was a delightful boss and colleague, unfailingly considerate and good humoured even when – as we always seemed to be – under heavy pressure. Jimmy was an athletics renaissance man. He had been a good runner, starting as a sprinter with Surrey AC in 1924, going on to represent the AAA and RAF at 880y, mile and 2 miles (he raced against Sydney Wooderson), and finishing up 29th in the AAA/Poly Marathon of 1948. As a starter he was one of the country's best. He had wide experience of administration at club and county level and helped organise many top class meetings. He was one of the first senior coaches. He appointed me as editor in 1968, concentrating instead on the business and advertising side, and in 1979 – on his 70th birthday – he was succeeded in those areas by his youngest son Tim. Jimmy continued to help out at AW for several more years and retained his love for the sport until the very end.

Another multi-faceted contributor to British athletics was Tony Ward, in his time a coach, administrator, announcer, writer, PRO and British Athletics spokesman. His latest incarnation was as an editor and publisher and in January I was delighted to be invited to be the statistician and proof reader of his new monthly magazine *Inside Track*. The first 100 page edition appeared at the end of February and its content and design were admirable. That launch issue featured an interview with Colin Jackson by Neil Allen, Dave Moorcroft's first 100 days as BAF's chief executive as told to Neil Wilson, and a profile of Mary Rand by Tony himself. Other contributors included Tony's former international high jumper wife Gwenda on the worrying subject of anorexia. The magazine was a very welcome addition to athletics journalism but, alas, there were only four issues, for the harsh economics of publishing proved too much for Tony. It was a brave venture and a sad loss.

The early part of the year was notable for world indoor records by Maurice Greene (6.41 and 6.39 60m), Haile Gebrselassie (4:52.86 2000m and 7:26.15 3000m), Daniel Komen (7:24.90 3000m and 12:51.48 5000m) and Gabriela Szabo (5:30.53 2000m), while the still under-developed women's pole vault record was raised in ten instalments from 4.41m to Emma George's 4.55m. There was one other world record, which I had the great pleasure of witnessing at the European Indoor Championships in Valencia.

It was a case of third time lucky for Ashia Hansen. The British triple jumper's two previous appearances at the European Indoor Championships had been a disaster: at Paris in 1994 she had failed to reach the final with a dismal distance of 13.30m and Stockholm in 1996 was just as traumatic. She did make the final that time (with 14.32m) but proceeded to foul three times. No one doubted her immense talent but there was a question mark over her competitive temperament, for she had flopped also outdoors at the 1994 European and 1995 World Championships. Her morale following the Stockholm demise was so low that she came very close to retiring at the age of 24. What a waste that would have been, for since then she has gone from strength to strength, placing fourth in the Olympics, and since her coaching was taken over by Aston Moore (himself a windy 17.02m performer in 1981) in September 1996 she has blossomed into one of the greats of the event, capped by her Grand Prix triumph last year with 15.15m. Now she is a world record holder indoors, having smashed Iolanda Chen's figures of 15.03m with 15.16m in Valencia.

There were two other British winners. John Mayock took the 3000m in 7:55.09 just ahead of three Spaniards. Britain's fourth fastest 1500m runner at 3:31.86 had to fend for himself to hold his ground on the last lap as tempers flared and some of the home fans whistled and jeered as he took the lead on the final turn to become Britain's first winner of this title since Ian Stewart in 1975. Jonathan Edwards (17.43m) became the first Briton to land the men's triple jump championship.

It was proving to be a notable year for the Irish. At the indoor Millrose Games in New York, Marcus O'Sullivan notched up his 100th sub-four minute mile, a feat achieved only by New Zealand's John Walker (124) and the USA's Steve Scott (136). Ever since illness ruined her Olympic chances in Atlanta, the 1995 world 5000m champion Sonia O'Sullivan had been struggling to recapture top form but at the World Cross Country Championships in Marrakech, Morocco she returned with a vengeance. On the first day she captured the 8km title, defeating Paula Radcliffe after a close battle, and next day she ran away with the 4km race. Catherina McKiernan, four times a World Cross Country runner-up, opted instead for the London Marathon in which she beat Liz McColgan in 2:26:26. In November she would win the Amsterdam Marathon in 2:22:23, while O'Sullivan would land a 5000/10,000m double at the European Championships.

The week before London, Kenya's tiny Tegla Loroupe had won the Rotterdam Marathon in a world best of 2:20:47. There were no official world marathon records in those days but the IAAF reported a double infringement of the rules then in force and would not have ratified the performance anyway because she was paced throughout by two male runners and was repeatedly advised by the elite race director from a motorbike. The Berlin Marathon saw Brazil's Ronaldo da Costa smash the men's world record with 2:06:05 after covering the second half in an astonishing 61:23, while Paul Tergat set new half marathon figures of 59:17 in Milan.

It wasn't only on the roads that new standards of excellence were being established. Haile Gebrselassie enjoyed another fabulous season. He posted the year's quickest 3000m time of 7:25.09 in Brussels and set world records at 10,000m with 26:22.75 in Hengelo (halves of 13:11.8 and 13:11.0!) and, just 12 days later, at 5000m with 12:39.36 in Helsinki. Swedish statistical guru Lennart Julin deduced from video scrutiny that his kilometre splits were 2:34.8, 2:31.6, 2:32.9, 2:32.8 and 2:27.3 with the final mile covered in 4:01.2. Hicham El Guerrouj was equally dominant at 1500m with the year's five fastest times crowned by a world record of 3:26.00 in Rome (Lennart's estimated splits were 54.3 at 400m, 1:50.7 at 800m, 2:45.9 at 1200m) followed by the second best ever time of 3:26.45 in Zürich.

I was in Nice to see El Guerrouj run his fastest mile yet of 3:44.60, second only to Noureddine Morceli's 1993 world record of 3:44.39. Third in that race in his best time of 3:51.90 was Anthony Whiteman, who the previous year had run 3:32.34 for 1500m. Amazingly, after retiring from international competition in 2004 he returned at club level six years later and set world masters records of 1:48.05 for 800m in 2014 (age 42) and 3:42.02 1500m and 3:58.79 mile in 2012. He continued in 2017 to be competitive against runners half his age, registering remarkable world age-45 bests of 1:49.86 for 800m and

3:48.72 for 1500m! Back to El Guerrouj, who narrowly missed another of Morceli's world records when he clocked 4:48.36 for 2000m at Gateshead, which all too typically was wet, windy and cool. Meanwhile, Daniel Komen went very close in Sydney to his own 2 miles world best of 7:58.61 with 7:58.91.

Another athlete who was generating much admiration was Marion Jones. In the May 13 issue I wrote: *One has the feeling with Marion Jones that we've seen nothing yet. What a start she has made to this year, only her second on the international circuit. Indoors, she tied Gail Devers' US 60m record of 6.95, a time bettered only by Irina Privalova. Outdoors, in Australia in February, she opened up with 11.01 and 21.98 into headwinds, while in California in April she made an exciting excursion over the full lap, clocking 50.36 in her first race at the distance since 52.91 as a 15 year-old in 1991. At Mito she long jumped a pb of 7.05m and four days later, still in Japan in Osaka, she ran a 10.79 100m into an 0.6m wind.*

In the May 27 issue I reported: *Racing at Chengdu in China, she moved into second place on the world all-time list at 100m with a time of 10.71. Only Flo-Jo has ever run faster in legal conditions, Jones has announced her ultimate goal: to win FIVE gold medals at the Sydney Olympics (100, 200, long jump and both relays)! Looking further ahead: "I want to be remembered as one of the greatest female athletes, but across the wider spectrum. I want a little boy to say 40 years from now 'I want to run like Marion Jones,' not Carl Lewis or Michael Johnson."*

If anyone remembers the name of Marion Jones now or in years to come it's more likely to be because she cheated her way to her huge collection of medals, most of which have had to be returned. Jones went on in 1998 to jump 7.31m, become the first woman since Stella Walsh (of ambiguous gender) 50 years earlier to win the 100, 200 and long jump at the US Championships in a sweltering New Orleans (it reached a high of 45.6°C out on the field), and at altitude in Johannesburg for the World Cup she was timed at 10.65 and 21.62.

Tragically, the only woman ever to have run faster at those distances died at the shockingly young age of 38. Florence Griffith Joyner (Flo-Jo) slipped away in her sleep at home in California, the cause of death being suffocation during a severe epileptic seizure. The glamorous 1988 Olympic champion was survived by her husband, 1984 Olympic triple jump champion Al Joyner, and a seven year-old daughter.

It was a good year for Britain's athletes. Ashia Hansen's indoor triumph paved the way and the men's team shone at the European Cup in St Petersburg. As jubilant team captain Roger Black explained: "In the end it was down to those who were expected to win delivering and those expected to come sixth or seventh performing above themselves" which enabled the team to confound everyone by retaining the trophy. The primary goal had been to finish second to Germany and thus qualify for the World Cup, but that target was surpassed. British winners were Doug Walaker (200m), Mark Richardson (400m), Colin Jackson, Jonathan Edwards and both relay teams.

The women's squad placed fifth, the only winner being Paula Radcliffe (who had earlier broken Liz McColgan's UK 10,000m record with 30:48.58 in her debut at the distance) in the 5000m. The star performer was Slough-born Fiona May who won the long jump with 7.08m and the triple jump with 14.65m, both Italian records. A notable performance was Judy Oakes' second place in the shot, her highest ever position in a record tenth Cup appearance and at the age of 40. Pound for pound, Judy was a remarkable shot putter and although her best of 19.36m in drug-infested 1988 ranked her only 32nd in the world behind 20 East Europeans, five Chinese, four West Germans and two Americans, that distance was bettered by just four athletes in 2017 and would have won her the bronze medal at the World Championships.

Doping raised its ugly head also at the Goodwill Games in Uniondale on New York's Long Island. The American team of Jerome Young (44.3), Antonio Pettigrew (43.2), Tyree Washington (43.5) and Michael Johnson (43.2) combined to set a stunning world record of 2:54.20 ... but in 2008 the record was annulled because of Pettigrew's subsequent doping admission. In 2010, aged 42, he committed suicide by a drug overdose.

The victim of one of the worst team selection judgements since Seb Coe's omission from the 1988 Olympic squad, Roger Black ended his stellar racing career at the British Grand Prix in Sheffield.

The meeting was to have been one of Roger Black's final stepping stones on the way to bidding for an unprecedented third European 400m title. Instead, as a result of a bewildering selectorial decision which left him out of the 400m trio named for Budapest, Black used the occasion to take leave of his doting public. It was an emotional farewell appearance by one of Britain's most successful, durable, reliable and charismatic of athletes, and he received a standing ovation after finishing third to Mark Richardson and Iwan Thomas. Those are the joint favourites to keep the European 400m crown in British hands, but after running 44.71 in the AAA Championships Black felt he was on course to recapture the form which won him an Olympic silver two years ago ... and few, other than the selectors it would seem, would have denied him the chance of achieving his last major target. As Black ("I'm devastated and mystified at the selectors' decision") explained when announcing his retirement: "I am a championship performer. I need championship goals. My own goal now no longer exists. In such circumstances you either reset your goals or you accept defeat. The selectors have at long last defeated me!" Consequently, he gave up his place as a member of the relay squad ("it doesn't need me to win the 4x400") and relinquished the team captaincy.

Britain did indeed win the European 4x400m title in Budapest, although by less than a stride's length ahead of Poland, but the anticipated 1-2-3 in the individual 400m did not materialise. Prophetically wearing the number 445, Iwan Thomas, a TV reporter these days, won in 44.52 but Mark Richardson paid the penalty for too fast a start and finished third, while Solomon Wariso – the man the selectors preferred to Black – faded to sixth and was disqualified for running out of his lane.

Britain won more gold medals (nine) than any other nation, eight of them in the men's events. Six years earlier, Linford Christie had labelled Darren Campbell as his most likely successor. He was lost to semi-professional football for two years but in 1997, under Christie's coaching, he progressed to 10.13 for 100m and in Budapest he succeeded his mentor as European champion, his 10.04 good for second place on the UK all-time list behind Christie. Dwain Chambers finished second but the 200m runners did even better by filling all three medal placings, led by Doug Walker's 20.53. Campbell and Walker picked up second golds in the 4x100m relay, surprisingly Britain's first ever European title in that event.

Colin Jackson became the first to win a third European 110m hurdles crown, clocking 13.02 in his semi and equalling that in the final 75 minutes later for easily the fastest ever one-day double. It was his quickest time for four years. Two other "old faithfuls" claimed gold. Jonathan Edwards triple jumped 17.99m, a distance only he and Kenny Harrison had ever surpassed, but it could all have ended in disaster in the qualifying contest when, with his first attempt, he landed his step on a loose sunken long jump board, his right ankle buckled and he aborted the jump. Fortunately, no damage was sustained and minutes later, given the attempt again, he qualified without further ado.

Steve Backley needed just two throws to notch up his third European javelin title. In the qualifying round he threw 87.45m and he opened his account in the final with an 89.72m delivery which, not surprisingly, withstood all assaults. Team-mate Mick Hill, who had only qualified for the final in tenth place with his last throw, was fifth at halfway but in round five he produced an inspired 86.92m for the silver medal. Second also was high jumper Dalton Grant, who cleared 2.34m on the second attempt, the same height as winner Artur Partyka who made it first time. A knee injury requiring pain-killing injections played havoc with Grant in the qualifying contest, needing 11 jumps before making the required 2.24m. Partyka had three failures at 2.36m but Grant, who hadn't previously jumped higher than 2.28m all season, bizarrely decided to sit it out and took three shots instead at the Commonwealth record height of 2.38m! He didn't succeed but he did earn his first major medal outdoors since silver at the 1990 Commonwealth Games.

On the women's side, Denise Lewis triumphed in the heptathlon with 6559 points. Benefitting from the extra strength training she underwent while restricted by an ankle injury, Denise raised her best shot put from 14.72m to 15.27m and good results also in the long jump and javelin enabled her to win by 99 points. The 4x400m team finished third, with Katharine Merry and Allison Curbishley clocking 50.4 and 50.6 on the last two legs. Talking of relays, there was an astounding run in the 4x100m.

This race will be remembered for a very long time on account of the most spectacular relay anchor ever run by a woman. When Irina Privalova [the 200m champion and runner-up in the 100m in 10.83] took over for the last leg in the lead for Russia just ahead of Germany (Andrea Philipp), with France way back, the medals looked to be decided. That Privalova was not at her best on this occasion was made obvious by the fact that Philipp (pb of 11.05) was able to get past her, but it was Christine Arron who drew gasps from the crowd. She started some 5-6 metres down on Privalova and yet finished a metre and a half ahead; you would not have thought it possible if you hadn't seen it with your own eyes! Arron, who had won the 100m in a sensational European record of 10.73 to rank third on the world all-time list, brought France home in 42.59.

Moscow was the venue for the IAAF Grand Prix Final and the big payout. There was heartbreak for one athlete in particular.

As Bryan Bronson approached the final hurdle with a clear lead, the dollar signs must have been flashing before his eyes. Unbeaten in 17 races this season, Bronson would already have calculated that victory would net him at least $250,000 as his share of the Ericsson Golden League Jackpot plus $50,000 for winning the race and the probability of $100,000 for placing second in the overall Grand Prix standings ... a total of $400,000. But the American metaphorically fell at that last barrier. He took it poorly, lost his forward momentum and was agonisingly powerless to prevent world champion Stéphane Diagana overtaking him on the run-in for victory in 48.30, a time which Bronson has bettered in 12 races this summer. He is fated to run and re-run that race in his mind for the rest of his life. To have one of the biggest prizes in athletics history slip from his grasp was bad enough but Bronson compounded the loss by giving up in the final strides, slipping from 2nd to 6th in 48.94, a lapse which cost him $23,000. He ended up winning $57,000.

My sympathy for Bronson evaporated in March the following year when it was belatedly revealed that he had tested positive at the Rome Grand Prix meeting on July 14 1998 (where he won in 47.76) and he was banned for two years. So really he should never have been allowed to continue racing and earning money during that summer season. Did he ever have to pay back that $57,000?

With Bronson out of the running early in the proceedings, the other three jackpot candidates – Hicham El Guerrouj, Haile Gebrselassie and Marion Jones – stood to gain $333,333.33 apiece if they could win for a seventh time in the Golden League/Grand Prix Final series of meetings. None was troubled. El Guerrouj sauntered to 1500m victory in 3:32.03; Gebrselassie romped home in the 3000m in 7:50.00; and Jones, who had earlier beaten Heike Drechsler and Fiona May in the long jump with 7.13m, was as dominating as ever in the 100m, running 10.83 despite the cool weather. Financially she emerged the big winner: on top of her third of a million dollars she pocketed $200,000 for heading the women's overall standings and $100,000 for two event victories – a total of over $633,000! El Guerrouj, the men's overall winner, was awarded $583,000 and Gebrselassie $483,000.

Jones added another $120,000 to her bank balance by winning the 100m (10.65) and 200m (21.62) and finishing second to Drechsler (7.07m) with 7.00m in the long jump – her only defeat in any event all year – at the IAAF World Cup at high altitude Johannesburg. Her efforts helped the USA win the women's contest, two points ahead of Europe, while the men's competition was even closer as Africa edged Europe by a single point. There were three British winners: Iwan Thomas (45.33), Steve Backley (88.71m) and the 4x100m team (38.09). That should have been four as Colin Jackson ran 13.11 with a legal 0.150 reaction time but Germany's Falk Balzer – who blatantly beat the gun (0.031) – disgracefully was allowed by the starter to get away with it to take the race in 13.10.

The international track season came to an end with the Commonwealth Games in the Malaysian capital of Kuala Lumpur. Iwan Thomas, representing Wales, added that 400m title (44.52) to his AAA, European and World Cup victories, but his compatriot Colin Jackson controversially rejected the chance of winning a third Commonwealth title, enabling Tony Jarrett (13.47) to take his first gold medal since the 1987 European Juniors after nine major silver or bronze medals. Other English winners were Julian Golding (20.18 200m), Dalton Grant (2.31m), Larry Achike (17.10m triple jump), Robert Weir (64.42m discus, 16 years after winning the hammer!), the men's 4x100m team (38.20), Joanne Wise (6.63m long jump), Ashia Hansen (14.32m triple jump), Judy Oakes (18.83m shot) and Denise Lewis (6513 heptathlon). Stars of the Games were Trinidad's Ato Boldon who ran 9.88 for 100m and South Africa's world javelin champion Marius Corbett who threw 88.75m to beat Steve Backley's 87.38m.

34. ATHLETES OF THE CENTURY (1999)

Officially the 20th century ended on December 31 2000, but most people – myself included – regarded 1999 as the final year of the century. At any rate it marked the conclusion of the 1900s and it was time to take stock. Two world wars made it a century of unprecedented global bloodshed, but what progress there had been in so many areas of life. Back in 1900 women were still many years away from getting the vote never mind equal opportunities in the workplace; the first powered flight didn't take place until 1903; cars were still a novelty and most vehicles remained horse-drawn; there was no radio let alone television, while short silent films were just starting and electrical appliances were in their infancy. Life expectancy at birth for a man in Britain was 47, for a woman it was 50 (it's now over 80).

As for athletic performance, the progress in all events has been staggering. Some examples of world records as at 1900 and as at the start of 2000: 100m – 10.8 / 9.79; 400m – 47.5 (47.8 440y) / 43.18; mile – 4:12.8 / 3:43.13; high jump – 1.97m / 2.45m; shot – 14.75m / 23.12m. There was a tiny amount of female athletic activity but nothing on an internationally organised basis until the early 1920s. Who could possibly have foreseen when the great Emil Zátopek set a world 10,000m record of 29:21.2 in 1949 that an Ethiopian woman would run quicker in 2016 or that a British female would, in 2003, run a marathon two minutes faster than Jim Peters' best?

Speaking of Jim Peters, he was among the athletics personalities who didn't quite survive the 20th century. He was close to death after collapsing in Vancouver in 1954, but survived to live on to the age of 80.

Although Jim Peters, who died of cancer on January 9 will forever be identified with that dramatic collapse so close to the finish of the 1954 Empire Games marathon, his final race, it is as a marathoning trail blazer that he deserves to be remembered. Peters was already nearly 30 when he represented Britain in the 1948 Olympics, and was so disappointed at finishing ninth in the 10,000m, lapped by Emil Zátopek, that he considered retirement. Instead his coach 'Johnny' Johnston prevailed upon him to train for the marathon. The world 'record' at that time was 2:25:39 and yet Peters and his coach knew that to run under 2:20 was a possibility. That they succeeded in transforming that leap of the imagination into actual deeds assured them of an honoured place in the history of athletic progress. By virtue of his harsh training and uncompromising racing tactics he did for marathon running what Zátopek had done for long distance track racing a few years earlier. In

1952 he first astounded the world as he covered the Windsor to Chiswick course in a revolutionary 2:20:43. As a teenager I was fortunate enough to witness the finish of that race and Peters' subsequent world bests on that course (2:18:41 in 1953 and 2:17:40 in 1954) and the feeling of awe and admiration I experienced never left me. That he failed to finish in his two most crucial races, at the 1952 Helsinki Olympics and in Vancouver in 1954, was a calamity but his immense contribution to the evolution of marathon running is for eternity.

He may only have been a modest long jumper in his youth but Italy's Dr Primo Nebiolo, who died of a heart attack in Rome on November 7 aged 76, transformed international athletics.

With the death of Dr Primo Nebiolo, president of the IAAF since 1981, international athletics has lost its most powerful leader. A controversial and autocratic figure, Nebiolo dramatically reshaped the sport. Many may have disagreed with his vision and objected to his methods but few could deny that he was responsible for making athletics one of the world's most successful and publicised sports. During his reign athletics at the highest level became openly professional, enabling an athlete like Gabriela Szabo to earn over a million dollars this year in prize money from IAAF-endorsed events. World Championships, which started in 1983, have been held every two years at his instigation since 1991 and among other initiatives to raise the profile of athletics worldwide throughout the year have been the creation of World Indoor Championships and the IAAF Grand Prix in 1985, World Junior Championships in 1986 and the Golden League in 1998.

Just days after Dr Nebiolo's funeral, the IAAF Council elected 66 year-old Lamine Diack as acting president until the next IAAF Congress, scheduled for 2001. Diack, from Senegal, was also a former long jumper … but a classy one. He won the French title in 1958 and ranked 21st in the world that year with 7.63m. Diack would remain IAAF president until 2015, the year he was arrested. A report by the World Anti-Doping Agency's independent commission stated: "Lamine Diack was responsible for organising and enabling the conspiracy and corruption that took place in the IAAF." At the time of writing, he is still awaiting trial in France.

Haile Gebrselassie was such a beautiful runner to watch and I, along with the rest of a capacity crowd in Birmingham's National Indoor Arena (now the Arena Birmingham), was privileged to watch him regain the world indoor 5000m record from Daniel Komen with the splendid time of 12:50.38. The previous day, in Dortmund, Gabriela Szabo set herself a 5000m target time of 14:47.5, over 15 seconds inside Liz McColgan's world indoor record, and crossed the finish line in 14:47.35!

Two more records were created in Stockholm where Maria Mutola ran 1000m in 2:30.94 (still unbroken) and Nicole Humbert vaulted 4.56m a few days after Emma George had raised the outdoor record to 4.60m in Australia.

The climax of the winter track and field season was the World Indoor Championships in the Japanese city of Maebashi. With championship records broken in 11 events, including world records in both 4x400m relays (USA 3:02.83 and Russia 3:24.25), the standard was the best yet. Gebrselassie (7:53.57/3:33.77) and Szabo (4:03.23/8:36.42) scored unique 1500m/3000m doubles, while Iván Pedroso had to produce the second longest jump in indoor history of 8.62m to overtake a startling European record of 8.56m by Yago Lamela and thus equal the record in any event of four consecutive titles. Jason Gardener broke Linford Christie's European 60m record with 6.46 for third place behind the American duo of Maurice Greene (6.42) and Tim Harden (6.43), but Christie had the distinction of coaching Jamie Baulch to victory in the 400m (45.73), the first Briton to win a global 400m title since Eric Liddell in 1924. Baulch's sparkling 44.78 anchored Britain to third in the relay. Another Welshman, Colin Jackson, finally won the 60m hurdles championship. Fourth in 1987, he had finished second 2/100ths behind Roger Kingdom in 1989 and Mark McKoy's flier in 1993 and won another silver in 1997, just 1/100th behind Anier García. This time he had 2/100ths to spare over Reggie Torian in 7.38. There was a third British gold medallist as triple jumper Ashia Hansen opened her account with 15.02m, third longest ever indoors, but was disappointed not to break her world indoor record of 15.16m.

Belfast was the venue for the World Cross Country Championships in which Paul Tergat won an unprecedented fifth consecutive title, leading Kenya to their 14th successive team gold medals. The course was in parts a quagmire, causing even some of the world's most accomplished cross country exponents to slip and slide, out of control, but Tergat always looked composed and elegant even on the heaviest of the muddy stretches. Who would have thought that the 16 year-old Ethiopian who placed ninth in the junior race, 49 seconds behind the winner, would one day surpass Tergat's record? His name: Kenenisa Bekele. Another youngster with a golden future was Kenya's 15 year-old Vivian Cheruiyot, runner-up in the junior women's race who at the time was reportedly just 1.46m (4ft 9 1/2in) tall. She won that title the following year and in 2016, by then all of 1.55m (5ft 1in) and 38kg, she would be crowned Olympic 5000m champion!

There was a very unforunate accident at those championships. My friend Lionel Peters, who was at the course to report on the junior events for his newsletter, sustained a heavy fall, severely injuring a leg. During an operation the following week he suffered two heart attacks and very nearly died, saved only by his devoted wife Sigrid insisting on a particular treatment, and he remained in hospital for several weeks. In effect he was given a 14-year reprieve but his health never fully recovered. He died at St Luke's Hospice in Harrow in 2013, aged 76.

It would be another momentous year for the marathon, starting with London in April.

Joyce Chepchumba earned more money for a single race than any other female athlete in history when she pocketed around one third of a million dollars for winning in what the organisers claim to be a world's best time of 2:23:22 in a women-only race on an approved course. The 28 year-old Kenyan was awarded a $125,000 bonus to go with her first prize of $55,000, a women-only course record payment of $25,000 and another $25,000 for breaking 2:24 ... plus an appearance fee variously reported as $100,000-120,000. The London Marathon organisers were happy to pay the world record bonus as it brought massive publicity for their campaign to bring the women's marathon record policy into line with other athletics events where competition against men precludes official recognition of a performance. "There is a common belief in the sport now that only women-only races should be eligible for records," declared Alan Storey, general manager of the London Marathon. "We're in a transitional period."

Another Kenyan woman ran much faster in a mixed marathon in September as for the second year running the Berlin Marathon produced a world record. In 1998 it was Ronaldo da Costa's 2:06:05; this time it was 2:20:43 by Germany-based Tegla Loroupe, cutting four seconds from her own figures set in Rotterdam in 1998. Halfway was reached in 1:09:47 but then she felt a slight pain in her left leg and had to slow down. Controversially, she was accompanied until 40km by three Kenyan men. That constituted pacing but she explained: "In a big mixed field I need them to protect me from other people stepping on my heels and pushing." It was the men's turn in October when Khalid Khannouchi ran 2:05:42 in Chicago. That was his third marathon – all of them on that course. He had run the then fastest ever debut marathon, 2:07:10, to win in 1997 and in 1998 was second in 2:07:19. This time Khannouchi, a Moroccan who was in the process of seeking US citizenship, received $165,000 for his win, including a $100,000 world record bonus.

In addition to producing *Who's Who in World Athletics 1999*, containing data on nearly 2500 leading athletes, I was involved, with Alain Billouin and Roberto Quercetani, in selecting and describing 100 great moments during the 20th century for the IAAF's *The Magic of*

Athletics publication, edited by Nick Davies. This was one of those challenging but fascinating historical projects so dear to my heart and my 34 contributions included Jim Thorpe's ill-fated all-round triumphs at the 1912 Olympics, Paavo Nurmi's "impossible" double at the 1924 Games, Fanny Blankers-Koen's four gold medals at the 1948 Olympics, Roger Bannister's pioneering sub-4 minute mile and the Chris Chataway v Vladimir Kuts classic later on in 1954, the captivating sprinting of Wilma Rudolph at the 1960 Olympics … and, rather more recently, Mary Decker's double at the 1983 World Championships, Steve Cram's barrier breaking sub-3:30 1500m in 1985, the Mike Powell-Carl Lewis duel at the 1991 World Championships, and Jonathan Edwards' astonishing triple jump exploits in 1995.

I was in Paris for the European Cup, but no British heroics this time as the men finished third and the women sixth, the only wins coming from Dwain Chambers (10.21 100m), Mark Richardson (44.96 400m), the relay teams (38.16 and 3:00.61) and Paula Radcliffe (14:48.79 5000m). Jonathan Edwards' bid for a fifth successive European Cup triple jump victory was foiled by his Russian rival Denis Kapustin, 17.40m to 17.24m.

The four-trial format in the throws and horizontal jumps proved as frustrating and ill-conceived as previously. For example, Edwards was just getting into his stride (16.89m and 17.10m from behind the board, 17.20m and 17.24m) when it was all over. With a speedier measuring procedure six rounds could probably be accommodated in no more time than at present, if that is considered to be so important. EAA, please reconsider! They haven't.

Less than 36 hours after returning by Eurostar from Paris I was flying out from Heathrow in the company of Sir Eddie (well, he was in first class, I was in economy!). Our BA flight was to Seattle, and then transferring to Alaska Airlines for the short hop to Eugene, Oregon. I was in the process of fulfilling a long-standing ambition: to experience the unique atmosphere of Tracktown USA. The occasion was the American Championships and the appreciative and knowledgeable crowd witnessed numerous excellent performances as athletes battled for a place in the top three to gain selection for the World Championships two months later in Seville.

Maurice Greene, who a week or so earlier had broken the world 100m record in Athens with a time of 9.79, gave that event a miss because as defending world champion he was given a wild card. Instead he ran the 200m where he would have faced Michael Johnson had the world record holder not withdrawn with an injury. Greene won in a wind assisted 19.93, leaving Dennis Mitchell – about to serve a two-year drugs ban – to take the 100m in a windy 9.97. Highlight of the men's field events was Jeff Hartwig's US pole vault record of 6.02m, going on to fail at the magical height of 20 feet (6.10m). Marion Jones was well beaten in the long jump, won by Dawn Burrell (Leroy Burrell's sister) with 6.96m, but returned to take the 200m in 22.10. Gail Devers, edged by 1/100th in the 100m by Inger Miller's windy 10.96, went on to win the 100m hurdles – an event she had not contested seriously for three years – in a barely wind assisted 12.54. Six days after collecting a $100,000 bonus for becoming the first American woman to vault 15 feet (clearing 4.59m), Stacy Dragila won with 4.45m. She would later win the inaugural world title with 4.60m, matching Emma George's world record.

In the lead-up to the World Championships, the first 9000 point decathlon came tantalisingly close when Tomás Dvorák of the Czech Republic produced his symphony of all-round athleticism in ten movements. Competing on home soil in Prague in the European Cup for Combined Events, he reeled off personal bests in the first three events – 100m in 10.54, 7.90m long jump and 16.78m shot – and followed up with a 2.04m high jump and 48.08 400m. Next day he clocked 13.73 in the 110m hurdles, threw the discus a lifetime best of 48.33m and, recovering from the traumatic experience of having his pole snap, he went on to vault 4.90m. He came up with another pb in the javelin (72.32m), so in order to match Dan O'Brien's world record score of 8891 he needed to run 1500m in 4:54.04. The real target, though, was 4:36.34 which would bring his score up to 9000. He fell just short with 4:37.20 and a score of 8994.

Three days later, on July 7, Hicham El Guerrouj ran a mile in the fabulous time of 3:43.13, a world record which stands to this day. My colleague Peter Matthews was present, commentating along with Steve Ovett for TV, and he reported for AI: "There were perfect conditions at Rome's Golden Gala meeting. It was warm and still, the pacemaking was superb, and the king of the middle distances took another huge chunk off a world record. But this time it was not just the sublime Moroccan against the clock, but we were privileged to see a terrific race, for he was pressed all the way by the prodigious Kenyan, Noah Ngeny, the young man who had taken him through the vital third lap of his 1500m world record a year ago. The three-quarter mile split was 2:47.9, at which point El Guerrouj led. But he had company, for just behind (2:48.2) was Ngeny, who at 18 in 1997 had taken Jim Ryun's world junior mile record by running 3:50.41. Now Ngeny was soaring into new territory and there was a terrific battle between the two men, with El Guerrouj (3:28.21 displayed as his 1500m time) managing to stay just those vital couple of strides ahead all the way to the line." Ngeny's time of 3:43.40 was almost a second inside the previous world record, while uniquely all 16 finishers clocked inside 3:56. Ten days later, in Nice, Ngeny became also the second fastest at 1000m. It looked as though Seb Coe's world record of 2:12.18 might fall when Ngeny (pronounced nee-yen) reached 800m in a personal best of 1:44.79, as against Coe's corresponding 1:44.56, but he fell just short with 2:12.66.

I caught up with Ngeny at the Golden League meeting in Paris, where he maintained his extraordinary form by setting a Commonwealth and world age-20 1500m record of 3:28.84. Only El Guerrouj and Noureddine Morceli had ever run faster, and Ngeny might have threatened the world record of 3:26.00 but for the pacemaker going much too quickly on the first lap (53.77!). Two days later I was in Birmingham for the UK World Trials & AAA Championships. No sensational performances but Colin Jackson notched up a record ninth 110m hurdles title in a windy 13.24 and Katharine Merry moved to third on the UK all-time list at 400m (50.62), becoming only the third woman after Nellie Halstead and Kathy Cook to win national titles at 100, 200 and 400m. The top UK meeting was the British Grand Prix at Crystal Palace, which saw six all-comers' records broken, including Steve Cram's mile and Steve Ovett's 2 miles marks. El Guerrouj ran 3:47.10, merely his fifth quickest time (!), while Haile Gebrselassie clocked 8:01.72 for double the distance.

Just days before the World Championships, the IAAF announced that three celebrated athletes had failed drug tests. Dennis Mitchell, a 9.91 sprinter, had actually been caught in April 1998 and his results from that date were annulled, including his 1999 US title win. High jump world record holder Javier Sotomayor was stripped of his Pan-American Games title after cocaine had been detected in his urine sample. The Cuban, who denied using cocaine, claimed he was the victim of sabotage. The case of Britain's 1992 Olympic 100m champion Linford Christie (39) was particularly perplexing. He had retired from international competition in 1997 in order to concentrate on coaching (notably of Darren Campbell, who succeeded him as European 100m champion in 1998), but in order to show his training group that he still had it as a sprinter he came back to run a few indoor races early in 1999. He clocked the impressive 60m time of 6.57 in Karlsruhe but after running 6.59 in Dortmund he tested positive. As I wrote in my book *All-Time Greats of British Athletics* (2006):

The news came as a bombshell to the British public for whom he was a sporting icon. His sample produced an adverse finding of metabolites of the prohibited steroid nandrolone. Christie stated: "I am completely innocent of any wrongdoing and any case against me will be vigorously defended." In September the UK Athletics Disciplinary Committee unanimously decided to lift his suspension (although he had by now retired from competition anyway) and cleared him of all charges, concluding that it could not be proven beyond reasonable doubt that the substance present in Christie's sample was derived from a prohibited substance. However, the ultimate authority – the IAAF – referred the case to its independent Arbitration Panel, which in August 2000 decided that UK Athletics had reached an erroneous conclusion and that Christie had committed a doping offence and was suspended for two years. It was a sad conclusion to a momentous career. Interviewed in 2005 for the 'Observer Sports Monthly' he stated: "The fact is I can sleep at night. I love all my kids dearly and I can swear on their lives that I would never and have never taken anything to enhance my performance. That's all I can say."

Another sprinting legend, Merlene Ottey, withdrew from the World Championships after her urine sample from Luzern in July was found to be positive for nandrolone. She declared: "This has been the most difficult and emotionally draining moment of my life. I have lived my personal and athletic life with the utmost honesty and integrity. I have always proclaimed fairness in sport and adamantly oppose all use of banned substances. I will do anything in my power to find the truth and prove my innocence." In November she was cleared of drug cheating charges by the Jamaican AAA but the IAAF imposed a two-year ban. However, in July 2000 the IAAF Arbitration Panel decided there were no grounds to maintain her suspension because of a flaw in the testing procedure and she was back in competition in time for the Olympics.

I wasn't in Seville for the World Championships, content to watch all the action live on BBC and Eurosport; in fact seeing everything that mattered in more close-up detail than if I had been in the stadium. Of course, I missed the atmosphere of being there and making contact with friends and colleagues, but increasingly this would be how I would cover the major championships for AI.

The overwhelming star of those Championships, as at the 1996 Olympics, was Michael Johnson.

Now there can be no hesitation over labelling Johnson the greatest 400m runner who ever lived. To justify that accolade he needed to break Butch Reynolds' 1988 world record of 43.29 to add to his Olympic and world titles, and at last, after so many near misses, the record is his. After pulling up in Stockholm a month earlier there was a question over his fitness but reports of his best ever set of 3x350m in training and references to going for the world record in the right circumstances suggested all was well. Drawn in lane 5 and finding *conditions ideal for a record (hot and no wind) Johnson was timed in 11.10 at 100m, 21.22 (10.12) at 200m and 31.66 (10.44) at 300m. That gave him a six metre lead and in the straight, covering the last 100m in 11.52, he stretched his winning margin to ten metres, the widest ever in a world or Olympic 400m. His time of 43.18 won him a $100,000 bonus on top of his $60,000 first prize.*

His 43.49 anchor leg helped the USA to 4x400m victory in 2:56.45, but as in 1997 the American team was disqualified years later because of Antonio Pettigrew's admission that he was doping at that time. Although originally the recipient of ten gold medals at World Championships (2 at 200m, 4 at 400m, 4 at 4x400m), Johnson had to settle for eight, equalling Carl Lewis's record haul.

Other highlights in the men's track events included a superb sprint double by Maurice Greene in times of 9.80 (second quickest ever despite an early stumble) and 19.90; a fourth 10,000m title by Haile Gebrselassie, who in very hot weather produced a 26.3 last 200m to outsprint Paul Tergat in 27:57.27; while, utilising his unrivalled dip to great effect, Colin Jackson (13.04 110m hurdles) became the first Briton to win a second world title. Particularly notable was the 1500m.

Never has there been a global championship 1500m to match the speed of this one. Seb Coe's Olympic record is 3:32.53, the World Championships record was Noureddine Morceli's 3:32.84, but Hicham El Guerrouj came up with the fifth quickest ever time of 3:27.65, slowing down to blow kisses to the crowd before the finish after slaughtering the opposition. To the dismay of the big-kicking Spanish trio, who would have liked a slow race, El Guerrouj's team-mate Adil El Kaouch offered himself as a sacrificial lamb, reaching 400m in 54.31 and 800m in 1:52.15 with El Guerrouj hitting the front some 50m later to pass the bell in 2:33.78. By 1200m (2:46.79) he was away and flying, covering the last lap in 53.87. "This guy is incredible," gasped Coe. "He made the others look ordinary and they are far from that." Indeed, Noah Ngeny in second place trimmed his Commonwealth record to 3:28.73.

Jackson was Britain's only winner, but there were six other medallists. The 4x100m squad of Jason Gardener, Darren Campbell, Marlon Devonish and Dwain Chambers (third in the 100m in 9.97, second only to Christie on the European all-time list) finished runners-up to the Americans in a European record of 37.73; while Denise Lewis (6724) placed second to Eunice Barber (6861) – yes, the Barber of Seville – in the heptathlon. Then there was Paula in the 10,000m.

They don't award medals for courage in athletics but if they did there should be one for Paula Radcliffe, who enabled this to be the greatest ever distance race for women. Despite 30°+ heat she led for most of the race at incredible speed for the conditions, smashed her Commonwealth record by over 13 seconds and destroyed such brilliant runners as Fernanda Ribeiro (who dropped out at 6km) end even Tegla Loroupe, who had to let go early on the last lap. The only problem was that despite Radcliffe's Herculean efforts she could not shake off world 8km cross country champion Gete Wami, who proceeded to outkick the Briton over the last 200m having not led for a single stride until then. Wami's African and Ethiopian record of 30:24.56 was the fifth fastest ever run, while Radcliffe's 30:27.13 ranks sixth. The first half was covered in a respectable 15:25.24, the second 5000m in a remarkable 14:59.32.

Britain's revelation of the year was chirpy 21 year-old decathlete Dean Macey, who had created a stir in May when he scored 8347 points from a previous best of 7480 when placing second in the 1996 World Junior Championships. This time he set a legal 100m pb of 10.69, was close to his best at long jump and high jump and cut his 400m time from 47.49 to 46.72, astonishing for a man whose best before May was 50.41! That gave him a first day score of 4546 for second place, close behind the new world record holder Tomás Dvorák's 4582. On day two Macey was still on a roll as he improved to 14.36 in the hurdles but despite overcoming a broken pole yet raising his best to 4.60m the Briton was back to fourth after eight events. Reduced to one attempt because of an elbow injury, Macey nevertheless threw the javelin a pb of 64.03m. That took him into third place and yet another pb in the 1500m (4:29.31) promoted him to the silver medal with a score of 8556, Dvorák winning with 8744. The other British medallist, and certainly not a happy bunny, was Jonathan Edwards, third in the triple jump with 17.48m. "I couldn't envisage not winning," he said. "It was a complete disaster." Not in comparison to Ashia Hansen, who followed two fouls with a despairing effort from a vast distance behind the board. It measured just 13.39m and she, so brilliant at the World Indoors, finished last of 12 in the final.

The women's sprints were fairly dramatic. Marion Jones retained her 100m title in her best ever low altitude time of 10.70, ahead of Inger Miller who improved at the meeting from 10.96 to 10.79, but after picking up a bronze medal in the long jump Jones suffered a spasm in her back during her 200m semi-final, collapsed and was stretchered off the track. The title went to her US team-mate Miller, whose Jamaican father, Lennox Miller, won Olympic 100m medals in 1968 and 1972. Inger made a huge step forward in this event too, from 22.10 to 21.77. In retrospect, one does not know what to believe in those sprint events, for Jones and the third (Ekateríni Thánou) and fourth (Zhanna Pintusevich) finishers in the 100m all subsequently served doping bans, while Miller received a public warning and retrospectively forfeited her third place in the World Indoor 60m earlier in the year after testing positive for caffeine.

From Seville most of the world's elite athletes made for the closing stages of the Golden League. First stop was Brussels where Wilson Kipketer, having claimed his third world title, ran the fastest 800m of the year with 1:42.27, El Guerrouj moved to second on the all-time list with his 7:23.09 3000m and a practically unknown Kenyan by the name of Charles Kamathi clocked the year's quickest 10,000m time of 26:51.49. Two days after winning the 1500m there in 3:29.19, Ngeny turned his attention back to the 1000m in Rieti and, despite his heavy racing schedule, reached a new peak by breaking Coe's world record with 2:11.96. He sped through the first 400m in 49.9 and reached 800m in his fastest time of 1:44.62. That record still stands.

So too does El Guerrouj's equally wondrous 2000m time of 4:44.79 in Berlin. With 400m splits of 57.9, 57.5, 57.0, 57.2 and 55.2 it's estimated that he reached the mile mark in 3:50.9 before covering almost another lap at faster speed. Fifth in that race, by the way, was 24 year-old Bernard Lagat, then of Kenya and later of USA, who is still competing at a high international level. With victories in the 800m (1:44.03) and 5000m (14:40.59), Wilson Kipketer and Gabriela Szabo shared the million dollar Golden League jackpot. Szabo enjoyed another super payday four days later in Munich when she scooped $250,000, as did steeplechaser Bernard Barmasai, as Grand Prix champions.

With the track season over, Pat and I took a week's vacation in the delightful Italian resort of Cattolica and in October I paid my second visit of the year to Las Vegas, having tacked on a few days there after the US Championships. It proved to be my final stay at the Stardust. It was an enriching experience, though not financially so, as Debbie Reynolds – of whom I had been a fan ever since *Singin' In The Rain* – was on stage for her entertaining, nostalgic and somewhat bawdy one-woman show and I even managed to exchange a few words after her performance. I was sad to hear of her passing at the end of 2016, the day after her daughter Carrie Fisher died.

So who were THE athletes of the 20th century? We asked AI readers to name their three greatest male and female athletes since the year 1900, and more than 200 responded. No fewer than 33 men and 33 women were nominated but two athletes were dominant, the same two who topped an IAAF poll.

1. Carl Lewis USA 304 points (76 first place votes). Born 1.7.1961. Won nine Olympic gold medals (100m, 200m, long jump, 4x100m), including all four of those events in 1984 and won long jump in four consecutive Games 1984-96; won eight world titles 1983-91; set world records at 100m and long jump (indoors); also unofficial world sea-level bests at 200m and long jump; was unbeaten at long jump for 10 years.

2. Paavo Nurmi FIN 214 (42). Born 13.6.1897; died 2.10.1973. Amassed nine Olympic gold medals between 1920 and 1928, including the 1924 1500/5000m double in the space of an hour, and set 31 world records between 1921 and 1931 at distances ranging from 1500m to 20,000m.

3. Jesse Owens USA (41). Born 12.9.1913; died 31.3.1980. Famed for two multi-event exploits. In 1935 he set six world records in 45 minutes (100y, a long jump record which stood for 25 years, 200m/220y, 200m/220y hurdles) and at the Berlin Olympics in 1936 he won gold medals for the 100m, 200m, long jump and 4x100m relay.

4, Emil Zátopek TCH 130 (16); 5, Sergey Bubka URS/UKR 92 (6); 6, Al Oerter USA 61 (6); 7, Michael Johnson USA 35 (4); 8, Haile Gebrselassie ETH 31 (4); 9, Ed Moses USA 22 (1); 10, Herb Elliott AUS 19 (3).

WOMEN

1. Fanny Blankers-Koen NED 357 (96). Born 26.4.1918; died 25.1.2004. Heroine of the 1948 Olympics with golds in the 100m, 200m, 80m hurdles and 4x100m relay, but that was late in her career and she had set the first of 20 world records in 1938; her world records came at 100y, 100m, 200m, 220y, 80m hurdles, high jump, long jump, pentathlon and relays!

2. Irena Szewinska POL 194 (27). Born 24.5.1946. She made her name (as Kirszenstein) at 18 in the 1964 Olympics with 4x100m gold plus 200m and long jump silvers; the following year she was a world record holder for 100m and 200m; in 1968 she won Olympic 200m gold and later (1974) she became the first sub-50 sec 400m runner and was crowned Olympic champion at that distance in 1976.

3. Jackie Joyner-Kersee USA 122 (18). Born 3.3.1962. Simply the greatest multi-event competitor in history. After finishing a close second in the 1984 Olympics she did not lose a completed heptathlon contest for 12 years! She won two Olympic and two world titles and in 1988 set a world record that has never been threatened. As a long jumper she tied the world record and won two world titles and an Olympic gold.

4, Marita Koch GDR 91 (16); 5, Iolanda Balas ROU 87 (14); 6, Florence Griffith Joyner USA 60 (9); 7, Wilma Rudolph USA 57 (8); 8, Heike Drechsler GDR/GER 41 (3); 9, Grete Waitz NOR 30 (2); 10, Ingrid Kristiansen NOR 28 (4).

35. RISE AND FALL OF MARION JONES (2000)

It was Olympic year with the athletics events in Sydney starting in late September. For most of the world's top athletes that was all that really mattered in the 2000 season. Everything beforehand was simply preparation for the supreme test. Unhappily, that preparation in all too many cases involved the use of performance enhancing drugs. The most acclaimed winner, and deservedly so, was Australia's own Cathy Freeman in the 400m, but at the time the star performer of the Games was Marion Jones. Her aim was to win five gold medals. She didn't succeed in achieving that but she still made Olympic history by becoming the first woman to pick up five medals in a single Games. She collected gold in the 100m, 200m and 4x100m relay, and bronze in the long jump and 4x400m relay. It was a fabulous display of talent ... and cheating. Were those years when, thanks to doping, she was the darling of track fans and media worth it? She finished up disgraced, jailed even, and the medals had eventually to be returned. Her cheating cost many an honest rival the fame and fortune they deserved, although it's an indictment of her range of events that so many of her contemporaries also received doping related bans at some stage of their careers. I'll return to the highs and lows of the Games later in this chapter.

Wilson Kipketer, who had set world indoor 1000m records of 2:15.25 and 2:14.96, gave the European Indoor Championships in Gent a miss, but the 800m was still notable for the victory of 18 year-old Yuriy Borzakovskiy, who had the previous month clocked the remarkable time of 1:44.35, a mark bettered indoors only by Kipketer. I was very impressed by the nature of his run in Gent, describing him as the most exciting young European middle distance runner in years. With ability and self confidence astonishing for someone so young and relatively inexperienced, and quite unawed by the occasion in his first major senior championship, he simply played with his rivals and left them for dead in the closing stages, not surprising as he covered the final 200m in close to 25 sec. His time was a modest 1:47.92 but the second 400m took him only 51.7/51.8. He would go on to enjoy a stellar career, the highlight of which would be his Olympic victory in 2004, and his usual tactic of running at even pace, overhauling flagging opponents in the finishing straight, always made for a thrilling spectacle. No sooner had he retired from racing at 33 than he was appointed Russian head coach.

I was pleased to witness British wins in the two sprints. Despite an early stumble, Jason Gardener equalled the 60m championship record of 6.49, while world junior champion Christian Malcolm took the 200m in 20.54. A distant last in the final, in 21.79, was a Greek by the name of Konstadínos Kedéris. Guess what ... seven months later he would be crowned Olympic champion!

The first major exploit outdoors came in March courtesy of Michael Johnson. Racing in high altitude Pretoria, he covered 300m in 30.85 which remained the world best until 2017. Apart from a couple of early season walking marks by a pair of Russians, neither of whom fared well at the Olympics, there were no other world bests by men in 2000. The women did better with Stacy

Dragila in the pole vault and Trine Hattestad with the new specification javelin claiming official world records – and both went on to earn Olympic glory.

It was delightful news in June that Mary Peters, now 60, had been made a Dame in the Queen's Birthday Honours for services not only to sport but to the troubled community in her adopted homeland of Northern Ireland (she was born in the outskirts of Liverpool and moved to the province when she was 11). Following her retirement from competition she raised a huge amount of money for what became the Mary Peters Track at Queens University, Belfast; she qualified as a senior coach, was British women's team manager at the 1980 and 1984 Olympics and served a term as president of the British Athletics Federation. An equally welcome, if belated, honour was accorded former world 880y and mile record holder Sydney Wooderson, who at 85 was created an MBE.

My collaboration with Larry Eder of *American Track & Field* magazine and Shooting Star Media, Inc brought forth two more books during the summer. One was *Who's Who in Olympic Track & Field 2000* containing biographical and statistical data on nearly 2500 athletes. The longest entries were for Michael Johnson, Daniel Komen, Haile Gebrselassie, Colin Jackson, Marion Jones, Merlene Ottey and Heike Drechsler. The other book was *History of Olympic Track & Field Athletics*, a revised and updated edition of my volume of four years earlier.

Speaking of Ottey, she started her comeback following the lifting of her questionable doping suspension by setting a good but unexceptional world over-40 100m best of 11.42. That was just a case of dipping her toe in the water as she clocked 11.09 in the Jamaican Championships to make her sixth Olympic team, 20 years after her first. Faster and faster she went, progressing to 10.99 into a 1.2m wind in Greece and with the wind not too far over the limit at 2.4m she was timed at 10.91 in an Australian pre-Olympic meeting!

The long drive from London to Gateshead and back in July for the European Cup was well worth it.

Despite the absence of such first choice selections as Jason Gardener, Colin Jackson, Jonathan Edwards, Mark Proctor, Steve Backley and Iwan Thomas (4x400m), the British men's team rose magnificently to the occasion as the Spar European Cup returned to Gateshead, scene of Britain's first victory in 1989. The home side held a two-point lead over Italy at the end of the first day, with cup holders Germany only sixth, but the formbook indicated that Germany – with so many strong events on the second day – would still emerge the winners. However, in the most dramatic of climaxes the Germans seriously under-performed in the 4x400m and Britain squeaked home by half a point for the narrowest win in European Cup history.

The British event winners were Darren Campbell (a very late substitute for Gardener who was injured warming up) in the 100m, Christian Malcolm 200m, Jamie Baulch 400m, Chris Rawlinson 400m hurdles, Larry Achike triple jump and the 4x100m squad. The women's team placed sixth, just clear of the relegation zone, with Russia retaining the trophy. The only (and unexpected) home winner was Helen Pattinson in the 1500m (she was later better known as UK steeplechase record holder Helen Clitheroe), but 42 year-old shot putter Judy Oakes also excelled herself by placing third in a record 12th Cup appearance.

Two days after getting home it was time to travel out with Sir Eddie to California.

As is inevitable with the "sudden death" formula for selection, the US Olympic Team Trials in a baking hot Sacramento provided one dramatic situation after another, climaxing in the final 200m event with neither Michael Johnson nor Maurice Greene even finishing the race. Thus Johnson (who did win the 400m by almost a second in 43.68) will be unable to go for a second Olympic 200m crown. He and 100m winner Maurice Greene [10.01 after a 9.93 heat] can now aspire to just one individual and one relay gold medal apiece, but Marion Jones' dream of winning five events in Sydney is still intact. She took the 100m in 10.88, 200m in 21.94 and long jump with 7.02m, and has ensured her place in both relays. Regina Jacobs was a double champion, winning a fine 1500m race against Suzy Favor-Hamilton in 4:01.01 and then setting an American 5000m record of 14:45.35; while on a particularly eventful final day there was also a brilliant US 100m hurdles record of 12.33 by Gail Devers and a world pole vault record of 4.63m by Stacy Dragila. Among so many other superlative performances mention must be made of John Capel's 19.85 200m, hurdling marks of 12.97 by Allen Johnson, 47.62 by Angelo Taylor and 53.33 by Sandra Glover, a 22.12m shot put by Adam Nelson and an amazing women's 800m race in which all three Olympic places were filled by members of the Clark family! Enthusiastic, sell-out crowds in excess of 23,000 each day brought the total attendance to 187,104, easily breaking the US Trials record.

For the first time ever in a 200m race with a negative wind reading three men broke 20 sec ... and practically nobody noticed! The occasion was the most hyped 200m duel in history and all eyes were on Olympic champion and world record holder Michael Johnson and world champion Maurice Greene, but neither man reached the finish. It was a dismaying, somewhat surreal, sight. First Johnson collapsed rounding the bend [hamstring cramp] and seconds later, early in the straight, Greene [hamstring tear] pulled up. While the packed stadium stared in disbelief at the two stricken superstars, the race for Olympic places continued. The race typified what the US Olympic Trials are all about. The rigid 1-2-3 formula had just claimed two of its most celebrated victims and the Sydney Olympic 200m will be much the poorer for their absence, and yet the system – almost unanimously backed by the athletes – prevailed. On an afternoon when the temperature out of the shade reached 118°F (48°C), 21 year-old Capel clocked 19.85 but had only 3/100ths to spare over Floyd Heard, the 1986 and 1989 US champion and 13 years his senior. His previous best of 19.95 was set in 1987.

A feature film, "Lean On Me", was made about the life of Joe Clark, a celebrated high school principal, played by Morgan Freeman. There could be a sequel, except that even Hollywood might consider the script too fanciful. First there was his daughter Joetta, who though she clocked her best time of 1:57.84 in 1998, aged 36, appeared to be over the hill this year. Another much younger daughter, Hazel (22), broke 2 minutes for the first time this year; while daughter-in-law Jearl Miles-Clark (who is married to J.J.Clark, coach to all three) is US record holder at 1:56.40. The objective was for all three Clarks to make the Olympic 800m team, an unprecedented family act ... and they did it! It was Hazel who prevailed in 1:58.97, equalling her best time, ahead of Jearl 1:59.12 and Joetta 1:59.49.

From Sacramento I flew to Las Vegas and for the first time stayed at the Flamingo Hotel, which when it opened in 1946 – owned by notorious mobster Bugsy Siegel – was the first luxury hotel on the Strip. Then it was a low-rise 105 room property; now it soared to 28 storeys with more than 3600 rooms. The Flamingo became my hotel of choice for the next 16 years. Not only did I love having breakfast adjacent to the wildlife habitat with swans, carp and of course flamingos very much in evidence, but after a few visits the extent of my play on the slot machines entitled me to free accommodation for up to five nights per visit. How could I resist?

Attention switched back to Europe and, in Oslo, Norway's own Trine Hattestad improved on her world javelin record of 68.22m from the previous month with 69.48m. With the centre of gravity moved forward and the surface area increased, the new specification javelin did not fly as far as the old model, which meant that Petra Felke's 80.00m throw from 1988 would never be approached. Two middle distance races of some significance: Noah Ngeny beat a star-studded 800m field in a personal best of 1:44.49 and Hicham El Guerrouj took the mile in 3:46.24. The two clashed a week later at the British Grand Prix at Crystal Palace.

It speaks volumes for El Guerrouj's talent and style that he made a sub-3:46 mile look disarmingly easy! While everyone else, including his only credible rival Noah Ngeny (clocking his second best time of 3:47.67), were visibly giving their all, the Moroccan appeared to float around the four laps of the celebrated Emsley Carr Mile. Towed through the first half in an even-paced 1:52, the world record holder moved ahead and reached three-quarters in 2:49.2 some 8m clear of Ngeny. "At the three-quarter stage he wasn't even breathing heavily; it was just astonishing," observed an incredulous Lord Coe. "He's the best I've seen, by a long way." His last 440y took 56.8 and the time of 3:45.96 was his fifth and the world's eighth quickest ever.

El Guerrouj and Ngeny crossed swords again in Zürich, this time over 1500m, and it was closer this time. El Guerrouj won in 3:27.21 with Ngeny setting a Kenyan record of 3:28.12 just ahead of his then compatriot Bernard Lagat (3:28.51). A 54.97 last lap carried the winner to the third fastest ever time, behind his own 3:26.00 and 3:26.45 in 1998, while Ngeny and Lagat's times had been bettered only by one other runner, Noureddine Morceli. In Brussels, El Guerrouj produced yet another cracking mile time of 3:47.91, followed in Berlin by 3:30.90 for 1500m There were no performances of that calibre at the British Olympic Trials and AAA Championships in Birmingham but there was one extraordinary record as Judy Oakes won her 17th and final outdoor national shot title over a 21-year period.

To mark the 50th anniversary of the founding of the Association of Track & Field Statisticians, the ATFS's inaugural president Roberto Quercetani and former ATFS secretary general Bob Phillips produced a marvellous 180-page publication, *The ATFS Golden Jubilee Book*. No fewer than 41 ATFS members from 20 countries contributed articles. Among them, Roberto described how the Association was formed during the European Championships in Brussels, Bob reflected on the 1950 athletics scene, Norris McWhirter wrote about Harold Abrahams, Peter Lovesey delved into the ancient history of athletics statistics, Peter Matthews explained how the ATFS Annual was prepared, Lennart Julin revealed eye-opening facts behind many official results … and so much more. My own contribution was a history of the NUTS, founded in 1958.

We modelled the NUTS structure on that of the ATFS – an organisation which we had always held in awe as well as esteem – and we counted ourselves fortunate that we had close links to the parent body through Harold Abrahams, our first president, and another icon in Norris McWhirter, the holder of that office since Harold's death in 1978. Several NUTS stalwarts have made important contributions to the ATFS – not least Bob Sparks, who as a long-serving and highly-respected chairman of the world body has continued to devote considerable time and energy to the organisation despite daunting medical problems affecting him and his wife. Bob Phillips, who does such a marvellous job in editing the lively and wide-ranging NUTS quarterly, "Track Stats", succeeded Norris as secretary-general of the ATFS in the late 1960s and was also responsible during his years with "World Sports" for editing the sacred "International Athletics Annual", while Andrew Huxtable (who became secretary-general in 1980) performed sterling work for many years as the ATFS bulletin editor.

During the 1970s Peter Matthews and Richard Hymans became increasingly more involved with the compilation of world lists, and when Peter began editing the ATFS annual in 1984 it evolved into the huge and comprehensive reference work which is so widely used and appreciated worldwide. In 1988 Dave Martin, who had succeeded Andrew Huxtable as NUTS secretary, did likewise as ATFS secretary-general and continued in that office until 1993. This year Les Crouch stepped in as acting president. There are so many other NUTS members who have laboured mightily over the years. People like Liz Sissons, Tim Lynch-Staunton, Ian Hodge, Alan Lindop, Peter Martin, Tony Miller, Keith Morbey, Ian Smith, Eric Cowe and Martin Rix are just some of the unsung heroes, as is computer wizard Rob Whittingham, who in recent years has been responsible for financing and publication of the 400-page annual.

Suspicions surrounding Chinese female runners surfaced again in September.

Controversial coach Ma Junren and six of the seven female long distance runners in his "Ma Family Army" squad who had been selected for the Olympics were axed just prior to departure for Sydney. The official Chinese Xinhua news agency stated that Dong Yanmei (second fastest ever 5000m performer with 14:29.82), Song Liqing (world age-17 best of 14:45.71), Yin Lili (3:53.91 1500m, 14:39.96 5000m, 30:39.98 10,000m), Lan Lixin (3:53.97, 14:45.33, 30:39.41), Li Linnan and Dai Yanyan had been deleted from the team roster. Only Li Ji (32:14.97) had retained her place. A Chinese official confirmed that some of the runners trained by Ma were axed from the team because of blood test problems. There has been intense speculation in the media that the action was not unconnected with the announcement that testing for EPO would be carried out in Sydney and that China, a strong candidate to host the 2008 Olympics, did not want to run the risk of embarrassing drug positives at the Games. A later report indicated that Yin Lili tested positive for a stimulant in the pre-Olympic doping tests and has been suspended for two years by the China AA. At the same time they have cleared all other Ma Junren's runners and they are free to compete at the Chinese Championships.

Li Ji, a junior, placed seventh in the Olympic 10,000m in 31:06.94 ... but it was revealed the following year that she had tested positive for testosterone in July 2000 and she received a two year doping ban, as did Song Liqing and Yin Lili. Dong Yanmei, Lan Lixin and Dai Yanyan did compete in the Chinese Championships but registered mediocre times.

And so to the Olympics, the athletics events being held between September 22 and October 1.

For the first time since 1948 there were no world records set at the Olympic athletics, but despite that and the fact that winning marks were inferior to those set in the unfairly maligned Atlanta Games in 26 of the 43 events common to both occasions (plus two the same), the Sydney Olympics proved wildly successful. Unprecedented crowds, with attendances between 85,806 and 97,432 for each of the morning sessions and from 99,428 to 112,524 for the evening sessions, totalling 1,597,104 in all (over 300,000 more than in Atlanta), provided a fantastic atmosphere and the athletes responded accordingly.

We had some superb competition and the fourth day was one of the greatest in the history of our sport. The highlight for the crowd was undoubtedly Cathy Freeman's victory at 400m [49.11] run in a massive roar of public support and illuminated by the flashing of thousands of cameras as she strode around the track. But there was much else besides, with victories for all-time greats such as Michael Johnson [43.84 400m], Jonathan Edwards [17.71m triple jump], Maria Mutola [1:56.15 800m] and Gabriela Szabo [14:40.79 5000m], the closest approach to a world record from pole vault attempts [at 4.65m] by Stacy Dragila and Tatiana Grigorieva, and above all one of the greatest races we have ever seen, the men's 10,000m which culminated in an epic sprint to the finish in which the sheer mental strength of Haile Gebrselassie [27:18.20], below par all year, overcame the challenge from Paul Tergat [27:18.29].

Based on points awarded for the first eight places, the British team finished fourth behind the USA, Russia and Germany, and the medal tally was two gold, two silver and two bronze.

Four years after he was expected to become Olympic champion, the world record holder finally fulfilled his destiny. Now 34 (thus becoming easily the oldest ever winner of this event), Jonathan Edwards has remained the world's no 1 for most of the time since Atlanta and, with the virtual retirement of Kenny Harrison, no truly outstanding challenger has emerged. Edwards went ahead with his second jump of 17.37m, minutes later Denis Kapustin responded with 17.46m, but in round 3 Edwards leapt to 17.71m, the world's longest of the year. With three in the top six [Larry Achike 5th with 17.29m, Phillips Idowu 6th with 17.08m] this was Britain's best ever performance in an Olympic field event.

With all three having been beset by injuries this year, no one quite knew what to expect [in the heptathlon] from world champion Eunice Barber, defending champion Ghada Shouaa and world silver medallist Denise Lewis. Shouaa pulled up almost immediately in the hurdles, but Barber looked to be in fine shape as she flew to a 12.97 win and Lewis performed well for 13.23. Barber kept up the pressure with the equal highest jump of 1.84m but Lewis made an error by passing 1.78m before failing at 1.81m and she dropped to 8th place after two events, 152 points behind Barber. Lewis made up with fine shot putting [15.55m] and the positions were transformed. Atlanta silver medallist Natalya Sazanovich led by 30 points from Lewis and for Barber it was the beginning of the end. The overnight placings were: 1, Sazanovich 3903; 2, Natalya Roshchupkina 3872; 3, Lewis 3852 [24.34 200m]; ... 7, Barber 3707.

Barber took only one long jump before retiring injured. Lewis, too, was having problems with her left achilles tendon but stayed in the hunt with a 6.48m leap. Disaster for Roshchupkina, who dropped from 2nd to 8th. After five events: Sazanovich 4910, Lewis 4853. As so often, the javelin came to Lewis's rescue. She threw 50.19m to take the lead with 5717 ahead of Sazanovich 5654 and Yelena Prokhorova 5571. All would depend on Lewis staying close enough to Sazanovich in the 800m to preserve her lead and hope that Prokhorova would not repeat the fabulous 2:04.27 she ran when winning the Russian title. Prokhorova went for it but could not sustain the pace this time and finished in 2:10.32, good enough to take the silver but Lewis [2:16.83] did enough to win by 53 points with a score of 6584. "It's not a great score," she admitted. "It was simply about winning." She revealed that a foot injury sustained in the long jump got progressively worse and she nearly didn't make it to the javelin. "I have a great team around me and the physios did everything possible to get me through. If it wasn't for them I wouldn't have made it."

The silver medals went to Steve Backley and Darren Campbell. Early in round two Backley threw an Olympic record (with the current model) of 89.85m, a distance which he might reasonably have expected to win gold – but Jan Zelezny, irritated at having to hold fire while the women's 100m victory ceremony was being staged, ploughed all his frustration as well as strength and skill into his third round effort. It landed at 90.17m and Backley knew he was destined once again to finish second best to the Czech who must surely be acknowledged as the greatest ever javelin thrower. Had Zelezny not been his contemporary, Backley would have won two Olympic golds and a silver plus a world title as well as the four European titles (effectively the global championship in those years) he had actually won. Instead he could console himself with the thought that once again he had raised his game on the big occasion (his season's best had been 86.70m) and had become the first Briton in any event to win an Olympic medal in three Games.

The absence of Michael Johnson and Maurice Greene made the 200m wide open ... but few would have predicted that Konstadínos Kedéris and Darren Campbell would take gold and silver. Prior to 2000 the Greek had a best of 20.50 and was better known as a 45.60 400m runner, while the European 100m champion was a 20.48 performer. They were drawn together in the quarter-finals with Campbell clocking 20.13 to rank as third fastest ever Briton behind John Regis and his own coach Linford Christie, while Kedéris's 20.14 was a national record. In the final, with the American hope John Capel left at the start, Campbell led into the straight but Kedéris inched past to become the first Greek man to win an Olympic running title since 1896. He improved to 20.09 with Campbell on 20.14. Kedéris went on to capture the world title in 2001 and become European champion in 2002 (clocking his best time of 19.85) but there has always been speculation over his successes as prior to the 2004 Olympics on home soil in Athens he failed to appear for a drugs test and was banned for two years.

Marion Jones took the 100m by close to four metres in 10.75 and went on to win the 200m in 21.84 ahead of Pauline Davis-Thompson of The Bahamas (22.27), place third in the long jump (6.92m) behind Heike Drechsler (6.99m) and Fiona May (6.92m), anchor the USA 4x100m relay team to bronze medals in a race won, heartwarmingly, by The Bahamas in 41.95, and run a 49.40 third leg for the winning 4x400m team (3:22.62). She was hailed as Superwoman but ultimately all of her medals had to be returned although the Court of Arbitration for Sport upheld an appeal by Jones' relay team-mates for their results to stand and their medals to be retained.

The situation in the 100m was complicated. Normally the runner-up to a proven drugs cheat like Jones would be promoted to gold medallist but because of Ekateríni Thánou's own doping history she has been denied that precious piece of metal by the IOC. Although Thánou is listed as the winner in 11.12, she and Tayna Lawrence (third across the line in 11.18) are officially bracketed as silver medallists with 40 year-old Merlene Ottey raised to bronze in 11.19. Merlene won a silver medal with Jamaica in the 4x100m, to become the most prolific female Olympic medallist with a total of nine spread over a 20-year period ... three silver and six bronze. That's a record which was equalled but in effect surpassed by Allyson Felix in 2016 as her nine comprised six gold and three silver.

Mark Butler explained the Sydney 100m situation in the IAAF's admirable *Athletics Statistics Book* which he compiled and edited prior to the 2012 Olympics. He wrote: "In October 2007, Marion Jones confessed to doping violations back to just before the 2000 Olympic Games. The following month, the IAAF Council annulled all of her results since September 1 2000. In December 2007, the IOC Executive Board decided to disqualify Jones from all events in which she had competed at the 2000 Games. It was not until December 2009 that the Board reallocated Jones's individual medals. Her 200m gold and long jump bronze went to those women who finished directly behind her, but this was not the case for the 100m where the runner-up was Thánou, who by then had served a two-year doping suspension to 2006. The IOC spokesman Mark Adams explained that Thánou 'disgraced herself and the Olympic movement by avoiding three doping tests ... she admitted anti-doping violations when she accepted a two-year suspension from the IAAF. The rankings in the actual race are a matter for the IAAF, and they are changed, but the actual awarding of any medal is not a right. Therefore, in this case, it will not happen. It is felt that with her conduct, she did not deserve to be honoured with this recognition.' Therefore, though Thánou effectively won the race, her reward remains the silver. Lawrence and Ottey were however elevated to silver and bronze. Which means that the title of 2000 Olympic 100m champion is vacant; there are two silver medallists."

Marion Jones' exploits in Sydney now count for nothing, but Cathy Freeman's 400m victory will forever be celebrated. Cathy, accorded the honour of lighting the Olympic cauldron at the opening ceremony, remains one of Australia's most famous and beloved citizens.

The dramatic departure from Sydney of reigning champion Marie-José Pérec, initially claiming she had feared for her safety but later admitting she had run away from the prospect of taking on Cathy Freeman, robbed the Games of what might have been one of the great Olympic duels ... but the vast majority of the 112,000 fans who packed the stadium for the 400m final could not have cared less. It was unthinkable that Freeman, an icon of modern Austtralia who has become a symbol of reconciliation between the white community and the indigenous population, could lose this race and – despite the unbearable pressure of all the public expectation – she rose to the occasion. Lorraine Graham ran hard to enter the finishing straight narrowly ahead of Freeman and Katharine Merry, and although the local heroine powered past for victory in 49.11, the world's fastest for four years, the Jamaican finished second four metres back in a pb of 49.58. Merry (49.72) and fast finishing Donna Fraser (49.79) became, after Kathy Cook in 1984, the second and third Britons ever to crack 50 seconds. "I don't think it can get any better than this," said Freeman, the first Aboriginal to win an Olympic athletics title. "First the opening ceremony and now an Olympic gold in front of the biggest crowd in the history of this sport. It is just incredible."

Britain's other bronze medallist was, totally unexpectedly, Kelly Holmes in the 800m. Her season's best before the Games was merely 2:00.35 whereas ten entrants had bettered 1:59.

It was an astonishing sight: Holmes, so short of training after her latest round of injuries that making the British Olympic team had for most of the year seemed a forlorn hope, was well clear of the field entering the finishing straight. It was the stuff of dreams. Okay, Maria Mutola and Stephanie Graf did steam past to take gold and silver but Holmes could not have been more delighted with her bronze. Holmes ("I had nothing to lose") took the field by surprise with an early strike and led until 50m out, finishing in a remarkable 1:56.80, second only to her 1995 UK record of 1:56.21. Mutola, still only 27 yet contesting her fourth Olympics, became the first athlete from Mozambique to win an Olympic title, the time of 1:56.15 being the world's best this year.

Frustrated as fourth place finishers were Dwain Chambers (10.08) in the 100m won by Maurice Greene in 9.97; Jon Brown (2:11:17) in the marathon, just seven seconds away from a medal; long striding Donna Fraser in that pulsating 400m (her pre-Games best was 50.85); and Paula Radcliffe in the 10,000m. Lacking the finishing powers of her main rivals, Paula's tactic was to make the pace so fast that the kickers would fall back exhausted. At the 1999 World Championships she burned off everybody except Gete Wami and this time she ran even faster with another Commonwealth record of 30:26.97 and yet came fourth as Derartu Tulu won in an African record of 30:17.49. There was some consolation later in the year when Paula won the Great North Run with a European half marathon best of 67:07 and the world title in Mexico three weeks later in 69:07 for her first global championship as a senior.

And then there was Dean Macey, fourth in a contentious Olympic decathlon. Erki Nool won the title with 8641 points ahead of Roman Sébrle (8606), Chris Huffins (8595) and Macey (8567), with injured world record breaker Tomás Dvorák finishing sixth.

Unfortunately, a controversial decision involving Nool in the discus cast a shadow over the proceedings. Following two fouls Nool faced oblivion when his third attempt was measured but was declared a foul. A protest by the Estonians, originated by his adviser Daley Thompson (like Macey, Nool is coached by Thompson's former British rival, Greg Richards), succeeded as the referee over-ruled the judges, but experts who viewed the video were in no doubt that Nool foot faulted and should have been awarded 'nool points' and it was amazing that the Jury of Appeal upheld the referee's decision when they examined the video evidence.

In other Olympic action, Nils Schumann defeated Wilson Kipketer in the 800m, 1:45.08 to 1:45.14; Hicham El Guerrouj, unbeaten at 1500m since falling at the 1996 Games, was outkicked by Noah Ngeny, 3:32.07 to 3:32.32; Angelo Taylor took the 400m hurdles in 47.50 from the inside lane (like Morgan Taylor in 1924 and John Akii-Bua in 1972); Robert Korzeniowski completed an unique 20km/50km walk double in 1:18:59 and 3:42:22; years later Nigeria were awarded the 4x400m relay title (2:58.68) after the USA were retrospectively disqualified because of doping violations by Antonio Pettigrew and Jerome Young; Gabriela Szabo (14:40.79) won a closely contested 5000m against Sonia O'Sullivan; former sprint star Irina Privalova made some kind of history by winning the 400m hurdles (53.02) in her first season at the event; and the ill-fated Kamila Skolimowska, with a world junior hammer record of 71.16, became at 17 the youngest Olympic athletics champion since high jumper Ukrike Meyfarth in 1972. Sadly, the Pole died during a training session in 2009 of a pulmonary embolism aged just 26.

Mihaele Melinte, the world record holder with 76.07m, was led away from the arena just prior to the qualifying round of this inaugural Olympic hammer contest, having been informed that she had failed a drugs test. Indeed, such was the extent of doping at the highest level that no fewer than 16 Sydney medallists either had or would in the future serve lengthy (i.e. minimum of 2 years) drug bans. Inducted into this hall of shame were Konstadínos Kedéris (1st 200m), Alvin Harrison (2nd 400m, 1st 4x400m), Tim Montgomery (1st 4x100m; ran in heat), Antonio Pettigrew (1st 4x400m), Calvin Harrison (1st 4x400m), Jerome Young (1st 4x400m; ran in heat); Marion Jones (1st 100m, 200m, 4x400m, 3rd long jump, 4x100m), Ekateríni Thánou (2nd 100m), Stephanie Graf (2nd 800m), Tatyana Kotova (upgraded 3rd long jump), Tatyana Lebedeva (2nd triple jump), Yanina Korolchik (1st shot), Irina Yatchenko (3rd discus), Olga Kuzenkova (2nd hammer), Chryste Gaines (3rd 4x100m) and Torri Edwards (3rd 4x100m).

Held a few days after the close of the Olympics, the IAAF Grand Prix Final in Doha (Qatar) was something of an anti-climax, though not for Angelo Taylor and Trine Hattestad who won $200,000 apiece, while Hattestad – along with Gail Devers and Tatyana Kotova – came away with a one-third share of the $500,000 Golden League jackpot.

Later in October, Pat and I returned to Florida, this time flying to Tampa and staying at St Pete's Beach, but Olympic year ended on a sombre note as one of the greatest of all Olympians, Emil Zátopek, died in November following a stroke. He was 78 and survived by fellow Olympic champion Dana, to whom he was married for 52 years. I paid this tribute in AI:

Emil Zátopek was an exceptional athlete, but transcending that was his humanity. He was the personification of all that is worthy in sport, and in life. He was ambitious and successful but never lost his humility and sense of wonder. He had the capacity to enjoy himself and enrich the lives of others but also a stoicism born of early hardship which carried him through the bad times when he found himself on the wrong side of the political fence. His courage, on and off the track, was remarkable.

As a runner Zátopek broke through the barriers of what was deemed humanly possible by dint of training much harder than anyone before him and by pushing himself closer to the limits than his rivals; he was an uncompromising opponent who could destroy the field from the front as in most of his 10,000m races or by summoning a fearsome kick as in the classic 1952 Olympic 5000m. He won every honour during a long career and yet remained an intensely modest man, always somewhat bemused that long after his retirement he would still be recognised and honoured wherever he travelled.

His tortured expression and torso-rolling action, each stride looking as though it would be his last before collapsing, endeared him to fans the world over. Even his closest rivals, like Alain Mimoun and Gordon Pirie, had enormous affection as well as respect for the man dubbed "The Human Locomotive" and "The Bouncing Czech". His open, friendly personality won over everybody; he was always happy to share his training "secrets" and even in Olympic heats he would encourage or joke with his fellow competitors in a bewildering variety of languages. Many an outstanding athlete is admired, hero worshipped even ... Emil Zátopek was universally loved.

For perhaps the best of Zátopek's character and generosity we turn to another legendary distance runner, Ron Clarke, a man who set a stack of world records but never managed to win a major title. Writing in "Athletics Weekly" in 1987, the Australian recalled the end of his first visit to Zátopek nearly 20 years earlier. "As he marched me through customs and onto the plane on my way out of Prague, he shook hands and, in so doing, secretly transferred a small package into my grip. When I opened it up it was his 1952 Olympic 10,000m gold medal. I thought back to the words he said as he passed it across to me, which at the time I did not understand. "Because you deserved it", he said. I wish I had. I do know no-one cherishes any gift more than I do, my only Olympic gold medal and not because of what it is ... but because of the man whose spirit it represents."

36. THE HORROR OF NINE-ELEVEN (2001)

It was a routine Tuesday afternoon. I was in my study, tapping away on the computer with Classic FM on in the background as usual when my attention was caught by a news flash. Something untoward was happening in my beloved New York. I went into the lounge, switched on the television, called out to Pat … and we watched, live, the appalling sight of the attack on the Twin Towers of the World Trade Center. It was like a Hollywood disaster movie, only this was all too real, and it just got worse as the second plane crashed into the building and both the 110-storey towers collapsed before our disbelieving eyes. As we discovered later, almost three thousand people perished. September 11 2001 – 9/11 – was a day to remember: for the pitiless fanaticism of the al-Qaeda terrorists, for the loss of so many innocent people who just happened to be in the wrong place at the wrong time, but also for the courage of all those firefighters and police oficers who at the cost of their own lives did not hesitate to attempt to rescue those trapped inside. Those horrific images will never leave me.

Months earlier we had booked a three-centre, three-week American holiday and were looking forward to recharging our batteries, and it was to a subdued yet defiant nation with heightened security that we travelled on October 7. We flew first to Las Vegas for a few days at the Flamingo; then it was off to Orlando. That proved to be a nightmare of a journey as we flew through a massive Texan storm and it was with some difficulty that we landed *en route* at Dallas-Fort Worth, the pilots being applauded by the passengers when we touched down shakily but safely. After our stay in Orlando we moved on to the Sunny Isles section of Miami Beach. While in Florida I went for 12 consecutive pre-breakfast 'runs' before it got too hot – my longest training sequence for years. How I yearned to be able to stride out again for mile after mile but by now, in my sixties, I had to settle for brisk jogging.

My first trip abroad that year had been to Lisbon for the World Indoor Championships. For the first time in the meeting's history, no world records were broken, although there was a stunning world junior best in the 60m by world junior 100m champion Mark Lewis-Francis, who finished third behind the American pair of Tim Harden (6.44) and Tim Montgomery (6.46). The 18 year-old Briton had ranked only 23rd among the entrants with a best of 6.65, so realistically all that could have been hoped for was a place in the semis. However, he won his heat in 6.61, improved to 6.56 in his semi and clocked 6.51 in the final! Maurice Greene, who had equalled his own (and still standing) world record of 6.39 at the US Championships, did not compete. The other indoor world record setters in 2001 were Gabriela Szabo (8:32.88 3000m in Birmingham but beaten by Olga Yegorova in Lisbon) and Stacy Dragila, who vaulted 4.70m at altitude in Pocatello but managed only 4.51m for fourth place at the Worlds.

One of the features of the weekend was the demise of so many newly crowned Olympic champions like Szabo and Dragila, confirming how difficult it is for an athlete to rise to the heights again so soon after fulfilling the ultimate ambition. Of the 13 gold medallists present, only Iván Pedroso (8.43m for his fifth long jump title), Maria Mutola (1:59.74 800m) and Tereza Marinova (14.91m triple jump) emerged successful.

Britain's only winner was Daniel Caines in the 400m. He came to Lisbon with an indoor personal best of 45.61 but found a time of 46.40 sufficed for victory. His mother was a formidable athlete also … Blondelle Thompson, these days a barrister, equalled the UK 100m hurdles record of 13.0 in 1974. Otherwise, the only other British medallists were Lewis-Francis, Christian Malcolm (2nd 200m, 20.76) and Jonathan Edwards (2nd with 17.26m).

No sooner had the indoor season ended than it was time for the World Cross Country Championships in Ostend … and this time there was a happier outcome for the top British runner in the Belgian town which had seen Mel Batty controversially awarded second place in 1965.

Ever since she beat Wang Junxia for the world junior cross country title back in 1992, Paula Radcliffe has striven to win the senior 8km championship. As in her track endeavours she has often come so close to the major prize. She was second in 1997, overtaken just before the line by Derartu Tulu; second again in 1998, this time defeated by Sonia O'Sullivan; third in 1999 to Gete Wami and Merima Denboba. Last year she ran herself to a state of collapse in fifth place, with Tulu the winner, and returned next day to finish fourth in the 4km event, just one second behind winner Kutre Dulecha. This year, at the eighth attempt, she finally realised her dream, in so doing becoming the first woman to win both junior and senior titles.

The Championships were staged in cold, windy conditions on a course which was exceptionally muddy in places. Strength rather than blazing speed was needed for success, and that played into Radcliffe's hands. One kilometre remaining and it was between Radcliffe and Wami, the much taller Briton desperately trying to pull away but the Ethiopian refusing to concede. Momentarily there was a sense of déjà vu when Wami moved ahead in sight of the finish, but it quickly became apparent to Radcliffe that her rival was at full stretch and not pulling away. She had enough left to produce a counterstrike and there was a beatific smile on her face as she crossed the line ahead, Wami giving up once she was overtaken. "This is the one I've always really wanted," said Radcliffe. "For me, winning this is as good as winning the Olympics." Next day, in the 4km race, Radcliffe and Wami slugged it out again. Radcliffe pulled clear of everyone else with 800m to run but this time Wami moved ahead with some 800m remaining and held Radcliffe at bay.

It's fascinating, looking back at the results in Ostend, to note that 18 year-old Kenenisa Bekele finished second in the senior 4km event the day before winning the junior title by the record margin of 33 seconds. The Ethiopian's time for the 7.7km course was 25:04 … while Britain's first scorer back in 59th place in 28:06, two days after his 18th birthday, was one Mohamed Farah! The gulf between them at that stage of their careers was equally wide on the track that summer: Bekele ran 7:30.67 for 3000m and 13:13.33 for 5000m, Farah 8:09.24 and 13:56.31 although Mo did have the distinction of winning the

European junior 5000m title. In a very close finish to the junior women's race, fith place was filled by Ethiopia's legend in the making, a 15 year-old Tirunesh Dibaba.

I don't often editorialise in AI but in April I took up two pages to demonstrate the ruinous effect of cutting the number of field event attempts should the IAAF go ahead with a proposed rule change.

Who could forget that fantastic contest for the 1991 world long jump title when, in the fifth round, Mike Powell overtook Carl Lewis with a world record breaking leap of 8.95m and we waited in suspense to see how Lewis would respond? Never in the history of athletics has there been a more dramatic duel. Well, under rule changes to be considered by the IAAF Congress in August, that competition would have been terminated after four rounds when Lewis led by 8.91m to 8.54m and the real excitement had yet to begin. Similarly, that immortal battle between Jesse Owens and Luz Long for the 1936 Olympic title would have been completed before either man produced his best jump. Lynn Davies would not have brought off his shock victory at the 1964 Olympics and Mary Rand would not have broken the world record as their longest jumps in Tokyo came in the fifth round.

Take the pole vault and the proposal to evict competitors after two instead of three failures. On that basis Cornelius Warmerdam's legendary 4.77m in 1942 would not have happened, and Sergey Bubka would not have won his single Olympic title and his tally of world titles would have fallen from six to four. High jump history would have been fundamentally changed too. Stefka Kostadinova's world record of 2.09m would not have occurred and the two Olympic winners in 1988 – Gennadiy Avdeyenko (2.38m) and Louise Ritter (2.03m) – would not even have reached the finals as they needed third attempts at 2.22m and 1.92m respectively in the qualifying competitions! Terminating Olympic discus finals after four rounds would have meant Al Oerter winning two, not four gold medals.

What I have attempted to show with these examples is how profound a difference they would make. By attempting to shorten contests the field events will not only be radically altered but damagingly downgraded. And for what purpose? The needs of television have been brought into the argument ... but they are almost irrelevant. Television never broadcasts a field event in its entirety anyway; it dips in and out or inserts highlights packages so it's immaterial to them how many attempts the athletes are given. Field events are not like sprints, which are over in a flash; they need to be savoured. Our sport of track AND FIELD is already in danger of becoming so "slick" in terms of presentation that the essence is lost. Some top meetings are evolving into pop concerts with athletics action thrown in, alienating the more traditional spectators.

I am not averse to change where it proves to be beneficial; for example the experiment with false starting zero tolerance is worth pursuing. But these field event proposals have no merit in my view and I would hope that the many men and women within the IAAF who know at first hand just what field event competition is about will throw them out. Surely they will not permit any further marginalisation of their beloved events.

Happily, the proposals were rejected and the traditional number of attempts continues at international championship level. Less happily, four attempts in the throws and horizontal jumps have increasingly become the norm in many other competitions with European Athletics in particular downgrading those events in the European Cup and its successor ... and the "music" just gets longer and louder.

One of the most tantalising of "barriers" was the 9000 point decathlon. Two prime candidates in Daley Thompson and Dan O'Brien never quite made it to 8900, while Tomás Dvorák came so very close with 8994 in 1999. It was the latter's Czech compatriot Román Sebrle who hit the target at the deservedly celebrated Götzis meeting in Austria in late May with a score of 9026 points.

Sebrle got off to a great start and never looked back. He was fastest in the 100m, equalling his personal best of 10.64, and extended his lead with a terrific lifetime best of 8.11m in the long jump, a world decathlon best. After decent shot and high jump marks of 15.33m and 2.12m he ended day one with a 47.79 400m for 4675 points, 30 points more than Dvorák when he set his world record. A 13.92 hurdles and pb discus of 47.92m stretched his lead still further before Erki Nool made up some ground in the vault (5.30m to 4.80m). A world record would be possible only if Sebrle could surpass his previous bests in the final two events, and that he did resoundingly by throwing the javelin 70.16m and clocking 4:21.98 for 1500m for a 422 point margin of victory over Nool, the man who – in very controversial circumstances – deprived him of Olympic gold.

Other early season world record breakers were Stacy Dragila, who unlike Sergey Bubka's centimetre at a time record progression, was happy to raise her pole vault best from 4.70m to 4.81m; Cuba's Osleidys Menéndez who threw the javelin 71.54m; and Poland's Justyna Bak who I witnessed knocking almost 15 seconds off the previous best for the still under-developed women's steeplechase with 9:25.31 in Nice, the first time the event had been staged at an IAAF Grand Prix meeting.

Another example of the folly of restricting throws to four rounds was provided at the British Grand Prix at Crystal Palace. Had the javelin contest been terminated after four throws, Steve Backley would have been the winner with a decent but hardly earth-shattering 85.07m with Breaux Greer second with 82.80m. However, in the final round Backley moved from third to first by unleashing a mighty throw of 90.81m. In the fifth round Eriks Rags had set a Latvian record of 86.47m and Greer finished up with 85.91m. Hicham El Guerrouj, who had clocked his fourth and the world's sixth quickest ever mile time of 3:44.95 a few weeks earlier, won the Emsley Carr Mile in an easy looking 3:49.41. Katharine Merry, whose 49.59 400m in June would prevail as the world's fastest time of the year, won in 50.67 in her first race for three weeks because of a viral infection. Her twin aims for the season were to win the world title and break Kathy Cook's long standing UK record of 49.43, but alas she had to withdraw from the Worlds. She explained: "I have been warned that if I had run three rounds in Edmonton I would have run the risk of rupturing the achilles. As a result of this advice, and having trained only twice in five weeks due to illness, I have taken the heartbreaking decision to withdraw from the championships. Despite my recent illness I felt that I could bring back a gold medal for Britain." Katharine, who was coached at the time by Linford Christie, never did hit the heights again as an athlete but she has retained a prominent position in the sport as a TV commentator and stadium presenter/interviewer, and on top of that she does a wonderful job each year hosting the England Athletics Hall of Fame awards.

It was good to revisit Edmonton, Alberta after all too long an absence (23 years) although on this occasion British athletes played only a modest role with just one gold medal (Jonathan Edwards) and one bronze (Dean Macey).

Controversy, disasters, upsets, breakthroughs, great competition, dazzling performances ... we had them all. The weather was fantastic (except for the long distance athletes) and the total attendance figure represented a daily average of 40,000, which was excellent for a non-Olympic athletics occasion held on North American soil. "It's the best ever," said IAAF general secretary István Gyulai. The outstanding performers? A difficult choice, but on the men's side two Czechs should feature at or near the top of anyone's list: Jan Zelezny, who demonstrated yet again why he is acknowledged as the greatest javelin thrower who ever lived [92.80m with Backley failing to make the final], and Tomás Dvorák, who came up with the third highest decathlon score of all time [8902]. Other claimants might include Maurice Greene for his 9.82 100m, the fastest ever time with a negative wind reading; Dmitriy Markov's 6.05m vault to equal the best ever non-Bubka mark; Jonathan Edwards' 17.92m triple jump; and Lars Riedel, winner of his fifth world discus title with the longest throw [69.72m] ever recorded in championship competition – not to mention memorable battles among the African distance runners. Of the women, Tatyana Lebedeva's 15.25m triple jump was perhaps the finest achievement, closely followed by Osleidys Menéndez's 69.53m javelin throw, the gripping pole vault duel between Stacy Dragila and Svetlana Feofanova [both 4.75m], Anjanette Kirkland's 12.42 hurdles and Zhanna Pintusevich-Block's dramatic 100m victory over Marion Jones [10.82 to 10.85].

More column inches of newspaper coverage must have been devoted to Olga Yegorova than any other athlete. Her controversial appearance in the 5000m elicited more boos than cheers and Paula Radcliffe and some of her British team colleagues were sufficiently incensed to display a banner proclaiming "EPO Cheats Out". Because of irregular procedure with her EPO test in Paris, Yegorova had her suspension overturned by the IAAF and was allowed to run, but few will have applauded her victory.

Yegorova did eventually get her comeuppance, out for four years from 2007 for an anti-doping offence, and so too did her runner-up Marta Domínguez, who was handed a three year ban. There were all too many Edmonton medallists who later (and in some cases at the time) were involved in doping. Among them was Tim Montgomery, 2nd in the 100m but retroactively disqualified, as was the winning USA 4x100m team of which he was a member. The American 4x400m squad also forfeited their gold medals because of the eventual disqualifications of Antonio Pettigrew and Jerome Young. Others who had to hand back their fraudulently gained medals were Ali Saïdi-Sief (2nd 5000m), Marion Jones (1st 100m, 2nd 200m), Kelli White (3rd 200m), Natalya Sadova (1st discus) and the USA women's 4x100m team. Keeping their medals but destined for future doping bans were Konstadínos Kedéris (1st 200m), Shawn Crawford (equal 3rd 200m), Zhanna Pintusevich-Block (1st 100m), Ekateríni Thánou (2nd 100m), Stephanie Graf (2nd 800m), Tatyana Kotova (2nd long jump), Tatyana Lebedeva (1st triple jump), Yanina Korolchik (1st shot), Vita Pavlysh (3rd shot), Olga Kuzenkova (2nd hammer) and Anastasiya Kapachinskaya (3rd 4x400m). A shocking list.

African athletes won all of the longer men's running events: Hicham El Guerrouj (3:30.68 1500m) of Morocco, Richard Limo (13:00.77 5000m), Charles Kamathi (27:53.25 10,000m) and Reuben Kosgei (8:15.16 steeplechase) from Kenya, Gezahegne Abera (2:12:42 marathon) from Ethiopia. In addition, thanks to the USA's subsequent disqualification, South Africa won the 4x100m relay. Africa's gold medal haul in the women's events was more diverse: Amy Mbacké Thiam of Senegal in the 400m (in 49.86, so spare a thought for the sidelined Katharine Merry), Maria Mutola of Mozambique (1:57.17 800m), Derartu Tulu of Ethiopia (31:48.81 10,000m), Nezha Bidouane of Morocco (53.34 400m hurdles) and Hestrie Cloete of South Africa (2.00m high jump).

Back to the two British medallists, but first a word of sympathy for Paula Radcliffe, who since her cross country triumph had set a formidable UK 3000m record of 8:26.97. She had high hopes for at least a medal in the 10,000m.

Paula Radcliffe changed her strategy as she attempted to defeat the Ethiopians for a global track title, but the result remained the same. Second to Gete Wami in the 1999 Worlds and fourth in the Olympics won by Derartu Tulu after leading most of the way, she decided this time to leave her bid until much later in the race. Too late, as it would be seen. Radcliffe held back, striking with three and a half laps remaining and the pace increased. With the three Ethiopians – Berhane Adere, Wami and Tulu – in ominously close attendance, Radcliffe covered the ninth kilometre in 2:58.80. But on the penultimate lap she was back to fourth and a 63.36 last lap carried Tulu to a narrow victory over Adere, while Wami just held off the Briton (31:50.06) for bronze. Tulu commented: "I was a little surprised by Paula's tactics; for her to pick up so late was not a good decision. I think had she pushed the pace I would not have been able to keep up."

Some may have thought that Jonathan Edwards only had to show up to have the gold medal draped round his neck, and indeed he did win with one of the longest ever jumps, but his path to the top of the podium was not that smooth. In the qualifying contest he was in deep trouble after wasting his first jump and reaching only 16.51m on his second for 16th overall. One last try ... the Edwards magic returned and he bounced out to 17.46m. In the final his third attempt was an Edwards special of 17.92m, his and the world's longest for three years. At 35 he was world champion again.

Right from the start, when Román Sebrle ran 10.91 and long jumped 7.67m, it was evident that the world record holder was carrying an injury and would be operating well below form. What was not obvious was that Dean Macey was also being hampered by a groin injury. Yet astonishingly, despite physical problems which intensified as the day wore on, the Briton was the overnight leader with 4638 after personal bests in the high jump (2.15m) and 400m (a scintillating 46.21). Just one point behind was Tomás Dvorák, who set a pb long jump of 8.07m, with Erki Nool 3rd 4531. Dvorák ran a fine 13.80 in the hurdles to open up a 68 point lead over Macey, who miraculously set a pb of 14.34 with his left thigh strapped and clearly in pain. After seven events it was Dvorák 6414, Macey 6376, Nool 6189. Nool came into his own by vaulting 5.40m to move into 2nd with 7224 to 7324 by Dvorák and 7195 by Macey, who was reduced to a pathetic javelin mark by an arm injury. The 1500m did not affect anything and Dvorák totalled a magnificent 8902 for his third world title. Nool raised his Estonian record to 8815, the highest ever non-winning score, and Macey held his body and spirit together for his best score of 8603.

The most resounding performance in the spate of top-class European meetings from mid-August was a world record in the steeplechase by Brahim Boulami, who had finished only tenth in Edmonton in 8:21.95, some 40m behind the Kenyan winner, Reuben Kosgei. He had set a Moroccan record of 7:58.50 ahead of Kosgei (8:03.22) in Zürich, and a week later in Brussels he clocked 7:55.28 with Kosgei (7:57.29) again second, while in third place Stephen Cherono of Kenya improved from 8:19.12 to 7:58.66 for a phenomenal world junior record. Three years later, now known as Saif Saaeed Shaheen of Qatar, Cherono would succeed the by then discredited Boulami as world record holder. Also in Brussels, Yuriy Borzakovskiy's even pace running (51.0 + 51.5) brought the reward of a Russian 800m record of 1:42.47, and a great 1500m saw Hicham El Guerrouj pressed hard all the way by Bernard Lagat, 3:26.12 (53.5 last lap) to the Kenyan's Commonwealth record of 3:26.34. Those times remain to this day the fastest ever behind El Guerrouj's 3:26.00 of three years earlier. Yegorova may have been the most unpopular athlete on the circuit but she continued to shine, posting a world leading 8:23.26 3000m in Zürich, winning again in 8:30.09 in Brussels and setting a European 5000m record of 14:29.32 in Berlin, a race in which Paula Radcliffe improved her UK record to 14:32.44.

The Grand Prix Final on September 9 was staged in Melbourne and the big winners were Switzerland's world 800m champion André Bucher and Romania's 1500m silver medallist Violeta Szekely, both of whom collected $150,000 for winning the overall Grand Prix plus a one-sixth share of the Golden League jackpot.

Three days later, IAAF president Lamine Diack sent this message to US president George W Bush: "On behalf of the International Association of Athletics Federations – which has 210 members in every corner of the world – I would like to send our most sincere condolences at the shocking and evil attacks on US soil yesterday. Our sport of track and field athletics is based on the principle of friendly and peaceful competition and tolerates no discrimination based on sex, or race or religion. Cold hearted, brutal terrorism is an affront to all civilised behaviour and cannot be tolerated. Our prayers are with the victims and their loved ones and we hope that your great nation will find the strength, and faith, to recover from this blow."

The autumn road racing season threw up a pair of marathon world records. The women's 2:20 barrier was breached by Japan's Naoko Takahashi, whose extreme training methods included covering up to 50 miles in a day. Running in Berlin, she clocked 2:19:46 (halves of 69:50 and 69:56), but her record lasted precisely a week for Kenya's Catherine Ndereba won in Chicago in 2:18:47 (70:15 and 68:32). Women were closing the gap. When Grete Waitz set her first world record of 2:32:30 in 1978 the corresponding men's record stood at 2:08:34 – a difference of almost 24 minutes. Ndereba's exploit narrowed the gap to barely 13 minutes. Ndereba commented: "When Takahashi broke 2:20 last Sunday, that made it so much easier. It was like she broke a barrier. Before, women didn't think we could go under 2:20. In the future, the next generation of women will run under 2:18. Maybe they will go 2:15."

Cue Paula – the woman who *would* run 2:15 just a couple of years later. She bounced back from her Edmonton disappointment with a superb victory in the world half marathon championship in Bristol in the European record time of 66:47.

37. IT'S PAULA IN THE LONG RUN (2002)

As a track runner Paula Radcliffe was close to being the world's best at 10,000m, but not quite. At cross country and half marathon she had won world titles but there were others just as successful. It was the marathon which would prove to be her forte and her impact on the event in 2002 was as profound as it was heart warming. Britain's most popular athlete had found the event to which she was best suited and it was entirely appropriate that the IAAF voted her world female athlete of the year.

She didn't put a foot wrong all year. Despite feeling "a little short of racing fitness" following a knee injury, she kicked off with a front running cross country win in Italy in January. The following month, seemingly oblivious to the 30°C heat and windy conditions in San Juan (Puerto Rico), she missed Liz McColgan's world 10km road best by just four seconds, clocking 30:43. It was back to cross country in March and on Dublin's Leopardstown Racecourse she retained her world title. In this her final race before her eagerly awaited London Marathon debut, she showed her speed as well as endurance was intact as she and Deena Drossin (later Kastor) battled it out. Pulling well clear at the start of the final lap of the 7.87km race, Paula won by nine seconds in 26:55.

The 2002 edition of the Flora London Marathon will go down in athletics history as the greatest marathon event yet witnessed. It had everything: a world record by Khalid Khannouchi in the men's race, a women-only race world best by Paula Radcliffe in a sensational debut at the distance, and a stack of other scintillating performances which made both the men's and women's races the best ever for elite quality. Race director Dave Bedford had spent a fortune assembling an incredible array of talent and the organisers had to pay out an equally unprecedented amount in record and time bonuses ... but it was worth every penny. The race attracted a record number of starters (33,297); the crowds, as always, were magnificent; and this year – for a welcome change – there was no wind to speak of, making the conditions (rising from 7 to 10°C) perfect for fast running.

The women started 45 minutes ahead of the men and the conventional wisdom was that Radcliffe would stay with the experienced runners in the lead pack until 20-22 miles before making a move if still feeling comfortable. That's not at all how it turned out! Paula felt so at ease that by 9 miles she was the only runner still in contact with the pacemaker and had built up an 11 sec margin over Susan Chepkemei, Derartu Tulu and the other main contenders. She reached halfway in 71:04, fully 50 sec clear. But we had seen nothing yet, for Radcliffe's second half provided arguably the most devastating display by any female marathoner, never mind one trying the distance for the first time. In her world record 2:18:47 in Chicago last October, Catherine Ndereba covered the second half in 68:32, aided and abetted by male athletes. Paula, absolutely alone, clocked 67:52 and various other splits were equally astonishing. She reeled off the 25th mile in 5:06 (even Khannouchi only ran that in 4:55) and her ten fastest miles added up to 51:39.

Paula's final time of 2:18:56 (17th overall in the race, fourth Briton!) broke every record in the book except for Ndereba's world and Commonwealth best. It easily surpassed Ingrid Kristiansen's 1985 European and London course record of 2:21:06, Véronique Marot's 1989 UK record of 2:25:56, the fastest ever women-only race best of 2:21:47 and the fastest ever debut time of 2:23:11. She even managed to break the Radcliffe family record, her dad Peter having run 3:30 in London in 1985! Altogether, she collected $255,000 in prize money and record/time bonuses, and when you add her appearance fee and shoe sponsor's bonus it's probable that she made over half a million dollars from this one race, the most by any female in athletics history.

All that would have been quite enough excitement for one day, but we were treated also to an amazing men's race which saw the world record broken and the next five places occupied in best ever times for those positions. Haile Gebrselassie, who was in effect making his marathon debut even if he did run 2:48 at age 15, had asked the pacemakers for an ambitious halfway time of 62:30, and they were not far off with 62:47. By 21 miles it was between Gebrselassie, Paul Tergat and Khannouchi. It remained anybody's race until, 3km from the finish, Gebrselassie developed muscle cramp in his left calf and fell back. With just under a mile to go Khannouchi succeeded in dropping Tergat and ran out the winner by 10 sec in 2:05:38. As a Moroccan he won in Chicago 1997 in 2:07:10, was 2nd in Chicago 1998 in 2:07:19, set a world and African record of 2:05:42 in Chicago in 1999 and placed 3rd in London 2000 in 2:08:36. Since becoming an American citizen he won again in Chicago in 2000 in a US record 2:07:01, dropped out of the World Championships in Edmonton with blisters and breathing problems, and now has run 2:05:38.

Although a great cross country and half marathon champion, Tergat once again finished second best. For the first time he defeated Gebrselassie but, as in his two previous marathons, he was runner-up. This time, though, he ran a superb 2:05:48 to become the second fastest ever marathoner. Gebrselassie became the fastest debutant in history with his Ethiopian record of 2:06:35, an indication that he could take the record below 2:05 on a future occasion.

For someone who had run the marathon three months earlier, Paula displayed impressive track speed in Monaco on July 19. Gabriela Szabo won the 3000m in a European record of 8:21.42, but she didn't have much to spare over Paula, who took 4.77 sec off her own British and Commonwealth record with 8:22.20 which ranked her third on the all-time list if one ignored five Chinese runners. To this day it remains the third fastest by a European. Nine days later, in Manchester, she threatened the world 5000m record of 14:28.09.

It's been a long time a'coming ... and all the sweeter for it. In senior international track championships between 3000 and 10,000m Paula had previously lined up on eight occasions since 1993, given her all each time and had just one silver medal to show for it. Now, in her Commonwealth Games debut, she was at last a winner – and with a fabulous run. In Manchester, close to her Cheshire birthplace, she came within 3.3 sec of the world record when lowering her Commonwealth record to 14:31.42. Edith Masai, who had run

8:23.23 behind Radcliffe in that fabulous 3000m in Monaco, was left 22 sec adrift as Radcliffe produced one of the most devastating front running displays ever seen – and how the capacity 38,000 crowd loved it! Indeed, had the first kilometre not been on the slow side at 2:59.91 the world record would surely have gone. Radcliffe, ahead from the second lap, was operating at sub-14:25 pace for the last 4km.

Another nine days after that exploit Paula produced an even greater run at the European Championships in Munich, this time at 10,000m.

"I knew I was capable of running under 30 minutes in perfect conditions in a perfect race," she said. "Initially I was disappointed, but I gave it everything I could and I can't be too disappointed breaking the European record by 12 seconds." Radcliffe's run was quite astonishing even if it had been obvious that she was ready to threaten Ingrid Kristiansen's 16 year-old European mark of 30:13.74. She quickly made her intentions clear: she was out to break 30 minutes. She was in front by the second lap, setting a devilish pace, and continued to splash her way around the track at devastating speed – the light drizzle in the early stages having given way to heavy rain which, in her words, "didn't help." She reached 5000m in 14:57.65, easily the fastest ever halfway split ... and way inside Sonia O'Sullivan's 1998 5000m championship record of 15:06.50! O'Sullivan was an isolated second over 20 sec behind. Having continually to run wide to lap competitors, Radcliffe clocked the glorious if frustrating time of 30:01.09. It was the second fastest ever behind the controversial 29:31.78 of Wang Junxia and an improvement of over 25 sec on her previous Commonwealth and UK records. It's a time which is less than 2 sec slower than when Emil Zátopek won the 1948 Olympic title.

Paula was by no means finished yet. In her next race, a 10km road event in London's Richmond Park in September, she broke Liz McColgan's European and UK best with 30:38, reaching halfway in a very fast 15:02 before the hilly course and windy weather slowed her down. That was just a tune-up before her final and most momentous race of the year: the Chicago Marathon.

For those of us who had the privilege of witnessing the last of the great Jim Peters' world marathon bests – 2:17:39.4 as it was then recorded back in 1954 – it was totally inconceivable that one day a woman would run faster. At the time, the longest Olympic race for women absurdly was just 200m; the world record for 800m stood at 2:07.3; the best time for 1500m, an event which would not receive official world record status for many years, was 4:37.0; while no women's races had yet been staged – or even considered – at 5000 or 10,000m. As for the marathon, Violet Piercy had reputedly clocked 3:40:22 in a solo time trial between Windsor and Battersea Town Hall in 1926, but it wasn't until 1971 that three hours was broken.

Now Paula has capped an incredible year by winning the Chicago Marathon in a stunning 2:17:18, chopping 1 min 29 sec from Catherine Ndereba's world record set on the same course a year ago. The time ranks Radcliffe as the fourth fastest British marathoner this year. That draws attention to the current dearth of men's marathon talent in Britain (she would have

369

ranked 45th with that time in 1983). A difference from London, where the women run alone, is that this was a mixed race and Radcliffe reaped the advantage of having a number of men around her for most of the race, including Weldon Johnson (USA). His role, in addition to running at around 2:18 pace for as long as he could, was to act as Radcliffe's "minder" and keep her informed of mile splits, which was much appreciated by Paula. [Weldon and his twin brother Robert later founded the LetsRun.com website].

But this was no one-woman show, even though Radcliffe never saw any of her rivals after the first few miles. She was up against Ndereba, so although it was always her intention to go for the world record she also realised that winning the race was the main priority. Up at 3.30 am for the 7.30 race start, the morning cool (6°C) but bright, Radcliffe dressed warmly for the conditions, sporting a blue hat and white gloves. At halfway Ndereba was given the same time as Radcliffe (69:05). The incessant head bobbing caused Radcliffe's hat to fly off at 15 miles, at the conclusion of another searing mile split of 5:08, but Ndereba was still only some 30m behind and herself well inside world record schedule. But Radcliffe continued to turn the screw. She reached 20 miles in an extraordinary 1:44:43, compared to Ndereba's 1:46:12 last year. She experienced a bad patch between 22 and 23 miles, but despite a strong headwind in the closing stages maintained her fantastic pace to the end. She has now narrowed the differential between the men's and women's records to an all-time low of 11 min 40 sec. Ndereba clocked the fourth quickest ever time of 2:19:26, the first time two women broke 2:20 in the same race. Radcliffe, who covered the second half in 68:13, is estimated to have earned at least half a million dollars from this race in prize money ($100,000), world record and time bonuses and participation fees. While Radcliffe grabbed all the headlines, Khalid Khannouchi's brilliant run must not be overlooked. He has now run back to back marathons this year in 2:05:38 (world record in London) and 2:05:56, and owns three of the four fastest times in history.

Back to the indoor season, the highlight of which was the best ever European Championships in Vienna, featuring world records in the women's 800m by Jolanda Ceplak (1:55.82) just ahead of Austria's own Stephanie Graf (1:55.85) and in the pole vault by Svetlana Feofanova with 4.75m, her fifth record – up a centimetre at a time à la Bubka – in four weeks. However, there is a cloud over the careers of the two 800m runners as Ceplak (in 2007) and Graf (in 2010) received bans for violating the anti-doping rules. The British team came away with seven medals, one fewer than the record haul of 1989, the golds being awarded to title holder Jason Gardener in the 60m (6.49) and Colin Jackson in the 60m hurdles (7.40).

Pat and I lost two good friends during the year: Sir Arthur Gold and his wife. Lady Marion went first, in January, aged 84 following a courageous 18-year fight against cancer which amazed her doctors at Barts Hospital in London. She was always such good company and we admired her indomitable spirit. Arthur (85) survived his wife of 59 years by four months.

Arthur Abraham Gold made an unparalleled contribution to his beloved sport. An international high jumper in 1937 (his pb was 1.90m at a time when the British record stood at 1.95m), he was among the pioneers of British coaching, qualifying in his early twenties. His most notable coaching success was with the legendary high jumper Dorothy Tyler. But it was as an administrator that Sir Arthur made his most indelible mark. At one time or another he filled practically every post of significance in British athletics. He succeeded Jack Crump as honorary secretary of the BAAB in 1965 and engineered many vital changes during his 12 years in office, his policy being "evolution not revolution". During that period he was athletics team leader at the Olympics of 1968, 1972 and 1976. In 1992, by now the elder statesman of British sport and chairman of the British Olympic Association, he was commandant of the entire team at the Albertville and Barcelona Olympics. His crowning achievement was presiding over the European AA from 1976 to 1987. In that post his diplomatic skills, encyclopaedic knowledge and a mission to protect the sport from the dangers of drug use and over commercialisation made him one of the most respected figures in world sport. Knighted in 1984 for his services to athletics, Sir Arthur was elected president of the AAA in 1995 but ill health caused him to cut back on his activities.

On a personal note, I first encountered Arthur way back in 1954 when I was competing for the school team in the 440 yards and he was high jumping for the "old boys". Three years later, as president of Grafton AC, he handed me a medal for winning the club's 4 miles road handicap. Later, when I was editing AW and he was BAAB secretary, he would always find the time to discuss matters with me. He was the most erudite man I've ever met, so knowledgeable about almost everything, and always so courteous to someone who knew rather less about everything. He loved to gossip also (off the record, of course) and it's a pity he never got around to writing what could have been an explosive book about the corridors of power within athletics. He represented the conscience of athletics, and the sport will be the poorer and more endangered with his passing.

The British men won the European Cup for a fifth time in a closely fought contest in Annecy, victory in the final event, the 4x400m relay, deciding the outcome. ... or so we thought. The team scored 111 points against 107 by Germany and 105 by France. There were wins for Dwain Chambers in the 100m, Marlon Devonish in the 200m (both also contributing to the 4x100m victory), Daniel Caines in the 400m, Colin Jackson in the 110m hurdles, Chris Tomlinson in the long jump and Jonathan Edwards in the triple jump. However, the maximum points scored in the 100m and 4x100m relay were subsequently cancelled when Chambers admitted he was then on drugs and the revised result was that Germany won the cup with Britain now down to fourth.

I was over 5000 miles away at the time, in my element savouring the US Championships at the Stanford University track in Palo Alto, California. Among the top performances were a wind aided 9.88 100m by Maurice Greene and a 22.22m shot put by Adam Nelson, who whipped up great crowd support by theatrically tearing off his T-shirt and flinging it to the ground before entering the circle each time. A pointer for the future was the 50.69 400m in the junior championship final by Jamaican-born Sanya Richards (17) who was destined to set an American record of 48.70 in 2006 and win the Olympic title in 2012.

Richards was expected to capture the World Junior title in Kingston, Jamaica but had to settle for second place. She later placed third, and another future great in Allyson Felix fifth, in the 200m won in 22.93 by Britain's Vernicha James who, for whatever reason, never raced seriously again. The most popular winner was a lanky Jamaican schoolboy in the 200m. At 15 years and 332 days Usain Bolt became the youngest ever male world junior champion, and set a world age best of 20.58 in his heat before taking the final in 20.61. That wasn't all. He received a silver medal for his part in the 4x100m relay and a bronze in the 4x400m where he was clocked at 45.5 for his leg At the end of the year he was presented with the IAAF "Rising Star" award for 2002. He was on his way!

David Barnett of Track & Field Tours organised excellent apartment accommodation for Pat and me during the Commonwealth Games in Manchester. Transport to and from the stadium (now the home of Manchester City FC) was laid on and Pat, as a member of a group of fans happily waving their flags, enjoyed these Games far more than the Edinburgh 1986 edition when the chilly weather caused her almost to suffer from hypothermia (in mid-summer)! Paula's 5000m produced a wall of noise which must have been the loudest ever experienced at a British athletics meeting – at least until the London Olympics ten years later – and there was so much else to enthuse over.

I have been fortunate enough to attend many major international championships since the 1958 Commonwealth Games in Cardiff, and I cannot think of any to equal Manchester's Games for sheer enjoyment. Of course, the standard of performance – particularly in terms of depth – does not compare with the Olympic Games or World Champs, but there were still plenty of world class achievements to rave about. Where Manchester scored so heavily was in its friendly atmosphere and unrivalled presentation. To be part of a capacity (38,000) crowd for each evening session was a delight. You would have to go back to the White City's heyday more than 40 years ago to find such an attendance at a British athletics meeting. And what a crowd! The spectators cheered, applauded and sang, and generally created the most welcoming and inspirational of stages for the athletes to perform on. Competitors lined up to pay tribute to the fans' support. Even the weather played its part. It was warm and sunny most of the time with only one day affected by Manchester's legendary rain.

The enormous success of the Games was not unconnected to the admirable showing by English athletes with gold medals being won by Michael East (3:37.35 1500m), Chris Rawlinson (49.14 400m hurdles), Nathan Morgan (8.02m long jump), Jonathan Edwards (17.86m triple jump with his eventual successor Phillips Idowu second at 17.68m), Mick Jones (72.55m hammer),

Steve Backley (86.81m javelin), both men's relay teams, Kelly Holmes (4:05.99 1500m), Paula of course, Ashia Hansen (14.86m triple jump) and Lorraine Shaw (66.83m hammer). Kim Collins from St Kitts & Nevis, then 26, won the 100m in 9.98 ... and remains a world class sprinter to this day.

No sooner had we recovered our breath from Manchester than it was time for the European Championships in Munich where Paula's record-breaking 10,000m was just one of seven British victories and 14 medals in total. Dwain Chambers won the 100m in 9.96, Colin Jackson and Steve Backley notched up their fourth consecutive titles with a time of 13.11 and a distance of 88.54m respectively, both men's relay teams ran out winners in 38.19 and 3:01.25, and Ashia Hansen took the triple jump with a wind assisted 15.00m. A word on her.

Watching Hansen competing for major titles could lead to extreme stress. Just 10 days after her heart-stopping last gasp victory in Manchester she was at it again. The challenge this time came unexpectedly from Finland's Heli Koivula, who entered with a pb of 14.36m yet in the first round landed at a remarkable 14.83m with the wind only just over the limit. Hansen, meanwhile, jumped 14.60m for a safe second place, but that wasn't what she was after. A run through in round 3 followed by two other fouls (the last looking around 15.20m from a marginal no-jump) meant that it was all down to Hansen's final jump. Now gloriously restored to peak physical and emotional strngth, she broke the sand at exactly 15 metres, the first time she has reached 15m outdoors for five long years. She is the first British woman to win a European jump title since Thelma Hopkins (high) and Jean Pickering (long) in 1954.

The men's triple jump fell well short of British expectations after the outstanding one-two in Manchester. Phillips Idowu led the qualifiers by over half a metre with his second longest ever jump of 17.54m and in the first round of the final he marginally fouled an effort of around 17.50m. He never recovered from that disappointment and placed fifth with 16.92m. Jonathan Edwards took the lead with his second round 17.32m but failed to improve upon that although his final attempt, a foul by just 1.5cm, was in the area of 17.70m. In the meantime, Charles Friedek briefly held the lead with 17.33m, to be superseded in turn by Christian Olsson with 17.44m and ultimately 17.53m, still 1cm short of Idowu's qualifier. Edwards' distinction of holding Olympic, world, Commonwealth and European titles simultaneously was terminated after just 11 days.

Another of the jumping events, the pole vault, produced a result of particular significance.

How poignant and symbolic was Alex Averbukh's victory, the first ever European outdoor title by an Israeli. Thirty years after the massacre of Israeli team members the strains of "Hatikvah" defiantly rang out in Munich's Olympic stadium. Despite his European indoor title of two years ago and World Championships silver medal in Edmonton, Averbukh was not considered the favourite as he had cleared no higher than 5.72m this season. The Russian-born athlete's prospects looked even shakier after the qualifying round, where he failed three times at 5.60m although his 5.45m eventually sufficed to advance.

After making his opening height of 5.60m second time in the final, he chose to pass 5.70m and took the lead with his first attempt clearance at 5.75m. He went over 5.80m at the second try and only he managed to go higher with a massive first time clearance at 5.85m.

How was it possible that Averbukh could become European champion when Israel geographically is an Asian country? Because of the political situation in the Middle East, Israeli sportsmen and women were barred from competing in any Asian Games or championships – despite that exclusion being against the rules. So, in order to solve the problem, the International Basketball Federation admitted Israel to membership of their European Association and other governing bodies followed. At the request of the IAAF, Israel was affiliated to the European Athletic Association in 1993 and since then Israeli athletes have competed in European championship and cup events.

Regrettably, one has to return to the subject of doping. They might in some cases have been clean at the time of the championships but European gold medallists who served bans at some time in their careers were Dwain Chambers (subsequently stripped of the title, which went instead to Francis Obikwelu), Konstadínos Kedéris (200m winner in 19.85, a European "low altitude" best), Alberto García (5000m), Antonio Jimenez (steeplechase), Yuriy Belonog (shot), Róbert Fazekas (discus), Adrián Annus (hammer), Francisco Fernandez (20km walk), British 4x100m team (because of Chambers they eventually forfeited the title which went instead to Ukraine), Ekateríni Thánou (100m), Jolanda Ceplak (800m), Süreyya Ayhan (1500m), Marta Domínguez (5000m), Tatyana Kotova (long jump), Irina Korzhanenko (shot), Olga Kuzenkova (hammer) and Olimpiada Ivanova (20km walk). What a shocking indication it was of the extent of cheating at the highest level. The most corrupt event was the women's shot where not only Korzhanenko but also Vita Pavlysh (2nd), Svetlana Krivelyova (3rd) and Nadezhda Ostapchuk (5th) have been caught doping.

So too was Brahim Boulami, the Moroccan who broke his own steeplechase world record of 7:55.28 when he ran 7:53.17 in Zürich. He was tested the day before and recorded a positive reading for EPO. He was banned for two years and his performance annulled. Another doping offender, although that was not known at the time, was Marion Jones and she – together with Ana Guevara, Felix Sánchez and Hicham El Guerrouj – shared the IAAF Golden League Jackpot of gold worth around $500,000 by winning at all seven meetings during the summer. The overall Grand Prix men's winner and its $100,000 award looked to be between Sánchez and El Guerrouj, but in the final in Paris they were pipped by Tim Montgomery on account of the bonus points he received for breaking the world 100m record with 9.78, his reaction time a just legal 0.104 sec. He collected a cheque for $250,000 which included $50,000 for the individual event win and $100,000 world record bonus. A metre behind him, Dwain Chambers equalled Linford Christie's European record of 9.87. Retroactively, both sprinters had those performances annulled when they were found guilty of doping. The women's winner, who received a total of $150,000, was Marion Jones, then Montgomery's girlfriend and the following year mother of his child. She too was heading for disgrace.

Four days after the Paris meeting, Bob Hayes – an American football as well as track and field legend – died at the age of 59.

Hayes was one of the all-time greats of sprinting even though he was only 21 when he ran his last – and greatest – race. That was at the Tokyo Olympics of 1964. After scorching to victory in his 100m semi-final in a heavily wind assisted 9.91, an amazing time on a cinder track, he won the final from a particularly soft lane by a full two metres in a legal 10.06, an unofficial world record as electronic times were not ratified by the IAAF until 1977. The official hand time of 10.0 tied the world record. He was even more dazzling on the anchor leg of the 4x100m relay. He was only fifth, some three metres down on the leader, when he took over ... but he powered past everybody within the first 30m and went on to win by three metres in a world record 39.06, his highly unofficial split being 8.6! A disgruntled rival said to lead–off man Paul Drayton, "you haven't anything except Hayes," to which the American, proudly displaying his gold medal, replied: "that's all we need, pal." On returning to the USA Hayes signed a professional football contract as a wide receiver with the Dallas Cowboys [Super Bowl winner in 1971] and became one of the game's greatest players.

One of my most pleasurable and nostalgic assignments during the year was writing a six-part history of *Athletics Weekly*. Long after the dark days of the early EMAP era and the battle for circulation between AT and AW, my relationship with the magazine was now perfectly cordial and in 1999, with Nigel Walsh as editor and Matthew Fraser Moat as publisher, Peter Matthews and I had begun compiling a more extensive overseas results section for AW and at year's end we started a mutually beneficial arrangement (which has continued ever since) whereby AW produces AI's world merit rankings and other statistical features within a well illustrated annual review issue. In the final part of the history series, I wrote that under Jason Henderson, who had joined the staff in 1997 and been promoted to editor in September 2001at the age of 32, "we are seeing a return to AW's core values ... I wish Jason and his colleagues all the luck in the world as new chapters in the history of AW unfold. There have been more than 2700 editions so far ... may there be thousands more to come!" Indeed, there have been another 800 or so under Jason's direction and the magazine is serving the sport well.

Once I had completed work on the annual review issue for 2002 I treated myself to another American casino adventure in December when I tried my luck in a decidedly chilly Reno (5000ft altitude). The machines were hot, though, and my winnings covered the cost of the trip. I would do even better the following year.

38. THE GREATEST WOMEN'S RECORD? (2003)

Although she still harboured track ambitions, circumstances dictated that Paula Radcliffe would race only on the road in 2003 and on that surface she topped even her extraordinary exploits of the previous year. Her season started with a bang in late February.

Paula Radcliffe has begun 2003 as she finished 2002 – breaking world records. Racing for the first time since her 2:17:18 marathon in Chicago last October, she won Puerto Rico's appropriately if immodestly named "World's Best 10k Road Race" in San Juan. In last year's event, while preparing for her London Marathon debut, she missed the $100,000 bonus on offer for breaking the then world best of 30:39 by Liz McColgan by 4 sec. This time the target was Asmae Leghzaoui's 30:29 and Radcliffe shattered that with 30:21 despite warm, humid and windy weather as well as a hilly course. Leghzaoui, who attempted to stay with Radcliffe in the early stages, finished second over 400m behind. Radcliffe said "I'm in way better shape than before London last year".

Contrasting fortunes: one month after that race, Leghzaoui, from Morocco, tested positive for EPO and was banned for two years; while on April 13 Paula produced what many observers (myself included) regard as the greatest of all women's world records – and with no hint of drug assistance. In the year 2000 the gap between the men's and women's world marathon records was 14 min 38 sec; now it was down to just 9 min 47 sec and it would never again be as close.

It was barely 18 months ago that Naoko Takahashi became the first woman to run a marathon inside 2:20. Now, astonishingly, Paula Radcliffe has broken through the 2:17 and 2:16 barriers, clocking the fabulous time of 2:15:25 in the Flora London Marathon to smash her own world record by close to two minutes. That new time is only seconds away from the world record equalling 2:15:17 by the legendary Abebe Bikila when winning his first Olympic title in 1960. And yet, despite all the hard training (including 140 miles a week at high altitude) and attention to detail by her support team, Paula's preparations could have been ruined by an accident which occurred at her US training base of Albuquerque on March 8. Nearing the end of a 24-mile run, she was involved in a collision with a young cyclist which left her with a dislocated jaw, cuts to her elbows and knees and grazed shoulders. Miraculously, she missed only two days training.

The elite women's race started at 9 am (45 minutes before the men's race) in near ideal conditions. The temperature was 10°C with 74% humidity; by the finish the temperature had risen to 16°C with 50-55% humidity. Lining up with the 15 women were eight male Kenyan pacemakers, all of whom have run marathons in the 2:09-2:14 range. On their backs were signs designating the pace at which they would be operating: two apiece at 2:16, 2:18, 2:20 and 2:22. It was an unique method of preserving a women-only race (mainly for the benefit of television) but enabling everyone in the field to benefit from pacing. After all, there is no woman in the world capable of usefully pacing Radcliffe even to halfway ... not that the supreme front runner needs any help in that department anyway. She said after the race that at no time did she speak to the two 2:16 hares, Samson Loywapet and Christopher Kandie, adding: "I don't think it made much difference having the pacemakers."

Radcliffe made no secret of her intentions. By 2 miles she was 14 sec ahead and a frightening third mile of 4:57 – the fastest ever by a woman in a marathon – took her to 3 miles in 15:15, which was close to 2:13 pace! She backed off after that but was still moving at a terrific lick to reach 10k in 32:01. She passed 10 miles in 51:48 and her halfway time was an awesome 68:02 as against 71:04 in her London debut and 69:05 in Chicago. At 30k Radcliffe's time of 1:36:36 shattered her own 1:37:40 in Chicago and Takahashi's official world best of 1:39:02 and she picked up another world best of 1:43:33 at 20 miles. She was showing no signs of slowing despite suffering from stomach cramps; her 24th mile of 5:03 was the second quickest of the race. A strong finish enabled her to cover the second half in an amazing 67:23. She now owns the first, second and fourth fastest ever marathons (averaging 2:17:13!), while Catherine Ndereba was second in 2:19:55, her third sub-2:20.

Paula, whose time was not bettered by any British man that year, did not race again until September. As she explained in her 2004 autobiography *Paula: My Story So Far*, "I had one problem, then another; an injury that almost drove me insane, then a bilateral pneumothorax (two partially punctured lungs), and when I fought my way through all of that to where, against the odds, it seemed I might be able to compete at the World Championships in Paris, a minor injury killed those hopes. I really believed I could win my first world track title. My heart was set on being in Paris. My heart was broken by not being there."

The 10,000m in Paris on August 23 turned out to be the greatest mass race in that event's history with Berhane Adere winning in an African record and third fastest ever time of 30:04.18. Paula's European record stood at 30:01.09.

Paula began her comeback in hilly Richmond Park on September 7 with a promising 30:50 for 10km. One week later she covered a twisting 5km course in Hyde Park in a world best of 14:51. Another week on and she not only won the Great North Run from Newcastle to South Shields by nearly two minutes from Adere but her time of 65:40 was another world best. Because the route is point to point with the finish more than 30% of the distance away from the start and the course drops 30.5m, which is more than the permitted maximum of one metre per kilometre, the time could not be considered as an official world record, but it was a stunning performance all the same.

Older readers might remember Diane Leather's world mile best of 5:02.6 at the White City in 1953; well, Radcliffe averaged around 5:01 for 13 consecutive miles! Her slowest was 5:18 on a particularly tough uphill stretch between 8 and 9 miles, while her fastest split was a fantastic 4:44 for the preceding downhill section. Her 5k splits were 15:26, 15:52, 15:23 (world best of 46:41 for 15k) and 15:40 (world best of 62:21 for 20k). She also ran the fastest ever 10 miles time of 50:01 en route. "I didn't set off with the intention of breaking the world best, but I was feeling good and really it was just like a very hard training run."

Her final flourish for 2003 was victory in the IAAF World Half Marathon Championship in Vilamoura on October 4, her third win in that event in four years. She had hoped to break Elana Meyer's legal world best of 66:44 but the scorching Algarve weather put paid to that and she came home in 67:35, her winning margin of 1 min 27 sec over Adere being the widest in the race's history.

In between Paula's last two races, the Berlin Marathon saw two Kenyans smash Khalid Khannouchi's world record of 2:05:38. Paul Tergat, winning a marathon at the sixth attempt, burst through the 2:05 barrier with a time of 2:04:55 but he had only one second to spare at the finish over Sammy Korir. His splits were 63:04 and 61:51. Tergat, now exclusively a road runner, was powerless to prevent Kenenisa Bekele eclipsing his cross country achievements. At the World Championships in Switzerland, the 20 year-old Ethiopian won both the 4km and 8km events for a second year to add to his junior victory in 2001 ... by 2008 Bekele's total of individual world cross country titles would number a staggering twelve. Bekele wasn't yet in world record breaking form on the track but he did beat Haile Gebrselassie for the World Championships 10,000m title in 26:49.57 with a second half covered in 12:57.24!

Not that Gebrselassie was doing too badly himself. Having being rewarded with a million dollar prize for setting a world road best of 27:02 for 10km in Qatar in December 2002, he clocked 8:04.69 in Birmingham for a world indoor best for 2 miles and won the world indoor 3000m title in 7:40.97. That race too was held in Birmingham, the highlight of the championships being a world indoor pole vault record of 4.80m by Svetlana Feofanova. There were two British victors: Marlon Devonish in the last ever 200m championship (20.62) and Ashia Hansen in the triple jump. As always with Ashia there was plenty of drama involved.

For Ashia Hansen to win the gold medal before her home crowd with one of the longest jumps in history was a dream result ... but on the way she had to live through more than one nightmare. It started in the qualifying round. Suffering from a heel injury, she could only compete after being injected with an anaesthetic, and even then was in pain. Injected again for the final, Hansen opened promisingly with 14.77m but Francoise Mbango concluded the first round with an African record of 14.88m. To add to Hansen's distress, she found that her runway marker had been moved (deliberately, she thought), causing a lengthy delay and much expenditure of nervous energy as she "dolly-stepped" her run-up again. She landed at around 14.90m but it was a foul. In round 5 everything came together. With just 2.5cm to spare on the board she leapt a world-leading 15.01m, a distance only she and Iolanda Chen have ever bettered.

There were medals for Jason Gardener (3rd 60m in 6.55), Daniel Caines (2nd 400m in 45.43), Jamie Baulch (equal 3rd 400m in 45.99), the 4x400m team

(3rd in 3:06.12) and Kelly Holmes (2nd 1500m in a UK record 4:02.66). It should be noted that the American 1500m winner Regina Jacobs, who the previous month had set a world indoor record of 3:59.98 at age 39, tested positive three months later and served a four year ban. Racing for the last time, Colin Jackson (36) wasn't able to add to his fabulous total of 25 major championship medals, placing fifth in the 60m hurdles, but he deservedly received a standing ovation from the crowd. Two years later he displayed other talents by finishing runner-up in *Strictly Come Dancing* (as had Denise Lewis in 2004) and he (and Denise) remain prominent figures in the sport as BBC TV pundits.

A few weeks before Paula's historic marathon, we mourned the passing of the man who made it possible for an athlete to set a world record through the streets of London, cheered on by a vast number of spectators.

Few men can have made such a splendid and varied contribution to British athletics as Chris Brasher, who died of pancreatic cancer on February 28, aged 74. He will be remembered with affection for three achievements in particular: his spot-on pacemaking during Roger Bannister's pioneering four minute mile, his sensational Olympic steeplechase victory at the Melbourne Olympics of 1956, and his creation of the phenomenally successful London Marathon. That would have represented an exceptional lifetime's endeavour, and yet there was so much more. As a mountaineer he was shortlisted for Edmund Hillary's historic Everest expedition; as a journalist he became sports editor of "The Observer" and an award-winning writer; he was prominent also on television both as a reporter and as BBC's head of general features. Still there was more. Together with his old steeplechase rival John Disley he introduced orienteering to Britain, and again with Disley he built up profitable sportswear and shoe companies. He was also a family man. He married tennis star Shirley Bloomer in 1959; their two daughters, Kate and Amanda, were promising tennis players while their only son, Hugh, followed his father into steeplechasing although his best of 8:54.59 in 1995 fell short of his dad's 8:41.35 in Melbourne. [Hugh is now the London Marathon's event director].

Leukaemia claimed the life of former NUTS chairman (1974-1979) and ATFS president (1977-2000) Bob Sparks on April 30, aged 65.

I am deeply saddened by the death of Bob, whom I had been privileged to know for more than 45 years. We were the two youngest founder members of the NUTS in 1958; he was 20, I was 19. Within a few years he was acknowledged as an outstandingly effective and knowledgeable announcer and deservedly attained Olympic and World Championship status in that field. All other statisticians owe Bob a great debt of gratitude; he was the most meticulous keeper of the sport's facts and figures and could always be relied upon when seeking to check a performance or record. His research into photo finish prints and automatic times was of huge significance. Bob will be remembered with affection and admiration by all who care about the documentation of our sport.

My Life in Athletics

As from May 26, when I turned 65, I may have become a pensioner but I was still more than happy to continue with all my various activities within athletics. A new departure was helping with a series of video histories. For a year or more I had been supplying former decathlete Rodney Charnock with various publications, clippings and statistics which he needed for research, and he appointed me consulting editor for the series. Having acquired Guy Butler's extensive film archive and much other visual material, Rodney's intention was to edit and market videos charting the history of such events as the mile, the careers of athletes like Sydney Wooderson and Roger Bannister, and stars of the 1940s and 1950s. Rodney was providing the commentary himself and was in the process of interviewing various personalities on camera. It was an ambitious and infinitely worthwhile undertaking and in December 2003 he placed a notice in AI advertising "Bannister and the Mile Greats" as the first in a visual history series to commence in 2004. Much dedicated work continued, contributors including Norris McWhirter, Doug Wilson, Arne Andersson and David Thurlow. Those compilations, so lovingly assembled, are terrific and anyone viewing them would be transported back to another era. But, for various reasons, Rodney has been unable to complete the project and offer the videos for sale. Let's hope he can before long, for they are treasure trove.

Speaking of treasure, I got lucky in Las Vegas in June, on the way to attending the US Championships at Stanford University. Playing the slots at Caesar's Palace I hit a jackpot paying out $2700. Mindful of possibly losing a quarter of it as happened in 1997 I pointed out to the manager who came over to pay me that there was no betting tax in the UK and I believed there was now a reciprocal arrangement between Britain's Inland Revenue and the USA's Internal Revenue Service (IRS). He checked, agreed that was the case and I was paid out in full. He also gave me a slip of paper confirming the arrangement.

In something of a daze I crossed Las Vegas Boulevard (The Strip) back to my hotel, the Flamingo, went up to my room and deposited my winnings in the safe. I still had other cash to play with, so I went down to the casino to try my luck again. Normally I would play 3 x 25 cents a spin but, suitably emboldened, I thought I would go this time for a one dollar machine ... and, would you believe, I almost immediately hit a jackpot of $6000! The manager this time wasn't aware of any reciprocal tax concession and in all the excitement I had managed to lose that slip from Caesar's Palace. I was told that 25% would have to be deducted, so I was paid $4500. To be honest, I was more than happy with that, but fortuitously a couple of weeks later back in London I received through the post an official certificate from the IRS confirming that I was excused paying tax under a treaty between the USA and UK. I faxed a copy of that document to the Flamingo and eventually, in October, I received a cheque for the $1500 which had been deducted in error. That $8700 windfall would pay for several more trips to Vegas! Incidentally, I carried that tax exemption certificate around with me on more than 20 subsequent trips to Las Vegas and Atlantic City in case I hit it big again ... of course I never did.

Back in Britain I travelled to Gateshead for a Grand Prix meeting and witnessed something, and someone, rather special.

The many spectators who left Gateshead's International Stadium straight after the final track event must be kicking themselves, for they missed participating in a piece of athletics history. The women's pole vault was nearing its climax (although you would never have known had you been watching the BBC's coverage, which totally ignored the event); the bar was at 4.64m. Yelena Isinbayeva cleared at the second attempt for victory. But we who stayed had seen nothing yet. Again on her second try she soared cleanly over 4.74m, a personal best. Up went the bar to a world record 4.82m and, following a reasonable first attempt, the 21 year-old Russian made it, even if the bar did bounce on the pegs. She had added a centimetre to Stacy Dragila's 2001 mark ... and, adding to her undisguised delight and surprise, she received a $50,000 world record bonus cheque.

The same day, at the IAAF World Youth Championships at Sherbrooke in Canada, another future all-time great was making waves. Usain Bolt, still only 16, won the 200m in 20.40 – and a week later, at the Pan American Junior Championships in Barbados, he tied the world junior record of 20.13. Back at the World Youth meeting another superstar in the making created rather less of an impression. It was 17 year-old Jessica Ennis. Leading by 100 points with two events remaining in the heptathlon, she slumped to fifth place with 5311 points. Fellow 2012 Olympic champion Mo Farah (20) was narrowly outkicked over 5000m in the European Under 23 Championships in Poland by team-mate Chris Thompson, 13:58.62 to 13:58.88.

Drug issues involving two celebrated American athletes, together with the truculent behaviour of a third, cast a shadow over what were otherwise a joyous nine days of great competition in the 9th IAAF World Championships in Saint-Denis (north of Paris). The Stade de France proved a worthy setting and, as at the 1998 football World Cup, inspired the home team to great heights. France's medal total (7) was exceeded only by the USA (20) and Russia (19), although subsequent doping disqualifications lowered the USA total to 16. Jerome Young was stripped of the 400m gold medal (and the 4x400m team also lost out), and Kelli White had her 100m/200m double annulled. Zhanna Block (formerly Pintusevich) lost her 100m bronze medal, while Britain's medal count fell from four to three as Dwain Chambers, originally 4th in the 100m, caused the 4x100m team to hand back their silver medals. Kelly Holmes (2:00.18) finished second to Maria Mutola in the 800m, Darren Campbell (10.08) was third in the 100m just 0.01 behind winner Kim Collins and Hayley Tullett set a Welsh 1500m record of 3:59.95 in placing third behind Tatyana Tomashova and Süreyya Ayhan, two athletes who would go on to serve doping bans.

Unhappily for the image of athletics, the abiding memory of Paris for countless millions of televiewers around the world will be of Jon Drummond's antics after being thrown out of his 100m semi for a false start. Whether the new starting rule is fair and effective needs to be the subject of continuing scrutiny, but what is not in dispute is that when an athlete is ruled out he must accept the decision. *As a professional athlete of immense experience he should not only know the rules but abide by them. By his actions, resulting in a long delay, he upset countless other competitors in his and other events and provoked an ugly crowd reaction that should play no part in athletics. The inability of officials to deal with the problem quickly and firmly only exacerbated the situation.*

Who were the stars of the meeting? Both men's walks were won with world best performances for Jefferson Pérez (1:17:21 20km) and Robert Korzeniowski (3:36:03 50km) but they received scant media coverage or public acclaim. Out in the stadium the athletes who attracted the most attention and plaudits were Carolina Klüft for a heptathlon (7001) as sparkling as her personality (though the greatest ovation was reserved for her vanquished rival Eunice Barber when she pulled off the winning long jump of 6.99m) and Hicham El Guerrouj, who came so agonisingly close to emulating Paavo Nurmi's immortal 1924 Olympic 1500m/5000m double in Paris. [After winning the 1500m in 3:31.77 he was narrowly beaten in the 5000m by 18 year-old Eliud Kipchoge, these days the world's top marathoner, 12:52.79 to 12:52.83, with Kenenisa Bekele a close third]. Indeed, all of the longer distance races were to be treasured, the men's and women's 10,000m races in particular being classics, while there has never been a steeplechase to rival the twists and turns of the Qatar v Kenya duel.

Here is how I reported on the men's 10,000m and steeplechase.

Remember when Haile Gebrselassie set his first world record – 12:56.96 for 5000m? Who would have imagined that nine years later someone would run practically the same time during the second half of a 10,000m race. That's what happened in this astonishing race, which resulted in a clean sweep of the medals by the Ethiopian trio. The formidable Kenyan opposition couldn't live with the relentless pace of the second half. Halfway was reached in 13:52.33. From here on the Ethiopians would show no mercy. Kenenisa Bekele threw in a 61.24 lap and proceeded to share pacemaking duties with Geb while 20 year-old Sileshi Sihine was always third. Geb led at the bell (25:54.54), and as in Hengelo in June [26:53.70 to 26:54.58] it was Bekele who had the stronger kick. He exploded past the master 150m out to complete the last 200m in 26.1, 400m in 55.0 and 1600m in 4:02.8! In just the second track 10,000 of his life, Bekele had run the last 5000 in a staggering 12:57.24 for a time of 26:49.57. Gebrselassie was a magnificent second with his fastest ever championship time (26:50.77), with splits of 13:52.4 and 12:58.8. "I am as happy for Kenenisa as I am for myself," he said.

The steeplechase has for so long been Kenya's parade event in the World Championships ... 1-2 in 1991, 1993 and 1995; 1-2-3 in 1997; 1-2 in 1999 and 1-3 in 2001. This time, the signs were ominous as the world's top exponent, the former Stephen Cherono (now Saif Saaeed Shaheen), had switched allegiance for financial considerations to Qatar. The race was both bizarre and totally enthralling. In their last encounter, in Zürich 11 days earlier, the athlete formerly known as S Cherono had beaten Ezekiel Kemboi in an eyeballs-out finish, 8:02.48 to 8:02.49. In Paris the result appeared somewhat more clearcut, 8:04.39 to 8:05.11, but it was just as hotly contested. Shaheen (20) bolted off at a terrific pace, something like 59 sec for the first lap. By the kilometre mark he had a huge lead, not surprising as the time was 2:38.24 – sub 7:49 speed! It was a potentially suicidal move, but he slowed to 2:43.34 for the second kilo, enabling Kemboi to close up to within five metres. Kemboi went ahead at the next water jump and then both slowed so drastically that by the bell the three top Europeans were almost breathing down their necks. It seemed possible that the two main contenders might have already shot their bolt, but that wasn't the case as they opened up 30m or so during a phenomenal last lap (water jump inside track) of 57.5. They took the last barrier together, Kemboi edging ahead momentarily before Shaheen summoned one last burst of speed for victory.

Other outstanding winners included Allen Johnson, 110m hurdles champion for the fourth time (13.12); Felix Sánchez with the fastest 400m hurdles time (47.25) for five years; Ana Guevara, whose 400m time of 48.89 was the quickest since 1996; and Hestrie Cloete, whose 2.06m high jump was a Commonwealth record and ranked her equal third on the world outdoor all-time list. Notable too was the 5000m victory (14:51.72) by Tirunesh Dibaba, who at 18 years and 36 days became the youngest ever world champion in an individual event. One of the most unchallenged winners was Christian Olsson in the triple jump, his leap of 17.72m being 44cm ahead of the silver medallist. Jonathan Edwards, who had been stretchered off after twisting his right ankle at the Crystal Palace meeting a couple of weeks earlier, recovered sufficiently to make the final but took only two attempts and finished last in what was his final competition. Jonathan went on to make a career in television and is currently Eurosport's lead presenter.

The IAAF Golden League climaxed in Brussels and the million dollar jackpot was scooped up by Maria Mutola, the only athlete to win all six designated events, in her case 800m (1:57.78). The Van Damme Memorial meeting traditionally included a high class 10,000m and in this edition Haile Gebrselassie came up with the third fastest ever time of 26:29.22. Despite tearing round the last two laps in 59.7 and 56.7 he won by less than a second from 19 year-old Nicholas Kemboi (26:30.03), a Kenyan whose only previous 10,000m was 28:19.77. Kemboi, who switched to Qatar in 2005, never came close to such form again.

The IAAF decided to replace its traditional Grand Prix Final with a two-day "World Athletics Final" in Monaco. The format was that at least the top seven in each event according to the points-based IAAF World Rankings would be invited to compete along with a limited number of "wild card" entries. Hicham El Guerrouj led the men's standings with 1461 points, while Carolina Klüft (1436) was just ahead of Hestrie Cloete (1434). Citing fatigue, El Guerrouj did not race in Monaco but still won the $100,000 award but, with Klüft absent, Cloete's high jump win at 2.01m was enough to boost her ranking score to 1441. Consequently, both El Guerrouj (for the third year running) and Cloete were hailed as World Athletes of the Year at the International Athletics

Foundation Gala held at the conclusion of the meeting, the highlight of which was an epic steeplechase duel in which Shaheen set an Asian record of 7:57.38 with Paul Koech just 0.04 sec behind. Peter Matthews and I strongly disagreed with the whole rankings-based concept.

We at AI feel that the true female World Athlete of the Year is Paula Radcliffe, whose world marathon best in London is arguably the greatest performance in women's athletics history, and whose previous world record at Chicago in October 2002 also falls within the one year to September 14 on which this award and the IAAF Rankings are based. The complex World Rankings are a mystery to many in athletics but they are fatally flawed because they take no account of road running and walking performances, an integral part of the sport and the IAAF's responsibility. By effectively debarring athletes like Radcliffe and fellow record breakers Robert Korzeniowski and Jefferson Pérez, these Rankings and the lucrative awards involved lose credibility.

The IAAF Council, meeting in April 2004, acted to redress the anomaly and agreed that the World Athlete of the Year should not be simply based on the athlete's position in the overall IAAF World Rankings as in 2003, but should be based on a vote by experts drawn from all sections of the Athletics Family. The claims of walkers and road runners would be considered.

Towards the end of 2003, the sport was rocked by revelations that the Bay Area Laboratory Co-Operative (Balco), a San Francisco Bay nutrition company founded by Victor Conte, had supplied tetrahydrogestrinone (THG or "The Clear"), a new performance enhancing "designer steroid", to several celebrated athletes. Amid much denial, and downright lying, eventually the names of the offenders became known and bans imposed. The guilty included sprinters Tim Montgomery, Marion Jones, Kelli White, Chryste Gaines, Michelle Collins and Britain's Dwain Chambers, 400m runner Alvin Harrison, 1500m/5000m performer Regina Jacobs and shot putter Kevin Toth. Dick Pound, then chairman of the World Anti-Doping Agency, stated: "This is a serious warning for cheaters. It shows that supposedly undetectable substances can be detected as new tests are developed."

39. THE IDEAL HOLMES EXHIBITION (2004)

The year is 1983. The English Schools Championships are being staged in Plymouth and among the winners is Sally Gunnell in the Senior Girls 100m hurdles (13.7w). Nine years later she will be crowned Olympic 400m hurdles champion. She is one of the stars of the meeting, which is more than can be said for Jonathan Edwards – ninth in the Senior Boys triple jump with 13.84m. Twelve years later he will astound everyone by setting a world record which looks like standing for a long time yet and another five years after that he takes the Olympic gold medal. But there is a third youngster on view in Plymouth who will take all of 21 years to realise her Olympic dream. Reporting for "Athletics Weekly", Barry Trowbridge wrote: "Kent's Kelly Holmes (who?) produced one of the major upsets of the meeting." She, an unknown 13 year-old, won the Junior Girls 1500m in 4:37.8.

That was my introduction to the Kelly Holmes chapter of my book, *All-Time Greats of British Athletics*. I went on to chronicle the ups and downs in the career of this daughter of a white English mother and Jamaican father ... as she put it in her autobiography *Black, White and Gold*, "an accident that no one wanted to happen." At 14 she watched the 1984 Olympics on TV and Seb Coe became her hero. "He was an aggressive runner who didn't give up and his determination was obvious. I identified with that even then."

She might have been lost to the sport when she joined the Army at 17 but fortunately Kriss Akabusi urged her to start training again and in 1993 she took athletics by storm. Short but well muscled after working hard on her upper body strength, she won the British 800m title and broke the English record. In 1994 she burst forth also as a world class 1500m runner and, in her first serious season at the event, took the silver medal at the European Championships. She went on that year to win the Commonwealth Games 1500m title, but that would prove to be her only gold medal for eight often frustrating years. Other medals would come her way, including 1500m silver at the 1995 World Championships and 800m bronze at the 2000 Olympics, but constant injuries prevented her from fulfilling her true potential.

The gold medal drought ended at the 2002 Commonwealth Games in Manchester when she reclaimed the 1500m title, but after a great indoor season in 2003 which filled her with the justifiable hope of becoming world 1500m champion that summer she suffered further injuries to her left knee and right calf. She couldn't even jog and, as she revealed in her book: "After one particularly frustrating day I suddenly felt as if I couldn't cope any longer. I stood in the bathroom, locked the door and stared in the mirror, feeling utterly miserable. I was crying uncontrollably. There was a pair of nail scissors on a shelf. To this day, I don't know what made me do this, but I picked them up, opened them and started to cut my left arm with one of the blades. One cut for every day that I had been injured." Happily, hope returned as gradually her injuries healed and rather astonishingly she finished second to training companion Maria Mutola in the 800m at that year's World Championships.

My Life in Athletics

I wasn't in Athens for the 2004 Olympics, instead taking copious notes as I watched on TV, but how wonderful it was to be able to report in AI on Kelly's double triumph.

It was in the original version of Athens' Olympic Stadium seven years ago that Kelly Holmes, an overwhelming favourite to win the world 1500m title having recently run 3:58.07, broke down injured. Ever since, although collecting five Olympic or World Champs medals, a global title had eluded her. One injury after another had conspired to frustrate her and, as a variation of her bad luck, she fell over in this year's World Indoor 1500m, a race she could have won. But perseverance finally paid off in her third Olympics and at 34 she became easily the oldest ever 800m champion. The key to her belated success? For almost the first time in her career she had been able to prepare free of injury. The 1500m title was always her goal but, having also been selected for 800m, she faced a dilemma. Should she run the 800 and thus probably have three races in her legs before embarking upon the heats of the 1500, or simply concentrate on what she considered to be her stronger event? Just days before the event a particularly good training session in Cyprus convinced her she was in form to double ... and the rest is history.

Barely out of breath after clocking the quickest semi-final time of 1:57.98, her best for three years, she ran a tactically astute race in the final. Content to run at the back (57.6) while Jearl Miles-Clark blazed through the first lap in 56.37, she followed Maria Mutola as she clawed her way towards the front along the back straight. Normally when Mutola moves ahead early in the final straight the race is over, but this was an occasion which saw Holmes in inspired form. The two women slugged it out but ultimately there was no resisting Holmes. Out in lane 3 she was even more resolute than the defending champion. She clocked 1:56.38, her fastest since setting the UK record of 1:56.21 back in 1995. TV pictures of her look of disbelief, turning to wonderment and delight when she realised she had indeed won, will long remain in the memory.

By capturing the 1500m to add to her 800m title Kelly Holmes established all sorts of British records, not least her winning time (which astounded her) of 3:57.90 – fastest in the world this year and 0.17 inside her previous UK record. She is now not only the first British female to win a second Olympic title but has completed the double which eluded even her hero Seb Coe as well as Steve Ovett. She also goes into the record books as the oldest man or woman to have won either of those titles. Since winning the 800m she has developed an aura of invincibility and it now seems unimaginable that leading up to the Games she was indecisive and lacking in self confidence. Only now has she become the truly great runner she might have been all this time given better luck. Having discovered the most effective way of racing, she ran with assurance in heat and semi, holding back until the finishing straight, and that's how she ran – and won – the final too. At the bell Holmes was lurking in eighth place. With 200 to go she was up to fifth and by the time Natalya Yevdokimova had led into the finishing straight the Briton was second and no power on earth was going to deprive her of a second golden moment. Running 59.8 for her last lap, she moved into the lead 60m from the finish, looked round to assess the danger, and held on resolutely.

The USA and Russia dominated the medal table but Britain came next with three golds and a bronze. That third place was occupied by Kelly Sotherton in the heptathlon in which she scored 6424 behind Carolina Klüft's outstanding 6952 and Austra Skujyté's 6435. The other gold went to the men's 4x100m relay team.

The year is 1912. The Titanic, on her maiden voyage from Southampton to New York, strikes an iceberg and sinks ... Woodrow Wilson becomes US president ... The Great War is two years away ... The world 1500m record is 3:55.8 and high jump 2.00m. That was the year when Britain won the inaugural Olympic 4x100m relay in 42.4. Since then it has been an American preserve with 15 victories. Everyone assumed that would become 16 considering that in their heat the USA ran 38.02 over five metres clear of Britain and for the final Justin Gatlin (best of 9.85) would replace Darvis Patton on the second leg and join Shawn Crawford (9.88), Coby Miller (9.98) and Maurice Greene (9.79) for a team fully capable of breaking the world record of 37.40. Well, life is full of surprises. While the 'dream team' suffered a dreadful exchange between Gatlin and Miller, the British runners – none of whom had made the 100m final – were making splendid progress. Jason Gardener, Darren Campbell and Marlon Devonish succeeded in handing the stick to Mark Lewis-Francis two metres ahead of the USA and even a storming anchor by Greene proved insufficient ... just. Lewis-Francis held on for a stunning victory by 0.01 in 38.07.

The Games, back in their Greek homeland, proved to be an outstanding success and, on a performance level, outranked Sydney. No world records were set at the 2000 Games for the first time since 1948, but here there were two: Liu Xiang, becoming China's first ever athletics gold medallist, equalled Colin Jackson's 110m hurdles record of 12.91, and Yelena Isinbayeva vaulted over 4.91m with plenty to spare. Olympic records are special too and they fell to Kenenisa Bekele (27:05.10 10,000m), Tim Mack (5.95m vault), Virgilijus Alekna (69.89m discus), Román Sebrle (8893 decathlon), Joanna Hayes (12.37 100m hurdles), Faní Halkiá (52.77 400m hurdles in a semi-final), Yelena Slesarenko (2.06m high jump), Olga Kuzenkova (75.02m hammer) and Osleidys Menéndez (71.53m javelin, just 1cm shy of her world record). The winning marks in Athens were superior to those in Sydney in 28 of the 46 events. Kelly Holmes wasn't the only double winner.

Fears that Hicham El Guerrouj would go down in history as the greatest middle distance runner never to be an Olympic champion have thankfully proved groundless. Rarely could there have been such a popular winner; even Bernard Lagat – a marvellous runner-up after a terrific duel – was happy for him. Now there can be no dispute: El Guerrouj is the supreme miler of all time. The Olympic crown was the one element missing from a career which has included four outdoor world 1500m titles, world records at 1500m, mile and 2000m, just five defeats in 89 1500m/mile races since 1996 and nine of the world's 14 sub-3:28 times and seven of the ten fastest miles. The start was disappointingly slow but the third lap was covered in a merciless 53.28, and that was just the curtain-raiser for El Guerrouj narrowly held Lagat at bay throughout a final 300m of 38.97 (51.91 last 400m). That final 700m had taken just 1:32.25 ... which represents 1:45.5 800m pace! The winning time was 3:34.18, with Lagat on 3:34.30.

The 5000m was a replay of last year's classic World Champs clash when Kenenisa Bekele and El Guerrouj were thwarted by the finishing kick of the junior Eliud Kipchoge. The same three lined up, again with Bekele (10,000m in 27:05.10) and El Guerrouj having already struck gold, but this time the finishing order was completely different. Thus Bekele was denied his ambition of joining those men who have won the 5000 as well as the 10,000, although only by the length of a stride, but El Guerrouj succeeded in emulating Paavo Nurmi's 1500/5000 double of 1924 ... although the Finn completed his within an hour! The first kilometre took all of 2:58.46. What were the others thinking about with the greatest ever 1500m runner in the field? The second kilo was better at 2:37.53 but it wasn't until Bekele hit the front with seven laps to go that the race came alive. The third kilo took 2:34.90 but then the pace slackened again to 2:37.73. On the last lap Bekele began his run for home along the back straight, but the Moroccan would not be denied and kicked past in the final straight, having covered his last lap in 52.6 (25.3 final 200m). Time for the last kilometre was 2:25.77. The winning time was 13:14.39 with Bekele clocking 13:14.59 and Kipchoge 13:15.10.

Other highlights included the closest ever three-way finish to an Olympic men's 100m as Justin Gatlin (9.85) outleaned Francis Obikwelu (9.86) and Maurice Greene (9.87). Gatlin, who won the 2017 world title and remains no stranger to controversy, failed a drugs test in 2001 only to be reinstated by the IAAF in 2002 as the amphetamines in his sample were from medication he took for a condition known as attention deficit disorder. However, in 2006 he tested positive for testosterone and received an eight year ban, which was subsequently cut to four years although many feel he should have been banned for life. It's probably forgotten now that he was once a hurdling star too, clocking 13.41 in 2002. An equally divisive figure, Greek icon Konstadínos Kedéris, was unable to defend his 200m laurels on account of having avoided (along with fellow sprinter Ekateríni Thánou) drugs tests before the Games. He was banned for two years and never raced again. The only downside to his absence was the outrageous conduct by many Greek spectators who in a misguided show of sympathy for their missing hero delayed the start of the 200m final, won by Shawn Crawford in an outstanding 19.79, the quickest time at sea level for seven years. Ironically, much later in his career the American was banned for two years for three whereabouts failures in an 18 month period – the anti-doping arrangement whereby elite athletes have to specify where they can be reached for testing at a specified time on any particular day. Usain Bolt, now just turned 18, experienced an unhappy Olympic debut as, racing for the first time since his world junior record of 19.93 in April, he was nowhere near fully fit after a hamstring injury and was eliminated in his heat in 21.05. The next three Olympics would prove rather more productive!

Running with a maturity which belied his 20 years, Jeremy Wariner – trained by Michael Johnson's coach Clyde Hart and mentored by the great man himself – won the 400m in 44.00, while even pace advocate Yuriy Borzakovskiy strung together laps of 52.2 and 52.3 for an 800m victory in 1:44.45. With Saif Saaeed Shaheen's Olympic eligibility blocked by his former country, Kenya scored a clean sweep of the medals in the steeplechase, won by Ezekiel Kemboi in 8:05.81. Nine years earlier, at the World Championships in Gothenburg when Jonathan Edwards set his world records of 18.16m and 18.29m, 15 year-old high jumper Christian Olsson (whose best triple jump that summer was a windy 12.20m) was an awed spectator. In Athens he succeeded Edwards as Olympic champion with a Swedish record of 17.79m. It was a great Games for Sweden, as Stefan Holm won the high jump the same day at 2.36m, while the previous day Carolina Klüft had struck gold in the heptathlon with 6952 points. Incidentally, the incomparable Merlene Ottey, now representing Slovenia and aged 44, missed making the 100m final by just 3/100ths of a second. It was her seventh Olympics, a record.

Dismaying as it is, the fact that three newly crowned world champions – Róbert Fazekas (70.93m discus), Adrián Annus (83.19m hammer) and Irina Korzhanenko (21.06m women's shot) – were stripped of their titles for drug testing offences is a heartening sign that although some athletes are still trying to gain an unfair advantage the chances of their being apprehended are increasing. I would like to see a rule introduced that anyone receiving a two-year ban for testing positive at an Olympics or World Championships is banned permanently from all future global events. I would go further. Surely the IAAF can amend its anti-doping regulations to warn that in addition to a two-year ban from competition any offender will be barred for life from the Olympics and World Championships. Better still, also from other financially lucrative IAAF competitions like the Golden League and World Athletics Finals. Now is the time to strike hard while the cheats may be having second thoughts. What will be the incentive to steal an advantage if those athletes are unable to bid for major titles or earn a good living on the circuit?

Those three throwers, plus Gatlin and Crawford, were not the only winners in Athens who would go on to serve doping bans. That applied also to shot putter Yuriy Belonog, who along with Korzhanenko defiled the sacred site of the ancient Games in Olympia where their competitions were staged, 400m hurdler Faní Halkiá, long jumper Tatyana Lebedeva, discus thrower Natalya Sadova, hammer thrower Olga Kuzenkova and walker Athanasía Tsoumeléka.

They say fourth is the worst place to be in, and that seemed to be the perpetual fate of UK 10,000m record holder Jon Brown. At the 2000 Olympics he had finished fourth in the marathon, just 7 seconds away from a medal, and this time he was fourth again, 15 seconds adrift. He must have been resigned to that position as he was fourth also at 5000m in the 1991 World Student Games and 1994 Commonwealth Games and at 10,000m in the 1998 European

Championships. Still he did win one major title: the 1996 European cross country. Even more frustrated was fellow marthoner Paula Radcliffe.

A combination of extreme heat, a merciless course and a murderous uphill charge by the winner in 2:26:20, Mizuki Noguchi, contributed to favourite Paula Radcliffe almost literally running herself into the ground 6k from the end. She was one of 16 competitors who failed to finish but as world record holder and previously unbeaten at the distance her demise made headline news. The TV pictures of her by the roadside in tears rank alongside Jim Peters' collapse in Vancouver as among the most heartbreaking images in marathon history. She felt she had "let everyone down". On the contrary, she had – as always – given it her all, but on this occasion the course and the conditions defeated her. It didn't help that the race was held on the hottest day of the Games (well over 30°C in the shade at the start and the road surface much hotter than that) and that, largely due to the demands of TV, it started at 6 pm rather than the early morning favoured by the athletes. But who cares about them?

In my opinion certain British sportswriters (the ones that know nothing about athletics but feel qualified once every four years to pontificate on Olympic competition) were an absolute disgrace. To accuse Paula of all people of being a quitter, of dropping out when the going got too tough or the prospect of a medal had disappeared, would be laughable if the comments had not been so hurtful, damaging and ignorant. Nobody in athletics can surpass Paula for sheer guts and determination, and the fact that she was unable to complete either the marathon or the 10,000m was because her body – not her spirit – would not permit her to. She was in such a bad way before she even started the marathon that had it been any competition other than the Olympics she would have withdrawn. The problem was that anti-inflammatories used in the treatment of a leg injury shortly before the Games upset her bowel so that she was unable to absorb enough energy and nutrients.

For several years now I had been advising professional gambler Tony Ansell on possible good bets at events like the Olympics and World Championships, the object being to take advantage of glaring errors of judgement by bookmakers when setting their odds. We did very well in Athens. My finest hour was predicting that Faní Halkiá in the 400m hurdles was a very promising each-way bet and even had a reasonable chance of winning. I based my assessment on (a) she had improved from a 2003 best of 56.40 to 54.88 when winning the Greek title, advanced to 54.16 winning at the European Cup, and reduced her pb again to 53.99 in a race close behind Jana Pittman and Yuliya Pechonkina, two of the favourites; (b) at the European Cup she ran a significant but largely overlooked relay leg in 49.75; (c) she would be performing in front of her own crowd. Those who advised the bookies clearly missed those pointers because initially she was quoted as a complete outsider at 20/1. Tony lost no time in placing an each-way bet of £500 with Ladbrokes. After winning her heat in 53.85 the price dropped to 16/1, still a bargain, but when she won her semi in an Olympic record and world-leading time of 52.77

the bookmakers realised too late they had made a colossal and potentially costly mistake. They had indeed, as Faní romped home by a good four metres in 52.82 … and Tony won a total of over £26,000! The second great choice had no input from me. Tony wanted to place a bet on the men's javelin and with eight entrants having thrown between 86.12m and 87.73m that season it was a totally open event. Quoted at a tempting 39/1, Tony decided to stake £500 on Andreas Thorkildsen. The Norwegian ranked only 13th with a season's best of 84.45m but he had won in Stockholm and London. He won too in Athens with a personal best of 86.50m – and Tony's hunch netted him £19,500. When Tony does well, his helpers benefit also with bonuses, and so everyone (other than the bookies) was happy.

It was a good year all round, for I always loved visiting America and I managed no fewer than four trips across the pond. The first was to New York in January.

As Duke Ellington and Billy Strayhorn urged in their jazz classic: "Take The 'A' Train". That's the subway line that will whisk you to the Washington Heights area of Upper Manhattan and a brand new attraction which will be of immense interest to all athletics enthusiasts visiting New York. I was honoured to be present at the opening of the US National Track & Field Hall of Fame, and what a glittering array of our sport's legends graced the event. Among those at the opening were such Olympic champions as Bob Beamon, Don Bragg, Billy Mills, Al Oerter, Frank Shorter and Mal Whitfield, together with other luminaries like Harold Davis (now aged 83, he tied Jesse Owens' world 100m record of 10.2 in 1941) and Grete Waitz, nine-time winner of the city's marathon which is celebrated in the Hall of Fame's Fred Lebow Marathon Hall. For many years obscurely housed in Indianapolis, the Hall of Fame has been greatly enhanced and now has a brilliantly designed home in the New Balance Track and Field Center at the Armory at 168th Street and Fort Washington Avenue.

Here are hundreds of photos of all the great American stars, arranged decade by decade from the 1880s onwards, and including such early shots as Charles Sherrill using a crouch start in 1884 and William Byrd Page clearing a world record 1.93m in 1887. Complementing the photos are a host of fascinating historic artefacts. You can see Al Oerter's four Olympic gold medals, Charley Paddock's silk singlet and shorts, one of Cornelius Warmerdam's bamboo poles etc. It's well worth boarding that 'A' Train.

Whenever in New York I would take in a Broadway show, and on this trip I was lucky enough to get tickets for two wonderful productions. Accompanied by my cousin Naomi I enjoyed a vibrant performance of *42nd Street* (in a theatre located on 43rd Street!), while Elliott Denman and I were stunned by the virtuosity of Hugh Jackman as *The Boy From Oz*. This was a musical based on the life of Australian Oscar winning songwriter and entertainer Peter Allen, who was married to Liza Minnelli for seven years before coming out as gay and dying of AIDS-related throat cancer in 1992, aged 48. Jackman deservedly won a Tony award for his dynamic acting, singing and dancing role which won him a lengthy standing ovation. In fact, when I phoned Pat in London that night I told her she had to come to New York to see that show because I knew she, already a Hugh Jackman fan, would love it. Pat had never been keen to visit New York with all of its hustle and bustle but I persuaded her (not quite dragging her screaming onto the plane) and in April we spent four sightseeing days in Manhattan ... and, yes, she adored the show.

Astonishingly, considering Pat never enjoyed long flights, that was our second transatlantic foray that month! We celebrated our 31st wedding anniversary on April 8 in Las Vegas where we met up with my sister Benita and husband Charlie who were out there for their 50th wedding anniversary. After five nights at the Flamingo we took a one-hour flight to Palm Springs to spend six nights in an American Indian hotel-casino. A highlight of our stay was taking a trip on the aerial tramway, a spectacular 12 minute rotating cable car ride starting at 2600 feet above sea level and propelling us up to 8500 feet during which time the Sonoran desert was replaced by alpine forest and the temperature plummeted some 30°F. I returned to Vegas on my own early in December, by which time so much had happened in the world of athletics.

Long before doping became such a problem, the sport was graced by such all-time greats as Gunder Hägg of Sweden (16 world records from 1500m to 5000m between 1941 and his disqualification as an amateur in 1945), Fanny Blankers-Koen of Holland (20 world records or bests at sprints, 80m hurdles, high jump, long jump and pentathlon between 1938 and 1952, not to mention a record four Olympic gold medals in 1948) and Shirley Strickland, later de la Hunty of Australia (11 world records and bests at sprints and 80m hurdles between 1952 and 1956, plus seven Olympic medals). They all crossed life's finishing line in 2004, aged 85, 85 and 78 respectively.

Two of the most respected names in British athletics also passed away. Norris McWhirter (78), a Scottish international sprinter (10.7 100m in 1950) who with his twin brother Ross made such a massive contribution to athletics documentation with the book *Get To Your Marks!* and the monthly magazine *Athletics World*, and found wider fame and fortune through the *Guinness Book of Records*, and Derek Johnson (71), who so very nearly won the 1956 Olympic 800m, was a highly competent performer at all distances from 100 yards to the 3000m steeplechase, and later became an influential figure in the International Athletes Club and the South of England AAA. Mourned also was New Zealand's Arthur Lydiard, aged 87.

One of the world's most celebrated and influential coaches, Arthur Lydiard, died of a suspected heart attack in Houston while on a typically demanding lecture tour of the USA. Twice New Zealand marathon champion, he became mentor to a remarkable collection of middle and long distance runners, his protégés including Olympic champions Peter Snell and Murray Halberg. His belief in heavy mileage training schedules for his runners, with even 800m runners like Snell (who ran a 2:41 marathon in 1961 just weeks before setting world records at the mile, 800m and 880y) covering a hilly 20 miles course during a certain period of their build-up, was widely copied. After his phenomenal success with fellow New Zealanders he spent most of the rest of his long life in other countries. He moved to Mexico in 1965, and two years later he started an appointment to Finland which led to the spectacular revival of that nation's long dormant middle and long distance running tradition. Long before the great distance running boom took off in the USA during the 1970s he advocated jogging for the masses and right until the moment of his death he remained hugely in demand the world over for his coaching philosophy and methods. He was awarded the Order of New Zealand, his country's highest honour, in 1990.

Months before his Olympic gold medal in the 4x100m relay, Jason Gardener tasted individual glory by becoming the first Briton to win the World Indoor 60m title, his time in Budapest being 6.49. Kenenisa Bekele, who had set a world indoor 5000m record of 12:49.60 in Birmingham, gave the World Indoors a miss in order to concentrate on the World Cross Country in Brussels, where he repeated his 4km/12km double and led Ethiopian clean sweeps in both races. Shortly before his 22nd birthday, Bekele produced two absolutely phenomenal runs back to back in Hengelo on May 31 and Ostrava on June 8, breaking world records held by Haile Gebrselassie. First he covered 5000m in 12:37.35, an average of 60.59 per lap, and then he combined halves of 13:14.42 and 13:05.89 for a 10,000m time of 26:20.31.

I first took real notice of the man who would develop into one of Bekele's greatest rivals, Mo Farah, in a mile race at Oxford's Iffley Road track on May 6. Ring any bells? Yes, it was exactly 50 years since Roger Bannister's epic run and the anniversary was celebrated with a match between the AAA and Oxford University, plus special races staged by the British Milers Club. The windy conditions held down the times but the elite race was won by Australia's Craig Mottram in 3:56.64 while 21 year-old Farah was second in a tantalising personal best of 4:00.07, just missing becoming Britain's 158th sub-4 minute miler. Never mind his mind-boggling collection of global titles at 5000m and 10,000m, Mo would advance to 3:56.49 in 2005 but that was small beer compared to his stunning European 1500m record of 3:28.81 in 2013, the miling equivalent of around 3:46!

On either side of her Olympic ordeal, Paula Radcliffe enjoyed some brilliant runs. Racing on a track for the first time since winning the European 10,000m title in August 2002, she was the star performer at the European Cup in Bydgoszcz in June, breaking her own Commonwealth 5000m record with 14:29.11, third fastest ever time to that point. A week later in Gateshead she defied the windy conditions, costing her at least a second a lap, to set a UK all-comers 10,000m record of 30:17.15. In November she demonstrated there was no lasting physical damage from the Athens marathon.

To the delight of her supporters and one hopes to the discomfiture of those who so unfairly and insensitively labelled her a quitter because of her Olympic nightmare, Paula Radcliffe bounced back triumphantly with a resounding victory in the New York City Marathon. In her first race since Athens, Radcliffe may have run the slowest of her four completed marathons

(2:23:10), but it was the win which mattered ... of huge importance to her morale as well as her standing as the greatest female marathoner the world has seen. She said later that she was always confident of finishing first but to anxious televiewers it looked as though it could go either way as she and Susan Chepkemei slogged it out stride for stride, mile after mile, after burning off the rest of a high class field. They fought body and soul as they entered Central Park and those energy sapping hills as the finish approached. Neither woman was in any state to actually sprint away; it was a case of who could hold the pace longer. The answer came some 200m from the end when Chepkemei faltered just sufficiently to allow Radcliffe to draw a few strides clear. It had been a war of attrition and Radcliffe had the physical resources and mental resolve to prevail, even though she was suffering a stomach upset and was perilously close to being sick three miles from the finish. The winning margin of 3 sec made it the closest women's finish in the race's history.

The most prolific world record breaker was Yelena Isinbayeva. She had raised the indoor pole vault best three times up to 4.86m, while outdoors she cleared 4.87m in Gateshead before being temporarily dethroned as her arch-rival Svetlana Feofanova made 4.88m in Greece. Three weeks later, in Birmingham, 'Isi' reclaimed the record with 4.89m and progressed to 4.90m in London, 4.91m winning the Olympic title and 4.92m in Brussels where Saif Saaeed Shaheen, barred from the Olympics, broke the world record for the steeplechase with 7:53.63.

The AAA Championships were staged in Manchester for the first time in 97 years. The meeting was held at the Manchester Regional Arena, a 6000-seat stadium which had been constructed around what had been the warming-up track for the 2002 Commonwealth Games. The revelation was 20 year-old Christine Ohuruogu, an England junior netball international whose best 400m time before that season was just 54.21. Having already improved in one go to 52.20, she beat the favourite, Lee McConnell, in chilly and windy conditions in 50.98. There can't be many other female 400m runners who never had a personal best in either the 53s or 51s.

The million dollar Golden League Jackpot, decided in Berlin, was split between Olympic champions Christian Olsson and Tonique Williams-Darling, both of whom won all six of their competitions in the series. Olsson signed off with a 17.45m triple jump and Williams-Darling set a Bahamian 400m record of 49.07.

It had been another hectic year, workwise, as I had one book published and was just starting to research a second. *Olympic Track & Field History*, another joint publishing venture with Larry Eder of Shooting Star Media, Inc (USA), updated my 1996 publication, while I was busy sorting out who to include in my upcoming *All-Time Greats of British Athletics* which eventually appeared in 2006.

40. TRACK NUTS' HEAVEN (2005)

This was one of my most fruitful years for travel. In April 2005 I revisited one of my favourite cities, Amsterdam, with its glorious art galleries, and took the opportunity to wander over to the 1928 Olympic Stadium to pay my respects. Over the years I've managed to visit all but three of the 23 Olympic host cities ... only Antwerp, Melbourne and Beijing have eluded me. In May, I drove with Pat to the historic city of Chester, making a diversion on the way to the Merseyside nature reserve in Formby in order to catch sight of red squirrels, a particular interest of ours. Early in June we spent a week in the delightful Italian resort of Viareggio. Well, it should have been a week but it turned out to be only five days as we hadn't noticed until we checked in at Gatwick that Pat's passport had recently expired. That was on a Saturday and the earliest we could arrange a new passport (to be collected in Peterborough, not London) was on the Monday, so it was Tuesday before we could fly out for our curtailed holiday. Frustrating to say the least!

Later in June I took a much longer flight to Los Angeles in order to attend the US Championships at the nearby city of Carson. I couldn't enthuse much over the star of those championships, Justin Gatlin, who became the first man for 20 years to complete the 100m/200m double, clocking 10.08 and 20.04 into the wind. Other top performances included a 44.20 400m by Jeremy Wariner, 12.99 110m hurdles by Allen Johnson, 47.24 400m hurdles by Trinidad-born Kerron Clement and such victories as Allyson Felix's 22.13 200m and Sanya Richards' 49.28 400m.

During my stay I took a fascinating tour of the famous British liner, the *Queen Mary*, which for the last 50 years has been moored at Long Beach as a hotel and museum. A group of fans who had booked through *Track & Field News* were staying aboard and it was a pleasure to bump into Cordner Nelson, who together with brother Bert founded that indispensable monthly magazine ("The Bible Of The Sport") in 1948. Bert died in 1994 at 72, but Cordner lived on to 2009 aged 91. I haven't missed an issue since the early 1950s and happily it survives, edited in California since 1973 by Garry Hill, an exuberant Canadian who has been an announcer at several Olympics and World Championships.

Another memorable visit – thanks to my friend Ken Nakamura, the world's foremost marathon statistician – was to the Amateur Athletic Foundation Sports Library in LA. It's housed in what used to be the Helms Athletic Foundation's sports museum (to which Dick Bank took me back in 1964), and it's just a heavenly place for any athletics enthusiast. I could have spent weeks, rather than a few hours, there.

It's every tracknut's dream. A library containing seemingly almost every athletics book and magazine ever published on shelf after shelf – and you're free to browse to your heart's content. I was knocked out by the range of the collection. I was able to view the very first issue of "Track & Field News", but there's no parochialism here. There is an almost complete run of "Athletics Weekly", and "Athletics Today" of blessed memory is also to be found, as is the old East German weekly, "Der Leichtathlet". I knew the library, financed by profits created by the Los Angeles Olympics of 1984, subscribed to "Athletics International" – but it was a surrealistic moment when, having left London on a Wednesday without seeing the latest printed issue, I spotted it on display in the library, nearly 6000 miles away, on the Friday morning! The library's treasures include the National Track & Field Research Collection comprising thousands of books, periodicals, videos and programmes, and more than 7000 Olympic publications. However, athletics and the Olympics constitute just a small part of the library's range; all sports are covered (7000 books on golf alone) and there are over 90,000 photographs and thousands of instructional and historical sports videos.

Talking of books, I spent a few days away on my own in Nice in the autumn, in pleasant surroundings and away from all distractions, to concentrate on completing the *All-Time Greats of British Athletics*, while in November it was back to the Big Apple to report on the closest and biggest New York Marathon. The race came down to a lung-bursting side by side sprint to the tape with world record holder Paul Tergat of Kenya prevailing by 32/100ths of a second in 2:09:30 as South Africa's defending champion Hendrick Ramaala crashed to the ground as he tried a Colin Jackson-like dip finish. The size of the field broke all records with 37,516 starters and 36,894 finishers. As was becoming my custom, I tacked on a few days trying my luck in Atlantic City, the Greyhound bus journey from New York reviving fond memories of my trans-America odyssey of over 40 years previously.

The London Marathon in April was also bigger than ever with 35,600 starters and 35,300 finishers, and notable for the fastest time to be registered in a women-only race. That was 2:17:42 by Paula Radcliffe, completing her post-Olympic rehabilitation which had started with her hard won victory in New York in November 2004. Winning, literally, by a mile, Paula covered the first half in 68:27 but stomach cramps slowed her to a second half of 69:15. She could now claim the three quickest ever marathon times and four of the top five, a degree of supremacy unprecedented in marathon annals. Four months later, in Helsinki, she demonstrated her ability to shine in a major marathon championship by capturing the world title.

She has of course won world titles at cross country and half marathon but it has been a long and arduous journey towards Radcliffe's first global championship in an 'Olympic' event at the age of 31. Since 1995 she had competed in three Olympics and four editions of the World Championships with only a single medal (silver in 1999 10,000m) to show for it and after last year's horrendous experience in Athens there were those who questioned whether she would ever be a "big time" winner. Now, to the delight of (but no surprise to) her loyal fans she has succeeded in one of her main competitive goals although the marathon in Beijing [2008 Olympics] remains the ultimate target. It was no occasion for world record attempting heroics and so Radcliffe contented herself with running the first half well within her comfort zone, which for her – uniquely – is around 70 minutes, and then be guided by how she felt. Leading from the outset she reached halfway in 69:49, started to pull away at 27k and was 64 seconds ahead of Catherine Ndereba by the finish which she reached in 2:20:57. That is easily the fastest ever time in a global championship race. Another distinction is that she is the first Briton of either sex to win a world or Olympic marathon title and now there can be no doubt about her status as the greatest distance runner Britain has ever produced.

There was no doubt, also, that Russian pole vaulter Yelena Isinbayeva was the world's top female athlete of 2005. Take her indoor season; four competitions and four world indoor records: 4.87m in Donetsk, 4.88m in Birmingham, 4.89m in Liévin and 4.90m when winning the European title in Madrid. She opened her outdoor campaign in Lausanne and, sure enough, she added her usual single centimetre (for bonus payment reasons like Sergey Bubka) to her world outdoor record with a clearance of 4.93m. Eleven days later, in Madrid, she raised the record again but … shock, horror … by TWO centimetres. The reason was that a few days earlier in Greece she had failed at 4.94m so had decided on a new target height of 4.95m, but her characteristically cautious approach was swept aside when she appeared at the London Grand Prix on July 22.

Although he has long been an admirer of Yelena Isinbayeva, Sergey Bubka once said he would not take women's pole vaulting really seriously until the world record reached five metres. Well, now it has … and the great man was not only present at London's Crystal Palace to witness this piece of history but was chosen to present a world record bonus cheque to the vivacious 23 year-old from Volgograd. Actually, there were two bonuses: $50,000 for an earlier clearance of 4.96m and another $50,000 for the landmark height, plus $10,000 first place prize. By the time she entered the competition on a warm evening before a capacity crowd of 18,500, only one rival remained ... hardly surprising as her starting height was 4.70m! Isinbayeva was faultless at that and 4.80m, and the bar went next to 4.96m. At her second attempt she soared well clear and although she nicked the bar on her descent it stayed up and she had set her 16th world record. Just as the gun fired for the start of the final track event, the 5000m, she sped down the runway for her first attempt at 5.00m ... and over she went clean as a whistle for no 17. Forty two years after the ill-fated Brian Sternberg opened the five-metre era with one of those new-fangled fibreglass poles, a woman had joined the club.

And still there was more from Superwoman, for at the World Championships on August 12 she went higher still.

How fortuitous it was for Isinbayeva's bank balance that the final was held over for two days because of the potentially dangerous conditions on the original date. Weather conditions for the postponed contest were at least reasonable, enabling her to aim for and attain her 18th world record and a $100,000 bonus on top of her first place prize money of $60,000. With her first world title won [no one else cleared 4.70m], Isinbayeva asked for 5.01m and at the second try she cleared with plenty to spare.

My Life in Athletics

Equally clearly, the male athlete of 2005 was Kenenisa Bekele. The year had started tragically for the Ethiopian, for on January 4 he was out training on the outskirts of Addis Ababa with his 17 year-old fiancée Alem Techale when she suddenly collapsed. He immediately carried her to his car, but she died of a suspected heart attack on their way to the hospital. An immensely promising athlete in her own right, having won the 1500m at the 2003 World Youth Championships, Alem had been due to marry Kenenisa in May. He returned for a couple of indoor races, beaten each time, but even though not at peak fitness he added two more world cross country titles, at 4k and 12k, to his already bulging collection. It was his fourth "double" and, including team awards, he now had 21 cross country medals ... and was still only 22! Outdoors, he was unstoppable. He opened up with a 26:28.72 10,000m, the fourth fastest ever, in cold and windy Hengelo; followed up with the fourth quickest ever 5000m time of 12:40.18 in Paris; won again over that distance in London in 12:55.55 (with one Mo Farah 16th in 13:48.46); retained his world 10,000m title in Helsinki in 27:08.33 thanks to a 26.15 final 200m; and brought his season to a climactic close by breaking his own world record for 10,000m with 26:17.53 in Brussels. He covered the first half in 13:09.19, the second in 13:08.34 ... and it wasn't until 1981 (Henry Rono 13:06.20) that anyone ran a single 5000m faster than that second split.

Of the other world records set that year, the most eye-catching was the 100m time of 9.77 in Athens by 22 year-old Asafa Powell, which I witnessed in a live Eurosport transmission.

He was away to a good start, but it was the second half of the race that was so phenomenal. He was up against a world class field but he finished two to three metres ahead of his closest challengers. Tim Montgomery's listed world record of 9.78 [later annulled due to an anti-doping rule violation] had been broken and Jamaica could hail her first ever world record breaker at the distance. Powell isn't the first sprint star in his family. Brother Donovan Powell, 11 years his elder, had a personal best of 10.07 as well as a hand timed 9.7. Asafa expects to go faster still this summer but even more important to him is to prove in Helsinki that he is a championship competitor. So far, in global events, he was disqualified in his quarter-final at the 2003 World Championships and placed fifth in the Olympic final last year.

As it turned out, Powell missed the World Championships through injury (Gatlin taking both sprint titles in 9.88 and 20.04) and although he remains a world class performer a dozen years later and astonishingly has dipped under 10.00 without wind assistance almost 100 times he has never been able to do himself justice on the most important occasions. His highest Olympic placing remains fifth and twice he has finished third in the World Championships, although it hasn't helped that from 2008 onwards he would always be in the shadow of a certain Usain Bolt.

One athlete who did come good at the Olympics, and how, was Kelly Holmes and in the Queen's New Year Honours she was made a Dame. Although recovered from the achilles tendon injury which kept her out of the

398

World Championships and selected for the Commonwealth Games in March 2006, she announced her retirement in December. "Nothing could ever top what I achieved in Athens last year," she explained. Happily, she was not lost to the sport she had graced for so long. She mentored several of Britain's most promising female middle distance runners, set up the Dame Kelly Holmes Trust to support disadvantaged young people and retired athletes, and served as president of Commonwealth Games England from 2009 to 2015, succeeded by Denise Lewis.

Top mark at the World Championships Trials and AAA Championships in Manchester was the 17.64m triple jump by Nathan Douglas. Rather less attention was paid to 18 year-old Greg Rutherford, winner of the long jump with 7.79m, but a better indication of his talent was provided a fortnight later when he captured the European junior title, 41cm ahead of his nearest rival, with a jump of 8.14m. He was fast, too, twice clocking 10.38 and reaching the AAA final. Mo Farah didn't survive his 1500m heat but did pick up a 5000m silver medal the following week at the European Under 23 Championships. The third member of the seven-years-away Olympic gold medal trio, Jessica Ennis, placed third at the Trials in the 100m hurdles and equal sixth in the high jump. Later in the season she became European junior heptathlon champion.

It was only a few days before the Trials that the above trio, and everyone else, knew that the 2012 Games would be contested in London, who edged out the favourites, Paris, by 54 votes to 50 in the IOC poll on July 6. London thus became the first city to host the four-yearly Olympics for a third time, having staged them at short notice in 1908 and 1948. There was much rejoicing throughout the UK … until the very next day (7/7) a series of Islamist terrorist bomb attacks in central London on the Underground and a bus killed 52 innocent people and injured hundreds more.

Natural causes claimed the lives of two highly respected British coaches. Stan Long of Gateshead, best known for guiding Brendan Foster's stellar career, died at 76 and Denis Watts passed away at the age of 84. Denis, the AAA long jump (1946) and triple jump (1946 and 1947) champion, was 28 when appointed as one of the AAA's professional coaches under Geoff Dyson and during his 30-year career he coached Dorothy Hyman, Ann Packer and Lillian Board, among many others, to the highest world class level. As was the case also with his long-time colleague John LeMasurier, his gentle but expert approach produced great results.

Colette Besson, the Frenchwoman who so narrowly deprived Lillian Board of the 1968 Olympic 400m title, died of cancer (as had Lillian), aged 59. She passed on while the World Championships were being staged in Helsinki, where the French team excelled itself by winning seven medals, including gold by the men's 4x100m squad (profiting from the heavily favoured American team failing to survive the heats) and by 110m hurdler Ladji Doucouré, who finished 1/100th ahead of China's Olympic champion and world record holder Liu Xiang in 13.07. The British team fared less well. As related earlier, Paula

Radcliffe triumphed in the marathon but there were only two other medals: bronze for the men's 4x100m and women's 4x400m teams.

Despite the sprint relay debacle, the US team dominated with 14 victories, including a 43.93 400m (the world's fastest for five years) by Jeremy Wariner, 47.30 400m hurdles by Bershawn Jackson (a remarkable personal best in heavy rain and strong winds), 8.60m long jump followed by five fouls from Dwight Phillips, 22.16 200m by 19 year-old Allyson Felix and 6.89m long jump by Tianna Madison, also 19, who under her married name of Tianna Bartoletta would be crowned Olympic champion in 2016. History was made when the Americans filled the first four places in the men's 200m, something which had only been possible since the IAAF decided that from 2001 defending champions could be automatic entrants in addition to a nation's three selected entrants. Among many other scintillating performances were a 70.17m discus throw, the first 70m delivery in a global championship, by Lithuania's Virgilijus Alekna; a 14:38.59/30:24.02 distance double by Tirunesh Dibaba thanks to last laps of 58.2 and 58.4; and women's world records (in addition to Isinbayeva's) by Cuba's Osleidys Menéndez in the javelin with 71.70m and by Russia's Olimpiada Ivanova in the 20km walk with 1:25:41. Usain Bolt, still just 18, contested his first senior World Championships and made the 200m final but, as I reported: "The gangling Jamaican prodigy, drawn in the tight lane 1, ran a surprisingly good turn and was a close fifth when he pulled up injured."

The downside of Helsinki was the number of athletes who were stripped of their medals, in some cases many years later when doping control samples were re-analysed using the latest advanced techniques. The cheating gold medallists were revealed as shot putter Nadezhda Ostapchuk and hammer thrower Ivan Tikhon of Belarus and Russian hammer thrower Olga Kuzenkova. Several other winners served doping bans of two years or more at other times in their careers: Justin Gatlin (100m & 200m) of the USA, Moroccan-born Rashid Ramzi (800m & 1500m) of Bahrain, Vadim Devyatovskiy (hammer, in place of Tikhon) of Belarus, Sergey Kirdyapkin (50km walk) of Russia and Tatyana Tomashova (1500m) of Russia.

Tatyana Lebedeva, a Russian who in 2017 was stripped of two silver medals from the 2008 Olympics after re-analysis of her samples (she has lodged an appeal), had been expected to win her third world triple jump title but, hampered by an achilles tendon problem, she withdrew from the final as a precautionary measure. Financially at least it proved a shrewd move, for at the Golden League finale in Berlin four weeks later she became the only athlete to win at all six meetings in the series and thus won the entire million dollar jackpot on offer. It was touch and go, though, for Lebedeva's second round 14.85m only just prevailed as Yamilé Aldama's final effort was measured at 14.82m, and she was lucky that Jamaica's London-based Trecia Smith, winner of the world title with 15.11m, was out with an ankle injury. Aldama may be unique in that she has represented three countries. She competed for her native Cuba when placing second in the 1999 World Championships and fourth in the 2000 Olympics; moved to London with her Scottish husband in 2001 and hoped to become eligible to jump for Britain at the 2003 Worlds (she achieved her best ever distance of 15.29m that year) and 2004 Olympics but, not being Zola Budd, she would have to wait for three years to get a British passport and so she opted to switch her allegiance to Sudan of all places and became an African as well as Caribbean record holder. She finally began to represent Britain in 2011 and her finest moment was winning the 2012 world indoor title in her 40th year.

December marked the 60th anniversary of the founding of *Athletics*, the monthly forerunner of *Athletics Weekly*, and I was kindly invited to attend a celebratory dinner in Peterborough. The magazine was again a 'must-read' publication and a splendid 100 page issue was produced to mark the Diamond Anniversary. There were complimentary messages from the likes of Brendan Foster ("a fundamental part of the British athletics scene"), Dave Bedford ("the magazine has done well to reach to its 60th birthday"), Dave Moorcroft ("it is at the heart of the sport") and Seb Coe ("AW has been part of my life since I started running"), and a feast of stimulating and nostalgic aricles. My contribution to this special issue included a concise history of AW, emphasising its importance to the athletics community, and profiles of McDonald Bailey, Ann Packer and Geoff Capes.

Quizzed, as were several other previous editors, as to "what's the one change you would like to see to improve the sport", I replied (citing two):

Much as I'm obsessed by records and statistics, I feel that meticulously orchestrated pacemaking has ruined middle and long distance running at the Golden League and Grand Prix level. Let's get back to true racing and tactics, hopefully providing fast times as a by-product. Also, I long for the day when athletes have to pledge they will not use performance enhancing substances, doping tests are so watertight that there can be no disputing the results, and that offenders are kicked out for life and to hell with "constraint of trade" legal threats.

41. A STROLL DOWN MEMORY LANE (2006)

Although I still enjoy reporting on the current athletics scene at home and abroad for AI, I have for some years now concentrated increasingly on our sport's history. If I have a 'mission', it is to commemorate the achievements of the champions of yesteryear. It is so important that today's athletes and enthusiasts should be aware of what has gone before. It's great that athletes like Mo Farah, Greg Rutherford and Jessica Ennis-Hill are household names but let's not forget such predecessors in their events as Alf Shrubb, Gordon Pirie, Chris Chataway, Dave Bedford, Ian Stewart, Dave Moorcroft, Lynn Davies, Mary Rand, Mary Peters and Denise Lewis – all huge stars in their day. Towards the end of 2004 I started to research and write what I hoped would be an appropriate salute to Britain's most successful athletes. The resulting book was published in May 2006 and in my introduction to *All-Time Greats of British Athletics* I explained why and how it had come about.

This book is my tribute to 78 of the all-time greats of British athletics ... in the hope that new generations of athletics followers will come to appreciate the brilliant achievements of men and women they may never have heard of before, and that older readers will rekindle fond memories of athletes and contests from their earlier days in this wonderful sport of ours. Over that half century of documenting the sport I have written countless profiles (and, regrettably, obituaries) of leading British athletes and some years ago I resolved to collect, expand and update them to form a book. It would be my retirement project. Well, as my long suffering but ever supportive wife Pat will testify, that retirement always tends to be deferred for just another year or two, so at the end of 2004 I decided I would get on with it while still involved with other work.

The most difficult aspect of this book was deciding who to include and exclude. How can you define who is, and who isn't, an 'all-time great'? The answer is that you can't; there is no definitive qualification. Ultimately it's a subjective choice based on facts, figures, historical perspective ... and a gut feeling. I would guess that most athletics enthusiasts with a grounding in the sport's history would agree with around 70 of my selections but vehemently disagree with the others. Believe me, I went through agonies before finalising my list.

The athletes I chose ranged alphabetically from Harold Abrahams to Sydney Wooderson and in terms of birthdate from Walter George (1858) to Paula Radcliffe (1973). The oldest life span was Jack Holden's at 96 years, the briefest was poor Lillian Board's, just 22. All of our Olympic champions from 1924 to 2004 were included, plus Arnold Strode-Jackson from 1912 and Albert Hill from 1920.

Seb Coe did me the honour of contributing a foreword which ended with the words: "He has lovingly and painstakingly chronicled those individuals who have left a nation with some of the most breathtaking moments in our sporting history like the four minute mile, great head to heads, Olympic glory and world records. I know that this book will relive those moments for everybody that reads it." It was my pleasure, Seb. My thanks also to my old AT co-editor Randall Northam, whose company, SportsBooks Ltd, published the 274 page volume which included 44 photos, mostly by the incomparable Mark Shearman.

My next major historical project appeared between October 2006 and March 2007 in *Athletics Weekly*. The objective was to decide the world's ten best athletes of all-time in each event. In my introduction to the series I explained that a perpetual area of discussion among enthusiasts is comparing one great athlete with another and that of course there is no totally objective method of ranking athletes of different eras. However, for want of anything more scientific, I had devised a points system which took into account Olympic and World Championship medals, world records (and their longevity) and world merit rankings. The system had its flaws, obviously, but I think the results were largely credible. At least the rankings provoked discussion and, again an important element of my work, drew attention to great names of the past.

By my reckoning the ultimate all-time greats as at the end of the 2006 season included three Britons: Colin Jackson, Daley Thompson and Sally Gunnell. Overall, Sergey Bubka and Jan Zelezny (tie) and Jackie Joyner-Kersee were the highest single event point scorers, with Carl Lewis (100m, 200m & long jump) and Fanny Blankers-Koen (100m, 200m, 80m hurdles, high jump, long jump & pentathlon!) earning the highest aggregate scores.

As a huge fan of marathon running, ever since as a schoolboy witnessing Jim Peters' groundbreaking runs from Windsor to Chiswick, I had the pleasure of being present for the Boston, London and New York classics in 2006. The stay in Boston was brief but fascinating, combining some hectic sightseeing with witnessing Robert Cheruiyot set a course record of 2:07:14. A few hours later I was on my way to Las Vegas, the highlight of my four days there being an exhilarating flight to and over the Grand Canyon in an aircraft so small that the passengers had to be weighed to make sure the plane was evenly balanced. I arrived home just in time to catch the London race which, for the first time in marathon history, had seven men inside 2:08. With Haile Gebrselassie hampered by cramp and finishing ninth, victory went to Felix Limo in 2:06:39 while Deena Kastor (née Drossin) won the women's race in an American record of 2:19:36. The New York race in November, again breaking all records for the size of the field, was won not by an African as in the previous nine editions but by Brazil's Marilson Gomes dos Santos in 2:09:58.

Despite the hiccup in London, Gebrselassie enjoyed a notable season. A great ambassador for Ethiopia with his cheerful countenance and sportsmanship as well as his exploits on track and road, he set his 20th world record by clocking 58:55 for a half marathon in January and ended his season with marathon victories in Berlin (2:05:56) and Fukuoka (2:06:52). His younger compatriot Kenenisa Bekele was also continuing to make history. By winning the world indoor 3000m championship in Moscow he became the first athlete to achieve gold medals at the Olympics, World Championships, World Indoors

403

and World Cross Country. Three weeks after his indoor triumph he won both the 4km and 12km cross country races in Fukuoka, his fifth and final such double as the 4km event would not be contested again. During the track season he topped the world 5000m list with 12:48.09 and in his first ever serious 1500m race clocked an impressive 3:33.08.

Voted by the IAAF and AI readers as athletes of the year were Asafa Powell and Sanya Richards. Powell was unbeaten at 100m until his final event in Japan when he was disqualified for a false start. Prior to that he had compiled the greatest ever series of 100m races: he won all 16, including the Commonwealth Games title in Melbourne, broke 9.90 seven times and equalled his own world record of 9.77 initially in Gateshead (the first time a world 100m record had ever been set in Britain) and then in a much more competitive race in Zürich. Richards, also born in Jamaica but a US citizen since 2002, won all 13 of her races at 400m, nine of them inside 50 sec and ending her campaign at the World Cup in Athens with an American record of 48.70, the world's quickest for ten years.

The Commonwealth Games drew huge crowds (83,000 one day) and vociferous support for the home athletes. Not surprisingly, the Australian team dominated with 36 medals, 14 of them gold. England provided six winners: Phillips Idowu (17.45m triple jump), Nick Nieland (80.10m javelin), Dean Macey (8143 decathlon), Christine Ohuruogu (50.28 400m), Lisa Dobriskey (4:06.21 1500m) and Kelly Sotherton (6396 heptathlon). Of the trio who would strike Olympic gold six years later, Jessica Ennis placed third in the heptathlon, Greg Rutherford eighth in the long jump and Mo Farah ninth in the 5000m. It was here that Jessica, at 20, indicated her exciting potential for she improved her best score from 5910 to 6269 (her target had been 6000) and her 1.91m high jump was equal to the winning height in the individual event.

Usually the European Championships are a happy hunting ground for British athletes. Nine gold medals were won in 1990 and 1998, but in Gothenburg 2006 there was just one victory, equalling the lowest ever return since the championships were instituted in 1938. As the solitary win was by the men's 4x100m relay team of Dwain Chambers, Darren Campbell, Marlon Devonish and Mark Lewis-Francis in 38.91, it marked the first occasion that no individual title was gained by a Briton. It wasn't all gloom, though, as ten other medals were achieved, including silver in the 5000m by Farah, who launched a prolonged strike for home with a kilometre to go but was pipped at the finish by Spain's Jésus Espana. Other runners-up were Rutherford, triple jumper Nathan Douglas, the men's 4x400m team and the women's 4x400m squad. Jessica Ennis improved slightly to 6287 but in eighth place. Dropped from the team was Christine Ohuruogu who faced a possible ban as she had missed three drug tests within an 18-month period. Although there was never any suggestion that she was seeking to avoid testing, a sanction had to be applied and she was suspended for a year from August.

There was plenty of activity on the anti-doping front. Justin Gatlin ran 9.77 for 100m in Doha in May to equal Asafa Powell's listed world record time but it later transpired that three weeks earlier he had tested positive for testosterone and thus the record was rescinded. Furthermore, he was banned for eight years. As a second doping offender the ban should have been for life, but the US Anti-Doping Agency cut it to eight years as Gatlin had promised to co-operate with USADA in its efforts to eradicate drug use. In fact the penalty was subsequently reduced to four years, Gatlin returned to competition in 2010 and has remained a controversial figure ever since. He clocked his quickest ever time of 9.74 in 2015, aged 33, and was crowned world champion in 2017.

The IAAF announced that another disgraced sprinter, Dwain Chambers, would have all of his results between January 1 2002 and August 1 2003 annulled after admitting drug use when he trained in the USA in 2002. That cost him not only his European Cup and European Championships 100m wins that year, but resulted in Britain being stripped of overall team victory in the European Cup (and consequently disqualification from the World Cup) while his 4x100m relay colleagues at the European Championships lost their gold medals too. A further sanction was that he would forfeit his 9.87 behind Tim Montgomery (another banned athlete) which had equalled Linford Christie's European and UK record. The personal best for Chambers, who returned to competition in 2006, reverted to 9.97 in 1999. His fastest subsequently was 9.99 in 2010 and at 39 in 2017, his final season, he clocked 10.31. Unlike many other offenders, Chambers has acknowledged his cheating and done his best to atone by campaigning for drug-free athletics.

The biggest fish of all in this ocean of drugs was Marion Jones, the most famous female athlete in the world. The net was closing. Traces of EPO were found in the A sample taken at the US Championships but she was cleared of any offence when the B sample proved negative. "I have always maintained that I have never, ever taken performance-enhancing drugs, and I am pleased that a scientific process has now demonstrated that fact." The following year we would see that she lied, and her carefully built world of acclaim and wealth would collapse around her.

THE performance of the year came in the 110m hurdles at Lausanne's Grand Prix meeting.

When Liu Xiang set world age records for 16 (13.94), 17 (13.32) and 18 (13.12) and at 21 tied Colin Jackson's 1993 world record of 12.91 when winning the Olympic title in Athens it seemed inevitable that he would become the first man to dip under 12.90. In Lausanne's superlative Athletissima meeting, the Chinese athlete would make an indelible mark in athletics history. Taking the barriers flawlessly, Liu was credited with 12.88. Interviewed by Chris Turner for the IAAF website, Renaldo Nehemiah (world record 12.93 in 1981) had this to say about Liu: "He is technically sound. His basic flat speed is not as good as the other guys which means that he can race the hurdles at his top speed without fear of going too fast. He is able to relax, and can just concentrate on his technique, clearing the hurdles low. His body is phenomenally flexible."

The pot of money for the IAAF Golden League was changed for the final meeting in Berlin. Instead of a million dollars to be shared by anyone winning at all six meetings, that was cut in half and Asafa Powell, Jeremy Wariner and Sanya Richards were awarded $249,999 each. That was made up of a one-third share of the main jackpot ($166,666 each) plus $83,333 apiece from the secondary jackpot of $500,000 – a sum won also by the three athletes who secured five wins: Kenenisa Bekele, Irving Saladino and Tirunesh Dibaba.

The international season ended the following weekend in Athens. The occasion was the IAAF World Cup and in the men's match Africa, winner at the previous four editions, had to settle for third this time well behind Europe and the USA. Russia retained the women's trophy. Representing the Americas in the 200m, Usain Bolt (19.96) was overtaken in the closing stages by the USA's Wallace Spearmon (19.87). Bolt, yet to race at 100m, had reduced his best time to 19.88 in Lausanne in a great race won by Xavier Carter (19.63) ahead of Tyson Gay (19.70). Gay won the Cup 100m in 9.88, while other highlights included an Australian 3000m record of 7:32.19 by Craig Mottram well clear of Kenenisa Bekele, a 12.96 110m hurdles (a world age 35 record) by Allen Johnson over Liu Xiang's 13.03, and Sanya Richards' 22.23 200m the day after her US record 48.70 400m.

As mentioned in the chapter covering 2004, my enjoyment of the major international championships has for several years been heightened by collaborating with professional gambler Tony Ansell (winonsports.com) with the object of taking advantage of any misjudged odds offered by the bookmakers. This amicable and profitable partnership was revealed to the readership of AW in October after Tony was interviewed for the magazine by Steve Landells. He explained the system. "We assess every event by allocating a percentage chance to each athlete where that chance represented at least 2%, and then allocate a percentage for all the rest of the field combined. The total of those percentages has to add up to exactly 100%. In this way we arrived at the true price of each athlete to compare with the bookmakers' prices. Where those prices exceeded ours by 20% I would have a bet."

Among those who died in 2006 was the pre-eminent women's athletics historian Eric Cowe (62). Another who passed away far too young, also at 62, was the IAAF's ever helpful general secretary István Gyulai, a former head of sport for Hungarian TV who competed at 400m at the 1964 Olympics. Mourned too as a friend and international colleague was that most intellectual of athletics writers, Robert Parienté (75) of *L'Equipe*. Among so many others of note I would make special mention of four very special people.

Len Gebbett *died at the age of 83. When we formed the NUTS in 1958 I was the youngest (at 19) of the eight founder members and Len (all of 35) was the father figure. Fittingly, he became our first chairman and, thanks to his enthusiasm and knowledge, our fledgling organisation quickly made its mark on the British athletics scene. Committee meetings were events to be treasured, for Len had the most wonderfully "Goonish" sense of humour and on many occasions business had to be suspended while we all collapsed in laughter.*

Happy times – as were the frequent occasions when the "nuts" would congregate at the White City, Motspur Park, Chiswick and other nostalgia-inducing venues. Len held a highly responsible position with the Greater London Council as a senior computer programmer and was for many years the UK correspondent for the East German weekly magazine "Der Leichtathlet". It was through that connection and his trips to the GDR that he met Anita who, despite appalling obstacles at the height of the Cold War, eventually became his wife.

Bob Mathias *lost his battle against cancer and died at the age of 75. Who would have predicted, when he was an anaemic young boy, that Bob would grow up to become the world's greatest all-round athlete. It was in May 1948 that his coach, Virgil Jackson, told him: "I've just heard about some event called the decathlon that will be included in a meet in Los Angeles about a week after you graduate. It'll give you something to do after you get out of school." Jackson was convinced that with sufficient work Mathias – at that time primarily a discus thrower – could make the Olympic decathlon team in 1952, but those calculations had to be revised after he won that decathlon on June 10/11. He went on to win the Olympic trial on June 26/27 and the Olympic crown [in London] on August 5/6. Kids of 17, even if they do stand 1.83m (6ft) tall and weigh over 84kg (185lb), are not supposed to be world beaters in the gruelling ten event test, but Mathias had no real weaknesses and coped brilliantly in difficult conditions with the accumulating fatigue and pressure. Asked how he would celebrate, he quipped: "I'll start shaving, I guess."*

Don Thompson*, the 1960 Olympic 50km walk champion, died after suffering an aneurysm, aged 73. After collapsing in hot weather at the 1956 Olympics in Melbourne, he set about acclimatising himself for the trying conditions anticipated for the Rome Games. For three months, in addition to his usual gruelling training, he performed exercises on the spot in his tracksuit in an improvised steam room at his parents' house with temperatures hovering around the 40°C mark. All the discomfort was worth it, for as a result he adapted to Rome's sultry climate without trouble and was able to perform to the best of his ability, finishing 17 seconds clear in 4:25:30, an Olympic record. The sight of Thompson, in sun glasses and a French Foreign Legion type head-dress, striding briskly towards the finish in the stadium was one that was not easily forgotten by the British supporters present, particularly as he was his country's only athletics gold medallist in those Games. His victory was celebrated also by local fans. Known affectionately as Il Topolino ("the little mouse") from winning a 100km race in Milan in 1955, he captured the hearts of everyone in the stadium as he wiggled around the final lap.*

Sydney Wooderson*, who died at the age of 92, achieved more than enough during his fabulous running career to rank among the very greatest of British athletes. Nevertheless, he was also one of the unluckiest. Had fate been kinder it's not inconceivable that he might have won two or three Olympic 1500m titles and beaten Roger Bannister by a full decade to the distinction of becoming the world's first sub-four minute miler. Visually, Sydney was the most* *unlikely of sporting heroes. He was short, light of build and bespectacled, looking every inch the studious solicitor he was. Clad in the all-black kit of his beloved Blackheath Harriers he would receive pitying glances from the less informed spectators when he lined up with his far more athletic looking opponents. That is until the race unfolded and Sydney displayed the surprisingly long stride, remarkable acceleration and deadly kick that made him the scourge of the world's top milers. Described by one American journalist as a "slight anaemic-looking chap who does not look capable of running round a corner without swooning", he was the most versatile runner of his or any other generation. His range was simply phenomenal. Here was a man who in 1938 ran 440y on a poor grass track in 49.3 – surely a time worth inside 48.5 for 400m on a modern synthetic track – and eight years later captured the European 5000m title in 14:08.6 for what was then the world's second fastest ever mark. He set world records at 800m (1:48.4), 880y (1:49.2), three-quarters of a mile (2:59.5) and mile (4:06.4) in 1937-8 but returned in 1945 to lower the British mile record to 4:04.2. By then retired from the track, he won the 1948 English 10 miles cross country title over a hilly course in 56:52. What an inspiration he was, and how outrageous that the most distinguished, popular and modest athlete of his time was so callously passed over for the honour of carrying the Olympic torch at the opening of the Wembley Olympics later that year.*

Just think of what Wooderson might have accomplished had the war and ill health not robbed him of what should have been his greatest years, between the ages of 25 and 30. He missed the chance of Olympic glory at the 1936 Games when, shortly after beating Jack Lovelock for that year's AAA mile title, he sustained a serious ankle injury – with the New Zealander going on to take the Olympic 1500m crown in world record time. The cancelled Games of 1940 and 1944 could have seen him at the peak of his powers and although he always dismissed the suggestion he would probably have been capable of breaking four minutes for the mile during that period. He was, after all, considerably faster than Bannister over 400/800m and his later efforts at 3 miles, 5000m and cross country showed him to have far greater reserves of stamina.

42. A BOLT FROM THE BLUE (2007)

It was an auspicious start to 2007. To celebrate his 75th birthday the previous month, I treated my brother-in-law Charlie to a week's holiday in Las Vegas in January. There had been occasions out there when I had endured temperatures above 110°F and been reluctant to leave the refreshingly cool air conditioning in the casinos but at that time of year the desert resort was decidedly chilly. A highlight of the stay was seeing the Cirque du Soleil show, *Love,* a spectacular and imaginative *homage* to The Beatles, featuring their actual recordings reworked by music directors Sir George Martin and his son Giles.

I was so impressed that, as had been the case with Hugh Jackman in *The Boy From Oz*, I phoned Pat back in London to tell her she just had to see this show some time later in the year. No that there was any great hurry. There are always several Cirque du Soleil productions playing in Vegas and the cost of staging them in vast and specially adapted theatres is such that they have to run for many years to recoup their investment. *Love,* which cost $125 million before it opened in 2006, is still going strong.

Anyway, I arranged for Pat and me to catch the show on October 8. Why that date? There has to be an athletics connection and it just happened to be the day after the Chicago Marathon. Having flown to the Windy City, we stayed overnight at an airport hotel so that I could watch the race live on TV. We took a late night flight to Vegas that Sunday, checking into the Flamingo at around midnight, and on the Monday evening we went to see *Love,* which Pat did indeed enjoy enormously. It was a good start to our five-night stay, but disaster was about to strike. Pat takes up the story:

"Much as I enjoyed the show (and everything else), I was beginning to be affected by exhaustion, partly from the long journey to the USA and partly by the fact that, as I have various eating problems, I hadn't been able to eat enough to replenish my forces adequately. It didn't help that the hotel is huge and just walking along corridors to the breakfast buffet on the ground floor and then standing in the long queue – even though I was drinking water – proved too much and I fainted.

"When I came to I found several policemen, security staff and ambulance men towering over me (all enormous!). Had I, when I had drunk enough water and come round, been able to go into the breakfast room and have tea and eat some of the lovely fare, I'm sure I would have been OK, but the men were all very kind to me and strongly urged me to go to hospital and get checked out. I didn't want to, but I agreed to go in the end for Mel's sake, to reassure him after the fright he had had!

"We were taken to the hospital, and as soon as I was admitted (and they had checked that we had medical insurance and a credit card!) I was subjected to a battery of tests over one and a half days (it seemed like years) ending with an MRI scan, which was one test too many. I couldn't stand the noise and had to scream and beg Mel to make the doctors stop the test, which they really didn't want to do. If it hadn't been for Mel I would have been totally lost! In the end, we got away, after giving them all our details.

"We will never know if any of our bills were paid, because the people in the hospital's office didn't seem very efficient and despite writing to my GP in England for a total medical history, which she gave them, we heard almost nothing more and our insurance company invited us to renew the next year on better terms than previously, without mentioning the colossal amount of $24,000 that the hospital had said my stay had cost."

The early months of 2007 featured several world indoor records. First to strike was Tirunesh Dibaba with 14:27.42 for 5000m in Boston; next came Meseret Defar with 8:23.72 for 3000m in Stuttgart in a thrilling race which saw Meselech Melkamu, in her first ever indoor race, finish just 2/100ths behind, while third was Jo Pavey in a Commonwealth and UK record of 8:31.50. As Joanne Davis she set a British under-15 1500m record of 4:27.9 in 1988 and here she was, at 33, breaking records ... and yet her best was still to come several years later! Yelena Isinbayeva notched up her 20th world pole vault record (11th indoors) by clearing 4.93m in Sergey Bubka's home city of Donetsk. Seven of those records had been set in Britain and a week later, at a Grand Prix meeting in Birmingham, she attempted 4.94m, but it was not to be. However, that city's new track in the National Indoor Arena was the scene of a 2000m world best of 4:49.99 by Kenenisa Bekele.

Birmingham was the venue for the European Indoor Championships and the British team fared admirably, winning the most gold medals (four) and finishing second to Russia in overall medal and placings terms. In the 60m Jason Gardener (6.51) collected his fourth consecutive title with his training companion Craig Pickering second, and in the triple jump Phillips Idowu (17.56m) and Nathan Douglas (17.47m) scored another one-two with both setting indoor personal bests. The British men's 4x400m team also struck gold, but arguably the finest performance of the meeting came from Nicola Sanders in the 400m.

With the Russians strangely subdued this winter, Sanders started as solid favourite. She was some six metres clear at 200m in the startling time of 23.31, easily a pb for that distance. At 300m Peter Matthews timed her at 36.0 and the only worry was whether she had misjudged her pace. She hadn't, for at the finish – looking remarkably unfatigued – she had almost a full second to spare in a brilliant 50.02. That time, fully 0.66 faster than her outdoor best, smashed Katharine Merry's UK record of 50.33 and moved her to fifth on the world all-time list. Only three Britons have run faster outdoors: Kathy Cook (49.43), Merry (49.59) and Donna Fraser (49.79).

Elsewhere in the British team, Mo Farah placed fifth in a slow 3000m and Jessica Ennis sixth in the pentathlon with 4716 points for a massive improvement over her previous highest of 4401. The youngest at 21 and much the smallest in the field, Jess equalled her outdoor high jump best of 1.91m. The British star here, though, was Kelly Sotherton who pressed Carolina Klüft hard all the way. The Swede prevailed with 4944 points with Kelly improving upon her UK record of 4733 with 4927. In her first heptathlon of the year, Jess raised her British under-23 record to 6388, jumping 31cm over her head to equal the British high jump record of 1.95m in the process. That score she increased to 6399 when winning the European Cup contest ahead of Kelly's 6229, Britain winning the team title for the first time.

The big road running news came from Kenya's Japan-based Sammy Wanjiru, who in 2005 while still a junior had set a world half marathon record of 59:16, a time reduced to 58:55 by Haile Gebrselassie in 2006. Racing in Ra's Al Khaymah (United Arab Emirates) in February, Wanjiru – still only 20 – was timed in 58:53, and the following month in The Hague he clocked a stunning 58:35, covering the first 10km in 27:27 and the second in 28:04 for a 20km world record *en route* of 55:31. His exciting potential at the marathon was confirmed in December when, in his debut, he won the Fukuoka race in 2:06:39.

Gebrselassie enjoyed quite a season too, although it didn't start well as stitch caused him to drop out of the London Marathon. Buoyed up by running 26:52.81 for 10,000m in his first track race for three years, he set new global figures of 56:25.98 for 20,000m prior to completing 21,285m in the hour in Ostrava. Out on his own after 12km, he averaged 67.65 per lap for 53 and a bit laps! Even more spectacular was his world record of 2:04:26 in the Berlin Marathon, reaching halfway in 62:29 and completing the second half (running the last 12km alone) in 61:57. It was the 34 year-old Ethiopian's 24th world record or world best. Meanwhile, Bekele recovered from blotting his world cross country copybook (he dropped out due to stomach problems and dizziness in the heat of Mombasa) by clocking fast times at 3000m and 5000m before notching up his third world 10,000m title. The heat (32°C) of Osaka had no effect on him this time and he sprinted home in 27:05.90. A couple of weeks later, in Brussels, he clocked the year's quickest time of 26:46.19.

Ethiopia's women were not to be outshone. Meseret Defar smashed her own world record for 5000m with 14:16.63, won the world title and clocked a barrier-breaking 8:58.58 for the admittedly rarely contested 2 miles distance in Brussels. She was unbeaten on the track, as was Tirunesh Dibaba who, despite falling and suffering from stomach pains, still managed to gain her third world 10,000m title. It was quite a year at the longer distances as in addition Kenya's Lornah Kiplagat posted a world half marathon record of 66:25.

Although conditions were far from ideal for great times at the US Championships in Indianapolis in June, Tyson Gay came up with the fastest sprint double up to that time. Gay, who had been timed in New York three weeks earlier at 9.76 with the wind just over the limit at 2.2m, first took the 100m in 9.84, equalling his legal personal best, and two days later, on a soggy track, he stormed to the second fastest ever 200m time of 19.62. Late in August, at the World Championships in Osaka, Gay would confirm his status as the world's top speed merchant.

The much anticipated 100m clash between Asafa Powell and Tyson Gay, with each man seeking his first global title, resulted in victory for the American and surrender for the Jamaican. The final was held in 30°C heat on a lightning fast track, and had there not been an 0.5m headwind the world record [Powell's 9.77] might have been threatened. Powell got the better start and was at least a metre clear at halfway but Gay was never flustered and, when he drew level with his rival, Powell – in his own words – "just panicked and tightened up." Gay went on to open a lead and Powell admitted: "When I saw I wasn't in gold medal contention I gave up; I just stopped running." The outcome was that Gay won in 9.85.

Gay's main rivals in the 200m were always likely to be Usain Bolt and Wallace Spearmon but Gay, in his eighth race of the meeting, left them far behind with the sixth sub-19.80 run of his career (19.76). Bolt held a narrow lead over Gay at halfway, but the giant Jamaican had shot his bolt, so to speak, and there was no holding the more relaxed Gay in the straight. Gay reflected: "I'm not used to not coming off the curve first. Usain Bolt gave me a run for my money. I want the world to know that Bolt's a great competitor. I've seen him put in the work, throwing up after practice."

Bolt, who had turned 21 a few days earlier, placed second in 19.91. Gay and everyone else recognised Bolt's immense potential at 200m but no one could have foreseen the impact Bolt would have on the 100m. It was on July 18 that Bolt lined up for the first serious 100m race of his life. A few weeks earlier his coach Glen Mills had suggested that in order to develop further at 200m he ought to work at another distance to increase his strength and speed stamina. He should take up the 400m again, a distance he had run in an outstanding 45.35 at age 16. Bolt was horrified. As he wrote in his 2013 autobiography *Faster Than Lightning*, "To me, that race was just plain bad news. The 400m meant pain, lots and lots of pain. 'Nah, Coach,' I said, thinking fast. 'Let's do the 100m instead.'" Mills disagreed; he felt that at 6ft 5in his pupil was too tall to be able to match his potential rivals at the start of the race. Usain, desperate to avoid the 400m, almost begged his coach. "One chance, that's all I want. Enter me into a meet. If I run a bad 100, I'll run the 400m next season. But if I run good, say 10.30 or better, then I'll do the 100m."

Coach Mills reluctantly agreed, but not until Bolt had broken Don Quarrie's long standing national 200m record of 19.86. That he did in the Jamaican Championships, clocking 19.75, and Mills upheld his side of the bargain by entering him in a relatively low pressure race in Crete. He won but the all important factor was the time. It was 10.03! Bolt's relief and happiness knew no bounds. He was now safe from having to undertake the merciless training necessary for success at the 400m. He didn't race again at 100m in 2007 and that time, remarkable for a debut, ranked him equal 12th on the world year list. A good three metres quicker was his compatriot Asafa Powell, who two weeks after his disappointment in Osaka lowered his world record to 9.74 in Rieti, running relaxed in a heat. In the final he clocked 9.78.

Led by Gay's three victories (the US quartet won the 4x100m relay in 37.78 ahead of Jamaica's 37.89 and Britain's 37.90), the American team dominated the World Championships, amassing 14 gold medals while the next best was five by Kenya. A great contribution to that total was made by Bernard Lagat.

Surely no one could have begrudged Lagat his 1500m victory. Here is a man who had the misfortune to race at his peak in the shadow of the event's all-time great, Hicham El Guerrouj. He finished second to him in the 2001 World Championships and 2004 Olympics and would have been world record holder (3:26.34 in 2001) but for the Moroccan's awesome presence. Another setback was missing the 2003 World Championships due to a 'positive' test for EPO which was later found to be incorrect. Kenyan-born but now an American citizen, Lagat (32) was representing the USA for the first time and by winning the world title he ended a 99-year drought ... the last American to lift a global 1500m championship was Mel Sheppard at the 1908 Olympics. After 700m world junior cross country champion Asbel Kiprop took over and continued to lead around the final bend but it was Lagat whose kick proved the deadliest as he sped through the last 100m in 12.65 for a time of 3:34.77. [Kiprop set a pb of 3:35.24 in fourth place]. This was the closest ever World Championships 1500m as the first eight finished within a second.

There have only been two previous 1500/5000m doubles in global championships: Paavo Nurmi in 1924 and Hicham El Guerrouj in 2004 at the Olympics. Now Lagat too has won both events. The rest of the field played into his hands by allowing the race to be run so slowly; every shuffling lap enhanced the prospect of his terrific finish proving the key factor. The first kilometre took 3:00.35, which was slower than in the women's race. With two laps to run it was still anyone's race. Mo Farah was ahead at the bell in 12:53.08. With just over 200m to go the 2003 champion Eliud Kipchoge sprinted ahead but Lagat had more fire power in the finishing straight and took the race by 0.13 in 13:45.87. Lagat's last 200 took 25.9 for a final 400 of 52.3. Farah (13:47.54) in sixth had the satisfaction of beating Jesús Espana, the man who outkicked him for the European title last year.

Another American star was Allyson Felix, who not only won the 200m in a big personal best of 21.81, but was a member of both victorious relay teams, in the 4x400m clocking a fabulous 48.0 on the second leg to take her team from fourth into a lead they would never lose. Other American winners included Jeremy Wariner, who took the 400m in 43.45, the world's quickest time since Michael Johnson's world record of 43.18 in 1999; and indicating the breadth of their talent there were also gold medallists in the 400m hurdles, pole vault, shot, 4x400m (with Wariner anchoring in 43.10), and women's 100m hurdles.

The British team came home with five medals: bronze by the 4x100m squad of Christian Malcolm, Craig Pickering, Marlon Devonish and Mark Lewis-Francis, the women's 4x400m team of Christine Ohuruogu, Marilyn Okoro, Lee McConnell and Nicola Sanders (who ran a blistering 48.76 leg) in the UK record time of 3:20.04, and by Kelly Sotherton (6510) in a heptathlon contest won by Sweden's Carolina Klüft with a European record of 7032, a score bettered only by Jackie Joyner-Kersee. Fourth was ever improving Jessica

413

Ennis, who "won" the 100m hurdles (12.97) and 200m (23.15) and finished with a score of 6469. The other two medals – gold and silver – came in the women's 400m. Many years later another bronze medal was added as Jo Pavey was promoted to third place in the 10,000m after runner-up Elvan Abeylegesse was disqualified retrospectively for doping.

Christine Ohuruogu's one-year ban for missing three drugs tests came to an end on August 5. Two days later the British selectors showed faith in her by selecting her for Osaka. On August 11 she lined up for her first race since July 2006, winning a 400m heat at the Scottish Championships in a modest 53.09; next day she won the 200m in 23.71w but scratched from the 400m final in order to catch her flight to Japan. There, on August 16, she clocked a startling 50.56 at a warm-up meeting in Osaka, close to her best of 50.28 when winning the Commonwealth title. Nevertheless, prior to the heats, Ladbrokes didn't rate her chances – pricing her at 50-1 [odds seized eagerly by yours truly!]. *Not that they expected much either from Nicola Sanders, offered at 40-1, whereas Jamaica's Novlene Williams was installed as 3-1 favourite.*

Williams did post the fastest time of the round on August 26 with 50.21, but Ohuruogu indicated she really was a force to be reckoned with by recording 50.46. Next day, Williams won the first semi in 49.66, Sanders the second in a pb 49.77 and Ohuruogu the third in a pb 50.16. It was beginning to look as though at least one of the Britons would gain a medal but what actually happened in the final on August 29 was the stuff of dreams for the British supporters. With 50m to run Sanders was third and her team-mate fourth but they found another gear. For a second or two it looked as though Sanders was the more likely to catch the flagging Williams but then Ohuruogu's superior strength came into play and both Britons produced a dip finish while Williams stayed upright. Shades of Kelly Holmes in Athens, Ohuruogu mouthed "is it me?" – it was indeed, and in another pb of 49.61. Sanders also ran faster than ever before with 49.65 to score only the second British 1-2 in World Championships history, Colin Jackson and Tony Jarrett in the 1993 110m hurdles being the first. Ohuruogu became the first British woman to win a global 400m title; the last British man was Eric Liddell in 1924.

The winner did all – and more – than could have been expected of her and her feat should not be devalued. Regrettably, instead of celebrating a remarkable achievement some ill-informed journalists have chosen to infer that Ohuruogu is a drugs cheat. That is absolutely NOT the case. She missed three tests, it is true, but as the Court of Arbitration for Sport noted, there was no suggestion of her taking drugs; it was a case of a "busy young athlete being forgetful."

Sanya Richards, who headed the world list with 49.52 prior to Osaka, was unable to defend her world title as she had finished only fourth in the US Trials although she did anchor the US team to victory in the relay in 3:18.55. Later she was financially well compensated for being one of only two athletes (Yelena Isinbayeva being the other) who won at all six IAAF Golden League meetings and received $500,000 each. Richards had the satisfaction of beating

Ohuruogu in Zürich (49.36), Berlin (49.27) and the World Athletics Final in Stuttgart (another 49.27) to rank as world number one at 400m for the year.

Paula Radcliffe was frustrated at having to miss the World Championships, where she believes she could have won a medal in the 10,000m, but her season was delayed because of giving birth to daughter Isla in January followed by a stress fracture of the sacrum related to childbirth. Racing for the first time since December 2005, she finished a creditable second to Kara Goucher (USA) in the Great North Run in 67:53 and then scored a notable victory over former world 10,000m champion Gete Wami in the New York Marathon in 2:23:09. That was her seventh victory in eight marathons, the only blot being that dnf at the 2004 Olympics.

Paula emerged as the top women's point scorer in my series of UK all-time rankings which AW published between October 2007 and February 2008. Points were awarded for European Championship and Commonwealth Games medals, AAA titles and UK records as well as Olympic/World Championship honours and world records and merit rankings. Paula's score incorporated points from the 3000/5000m, 10,000m, marathon and cross country, while Sally Gunnell in the 400m hurdles earned the highest score in any one event. Top ranked men were respectively Seb Coe (400m, 800m and 1500m accumulation) and 110m hurdler Colin Jackson.

The biggest athletics news of the year broke in October. Under the heading "Marion Jones: A Liar And A Cheat" I wrote a long report in AI. Some extracts:

Although it hardly came as a complete shock, Marion Jones' admission that she took performance enhancing drugs has further damaged a sport that has long been struggling for credibility in the general public's eyes. The widely held, if (hopefully) inaccurate, belief that most top athletes are using drugs will have gained even further acceptance now that Jones has hit the headlines in the highest profile case since Ben Johnson nearly 20 years ago.

Jones has never actually tested positive and in her 2004 autobiography took a whole page to proclaim in large red letters "I have always been unequivocal in my opinion: I am against performance enhancing drugs. I have never taken them and I never will take them." But that was a lie. Now she has admitted that she took drugs from 1999. What is disturbing is that in all that time, during which she must have taken dozens of tests, the results were always reported as negative. On the one occasion, at the 2006 US Championships, when the 'A' sample tested positive (for EPO), the 'B' sample produced a negative result and she was exonerated. In these matters I always try to give the athlete the benefit of the doubt but, when it is proved beyond doubt (or in this case a confession) that Jones was indeed a cheat, I feel betrayed – as surely do all the others who admired a seemingly exceptional athlete only to find themselves duped.

She pre-empted a court appearance on October 5 with a widely published letter to family and close friends. In it she disclosed that she planned to plead guilty to two counts of lying to federal agents and stated: "In 1999, my track coach Trevor Graham provided me with some nutritional supplements. There is one in particular that he called 'flaxseed oil'. He told me that it was necessary to add this to my diet so that I could be in peak running shape. I, unfortunately, never asked him any questions about it. I trusted him and never thought for one second that he would jeopardise my career, nor his own. He supplied me this for the 1999 and 2000 seasons. It was not until after I left Trevor at the end of 2002 that I began to wonder to myself whether or not Trevor had given me something to enhance my performance."

She went on to mention that in 2003 she was interviewed by federal agents regarding the Balco scandal. When shown a substance called the 'clear' [THG, a powerful anabolic steroid], which she recognised as the supplement she had been taking for nearly two years, she told the agents she had never seen the substance before. She admitted: *"I lied because I panicked. I lied to protect my coach at the time. I lied to protect all that I had worked so very hard for in my life and career. And lastly, I lied to protect myself. It was an incredibly stupid thing to do. I made the decision to break the law and have to take full responsibility for doing so."* Despite a plea to the judge for leniency, not wishing to be parted from her two young sons, Jones was sentenced on January 11 2008 to six months in prison, plus 800 hours of community service spread over two years.

As a consequence of her admission of guilt, all of Jones' results from September 1 2000 onwards were annulled by the IAAF. Publicly disgraced, she returned her five Olympic medals from Sydney and forfeited numerous other titles and medals as well as being ordered to return money won in IAAF competitions. As for Graham, a member of Jamaica's 1988 Olympic 4x400m silver medal team who, ironically, was a whistleblower in the Balco doping scandal, he was found guilty of perjury, sentenced to one year of house arrest and five years of probation, and banned for life from coaching by the US Anti-Doping Agency. Former world record holder for 100m (but stripped of that distinction) Tim Montgomery was in even more serious trouble. Marion Jones' former partner and father of her son not only pleaded guilty in 2007 to cheque fraud and sentenced to 46 months in jail but the following year was found guilty of possession and distribution of heroin, the punishment being a further five years in prison.

Having attended his funeral in January, I was one of a large congregation in West Wickham Parish Church in Kent in September for a moving yet joyful service of thanksgiving and celebration for the life of Sydney Wooderson. Many of his fellow Blackheath Harriers were there as well as several stars of the early post-war era like Doug Wilson, John Parlett, Bill Nankeville, Peter Hildreth, John and Shirley Disley and Eric Shirley. Among the apologies for absence was one from Steve Ovett, now resident in Australia, who wrote that Wooderson was "a source of inspiration and a hero of mine."

Among those who died in 2007 were two of my most valued former overseas correspondents in Richard Ashenheim (80) of Jamaica and Peter Heidenstrom (77) of New Zealand, the ever controversial Andy Norman (64) and all too many all-time great athletes, including 1936 Olympic 800m champion John Woodruff (92), Parry O'Brien (75) and Al Oerter (71). One I mourned in particular was one of my boyhood heroes.

Just imagine the excitement, disbelief even, if Jeremy Wariner were to run a 400m relay leg timed at a shade inside 42 seconds! Yet that was the sort of peep into the future of athletic performance provided by Herb McKenley – who died in a Kingston hospital aged 85 – at the Helsinki Olympics of 1952. At a time when the world 400m record stood at 45.8, he was clocked at what was then regarded as a totally phenomenal 44.8 on the third leg of that fabulous relay race when Jamaica defeated the USA in a world record 3:03.9. It was the crowning moment of McKenley's brilliant yet slightly frustrating career; he was at last, after many near misses, an Olympic gold medallist.

Two days after placing fourth in the 200m, "Hustling Herb" lined up as a solid favourite to win the 400m at the London Olympics of 1948 but he made a fatal error of pace judgement as well as being over confident. Attempting to run the legs off his giant compatriot Arthur Wint, and shooting for a time of 45.6 or quicker [his world record was 45.9], he went off too fast in the early stages, particularly in view of the heavy state of Wembley's cinder track. At halfway he was some seven metres up on Wint in 21.4 but began to tie up when the finishing straight was reached. Hardly daring to believe his luck, Wint caught his flailing rival 20m from the finish to become Jamaica's first ever Olympic gold medallist in his fastest ever time of 46.2 with McKenley second in 46.4. A fellow Jamaican, George Rhoden, succeeded him as world record holder with 45.8. That year (1950) McKenley, in effect a full-time professional athlete in an era when the sport was supposedly strictly amateur, ran no fewer than 94 individual races (51 at 400m/440y)!

It was Rhoden who triumphed in the 1952 Olympic 400m. For once McKenley decided to ditch his blazing first 200m strategy; this time he hung back (22.7 at 200m) but despite closing along the finishing straight he had to settle for another second place (45.9 each on hand timing). That was in fact his third Olympic silver as four days earlier he had so nearly captured the 100m title, failing to catch Lindy Remigino by just 1/100th. McKenley himself thought he had won and the American outsider was almost apologetic about the judges' decision. "Gosh, Herb, it looks as though I won the darn thing."

There was one more golden opportunity: the 4x400m relay. The chances appeared slim by the time the baton reached him for the third leg as Jamaica were some 13-14 metres behind the Americans. It was then that 30 year-old McKenley displayed the full extent of his talent. The McKenley who stormed round was not just a man in form; it was a man inspired. Olympic 400m hurdles champion Charles Moore wasn't exactly dawdling as he covered his lap in 46.3, but McKenley not only cut back that huge deficit but managed to hand over just ahead and Rhoden, with Mal Whitfield breathing down his neck, completed the job as the world record was smashed.

43. "SIMPLY THE BEST" (2008)

How was it possible? On May 26 2008 I turned 70; the years had just flown by. In addition to family celebrations Pat and I organised a lunch for close friends at one of our favourite restaurants, the Oslo Court, near Regent's Park, and AW featured a two page interview with me. In answer to the question "When will you retire?", my reply was: "As athletics writing, statistics and historic research would be my hobby if it had not been my life's work (and how lucky I have been), it's not my intention to give that up. However, after the end of this year, I shall be cutting back on my work for *Athletics International* and scaling down on other projects. But, not complete retirement as long as I have the ability to contribute to the sport's documentation." So here I am, almost a decade later, still writing about my beloved sport!

Having watched top class athletics for close to 60 years I thought I had seen everything. I hadn't, for in 2008 Usain Bolt not only astonished everyone with his times at 100m and 200m but captivated the general public in a way never known before. No athlete in history, and few in any sport, became as universally famous as the lanky Jamaican with the sparkling personality. Many sprinters display either aggression or seeming indifference as they prepare to start a race, but the laid-back Bolt put on a show for the crowd and they lapped it up. They loved it even more when he hurtled down the track at unprecedented speed. Indeed, the whole Usain Bolt experience became a mutual love affair.

In February we printed in AI a three-line brief: "According to Jamaican sources, Usain Bolt – who ran 10.03 in his first 100m race last year – plans to take the event more seriously this summer." Little did we know what was in store! The first indication came in Kingston on May 3.

This time last year Usain Bolt had never registered an official time for 100m – yet now he is the second fastest man in history! He made an auspicious debut in Greece last July with 10.03, while in his native Jamaica on March 8 this year he replicated that time, asserting he would run only the 200m in Beijing. But after clocking an amazing 9.76 in the Jamaica Invitational he must now consider going for the double. With a kindly 1.8m/sec wind at his back the 1.96m (6-5) tall 21 year-old was credited with a time which only his compatriot Asafa Powell (9.74) has ever bettered. "I was definitely surprised when I saw the time," said Bolt. "I thought I was in shape for a 9.85." His coach, Glen Mills [who had originally wanted Bolt to link the 200m with 400m not 100m], remarked: "This is just the beginning."

That it was, for after clocking 9.92 from a bad start in Port of Spain, his fifth race at the distance – at an IAAF Grand Prix meeting in New York on May 31 – resulted in his becoming world record holder!

There is nothing in sprinting history to compare with Usain Bolt's meteoric rise. Previously a 200m specialist who had displayed tremendous potential also at 400m, he succeeded Asafa Powell as world record holder with 9.72, leaving Tyson Gay a metre and a half behind even though the world champion missed his pb by just 0.01. The large number of Jamaicans in the capacity crowd went wild when it became clear that their man had not only beaten the American star but broken the world record into the bargain. However, Bolt – although excited – was quite philosophical. "The world record means nothing without gold medals in the World Championships or the Olympics. You've got to be Olympic champion or world champion to really count."

Bolt's next two 100m races resulted in a win at the Jamaican Championships in 9.85 and a narrow defeat by Powell (9.88 to 9.89) in Stockholm. At 200m he was unbeaten, setting a Commonwealth record of 19.67 in Athens before appearing in the London Grand Prix at Crystal Palace.

It was Usain Bolt who stole the show. With no disrespect intended to his rivals, he was like a giant among pygmies as he powered along the straight to clock a UK all-comers 200m record of 19.76 into an 0.4m wind. He will go to Beijing as overwhelming favourite for the 200m but still he doesn't know if he will run the 100m. "I'm still not sure about doubling. My coach will make the decision. I'd definitely like to double; I think I could do well in both. But my coach hasn't made a bad decision in five years so if he says I can only do one, I'll do one."

Happily, he was given the green light and the world was able to witness one of the most breathtaking and memorable moments in the annals of athletics. After sauntering through the rounds he lined up for the 13th 100m race of his life. Exhibiting no signs of nerves before the race – indeed relishing every minute of the occasion – he built up a three metre lead before shutting down over the last 20m, looking round, dropping his arms and then raising them aloft at the finish. Despite coasting for those last seven giant strides he was timed at a world record 9.69 in absolutely still conditions. As an awestruck Michael Johnson gasped: "I've never seen anything like that before. He could have run 9.66." [Coach Glen Mills believed he could have run 9.52 had he not eased up!] Bolt, five days away from his 22nd birthday, was not bothered about missing an opportunity to have run a considerably faster time. "I came here just to win." Why didn't he just concentrate on sprinting full out until the finish? "I just wanted to have fun." Bolt will also forever be remembered as the first Jamaican to win this most coveted of Olympic titles. Jamaican-born Linford Christie and Donovan Bailey won in 1992 and 1996 but in the colours of Britain and Canada respectively.

They say lightning doesn't strike twice. Not true in the case of this Bolt. Having played around in the 100m final, yet emerging with a world record of 9.69, Bolt decided to go for broke in the event (200m) which had always been his long-term target. No one could doubt he was going to win. The question was whether he could, or would attempt to, break Michael Johnson's hitherto unapproached 12 year-old world record of 19.32. The answer came in breathtaking fashion. Drawn in lane 5 he got away to a fast start even though his reaction time of 0.182 was nothing special. Everything else about his race was. He ran a fantastic bend, reportedly taking 9.96 for the first 100m (as against 10.12 by Johnson in Atlanta), and entered the straight two or three metres up on defending champion Shawn Crawford. He then proceeded to cover the second 100m in 9.34 for an overall time of 19.30. There was no playing to the crowd this time; he ran as hard as he could all the way, his huge stride devouring the track, and he dipped at the finish even though he won by around seven metres, the widest margin in the event's Olympic history.

It was a run which will never be forgotten by the 91,000 in the stadium and the countless millions who watched on TV. He had become the first to land the Olympic 100/200 double since Carl Lewis in 1984 and the first man ever to win two Olympic titles at the same Games with a world record in each. "It was an amazing performance," said Johnson himself. "He had a phenomenal start out of the blocks. Drive phase, transition, everything was great." Bolt said: "I knew the track was fast but I didn't think this was possible. I'm shocked. I have been aspiring to the world record for so long. It is a dream come true."

He wasn't finished yet in the "Bird's Nest" Stadium. There was still the 4x100m relay to come.

Jamaican sprinters continued their shock and awe campaign by breaking a world record which had stood for 16 years. No they didn't just break it; they smashed it to smithereens. Ever since 1977 when the IAAF started ratifying 4x100m relay records to 1/100ths the times have come down gently: 38.03, 37.86, 37.83, 37.79, 37.67, 37.50, 37.40. Now Nesta Carter, Michael Frater, Usain Bolt and Asafa Powell have contrived to take 0.30 off in one go with a startling 37.10. Thus, Bolt made further history by winning three Olympic gold medals, each in world record time – a feat which may stand for eternity. There were safe change-overs from the Jamaicans with the first two men handing Bolt a lead that he substantially enhanced with another stupefying bend run (8.98) and then there was the glorious sight of Powell in full flight on the anchor leg (8.73).

That historic feat of three Olympic golds, all in world record times, did not in fact stand for eternity … just until January 2017 when Bolt and his relay team-mates had to hand back their medals because of a doping offence at the Games by Nesta Carter which showed up when his sample was re-tested in 2016. How selfish can an athlete get? If you cheat when competing as an individual and get found out eventually then you alone face the consequences. But, as a member of a relay team, your doping can lead as in this case to three innocent colleagues being penalised too. I hope that weighs on his conscience.

Although of course Usain ("Simply The Best") Bolt was the star of the show, there was plenty of action in other Olympic events to savour. LaShawn Merritt won the 400m by almost a second in his best time of 43.75; in hot weather Sammy Wanjiru ran by far the quickest ever marathon time (2:06:32) in a global championship; Dayron Robles took the 110m hurdles in 12.93 (sadly, China's defending champion Liu Xiang was injured and unable to finish his heat); Angelo Taylor not only regained the 400m hurdles title he had won in 2000 but lowered his best time to 47.25; Jamaican speedsters Shelly-Ann Fraser (10.78) and Veronica Campbell-Brown (21.74) won their events; Pamela Jelimo set a world junior and Commonwealth record when winning the 800m in

1:54.87; Gulnara Galkina clocked a barrier-breaking world record of 8:58.81 to claim the inaugural Olympic women's steeplechase; Yelena Isinbayeva vaulted 5.05m for her 24th world record (having earlier in the season cleared 5.03m and 5.04m); and Barbora Spotáková won the javelin with a European record of 71.42m. And then there were the Ethiopian distance runners.

Still only 26, Kenenisa Bekele has joined the Olympic immortals of the event by winning a second 10,000m gold medal, thus emulating Paavo Nurmi (1920/1928), Emil Zátopek (1948/1952), Lasse Viren (1972/1976) and Haile Gebrselassie (1996/2000). There was a sense of déjà vu when, as in Athens and also at the 2005 and 2007 World Championships, Bekele sprinted home chased by Sileshi Sihine, the Alain Mimoun of our days. Bekele dashed ahead just before the bell and produced a majestic last lap of 53.42, easing up to savour his victory, and clocking the Olympic record time of 27:01.17.

A magisterial display by Bekele [in the 5000m six days later] enabled him to join one of the world's most illustrious clubs: runners who have landed an Olympic 5000/10,000m double at the same Games. The founder member back in 1912 was Hannes Kolehmainen. Emil Zátopek joined in 1952 (what a show-off, he won the marathon too!), Vladimir Kuts in 1956, Lasse Viren in 1972 (reapplying in 1976) and Miruts Yifter in 1980. Now, after 28 years, there are two new members: Bekele and, no discrimination allowed in this club, Tirunesh Dibaba. Even Eliud Kipchoge, the 2003 world champion, was left for dead when Bekele launched his finishing kick. It was an awesome display as Bekele ran 53.87. Clocking 12:57.82 to shatter Said Aouita's Olympic record, Bekele covered the last mile in 3:58.7.

As for Dibaba, she moved to second on the world all-time list for 10,000m with 29:54.66, taking 15:09.98 for the first half and a sizzling 14:44.68 for the final 5000m, clocking just 2:04.1 for the last 800m. She had to finish fast to stay clear of the Ethiopian-born Turk, Elvan Abeylegesse, whose time of 29:56.34 broke Paula Radcliffe's European record. However, in 2017 following retesting of samples taken at the 2007 World Championships, Abeylegesse was retroactively disqualified and her results from 2007 to 2009 were annulled, including her Olympic medals (silver also in the 5000m) and that European record.

The 10,000m gold medallist Tirunesh Dibaba made history by winning a second Olympic title, this time over 1000m. Well, officially it was the 5000m she won, but disappointingly the field ambled around until the 11th lap and only then did the race really start. The kilometre splits were absurd: 3:39.20, 3:06.21, 3:12.72, 3:06.64 and, wait for it, 2:36.63! The race was one of the most eagerly anticipated of the Games, bringing together Ethiopia's two superstars, world record holder Dibaba and defending champion Meseret Defar, for their first encounter for two years. They are the two fastest ever at 14:11.15 and 14:12.88 respectively. Considering the well known finishing speed of the pair, not to mention Abeylegesse, one might have thought someone would ensure a fast pace in an attempt (admittedly doomed probably) to blunt those fearsome kicks. But no, the first lap took 82.6 and it got slower still during the opening five minutes of the race. At the bell Dibaba led narrowly from Defar and Abeylegesse. That was still the order with 200 to go but over the last half lap Dibaba kicked away, covering the final 400 in 59.54 and 800 in 2:03.96, while around the final turn Abeylegesse overtook Defar.

How did the British team get on in Beijing? Although her preparation had been hampered by injuries, Tasha Danvers produced a timely personal best of 53.84 for third place in the 400m hurdles. Silver medals were gained by Germaine Mason in the high jump and Phillips Idowu in the triple jump. Mason, who previously competed with distinction for Jamaica but became a British citizen in 2006 (British father, Jamaican mother), had not been expected to challenge for a medal but rose splendidly to the occasion by jumping 2.34m to tie his personal best from five years earlier and move to third on the UK all-time list behind Steve Smith and Dalton Grant. A close friend of Usain Bolt, tragically he was killed in a motor cycle accident in 2017 aged only 34. As world indoor champion, Idowu entered the competition as favourite but despite producing an outdoor best of 17.62m he finished 5cm behind Nelson Évora. The star of the team, though, was Christine Ohuruogu.

Just seven British women have been crowned Olympic champion: Mary Rand and Ann Packer in 1964, Mary Peters in 1972, Tessa Sanderson in 1984, Sally Gunnell in 1992, Denise Lewis in 2000 and Kelly Holmes in 2004. Make that eight. Going one better than Packer in 1964 and Lillian Board in 1968, both of whom finished an agonisingly close silver medallist at 400m, Christine Ohuruogu ran a brilliantly judged race to add the Olympic title to her 2006 Commonwealth and 2007 world titles. The winner, who was 6th at 250m and 4th at 300m, overtook the flagging Sanya Richards some 30m from the finish to clock 49.62 [having ranked 9th with 50.80 prior to the Games]. "My coach Lloyd Cowan has always said to me that the race is going to be won in the last 50m. If you can just keep your cool, keep your composure for the last 50m, that's when people start dying and he knows that I don't start dying – that's how I run and it works for me. It's not about who's fastest or strongest, it's about greatest will – that's what my coach says."

What about the three Britons destined to strike gold in London four years hence? Mo Farah didn't get through his 5000m heat (13:50.95), Greg Rutherford jumped 8.16m in qualification but only 7.84m for 10th place in the final, while Jessica Ennis suffered a stress fracture in May and to her huge disappointment had to miss the Games. In her event, the heptathlon, Kelly Sotherton placed fourth with 6517 points, only to be upgraded to bronze medal status in 2017 when Russia's Tatyana Chernova was retrospectively disqualified. Also promoted to bronze years later were the British 4x400m team of Andrew Steele, Robert Tobin, Michael Bingham and Martyn Rooney (anchoring in 43.73) in 2:58.81 after the Russian team's result was annulled; Goldie Sayers in the javelin with a UK record of 65.75m when another Russian was disqualified; and the women's 4x400m squad of Ohuruogu, Sotherton, Marilyn Okoro and Nicola Sanders (3:22.68). How ironic that Dave Collins, UK Athletics' performance director at the time, had to quit his job because

Britain's four medals was short of the target figure ... but now that medal haul from the 2008 Games has, mainly due to Russian cheats, risen to the impressive total of eight!

It had been a productive year for world records. Indoors, Bekele ran 2 miles in 8:04.35 in Birmingham, Defar clocked 9:10.50 for the same distance in Boston, Susanna Kallur was timed at 7.68 for 60m hurdles in Karlsruhe and Yelena Isinbayeva vaulted clear at 4.95m in Donetsk. Outdoors, in addition to the Olympic exploits, Robles posted a sprint hurdles time of 12.87 in Ostrava, Dibaba ran 14:11.15 for 5000m in Oslo and Spotáková threw the javelin 72.28m in Stuttgart. The king of the road runners was Haile Gebrselassie. In Dubai in January he posted the second quickest ever marathon time of 2:04:53, 27 seconds outside his own world record, while in Berlin in September he achieved his goal of being the first runner to break 2:04, which he did with one second to spare.

There was one British winner at the World Indoor Championships in Valencia. Triple jumper Phillips Idowu served his international apprenticeship in the shadow of Jonathan Edwards but on this occasion he finally came into his own.

For several years Idowu has flattered to deceive on the world stage. He has the physical ability to jump close to 18m and victories in the 2006 Commonwealth Games and 2007 European Indoors indicated he could be a good championship competitor, but his record in the Olympics (6th in 2000, fouled out in 2004) and World Championships (9th in 2001, 6th in 2007) was acutely disappointing. However, at 29 the Londoner finally came good – very good – at the opportune moment. In the second round he produced a stupendous leap of 17.75m. That was not only in excess of his 2002 outdoor best of 17.68m but it broke Jonathan Edwards' UK indoor record of 17.64m. Although Ashia Hansen twice won the women's triple jump title, Idowu became the first British man ever to win a world indoor gold medal in a field event.

Already acknowledged as the greatest cross country runner of all time, Kenenisa Bekele made further history in Edinburgh's Holyrood Park by becoming the first man to notch up a sixth world title at 12km. That was despite being beset by stomach problems the day before the race and losing dozens of places when after just 2km his left shoe was almost ripped off and it took him around 15 seconds to adjust it. He didn't panic and gradually worked his way back to the leaders. Kenya beat Ethiopia in the team race but Kenenisa (whose younger brother Tariku won the world indoor 3000m title three weeks earlier) brought his total of world cross country medals to a staggering 27. The Dibaba family weren't doing badly either as Tirunesh overcame a mid-race attack of stitch to win her third senior title and her 17 year-old sister Genzebe triumphed in the junior race. It was quite a year for Tirunesh, for a few weeks after her Olympic double she married 10,000m silver medallist Sileshi Sihine.

On the very day (April 6) that the NUTS held a Golden Jubilee celebration, attended by five of the six founder members, one of the foremost athletics historians and statisticians, Ian Buchanan, died at the age of 76. Later in the year I attended the funeral of a remarkable coach.

Peter Coe, who guided his son Sebastian to the highest honours in athletics, died in London on August 9, aged 88. At the funeral, a day after his return from Beijing, Seb paid an affectionate tribute to his father, who despite having had no background in athletics (cycling had been his chosen sport) used his skills as an engineer, his self taught knowledge of bio-mechanics and intensive research into training methods to develop into one of the most knowledgeable, analytical and respected of coaches. Allied to the exceptional ability and capacity for hard work of his son, theirs became one of the most celebrated partnerships in athletics history. Peter once described his son as "a hell of an athlete", adding "but then, he had a hell of a coach." Too true.

The European Cup, inaugurated back in 1965, had long been one of my favourite fixtures and it was sad that the 2008 edition in the picturesque French town of Annecy would be the last before European Athletics introduced its unwieldy and less attractive successor, the European Team Championships, in 2009. As a member of the Track & Field Tours group I spent a very pleasant weekend, made all the more enjoyable because the British men's team lifted the cup by one of the widest margins in the event's history. Another bonus was the opportunity on the homeward journey to visit the fascinating Olympic Museum in Lausanne.

It proved to be just the tip of the iceberg as regards doping in Russia, but an early indication of the scale of the problem was the announcement by the IAAF in July that it had provisionally suspended seven prominent Russian female athletes, charged for a fraudulent substitution of urine when being tested. The rule violations were established following the storage of samples and re-analysis using comparative DNA techniques. All were later banned. In addition, five top male Russian walkers, all coached by the notorious Viktor Chegin in Saransk, were banned for EPO usage, and other cases followed. Referring to the seven women, IOC medical chief and World Anti-Doping Agency vice-president Arne Ljungqvist commented: "I find it frustrating that such planned cheating is still going on. I am very disappointed."

The million dollar Golden League Jackpot went to Kenya's Pamela Jelimo. Hers was a remarkable rags-to-riches story.

Until April of this year she was just a so-so runner who in Yves Pinaud's African lists for 2007 ranked 77th at 200m with 24.68 and 51st over 400m with 54.93. Now, not only has she become at 18 the youngest ever Olympic 800m champion but has scooped the entire million dollar jackpot. In Brussels, the final meeting of the series, she clocked her fifth quickest time of 1:55.16 and now has the eight fastest times of the year, from 1:54.01 to 1:55.76.

One of the most pleasurable if challenging appointments in my career was being invited to be a member of the independent panel to select inductees for the newly created England Athletics Hall of Fame, a project dear to my heart. My fellow judges that first year were Darren Campbell (chairman), Dame Tanni Grey-Thompson, Paul Dickenson, Jason Henderson and Frances

Ratchford, and I was happy to provide them with biographical details of athletes to be short-listed. With Scott Grace of England Athletics presiding, we held our first discussion meeting in April, and the inaugural awards evening, organised so well, as on all subsequent occasions, by Alison Potts of England Athletics, was held in October. Influenced by a public vote, the first inductees were Sir Roger Bannister, (Lord) Sebastian Coe, Sally Gunnell, David Hemery, Steve Ovett and Daley Thompson. The panel also inducted three distinguished personalities for their very special contribution to the sport: Geoff Dyson (chief national coach 1947-1961), Chris Brasher (Olympic gold medallist and co-founder of the London Marathon) and David Coleman (BBC television's voice of athletics for so many years), while David Holding was included for his achievements as a wheelchair racer. I had the privilege of addressing the audience on the subject of Geoff Dyson.

Unless you are about my age, or you are a coach who has a good knowledge of the sport's history, you may not be familiar with the name. Well, there's a very good reason why Geoff Dyson is being honoured tonight, because it could be argued that he made a greater individual contribution to British athletics than anyone. He laid the foundations for a national coaching scheme that was the envy of the world. As a young reporter for "Athletics Weekly" I met Geoff a few times and sat in on some of his lectures and demonstrations. He was a dynamic, charismatic and inspiring coach.

All credit to England Athletics for their initiative, but really UK Athletics should have set up a British Hall of Fame, so that stars like Eric Liddell, Allan Wells and Liz McColgan from Scotland, Colin Jackson and Lynn Davies from Wales and Mary Peters from Northern Ireland could also be honoured.

I was in New York in November for the marathon and was delighted to see the return to winning ways of Paula Radcliffe after her second mortifying Olympic marathon experience. In Beijing, Paula pluckily completed the race in 23rd place (2:32:38) despite acute leg problems arising from the stress fracture to her left thigh which severely curtailed her preparations three months earlier.

For the third time in her career the New York City Marathon has re-established Paula Radcliffe as the queen of road racing. Eleven weeks after her traumatic experience at the Athens Olympics she disproved her doubters by winning in 2:23:10. Last year, in her first marathon for 26 months, having given birth to daughter Isla in January 2007, she outsprinted Gete Wami in 2:23:09. This time, again exactly 11 weeks after another Olympic disappointment (when she was far from ready to compete at such a level) she destroyed one of the most talented fields ever assembled in New York to run out the winner by almost two minutes in 2:23:56. Forget the time. The race was run on such a cold, blustery morning that the opening uphill mile took all of 6:31. Effectively, Radcliffe led all the way. Easing through the first half in 73:23 she covered the second half in an outstanding 70:33. "It makes the Olympics even more frustrating. Why can I get it right in New York all the time and I can't get it right there? But sometimes you have to take what life deals you, I guess, and just do the best you can."

From New York I added on a few days in Atlantic City and there I met up with a family member of whom I had no knowledge until a few months earlier. I have various cousins dotted around the USA but only recently had I become aware of one living in Albuquerque by the name of Joy Watnik Saul. We emailed each other and she informed me that her father had been a soccer international. Sure enough, I discovered that Ben Watnik (né Watman) had been a fullback in the US World Cup squad of 1949/50! He played in the qualifying matches against Mexico and Cuba in Mexico City although he was not in the team which famously (okay, embarrassingly) beat England 1-0 in the finals. How come his name was Watnik? Ben's father, Noah (who was a brother of my grandfather Jack Watman), moved from Pinsk to Argentina in 1926 before emigrating with Ben to the USA in 1944 where officials mistakenly documented their name as Watnik instead of Watman!

Ben, who lived in New Jersey and was well into his eighties, regularly patronised the casinos of nearby Atlantic City and through Joy and her twin sister Alicia I arranged to meet him. We spent time together at his hotel, me being somewhat starstruck that I actually had an international footballer as a cousin.

44. A LEGEND IN THE MAKING (2009)

There was a major development with *Athletics International* at the start of 2009. Peter Matthews and I had decided it was time for AI to be published solely in email form and so after 440 printed issues since 1993 we embraced the new technology, a move which was welcomed by the vast majority of our subscribers. By eliminating the heavy costs of printing and postage we were able to reduce the price of an annual subscription for the electronic version, and our readers could receive the latest issue with the weekend's results on a Monday evening or Tuesday morning. The printed version would normally be mailed on a Tuesday, delivered in the UK on Wednesday at the earliest – and of course later in the week for overseas subscribers. Another advantage was frequency of publication. We had usually published 26 issues a year but in 2009 that rose to 36, a minimum level we have maintained ever since (39 in 2016).

I was critical in the year's first edition of the events which qualified for the IAAF's million dollar Golden League jackpot. I pointed out that this would be the 12th year of the Golden League but the men's hammer and women's steeplechase, shot, discus and hammer had never been selected, while only once had the men's shot and discus and women's long jump been on the schedule – thus depriving athletes in those disciplines from contesting the jackpot. To this day the hammer throwers are ignored by the Diamond League, successor to the Golden League, although – unsatisfactorily – they have their own segregated Challenge series. Our sport is known as track and field but in all too many ways the field element is discriminated against.

Doping continued to be the sport's most pressing problem and under the heading "The Athletics Hall of Shame" I wrote:

Practically never an issue of AI goes by without reference to doping positives or sanctions, and in this edition we report that three Bulgarian women have been suspended for two years. Bulgaria appears to have a particularly dismal record for drug offences, and so I researched which countries have produced the most cheats since the IAAF brought in doping bans in 1975. I counted only those athletes who have been banned for a minimum of 18 months. Sure enough, Bulgaria (population of only 7 million) ranks seventh on the list with 33 offenders (fifth worst counting women only with 22), although neighbouring Romania (22 million) also set a shocking example, ranking fourth with 44 (40 of them women!) behind Russia (142 million) 113 + 34 from the USSR, USA (300 million) 95 and China (1.3 billion) 76. Dismayingly, more than 90 countries have had athletes banned for 18 months or longer. Britain ranked equal 16th with 21. Take a bow, Japan, the only major power with a clean sheet. I also took the opportunity to count "serious" doping offenders on a year by year basis, and the figures reveal that the situation is going from bad to worse, with 2008 the worst on record with 77 offenders (44 men, 33 women), and that will surely increase with later information.

The figure for 2008 eventually rose to 92. In 2010 is was 96, in 2011 it reached 123, while in 2012 there were no fewer than 161 athletes banned for two years or longer with India (35) and Russia (24) the worst offenders. Those were just the ones who were caught and shamed ... how many others were not detected at the time? To the credit of athletics, at least the issue was being tackled and the cheats ousted, in contrast to the denial of any problem by many other major sports.

One former drug offender who served his time and expressed remorse at his behaviour was Dwain Chambers. Whether his drug use had beneficial long-term effects cannot be ascertained, but the sprinter was certainly in fine fettle at the European Indoor Championships in Turin. He was one of two British gold medallists.

Whatever one's views on Chambers, as to whether he should still be competing, there is no denying that despite his lack of top class competitive opportunities he is currently in fantastic form. Before this winter his best 60m time was 6.54 when dead-heating for the silver medal at last year's World Indoors. This season he reduced that to 6.51 and he travelled to Turin as clear favourite. He opened with an impressive 6.53 but then shocked everyone, himself included, by running 6.42 in his semi. That broke every record in the book other than Maurice Greene's world record of 6.39. Chambers (30) was not quite so outrageously quick in the final but still ran a scorching 6.46.

Mo Farah (25) became the fifth Briton to be crowned European indoor champion at 3000m, upholding the tradition established by Ian Stewart (1969 & 1975), Ricky Wilde (1970), Peter Stewart (1971) and John Mayock (1998), and he did it the hard way by grinding it out from the front. Farah went ahead before the kilometre mark (2:33.54) and reached 2000m in 5:06.63. Farah's final kilometre of 2:33.54 proved too much for France's Bob Tahri and he crossed the line in a championship record of 7:40.17.

The two stars of the indoor season were Meseret Defar and Yelena Isinbayeva. On successive weekends the Ethiopian set world indoor records of 14:24.37 for 5000m and 9:06.26 for 2 miles, while the Russian vaulted 4.97m and 5.00m in the same competition, her 25th and 26th world records. The most astonishing exploit of the indoor season came in the men's long jump in Turin.

This appeared to be a very open but rather modest event with any one of half a dozen men capable of victory with a jump in the 8.10-8.20m range. No one could have predicted that someone would produce a monster leap to win by almost half a metre! That someone was Germany's Sebastian Bayer (22), silver medallist in the 2005 European Juniors a long way behind Greg Rutherford. This winter he had progressed to 8.17m and in the first round he came up with a resounding 8.29m, the world's longest this year. That looked like being the winning jump. Bayer passed three times followed by a foul in the fifth round. With the title already won, Bayer took his final jump in a completely relaxed mode ... and landed at 8.71m! It was a distance he could not have dreamt about; suddenly he was not just European record holder, but only Carl Lewis with 8.79m in 1984 has ever jumped farther indoors. "I knew it was far and hoped for 8.30m to maybe 8.4m0, but I did not expect 8.7m1. I was speechless."

Rather like Bob Beamon 40 years earlier, Bayer never subsequently got anywhere close to replicating his huge jump. He did win the German outdoor title that year with 8.49m but thereafter his best was 8.34m in 2012. However, he did retain the European indoor title in 2011 and outdoors was crowned European champion in 2012 … but Greg Rutherford, sixth in Turin with 8.00m, went on to become Olympic and world champion.

A poignant event in March was the death of one of the finest of all athletics writers in John Rodda, aged 78. John, the former athletics correspondent of *The Guardian*, was a well respected and immensely knowledgeable reporter who was also a most acute observer of international sports politics and in particular the workings of the International Olympic Committee. He was a valued columnist for *Athletics Today*, and we enjoyed a very good working and personal relationship over many years.

Three weeks after John's passing, a much happier event took place in London. The day after celebrating his 80th birthday on March 23, Sir Roger Bannister hosted a luncheon primarily for friends and acquaintances in athletics, organised by noted sportswriter David Miller. I was privileged to be one of around two dozen people to be invited to this magical, nostalgic occasion. Of those present, apart of course from the birthday boy himself and pacemaker Sir Chris Chataway, the only athletes who were actually at Iffley Road on May 6 1954 were John and Sylvia Disley, distance runner Phillip Llewellyn Morgan plus journalists Neil Allen and Terry O'Connor. Others present included world record breakers Derek Ibbotson, Steve Cram and Dave Bedford, and Britain's other outstanding miler of the Bannister period, Bill Nankeville. It was Bill's 84th birthday and his son, comedian Bobby Davro, popped in for a surprise visit. It was a truly lovely occasion.

To mark his 100th birthday on May 14 *Athletics Weekly* published my two-page tribute to Godfrey Rampling. The Olympic 4x400m relay gold medallist, father of acclaimed film actress Charlotte Rampling, lived just up the road from me in a care home in Bushey and I had hoped to visit him for a chat. Unfortunately I chose a day when he wasn't feeling too well, so I left a copy of the article with one of the staff. He died a month later.

Great as Usain Bolt had been in 2008, he was even more amazing in 2009. His first international appearance of the season was in Manchester … and he was just sensational.

An indication of what Usain Bolt might serve up for our delectation this summer was provided on a damp afternoon in the centre of Manchester on May 17. The BUPA Great City Games 150 metres may have been an experiment to see whether there is a public for street racing but by attracting Bolt the event proved not only wildly successful, with big crowds lining the specially constructed straight track in Deansgate despite the weather, but will go down in athletics history. It's a distance that is rarely contested but by any measure Bolt's time of 14.35 was remarkable. The previous 'world best' was a hand timed 14.8 by Pietro Mennea in 1983, while Linford Christie clocked a windy 14.74 in 1994. Most astonishing were Bolt's 50m splits. A stumble soon after the start slowed him to an unexceptional 5.65 for the first 50m, but then he really took off. He flashed past the 100m mark in 9.91 for a flying 50m split of 4.26 – surely representing the fastest speed ever recorded by a human – and then finished with a 4.44. He thus covered the last 100m in a phenomenal 8.70, and all that on a chilly early season day on a sodden track in what was essentially an exhibition run by a man who declared "I'm not in the best of shape." How fast will Bolt go this year? He recently reckoned that he could have run 9.56 in Beijing has he not slowed down to celebrate 20m from the line. Already, at 22, the world's most famous and popular athlete, Bolt has a precise ambition. "My main goal is to make myself a legend."

He certainly achieved legendary status at the World Championships in August in Berlin, the very stadium in which Jesse Owens made Olympic history in 1936.

The conjecture is over. Ever since Bolt clocked 9.69 easing up in Beijing the main topic of conversation within athletics has been just how fast could he have run. The consensus was something inside 9.60 ... and now he has actually recorded 9.58. You cannot discuss Bolt's achievements in normal terms; all the superlatives lavished on his predecessors as the world's fastest human seem inadequate. Here is a man who, when logically world records should become progressively tougher to break and then by minute margins, has now carved the biggest chunk off the 100m mark since electrical timing became mandatory. An IAAF bio-mechanical analysis of the 20m splits show that Bolt clocked 1.61 sec between 60m (6.31, as compared to Maurice Greene's world indoor record of 6.39) and 80m (7.92), for the highest speed on record. He covered the 20m segments in 2.89, 1.75, 1.67, 1.61 and 1.66. Tyson Gay, whose new American record of 9.71 is the third quickest ever time, lost ground at every stage of the race. Gay needed 46 strides to complete the race, Bolt just 41.

Although he declared he wasn't in the same shape as he was in Beijing, and was tired after his 100m exertions, Bolt treated himself to a 23rd birthday present a day early when he posted the extraordinary time of 19.19, swelling his bank balance by another $160,000 (as in the 100m) in the process. Reacting well to the gun he ran a bend which Michael Johnson, commenting on BBC television, described as "unbelievable" and although there were some tremendous times behind him he won by some seven metres, the biggest ever margin of victory in the event's World Champs history. "I didn't expect a world record," he declared. "It wasn't a good race, but it was a fast one!"

Bolt picked up a third gold medal in the 4x100m relay. The US team was disqualified in the heats, leaving the Jamaican foursome to romp home in 37.31, the second fastest ever time. The Jamaicans had a wonderful championships, for in addition to those three golds in the men's sprints there were victories also for the petite Shelly-Ann Fraser in the 100m (10.73), Brigitte Foster-Hylton in the 100m hurdles (12.51), Melaine Walker in the 400m hurdles (52.42) and the 4x100m team (42.06 after a 41.88 heat). The Americans as usual topped the table with 22 medals, ten of them gold.

The British team came away with six medals, but thanks to a retrospective Russian disqualification that total years later rose to seven. Three of them were bronze, awarded to the men's 4x100m (38.02) and women's 4x400m (3:25.16) relay squads and to Jenny Meadows (1:57.93) in a race won by the controversial 18 year-old South African, Caster Semenya, in 1:55.45. Silver went to Lisa Dobriskey, who ran the race of her life to finish just 1/100th behind the 1500m winner in 4:03.74, Bahrain's Ethiopian-born Maryam Jamal, and the men's 4x400m team (3:00.53). Two Britons made it all the way to the top of the podium.

"It's been a long time coming," admitted an exultant but relieved and emotional Phillips Idowu (30) after gaining the global title he had yearned for over so many years. He may have won world indoor, European indoor and Commonwealth Games gold medals, but the only ones that really mattered to him were the Olympics and outdoor Worlds – the ultimate tests in athletics. Last year in Beijing he came close, jumping an outdoor pb of 17.62m, only to be overtaken by Nelson Évora's 17.67m, and that hurt. It was an admirable performance but he had been convinced he would win and thus it ranked as a disappointment. This time, in Berlin, he fulfilled everyone's highest expectations, his own included, at last. The breakthrough came in the third round when Idowu summoned up the leap of his life. It was measured at a world-leading 17.73m, an outdoor pb (he jumped 17.75m indoors last year), but as his toes weren't quite on the board he gave away fully 20cm, actually covering 17.93m from take-off to landing. He became the first Briton to win a men's world title since, appropriately enough, Jonathan Edwards in 2001.

Like Daley Thompson, the only other Briton to win a multi-events title at the World Champs, Jessica Ennis (23) has the advantage of starting with her two strongest individual events. In Thompson's case it was the 100m and long jump, for Ennis it's the hurdles (equal 2nd on the UK all-time list with 12.81) and high jump, at which she is joint UK record holder at 1.95m. In Berlin she capitalised to the full by clocking 12.93, her fastest in a heptathlon, and clearing her season's best of 1.92m, so that after two events she led by 181 points. In the shot, after two poor efforts, Ennis came through with a timely pb of 14.14m. A season's best of 23.15 for 200m widened her overnight advantage to a colossal 307 points. Her first day score of 4124 has only ever been bettered by Jackie Joyner-Kersee and Carolina Klüft – select company indeed! Having had to change her take-off foot this year after three stress fractures of her right ankle terminated her season early last summer, Ennis has yet to fulfil her potential in the long jump but 6.29m with 17cm to spare on the board was an acceptable result. Ennis has worked hard on the throws this year and her 43.54m ensured she didn't concede too much in the penultimate event, the javelin. She enjoyed a cushion of around 12 seconds going into the 800m where her pb of 2:09.88 was the fastest of any of the medal contenders. She could have sauntered around, but instead nerves and adrenalin took over and she went off too fast, leading through 400m in 61.12. Later she began to tread water but she was not to be denied and fought back to win the race in 2:12.22 for a world

431

leading score of 6731, an improvement of 144 points over her previous best and the third highest ever score by a Briton behind Denise Lewis's 6831 and 6736.

Next to Bolt, the star of the championships was Kenenisa Bekele, who became the first man to complete a 5000/10,000m double at the Worlds. The 10,000m came first.

How do you beat Bekele? The answer is, if he's fit and healthy, you can't. Zersenay Tadese ran a blinder of a race from the front, setting an almost inhuman pace for the final 6k, and yet far from being broken the 27 year-old Ethiopian took it all in his silken stride and still sprinted away with a 57.4 last lap. By winning a fourth world title at this event he matched Haile Gebrselassie and he brought his career record of 10,000m victories to 12 out of 12. At 5000m the time was 13:40.45. From then on the pace, with Tadese in charge, was relentless as lap after lap was covered in 64 sec or faster. The gallant but doomed Tadese led at the bell, the signal for Bekele to cut loose and open up a winning margin of 25m. His time was 26:46.31, the second 5000m run in 13:05.86.

The manner of Bekele's 5000m victory was reminiscent of Lasse Viren in Montreal when the world's best lined up behind him but nobody could get past as he remorselessly tightened the screw. At the bell it was Bekele and Eliud Kipchoge with defending champion Bernard Lagat next. As Kipchoge dropped back it was Lagat (with a severe spike wound in his left foot from the 1500m) who mounted the most severe challenge, and these two great competitors raced neck and neck along the final straight. It was a titanic struggle and it was Bekele whose legs, lungs, heart and will were stronger. Completing the last 200m in 26.1 Bekele finished just 0.24 ahead in 13:17.09 to become Ethiopia's first winner of this event. Kenyan-born athletes took the other medals through Lagat (USA) and James Kwalia (Qatar). Mo Farah placed 7th, the first European finisher, in 13:19.69.

Another highlight was the world record hammer throw of 77.96m by Poland's Anita Wlodarczyk, a worthy successor to her compatriot Kamila Skolimowska, the 2000 Olympic champion, who in February at a training camp in Portugal died of a pulmonary artery embolism at the shockingly young age of 26. The downside was that four gold medallists were later found to have cheated when their samples were re-tested years later using more sophisticated equipment. The guilty parties, and rightfully stripped of their medals and reputations, were Russia's Valeriy Borchin (20km walk), Sergey Kirdyapkin (50km walk) and Olga Kaniskina (20km walk), and Spain's Marta Domínguez (steeplechase). The International Olympic Committee announced in November that Moroccan-born Rashid Ramzi of Bahrain had been stripped of the 2008 Olympic 1500m title after a re-test indicated the presence of CERA, an advanced version of blood-boosting EPO.

The biggest shock in Berlin was the demise of Yelena Isinbayeva in the pole vault. She may have paid the penalty for being over confident. While all her main rivals entered the competition at 4.40m and then vaulted at 4.55m and 4.65m, she elected to come in at 4.75m no less! That might have been

432

understandable had she been in proven 5 metre form but her summer season had been undistinguished by her own standards and in her two most recent contests she had won in Paris with a modest 4.65m and lost to Anna Rogowska in London on countback at 4.68m. After seeing Rogowska clear what proved to be the winning height of 4.75m at the first attempt, Isinbayeva went under the bar at her first try and then missed twice at 4.80m, finishing in tears. But her misery didn't last long, for in her next competition 11 days later in Zürich she made first time clearances at 4.71m, 4.81m and 5.06m – her 15th outdoor world record to add to the 12 she has set indoors! There was further joy for the Russian in Brussels where she, Sanya Richards and Kenenisa Bekele shared the Golden League's million dollar jackpot.

The most damaging innovation of the year was the rebranding of the popular, long established European Cup as the European Team Championships. Instead of eight or nine teams with separate men's and women's scores, the new format featured an unwieldy twelve teams with men's and women's scores combined. More damaging was the reduction of attempts in the field events and the introduction of such gimmicks as "devil take the hindmost" which made a farce of the longer track races. Writing in AI, Peter Matthews was scathing in his criticism of the governing body, European Athletics, and I agreed with his trenchant views. Some of the more outlandish features were dropped the following year but the damage had been done.

Peter, incidentally, was a deserving recipient of that year's Ron Pickering Memorial Award for services to athletics. The presentation by Ron's widow, Jean Pickering, at the British Athletics Writers' Association dinner, left him stunned. As someone who has known Peter for around 50 years and been a close colleague as co-editor of AI since 1993, I have no hesitation in describing him as Britain's, and probably the world's, foremost athletics statistician and analyst. He has been a prominent member of the ATFS since 1970, has edited the invaluable *International Athletics Annual* since 1984 and for several years has been chairman of the NUTS … all that in addition to his announcing and TV commentating activities.

A gloriously nostalgic evening was enjoyed by those present at the second England Athletics Hall of Fame awards with 89 year-old Dorothy Tyler, Jonathan Edwards, Steve Backley, coach Malcolm Arnold and multu-Paralympic champion Noel Thatcher inducted in person. The other inductees were Mary Rand and Ron Pickering (both awards accepted by Jean Pickering), Alf Shrubb (by his Canadian grand-daughter), Lord Burghley (by his daughter Lady Victoria Leatham), Harold Abrahams (by his daughter Susan Pottle), Sydney Wooderson (by his widow Pamela Wooderson), Steve Cram (by Paul Dickenson) and Ann Packer (by yours truly).

45. MO AT THE DOUBLE (2010)

Mo Farah can look back to 2010 as the year when it all began to click for him; the year of his first major championship double. It had been a long journey. Born in Somalia, he arrived in London in 1993 at the age of ten, speaking no English. From his early teens his running talent was obvious. At 14 he was English Schools cross country and 1500m champion in his age group; at 16 he finished sixth over 3000m at the World Youth Championships and at 18 he was crowned European junior 5000m champion. That he had speed as well as endurance was made clear in 2003 when he ran 800m in 1:48.69 and two years later he ran the mile in 3:56.49. In 2006 he won a silver medal at 5000m in the European Championships and ended the year as European cross country champion, but at the global level he hadn't yet cut it: sixth at 5000m in the 2007 World Championships after leading at the bell; eliminated in his heat at the 2008 Olympics; and seventh in the 2009 World Championships although he did win the European indoor 3000m title that year.

After getting married to Tania in April 2010, Mo's running career started to take off. He won a 10km road race in London in the swift time of 27:44, covering the second half in a spectacular 13:34, and the following week won the European Cup 10,000m (in only his second track race at the distance) in 27:28.86 for third place on the UK all-time list. He ran almost a minute slower in Barcelona at the European Championships but that sufficed for victory with team-mate Chris Thompson second.

Despite all the nation's great long distance track runners, Britain had never won a men's 10,000m title at Olympic, world or European level. Now at last there is a champion to acclaim in Mo Farah (27). Beaten so narrowly over 5000m at the 2006 Europeans, he has had to wait four long years for the chance to go one better and he fully justified his status as favourite for this title. The winning time, 28:24.99 in 25°C, was the slowest since 1974 but it was an intriguing race, infinitely preferable to the carefully paced time trials arranged for the leading East Africans when they compete in Europe. The British duo were content to hold back in midfield at halfway (14:38.10) but by 6000m Thompson was in front of Farah and the pace started to pick up – the second half would be covered in 13:46.89. Before 8000m Farah moved in front and only Ayad Lamdassem, a former Moroccan representing Spain, was able to stay with him. In complete control of the proceedings, Farah invited Lamdassem to take the lead shortly before 9000m ... which he did. It would prove to be his undoing for now Farah could simply shadow an increasingly anxious opponent, ready to strike when it suited him and he did so with 300m to go. It was all over as Farah ran the final lap in 57.6.

Farah made further history by completing a momentous double in the 5000m. The victory gave Farah immense satisfaction for four years ago he was beaten by 0.09 by Spain's Jesús España in a furious sprint for the finish. This was payback time and on this occasion Farah's finishing powers were so superior that he crossed the line almost 2 sec clear of España in 13:31.18 after a tremendous final kilometre from the front of 2:25.24 with the last three laps in 61.42, 59.15 and 55.70.

In Mo's next race, at Crystal Palace, he was himself outkicked by the ever formidable Bernard Lagat, the former Kenyan now American, who beat him over 3000m: 7:40.36 to 7:40.75. But in his final track race of the year, in Zürich, Mo achieved one of his major goals of the season: to break Dave Moorcroft's UK (and former world) 5000m record of 13:00.41. In fact he smashed it with 12:57.94 although an indication that he still wasn't yet in world-beating mode was that he finished fifth in the race, won by Tariku Bekele (Kenenisa's younger brother) in 12:55.03. The full extent of Mo's talent would emerge the following year.

I combined one of my usual jaunts to Las Vegas (now even more enjoyable as I had discovered cousins who actually lived there!) with a few days tacked on in order to visit another cousin, Joy, in Albuquerque, New Mexico. The US Indoor Championships were being staged in the high altitude city and several competitors there went on to individual victories at the World Indoors in Doha: Bernard Lagat in the 3000m, Christian Cantwell in the shot, Bryan Clay in the heptathlon, Debbie Dunn in the 400m, Lolo Jones in the 60m hurdles and Brittney Reese in the long jump. Other highlights of my stay were accompanying Joy and Elliott Denman on a car trip to fascinating Santa Fe and riding the Sandia Peak Tramway (cablecar), the world's second longest aerial tramway (2.7 miles), up to an elevation of 10,300 feet. It was mighty cold at the top!

Those World Indoor Championships featured a world record right at the end of the three-day programme by Teddy Tamgho. In the absence of title holder Phillips Idowu, a lifetime best first round leap of 17.69m appeared to ensure victory for Cuba's Yoandris Betanzos, but with the penultimate jump of the contest the 20 year-old Frenchman landed at 17.90m no less. Britain came away with four medals. The men's 4x400m team placed third and Jenny Meadows clocked a UK 800m record of 1:58.43 very close behind the Russian winner, Mariya Savinova (1:58.26). Throughout her career, Jenny lost valuable placings and financial rewards because of doping cheats (usually of the Russian persuasion) and Savinova was a case in point. In 2017 the Court of Arbitration for Sport upheld a four year ban and disqualified all of her results from July 2010 to August 2013, thereby stripping her of gold medals at the 2010 European Championships, 2011 Worlds and 2012 Olympics. Unfortunately, this cheat rather than Jenny remains in the record books as 2010 world indoor champion. However, there were two undisputed British gold medallists even if one of them does have a tainted reputation.

Thirteen years after setting a world junior 100m record of 10.06, and four years after his controversial return to the sport following a two-year drugs ban, Dwain Chambers captured his first global title. The third quickest of all-time with his 6.42 60m at last year's European Champs he went one better than his World Indoors silver medal of 2008 by winning in the year's fastest time of

435

6.48. Chambers became the second Briton to win this title, after Jason Gardener in 2004, and at 31 supplanted his compatriot as the oldest winner.

Not that any further proof was necessary, but Jessica Ennis (24) demonstrated again what a superb major championship competitor she is. In Berlin last summer she won the world heptathlon title with a big pb of 6731 and now, in Doha, she not only broke Kelly Sotherton's UK and Commonwealth pentathlon record of 4927 but also the great Carolina Klüft's championship record of 4933. Her score of 4937 has only ever been surpassed by Irina Belova (4991 in 1992) and Klüft (4948 in 2005 and 4944 in 2007). It was a huge leap forward from her previous best, 4716 for 6th in the 2007 European Indoors. She led from the outset, clocking the fine 60m hurdles time of 8.04. She faced a setback in the high jump when she failed twice at 1.90m but she just got over at the third attempt. Nataliya Dobrynska's big opportunity to go ahead came in the shot where her lifetime best is 17.29m as against the Briton's 14.14m but the Ukrainian managed "only" 16.43m to her opponent's indoor pb of 14.01m and Ennis remained in front, 3021 to 3003. In the long jump Ennis produced an absolute pb of 6.44m and with victory assured, barring accidents or injury, attention switched to her record breaking prospects. She needed to run 800m in 2:13.18 or faster to break the UK record and she finished in 2:12.55, an indoor pb.

Jessica was clearly the world's foremost female all-rounder in 2010. Despite horrendous weather conditions on the second day in Götzis, she put together marks of 12.89 hurdles, 1.91m high jump, 14.25m shot (a pb), 23.31 200m, a disappointing 6.13m long jump, 43.40m javelin and 2:11.19 800m for her second highest score of 6689. She went on to total a personal best of 6823 when winning the European title.

Ennis started in supreme form with 12.95 hurdles into a 1.0m wind and also "won" the high jump, although she would have expected to go higher than 1.89m. The shot would be the key event. However, far from her best, Dobrynska reached 15.88m while Ennis, with only 13.49m on the card after two tries, rallied to finish with 14.05m. She had lost only 123 points and was still ahead after three events: 3022 to 3011. Ennis moved into a much more substantial overnight lead as she ran a near pb of 23.21 for 200m. Day one scores: Ennis 4080, Dobrynska 3970. The long jump was the other event where Dobrynska could make up ground but again the damage was limited. Ennis jumped 6.43m while Dobrynska managed 6.56m. Both threw lifetime bests in the javelin: Dobrynska 49.25m, Ennis 46.71m. So, with the 800m to go, Ennis was on 5861, Dobrynska 5843. Dobrynska (pb of 2:12.96) thus had the unenviable task of having to finish just over a second ahead of Ennis (2:09.88) to take the gold medal. She gave it her best shot, moving ahead briefly at 600m, but Ennis sprinted past to win the race by almost 2 sec, 2:10.18 to 2:12.06, and become European champion with 6823. That broke Klüft's championship record of 6740 and was just 8 points short of Denise Lewis's UK and Commonwealth record. Dobrynska's pb 800m enabled her to score her highest total of 6778.

The British team overall performed splendidly at those European Championships, winning 19 medals at the time to rank second to Russia's 24. Subsequent re-testing of samples has resulted in several Russian athletes being stripped of their medals and Britain now tops the table with 20 (six gold, eight silver, six bronze) to Russia's 19. In addition to Jessica's success and Mo's double, there were three other British gold medallists. Andy Turner took the 110m hurdles in 13.28; Dai Greene won the 400m hurdles in 48.12 (joining David Hemery as the second fastest ever Briton) with Rhys Williams second, both men being coached by Malcolm Arnold; and Phillips Idowu produced the longest leap of his life, 17.81m (17.92m from take-off) to defeat a world class triple jump field.

One of the most impressive winners in Barcelona was Croatia's vivacious Blanka Vlasic who high jumped 2.03m but an even better moment awaited her in her native Split on the occasion of the inaugural IAAF Continental Cup, a more streamlined successor to the World Cup. Instead of five continental and three national teams as previously, now there were just four teams – Africa, Americas, Europe and Asia-Pacific – with two representatives per event (three in races of 1500m upwards). Two of those teams dominated and after a close contest Europe (429 points, men and women combined) won ahead of the Americas (419.5) … or so we thought. The ugly face of doping became apparent years later when re-testing resulted in the retrospective disqualification of several athletes and the revised team result meant the Americas had in fact beaten Europe, 422.5 to 413. Among several sparkling performances were a 1:43.37 800m by David Rudisha, of whom more later; a Welsh record of 47.88 by Dai Greene (just short of Kriss Akabusi's UK record of 47.82); and an Asian triple jump record of 15.25m by Olga Rypakova.

There cannot have been many more emotional moments in athletics than when Blanka Vlasic, truly a Split personality as that city's favourite and most celebrated daughter, cleared 2.05m. The crowd of 27,500, mostly Croatians of course, had clapped and cheered her from the moment she walked into the arena and each of her faultless clearances was greeted by roars of approval. Emma Green was her only real competition and after the Swede's final failure at 2.02m it was evident that Vlasic had gained her 17th victory this year from 19 contests. That Cup record clearance at 2.05m was the icing on the cake as it matched Chaunté Lowe's world outdoor lead (Vlasic jumped 2.06m indoors in February) and it brought her tally of 2m or higher competitions this year to 16. She wasn't close as she took her 58th, 59th and 60th attempts at a world record 2.10m, but it didn't matter. She was in tears as she ran over to hug her father [who set a Croatian decathlon record of 7659 in 1983] and then sank to the track, sobbing. "This today made everything worth it," she said. "I could retire tomorrow and I would have no regrets."

Vlasic was voted female athlete of the year by the IAAF and readers of AI, and the men's accolade went to David Rudisha, winner of all 12 of his 800m races including a pair of world records.

Wilson Kipketer's reign as world 800m record holder is over. Two days short of 13 years since the Kenyan-born Dane ran 1:41.11, David Rudisha was timed at 1:41.09 at Berlin's ISTAF meeting to become at 21 the youngest holder of this record (as ratified by the IAAF) since Ted Meredith back in 1912. "I told my pacemaker [Sammy Tangui] to run the first lap under 49 sec; he did a great job," said Rudisha. Tangui reached halfway in 48.68 and Rudisha, close behind at that point, went on to pass 600m in 74.54. "In the last 200m I had to push really hard, but when I saw the clock at the end it was amazing, a fantastic feeling." Rudisha, a Masai, always seemed destined for greatness as an 800m runner. His genes helped, for his father Daniel Rudisha ran a 44.4 anchor leg for Kenya's 4x400m silver medal team at the 1968 Olympics. David himself is no slouch at one lap (pb of 45.50 this February), but his talent was always at 800m. He started at 400m and decathlon but found his true event as a 17 year-old in 2006 with a time of 1:46.3 and victory in the World Juniors. The following year, still a junior, he ran 1:44.15; in 2008 he progressed to 1:43.72 and last year to an African record of 1:42.01 although he failed to reach the World Champs final on the same Berlin track on which he would make history a year later.

David Rudisha completed one of the most amazing weeks in athletics history with another fantastic 800m on Rieti's miraculous track. In Berlin on Aug 22 he had lowered the world record to 1:41.09; in Brussels on Aug 27 he disposed of his main rival Abubaker Kaki in 1:43.50; and in Rieti on Aug 29 he improved again to 1:41.01. Setting two world outdoor records at 800m in such a short period of time is unprecedented. "The conditions were perfect," said Rudisha, who was paced by training partner Sammy Tangui. The 400m split was 48.20. Jackson Kivuva then took over for the next 100m before Rudisha moved ahead. The 600m split was 74.59 compared to 75.0 by Seb Coe in his record 1:41.73, 74.6 by Kipketer in his 1:41.24 and 1:41.11, and 74.54 by Rudisha in Berlin.

How did Usain Bolt get on in a year when there was no global championship for him to aim at? He raced only seven times, topping the world list at 200m with 19.56 and at 300m with the fastest ever time (30.97) at or near sea level. At 100m, though, his best mark of 9.82 ranked only equal third and the top man was Tyson Gay who decisively beat Bolt in Stockholm, 9.84 to 9.97, before clocking 9.78 in London and 9.79 in Brussels.

Bolt, like so many other leading eligible athletes, opted to miss October's Commonwealth Games in Delhi. Other notable absentees included Asafa Powell, Yohan Blake, Rudisha, Asbel Kiprop, Farah, Idowu, Veronica Campbell-Brown, Shelly-Ann Fraser and Ennis, and the standard in too many events was weak even by Commonwealth standards. Kenya won the most medals with 29 (11 gold), followed by England's 23 (6 gold). The English winners were Leon Baptiste (200m), Andy Turner (110m hurdles), Louise Hazel (heptathlon), Johanna Jackson (20km walk) and both 4x100m relay teams – not forgetting Dai Greene's 400m hurdles victory for Wales.

It was my sad duty during the year to record the deaths of several friends and acquaintances in the sport. *Wilf Paish* (77) coached Tessa Sanderson, Peter Elliott and Mick Hill among many others and his services to athletics were recognised by the award of the MBE in 2005, while in 2008 he was presented with a lifetime achievement award from England Athletics. As Elliott remarked: "He was a great coach and motivator. He may have been short in stature but he was huge in character and personality." *Janet Clerc (née Simpson)*, a member of the British 4x400m team which won the 1969 European title in world record time, passed away at 65. She and her mother, the former Violet Webb, remain unique in British athletics history as the only mother and daughter to win Olympic medals: Violet in the 1932 4x100m and Janet likewise in 1964. She placed fourth in the 1968 Olympic 400m in 52.57 and was married for 24 years to Switzerland's 1969 European 200m champion Philippe Clerc. *Scott Davis* (67) was a larger than life American statistician, meeting director, public address announcer and ATFS secretary general who brightened up every meeting he attended with his genial personality. *Doug Wilson*, who was once Britain's second fastest ever miler behind Sydney Wooderson and a long serving athletics correspondent for the "News of the World", at least reached the grand old age of 90. I never forgot that when I was 15 Doug was kind enough to respond to my letter asking for advice on how to get into journalism. I still have his letter. *Tony Ward* (79) was a pioneer in many facets of the sport, including the introduction of 'Tartan' tracks and the British Athletics League. A prolific writer, he was also a leading public address announcer and worked as public relations officer for British Athletics. I hadn't seen him for many years but I was saddened also to hear that *Charles Elliott* (78) had died. He was an early member of the NUTS, organising their track and field meetings, became a well regarded coach and published the lively "Athletics Arena" monthly magazine between 1963 and 1971.

Inducted into the England Athletics Hall of Fame were Walter George, Albert Hill, Linford Christie, Brendan Foster, Dame Kelly Holmes, former Principal National Coaches John Le Masurier and Denis Watts, and AW founder Jimmy Green, myself happy to present the award to Jimmy's son Tim. There was also an award for Paula Radcliffe as England's athlete of the decade (2000-09) following a public vote organised by England Athletics. Having given birth to her second child a month earlier, Paula was unable to be present at the ceremony and the award was received on her behalf by her proud parents.

On the personal health front, I was somewhat shocked in September, following various tests and a biopsy, to find that I had been diagnosed with MALT lymphoma, a form of blood cancer. In November, at London's University College Hospital, I underwent ten sessions of radiotherapy directed at my neck and – fingers crossed – that appeared to do the trick. I have been in remission ever since.

46. THE YEAR OF THE BOOK (2011)

It was late in 2004 that I started to research and write the *All-Time Greats of British Athletics*. It was a project close to my heart, indeed a labour of love as the income generated was exceedingly modest and it took me some 18 months to produce the manuscript. When it was finally published in May 2006, round about my 68th birthday, I decided that would be my last book. Not counting the little booklet on Derek Ibbotson, my first proper book had appeared in 1964, so my span as an author was in excess of 40 years. My writing for and editing of magazines had always taken precedence and the work involved in producing a book had somehow to be slotted in to an already time consuming routine. I thought enough is enough.

That is until I was approached in the autumn of 2009 to write *The Official History of the Amateur Athletic Association*. Chris Carter, the former UK 800m record holder who was then chairman of the AAA, honorary secretary Walter Nicholls and former chairman George Bunner were particularly keen, as a significant part of the AAA's legacy, to commission a history of the world's oldest athletics governing body as it approached its 130th birthday in 2010. It was an offer I couldn't refuse!

I tried to avoid duplicating the content in Peter Lovesey's magnificent *Official Centenary History of the AAA*, published in 1979, and came up with a different format. Although covering in some detail the Association's evolution and decision making since its formation in 1880, I concentrated on a year by year account of the highlights of each year's Championships from its inception until 2010 although regrettably the last meeting to incorporate the title of AAA Championships was the one staged in 2006. It was wonderful to be able to summarise all those historic meetings, drawing attention to distinguished athletes of their time who in many cases had long been forgotten.

The book ran to 388 pages and I was delighted that one of my heroes, Sir Chris Chataway, agreed to contribute a foreword. It was an amusing and thoughtful piece of writing. Describing himself as "the most persistent loser of middle distance races in the history of the AAA Championships", having been edged out by inches in the 3 miles on three occasions ("even in 1954 when I broke the world record I was beaten by Freddie Green"), he regarded the story of the AAA as a fascinating part of British social history. "It was founded for gentlemen amateurs, who did not wish to mix with professional runners; nor since they were generally faster did the gentlemen wish to compete against them. As social attitudes changed so did the sport and the governing body – usually as a result of fiercely fought controversies. In due course the gentlemen were prepared to compete against tradesmen and artisans just as long as they gained no material reward from the sport. It seems extraordinary now that amateurism should have been seen as something grand and noble by otherwise sensible people. Would Shakespeare or Leonardo da Vinci really have been so much better if they had not been paid? But for athletics as for other sports it was a long and bruising struggle before the organisation came to terms with the fact that the first word of its title was no longer operative."

By the time the book was launched at the English Championships in July 2011 I was already working on a companion volume: *The Official History of the Women's AAA*. And that wasn't all, because simultaneously I was heavily involved with a major IAAF publication, necessitating several editorial conferences in Monaco. No complaints! More about this project in the next chapter.

Still on the subject of books, the year saw the publication of two outstanding biographies with which I had been pleased to be of some assistance to the authors. Reviewing Mark Ryan's masterly biography of Harold Abrahams, *Running With Fire*, I began:

Having been something of a father figure to me when I was a young man, I thought I knew Harold fairly well. I was wrong. Mark Ryan's 389-page hardback volume provides one revelation after another thanks to fascinating reminiscences by members of Harold's family and a good deal of meticulous detective work on the part of the author. It's common knowledge that the portrayal of Harold in the Oscar-winning film was somewhat distorted for dramatic effect, and this book seeks to redress the balance. It's subtitled "The true story of Chariots of Fire hero" and it lives up to that claim as the complex nature of the 1924 Olympic 100m champion is unveiled. I would rate this as the best athletics biography I have ever read. It has everything. Whether you are interested just in Abrahams the athlete (some 50 pages alone are devoted to a classic account of his experiences at the Paris Olympics) or a rounded warts-and-all portrait of a remarkable man who, despite what his critics might argue, did more to popularise British athletics than any other individual.

Who are British athletics' most successful married couple? You have to go back nearly half a century to their days of glory on the track but it's Mr and Mrs Brightwell – Robbie and his wife, the former Ann Packer. Ann won Olympic gold (800m) and silver (400m) medals at the Tokyo Olympics of 1964, while Robbie – European 400m champion in 1962 – heroically anchored the British team to silver in the Olympic 4x400m. Now at last their inspiring story is available ["Robbie Brightwell and his Golden Girl"], not as a conventional printed book but electronically on the Amazon Kindle internet site. It's a fascinating tale of how two romantically entwined athletes struggled to reach the top, set against the background of a largely vanished amateur athletics scene.

Road running featured prominently throughout the year, with Mary Keitany setting the tone with a world record half marathon time of 65:50 in February at Ra's Al Khaymah in the United Arab Emirates. It was ten seconds slower than Paula Radcliffe's time in the 2003 Great North Run but that was on a slightly downhill course which disqualified it for record purposes. The tiny Kenyan's next race was the London Marathon in April.

The previous time Mary Keitany (29) ran in the London Marathon was as a pacemaker in 2007, reaching halfway in 69:58 before dropping out at 25k.

Since then she has built up a formidable reputation as a half marathoner, winning six on the trot and setting a world record. She had a tough time in her first completed marathon, in New York last November, suffering through the final hilly miles as she finished third in 2:29:01. However, she learned much from that experience and having modified her training accordingly she was fully prepared this time. After a first half in 70:37 she cut loose with a second half in an outstanding 68:42 to clock a world-leading 2:19:19, equalling Irina Mikitenko as the fourth quickest ever marathoner behind Paula Radcliffe (2:15:25), Catherine Ndereba (2:18:47) and Mizuki Noguchi (2:19:12).

The London winner in 2010, Liliya Shobukhova finished second in 2:20:15, breaking her own Russian record, but that performance has been annulled along with the 2010 victory and several other fast and lucrative wins, including 2:18:20 in Chicago in October 2011, because of drug use. It was announced in 2014 that abnormalities were discovered in her athlete biological passport and that all of her race results since October 2009 would be struck off. Efforts are still being made for her to repay the huge amount of money she won during that period, including almost £378,000 plus costs to the London Marathon and a million dollars for twice winning the World Marathon Majors series.

The men's race in London saw a course record of 2:04:40 by Kenya's Emmanuel Mutai for fourth on the world all-time list, but an even quicker time was registered the following day in Boston ... but it couldn't count as a world record.

Perfect weather, a generous tailwind and fabulous competition made the 115th Boston Marathon the fastest marathon ever run. Geoffrey Mutai of Kenya (no relation to London winner Emmanuel Mutai) ran a spectacular 2:03:02, outsprinting countryman Moses Mosop (2:03:06). Both times were nearly a full minute better than Haile Gebrselassie's world record of 2:03:59, but due to the elevation drop and point-to-point measurements of the Boston course the performances are not record-eligible. The runners were assisted by winds of roughly 10 mph. The speed of the closing stages was amazing with splits of 14:11 for the 5k from 30-35k and 14:13 from 35-40k – that's 28:24 for 10k! Mutai's second half split of 61:04 is the fastest ever recorded.

Much later in the year, in Berlin in September, the world record was broken officially. The pacemakers reached halfway in a promising 61:44 and at 26km it was between Kenya's Patrick Makau and Ethiopia's Haile Gebrselassie. Shortly afterwards 'Geb' stopped, bent double with breathing difficulties (he suffers from exercise-induced asthma), but he got back into the race and was in second place when he dropped out soon after 35km. Makau, meanwhile, sped on and covered the second half in 61:54 for a time of 2:03:38. Completing a marathon for the first time, his compatriot Florence Kiplagat won the women's race in 2:19:44 with Paula Radcliffe (37), in her first marathon since placing fourth in New York in 2009 in 2:29:27, having given birth to son Raphael in September 2010, finishing third in 2:23:46 – her fastest for four years. It would prove to be her last world class performance. As for Gebrselassie, he would finish only one more marathon: fourth with 2:08:17 in Tokyo in 2012. A glorious era was ending.

The year saw the tragically early deaths of two of the most distinguished names in marathon running. Following a six-year battle against cancer, Grete Waitz succumbed in April at the age of 57. The Norwegian was the inaugural world champion in 1983, Olympic silver medallist in 1984 and won the New York Marathon a staggering nine times between 1978 and 1988. She set four world bests between 1978 and 1983, bringing the record down from over 2:34 to under 2:26, her fastest time being 2:24:54 when winning London in 1986. Sammy Wanjiru died in May after falling in unexplained circumstances from the balcony of his home in Kenya. He was merely 24. At the age of 18 he had set his first world record for the half marathon, and he made a successful marathon debut in 2007 by winning in Fukuoka in 2:06:39. Next year he improved to 2:05:24 when placing second in London and went on to become Kenya's first Olympic marathon champion, clocking easily the fastest ever major championship time of 2:06:32 in Beijing's sweltering conditions. Further victories followed in 2009 – London in 2:05:10, Chicago in 2:05:41 – and finally in 2010: Chicago in 2:06:24.

Nearer home, I was sorry to lose the company of Peter Hildreth (82), a leading British high hurdler throughout the 1950s and as athletics correspondent of the *Sunday Telegraph* for over 30 years a long-time journalistic colleague, and Mel Batty who died following a heart attack aged 71.

Mel Batty, one of the most popular and amiable characters in British athletics, was one of the most successful cross country, road and track runners of his day. Coached by long distance walker and distance running enthusiast Colin Young, whose inspiration was Emil Zátopek, Mel broke through to the big time in 1962 when he placed third in the International Cross Country Champs. Always a committed front runner, his greatest moment on the track came early in 1964 when he smashed Basil Heatley's world record for 10 miles (Zátopek was a previous record holder) with 47:26.8. He had the previous month fulfilled every English distance runner's ambition by winning the "National". He retained that title in 1965, going on to be controversially placed second in the International Cross Country in Ostend. Observers, including myself, felt that at worst a dead heat should have been declared. He later became a successful coach, his star being Eamonn Martin, who became UK 10,000m record holder and won the London and Chicago Marathons. He was associated with Brooks [the shoe firm] for many years, signing up the barefoot runner Zola Budd (!), and worked for television and the press as a "quotes man".

This was the year when Mo Farah, having served a long apprenticeship, finally emerged as a master craftsman of distance running. Now coached by Alberto Salazar in Oregon, Farah displayed his versatility in March by sprinting to victory over 3000m at the European Indoor Championships and two weeks later making his half marathon debut in New York, winning in the British record time of 60:23. In outdoor track races he posted his quickest ever times of 26:46.57 (European record) for 10,000m in June and 12:53.11 (UK record) for

5000m in July. It was in the 5000m at the World Championships in Daegu on September 4 that he began his incredible sequence of global title wins, but first came the 10,000m on August 28.

At 9000m there were still eight in contention. Farah, 8th at 5000m in 13:53.6, moved ahead with 600m to go and launched his prolonged finish at the bell. He quickly opened a 10m advantage over Ethiopia's Ibrahim Jeylan and Imane Merga. The latter couldn't match Farah's speed along the back straight but Jeylan could. Some 5m down with 200m remaining, he chased after Farah, gradually closed the gap and edged past some 30m out for victory in 27:13.81. Maybe Farah went too soon (or perhaps too late!) but he ran the last lap in 53.36 ... only for the unheralded Jeylan to run 52.8. So who is Jeylan? Only 22, he was an outstanding teenager, winning the world junior 10,000m in 2006 and the cross country title two years later. He ran his best time of 27:02.81 (the world youth record) in 2006, aged just 17.

Seven days later, having in the meantime run a 13:38.03 heat, Mo lined up for the 5000m final.

It has been a long wait. No male British distance runner had ever been a global gold medallist. The distinction fell to Mo Farah (28), who after his so-close silver medal in the 10,000m came up trumps at half the distance. The winning time of 13:23.36 might look ordinary but it was a most exciting race with the outcome in the balance until the last few seconds. As usual, Farah was happy to run right at the back in the early stages. At 2000m he began to take closer order, and it was from this point that the race began to hot up – the final 3000m took 7:47.75. At the bell it was still anyone's race and with 200m remaining Farah and Dejene Gebremeskel were abreast with Imane Merga and and Bernard Lagat breathing down their necks. Farah held a narrow lead entering the final straight and, gritting his teeth, this time he held on although Lagat, veering out into the third lane after being boxed briefly earlier, fought mightily to catch his man. At the finish Farah was a stride clear of the 2007 champion, having run the last lap in 52.61. Farah became the first European winner of this title since Eamonn Coghlan at the inaugural championships in 1983.

Britain's other victory in Daegu came in the 400m hurdles.

The curious aspect of the final was the winning time. It was breezy but following straight after the women's event in which Lashinda Demus ran a superb 52.47 it could have been assumed that a time of under 48 sec would be required for a chance of victory. That wasn't the case as 48.26 sufficed, the previous slowest winning time being 47.98. Not that gold medallist Dai Greene cared. He would love to break Kriss Akabusi's UK record of 47.82 but winning was all that mattered. His high level of self confidence proved completely justified as he put together an exquisitely judged race. Greene, striding 14s to hurdle six and then 15s home, bided his time. Javier Culson led over the final barrier but while he ran out of steam Greene charged past him on the run-in. Greene's triumph adds further lustre to the coaching skills of Malcolm Arnold for the 25 year-old Welshman is the fourth hurdler Arnold has guided to a global title after John Akii-Bua, Colin Jackson and Mark McKoy.

We didn't know it at the time but Jessica Ennis would also be crowned world champion, retaining the heptathlon title she had won in 2009. In Daegu she finished second with 6751 points to Tatyana Chernova's 6880 but belatedly in 2017 the now retired Dame Jessica received her well deserved gold medal after the Russian was retrospectively disqualified for doping – as were her equally "victorious" team-mates Valeriy Borchin (20km walk), Sergey Bakulin (50km walk), Mariya Savinova (800m), Yuliya Zaripova (steeplechase) and Olga Kaniskina (20km walk). What an indictment of Russia's wholesale cheating – a policy which, despite constant denials, must surely have been condoned if not actively encouraged at the highest political level. My report for AI, of course, could not anticipate future developments.

Daegu 2011 carried echoes of Tokyo 1964. Remember the Olympic pentathlon of 47 years ago, won by Irina Press with a world record 5246? On that occasion Britain's Mary Rand finished second 211 points behind although she outscored her Russian rival in three of the five events. One event made all the difference as Press put the shot 17.16m and Rand 11.05m – a massive turnaround of 384 points. How reminiscent that situation was when you consider what happened in the Daegu heptathlon. Britain's Ennis "beat" Russia's Chernova in five of the seven events but – conceding 251 points in the javelin – she lost by 129. Ennis set pbs in the shot (14.67m), long jump (equal at 6.51m; 6.66m from take-off to landing) and 800m (2:07.81) and scored more points than when she won the world title in Berlin but was defeated for the first time in a completed heptathlon since 2007.

Britain had two silver medallists in Phillips Idowu, who produced his second longest ever triple jump of 17.77m in reply to Christian Taylor's winning effort of 17.96m, and Hannah England – mentored by Kelly Holmes – who in a 1500m final marred by falls moved from seventh to second along the finishing straight in a race won by US steeplechase record holder Jenny Simpson in 4:05.40. Andy Turner picked up a bronze in the 110m hurdles. The shock of the meeting was the disqualification for a false start of the previously all-conquering Usain Bolt in the 100m final.

Earlier this year we collectively licked our lips in anticipation of a three-way battle for the world title involving Usain Bolt, Asafa Powell and Tyson Gay. When Gay dropped out with an injury we consoled ourselves with Bolt v Powell. Then on the eve of the championships, Powell – world's fastest this year with 9.78 – dropped out too due to a groin strain. Okay, there was still Bolt against the rest to savour, and the heats and semis with Bolt easing off drastically each time in 10.10 and 10.05 suggested the great man was getting close to his best form. We never found out. Of course it was a huge disappointment to Bolt, the thousands in the stadium and the millions watching on TV worldwide, but Bolt had only himself to blame for his lack of control. Reacting legitimately at the start is part of a sprinter's discipline and the almost hysterical clamour in some sections of the press that the no-tolerance rule should be thrown out is quite unjustified. The present rule is much fairer than its predecessor. Many will feel that Yohan Blake's victory was a hollow one, but that is grossly unfair to the Jamaican, who at 21 became the youngest ever world 100m champion. Blake, who trains with Bolt, was a worthy champion in his own right as he won by the yawning margin of 0.16 and his time of 9.92 into a 1.4m wind was highly creditable, worth 9.84 with zero wind and 9.74 with a 2m following wind according to "Track & Field News" tables.

After the 100m embarrassment there was enormous pressure on Bolt to redeeem himself with an outstanding performance in his favourite event and he didn't let down his millions of fans. Despite understandably registering the slowest reaction time he was quickly into his running and extended his advantage over Walter Dix to over 3m by the finish which he reached in a resounding 19.40. His time has only ever been bettered by himself (19.19 and 19.30) and Michael Johnson (19.32) – all world record marks – and he extended a win streak at 200m that began in June 2008.

It had been a marvellous championships, lacking just one element – a world record – and that was rectified when in the very last event the Jamaican squad of Nesta Carter, Michael Frater, Bolt and Powell carried the baton around in 37.04, fully 6/100ths inside the record set at the Beijing Olympics. The only team with any possibility of challenging the Jamaicans, the Americans, suffered another disaster. This time they won their heat in 37.79 but failed to finish in the final.

Bolt didn't run another 200m that season but despite a poor start he clocked a 9.85 100m in Zagreb and then three days later was even faster in Brussels.

Who would have thought that, just a few minutes after Bolt had raised the roof by running the world's quickest 100m time of the year with 9.76, his training partner Yohan Blake would totally upstage him. Blake (21) had not run 200m faster than 20.60 before last year, when he improved drastically to 19.78. This year, while shining at 100m, his 200m times were modest with 20.39, 20.33 and 20.38. In Brussels, but for a remarkably lethargic reaction to the gun, he might have broken Bolt's world record! He took all of 0.269 sec to press against his blocks, whereas had his reaction time been the same as runner-up Walter Dix (still a slowish 0.185) his finishing time could have been 19.18, shading Bolt's world record of 19.19. As it is, Blake's 19.26 is the second quickest ever.

The latest batch of inductees to the England Athletics Hall of Fame comprised Kathy Cook, Tom Hampson, Dorothy Hyman, Derek Ibbotson, Denise Lewis, Ken Matthews, Jean Pickering, Harold Whitlock and coaches Bruce Longden, Sam Mussabini and Mike Smith. How rewarding it was to have played a part in honouring these legendary figures.

47. AN OLYMPICS TO DIE FOR (2012)

What a fantastic Olympic year 2012 turned out to be. Those magnificent Games in London exceeded all expectations ... two books I worked on were published ... it was a vintage year for travel ... and I received a coveted award.

Let's start with an eventful indoor season. Holly Bleasdale (now Bradshaw) got me all excited when she raised her UK indoor pole vault record to 4.87m in January, ranking her second only to Yelena Isinbayeva on the world indoor all-time list and the highest ever clearance by a 20 year-old. She confirmed her new status by winning a bronze medal with 4.70m at the World Indoor Championships in Istanbul in March, victory going at 4.80m to a rejuvenated Isinbayeva, her first major title since 2008. A few weeks earlier the Russian had raised her world indoor record to 5.01m – her 28th world record indoors or out. The World Indoors were highlighted by world records in both the multi-events contests.

Who will be the next decathlete to surpass 9000 points and challenge Roman Sebrle's world record of 9026? Don't bet against Ashton Eaton. Last year he topped the world list with 8729 and his form this winter suggests another big gain in points is imminent this summer. Here he collected his third world record, compiling the stunning score of 6645 points – and it could have been considerably more had he been able to make a decent start to the 60m. His reaction time was 0.277, around a tenth slower than might have been expected, and had he run 6.69 rather than 6.79 (his pb is 6.66) he would have added 37 points to his score. He long jumped a colossal 8.16m, an absolute pb and multi-events "world record", and he followed with a 14.56m shot and 2.03m high jump. A 13.35 hurdler outdoors, Eaton has an indoor best of 7.60 and he wasn't far off that with 7.66. After the pole vault (5.20m) his lead had grown to 466 points. In the 1000m, needing 2:39.54 for a world record, he led throughout, looking serene and undistressed, for a time of 2:32.77, bringing his winning margin to an unprecedented 574 points.

Much was written about the impending pentathlon clash between defending champion Jessica Ennis and the world heptathlon champion Tatyana Chernova. As it turned out, Chernova seriously under-performed and the contest became a duel between Ennis and Olympic champion Nataliya Dobrynska. Ennis got away to a perfect start, clocking 7.91 for the hurdles, smashing the world's quickest ever in a pentathlon. Dobrynska was quite close to her best with 8.38. On paper Ennis was the leading high jumper at 1.95m but wound up only third with 1.87m. Dobrynska cleared 1.84m. Ennis performed exceptionally well in the shot for an absolute pb of 14.79m. It was a damage limitation exercise as Dobrynska (pb of 17.29m) registered 16.51m. Ennis still led, but only just, after three events. It was the long jump which essentially decided the destination of the medals. Ennis, who has a pb of 6.51m, reached only 6.19m while Dobrynska's final jump was measured at 6.57m and propelled her into the lead for the first time. The situation was that Dobrynska needed to run the 800m in 2:12.69 for a world record, while Ennis (pb of 2:07.81) would need to finish around 6.5 sec ahead of the Ukrainian (pb 2:11.34) to snatch the gold medal. Both women ran their hearts out with Ennis clocking 2:08.09 and Dobrynska 2:11.15. Unforgiveably, the electronic scoreboard at first indicated Ennis in first place with a UK record 4965, prompting Jess to celebrate (she did not know how far ahead of her rival she had finished), but that was before Dobrynska's time was registered. A few seconds later Ennis was devastated to discover that she was second and Dobrynska the new champion with a world record score of 5013.

Nonetheless, there were two British gold medals to celebrate. In a thrilling finish, the 4x400m relay team of Shana Cox (52.82), Nicola Sanders (52.48), Christine Ohuruogu (51.98) and Perri Shakes-Drayton (51.48) held off the strong American challenge for victory in 3:28.76, while there was a remarkable result in the women's triple jump.

Just three jumps (literally a triple jump) won an unlikely gold medal for Yamilé Aldama, who will turn 40 in August! She created the first sensation in the qualifying by reaching 14.62m, breaking her own world over-35 best of 14.51m (outdoors) in 2008. Aldama's opener in the final was only 14.10m but as she fell back on her hand that wasn't a true indication of her form. That came in the second round when she sailed out to an extraordinary 14.82m, a distance few men in the world could expect to match at age 39. It was her longest jump for six years. She ran through in the third round and, feeling a hamstring twinge, sat out the rest of the contest. The only serious challenge was mounted by Olga Rypakova but her 14.63m fell short. Aldama was appearing in her seventh World Indoors. She was 6th in 1997 and 7th in 1999 for Cuba, 2nd in 2003, 3rd in 2006, 5th in 2008 and a non-qualifier (19th) in 2010 for Sudan, and now a winner in British colours. As she commented: "Better late than never."

The other British medallists were: silver – the 4x400m team of Conrad Williams, Nigel Levine, Michael Bingham and Richard Buck (3:04.72) and Tiffany Porter, 60m hurdles in 7.94; bronze – Dwain Chambers, 60m in 6.60; Andrew Osagie, 800m in 1:48.92; Shara Proctor, a UK indoor long jump record of 6.89m; and the afore mentioned Holly Bleasdale. Near misses (fourth place) for Mo Farah (7:41.79 3000m, less than two strides behind winner Bernard Lagat) and Andy Pozzi (7.58 60m hurdles).

Nothing went right for Nataliya Dobrynska during the outdoor season, understandable as she had recently been widowed, whereas Jessica Ennis couldn't put a foot wrong. The first big heptathlon test was in Götzis, where the Ukrainian placed ninth with 6311 points (and would fail to finish in the Olympics) while the Briton scaled new heights.

Jessica Ennis assumed the mantle of Olympic favourite by smashing Denise Lewis's 2000 Commonwealth and UK record of 6831 with the magnificent score of 6906. Ennis, whose previous best was 6823 in 2010, clocked her second fastest ever hurdles time of 12.81, was close also to her outdoor shot pb with 14.51m, reduced her 200 pb from 23.11 to 22.88, equalled her best ever legal long jump of 6.51m, improved her javelin pb from 46.71m to

47.11m and ended with a 2:09.00 800, not far off her best of 2:07.81. Ironically, the one weak link was the high jump, which used to be her strongest individual discipline, having tied the UK record of 1.95m five years ago. On this occasion she managed only 1.85m. Nevertheless, she turned the tables on her Daegu conqueror Tatyana Chernova, winning by 132 points. Dafne Schippers, a 11.19/22.69 sprinter last year as a junior, improved her pb from 6172 to 6360.

There was an even more impressive all-round display at the US Olympic Trials in Eugene when Ashton Eaton broke the world decathlon record with a score of 9039 in cold and wet conditions. Performing in front of a veritable who's who of great American decathletes (Milt Campbell, Rafer Johnson, Bill Toomey, Bruce Jenner, Dan O'Brien, Bryan Clay) he began with a 10.21 100m, the fastest ever time in a decathlon. He followed that up with another decathlon "world record" of 8.23m in the long jump, giving him an astonishing two-event score of 2164 points. Next came a 14.20m shot put and 2.05m high jump in the slippery conditions, and he ended the day with a solid 46.70 400m although that fell far short of his remarkable early season mark of 45.68. His halfway score was 4728. Cold weather and a headwind slowed him to 13.70 in the hurdles, but after throwing the discus 42.81m he vaulted a personal best of 5.30m. A 58.87m javelin throw kept him on track for a shot at the world record and he gave it everything in the 1500m, reducing his pb from 4:18.94 to a gutsy 4:14.48.

As always, the 100m was the marquee event at the US Trials and it didn't disappoint as Justin Gatlin, the tainted 2004 Olympic champion, clocked a personal best of 9.80 ahead of Tyson Gay's 9.86. Shock, sensation at the Jamaican Trials in Kingston the following week as Yohan Blake beat Usain Bolt in both the 100m (pb of 9.75 to 9.86) and 200m (19.80 to 19.83). Bolt didn't race again until the Olympics but Blake won in Luzern in 9.85, while Gay beat Gatlin, 9.99 to 10.03 in Paris. The stage was set for some sprinting fireworks in London!

Before those Games there were European Championships to be staged in Helsinki. It was a controversial move as the Europeans had never before been held in an Olympic year, and many leading athletes saved themselves for the ultimate test. However, it didn't do any harm to Mo Farah, who became the first man to retain a European 5000m title (13:29.91). The other British winners were Rhys Williams in the 400m hurdles (49.33) and Robbie Grabarz in the high jump (2.31m).

From a British perspective at least the London Olympics, the Games of the 30th Olympiad, exceeded all expectations with medals from a wide variety of sports pouring in on a daily basis. Athletics certainly played its part in this overwhelming success. Who will ever forget "Super Saturday" (August 4) when THREE gold medals were won by British athletes within the space of 44 minutes! Certainly none of the 80,000 fans in the stadium who created the loudest noise I have ever experienced, or the millions watching on TV. Sitting next to Stan Greenberg in the press tribune, I murmured "I can die happy now".

First up, the day before, was Jessica Ennis for the first four events of the heptathlon. Pat had always wanted to sample the Olympic experience and this was her one opportunity, so I bought tickets for the two of us for that opening morning session. The stadium was packed, the atmosphere invigorating, and what a reception there was for Jess. No wonder she was inspired.

There was a sensational start to the contest when Ennis flew to a 12.54 clocking in the hurdles, breaking Tiffany Porter's UK record of 12.56 and shattering her own pb of 12.79. It was a "world heptathlon record", the previous quickest being 12.64. That earned her 1195 points and gave her an instant 142 point advantage over Tatyana Chernova. That was a dream start but her high jump was disappointing and a 1.86m clearance was 3-6cm lower than anticipated. Another "world heptathlon record" was set when Austra Skujytė sent the shot 17.31m. That enabled her to take the lead after three events with 3126 to 3062 by Ennis (14.28m), but there was an even wider discrepancy between them after the 200m as Ennis ran a sparkling pb of 22.83 (inches behind Dafne Schippers). The overnight positions were: 1, Ennis 4158 (her highest score); 2, Skujytė 3974.

Ennis's first long jump was a paltry 5.95m but all went well after that with leaps of 6.40m and 6.48m. After five events: Ennis 5159, Skujytė 4901, Chernova 4869. Chernova was unable to take advantage of her supposed superiority in the javelin. A 54.49m thrower, as against Ennis's best of 47.11m, Chernova managed only 46.29m whereas Ennis came up with a splendid 47.49m pb. So, with just the 800m to go, the scores were: Ennis 5971 and Skujytė 5783, with Chernova sixth on 5657. Short of falling over, getting injured or blowing up, the gold medal was Ennis's. She could have taken it easy in the 800m but that's not her style. She was hungry for a big score, needing 2:12.00 to break her Commonwealth record of 6906, 2:05.69 to reach 7000 points. She went for it, reaching 400m in 61.89, and to the huge and noisy crowd's delight she won the race in 2:08.65. Her final score was 6955 and only Jackie Joyner-Kersee has ever matched her achievement of scoring over 6900 twice in the same year. There was a long delay before the emotional medal ceremony as Lilli Schwarzkopf, who had finished second with a pb score of 6649, was initially disqualified for leaving her lane too early. An appeal was lodged and she was reinstated as silver medallist with Chernova taking bronze with 6628. In 15th place there was an immensely promising performance by Katarina Johnson-Thompson, whose 6267 broke her own UK junior record of 6248, a mark previously held by Ennis with 5910 in 2005.

It may have been the shortest winning distance since 1972 but that was of no consequence to Greg Rutherford. He was Olympic champion, the first Briton to win this event since Lynn Davies in 1964 ... and the first Englishman. He came in as one of the favourites, sharing the 2012 world leading mark of 8.35m, and his prospects were enhanced when defending champion Irving Saladino failed to register a valid jump in the qualifying round. The first round leader at 8.06m was Chris Tomlinson, co-holder with Rutherford of the UK record of 8.35m. Early in the second round Rutherford took the lead with 8.21m and for a few surreal moments at around 8.20 pm Britain were 1-2! However, the next jumper up was Will Claye, who moved into second with 8.07m. Rutherford kept up the pressure with a third round 8.14m while Michel Tornéus moved into a medal place with 8.07m. The fourth round saw Sebastian Bayer become runner-up with 8.10m and Tomlinson briefly claim third place on countback with 8.07m, but then Tornéus reached 8.11m, Claye 8.12m and Rutherford brought the fourth series of jumps to a close with 8.31m, the third longest of his injury-strewn career. The only jump of significance in the fifth round came from Mitchell Watt. He landed at 8.13m to supplant Claye in second place and with his final jump the Australian improved to 8.16m. Rutherford, one of the fastest men on the runway with his 10.26 100m speed, reflected: "This is what I've dreamt of all my life. When I chose athletics all I wanted was to be an Olympic champion."

It was a fitting finale to the most remarkable evening in British athletics history as Mo Farah followed Jessica Ennis and Greg Rutherford in being crowned Olympic champion. The noise levels as the overwhelmingly British crowd of 80,000 cheered him to victory in the 10,000m must have broken all decibel records for an athletics stadium! What a triumph not just for Farah but for his coach, Alberto Salazar, for in second place less than half a second behind was his training companion Galen Rupp, the first American medallist in this event since Billy Mills' shock victory in 1964. Farah became the first Briton – male or female – ever to win an Olympic distance running event. It was a typical championship 10,000m, with no dramatics during a slow first half (14:05.79). As usual Farah was content to run unobtrusively well back from the leaders but ready to cover any break. With two laps remaining it was Tariku Bekele and Farah just ahead of Rupp, while at the bell Farah showed just ahead ... and he remained in front throughout a pulsating last lap of 53.48 for a time of 27:30.42. Rupp got past Bekele the younger for the silver with Kenenisa – bidding for a record third consecutive title – out of the medals.

Seven days later, Mo lined up for the 5000m final.

Any doubts as to whether Farah would be fully recovered after his wonderful 10,000m victory and a 13:26.00 heat were swept away when, to a deafening roar from the 80,000 spectators, he moved into the lead with 700m to run. The other runners had played into his hands. Instead of ensuring a punishing pace which might have been too much even for Farah's powers of recovery the Ethiopians and Kenyans allowed the race to be conducted at a ridiculously slow tempo. The second heat, won by co-favourite Dejen Gebremeskel in 13:15.15, was by far the quickest in Olympic history but the winning time in the final of 13:41.66 was the slowest since the high altitude Games of 1968. An opening kilometre in 2:55.40 was foolish enough and that error was compounded by a second kilo of 3:01.30, not even a decent women's race pace. Yenew Alamirew went ahead shortly before 3000m and from then on the race really hotted up. With Farah now in front the penultimate lap took 61.10 with almost the entire field still in contention. Reminiscent of Lasse Viren in 1976 Farah just kept running faster and faster, resisting all challenges through a last lap covered in a fantastic 52.94. Farah, described by Seb Coe as "arguably the best British runner of all time", gasped: "It's unbelievable! Two gold medals. Who would have thought that?"

Lord Coe, the man most responsible for bringing the Games to London, was certainly impressed by Farah, but his man of the Games – a view shared by this writer – was Kenya's 800m champion David Rudisha.

It was clear from earlier races that David Rudisha was so superior to his opposition that he could go out hard and literally run his rivals into the ground. Easy to say, not so easy to do ... but he did. Normally Rudisha has a friendly pacemaker to tow him around the first lap in close to 49 sec but this time the onus was on him, and how magnificently he undertook the task. He sped through the opening 200m in a sensational 23.5 and reached halfway in 49.28 with only Abubaker Kaki attempting to stay close, and he would pay for that. Then the third 200m set Rudisha up for a crack at the world record; he covered that stretch in an exceptional 25.02 for a 600m split of 1:14.30 as against 1:14.54 when he set his first world record of 1:41.09 and 1:14.59 in his 1:41.01. In as thrilling a display of front running as has ever been witnessed he maintained that long elegant stride to stop the clock at 1:40.91. Coe remarked: "It was the most extraordinary piece of running I have probably ever seen. It was the performance of the Games, not just of track and field, but of the Games. David Rudisha showed supreme physical and mental confidence to run like that in an Olympic final. Instead of just doing enough to win the race he wanted to do something extraordinary and go for the world record as well. Rudisha's run will go down in history as one of the greatest Olympic victories."

Historic also was Usain Bolt's massive contribution to these wonderful Games. First came the 100m.

Would Bolt be at his unmatchable best or, as in the Jamaican Champs when he lost to Blake, would he show signs of vulnerability as he sought to become only the second man (after Carl Lewis) to win two quadrennial Olympic 100m titles? Although the temperature was nowhere near the sprinters' ideal, the combination of a super-fast track and a 1.5m tailwind combined to make this the greatest mass sprint race of all-time. Bolt got a reasonable start but it was only at halfway that he began to draw clear. His final 40m were awesome as he left his nearest challenger, Blake, nearly a metre and a half behind. The time of 9.63 broke his own Olympic record of 9.69 and was the second fastest in history behind his 9.58 of three years ago. World champion Blake tied his pb of 9.75 to underline Jamaica's sprinting supremacy in the island's 50th year of independence. Gatlin was third in 9.79, his "legal" best although he ran 9.77 in 2006, a mark which was retrospectively annulled as a consequence of his drugs ban.

More Olympic history was made by Bolt, who became the first man to complete the 100/200m double twice. He fully deserved the crowd's acclaim that greeted his 19.32 victory and few would disagree with his statement that "I'm now a legend." However, discerning followers of the sport would not necessarily concur with his boast: "I'm also the greatest athlete to live." That is for others, not the athlete himself, to judge. The final was as good as over by the time the runners swept into the straight. Bolt held a substantial lead and no one could possibly catch him. His margin dwindled somewhat towards the end as Blake chased hard and Bolt eased off a little, possibly costing him a new world record. Bolt's time equalled that of his hero Michael Johnson when winning the 1996 Olympic title but he missed his own Olympic record from Beijing by 0.02. It's the joint fourth quickest ever and his seventh clocking inside 19.60. No one else had ever bettered 19.60 more than once until Blake's 19.44 for the silver medal.

Bolt hadn't finished yet, for there was still the 4x100m relay to come, and that turned out to be some race.

What a finale to the track programme in the stadium! It was clear from the heats that the clash between the two sprinting superpowers could be something special. Jamaica, with Bolt rested, won the first heat in a world-leading 37.39, only for the USA (without Tyson Gay and Ryan Bailey) to take the other race in 37.38, breaking the American record. The Canadians were celebrating like crazy after crossing the line third in the final, so you can imagine their feelings when it was revealed that they had been disqualified and the medals were going instead to Trinidad & Tobago. All that happened while the stadium was erupting to laps of honour by the Jamaicans and Americans. The US team had just run 37.04 to equal Jamaica's listed world record from Daegu last year ... only they had finished over two metres down as Nesta Carter, Michael Frater, Blake and Bolt stormed home in a fabulous 36.84!

There was a world record also in the women's sprint relay, only this time it was the Americans who triumphed. That the GDR's 1985 mark of 41.37 would come under fire became clear when the US squad won their heat in 41.64 … and they still had Carmelita Jeter (runner-up to Shelly-Ann Fraser-Pryce's 10.75 100m in 10.78) and 200m champion in 21.88 Allyson Felix to bring in for the final. Prospects of a close race with Jamaica had ended by halfway and Jeter brought the baton home fully six metres clear after a brilliant display of fast running and slick baton passing. The time was an almost unbelievable 40.82. Remember, the last time the Olympics were held in London, in 1948, the USA won the MEN'S relay in 40.6 with Britain second in 41.3!

Felix brought her London tally of gold medals to three by contributing a 48.1 leg on stage two for the winning US team's 3:16.87, the world's fastest time for 19 years. The squad was anchored by Sanya Richards-Ross, winner of the individual 400m title in 49.56 over Christine Ohuruogu (49.70), who in that race moved from sixth to a fast closing second in the home straight. Britain's other medallist was Robbie Grabarz, equal third in the high jump with 2.29m.

Doping continued to cast its shadow over the Olympics. A number of top athletes failed to turn up following positive tests before the Games and shortly afterwards the IOC announced the disqualification of women's shot "champion" Nadezhda Ostapchuk from Belarus. She had been tested the day before the event and again after winning it with a put of 21.36m and both samples indicated the presence of metenolone, classified as an anabolic agent. The title went instead to New Zealand's defending champion Valerie Adams with 20.70m but the proud moment of standing on the top of the podium and hearing her national anthem played was denied her – as it was for several others who, following further disqualifications resulting from the re-testing of samples, were belatedly promoted to gold medal status. In addition to Ostapchuk, the disgraced London "winners" who brought the sport further into disrepute and in my opinion have forfeited the right to compete again were Russia's Sergey Kirdyapkin (50km walk), Mariya Savinova (800m), Yuliya Zaripova (steeplechase) and Tatyana Lysenko (hammer) and Turkey's Asil Cakir (women's 1500m). The 20km walk winner, Yelena Lashmanova, has kept her title but was banned from 2014 to 2016, while fellow Russian, high jumper Anna Chicherova, was stripped of her bronze medal from the 2008 Ganes.

Back to those who play by the rules … and one of the outstanding London winners. Aries Merritt had never run faster than 13.09 for the 110m hurdles prior to 2012 but in his last three races before the Games had clocked 12.93 each time. In his semi he ran 12.94 and in the final he lowered his pb to 12.92. But that wasn't his peak for the year, for in his final race of the season, in Brussels, he produced a sensational performance … and that wouldn't be the last time he amazed the world of athletics.

Prior to the 36th edition of the Ivo Van Damme Memorial, there could have been little dispute over what constituted the greatest individual performance of the year: David Rudisha's 1:40.91 800m. But in Brussels the capacity crowd of 47,000 was treated to arguably an even more astonishing feat when Aries Merritt skimmed over 110m hurdles in 12.80! That took 0.07 off Dayron Robles' world record, the biggest improvement since 1981. Colin Jackson described Merritt's performance as "fantastic, sheer magic, perfection", adding "he made it look so effortless." Interviewed shortly after the race, in which he did not hit any of the hurdles, Merritt gasped: "I'm still in shock"

Two figures who in their different ways were major influences on me had blue plaques erected in their memory, and I was pleased to attend both ceremonies. The first locality was of particular significance. It was 30 Rutland Road, Bedford – a few steps away from my wartime home – and the plaque erected by The Heritage Foundation and Bedford Borough Council read: "HAROLD ABRAHAMS 1924 Olympic 100 metres champion, whose deeds were immortalised in the award-winning film Chariots of Fire, was born in a house on this site on 15th December 1899." The plaque was the initiative of Dennis Johnson and the ceremony was conducted by fellow coach Tom McNab, technical director and script advisor for *Chariots*, with the actual unveiling undertaken appropriately by Allan Wells, the first Briton after Abrahams to win the Olympic 100m. The other plaque was unveiled at 22 Philbeach Gardens, in the Earls Court area of London, the home of Arthur Wint from 1949 to 1960. Those present included his two daughters, one of his greatest rivals and friends in John Parlett and British international 400m team-mate Lord (Terry) Higgins.

Another nostalgic occasion was the 50th annual awards function of the British Athletics Writers' Association, the guest of honour being 1964 Olympic steeplechase silver medallist Maurice Herriott, who had been BAWA's inaugural male athlete of the year in 1983. Apart from myself, the only other founder member able to attend the lunch was Neil Allen. The previous year, at the Association's AGM, I had been elected honorary president with Neil as vice-president. To my complete surprise, even though I was a member of the organising committee for the lunch, I was presented with the Ron Pickering Memorial Award by Ron's son Shaun (the 1998 Commonwealth Games shot put bronze medallist representing Wales) on behalf also of Jean Pickering. I was deeply touched to have my work recognised in this way, particularly as Ron and Jean had been such good friends for so many years and I even remembered Shaun as a little boy!

More fond memories were revived at the England Athletics Hall of Fame Awards, the ten new inductees being Sir Chris Chataway, Don Finlay, Douglas Lowe, Dave Moorcroft, Tessa Sanderson, Fatima Whitbread, Dame Marea Hartman, and coaches Fred Housden, Wilf Paish and Capt F.A.M.Webster.

Prior to the awards evening in Birmingham a book signing was organised by the AAA. It marked the launch of *The Official History of the Women's AAA*, the second book commissioned by the AAA as part of its legacy. I was delighted that Dame Mary Peters consented to write a foreword to the volume which she described as "a glorious nostalgic wallow." In my introduction to the 400-page work I wrote:

After more than 40 years I am making amends. Back in 1968 I wrote a book, "History of British Athletics", which was well received but which caused me considerable embarrassment. The problem was that because of publishing deadlines and the amount of time I had spent researching and writing about the men's side of the sport I was able to include only a quickly assembled and cursory outline of British women's athletics history ... 213 pages devoted to the men, a mere 14 to the women. Now, thanks to the AAA, I am able to rectify a situation that has bugged me for decades.

As I researched this work, so my admiration grew for the female pioneers of the sport. The First World War and its aftermath fundamentally changed society at every level and during the 1920s the role and status of women were enhanced in many ways ... but not without a struggle against deeply entrenched male chauvinist attitudes. Remember, it was only in 1928 that women were accorded the same voting rights as men. It was during this period of campaigning for female emancipation that the Women's AAA came into existence in 1922. It could not have happened without the drive and vision of a few enlightened men, but from the outset the WAAA – having been rebuffed by the AAA – decided it would be better anyway to go it alone. That policy served them well for many years, but after the Second World War the WAAA became a curiosity as the only governing body exclusively for women. That independence was fiercely guarded ... but slowly – ever so slowly – the more progressive elements in the WAAA who felt the sport would be better served by

amalgamating the men's and women's governing bodies won the day and
marriage with the AAA took place in 1991.

At the same time that I was working on the WAAA book, I was also involved with a massive book celebrating the IAAF's centenary. This was the most elaborate literary project I had ever handled. My old *Athletics Today* colleague Nick Davies, at that time deputy general secretary of the IAAF, invited me to become editor and he, Chris Turner, Laura Arcoleo, Nathalie Renevier-Durot and myself held our first meeting in Monaco in September 2010, discussing what articles to include in the book which needed to be published by November 2012 in time for distribution at the IAAF Centenary Gala to be held in Barcelona. Alberto Casella, responsible for the printing, joined us for the second meeting in December 2010 and during 2011 I commissioned numerous articles to be updated in the summer of 2012 where applicable. Alain Billouin, formerly of *L'Equipe*, joined us as editor of the French text and all was finalised in time for our 2012 deadline. It was hard but hugely enjoyable work: editing the articles, writing my own contributions, selecting around 200 photos from the fabulous Getty Images archive and helping with the layout of the 429 large format, profusely illustrated pages. It was, even if I say so myself, a stunning production, but all credit to my IAAF colleagues, the printers and a dream team of contributors.

The contents included an account by Roberto Quercetani of the development of the IAAF over 100 years from its formation in 1912; profiles by David Miller of the five IAAF presidents (Sigfrid Edström 1912-1946, Lord Exeter, the former Lord Burghley 1946-1976, Adriaan Paulen 1976-1981, Primo Nebiolo 1981-1999 and Lamine Diack from 1999) although the biography of the last named certainly now needs intense revision owing to later developments; history of IAAF rules by Dave Johnson; 100 years of athletics development by Sergey Bubka; the fight against doping by Professor Arne Ljungqvist; the world's fastest humans by Richard Hymans; the mile by Alain Billouin; the evolution of women's athletics by Peter Radford; distance running by Pat Butcher; cross country by Mark Butler; walking by Paul Warburton; indoor athletics by Doug Gillon; and teenage talent by Phil Minshull. There were also features on athletics in the various continents and I wrote an account of the Stockholm Olympics of 1912, imagined a dream decathlon featuring the likes of Daley Thompson, Dan O'Brien and Ashton Eaton, and (just before the deadline) a report on the 2012 London Olympics.

The star-studded centenary gala was a glamorous affair, a highlight of which for me was having a conversation with one of my all-time heroes in 89 year-old Harrison Dillard. That trip to Barcelona and the regular working visits to Monaco, plus transatlantic journeys to Las Vegas in March and New York combined with Atlantic City in October made it another travel year to cherish.

48. A TOAST TO ABSENT FRIENDS (2013)

Although it wasn't all gloom and doom, 2013 was a year I shall remember with sadness because of the passing of so many prominent figures in our sport, several of them personal friends.

The first to go, in February, was 1970 Commonwealth Games 1500m champion Rita Ridley (66). "It was my pleasure to report on dozens of her races," I wrote for AW, " and I was captivated both by her determination on the track and her beaming demeanour off it." The following month I was devastated to hear of the death of Jean Pickering (83), who had been a fixture in my life ever since, at age 13, I had first watched her (as Jean Desforges) running 80m hurdles at the White City.

*If you compiled a list of the individuals who have made the greatest contribution to the well-being of British athletics, the name of Jean Pickering would be at the very top. A brilliantly successful athlete herself, she financially helped and encouraged countless young athletes at a crucial stage of their careers through the Ron Pickering Memorial Fund, many of them going on to become stars themselves. There are many figures in British athletics who are admired and respected, but Jean was also **loved** by all who knew her. After so many years bravely fighting illness and infirmity, may she now rest in peace.*

Generations of athletes who have made a good living out of the sport are in the debt of Robert Stinson, who died in April at 82. A former general secretary of the British Amateur Athletic Board and chairman of its finance committee, he paved the way to full blown professionalism by instituting trust funds controlled by the governing body as a cautious first step. From 1984 to 2003, years in which the sport at international level was transformed, he served as IAAF treasurer.

Two of Britain's finest one-lap runners, both born in Southampton and coached by Mike Smith, passed away at far too early an age. Donna Murray (58), the golden girl of British athletics in the 1970s, set British records at 200m and 400m and was Commonwealth 400m champion in 1978. She was married first to 400m hurdles star Bill Hartley and later to comedian Bobby Knutt. She died in June, and was joined the following month by Todd Bennett, a cancer victim at 51. At his best in relays and at 1.70m (5-7) ideally suited to racing indoors he set a world indoor best when winning the European title in 1985. Two days after Todd, Pat and I mourned Lionel Peters, aged 76.

He had been a close friend for over 30 years and it was painful to observe his deterioration in recent months. All who knew Lionel, that gentle giant, will join in offering their condolences to Sigrid (happily they were able to celebrate their golden wedding anniversary last September when Lionel was still in reasonable health) and their son Neil. Athletics was what brought us together in the 1980s, the decade during which he became a member of the ATFS and of the NUTS executive committee. Frustrated by the paucity of junior results to appear in print, he corrected that deficiency by publishing "World Junior Athletics News" from 1994 to 2001, supplementing that newsletter with a dedicated website in 1999. Lionel also made an invaluable contribution to the sport's documentation of statistics and historic material with the compilation and publication of numerous annuals and other booklets during a 20-year period.

One of my athletic gods, McDonald Bailey, died in his native Trinidad in December just four days before his 93rd birthday.

Although born and raised in Trinidad, Emmanuel McDonald Bailey lived in London and represented Britain throughout his sparkling international career and those of a certain age, like myself, will never forget the wondrous sight of this tall, elegant sprinter outclassing almost all of his opponents at the White City year after year. He, along with Arthur Wint, was the first of my track idols when I got hooked on the sport at the age of 12 and although I have subsequently watched and reported on much faster men like Bob Hayes, Carl Lewis and Usain Bolt, no one has ever surpassed him in my personal galaxy of sprinting heroes. If any sprinter personified "poetry in motion" it was McDonald Bailey. His high-level consistency over a long period was astonishing; more often than not running against mediocre opposition on sluggish cinder or grass tracks and in unfavourable weather conditions he turned in dozens of clockings in the range of 9.6-9.8 for 100 yards and 21.2-21.5 for 220 yards and one wonders what he might have achieved had he been resident in the United States, with the good tracks, weather and competition he would have encountered there. As it was, he almost invariably recorded his fastest times abroad, notably his world record equalling 10.2 for 100m in 1951.

Just before Christmas, the BBC television commentator who for some 40 years was the voice of athletics, died aged 87 … David Coleman. I worked with him a few times, deputising as statistician for Stan Greenberg, and as an admirer of *Athletics Weekly* he respected my contribution and we got on well together. I realised that he thrived on pressure in a live broadcasting situation, which could make life difficult for some of his colleagues, but he was brilliant at his job.

He commentated on every Olympics from 1960 to 2000, and such was the quality of his work that in 2000, the year he retired, he became the first broadcaster or journalist to be awarded the Olympic Order, the highest honour to be bestowed by the IOC. Eight years earlier he was awarded the OBE and in 2008 he was among the first "legends" to be inducted into the England Athletics Hall of Fame. Coleman was himself a useful runner, winner of a team bronze with Manchester A&CC in the 1952 National Cross Country Championships before an achilles tendon injury cut short his career. He was a successful journalist before turning to television. In 1954 he joined the BBC. He rose rapidly through the ranks and with his encyclopaedic knowledge and distinctive delivery he developed into the country's foremost sports presenter. Perhaps his finest, but most poignant, moment as a broadcaster was his marathon stint describing the 1972 Munich Olympic siege as it unfolded, bringing into play his journalistic background. According to Stuart Storey, his co-commentator from 1974, "David always said he would give up everything to be an Olympian like the rest of us in the commentary box; well, he was. He was an Olympian of television. As an all-round broadcaster I think he was the greatest."

Usain Bolt enjoyed another fabulously successful season, winning both the 100m and 200m (plus 4x100m relay) at the World Championships in Moscow, although he wasn't flawless at 100m as Justin Gatlin edged him in one race. Bolt had a best time for the year of 9.77 and Gatlin 9.85, both at the World Championships, but faster still was Tyson Gay with 9.75. However he missed the World Championships as he had tested positive for an anabolic steroid in May, disappointing everyone in the sport who had looked up to him as a "clean" athlete. It transpired that, in Gay's words, "I basically put my trust in someone and was let down." That someone turned out to be his former coach and Olympic relay gold medallist Jon Drummond, who at the end of 2014 was banned from all coaching activity for eight years. Gay would normally have been banned for two years but the penalty was reduced to one year because of the help he gave the US Anti-Doping Agency in their investigation into Drummond. Gay went on to resume his sprinting career but suffered a grievous loss when his 15 year-old daughter, Trinity, herself a promising sprinter, was killed in 2016 by a stray bullet.

A major weapon in the war against dopers was revealed when six medallists – four from Belarus and two from Russia – were faced with bans when their samples from the 2005 World Championships were re-tested using the latest analytical techniques. Ironically in view of later developments, 80 year-old IAAF president Lamine Diack stated: "The IAAF's message to cheaters is increasingly clear that, with constant advancements being made in doping detection, there is no place to hide. This re-testing is just the latest example of the IAAF's firm resolve to expose cheating in our sport. The IAAF will continue to do everything in its power to ensure the credibility of competition, and where the rules have been broken, will systematically uncover the cheats." Fine words ... but Diack himself would, two years later, be arrested and investigated over alleged corruption involving drug tests among other issues. One welcome development was the IAAF's approval of bans of four years rather than two for first-time serious doping offenders.

With the World Cross Country Championships now being staged every other year instead of annually, and the "National" no longer one of the highlights of the winter season that it used to be years ago, it was the indoor campaign which kept me absorbed until the spring. The most meritorious result of the 2013 season came in the women's pole vault. Yelena Isinbayeva's world indoor record of 5.01m was bettered by a centimetre ... but not this time by the Russian. Competing in the US Championships in high altitude Albuquerque, Jenn Suhr added 10cm to her previous personal best by clearing 5.02m, a height surpassed outdoors only by Isinbayeva.

The British team excelled at the European Indoor Championships in Gothenburg, finishing second on the medals table to Russia. The pole vault featured heavily there too as Renaud Lavillenie not only cleared 6.01m but thought he had succeeded at the dizzy height of 6.07m. As I described his final attempt: "He wriggled over, celebrating wildly on his way down. Seconds later, joy turned to despair as a red flag was raised. The vault had been declared a failure as the dislodged, wobbling bar would have fallen had it not come to rest on another part of the frame. Initially tearful, Lavillenie later came to terms with what he had achieved."

For Holly Bleasdale there was only joy as with a relatively modest clearance of 4.67m – after a jump-off against Anna Rogowska – she became the first Briton, male or female, indoors or out, to win a senior European vault title. There was glory, and not a little satisfaction too, for Perri Shakes-Drayton who despite having been dropped from the UKA's highest level of lottery-supported elite funding won the 400m in grand style in a world-leading 50.85, with fellow 400m hurdler Eilidh Child runner-up. Later they were joined by Shana Cox and Christine Ohuruogu in winning the relay in a UK record 3:27.56, the men's team taking their race in 3:05.78.

April 15 2013 was the date of the 117th edition of the Boston Marathon, a race which will be remembered only for the terrorist attack. The event made the world's headlines for all the wrong reasons when two bombs were detonated near the densely packed finish line. Three spectators were killed and an estimated 264 injured, 16 of whom lost limbs. Two Chechen-American brothers, motivated by extremist Islamist beliefs, were responsible. One died when his brother ran him over while trying to escape from the police in a stolen car, the other was captured and sentenced to death.

Berlin in late September was the setting for a much happier marathon occasion when Wilson Kipsang put together halves of 61:34 and 61:49 for a time of 2:03:23, knocking 15 seconds off Patrick Makau's 2011 world record, with Eliud Kipchoge second in a personal best of 2:04:05.

The first shock of the outdoor season, early in June, was the defeat of Bolt at the hands, or rather feet, of arch-rival Gatlin. The occasion was Rome's Golden Gala Pietro Mennea (named after Italy's former world record holder for 200m) and although Bolt unusually got away to an excellent start he stumbled early in the race and the American took advantage to win by 1/100th in 9.94. That proved just an aberration as Bolt won all his remaining races, including another three gold medals at the World Championships. It took him some 70m to overhaul Gatlin but he went on to regain his 100m title in 9.77, and then proceeded to win the 200m in 19.66 and anchor the Jamaican relay squad to a clearcut relay victory over the Americans in 37.36.

The "pocket rocket" known as Shelly-Ann Fraser-Pryce matched her team-mate's triple crown. Always lightning fast out of the blocks and into her running, the rapidity of her stride was quite remarkable and she took the 100m in 10.71, 200m in 22.17 and anchored the relay team to a Commonwealth record of 41.29, second quickest ever. Tiny Jamaica with its population of less than 3 million (most of whom appear to be either sprinters or sprinting fans) equalled the total of six gold medals won by the USA (population of around 320 million). Only Russia (over 140 million) appeared to do better with seven victories, but a retrospective disqualification of the women's 4x400m team brought that tally down to six also ... and two of those winners, hammer thrower Tatyana Lysenko and walker Yelena Lashmanova, have at some time or other been sanctioned for doping violations.

Two of Britain's most dependable athletes struck gold again.

It's not often a race pans out almost exactly as imagined, but this memorable women's 400m final did. Two contenders stood out: defending champion Amantle Montsho, world leader this year with a Botswana record of 49.33, and the 2007 world and 2008 Olympic champion Christine Ohuruogu who signed off with a 50.00 win in London, her fastest ever outside a major championship. The scenario was obvious. Montsho would run a swift first 300m to enter the straight several metres up on her British rival and Ohuruogu would narrow the deficit all the way to the finish ... as in their Birmingham clash when the home runner beat the visitor by 0.01 in 50.63. It turned out to be even closer than that!

In the final Natasha Hastings went out fast, as did Montsho, and between them Ohuruogu in lane 4 was drawn to a slightly quicker 200m than usual. Nevertheless, Montsho held a 3m lead at 300m with Ohuruogu worryingly adrift ... whereas in fact she was judging her effort perfectly. Along the finishing straight she set out in pursuit of Montsho. For several seconds, despite the deficit being reduced at every stride, it looked as though the finish line would intervene in Montsho's favour, but Ohuruogu's long stride never faltered and she drew almost level a metre or two from the end. What decided the race was that Montsho, head up, crossed the finish line upright whereas her opponent lunged forward. The margin: 4/1000ths of a second! The time for both was 49.41, which for Ohuruogu was the icing on the cake. At last she had fulfilled a long standing ambition by breaking Kathy Cook's UK record of 49.43 set at the Los Angeles Olympics in 1984, the year of Christine's birth. The British team captain, leading by example, joined illustrious company for the only other women to win a pair of world 400m titles are Marie-José Pérec and Cathy Freeman, and she also claimed the distinction of being the first British woman to win two world titles in any event.

And then of course there was Mo, whose double – replicating what he had achieved at the previous year's Olympics – hoisted him into a place among the all-time greats of distance running. The 10,000m came first.

For one awful moment Mo Farah might have thought that history was about to repeat itself when Ibrahim Jeylan chased him around the final turn and into the straight. It was two years ago, in Daegu, when the Ethiopian overtook the Briton some 30m from the finish, a defeat that devastated Farah and created the resolve never to be outkicked again in a major event. He never has been. Any notion that victory would be handed on a plate to Farah proved unfounded. He had to work hard for his win as he covered the second half of the race in 13:29.3 (13:52.4 first half) for his third fastest time of 27:21.71. Knowing his finishing speed, it was surprising that not one of the five sub-27 performers from Africa decided to make the race a really fast one in the hope of diminishing that famous kick. Farah hit the front for good with 800m to go, and covered the last two laps in 60.62 and 54.49.

How do you beat Farah? In his present vein of form perhaps there is no way, but it was astonishing in the 5000m that the combined ranks of East African talent played completely into his hands yet again. Perhaps the Kenyans and Ethiopians thought that they, fresh for the race while Farah had already pulled out all the stops to win the 10,000m, could capitalise on that, but if so why on earth didn't one of them at least set such a testing pace that Farah's legendary sprinting powers might be affected? Instead they made it a slow race, which was perfect for the man who is now being considered the greatest ever British athlete with five global titles to his name over the last two years. Only Kenenisa Bekele before him had ever won the Olympic and world 5000m/10,000m double. Farah took off with just over 600m to go, and throughout the last lap he fought off every challenge. "They shall not pass" was his mantra. His unremarkable winning time of 13:26.98 disguised an amazing set of figures for the later stages of the race. Farah covered the last 400m in 53.44, 800m in 1:50.75 and kilometre in 2:22.12.

For the record, the other British medallists were the women's 4x400m team (silver in 3:22.61 with Christine O anchoring in 49.43), Tiffany Porter in the 100m hurdles (bronze in a pb of 12.55) and the women's 4x100m team (bronze in 42.87).

During the summer I attended five meetings, starting with the European Team Championships in Gateshead. The weather wasn't helpful, blustery on day one and rainy on day two, but Perri Shakes-Drayton clocked a personal best of 50.50 when winning the 400m – a time approached closely by Mo Farah (50.89!) on the last lap of his 14:10.00 5000m. The following weekend I was in Birmingham for the IAAF Diamond League meeting where Mo scored a significant victory over key Ethiopian rivals in a 13:14.24 5000m (53.39 last lap) and Perri shaped up as a potential world medallist at 400m hurdles with her time of 53.82. It was back to Birmingham for the British Championships, the almost tropical weather being most appreciated by the sprinters and particularly by James Dasaolu who improved his best 100m time from 10.03 to 9.91. That made him not only the second fastest ever Briton behind Linford Christie (9.87) but the quickest ever native European as Christie was born in Jamaica. Dasaolu has remained one of the country's top sprinters but in subsequent seasons has not legally broken 10 sec again.

My next venue was even more glamorous than Gateshead or Birmingham ... Monaco! The Herculis meeting, part of the IAAF Diamond League, is always a brilliant occasion and this edition featured a monumental middle distance race.

It wasn't even a track record as Hicham El Guerrouj ran 3:27.34 in 2002, but the 1500m produced one of the most startling races in the event's history. The event had seen 22 men run inside 3:34 this season but the year's top mark was a relatively modest 3:31.13 by Asbel Kiprop. However, the Kenyans had hatched a plan for a super-fast race. Andrew Kiptoo raced through 400m in 52.95 and 800m in 1:50.40, while James Magut kept the devilish pace going on the third lap. Kiprop, out on his own from the kilometre mark, reached 1200m in a staggering 2:45.91, as compared to 2:46.4 when El Guerrouj set the current world record of 3:26.00! The 2008 Olympic and 2011 world champion doesn't always deliver, but on this occasion he did – and how! The times were just sensational. Kiprop, with a previous best of 3:28.88, became the fourth fastest ever with 3:27.72. An amazingly quick Mo Farah, with a previous best of 3:33.98, was hoping to sharpen up for his forthcoming 3000m in London and 5000/10,000m in Moscow. "I will just be hoping to stay in with the guys and see what I can do," he said, feeling that 3:30 might be his limit. Well, what he proceeded to do was close a little on Kiprop with a last lap of 55.1 to the Kenyan's 55.3 and break not only Steve Cram's hallowed UK and former barrier-breaking world record of 3:29.67 just across the bay in Nice in 1985 (a shocked Cram was commentating on the race!) but also Fermin Cacho's 1997 European record of 3:28.95. Farah (3:28.81) joined Paavo Nurmi and Sándor Iharos as the only men to hold European records at 1500m and 10,000m at the same time.

Next stop was London's Olympic Stadium for the Anniversary Games, the last Diamond League fixture before the World Championships. Among many fine performances, Bolt completed his preparations for Moscow by winning the 100m in 9.85 despite what he termed a "horrifying" start. Mo clocked an outdoor best of 7:36.85 for 3000m and Perri, though well beaten by Zuzana Hejnová, improved to 53.67, a time bettered among Britons only by Sally Gunnell. The Czech went on to capture the world title in 52.83, while the silver medal went at 54.09. Perri won her semi in 53.92 but in the final she sustained such a serious knee injury early in the race that not only did she struggle to finish at all but she was out of the sport for three years and has never been able to race over the hurdles again. What a pity.

The last major event to be staged in Britain in 2013 was the Great North Run and the race founder Brendan Foster couldn't believe his luck as this half marathon brought together three of the all-time greats of distance running in Kenenisa Bekele, Haile Gebrselassie and Mo Farah.

Any fears that Bekele's glory days were behind him, never to return, were allayed when in his debut at half marathon the 31 year-old Ethiopian stole a march on Farah. It was a great race on a chilly, windy and, in the latter stages, rainy morning. Gebrselassie (40) led for much of the race, setting a pace which was honest if not super-fast, and his reward was a world masters best of 60:41 although it should be noted that the race is not eligible for official records. By the 12 miles point Bekele – making good use of his cross country prowess in running fast downhill – had opened up a 20m gap over Farah. Bekele repeatedly looked back along the final mile along the South Shields seafront and Farah began to close rapidly over the last 600m but he had left his effort just too late and in a thrilling finish Bekele held on to win by a second in 60:09 in his first race beyond 15k. Farah's 60:10 was a UK best.

My Life in Athletics

On a personal note, the year was a memorable one. In April, Pat and I celebrated our 40th wedding anniversary with parties for family and friends, and in October I was inducted into the England Athletics Hall of Fame (with Robbie Brightwell kindly making the presentation) along with Jack Holden, Diane Leather (Charles), Sheila Lerwill, Alan Pascoe, Jim Peters, Gordon Pirie, Don Thompson and Professor Sir Ludwig Guttmann, founding father of the worldwide Paralympic movement. I should declare an interest here as I am a member of the panel which determines who should be inducted each year, but I can assure you that I took no part in that vote and I was humbled to be so honoured. All I have done over the years is to write about athletics … I have never competed at a high level, officiated or coached.

My year ended on another high note with attendance at the star-studded Gala in Monaco. There I renewed acquaintance with 90 year-old Harrison Dillard and met up with another 1952 Olympic champion in Marjorie Jackson-Nelson, a sprightly 82. What a remarkable lady she is. After her husband died of leukaemia at age 45, leaving her with three young children to bring up on her own, the legendary sprinter raised six and a half million Australian dollars for a leukaemia charity and between 2001 and 2007 served as the Queen's representative in that state as the Governor of South Australia. Yes, there is life after athletics.

49. IT'S A HARD LIFE! (2014)

If anyone is surprised that I'm still working almost full-time in my late seventies, it's because I love what I'm doing. It's no wonder when, as in 2014, I was handed a free trip out to The Bahamas to report on the inaugural IAAF World Relays. Oh, it's a hard life!

The IAAF is always keen to popularise the sport worldwide and an imaginative decision was taken to introduce a high calibre all-relays meeting, and where better to stage it than Nassau, capital of The Bahamas – a string of islands with a tiny population but which has produced Olympic gold medal winning relay teams in the men's 4x400m (2012) and women's 4x100m (2000). I was invited to edit a 95-page book entitled *A World History of Relays*, published by the International Athletics Foundation, with contributions by Mark Butler, Ottavio Castellini, Imre Matrahazi, David Miller and Roberto Quercetani, and part of my reward was a return flight and four nights in a splendid beach hotel. And to make the trip even more special I won $5000 in a nearby casino!

The inaugural IAAF World Relays proved a huge success, in no small part due to the venue. For such a small country, with a population of barely 350,000, The Bahamas have a remarkable level of achievement in athletics, and particularly the relays, and Nassau was an inspired choice to stage this event. The splendid new Thomas A. Robinson stadium [named after the 1958 Commonwealth Games 220y champion] was almost full for both evenings, the crowds could not have been more enthusiastic (the Jamaican fans were outnumbered by Bahamians but their vocal support was not surpassed), the presentation was slick, the weather (29-30ºC) was beautiful, and the athletes performed brilliantly with world records set by Jamaica in the men's 4x200m (1:18.63) and by Kenya in the men's (14:22.22) and women's (16:33.58) 4x1500m. The IAAF has come up with a winner here.

The British contribution to this joyful festival was restricted to the shortest events. On the men's side there were third (4x100m) and fourth (4x400m) places, while the women's teams finished fifth in the 4x100m, second in the 4x200m and seventh in the 4x400m. It was a blinkered decision by UK Athletics not to select teams for the longer races. Why ever not? That decision prevented good 800m and 1500m runners from earning considerable amounts of prize money as well as experiencing highly enjoyable warm weather competition at an ideal time of year (late May).

It was a good year for family celebrations as my sister Benita reached her 80th birthday, looking nothing like that age, and she and Charlie received a congratulatory card from The Queen on the occasion of their Diamond Wedding anniversary. However, it wasn't the greatest of years for me medically. I was still in remission from lymphoma but in February I suffered a severe attack of sciatica which affected my legs and effectively ended my serious running days, although in 2017 I was still managing the occasional shuffle.

None of this affected my travelling and during the year in addition to my Bahamian jaunt I fitted in two more trips to Las Vegas, bringing my total to 30 since 1987, and I was in Monaco for another wonderful Herculis Diamond League meeting which featured an 800m where David Rudisha ran 1:42.98 in FIFTH place (Nijel Amos winning in 1:42.45) and an even more astonishing in-depth 1500m, won by Silas Kiplagat in 3:27.64, in which seven men dipped under 3:30. Never before had more than three broken that barrier in the same race. Another intriguing event was the high jump with five men still in contention with the bar at 2.40m. Bohdan Bondarenko was the only one to clear that height but both he and Mutaz Essa Barshim went so close at 2.43m.

It turned out to be a vintage year for high jumping, starting during the indoor season. Olympic champion Ivan Ukhov set a Russian record of 2.41m in January and equalled the European record of 2.42m in February, just 1cm below Javier Sotomayor's world indoor record dating back to 1989. Ukhov's declared intention was to jump 2.44m at the World Indoor Championships in the Polish city of Sopot, but had to settle for second place at 2.38m as the gold medal, on countback, went to the pencil-slim Qatari, Barshim. Outdoors, no fewer than five men cleared 2.40m or higher. Barshim topped the world list with 2.43m, a height exceeded only by Sotomayor, but Bondarenko (best of 2.42m, equalling the European record) was voted number one for the year in our world merit rankings as he held a 4-3 win-loss advantage against Barshim and won ten international competitions to his opponent's five.

The high jumpers weren't the only athletes to set the indoor season alight. Emerging further from the shadow of her sister Tirunesh, Genzebe Dibaba smashed two world indoor records with 3:55.17 for 1500m and, five days later, 8:16.60 for 3000m. Nine days after that, in Birmingham, she set a world best of 9:00.48 for 2 miles. On the same day (February 15), over in the Ukrainian city of Donetsk, a Frenchman rocked the world of pole vaulting.

While Renaud Lavillenie has been the world's top pole vaulter for the past four years, and has been in superb recent form, could one have thought that Sergey Bubka would lose his absolute world record? But it came to pass in the competition organised by Bubka himself in his home city of Donetsk. The 27 year-old Frenchman cleared 6.16m on his first attempt at the height and did so comfortably. Thus he added 1cm to the mark that Bubka set in this very city 6 days short of 21 years ago. Lavillenie said: "I think it's going to take me some time to come back to earth because it's incredible. This is a world record that is so mythical." Bubka, watching in the stands, was quick to praise his successor. "I'm very happy and proud for him, because he's a great athlete and a fantastic role model."

That vault of 6.16m was ratified by the IAAF as not only a world indoor record, replacing Bubka's 6.15m, but as the definitive world record as since 1998 IAAF rules have stated that world records can be set in a facility "with or without a roof". Bubka's outdoor world record of 6.14m in 1994 was set before this rule came into effect, but now there is only one world pole vault record.

Lavillenie did not compete in the World Indoor Championships, where the most surprising winner was a British sprinter.

Richard Kilty's best 60m time before this year was 6.61 in 2012. It wasn't until February 8 this year that he emerged as a 60m runner of world class. That was at the UK Championships where he finished third in 6.53 behind James Dasaolu (6.50) and Dwain Chambers (6.53). He consolidated that breakthrough in Birmingham with 6.57 in a race won by Dasaolu (6.50 after a world leading 6.47 heat) but he would not have been selected for Sopot had Dasaolu not injured himself at the finish of that race. Kilty was equal fourth (on non-altitude times) of the Sopot entries, but such was his low profile that one well known British bookmaker offered insulting odds of 33/1 against Kilty winning the world title – a bet that this writer could not resist! Kilty matched his pb of 6.53 for the fastest heat time, prompting an anxious bookmaker to slash his odds to 3/1. Next day in the semis he progressed to 6.52. In the final Kilty capitalised on his brilliant starting. Posting the fastest reaction times of 0.122 in the heats and semis, he nailed it again in the final with 0.120 and was never headed. He sped to a new pb of 6.49, while just 2/100ths covered the next five.

There were silver medals for the British men's 4x400m relay team and Katarina Johnson-Thompson, who would have preferred to compete in the pentathlon but came up with her longest ever jump of 6.81m. Bronze medals went to Andrew Osagie in the 800m, Tiffany Porter in the 60m hurdles and the women's 4x400m relay team. "KJT" displayed her all-round skills early in the outdoor season by winning in Götzis with a score (6682) which remained the highest in the world that year. She beat Brianne Theisen-Eaton and Dafne Schippers, who set Canadian and Dutch records of 6641 and 6545, with 19 year-old Nafi Thiam fifth with a Belgian record of 6508. Theisen-Eaton, married to decathlon great Ashton Eaton, would improve to 6808 when winning at Götzis the following year and go on to win a second World Championships silver medal in 2015 and Olympic bronze in 2016; Schippers would give up the heptathlon to specialise in the sprints, becoming world 200m champion in 2015 and 2017; while Thiam would develop into one of heptathlon's all-time greats by winning the 2016 Olympic and 2017 world titles as well as scoring 7013 points. By comparison, for all her huge potential, KJT's heptathlon career has stalled since that Götzis victory, her highest score having crept up only marginally to 6691, although as we shall see in the next chapter she has excelled at the indoor pentathlon.

Two of history's greatest track runners made their marathon debuts on successive weekends in April – one conspicuously more assured and successful than the other. Racing in Paris, Kenenisa Bekele became the fastest ever first-time marathoner over the age of 30 with his victory in 2:05:04. Mo Farah acquitted himself less brilliantly in the London Marathon although his time of 2:08:21 in eighth place was an English record and among UK runners only Welshman Steve Jones has ever run faster. Bekele would develop into the world's second fastest ever marathoner while Farah would add to his astonishing collection of global titles on the track before carrying out his intention of becoming a marathon specialist from 2018.

Only two years after the fabulously successful Olympic Games in London, the UK hosted another athletics jamboree with the Commonwealth Games being staged at Glasgow's national football stadium, Hampden Park. It was a highly entertaining and stimulating meeting to attend, although the weather could have been kinder and it was a pity that the Scottish fans had no home winners to acclaim although Lynsey Sharp in the 800m and Eilidh Child in the 400m hurdles came close with their silver medals. Even England's massive team captured only three gold medals, far behind the ten accumulated by Kenya and Jamaica. They went to pole vaulter Steve Lewis, long jumper Greg Rutherford (who had lengthened the UK record to 8.51m at the start of the season) and the men's 4x400m relay team.

Disappointment in Glasgow turned into elation in Zürich as British athletes enjoyed their most successful ever European Championships, winning no fewer than 12 gold medals. They swept all before them in the men's sprints as James Dasaolu took the 100m in 10.06, Adam Gemili the 200m in 19.98 and Martyn Rooney the 400m in 44.71, and both relays in 37.93 and 2:58.79 with Rooney anchoring in 43.93. Gemili's time, equalling his pb, was achieved despite the cold (13°C), rain-sodden track and a 1.6m headwind in the straight. It must rank instrinsically as the best 200m ever by a Briton as the only quicker times have been John Regis's 19.87 (+1.8m wind) at high altitude and 19.94 (+0.3m wind). Greg Rutherford leapt 8.29m and was presented with his medal by the only other man to have won Olympic, Commonwealth and European long jump titles … Lynn Davies, an impossibly youthful looking 72. Mo Farah, meanwhile, collected yet another 5000m/10,000m double in slow overall times of 14:05.82 and 28:08.11 but with last laps of 52.23 and 54.41. One week later he celebrated his twin daughters' second birthday by breaking Steve Ovett's UK (and former world) 2 miles best in Birmingham with a time of 8:07.85, covering the second mile in 4:00.1. The four women's event victories in Zürich came courtesy of Tiffany Porter in the 100m hurdles (12.76), Eilidh Child (54.48 400m hurdles), the 4x100m relay team in a UK record of 42.24, which they reduced to 42.21 in a later race, and – most remarkably – by Jo Pavey in the 10,000m (32:22.39).

Life begins at 40 … or at least it does for Jo Pavey, who after striving for nearly two decades as an international to win a major title has finally done so. She can look back on an extraordinary career – and clearly it's by no means over. As Joanne Davis she set a UK under-15 1500m record of 4:27.9 in 1988 and competed in her first World Championships in 1997, reaching the 1500m semis. It was several years later, in 2003, that she reached world class level at that distance with 4:01.79 and her other track pbs include 8:31.27 3000m (2002), 14:39.96 5000m (2006) and 30:53.20 10,000m (2012), while on the road she has run a 68:53 half marathon (2008) and 2:28:24 marathon (2011). Along the way she picked up silver medals at the 2006 Commonwealth Games (5000m) and 2012 Europeans (10,000m). It all added up to a career of great distinction but just short of complete fulfilment – and overshadowed by Paula Radcliffe. When Pavey gave birth at 39 to her second child in September 2013 she might reasonably have considered retirement, but happily she decided to continue ... and the bridesmaid at last became the bride. She began her comeback in May 2014 with victory in the UK 10,000m championship and set a world age-40 best at 5000m of 15:04.87 prior to her heart warming bronze medal at the Commonwealth Games. Now she is European 10,000m champion! The winning time of 32:22.39 is the slowest in the history of this championship, hardly surprising after the funereal pace of the first eight kilometres. At a month short of her 41st birthday she became the oldest female European champion in any event.

The European track and field season went out with a bang as Polish hammer thrower Anita Wlodarczyk crept ever closer to the 80m barrier with a world record throw of 79.58m in Berlin while in the Diamond League finale in Brussels the fastest one-day sprint double in history was performed by Justin Gatlin with 9.77 and 19.71, and Barshim high jumped 2.43m for an Asian record.

The German capital regained the spotlight when Dennis Kimetto smashed through the 2:03 barrier in the Berlin Marathon. Clocking 2:02:57 for the sixth successive world record on this course, he took 26 seconds off the previous year-old mark with halves of 61:45 and 61:12. The Chicago Marathon was noteworthy too as Eliud Kipchoge put together splits of 62:11 and 62:00 for a time of 2:04:11. But there was shame as well as glory for Kenyan marathoners. Rita Jeptoo won the women's race in a routine 2:24:35 but the shocking news emerged that in an out of competition test in Kenya the previous month her sample had proved positive for blood-boosting EPO. She was eventually banned for four years starting from October 2014, her Boston and Chicago victories annulled.

Three particularly significant figures from my life in athletics passed away during 2014: a boyhood running hero of mine, a wonderfully *simpatico* coach and a legendary high jumper.

No athlete was more popular among the crowds who flocked to the White City Stadium in the mid-1950s than Sir Chris Chataway, who died in his native city of London in January at the age of 82. Not only was he a lion hearted competitor, armed with a deadly kick, but the barrel-chested redhead was the epitome of the gifted amateur. He was the opposite of his equally successful contemporary, Gordon Pirie, whose legendary training regime involving between two and four hours of running every day made him a forerunner of later generations of distance runners. Chataway claimed to train for half an hour three or four times a week – and was often to be seen smoking!

At the age of 17 he was among the spectators at Wembley for the 1948 Olympics and (like Pirie, ten days the younger) his imagination was captured by the 5000m struggle between Gaston Reiff and Emil Zátopek. Little did the schoolboy miler imagine then that at the next Olympics he would find himself ahead of Zátopek on the last lap of the 5000m. At those 1952 Games, Oxford undergraduate Chataway made an audacious bid for victory with over 200m to go. He accelerated into the lead but on the crown of the last bend, just after three runners had swept past, he tripped over the raised track kerb and went sprawling, finishing fifth. Coached by Franz Stampfl, he played an invaluable training and pacemaking role in Roger Bannister's historic sub-four minute mile in May 1954, ran the second fastest ever 2 miles with 8:41.0 in June, while in July he broke Gunder Hägg's world record for 3 miles with 13:32.2 at the AAA Championships, only to find himself second in the same time as the winner, Freddie Green. The following month he won the Commonwealth Games 3 miles and finished ahead of Zátopek over 5000m in the European Championships ...the only trouble being that Vladimir Kuts had snapped the tape some 80m ahead in a world record 13:56.6. Revenge was exacted by Chataway during October's London v Moscow floodlit meeting, edging past 5m from the tape in a thrilling finish and breaking the world record with 13:51.6.

John Le Masurier, the distinguished coach who died in August aged 97, was quite unlike his mentor, the dynamic and extrovert Geoff Dyson. Although like Dyson he rose to the rank of Major during the War – as a Royal Marine – John Le Mas (as he was always affectionately known) preferred a mild, laid-back approach to coaching ... and just how effective that was can be gauged from the imposing list of athletes he advised. He was appointed AAA National Coach for the South of England in 1949 and in 1961 he and Denis Watts became joint AAA Principal National Coaches and both served the sport well in that capacity until their retirement in 1978. One of the most versatile of coaches, his crowning glory was Mary Rand, a prodigiously gifted athlete he began coaching after the 1958 season. She went on to become the sport's "golden girl", winning the long jump with a world record 6.76m, finishing second in the pentathlon (becoming only the second woman to exceed 5000 points) and third in the 4x100m relay at the Tokyo Olympics of 1964. Other pupils who made their mark included British record setters in the sprints, 800m, hurdles, triple jump, discus and javelin. He was British team coach at the five Olympics between 1960 and 1976.

Dorothy Tyler (née Odam), who died in September at the age of 94, gained the distinction of becoming the first British woman to gain an Olympic athletics medal in an individual event when, at 16 and on her first trip abroad, she placed second in Berlin in 1936 in the high jump. In fact she was unlucky to come away with the silver rather than the gold medal for she cleared the winning height of 1.60m at the first attempt, while Hungary's Ibolya Csák managed it only at the second try. Under the present rules Dorothy would have been declared the winner but a jump-off was decreed and Csák, who succeeded at 1.62m whereas Dorothy could go no higher than 1.60m, claimed victory. A few days later the IAAF passed a new rule governing ties and, had that been in force in Berlin, Dorothy would have been hailed as Britain's first female Olympic champion fully 28 years before Mary Rand.

Earlier in 1936 she had become the youngest ever British record holder (at 16 years 39 days) with a clearance of 1.65m and was still only 17 when she

470

won the 1938 Empire Games title. The following year she cleared 1.66m for what was eventually recognised as a world record. At the time the listed world record was 1.70m by one Dora Ratjen of Germany, but 'she' turned out to be 'he' and the record was eventually deleted. Dorothy married in 1940, served during the War in the Women's Auxiliary Air Force and gave birth to sons in 1946 and 1947. She then proceeded to make an astonishing comeback after an absence of eight years and again went so tantalisingly close to Olympic victory, this time in her native London in 1948. She was in the lead after clearing 1.66m, equalling her British record, but needed two attempts at 1.68m while Alice Coachman succeeded first time and Dorothy had to settle again for silver. In 1950 she retained the Empire Games title after a gap of 12 years and placed second in the European Championships with the same height as the winner, her team-mate Sheila Alexander (later Lerwill). Now coached by Arthur Gold, she changed her style from the outmoded scissors to the western roll in 1951. She placed equal seventh at the 1952 Olympics and equal 12th at the 1956 Olympics and as late as 1961, aged 41, she ranked fifth in Britain with 1.63m! She was belatedly awarded the MBE in 2002.

Speaking of Sir Arthur Gold, he was one of nine inductees into the England Athletics Hall of Fame and I had the pleasure of handing the award to his son Jonathan. Others honoured were Darren Campbell, Ashia Hansen, blind multiple Paralympic champion Bob Matthews, coach George Gandy, Ron Hill, Guy Butler (quadruple Olympic medallist from 1920 and 1924), Muriel Cornell, who set a world long jump record in 1926, and former AAA chairman George Bunner. George, the founder of Sportshall Athletics and other imaginative initiatives aimed at encouraging young athletes, was reluctant to be nominated … but the voting panel of which I was a member was insistent that his vast contribution to the sport be recognised.

The year ended on a profoundly disturbing note as I reported allegations in a German TV documentary, entitled *Top-secret doping: how Russia makes its winners*, that not only were athletes from that country taking performance-enhancing drugs on an industrial scale not seen since the days of the wretched GDR state sponsored system but that top officials could be implicated. Subsequent investigations by the World Anti-Doping Agency and other bodies endorsed the documentary's findings – leading eventually to Russia being excluded from the athletics events of the 2016 Olympics and beyond. We knew cheating went on, but not to such an extent, and encouraged it would seem by officials appointed to protect clean athletes. It was all very demoralising, and even more damaging revelations were to come.

50. THE BEST AND WORST OF TIMES (2015)

"It was the best of times, it was the worst of times, it was the age of wisdom, it was the age of foolishness, it was the epoch of belief, it was the epoch of incredulity, it was the season of Light, it was the season of Darkness, it was the spring of hope, it was the winter of despair, we had everything before us, we had nothing before us, we were all going direct to Heaven, we were all going direct the other way." Charles Dickens, in *A Tale of Two Cities* (1859), could have been describing the state of athletics in 2015.

Let's start with the positive aspects of the sport that year, beginning with the indoor season. The star turn was Genzebe Dibaba who, running alone for the last 3000m, sped around 25 laps of the Globe Arena in Stockholm to register a world indoor 5000m record of 14:18.86. Two days later, Birmingham's splendidly redeveloped National Indoor Arena, now known as the Barclaycard Arena, was the setting for Mo Farah's first "world record" – actually an unofficial world indoor best. The target was Kenenisa Bekele's 2 miles time of 8:04.35 but the first paced mile of 4:03.9 wasn't quick enough and Mo went ahead with seven laps to run. Covering the second mile in 3:59.5 he finished in 8:03.40, picking up a UK indooor 3000m record of 7:33.1 on the way. Finishing third in 8:17.05 was the ever remarkable Bernard Lagat, now 40. He set world masters (age 40+) records practically every time he set foot on a track, including indoor marks of 3:40.20 1500m, 3:54.91 mile and 7:37.92 3000m, while outdoors he ran 13:14.97 for 5000m and 27:48 for 10km on the road. Quite astonishing ... and he wasn't the only "golden oldie" for Kim Collins topped the world list at 60m with his fastest ever time of 6.47 and outdoors ran 9.98 for 100m. Amazingly, Kim was even quicker the following year, clocking a lifetime best of 9.93 aged 40!

The indoor season saw Katarina Johnson-Thompson at the height of her powers. She couldn't put a foot wrong as on successive weekends she set UK indoor records for the high jump, clearing 1.97m (1cm higher than the outdoor record) by such a margin that she was disappointed that 2.00m was beyond her, and for the long jump with 6.93m. It all came together for her in the pentathlon at the European Indoor Championships in Prague, but still she wasn't satisfied.

It should have been the happiest moment in her athletic life as she crossed the finish line of the 800m in the knowledge that she had won her first important senior title and beaten Jessica Ennis-Hill's Commonwealth and UK record ... but the look on her face as she glanced at the trackside clock revealed her disappointment and frustration. Johnson-Thompson, at age 22, had just completed one of the finest displays in multi-event history with a score of exactly 5000 points, but the clock showed 2:12.78 and she was looking for 2:11.86 to break the world record of 5013 set in 2012 by Nataliya Dobrynska. So near and yet so far. If only she had run just that little bit quicker or, looking back, had she long jumped an extra 4cm or put the shot 12.52m rather than 12.32m. By any standards it was a terrific day's work as she moved into second place on the world all-time list. She made a great start by clocking a pb of 8.18 in the 60m hurdles and her second "win" came in the high jump where she cleared 1.95m. The shot is her weakest event, placing 13th and last, but the next event, the long jump, saw KJT at her marvellous best, leaping 6.89m – longest ever in a pentathlon. 'The Kat' ran 2:12.78, easily an indoor pb but short of the 2:07.64 she has run in heptathlons. But then here she was running a virtual solo time trial on a 200m track and on tired legs in her fifth event of the day as compared to the third event of the day in a heptathlon. The winning margin of 304 points (over Nafi Thiam) was the widest ever at the European Indoors.

The British team accumulated nine medals in Prague, as against Russia's eight, including a gold by Richard Kilty in his second fastest ever time of 6.51. Another to excel was world junior 100m champion Dina Asher-Smith, a close second to Dafne Schippers (7.05) in the 60m in 7.08, equalling the UK record and a world age-19 best. The pair would clash again, outdoors over 100m in Hengelo in May, with Schippers smashing her Dutch record of 11.03 with 10.94 and Asher-Smith clocking the UK record time of 11.02.

The London Marathon in April brought together world record holder Dennis Kimetto and his predecessor Wilson Kipsang but they were upstaged by Eliud Kipchoge who covered the first half of the race in 62:20 and the second in 62:22 for a time of 2:04:42. Kipchoge, who at 18 brought off a sensational victory at 5000m at the 2003 World Championships and the following year ran a 3:50.40 mile, was in the process of assembling perhaps the greatest series of races in men's marathon running history: 2013 – 1st 2:05:30 in his debut, Hamburg, and 2nd Berlin 2:04:05; 2014 – 1st Rotterdam 2:05:00 and 1st Chicago 2:04:11; 2015 – 1st London 2:04:42 and 1st Berlin 2:04:00. Better still was to follow.

While on the subject of distinguished distance runners, I was saddened to hear of the death at the age of 78 of one of the very greatest trailblazers in Ron Clarke.

Journalists are supposed to be impartial observers but I have to admit having "favourites", athletes whose exploits and demeanour have made me particularly appreciative of their achievements and personal qualities. Emil Zátopek is one example. Another is Ron Clarke. You look in vain for Ron's name in the roll of Olympic champions but he made a greater contribution to the development of distance running than almost anybody. As at November 1963 the best times ever recorded for 5000m and 10,000m were 13:35.0 and 28:18.2, yet Ron – an exuberant front runner – went on to produce times of 13:16.6 and 27:39.4.

I was privileged to report on many of Ron's races. Some were triumphant affairs like his barrier-breaking 3 miles at the 1965 AAA Championships when I could hardly believe what my stopwatch was telling me; others were acutely disappointing as when he was sensationally beaten in the 1964 Olympic 10,000m in Tokyo. Worst of all was his experience at the Mexico City Olympics four years later when he almost literally ran his heart out, having no chance of success at high altitude. All these years later I still seethe at the folly of staging Olympic endurance events at such a venue.

I got to know Ron off the track also and he was always cheery, stimulating company. He wasn't just an outstanding runner. He was a distinguished writer and commentator on the sport, successful businessman and he served from 2004 to 2012 as Mayor of the Gold Coast, which will be the venue for the 2018 Commonwealth Games. Honours deservedly came his way: he was appointed MBE in 1966 for services to athletics and in 2013 he was made an Officer of the Order of Australia for his distinguished service to the community. As Gold Coast resident Sally Pearson tweeted: "Ron Clarke ... star on the track, a great man off the track. Athletics has lost a true statesman, RIP Ron."

It was another good year for travelling. Pat and I spent a pleasant week in Tenerife, our first holiday there since our honeymoon 42 years earlier, and I criss-crossed the Atlantic three times: twice heading for Las Vegas to meet up with American cousins among other activities, plus a return visit to Nassau early in May.

The second edition of the IAAF World Relays was as "Bahamazingly" successful as last year's inaugural celebration. It was another joyful occasion, the stadium packed both nights with a Bahamian public (not to mention a hugely vocal Jamaican contingent) who are in love with this particular form of athletics competition. Last year there were three world records, this time two as the IAAF made the distance medley an official world record event. Quartets from the USA set worthy inaugural marks of 9:15.50 and 10:36.50 and indeed the massively strong American team won seven of the ten events and might well have triumphed in nine but for baton passing disasters in the men's and women's 4x200m.

If 2014 was the year of the high jump, then 2015 celebrated the triple jump as Christian Taylor and Pedro Pablo Pichardo fought it out for the top world ranking. First blood to the Cuban in Doha. Taylor achieved his ambition of jumping over 18 metres with 18.04m in the final round but had to settle for second as Pichardo had in the third round touched down at 18.06m for the third best performance in history behind Jonathan Edwards (18.29m in 1995) and Kenny Harrison (18.09m in 1996). In his next competition, the Cuban Championships, Pichardo improved to 18.08m, but the American evened the score when they clashed next in Lausanne. Pichardo reached 17.99m, only to be overtaken by Taylor who jumped 18.02m and 18.06m. From this point on, Taylor always held the upper hand. In Monaco he scraped by, 17.75m to 17.73m, but at the World Championships in Beijing he destroyed his opponent.

After gaps of 2cm, 7cm and 2cm the difference this time was an extraordinary 48cm! It wasn't so much that Pichardo under-performed, as his final round 17.73m is a fine performance by any standards, but Taylor landed a jump he could only have dreamed of. He had made it known earlier this year that he was chasing the world record, but even he must have been shocked at how close he came. Edwards, a member of the BBC presentation team, looked on anxiously and smilingly signalled his relief when the measurement flashed up. It was 18.21m, and as the second longest ever legal mark and with an assisting wind of only 0.2m/sec it might just have been superior to Edwards' jump with its 1.3m reading. What's more, Taylor took off with 11.5cm to spare on the board so he actually travelled 18.32m!

Taylor was one reigning Olympic champion from 2012 to strike gold also at the World Championships, but there were several others: Usain Bolt (100 & 200m), David Rudisha (800m), Mo Farah (5000m & 10,000m), Ezekiel Kemboi (steeplechase), Greg Rutherford (long jump), Ashton Eaton (decathlon), Shelly-Ann Fraser-Pryce (100m), Allyson Felix (Olympic 200m but World 400m), Anita Wlodarczyk (hammer) and Jessica Ennis-Hill (heptathlon).

Ever since he won the Olympic 100m title in this stadium seven years ago it has been a case at global championships of not will Bolt win but by how much and what time will he do. This time the question was could 29 year-old Bolt possibly retain the title against a man whose credentials this season were so much superior? Justin Gatlin, at 33 running faster than ever before, has successively run 9.74 (pb), 9.75, 10.02, 9.75 and 9.78, while Bolt had times of 10.12, 9.87 and 9.87. For the first time, Bolt would line up for a major title as the underdog. What a dramatic final it proved to be, with just 13/1000ths separating Bolt (9.784) and Gatlin (9.797). At last Bolt got away to a decent start but it was Gatlin who led for most of the race. However, having won all his races this year without serious opposition and able to relax on the way to his super-fast times, on this occasion he was aware of Bolt closing and the result was that he lost his usually impeccable form, flailing as he strove too hard to stay in front. Bolt ran a season's best of 9.79, equalling his tenth quickest time but arguably the most satisfying 100m of his career.

Bolt was never in any doubt about retaining the title at his favourite distance [200m]. Since he finished second at the 2007 World Championships he has never been beaten in a global 200m final. In contrast to the close race offered by Gatlin in the 100m, Bolt won this clash with some ease. Gatlin's only chance was to hit the straight with a big enough lead to withstand Bolt's finish, but in fact it was Bolt who ran the swifter turn and Gatlin (19.74) was powerless to prevent Bolt (19.55) extending his advantage to a good two metres by the finish.

Bolt went on to win a third gold medal by anchoring Jamaica to victory in the 4x100m relay in 37.36. Jamaica finished up with seven titles, including two for the dynamic Fraser-Pryce who anchored the relay team to the world's second fastest ever time of 41.07 after taking the 100m in 10.76. She was a little disappointed with her time, but that certainly wasn't the case for runner-up Dafne Schippers whose new Dutch record of 10.81 was the fastest by a European for 11 years. The Flying Dutchwoman fared even better in the 200m, winning a close race with Elaine Thompson with a European record of 21.63. Only controversial Flo Jo and convicted drugs cheat Marion Jones have ever run faster.

Kenya also garnered seven titles, as against only six by the USA. The wins by Rudisha in the 800m (1:45.84), Asbel Kiprop in the 1500m (3:34.60), Kemboi (8:11.28 steeplechase), Vivian Cheruiyot (31:41.31 10,000m) and

Hyvin Jepkemoi (9:19.11 steeplechase) came as no great surprise, but that certainly was not the case in the 400m hurdles won by Nicholas Bett in a national record of 47.79, while in the javelin Julius Yego – who had suddenly improved from 87.71m to 91.39m before the championships – proved that was no fluke as he threw 92.72m for an African record.

Britain's three heroes from the London Olympics all won again.

Daley Thompson, Linford Christie, Sally Gunnell, Jonathan Edwards. These four all-time greats of British athletics had one thing in common: all had completed the grand slam of Olympic, World, European and Commonwealth titles. Now they have been joined by 28 year–old Rutherford, under-rated by some because the current world standard of long jumping is not that high, but there is no disputing that he is one hell of a competitor. In the fourth round he produced a beauty of a jump. He landed at 8.41m, the second longest of his career, and passed up his last two attempts. For Rutherford it was triumph at the fifth attempt, having failed to qualify for the final in 2007, 2011 and 2013, and placing fifth in 2009.

The last time Farah competed in the Bird's Nest Stadium he finished a bitterly disappointed non-qualifying sixth in his 2008 Olympic 5000m heat in 13:50.95. Since then he has accumulated a stunning collection of gold medals. Now he has won his third global 10,000m title but had to work very hard for it. No one since 2011 has outkicked Farah in a major championship and this time a very strong Kenyan trio pooled their resources to ensure a fast race in an attempt to draw the sting out of the Briton's renowned finish. It was to no avail, but the tactics were commendable as Farah – with a 5000m to come against fresh Kenyans – was obliged to run 27:01.13 in the hot, humid conditions. Farah went ahead with 500m to go and held everyone at bay throughout a 54.14 last lap.

There was much speculation over a Kenyan plan for defeating Farah [in the 5000m] but, whatever it might have been, it didn't work as he went on to score another Mo-mentous victory. The long striding Farah survived a number of tripping incidents in both heat and final, and it looked as though a fall would be the only way he could lose. Surely, Farah having won a gruelling 10,000m on August 22 and obliged to run a quick 5000m heat in 13:19.44 on August 26, the East Africans – running on fresher legs – would ensure the final on August 29 would be very fast. Not so. The event turned into what was effectively a 2000m race ... and who would bet against a man who has twice broken 3:29 for 1500m? Caleb Ndiku threw down the gauntlet with 800m to go. That 11th lap was covered in 58.39. It got faster and faster, with Ndiku staving off Farah's challenge as he raced through the next 200m in 28.16 to hit the bell in 12:57.71, four metres clear. Ndiku clocked 26.08 for the penultimate 200m; it was murderous speed (54.24 for that 400m) but Farah could not be dropped and with some 80m remaining he sprinted past the Kenyan for another glorious victory. The winning time of 13:50.38 may have been the slowest in World Championships history, but the finishing splits were simply phenomenal: 26.59 200, 52.67 400 (possibly 52.2 for Mo), around 1:48.6 800, 2:19.22 1000.

Perhaps the most remarkable of the four British wins was that of Jessica in the heptathlon. Because of injury she competed in only two meetings all season in 2013, the year she married her childhood sweetheart Andy Hill. In July 2014 their son Reggie was born and Jessica found it tough going when she resumed training under Toni Minichiello, her coach since she was 13. She wanted to get to the World Championships, although with no thought of winning, and her competitive comeback began in May 2015. Her first big test was the heptathlon in Götzis.

Ennis-Hill, whose training so far has been well below her previous levels, produced a magnificent performance to finish fourth with 6520, far in excess of her Rio Olympic qualifying standard target of 6200. It was her first heptathlon since her 2012 Olympic triumph. Only in the 800m, in which she demonstrated all her old competitive qualities to beat Brianne Theisen-Eaton in 2:09.21, did she get near her best mark but if she can progress in the next month or two and consider she has the chance of a medal she will compete in Beijing. Theisen-Eaton won with a world leading 6808, smashing her Canadian record of 6641.

Fast forward three months to Beijing … and further evidence that Jessica Ennis-Hill is one of the most accomplished athletes Britain has ever produced. Short in stature but long in talent and the desire to succeed.

It started so well for Theisen-Eaton and Johnson-Thompson as they recorded pbs of 12.98 and 13.37 in the 100m hurdles, while Ennis-Hill opened with a solid 12.91. The high jump was full of drama, Theisen-Eaton could manage only 1.80m, while 1.97m performer Nafi Thiam ruined her chances by clearing just 1.86m. That was the height achieved by Ennis-Hill, propelling her into the lead. Leaping up from ninth to second was KJT with her 1.89m clearance. Johnson-Thompson produced her second pb but it didn't help her much as it was a shot put of 12.47m and her overall position dropped to ninth. A more acceptable 13.73m gave Ennis-Hill a score of 2968. While Ennis-Hill maintained her stately progress with a 23.42 200m, KJT completed her roller coaster of a day by winning that race in 23.08. Scores after four events: Ennis-Hill 4005, KJT 3925, Nadine Visser 3871, Theisen-Eaton 3865.

The battle for the gold medal between the two Britons was won and lost in the long jump where Ennis-Hill produced a season's best of 6.43m. This is KJT's strongest event, having jumped 6.93m indoors, and this was her opportunity to seize the lead. At her first attempt she landed at close to 6.80m but it was a foul by 5cm; on her second try she went even further but fouled by 6cm. Now came the dilemma: should she go for safety, taking off before the board if necessary, or go for broke again. She chose the latter option and it proved to be her undoing. It was a massive jump, measured at 6.82m and, for a second or two, she was elated ... until she saw no white flag raised and officials closely inspecting the take-off board. By the tiniest of margins (1cm) it was declared a foul and it was game over. Scores after five events: Ennis-Hill 4990, Theisen-Eaton 4888. Ennis-Hill was content to throw the javelin 42.51m as her Canadian rival managed little more, so with one event to go: Ennis-Hill 5706,

Nadine Broersen 5620, Theisen-Eaton 5612. Barring a fall or injury, Jessica was now assured of victory. Theisen-Eaton went off too fast and Ennis-Hill overhauled her in 2:10.13 and thus regained the title she won in 2009 and – if Tatyana Chernova is eventually disqualified [she was, but not until 2017] *– won again in 2011. Her score of 6669 is her best for three years and ranks second on this year's world list behind the 6808 by Theisen-Eaton who here scored 6554 in second place.*

The Canadian's American husband, Ashton Eaton, went one better in the decathlon. Amid so many wonderful performances in Beijing, surely the greatest of them all was his world record score of 9045, adding six points to his 2012 figures. It was close. He started the 1500m knowing he would have to run 4:18.25 for the record ... and, leaving nothing on the track, he clocked 4:17.52. He was up against a worthy opponent in Damian Warner, yet his winning margin was a colossal 350 points, the widest in World Championships history. Contesting his first decathlon for two years (having run 48.69 for 400m hurdles in 2014!), he got away to a super start by clocking 10.23 for 100m. He followed up with a 7.88m long jump, 14.52m shot put and 2.01m high jump before producing one of the greatest individual performances ever witnessed in a decathlon. Bill Toomey held the world decathlon 400m 'record' of 45.68 ... but Eaton ran a staggering 45.00, yelling in delight when he saw those figures light up. His halfway score was 4703 and on the second day he clocked 13.69 in the hurdles, threw the discus 43.34m, vaulted 5.20m and threw the javelin 63.63m. With a gutsy last lap of inside 63 sec in the 1500m, the world record was his. Warner finished second with a Canadian record of 8695.

Although the US team collectively was not as dominant as usual, Eaton was not the only American superstar to shine. Allyson Felix, celebrated for her speed and grace on the track, added further lustre to her long and dazzling career. At Olympic Games and outdoor World Championships since 2004 she had amassed 16 medals (12 of them gold) at 200m, 400m and both relays, and in Beijing she added another three, winning the 400m in a personal best of 49.26 and collecting silver medals in both relays, clocking an outstanding 47.72 on the third leg of the 4x400m. More would follow in 2016 and 2017.

Among other impressive winners was Wayde van Niekerk, whose 43.48 400m elevated him to fourth on the world all-time list. For the first time ever, three men broke 44 sec in the same race, the other medals going to defending champion LaShawn Merritt and Olympic champion Kirani James. Another athlete to reach new heights was Sergey Shubenkov, the 110m hurdles champion with a Russian record of 12.98. However, it was the man who finished third in that race who captured more attention.

These Championships have been graced by so many great performances, but taking into consideration the exceptional circumstances none was as stunning as Aries Merritt's bronze medal in 13.04, his quickest since that glorious season in 2012 when he won the Olympic title and set a fantastic world record of 12.80. He had fallen well short of that level since, with a best of 13.09 in 2013 and 13.27 last year. There were vague rumours about health problems but it was only last week that Merritt made public the news that in 2013 he was diagnosed as suffering from a rare kidney disorder and told he would never run again. He confounded the doctors by continuing to compete, albeit to a lower standard. He revealed: "The more I train the worse my kidneys get and that's why I am getting a transplant. It hurts so much on the inside to know you are the best but you're struggling with this illness and you are just trying to fight through." On September 1, four days after this final, he was due to receive the transplant from his sister. For determination and bravery, Aries certainly deserves an Order of Merit as well as his bronze medal.

A month before the Championships I was lucky enough to be in Monaco to see a phenomenal performance by Genzebe Dibaba.

At last one of those controversial Chinese world records from 1993 has been broken. That 1500m record (Qu Yunxia was timed at a stunning 3:50.46) has for so many years looked impregnable, the nearest approach since by any non-Chinese athlete being 3:55.33 by the subsequently banned Süreyya Ayhan in 2003. Enter Genzebe Dibaba. In February 2014 she set a world indoor record of 3:55.17 and in Barcelona earlier in July she ran 3:54.11. She knew then that the world record was feasible. She enlisted the aid of world indoor 800m champion Chanelle Price to take her through 800m. The first lap was covered in 60.31 with Dibaba (60.5) in close pursuit. Price dropped out shortly after reaching 800m in 2:04.52 (Dibaba 2:04.7) and it was an astonishing third lap by Dibaba that brought the record within reach. She covered it in under 60 sec for a 1200m time of 3:04.62. It still needed an amazing last lap for the record to be broken and Dibaba, a beautiful runner in every sense, delivered by covering the final 400m in 59.79. Her time of 3:50.07 was described by Steve Cram, commentating for the BBC, as "stunning, almost beyond words."

There were great place times in Dibaba's wake. Ethiopian-born Sifan Hassan set a Dutch record of 3:56.05, Shannon Rowbury broke Mary Slaney's American record with 3:56.29 and up and coming Laura Muir produced a Scottish record of 3:58.66 to become the second fastest ever Briton behind Kelly Holmes. The men's 1500m wasn't bad either as Asbel Kiprop reached 1200m in 2:45.78, some 25m clear of Mo Farah. He finished in a magnificent 3:26.69, a time only Hicham El Guerrouj and Bernard Lagat have ever surpassed. Farah finished fourth in 3:28.93, second in European annals only to his 3:28.81 on this track in 2013, as a record ten men broke 3:31. Kiprop went on to take the world title in 3:34.60 thanks to a 51.53 last lap, while Dibaba triumphed in Beijing in 4:08.09, seeking to destroy the opposition by speeding around the third lap in an extraordinary 57.22, her last 800m covered inside 1:57! Dibaba sought to complete a double but although she clocked a meritorious 14:44.14 for third place in the 5000m (her fifth race of the Championships) she was no match for her fresh team-mate Almaz Ayana, the winner by over 100m in 14:26.83. After a slow start to the race, the former world junior record holder for the steeplechase completed the final 3000m in 8:19.91 – quicker than Hellen Obiri's non-Chinese world best of 8:20.68!

Other remarkable exploits abounded. Ghirmay Ghebreselassie (2:12:28) became at 19 not only Eritrea's first ever gold medallist but the youngest global marathon champion; Ezekiel Kemboi whizzed around the last lap of the steeplechase in 56.81 – and that despite easing up and veering into lane three to start his victory celebration; and Anita Wlodarczyk followed up a barrier-breaking world hammer record of 81.08m earlier in the month by producing the second longest throw of 80.85. The British team came away with a silver (Shara Proctor with a UK record long jump of 7.07m) and two bronze medals (in the 4x400m relays) in addition to the four victories, plus an honourable mention for fourth placed hammer thrower Sophie Hitchon, just 16cm away from a bronze medal with her UK record of 73.86m – some performance by an athlete who had ranked 18th among the entrants on personal bests.

A few days prior to the Championships a very significant event took place in Beijing as by a vote of 115 to Sergey Bubka's 92, 58 year-old Seb Coe was elected the new president of the IAAF, only the sixth man to hold this office since the IAAF was founded in 1912. He succeeded Lamine Diack, the president since 1999, but little did we (or Lord Coe) know at the time of the catastrophic revelations soon to emerge. Shortly before the vote, he told the IAAF Congress: "There is no task in my life for which I have been better prepared, no job I have ever wanted to do more nor would be more committed to." After being elected, he said: "I am deeply honoured that our sport has placed its trust in me. This is the pinnacle of my career." But his honeymoon period in office was short lived as one problem after another surfaced.

For a start it was just about the worst year on record in terms of doping bans. Russians weren't the only offenders but they constituted by far the most prominent group and hardly an issue of AI was published without news of yet further Russian cheating. Early in February I compiled "Russia's Hall of Shame", listing Russian winners of global titles during the last decade who have served doping bans. It was a wake-up call, underlining the extent of the problem.

2004 Olympics: Irina Korzhanenko (shot), Natalya Sadova (discus), Olga Kuzenkova (hammer). *2005 World Championships:* Sergey Kirdyapkin (50km walk), Tatyana Tomashova (1500m), Kuzenkova, Olimpiada Ivanova (20km walk). *2006 World Indoor:* Yuliya Chizhenko (1500m), Tatyana Kotova (long jump); *2007 World:* Olga Kaniskina (20km walk). *2008 World Indoor:* Yelena Soboleva (1500m). *2008 Olympics:* Valeriy Borchin (20km walk), Gulnara Galkina (steeplechase), Kaniskina. *2009 World:* Borchin, Kirdyapkin, Kaniskina. *2011 World:* Borchin, Sergey Bakulin (50km walk), Yuliya Zaripova (steeplechase), Tatyana Lysenko (hammer), Tatyana Chernova (heptathlon), Kaniskina. *2012 Olympics:* Kirdyapkin, Zaripova, Lysenko, Yelena Lashmanova (20km walk). *2013 World:* Lysenko, Lashmanova, women's 4x400m team which included Kseniya Ryzhova. *2014 World Indoor:* Yekaterina Koneva (triple jump).

As though that list wasn't bad enough, an indictment of the cheating by female athletes and walkers of both sexes in particular, the situation would get worse as continual retroactive testing of samples from previous Olympics and World Championships and anomalies discovered in athletes' biological passports threw up many more transgressors.

It was early in November that the sport was rocked to its foundations with the news that the IAAF's recently retired president, Lamine Diack, had been arrested and questioned by French police about allegations that he took bribes to suppress positive doping tests, with other senior figures also under investigation. Diack was taken into custody, released on bail of around $550,000 and ordered to surrender his passport. At the time of writing he is still awaiting trial. At around the same time, the World Anti-Doping Agency (WADA) produced a damning report highlighting systemic cheating and corruption within Russian athletics and recommending that the IAAF suspends the Russian Athletics Federation (RusAF). Here are extracts from my day-by-day summary in AI:

November 4: It was revealed that the French police had opened a criminal investigation into Lamine Diack (82) for alleged corruption and money-laundering. Also under investigation were Diack's legal adviser Habib Cissé and the former director of the IAAF's anti-doping department Gabriel Dollé.

November 5: British newspapers reported that Diack was accused of taking bribes in 2011 from RusAF to cover up positive doping tests. According to the office of France's national financial prosecutor, Eliane Houlette, he is alleged to have received more than one million euros in bribes since 2011. He denied all charges. Daley Thompson suggested the scandal was "worse than anything Sepp Blatter has done at FIFA" and that prison sentences should be imposed if the allegations are proven.

November 6: Prosecutor Eliane Houlette said that although investigators could not confirm that all of the bribes came from Russian payments … "what is certain is that Mr Cissé, the legal adviser to Mr Diack, travelled to Russia and gave to the All-Russian Federation the list of Russian athletes suspected of doping and, in exchange for sums of money, these athletes weren't sanctioned." The IAAF Ethics Commission recommended that disciplinary charges be brought against Papa Massata Diack (Lamine's son and former consultant to the IAAF), Valentin Balakhnichev (former president of RusAF and former IAAF treasurer), Aleksey Melnikov (former Russian chief coach for walkers and distance runners) and Gabriel Dollé for various alleged breaches of the IAAF code of ethics.

November 7: IAAF President Sebastian Coe spoke of his shock, anger and sadness, adding: "That people in our sport have allegedly extorted money from athletes guilty of doping violations is abhorrent." He said he is "more determined than ever to rebuild this sport and restore trust. However, this is a long road to redemption."

November 8: According to *The Sunday Times*, "gold and silver medal winners at the 2012 Olympics are on a list of eight athletes who are alleged to have escaped bans for doping after huge bribes were paid to the heads of world athletics so they could compete at the London Games." The report continued:

"Senior figures in RusAF are alleged to have paid Lamine Diack, then IAAF president, one million euros with a further 200,000 euros going to Dr Gabriel Dollé, the body's former anti-doping chief."

November 9: In response to WADA's Independent Commission report issued today, the IAAF president took the urgent step of seeking approval from his fellow IAAF Council members to consider sanctions against RusAF. These sanctions could include provisional and full suspension and the removal of future IAAF events. Commenting on the report, Coe said: "The information in WADA's Independent Commission's Report is alarming. We need time to properly digest and understand the detailed findings included in the report. However, I have urged the Council to start the process of considering sanctions against RusAF. This step has not been taken lightly. Our athletes, partners and fans have my total assurance that where there are failures in our governance or our anti-doping programmes we will fix them. We will do whatever it takes to protect the clean athletes and rebuild trust in our sport. The IAAF will continue to offer the police authorities our full co-operation into their ongoing investigation." He added: "The allegations are deeply shocking and I accept that the sport's credibility is on the line."

Following the documentary *Top Secret Doping: How Russia Makes Its Winners*, aired on the German TV channel ARD on December 3 2014, WADA set up an Independent Commission "to conduct an independent investigation into doping practices; corrupt practices around sample collection and results management; and other ineffective administration of anti-doping processes that implicate Russia, the IAAF, athletes, coaches, trainers, doctors and other members of athletes' entourages; as well as the accredited laboratory based in Moscow and the Russian Anti-Doping Agency (RUSADA)." The IC's report ran to 323 pages, and here are some of the findings.

"The IC has turned over considerable data and information to Interpol that tends to demonstrate criminal conduct on the part of certain individuals and organisations. The IC has identified systemic failures within the IAAF and Russia that prevent or diminish the possibility of an effective anti-doping programme, to the extent that neither RusAF, RUSADA, nor the Russian Federation can be considered Code-compliant. The IC has recommended that WADA declare RusAF and RUSADA to be Code noncompliant. The IC has recommended that WADA withdraw its accreditation of the Moscow laboratory as soon as possible and that its director be permanently removed from his position. The Moscow laboratory is unable to act independently. The IC has recommended that the IAAF suspend RusAF.

"The investigation has confirmed the existence of widespread cheating through the use of doping substances and methods to ensure, or enhance the likelihood of, victory for athletes and teams. The cheating was done by the athletes' entourages, officials and the athletes themselves. Evidence of extensive doping use is supported and confirmed by audio and video evidence, scientific evidence, corroborative statements, cyber analysis and related reporting documents. Numerous statements corroborate the original allegations and further detail the extensive use of doping substances and blood doping within Russian athletics.

"In addition, evidence exists that confirms that coaches have attempted to manipulate or interfere with doping reports and testing procedures. They are also the source and counselling of athletes' use of PEDs (performance-enhancing drugs). The coaches are supported in their doping efforts by certain medical professionals. Moreover, it is particularly alarming that there appears to be a collective disregard for the athletes' current or future state of health.

"The investigation indicates that the acceptance of cheating at all levels is widespread and of long standing. Many of the more egregious offenders appear to be coaches who, themselves, were once athletes and who work in connection with medical personnel. This 'win at all costs' mentality was then passed to current athletes, whether willing to participate or not. As a result of this mindset, an open and accepted series of unethical behaviours and practices has become the norm. This Report confirms allegations that some Russian doctors and/or laboratory personnel acted as enablers for systematic cheating along with athletics coaches.

"Grigory Rodchenkov, director of the Moscow accredited laboratory, was specifically identified as an aider and abettor of the doping activities. Rodchenkov ... requested money in order to execute the concealment of positive test results. Rodchenkov admitted to intentionally destroying 1417 samples ... to reduce any potential adverse findings from subsequent analysis by another WADA accredited laboratory.

"Although the IC report and recommendations are confined to Russia and athletics, the IC wishes to make it clear that, in its considered view, Russia is not the only country, nor athletics the only sport, facing the problem of orchestrated doping in sport."

November 13: The IAAF Council voted to provisionally suspend RusAF as an IAAF Member with immediate effect. The meeting voted overwhelmingly to sanction the Russian governing body. There were 22 votes in favour, one against, while the Russian member was not eligible to participate. The consequence is that Russian athletes are barred from international competition (including the Olympics) until the Russian authorities can comply with the WADA Code. To regain membership to the IAAF the new federation would have to fulfil a list of criteria. An inspection team will be led by Rune Andersen, an independent Norwegian international anti-doping expert.

More on the Russian saga in the next chapter, but let's leave 2015 on a brighter note. With Katharine Merry hosting the event in her usual breezy style, the latest batch of inductees into the England Athletics Hall of Fame comprised Joan Allison, McDonald Bailey, Roger Black, Lillian Board (a particularly poignant moment as I made the presentation to her former fiancé, journalist David Emery), Peter Coe, Peter Elliott, Basil Heatley, Emil Voigt (as Olympic 5 miles champion in 1908 the last British distance runner to win an Olympic gold medal until Mo Farah in 2012) and Paralympic champion Danny Crates.

51. EXPULSION OF RUSSIAN CHEATS (2016)

Ever since the Helsinki Games of 1952, Russian athletes have played a prominent role in the Olympics, but in 2016 only one Russian – Florida-based long jumper Darya Klishina – was permitted to compete in Rio. The scale of doping in Russian athletics, encouraged or at least condoned it would seem at the highest state level, led to the IAAF making the decision to suspend the Russian governing body and thus rule its athletes ineligible for international competition.

The IAAF Council, meeting in Vienna on June 17, took the momentous decision to bar Russia from the European Championships in Amsterdam and the Olympic Games in Rio as a consequence of the Russian Athletics Federation (RusAF) failing to satisfy the reinstatement conditions for IAAF membership. Rune Andersen, the independent chairman of the IAAF Task Force monitoring the verification process, delivered a report which made four separate unanimous recommendations to Council, and all four were unanimously accepted.

1. RusAF should not be reinstated at this stage because "the deep-seated culture of tolerance (or worse) for doping that led to RusAF being suspended in the first place appears not to have changed materially to date; a strong and effective anti-doping infrastructure capable of detecting and deterring doping has still not been created; there are detailed allegations ... that the Russian authorities, far from supporting the anti-doping effort, have in fact orchestrated systematic doping and the covering up of adverse analytical findings."

2. While RusAF remains suspended, no other representatives of RusAF (i.e. officials, athlete support personnel, etc) should take part in international competition or in the affairs of the IAAF.

3. If there are any individual athletes who can convincingly show they are not tainted by the Russian system because they have been outside the country, and subject to other, effective anti-doping systems, they should be able to apply for permission to compete internationally, not for Russia but as a "neutral" athlete.

4. Any individual athlete who has made an extraordinary contribution to the fight against doping should also be able to apply for such permission. In particular, the case of whistleblower Yuliya Stepanova, an 800m runner, should be considered favourably.

On the vexed subject of innocent athletes being denied their Olympic chance, the report stated: "Undoubtedly, non-reinstatement of RusAF would mean that some clean Russian athletes will miss out on Rio. But while that is unfortunate, it is nothing compared to the injustice that so many athletes have suffered in the past in being cheated out of medals, prize money and glory by their Russian competitors, and that so many more could suffer in the future if this opportunity to solve the problem is wasted. In short, this is the price that has to be paid for the failure of the Russian authorities to fix the problem before now, and the Russian authorities alone are to blame for that."

I felt the IAAF decision was fully justified. Despite a high incidence of denial by leading personalities in Russian athletics, the investigation proved beyond any reasonable doubt that cheating was accepted as normal. That had been the case also with the GDR in its heyday, but the East Germans got away with it. Their numerous world records and global medals remain intact because, despite all the suspicion, there was at that time no concrete proof of state-sponsored doping. It's a pity that when that proof was revealed no retrospective action was taken by the IAAF or IOC. The case with Russia is different. The evidence is there for all to see and this time the IAAF has acted decisively. The IOC, which historically has made so many poor decisions, added to its list of blunders by refusing to ban all Russian competitors from other tainted sports, copping out by leaving the decision to each individual governing body. What happened to the IOC's commitment to fair competition?

Despite the IAAF being applauded over its stance in this matter, the organisation remained in crisis. The second part of WADA's Independent Commission Report, released in January, accused Lamine Diack of being "responsible for organising and enabling the conspiracy and corruption that took place in the IAAF. He sanctioned and appears to have had personal knowledge of the fraud and extortion of athletes carried out by the actions of the informal illegitimate governance structure he put in place." The Report stated: "In the course of its investigation, the IC discovered evidence that the conduct of certain individuals within or associated with the IAAF went beyond mere sporting and corporate misconduct. Some of the evidence revealed was of a criminal nature." Earlier, the IAAF Ethics Commission charged Valentin Balakhnichev, Papa Massata Diack (Lamine's son, whom Interpol wish to extradite from Senegal to France), Aleksey Melnikov and Gabriel Dollé with violations of the IAAF's Code of Ethics. The first three were banned from any involvement in athletics for life, while Dollé was banned for five years. The charges related to the Russian marathoner Liliya Shobukhova who was blackmailed into paying hundreds of thousands of dollars to avoid a doping ban and enable her to compete at the 2012 Olympics.

Shobukhova, who was retrospectively stripped of her wins in the 2010 London Marathon and the 2009-2011 Chicago Marathons (clocking 2:18:20 in 2011) following the discovery of biological passport abnormalities, did get to race in the London Olympics after all but was a non-finisher. An addition to Russia's Hall of Shame printed in the previous chapter was Mariya Savinova, 2010 world indoor, 2011 world and 2012 Olympic 800m champion, while justice was served at last when Viktor Chegin, who operated the notorious Saransk race walking centre, was banned for life due to his involvement with doping which saw more than 20 athletes who trained at the centre failing drug tests.

The first major meeting without Russian representation was the World Indoor Championships in Portland, Oregon, which saw the US team achieve a record number of 13 gold medals from the 26 events. The first home victory was by Jenn Suhr, who at a minor meeting in January had raised her world indoor pole vault record to 5.03m, and on this occasion found 4.90m sufficed. The other significant world record breaker during the indoor season was Genzebe Dibaba, who in Stockholm had run the mile in 4:13.31, smashing a record which had stood for 26 years and a time second only to Svetlana Masterkova's hitherto unapproached outdoor record of 4:12.56 in 1996. The Ethiopian opted for the 3000m in Portland where she destroyed four-time winner of this title, team-mate Meseret Defar, in 8:47.43. The first kilometre took all of 3:15.73 but Dibaba whizzed through the final 2000m in 5:31.70, close to the world indoor record for that distance of 5:30.53! Britain came away with just three medals: silver for high jumper Robbie Grabarz (2.33m) and bronze for Tiffany Porter in the 60m hurdles (7.90) and Lorraine Ugen, whose long jump of 6.93m equalled the UK indoor record. Of the 24 individual winners only Matthew Centrowitz (1500m), Omar McLeod (60m hurdles), Ashton Eaton (heptathlon) and Michelle Carter (shot) went on to strike gold at the Rio Olympics five months later. Conversely, the most unlikely Olympic champion-to-be on display was Brazilian vaulter Thiago Braz da Silva who placed equal 12th with 5.55m.

The London Marathon was tinged with sadness as John Disley, who along with his old steeplechasing rival Chris Brasher founded the race in 1981, had died two months earlier at the age of 87. John, a Welshman who under the coaching of Geoff Dyson reduced the British record from 9:18.4 in 1950 to 8:44.2 in 1955, was the Olympic bronze medallist in 1952. The latest edition of the race was particularly notable on three counts: completing the halves in 61:24 and 61:41, Eliud Kipchoge clocked the second fastest ever marathon on a legitimate course of 2:03:05 (for a record seventh sub-2:06 time); it was the biggest London Marathon yet as 39,091 entrants completed the course; and a 39 year-old woman police officer became the event's one millionth finisher.

Kipchoge would confirm his standing as the world's outstanding marathoner by winning the Olympic title in Rio, but even he could not envisage winning the Olympic 5000m and 10,000m prior to a third gold medal in the marathon ... but that's what Emil Zátopek achieved in Helsinki 64 years earlier. Back in 2002 Bob Phillips wrote the definitive book on the Czech's astonishing running career with detailed description of his key races, but in 2016 three in-depth biographies were published. All were admirable accounts of his life on and off the track, and Richard Askwith and Pat Butcher are to be congratulated on their research and writing. However, declaring a personal interest as I helped a little with his research, I was particularly impressed by *Endurance: The Extraordinary Life & Times of Emil Zátopek* by Rick Broadbent of *The Times*.

The author interviewed Emil's widow Dana (the 1952 Olympic javelin champion) and several other Czechs who played a significant role in his life, resulting in a fascinating and often disturbing account. Emil, who ran his last race in 1958, reached the heights as an athlete, a national hero feted everywhere, but even his fame and popularity could not save him from the injustices of a ruthless Communist state which had tortured and imprisoned fellow athlete Jan Haluza, in effect Emil's coach in the early days, on trumped-up charges of espionage. When Alexander Dubcek was appointed first secretary of the

Czechoslovak Communist Party in 1968 he promised reforms that would improve life for the people and Emil and Dana signed up to a manifesto which called for the totalitarian regime to be liberalised. However, the Soviet Union would not tolerate any such reforms, Prague was occupied and Dubcek was removed. Lieutenant Colonel Zátopek broadcast messages of defiance, the consequence being that he was expelled from the Communist Party and sacked from the army. For years afterwards he was forced to work in menial jobs and it was not until the Velvet Revolution of 1989, when communism collapsed and free elections took place for the first time in 44 years, that Emil became fully rehabilitated. In 1998, two years before his death at 78, he was awarded the nation's highest honour, the Order of the White Lion, by President Václav Havel.

The issue of Russian cheating persisted throughout the year and, in May, the names of 11 athletes were revealed as having tested positive when samples from the 2008 Olympics were re-analysed. They included Yuliya Chermoshanskaya, a member of the winning 4x100m relay team which was therefore disqualified; javelin silver medallist Mariya Abakumova (world champion in 2011); steeplechase bronze medallist Yekaterina Volkova (2007 world champion); and high jump bronze medallist Anna Chicherova who went on to become world champion in 2011 and Olympic champion in 2012. Re-testing of 2012 Olympic samples led to Tatyana Beloborodova (née Lysenko) being stripped of the hammer title.

It wasn't only Russians who were exposed. Re-testing from the 2008 Games yielded an adverse analytical result (for a banned stimulant) for Jamaican 9.78 sprinter Nesta Carter and as a consequence Usain Bolt ("it's heartbreaking") had to return one of his precious gold medals. The 4x100m relay team of Carter, Michael Frater, Bolt and Asafa Powell, first in a world record 37.10, was disqualified and victory awarded instead to Trinidad & Tobago in 38.06.

British athletes fared extremely well at the European Championships, staged in Amsterdam's 1928 Olympic stadium, sharing the highest number of medals (16) with Germany although Poland with six were ahead of Britain and Germany (five) in terms of gold medals. The British winners were Martyn Rooney at 400m (45.29), long jumper Greg Rutherford (8.25m), the men's 4x100m team (38.17), Dina Asher-Smith in the 200m (22.37) and the women's 4x400m squad (3:25.05). With bigger fish to fry, Mo Farah – who had broken Dave Moorcroft's UK 3000m record with 7:32.62 a few weeks earlier – did not defend his 5000m and 10,000m titles.

A controversial aspect of the championships was the number of medals won by 'transferees' – athletes who for mainly financial benefits were representing countries to which they had only recently transferred allegiance. Turkey were the worst offenders in terms of recruiting athletic mercenaries. All of their four gold medals were won by imports: Polat Kemboi Arikan (10,000m) and Yasemin Can (5000m and 10,000m) are former Kenyans and Yasmani Copello (400m hurdles) is from Cuba. Winners of silver medals were Jak Ali

Harvey (100m) from Jamaica, Ramil Guliyev (200m) from Azerbaijan, Ali Kaya (10,000m), Aras Kaya (steeplechase) and Kaan Kigen Özbilen (half marathon) from Kenya. Turkey's doping record is deplorable also, with several of their most successful athletes being banned. Among them were distance runner Elvan Abeylegesse, originally from Ethiopia, who forfeited medals from the 2007 World Championships and 2008 Olympics, while the suspicion surrounding Turkish-born Asli Cakir and Gamze Bulut when finishing first and second in the 2012 Olympic 1500m proved to be fully justified.

Curiously, the only male competitors in Amsterdam to strike Olympic gold in Rio did not exactly shine at the European Championships. Discus thrower Christoph Harting placed fourth and German team-mate Thomas Röhler was fifth in the javelin. However, on the women's side 37 year-old high jumper Ruth Beitia, pole vaulter Ekateríni Stefanídi, discus thrower Sandra Perkovic and hammer thrower Anita Wlodarczyk won at both meetings.

Highlight of the Diamond League meetings in Europe as the Olympics approached was a dazzling new women's world record.

By finishing only sixth in the US Trials, Keni (Kendra) Harrison has missed her opportunity for glory in Rio but at the Müller Anniversary Games in London's Olympic Stadium she became world record holder for 100m hurdles. Back in May she clocked the equal second quickest ever time of 12.24, just falling short of the 1988 world record of 12.21 by Bulgaria's Yordanka Donkova, but in the Trials she could manage only 12.62 and her Olympic dream was over. All she could do now to salvage the season was to chase that world record, set four years before she was born. Conditions were perfect and there was an enthusiastic crowd of around 40,000 fans to voice their appreciation. Initially it was a disappointment when, as she crossed the finish line, the trackside clock displayed 12.58. Seconds later that was rectified, because as so often happened when Colin Jackson dipped low under the beam when winning his races the time shown was actually that for the second placed athlete. The correct time was in fact a stunning 12.20! Harrison's face was a picture of astonishment as the time was pointed out to her, followed by smiles and tears.

Subsidiary highlights of the two-day meeting included Usain Bolt's 19.89 200m in his last race before Rio, UK records by Laura Muir with a 3:57.49 1500m which broke Kelly Holmes' mark of 3:57.90 and by the women's 4x100m team with a time of 41.81, and a 12:59.29 5000m by Mo Farah, his fastest for four years. Katarina Johnson-Thompson shaped up promisingly for her Olympic heptathlon challenge with a high jump of 1.95m and long jump of 6.84m but Jessica Ennis-Hill was unhappy with a long jump of only 6.19m after clocking a heartening 12.76 hurdles. Unfortunately, 40 year-old Kim Collins was injured in the 100m final and unable to demonstrate the amazing form he had shown earlier in the season when he set a world masters (and St Kitts & Nevis national) record of 9.93!

The day before this meeting, the Court of Arbitration for Sport announced that it had rejected an appeal by 68 Russian athletes and the Russian Olympic Committee to overturn the IAAF's blanket ban. Unequivocally, with one exception (Darya Klishina), there would be no Russian athletes competing in Rio. Three days later the IOC announced its compromise, or rather cop-out: individual sports governing bodies would decide which Russian competitors would be eligible.

The decision may have been welcomed by IOC president Thomas Bach's friend, president Vladimir Putin, but it was condemned by many outside Russia. Travis Tygart, president of the US Anti-Doping Agency, may have summed it up best. "In response to the most important moment for clean athletes and integrity of the Olympic Games, the IOC has refused to take decisive leadership. The decision regarding Russian participation and the confusing mess left in its wake is a significant blow to the rights of clean athletes. The conflict of interest is glaring." Paula Radcliffe: "A sad day for clean sport. A decision that shows that the IOC's primary concern is not to protect the clean athletes and do all they could to ensure a level playing field." Cycling legend Sir Chris Hoy: "What sort of message does this send out? Surely the IOC's job is to make crucial decisions rather than passing the buck." Greg Rutherford: "Spineless."

I don't often editorialise in AI but this was my take on the situation in the issue of July 26.

Three cheers for the IAAF. They alone (so far) among the world's sports federations have had the guts to ban a Russian team from competing in Rio. With the totally corrupt state-inspired doping regime in Russia laid bare, the IAAF acted prudently so that the world's clean athletes would not have to compete against the products of a system based on cheating. There may be some Russian athletes who have not resorted to doping but they would find it impossible to prove their innocence. It's no good claiming they have never failed a doping test when it's clear that immense numbers of samples were falsified or thrown away. Those who really have reached the top honestly should not blame the IAAF or WADA or the CAS. They should blame their own administrators, coaches, medics etc who for years have enabled dozens of Russian athletes to cheat their way to records, medals and financial rewards.

Predictably, alas, the IOC fudged the issue. Here at last was the opportunity to make an example of a member country lacking any moral compass. Investigations proved that many Olympic sports, not just athletics, were involved and surely a blanket ban was called for. Instead the IOC have failed to face up to their responsibilities to safeguard honest competition by requesting individual sports federations to make decisions regarding the eligibility of Russian competitors. Few of those federations have ever displayed the willingness, shown by the IAAF over the years despite the recent damaging revelations, to tackle the problem of doping and so it's probable that hordes of Russians will be prominent in Rio.

And so to the Rio Games … and what an Olympics they turned out to be. The London Games were truly memorable, but Rio proved even greater as the winning marks were superior to London's 24-22 with one event tied, and three individual world records were broken as compared to London's one. The

Games got off to a sensational beginning with the women's 10,000m and never looked back.

What a start to the Rio athletics programme! In this, the first final of the Games on August 12, Almaz Ayana produced what can be regarded as the most phenomenal of all women's track running records. The world record time of 29:31.78 by Wang Junxia back in 1993 was regarded by many, this writer included, as too good to be true and one wondered whether it would ever be approached. The nearest anyone came was Meselech Melkamu's 29:53.80 in 2009 while even Tirunesh Dibaba, the outstanding distance runner of her generation, had not run faster than the 29:54.66 she clocked when winning the 2008 Olympic title. But now Ayana, in only her second race ever at the distance (she debuted with 30:07.00 in June), has smashed that record to smithereens with the amazing time of 29:17.45. What a sobering thought that Emil Zátopek's first world record, in 1949, was 29:21.2 and he won his Olympic titles with times of 29:59.6 (1948) and 29:17.0 (1952). The race was remarkable in many ways. Just look at the splits: Ayana reached 5000m in 14:47.1, so the second half – with Ayana ahead from 5200m – took just 14:30.4! All credit too to Vivian Cheruiyot who finished in 29:32.53, which not only broke the Kenyan record but also Paula Radcliffe's Commonwealth record. Tirunesh Dibaba, seeking an unprecedented third Olympic title in this event, also ran faster than ever before with 29:42.56 for the bronze. All of the first 13 finishers set personal bests while worthy of special mention was Jo Pavey's 31:33.44 in 15th place, a world age-42 best. She is the first Briton to run at five Olympics and hasn't ruled out the possibility of attempting selection for Tokyo 2020.

The 400m final (August 14) will long be remembered and treasured by all who saw it, either in the stadium or via TV. An epic battle was anticipated, involving defending champion Kirani James (pb of 43.74), 2008 champion LaShawn Merritt (43.65) and world champion Wayde van Niekerk (43.48). Well, there was a closely fought duel between James (43.76) and Merritt (43.85), but van Niekerk probably never saw either of them during the race. Drawn in the outside lane, he was clear of the other two at 300m (31.0) and simply powered away (i.e. decelerated less than the others) along the straight to win by a good six metres in an astounding 43.03 – 0.15 inside Michael Johnson's legendary world record from 1999! Here is our sport's new superstar – a man who has run inside 10 sec for 100m, 20 sec for 200m and quite possibly in the near future 43 sec for 400m.

Poland had two "certain" hammer winners, but one failed to qualify for the final [Pawel Fajdek] and the other – Anita Wlodarczyk – not only took the gold medal but smashed her world record into the bargain. It just went to confirm the glorious unpredictability of sport. Her winning margin of 5.54m was the widest in Olympic hammer history since 1912. In round two she effectively ended the race for the gold medal with an Olympic record of 80.40m, but that was only an appetiser because in the next round she served up a delicious world record of 82.29m. Her joy was evident as she jumped up and down in excitement in the circle while the implement was flying towards its distant destination. The ever consistent Zhang Wenxiu added another silver to her collection. The fight for the bronze was lively indeed and proved historic in terms of British hammer throwing. Entering the circle for her final throw in fifth place former world junior champion Sophie Hitchon summoned up all her strength, technique and determination ... and, almost disbelievingly, watched her hammer wing its way close to the 75m line. The distance was 74.54m (her 13th UK record) and Britain had her first Olympic hammer medallist since Malcolm Nokes in 1924. The former ballet dancer weighs just 74kg as compared to Wlodarczyk's 94kg and Zhang's 108kg.

There were three other British bronze medallists: Greg Rutherford in the long jump (8.29m) and both women's relay teams (UK record of 41.77 and 3:25.88). For Jessica Ennis-Hill, in what would prove to be her final heptathlon, the reward was a silver medal.

Ranked seventh on scores this year with 6491, Nafi Thiam was not expecting a medal in Rio. However, the 1.87m tall Belgian (born of a Senegalese father) just couldn't put a foot wrong and ended up, to her astonishment, as Olympic champion with a massive new pb score of 6810. On the way she set individual lifetime bests in five of the seven events! Ennis-Hill put up a typically gritty fight in her bid to become the first British woman to retain an Olympic title, falling just 35 points short with 6775, her highest score since London 2012. Her one disappointing event was the shot where her 13.86m earned 785 points, whereas she had been hitting around 14.50m (worth 827 points) in training, and that would have made all the difference. Normally Ennis-Hill would consolidate her overall lead (after a 12.84 hurdles) with the high jump but here, despite her delight in jumping 1.89m, her best for four years, she found herself third after two events. As a result of clearing the greatest height in heptathlon history, Katarina Johnson-Thompson led ahead of Thiam. At 1.98m Thiam went over first time for a pb and KJT at the second attempt set a new UK record. Note that the individual event was won with 1.97m! The Briton's euphoria evaporated in the shot where she could manage only a woeful 11.68m but bounced back with a 23.26 200m. Day one totals: Ennis-Hill 4057, Thiam 3985, Akela Jones 3964, KJT 3957.

The long jump was where KJT might have expected to make up ground on her rivals and her 6.51m surpassed Ennis-Hill's 6.34m (tantalisingly 6.56m from take-off) but an inspired Thiam added 7cm to her pb with 6.58m and was back in the lead with 5018, followed by Ennis-Hill 5013 and KJT 4967. The javelin effectively determined the medallists. KJT lost any chance of mounting the podium by throwing just 36.36m while Ennis-Hill's 46.06m paled by comparison with Thiam's mighty new pb of 53.13m, achieved despite carrying an elbow injury which caused her to scream out in pain. The gold medal was almost certainly destined for Thiam as Ennis-Hill would need to finish nearly 10 sec ahead of her in the 800m. She tried so valiantly, but 2:09.07 proved insufficient against Thiam's 2:16.54, yet another pb. KJT filled sixth place with her second highest score of 6523.

The golden lining for Britain was provided, yet again, by Mo Farah. By completing another 10,000/5000m double he made all sorts of history. He joined the illustrious company of Paavo Nurmi, Emil Zátopek, Lasse Viren, Haile Gebrselassie and Kenenisa Bekele as double Olympic 10,000m champions and became the first British athlete to win three individual Olympic gold medals. Seven days after that triumph, his 5000m win on August 20 enabled him to emulate Viren's "double double" and pushed his British "golds record" out to four.

The last time Farah was beaten at 10,000m was at the 2011 World Championships when Ibrahim Jeylan had to produce a 26.3 final 200m to win by a stride. Farah went on to victories in the 2012 Olympics, 2013 Worlds and 2015 Worlds, the Kenyans and Ethiopians having never found a way to get the better of him. It was the same again in Rio ... when it came down to the final sprint no one could live with the 33 year-old Briton. What's more, shades of Viren in 1972, Farah was inadvertently tripped just before 4000m by training mate Galen Rupp and fell to the track, coming close to being trampled before he regained his feet and chased after the leaders. Astonishingly, given what happened in the past where Farah has always managed to outkick his opponents, once again no one was prepared to cut out a savage pace. The first 5000m took 13:53.11. At 9000m Farah went ahead for the first time and led at the bell, but along the back straight Paul Tanui hit the front and was still just ahead entering the final straight. It was a brave attempt, but doomed to failure as Farah found another gear to pull away for victory in 27:05.17. The last 400m had taken 55.36, the final mile covered in around 4:03 and the second half of the race in 13:12.06.

Farah hasn't lost a championship 5000m since 2009 and his East African rivals, usually with faster times to their credit, are still puzzling over how to beat him. Basically, if Farah is still in contention at the bell it's all over, for no one has been able to outkick him. Farah went ahead at around 3150m and after 4000m the pace quickened considerably. With Farah dictating the race, the penultimate lap was covered in 59.82 and he and Hagos Gebrhiwet were neck and neck at the bell. They matched strides along the back straight but crucially Farah stole a 2m advantage by the 200m mark and once he hit the straight in front the result was never in doubt. The surprise was that the man who chased him home was not Gebrhiwet but Paul Chelimo, a Kenyan who now represents the USA. Farah's time was 13:03.30 with a last lap of 52.83 and final kilometre of 2:23.92! "I can't believe I did it," said Farah. "It's definitely my most satisfying win." The ever amazing Bernard Lagat (41) reduced his world M40 record from 13:14.96 to 13:06.78 and there was a great breakthrough by Andrew Butchart who reduced his Scottish record from 13:13.30 to 13:08.61 for third on the UK all-time list behind Farah and Dave Moorcroft.

Of course, the main attraction of the Games, as ever, was Usain Bolt and although not in vintage form he did not disappoint his legion of fans. He made history in the 100m by becoming the first athlete to win that title three times, indeed the first to complete an Olympic treble in any track event. He had a close call against Justin Gatlin in the 2015 World Championships but this time it was clear-cut. As usual Gatlin got away brilliantly and held a substantial lead until Bolt's giant strides caught him at around 80m. From that point it was no contest and despite relaxing in the last few strides Bolt had an 0.08 margin as he crossed the line in 9.81. Once again he had timed his peak to perfection. Four days later in the 200m he completed his third straight Olympic sprint double, an achievement which will surely never be equalled. The wraps came off in the semis with Bolt clocking 19.78 so comfortably that he was able to turn and share a laugh with an equally relaxed Andre De Grasse (Canadian record of 19.80!) in the closing stages. As all eight finalists were sub-20 sec performers it was surprising that Bolt alone bettered that time in the final, winning from De Grasse by an 0.24 margin in 19.78. The bronze went to Christophe Lemaitre, agonisingly for Adam Gemili by a margin of 3/1000ths of a second. Bolt brought his fabulous Olympic career to a close by anchoring the Jamaican team to victory in the relay in 37.27, coming from behind to overtake an inspired Japanese quartet. He had completed the "triple triple" although because of Nesta Carter's doping positive his final gold medal tally dropped to eight.

Among a wealth of other glittering performances were David Rudisha's successful defence of his 800m title in 1:42.15, a 50.62 last lap which enabled Matthew Centrowitz to become the first American winner of the 1500m for 108 years albeit in the slowest time since 1932, Eliud Kipchoge's seventh win in eight marathons (2:08:44 in humid conditions), and Olympic records by Conseslus Kipruto in the steeplechase (8:03.28), Ryan Crouser in the shot (22.52m), Ashton Eaton in the decathlon (8893), Vivian Cheruiyot in the 5000m (14:26.17), and a wildly acclaimed Brazilian victory in the pole vault as Thiago Braz da Silva soared over 6.03m. Other standout achievements included Elaine Thompson's 10.71/21.78 sprint double, Caster Semenya's South African 800m record of 1:55.28, Faith Kipyegon's 1:57.2 final 800m when winning the 1500m ahead of Genzebe Dibaba in 4:08.92 and three more medals for Allyson Felix (second to Shaunae Miller at 400m, 49.44-49.51, and golds in both relays), bringing her grand total to nine, equalling Merlene Ottey's women's record.

Post-Olympic activity is by definition anti-climactic but there were several exceedingly worthy performances, chief among them being a world steeplechase record of 8:52.78 by Bahrain's Kenyan-born Olympic champion Ruth Jebet in Paris, a meeting where Scotland's Laura Muir ran away from Olympic champion Kipyegon in a Commonwealth 1500m record of 3:55.22. Only Genzebe Dibaba has run faster during the past 20 seasons. Muir may have placed a weary seventh at the Olympics but that was because rather than settle for a likely bronze medal she tried to win the race by attempting to stay with Dibaba and Kipyegon in a third lap covered in a killing 56.79, a tactic she does not regret. I love her uncompromising attitude to racing! Appropriately in Warsaw, at a meeting dedicated to the memory of 2000 Olympic hammer champion Kamila Skolimowska, Anita Wlodarczyk extended her world record to 82.98m.

Highlight of the autumn marathon season was Kenenisa Bekele's Ethiopian record of 2:03:03 in Berlin, 10 seconds ahead of Wilson Kipsang. It was the second fastest time ever on a record-eligible course and was made up of halves of 61:11 and 61:52. The New York Marathon broke all participation records with 51,394 finishers from 51,999 starters.

Autumn also marked the awards season. Inducted into the England Athletics Hall of Fame were Judy Oakes, Peter Radford (it was my privilege to hand the award to the NUTS president and former 200m world record holder), Joyce Smith, coaches Bud Baldaro and Ron Roddan, Kriss Akabusi and the 1991 world title winning 4x400m team of Roger Black, Derek Redmond, John Regis, anchorman Akabusi plus Ade Mafe and Mark Richardson who played their part by running in the heats. Journalist and Surrey Athletics chairman Tom Pollak was presented with the Cliff Temple Memorial Award by the NUTS for his long-time services to athletics.

As a friend of his for over 60 years I can assure readers that Stan Greenberg is not often at a loss for words, but he was almost struck dumb when, to his complete surprise at the British Athletics Writers' Association lunch in November, he was presented with the prestigious Ron Pickering Memorial Award for his services to athletics. As honorary president and a founder member of the BAWA, I had put forward Stan's name as a deserving award winner, particularly in view of his close friendship with Ron, and that was endorsed by the committee and by Ron's son and daughter, Shaun and Kim, who made the presentation. NUTS founder member Stan, who was BBC Television's athletics statistician for 26 years until 1994, attended his first Olympics in 1948, and was sports editor of the *Guinness Book of Records* before leaving to work with the much praised commentary team led by David Coleman, Ron Pickering and Stuart Storey. He has written a number of books, primarily about the Olympics, and remains active compiling UK and Commonwealth lists, writing letters to *Athletics Weekly* (he must surely hold the record for the number published, mainly critical in recent years of British coaching) and watching major events in the company of yours truly, for whom he acted as best man in 1973.

The day after that delightful function I was off to Las Vegas for what has turned out to be the very last time. It may or may not be a coincidence that my decision to end my trips there came while I was watching – shocked and horrified – as it became clear from my hotel room TV that Donald Trump was to become president. My American cousins and friends were even more aghast. However, the main reason was that, much as I still enjoyed the glitter, familiarity and absurdity of Vegas, the long flights followed by seemingly endless queues to get through US border control were becoming too much of a physical challenge. Besides, I could now indulge my weakness for American-style slot machines at the Aspers casino close to London's Olympic Stadium. I no longer required an expensive 11,000 miles round trip with Virgin Atlantic; I could travel for free the length of the Jubilee Line from Stanmore to Stratford in one hour!

52. STILL HOOKED AT 79 (2017)

I recall as a young reporter marvelling at the sight of Joe Binks in the press box at the White City, still reporting for the *News of the World* in his eighties. How amazing ... and how could I have envisaged in those early days that, if I'm around for a little longer, I too will be covering the sport as an octogenarian! Yes, I'm still hooked!

This year (2017) got off to an auspicious start with the news that Britain's two most successful and popular athletes featured prominently in the Queen's New Year Honours List. Under the heading "Arise Sir Mo and Dame Jess", AI (entering its 25th year of publication) stated:

"A dream come true" was Mo Farah's reaction to being awarded a knighthood, the first active athlete to be so honoured. "I am so happy to be awarded this incredible honour from the country that has been my home since I moved here at the age of eight. Looking back at the boy who arrived here from Somalia, not speaking any English, I could never have imagined where I would be today. I am so proud to have had the opportunity to race for my country and win gold medals for the British people, who have been my biggest supporters throughout my career." This will be the last year of track racing for Farah (33) before he moves up to the marathon. Jessica Ennis-Hill (39), who announced her retirement in October, has been made a Dame, following in the footsteps of Kelly Holmes who was similarly honoured in 2005, the year after her Olympic double. Sir Roger Bannister (87) has been made a Companion of Honour, bringing the total of distinguished athletes on that list to four: Lord (Seb) Coe was so honoured in 2012, Sir Menzies Campbell in 2013, Dame Mary Peters in 2015. Others in that select group, which is restricted to 47 UK citizens, include Stephen Hawking, Sir David Attenborough, Dame Judi Dench, Dame Maggie Smith and Dame Vera Lynn.

The year was only 15 days old when the first world record was created. The IAAF had announced that as of January 1 any performance of 4:30:00 or better would be accepted as an inaugural world record for the women's 50km walk and Ines Henriques from Portugal lost no time in staking her claim with the exceptional time of 4:08:26, which would have won every Olympic title prior to 1972.

The first notable indoor mark of the 2017 campaign occurred even earlier when in Glasgow on January 4 Laura Muir clocked 14:49.12 for 5000m, the fastest ever – indoors or out – by a Scot and no one in the world was quicker that winter. Her only previous race at the distance was in 2013 when she ran 15:53.68. Laura, combining her running career with studying to be a vet, went on to enjoy a fabulous season. She topped the world list also at 3000m with a European indoor record of 8:26.41 in Karlsruhe, for another absolute Scottish best, leaving the redoubtable Hellen Obiri 20m behind. Next came a European indoor 1000m record of 2:31.93 in Birmingham and she ended her campaign on a glorious note by winning two gold medals at the European Championships in Belgrade.

Laura Muir completed the first part of her projected double in great style. Less than five hours after running 8:55.56 to qualify for the 3000m final she lined up for her 1500m heat, winning that in 4:10.28. Next day came the 1500m final and after a slow start she shot into the lead just before 300m. In winning her first ever international medal (apart from her bronze in the 2013 European U23 1500m) she broke another of Kelly Holmes' UK records. Laura's time was 4:02.39, a championship record. After winning her first gold medal, Laura managed to grab five hours' sleep before it was time to get up and prepare for the 3000m final. It was with just over 300m to go that Muir surged away from Yasemin Can ... and how. By the finish she was 50m clear and her time of 8:35.67 bettered the championship record. Fellow Scot, Eilish McColgan, finished amazingly fast to place third.

There were three other British winners in Belgrade. Richard Kilty, yet to really make his mark outdoors but always a formidable competitor at 60m, retained that title in 6.54; an injury-free at last Andy Pozzi, who topped the world year list with 7.43, took the 60m hurdles in 7.51; and Asha Philip set a UK record of 7.06 when winning the 60m. It was a wholly deserved triumph for Asha, the world youth 100m champion back in 2007. She ruptured her knee later that year when trampolining and her career in sprinting was on hold for some years. It wasn't until 2011 that she was able to compete effectively again. High jumper Robbie Grabarz added to his medal collection with a silver (2.30m) and placed second also were Shelayna Oskan-Clarke in the 800m, losing by just 1/100th with her time of 2:00.39, long jumper Lorraine Ugen with a UK record of 6.97m, and the women's 4x400m team. Mo Farah chose not to compete but marked his presence in Birmingham with a European indoor 5000m record of 13:09.16.

It was quite a year for road racing. Kenya's Peres Jepchirchir (23), the 2016 world half marathon champion, set a world record of 65:06 at the RAK race on February 10, while 35 year-old Mary Keitany – a close second in 65:13 – proceeded to win the London Marathon on April 23 in 2:17:01 to break Paula Radcliffe's women-only race world record of 2:17:42.

The most impressive feature of Mary Keitany's extraordinary run was that she didn't blow up after covering the first half at sub-2:14 pace. When Paula Radcliffe set her mind-blowing world record of 2:15:25 on this course she reached halfway in 68:02 and when she clocked 2:17:42 her split was 68:27. Keitany went through in 66:54! The BBC commentators – Paula, Steve Cram and Brendan Foster (covering the race for the 37th and last time) – all thought with good reason that she would pay for such impetuosity, but even when super-hare Caroline Kipkirui dropped out she maintained a decent tempo, covering the second half in 70:07. Runner-up Tirunesh Dibaba, whose one previous marathon was when she placed third in London in 2014 in 2:20:35, is now the third fastest of all time with her Ethiopian record of 2:17:56, and that despite a bout of stomach trouble which caused her to stop briefly.

That women's half marathon record didn't last long, for in Prague on April 1 (no joke) Joyciline Jepkosgei – a 23 year-old Kenyan who had placed third in the RAK race in a big personal best of 66:08 – ran 64:52, picking up other world records at 10km (30:04), 15km (45:37) and 20km (61:25) on the way! Later, back in Prague on September 9, she smashed that 10km record with an outstanding 29:43, picking up another world road best with 14:32 *en route*. It wasn't all good news for Kenyan runners, though, as it was revealed that Olympic marathon champion Jemima Sumgong had tested positive for EPO in a no-notice test conducted by the IAAF in Kenya.

Overshadowing all other marathon news and comment was Nike's massively funded and painstakingly orchestrated attempt on a sub-two hour marathon. It was an interesting but cold-blooded experiment which had nothing whatever to do with legitimate marathon racing.

It wasn't a proper race and so it won't be forwarded for ratification as a world record, but Eliud Kipchoge's marathon exploit on the dead flat Monza motor racing circuit in Italy early on the morning of May 6 (a date inextricably linked with the breaking of running barriers) was simply phenomenal. He may have failed in achieving the "Breaking2" objective, but what a fantastic run it was for him to cover the distance over two and a half minutes faster than the official world record of 2:02:57 set in Berlin in 2014 by his fellow Kenyan, Dennis Kimetto. The time was a mind-boggling 2:00:25!

Nike has spent millions of dollars on this project, aimed at boosting a revolutionary new road racing shoe as well as achieving a milestone in athletic performance. Three runners were recruited, and no doubt paid handsomely, to participate in the seven-month process undergoing a multitude of treadmill tests as well as their usual arduous training. No stone was left unturned in preparing the runners: experts in coaching, bio-mechanics, shoe design, nutrition, hydration and psychology among other aspects were brought on board.

Kipchoge was the man nominated to challenge the 2 hour barrier. Now aged 32 he is at the peak of his powers, having last year won the London Marathon in 2:03:05 and the Olympic title. His support would come from Ethiopia's Lelisa Desisa (27), the 2013 World Champs silver medallist and two-time Boston winner, and Eritrea's Zersenay Tadese (35), four times world half marathon champion. The attempt was a cold, clinical affair and against the rules as well as the spirit of racing as a posse of Nike-sponsored pacemakers took turns, usually six at a time, to shield Kipchoge from any wind and closely follow an electric car which was programmed to operate at the 14:13 per 5k speed required to break 2 hours. The pacemakers ran one or two of the 17 ½ laps of 2.4k, recovered and then returned for another stint, so there was always a phalanx of runners guiding Kipchoge towards his goal. The time at 10k was 28:21, 20k 56:49, halfway in 59:57.

Desisa surprisingly was dropped as early as 18k and even Tadese started to fall back just before halfway, although he made a big breakthrough as – helped along by another set of pacemakers – he completed the distance in 2:06:51. Kipchoge, serene and metronomic, kept to his task in magnificent fashion even though the battle against the clock began to be lost. The 30k mark was reached in an extraordinary 1:25:20 as against Kimetto's 1:27:38 during his world record, and 40k in 1:54:04. Kipchoge's halves were 59:57 and 60:28; he averaged around 4:36 per mile and finished in a remarkably fresh state.

That marathon wasn't part of the real flesh and blood world of athletics, and nor was a fantasy decathlon duel I concocted for AI between Dan O'Brien and the now retired Ashton Eaton.

*Who has the better set of individual personal bests? It's very, very close! This is how a contest between them would unfold if both matched their pbs. **100m**: Eaton 10.21 (1044 points) takes an early lead over O'Brien 10.32 (1018). **Long Jump**: Eaton goes further ahead (2164-2009) with 8.23m to 8.08m. **Shot**: O'Brien edges in front (2993-2978) thanks to 16.69m against 15.40m. **High Jump**: O'Brien greatly extends his lead (3985-3884) after clearing 2.20m to his opponent's 2.11m. **400m**: Eaton claws back valuable points with 45.00 to 46.53, leaving O'Brien the overnight leader with 4967 to 4944. **110m Hurdles**: Both men are brilliant hurdlers, Eaton having the edge with 13.35 to 13.47, and now there are only 7 points between them: O'Brien 6011, Eaton 6004. **Discus**: It's all over, surely, as O'Brien is in a different class: 55.07m against 47.36m and the scores are now 6988-6820. **Pole Vault**: Eaton narrows the deficit a little with 5.40m to 5.25m but O'Brien is still comfortably clear: 7976-7855. **Javelin**: Nothing in it here with O'Brien (66.90m) scoring 4 more points than Eaton (66.64m), so going into the final event O'Brien leads by a whopping 125 points (8818-8693). **1500m**: Would you believe it? Eaton (4:14.48) is so superior to his rival here (4:33.19) that he picks up 126 more points to win the contest by a single point: 9543 to 9542!*

Back to a real-life multi-events competition and an outstanding performance in Götzis by Nafi Thiam whose heptathlon score of 7013 moved her to third on the world all-time list. She began with her fastest ever hurdles time of 13.34 and then high jumped 1.98m to equal her (and Katarina Johnson-Thompson's) world heptathlon best. Next came a 14.51m shot put and a modest but personal best 200m time of 24.40. That gave her a first day score of 4056 but the leader with 4059 was KJT who had set a pb of 13.29 in the hurdles, cleared 1.95m and made up for a feeble 12.72m with the shot with a mightily impressive 22.81 200m into a 2.9m wind. It looked as though her move to a new coaching set-up in the South of France was paying off but a 6.53m long jump was disappointing, particularly as Thiam was close to her best with 6.56m. Carolin Schäfer made a huge improvement to her pb, from 6.31m to 6.57m, and after five events she and Thiam were tied for the lead on 5083 points with KJT a close third on 5076. All that changed with the javelin, for whereas Thiam created a sensation by improving from 53.13m to a Belgian record of 59.32m, and Schäfer threw a respectable 49.80m, the Briton could manage only 39.98m, conceding third place to Laura Ikauniece-Admidina (56.17m pb). Thiam ran the 800m faster than ever before with 2:15.24; and the next five finishers also produced lifetime best scores with Schäfer on 6836, Ikauniece-Admidina setting a Latvian record of 6815 and KJT totalling 6691, the highest ever fourth place score.

The same late May weekend saw many great performances at the Prefontaine Classic in Eugene. Mo Farah outkicked some of his main East African rivals in a 13:00.70 5000m; in a marvellous triple jump contest Christian Taylor jumped a legal 18.11m pushed all the way by Will Claye's wind aided 18.05m; and Tori Bowie clocked a personal best of 21.77 for 200m. Kenya's Celphine Chespol, world youth champion in 2015 and world junior champion in 2016 and still only 18, won the steeplechase in the second quickest ever time of 8:58.78 for a world junior, Commonwealth and African record … and that despite having to stop to adjust a loose shoe after the penultimate water jump and losing close to 20 metres in the process. And yet there was an even more precocious mark in the mile 'B' race when in 11th place Norway's Jakob Ingebrigtsen became the first 16 year-old to break four minutes, clocking a remarkable 3:58.07. The brother of Henrik, the 2012 European 1500m champion who has best marks of 3:31.46 and 3:50.72, and Filip, the 2016 European 1500m champion with pbs of 3:32.43 and 3:53.23, continued to astonish all summer. He improved his mile time to 3:56.29 (that's faster than the 1957 world record of 3:57.2 by Derek Ibbotson who sadly died in February aged 84) and ran 1:49.40 for 800m, 3:39.92 for 1500m, 8:00.01 for 3000m, 13:35.84 for 5000m and 8:26.81 for the steeplechase. What a talent and all before his 17th birthday on September 19! Another remarkable Scandinavian youngster to emerge was pole vaulter Armand Duplantis, who at 17 cleared a world junior record of 5.90m. He competes for Sweden, his mother's native land, although he was born and lives in the USA. His American father Greg Duplantis vaulted 5.80m in 1993, Armand's older brother Andreas cleared 5.42m in 2013, and his mother Helena (née Hedlund) was a 5314 point heptathlete in 1983. What a family!

Among many outstanding performances in Europe as athletes prepared for the year's ultimate test, the World Championships in London, was a world best for 300m by Wayde van Niekerk in Ostrava. He had already enjoyed a fruitful season, clocking a South African 200m record of 19.84 and a personal best of 9.94 for 100m, and in the Czech city he sped to a time of 30.81, surpassing Michael Johnson's altitude-assisted best on record of 30.85 and Usain Bolt's 30.97. Van Niekerk thus became the only man ever to run sub-10, sub-20, sub-31 and sub-44. He dearly wished to race Bolt over 200m but that was never going to happen as the Jamaican legend, in his final season, had made it clear that he would be racing only at 100m and 4x100m relay. Bolt's form was a little troubling as in his first two starts his times were among his slowest ever at 10.03 and 10.06, although he improved to 9.95 in Monaco a couple of weeks before the Worlds, a meeting which would signal his retirement. As for van Niekerk, he ran a world leading 43.62 400m in Lausanne before winning a close race against Isaac Makwala, 43.73 to 43.84, in Monaco. Makwala, from Botswana, had one week earlier completed an historic double in Madrid. First he produced what was then his second quickest ever 400m time of 43.92 (he ran 43.72 in 2015) and then, little more than an hour later, he smashed his 200m pb with 19.77 to become the first ever to crack 20 and 44 on the same day.

In London it was most unfortunate that after winning his semi-final in 44.30 Makwala was barred from taking his place in the 400m final two days later on medical grounds as he had been affected by an outbreak of gastroenteritis at his hotel and was placed in quarantine for 48 hours. Van Niekerk was thus never seriously challenged as he retained his title in 43.98 ahead of promising Steven Gardiner, who had set a Bahamian record of 43.89 in his semi-final. Following his exclusion from the 400m final Makwala endured further frustration when he was not permitted to contest the 200m heats as they came within the 48 hour ban but the authorities relented to the extent that they allowed him to run a solo time trial to determine his fitness, needing to run 20.53 or faster. In fact he clocked 20.20 and was added to the semis, although in the previously unused and waterlogged lane one. He sailed through that test but ran out of steam in the final, placing sixth in 20.44. Van Niekerk, attempting to emulate Michael Johnson, fell just short of completing the double as he placed second in 20.11 to the Turkish outsider, Ramil Guliyev (20.09).

The main attraction for the capacity crowds for each evening session (and gratifyingly close to a full house also in the mornings) was the appearance of two gods of the track, Bolt and Mo Farah. Both would be ending their fabulous track championship careers … Mo had a couple more races lined up before turning exclusively to the road, while Usain was definitely hanging up his spikes. It was going to be an emotional week!

In his vintage years Usain Bolt would win races no matter how slowly he got away, but that is no longer the case and a poor getaway cost him the glorious finale to his championship career at 100m which practically all of the 56,000 spectators were anticipating. Way down at halfway, he came close to salvaging the race but his top-end speed isn't what it used to be and with a time of 9.95 he fell 3/100ths short. Inches ahead of him was the new American hope Christian Coleman, the world's quickest this year at 9.82. That was bad enough for Bolt's supporters; worse by far was that the winner in a season's best of 9.92 was Justin Gatlin. The 35 year-old American, winner of this title as far back as 2005, was booed when introduced and again when the result was announced. Clearly his doping history was well known and fans were entitled to their opinion, but booing was too extreme a reaction, best left to the football fanatics who usually inhabit this stadium.

Still, there was the relay to come with a good chance that Bolt would leave the track with one more gold medal for his collection. What happened in that race caused the fans to experience mixed emotions: elation and sorrow.

Britain's male 4x100m relay teams, conquerors against the Americans at the 2004 Olympics, have built up a dreadful record in global championships in recent years: non-finishers in the 2011 final, disqualified in their heat in 2012, disqualified in the 2013 final, non-finishers in the 2015 final, fifth in Rio 2016. A lot of money and effort invested with little to show for it … until now! The heats were encouraging as Britain finished only just behind the USA (37.70) in 37.76, just 0.03 outside the European record. In the other semi, Jamaica – anchored by Usain Bolt in what would prove to be his last completed race – ran 37.95 but with Omar McLeod [the 110m hurdles champion] and Yohan Blake rested for the final, in which thanks to super sprinting and slick baton passing the British squad was narrowly ahead of the USA at the last change.

Amid a wall of noise Nethaneel Mitchell-Blake managed to hold off Coleman in the superb time of 37.47, a European record that only Jamaican and American teams have ever surpassed. Approximate splits: C J Ujah 10.3 (turn), Adam Gemili 9.0 (straight), Dan Talbot 9.2 (turn) and Mitchell-Blake 9.0 (straight). When Bolt seized the baton his team was too far behind for him to surge through for victory although certainly a bronze medal was likely ... but to universal consternation his left hamstriong cramped early on and he fell to the track in pain and frustration. It was not the finale that anyone would have wished for the world's most celebrated athlete. There was a more fitting farewell appearance the following night: a slow walking, emotional lap of honour to a standing ovation with Usain stopping to reflect at the start lines of the 100m and 200m. He is indeed the legend he always wanted to be and he will never be forgotten.

Nor will Mo Farah, Britain's only individual medallist at these superb championships as the total medal count reached the minimum target of six thanks to bronze by the men's 4x400m squad (2:59.00) and silvers by the women's relay teams in 42.12 (41.93 heat) and 3:25.00 (3:24.74 heat).

How could we have doubted him? With the cream of East African distance running talent lined up behind him at the bell in the 10,000m, one wondered whether Mo could work his magic one more time at this distance, an event in which he has been unbeaten for six years. He could ... and he did. When Paul Tanui edged ahead with 200m to go it was looking ominous but once again Mo found that extra gear to pull away in the final straight for victory by 0.43 over Joshua Cheptegei of Uganda in a world leading mark of 26:49.51. His winning margins in his previous four global 10,000m titles have been similarly slim yet totally decisive: 0.48 in London 2012, 0.52 in Moscow 2013, 0.63 in Beijing 2015 and 0.47 in Rio 2016. Five gold medals won by a total of barely two and a half seconds!

In none of those previous victories has Farah needed to break 27 minutes, playing into the hands of the world's fastest finisher, but this time the Kenyans and Ugandans appeared to have come to some arrangement to make the pace a hot one. The outcome remained the same but on this occasion he had to go very close to his European record of 26:46.57. At the age of 34 this was the final 10,000m track race of his career, and what a way to bow out. It was a magnificent race, exciting throughout, and seven men broke 27 minutes, a record for a championship race. For much of the first half Farah was content to run in mid-field (13:36.20) and launched a long run for home from over 600m out. A penultimate lap of 61.92 took Farah to the bell in 25:53.88 but Tanui was just ahead with 200m remaining after Farah twice stumbled during a fiercely fought final lap, finishing up bleeding and bruised. Farah covered the last lap in 55.63, and 5000m in 13:13.31.

Just as Usain Bolt was denied a golden finale to his 100m career, so Mo Farah was beaten at last over 5000m, ending a fabulous series of global championship victories ... 2011 Worlds, 2012 Olympics, 2013 and 2015 Worlds, 2016 Olympics. At the end of a slowish race he was finally outkicked by an Ethiopian, Muktar Edris. The crowd were thrilled to see Farah and Andrew Butchart sharing the lead with some 600m remaining but the Scot would fall back to eighth by the finish and at the bell (12:40.17) Yomif Kejelcha led from Edris and Farah. The pace was furious now, the lap to 4800m covered in 54.24, and Kejelcha led into the final straight. Just five metres covered the first four at the finish with Edris the winner in 13:32.79 and Farah (13:33.32), gritting his teeth, coming through on the inside of Kejelcha to snatch second just ahead of Paul Chelimo. Terrific splits: the last 200m was covered in 26.34, 400m in 52.62. Edris ran 2:21.04 for his final kilometre.

Although Britain's haul of six medals was relatively modest compared to the USA's 30, while Kenya (11), Poland (8) and China (7) won more also, the points scores for top eight placings saw the British team finish as high as third behind the Americans and Kenyans. Mitchell-Blake (200m), surprising Kyle Langford (800m), Callum Hawkins (marathon), Dina Asher-Smith (miraculously in the 200m considering how soon it was after a serious foot injury) and Laura Muir (1500m) all finished in that most worthy but frustrating of positions ... fourth.

One world record was broken. That came in the inaugural women's 50km walk event where Ines Henriques pocketed $160,000 for winning in the astonishing time of 4:05:56, while in the men's race at that distance Yohann Diniz won by a margin of eight minutes in 3:33:12, second only to his own world record of 3:32:33. The only other championship record came in the women's steeplechase where Emma Coburn brought off a shock victory in 9:02.58 with US team-mate Courtney Frerichs still hardly able to believe she finished as high as second.

Nineteen Russians, designated 'authorised neutral athletes', were permitted to compete in London, having satisfied the IAAF that they had adhered to an approved anti-doping programme, with defending champion Mariya Lasitskené (née Kuchina), who high jumped 2.03m, winning their only gold medal. But doping and Russian athletes continued to be intertwined as further renowned athletes were stripped of major medals during the year as a result of continuing re-analysis of doping samples from previous Olympics.

One of the most notable was Tatyana Lebedeva who lost her silver medals from the long jump and triple jump at the 2008 Games. That positive test cast a shadow over a career which saw her become 2004 Olympic and 2007 world long jump champion and 2001 and 2003 world triple jump champion. Following a lengthy process of appeals, Tatyana Chernova was finally stripped of the world heptathlon title from 2011, that honour belatedly transferred to Dame Jess.

Biological passport irregularities brought about the downfall of Mariya Savinova, the Court of Arbitration for Sport ruling in favour of the IAAF's four year ban and annulling all of her results between July 26 2010 and August 19 2013. As a consequence she has lost the 2010 European, 2011 world and 2012 Olympic 800m titles, with Caster Semenya succeeding her as gold medallist in those last two races. Semenya, who won the 800m in London in a South African record of 1:55.16 (plus third in the 1500m) and subsequently set a world best of 1:21.77 for 600m, now has five global titles to her name, having also triumphed at the World Championships of 2009 and the Olympics of 2016. However, she remains a divisive figure on account of her suspected hyperandrogenism, a medical condition involving excessive levels of testosterone. One gets the impression that at 800m she runs only as fast as she needs to in order to win; if she really cut loose, Jarmila Kratochvilová's 1983 figures of 1:53.28 (the oldest of all world records) would be at her mercy.

Thanks to the good offices of head of press operations, Jayne Pearce, I had probably the best seat in the stadium for the World Championships, almost over the finish line and at just the right height level. The company was stimulating, too, with Stan Greenberg on one side of me and Richard Hymans on the other. I could have done without the non-stop over-amplified sound and the unnecessary antics of the mascots (what purpose do they serve other than delight any four year-olds in the audience?), but I thoroughly enjoyed ten days of superlative and dramatic athletics competition ... the last outdoor global championships I expect to attend.

It was a great way to finish.

53. WORLD ALL-TIME RANKINGS

A perpetual area of discussion among enthusiasts is comparing one great athlete with another. Of course, there is no totally objective method of ranking athletes of different eras but, for want of anything more scientific, I have devised a points system to attempt a world all-time ranking in each event.

The biggest single awards (30 points) are for winning an Olympic gold medal (starting from 1908) or becoming a world record holder. An Olympic silver medal is worth 15 points and bronze 10. IAAF World Championships provide the same level of competition as the Olympics but as they are now held every two years rather than four for the Olympics and were instituted only in 1983, thus putting athletes of earlier generations at a disadvantage, the values are 15 for gold, 8 for silver and 5 for bronze. World Indoor Championship medals and world indoor records have not been taken into account as there are also overall as well as event by event all-time rankings and therefore athletes in such events as the 400m hurdles, discus etc would be disadvantaged.

As stated, 30 points are awarded to any athlete who broke or equalled a world record from 1900 onwards (normally as ratified by the IAAF but in some cases superior performances accepted by the ATFS have been considered), but it's 30 points per athlete not per record or otherwise Sergey Bubka for instance would reach a score totally beyond the possibilities, say, of a 10,000m runner. Instead there is a reward for longevity as a world record holder: 3 points for every two year period.

Another recognition of a long and consistent career at the top is the award of 2 points for each year an athlete was world ranked no 1. In this context that is for achieving the best mark in the world for the years 1921-1946, per *Track & Field News* world merit rankings 1947-1987 & *Athletics Today/Athletics International* world merit rankings since 1988. There is also a bonus of 2 points per occasion for any athlete who achieved the ultimate in athletic performance: winning an Olympic or world title with a world record. Doping bans of 18 months or longer are noted, which is not to say that all others in these lists were 'clean' throughout their careers. Here are the top three in each event as at September 2017, but first an example of how the points are accumulated.

Usain Bolt (100m) 1st 2008, 2012 & 2016 Olympics (90 points); 1st 2009, 2013 & 2015 World (45), 3rd 2017 (5); world records: 9.72 on 31.5.2008, 9.69 on 16.8.2008, 9.58 on 16.8.2009 (record holder for 9 years) (42); world record bonus: 2008 Olympics (9.69) & 2009 World (9.58) (4); world ranked number one: 2008, 2009, 2011, 2012, 2013, 2015, 2016 (14) = 200 points.

100m: 1, Usain Bolt JAM 200; 2, Carl Lewis USA 163; 3, Maurice Greene USA 133; **200m:** 1, Usain Bolt JAM 220; 2, Michael Johnson USA 132; 3, Pietro Mennea ITA 105; **400m:** 1, Michael Johnson USA 196; 2, Lee Evans USA 97; 3, LaShawn Merritt USA 100 (doping ban 2009-2011); **800m:** 1, David Rudisha KEN 143; 2, Wilson Kipketer DEN (ex-KEN) 130; 3, Peter Snell NZL 113; **1500m:** 1, Hicham El Guerrouj MAR 184; 2, Noureddine

Morceli ALG 125; 3, Sebastian Coe GBR 94; **5000m:** 1=, Kenenisa Bekele ETH & Mo Farah GBR 123; 3, Paavo Nurmi FIN 114; **10,000m**: 1, Haile Gebrselassie ETH 184; 2, Kenenisa Bekele ETH 180; 3, Paavo Nurmi FIN 125; **Marathon:** 1, Abebe Bikila ETH 103; 2, Sohn Kee Chung KOR aka Kitei Son JPN 79; 3, Waldemar Cierpinski GDR 69; **3000m Steeplechase:** 1, Ezekiel Kemboi KEN 150; 2, Moses Kiptanui KEN 116; 3, Volmari Iso-Hollo FIN 113; **110m Hurdles:** 1, Colin Jackson GBR 114; 2, Roger Kingdom USA 111; 3=, Lee Calhoun USA & Liu Xiang CHN 107; **400m Hurdles:** 1, Ed Moses USA 174; 2, Kevin Young USA 119; 3, Glenn Davis USA 110; **High Jump:** 1, Javier Sotomayor CUB 179; 2, Valeriy Brumel URS 97; 3, Patrik Sjöberg SWE 94; **Pole Vault:** 1, Sergey Bubka URS/UKR 218; 2, Renaud Lavillenie FRA 118; 3, Bob Richards USA 86; **Long Jump:** 1, Carl Lewis USA 180; 2, Mike Powell USA 139; 3, Dwight Phillips USA 105; **Triple Jump:** 1, Jonathan Edwards GBR 169; 2, Viktor Saneyev URS 161; 3, Christian Taylor USA 115; **Shot:** 1, Parry O'Brien USA 128; 2, Ralph Rose USA 105; 3, Randy Matson USA 97; unranked: Randy Barnes USA 129 (positive drug tests in 1990 & 1998 led to lifetime ban); **Discus:** 1, Al Oerter USA 165; 2, Jürgen Schult GDR 159; 3, Lars Riedel GER 133; **Hammer:** 1, Yuriy Sedykh URS 194; 2=, Pat O'Callaghan IRL & Sergey Litvinov URS 116; **Javelin:** 1, Jan Zelezny CZE 242; 2, Andreas Thorkildsen NOR 111; 3, Jonni Myrrä FIN 107; **Decathlon:** 1, Ashton Eaton USA 144; 2, Daley Thompson GBR 129; 3, Roman Sebrle CZE 127; **10km/20km Walk:** 1, Jefferson Pérez ECU 155; 2=, John Mikaelsson SWE & Vladimir Golubnichiy URS 117; **50km Walk:** 1, Robert Korzeniowski POL 192; 2, Ronald Weigel GDR 91; 3, Andrey Perlov URS/RUS 89; **Top single event scorers:** 1, Zelezny 242; 2, Bolt (200m) 220; 3, Bubka 218; **Top aggregate events scorers:** 1, Bolt 420 (100m, 200m); 2, Lewis 397 (100m, 200m, Long Jump); 3, Johnson 328 (200m, 400m).

Women – 100m: 1, Shelly-Ann Fraser-Pryce JAM 123; 2, Wyomia Tyus USA 105; 2, Florence Griffith Joyner USA 104; **200m:** 1, Florence Griffith Joyner USA 129; 2, Allyson Felix USA 120; 3, Irena Szewinska POL 110; **400m:** 1, Marita Koch GDR 125; 2, Marie-José Pérec FRA 100; 3, Cathy Freeman AUS 81; **800m:** 1, Maria Mutola MOZ 116; 2, Caster Semenya RSA 111; 3, Jarmila Kratochvilová CZE 99; **1500m:** 1, Tatyana Kazankina URS 120 (served ban for refusing drugs test in 1984); 2, Qu Yunxia CHN 72; 3, Lyudmila Bragina URS 69; **3000m/5000m:** 1, Meseret Defar ETH 166; 2, Tirunesh Dibaba ETH 132; 3, Wang Junxia CHN 91; **10,000m:** 1, Tirunesh Dibaba ETH 135; 2, Derartu Tulu ETH 99; 3, Wang Junxia CHN 97; **Marathon:** 1, Catherine Ndereba KEN 112; 2, Grete Waitz NOR 100; 3, Paula Radcliffe GBR 86; **3000m Steeplechase:** 1, Gulnara Galkina RUS 84; 2, Ruth Jebet BRN 62; 3, Habiba Ghribi TUN 55; **80m/100m Hurdles**: 1, Yordanka Donkova BUL 113; 2, Shirley de la Hunty (née Strickland) AUS 109; 3, Fanny Blankers-Koen NED 88; **400m Hurdles**: 1, Sally Gunnell GBR 93; 2, Yuliya Pechonkina (née Nosova) RUS 91; 3, Kim Batten USA 80; **High Jump:** 1, Stefka Kostadinova BUL 164; 2, Iolanda Balas ROU 126; 3, Ulrike Meyfarth GER 104; **Pole Vault:** 1, Yelena Isinbayeva RUS 188; 2, Stacy Dragila USA 101; 3, Svetlana

Feofanova RUS 92; **Long Jump**: 1, Heike Drechsler GDR/GER 169; 2, Brittney Reese USA 119; 3, Jackie Joyner-Kersee USA 118; **Triple Jump**: 1, Inessa Kravets UKR 114 (doping ban 2000-2002); 2, Caterine Ibargüen COL 96; 3, Francoise Mbango CMR 78; **Shot:** 1, Valerie Adams NZL 159; 2, Natalya Lisovskaya URS/RUS 139; 3, Tamara Press URS 116; **Discus:** 1, Nina Romashkova (née Ponomaryova) URS 114; 2, Sandra Perkovic CRO 110; 3, Evelin Jahl (née Schlaak) GDR 98; **Hammer**: 1, Anita Wlodarczyk POL 158; 2, Olga Kuzenkova RUS 115 (doping ban 2013-2015 & lost 2005 world title); 3, Betty Heidler GER 84; **Javelin:** 1, Barbora Spotáková CZE 176; 2, Osleidys Menéndez CUB 119; 3, Trine Hattestad NOR 113; **Heptathlon:** 1, Jackie Joyner-Kersee USA 196; 2, Jessica Ennis-Hill GBR 100; 3, Carolina Klüft SWE 87; **10km/20km Walk:** 1, Liu Hong CHN 120; 2, Yelena Nikolayeva RUS 105; 3, Olimpiada Ivanova RUS 93 (doping ban 2007-2009); **Top single event scorers:** 1, Joyner-Kersee (Heptathlon) 196; 2, Isinbayeva 188; 3, Spotáková 176; **Top aggregate events scorers:** 1, Blankers-Koen 381 (100m, 200m, 80m Hurdles, High Jump, Long Jump, Pentathlon!); 2, Joyner-Kersee 314 (Long Jump, Heptathlon); 3, T Dibaba 267 (5000m, 10,000m).

54. UK ALL-TIME RANKINGS

I have used a different set of values to determine who are the most successful British athletes in history. Points are awarded for the top four places in the Olympics (30 for a gold medal), top three in the World Championships (20 for a gold medal), European Championships (10 for a gold medal) and Commonwealth Games (6 for a gold medal). A world record merits 15 points plus an extra 2 points for each full year the athlete holds that record, and other points winners relate to UK records, world merit rankings, AAA/UK championship titles and a bonus for anyone who wins a global title with a world record. Indoor performances have not been considered. Here are the top three in each event as at September 2017.

100m: 1, Linford Christie 176; 2, McDonald Bailey 61; 3, Allan Wells 55; **200m:** 1, John Regis 62; 2, Willie Applegarth 55; 3, Allan Wells 48; **400m:** 1, Roger Black 73; 2, Godfrey Brown 47; 3, Eric Liddell 46; **800m:** 1, Seb Coe 165; 2, Douglas Lowe 85; 3, Tom Hampson 84; **1500m/Mile:** 1, Steve Cram 156; 2, Seb Coe 111; 3, Steve Ovett 74; **5000m:** 1, Mo Farah 199; 2, Gordon Pirie 61; 3, Dave Moorcroft 53; **10,000m:** 1, Mo Farah 182; 2=, Brendan Foster & Dave Bedford 41; **Marathon:** 1, Jim Peters 54; 2, Steve Jones 48; 3=, Sam Ferris & Basil Heatley 44; **3000m Steeplechase:** 1=, Chris Brasher & Maurice Herriott 42; 3, Percy Hodge 41; **110m Hurdles:** 1, Colin Jackson 245; 2, Don Finlay 71; 3, Tony Jarrett 58; **400m Hurdles:** 1, David Hemery 89; 2, Lord Burghley 78; 3, Kriss Akabusi 53; **High Jump**: 1, Steve Smith 50; 2, Robbie Grabarz 44; 3, Alan Paterson 40; **Pole Vault:** 1=, Geoff Elliott & Mike Bull 29; 3, Steve Lewis 24; **Long Jump:** 1, Greg Rutherford 114; 2, Lynn Davies 95; 3, Harold Abrahams 21; **Triple Jump:** 1, Jonathan Edwards 261; 2, Phillips Idowu 84; 3, Keith Connor 55; **Shot:** 1, Geoff Capes 53; 2, Arthur Rowe 37; 3, Robert 'Bonzo' Howland 32; **Discus:** 1, Bill Tancred 31; 2, Robert Weir 25; 3, Mark Pharaoh 18; **Hammer:** 1, Malcolm Nokes 57; 2, Howard Payne 40; 3, Martin Girvan 29; **Javelin:** 1, Steve Backley 206; 2, Dave Ottley 41; 3, Mick Hill 39; **Decathlon:** 1, Daley Thompson 216; 2, Dean Macey 33; 3, Peter Gabbett 13; **20km Walk:** 1, Ken Matthews 60; 2, Paul Nihill 52; 3, Ian McCombie 27; **50km Walk:** 1, Harold Whitlock 59; 2, Don Thompson 51; 3, Tommy Green 37; **Top single event scorers:** 1, Edwards 261; 2, Jackson 245; 3, Thompson 216; **Top aggregate events scorers:** 1, Farah 388 (1500m, 5000m, 10,000m, Marathon); 2, Coe 277 (400m, 800m, 1500m); 3, Edwards 261.

Women – 100m: 1, Dorothy Hyman 64; 2, Andrea Lynch 24; 3, Kathy Cook (née Smallwood) 23; **200m:** 1, Kathy Cook 50; 2, Dorothy Hyman 43; 3, Audrey Williamson 20; **400m:** 1, Christine Ohuruogu 117; 2=, Lillian Board & Kathy Cook 32; **800m:** 1, Kelly Holmes 95; 2, Ann Packer (later Brightwell) 64; 3, Diane Leather (later Charles) 32; **1500m:** 1, Kelly Holmes 88; 2, Diane Leather 42; 3=, Anne Smith & Lisa Dobriskey 24; **3000/5000m:** 1, Yvonne Murray 51; 2, Wendy Sly (née Smith) 30; 3=, Paula Fudge (née Yeoman), Zola Budd & Paula Radcliffe 28; **10,000m:** 1, Liz McColgan (née Lynch) 69; 2, Paula Radcliffe 50; 3, Jo Pavey 19; **Marathon:** 1, Paula Radcliffe 102; 2=,

Joyce Smith & Veronique Marot 15; **3000m Steeplechase:** 1=, Hatti Dean & Helen Clitheroe (née Pattinson) 8; 3, Tara Krzywicki 7; **80/100m Hurdles:** 1=, Maureen Dyson (née Gardner) & Shirley Strong 44; 3, Betty Moore 37; **400m Hurdles:** 1, Sally Gunnell 146; 2, Eilidh Doyle (née Child) 25; 3, Natasha Danvers 18; **High Jump:** 1, Dorothy Tyler (née Odam) 119; 2, Thelma Hopkins 77; 3, Sheila Lerwill (née Alexander) 74; **Pole Vault**: 1, Janine Whitlock 16; 2, Holly Bradshaw (née Bleasdale) 12; 3, Kate Dennison 10; **Long Jump:** 1, Mary Rand (née Bignal) 115; 2, Sheila Sherwood (née Parkin) 38; 3, Shara Proctor 28; **Triple Jump:** 1, Ashia Hansen 53; 2=, Michelle Griffith & Laura Samuel 9; **Shot:** 1, Judy Oakes 69; 2=, Sue Allday & Mary Peters 22; **Discus:** 1, Meg Ritchie 33; 2, Rosemary Payne 30; 3, Sue Allday 29; **Hammer:** 1, Lorraine Shaw 32; 2, Sophie Hitchon 25; 3, Zoe Derham 6; **Javelin:** 1, Fatima Whitbread 125; 2, Tessa Sanderson 90; 3, Goldie Sayers 30; **Pentathlon/Heptathlon:** 1, Jessica Ennis-Hill 154; 2, Denise Lewis 112; 3, Mary Peters 90; **Walks:** 1, Marion Fawkes 40; 2, Carol Tyson 36; 3, Lisa Kehler (née Langford) 34; **Top single event scorers:** 1, Ennis-Hill 154; 2, Gunnell 146; 3, Whitbread 125; **Top aggregate events scorers:** 1, Holmes 183 (800m, 1500m); 2, Radcliffe 180 (5000m, 10,000m, Marathon); 3, Ennis-Hill 173 (100m Hurdles, High Jump, Heptathlon).

55. WORLD RECORD PROGRESSION

Here is how the world record in events on the Olympic programme has dramatically progressed since my involvement in the sport started in 1950, in which year none of these subsequent performances could have been considered humanly possible!

	1950	2017		
100m	10.2	9.58	Usain Bolt JAM	2009
200m	20.7	19.19	Usain Bolt JAM	2009
400m	45.8	43.03	Wayde van Niekerk RSA	2016
800m	1:46.6	1:40.91	David Rudisha KEN	2012
1500m	3:43.0	3:26.00	Hicham El Guerrouj MAR	1998
(Mile)	4:01.3	3:43.13	Hicham El Guerrouj MAR	1999
5000m	13:58.1	12:37.35	Kenenisa Bekele ETH	2004
10,000m	29:02.6	26:17.53	Kenenisa Bekele ETH	2005
Marathon	2:25:39	2:02:57	Dennis Kimetto KEN	2014
Steeplechase	8:59.6	7:53.63	Saif Saaeed Shaheen QAT	2004
110m Hurdles	13.5	12.80	Aries Merritt USA	2012
400m Hurdles	50.6	46.78	Kevin Young USA	1992
High Jump	2.11	2.45	Javier Sotomayor CUB	1993
Pole Vault	4.77	6.16	Renaud Lavillenie FRA	2014
Long Jump	8.13	8.95	Mike Powell USA	1991
Triple Jump	16.00	18.29	Jonathan Edwards GBR	1995
Shot	17.95	23.12	Randy Barnes USA	1990
Discus	56.97	74.08	Jürgen Schult GDR	1986
Hammer	59.88	86.74	Yuriy Sedykh URS	1986
Javelin	78.70	98.48	Jan Zelezny CZE	1996
Decathlon	7287	9045	Ashton Eaton USA	2015
20km Walk	1:31:44	1:16:36	Yusuke Suzuki JPN	2015
50km Walk	4:23:40	3:32:33	Yohann Diniz FRA	2014
4x100m	39.8	36.84	Jamaica	2012
4x400m	3:08.2	2:54.29	United States	1993

WOMEN

	1950	2017		
100m	11.5	10.49	Florence Griffith Joyner USA	1988
200m	23.6	21.34	Florence Griffith Joyner USA	1988
400m	56.7	47.60	Marita Koch GDR	1985
800m	2:13.0	1:53.28	Jarmila Kratochvilová CZE	1983
1500m	4:37.8	3:50.07	Genzebe Dibaba ETH	2015
(Mile)	5:15.3	4:12.56	Svetlana Masterkova RUS	1996
5000m	-	14:11.15	Tirunesh Dibaba ETH	2008
10,000m	-	29:17.45	Almaz Ayana ETH	2016

Marathon	-	2:15:25	Paula Radcliffe GBR	2003
Steeplechase	-	8:52.78	Ruth Jebet BRN	2016
100m Hurdles	-	12.20	Kendra Harrison USA	2016
400m Hurdles	-	52.34	Yuliya Pechonkina RUS	2003
High Jump	1.71	2.09	Stefka Kostadinova BUL	1987
Pole Vault	-	5.06	Yelena Isinbayeva RUS	2009
Long Jump	6.25	7.52	Galina Chistyakova URS	1988
Triple Jump	-	15.50	Inessa Kravets UKR	1995
Shot	15.02	22.63	Natalya Lisovskaya URS	1987
Discus	53.25	76.80	Gabriele Reinsch GDR	1988
Hammer	-	82.98	Anita Wlodarczyk POL	2016
Javelin	53.41	72.28	Barbora Spotáková CZE	2008
Heptathlon	-	7291	Jackie Joyner-Kersee USA	1988
20km Walk	1:59:02	1:24:38	Liu Hong CHN	2015
4x100m	46.4	40.82	United States	2012
4x400m	-	3:15.17	Soviet Union	1988

Lightning Source UK Ltd.
Milton Keynes UK
UKHW01f1100260718
326328UK00002B/131/P

9 781907 953699